Frommer's

New Zealand
day BY day

1st Edition

by Adrienne Rewi

WILEY
John Wiley and Sons, Inc.

> Canoe paddling with Waka
Taiamai Heritage Tours.

Contents

PAGE 4

PAGE 30

PAGE 55

PAGE 268

PAGE 306

PAGE 327

PUBLISHED BY
John Wiley & Sons, Inc.
111 River St., Hoboken, NJ 07030-5774

ISBN 978-0-470-89457-6

Frommer's®

Editorial by Frommer's

EDITOR	PHOTO EDITOR
Christine Ryan	Cherie Cincilla
CARTOGRAPHER	CAPTIONS
Roberta Stockwell	Adrienne Rewi
COVER PHOTO EDITOR	COVER DESIGN
Richard Fox	Paul Dinovo

Produced by Sideshow Media

PUBLISHER	MANAGING EDITOR
Dan Tucker	Megan McFarland
PROJECT EDITOR	PHOTO EDITOR
Alicia Mills	John Martin
PHOTO RESEARCHER	DESIGN
Tessa Perliss	Kevin Smith, And Smith LLC
SPOTLIGHT FEATURE DESIGN	
Em Dash Design LLC	

For information on our other products and services or to obtain technical support, please contact our Customer Care Department within the U.S. at 800/762-2974, outside the U.S. at 317/572-3993 or fax 317/572-4002.

Wiley also publishes its books in a variety of electronic formats. Some content that appears in print may not be available in electronic formats.

MANUFACTURED IN CHINA

5   4   3   2   1

How to Use This Guide

The Day by Day guides present a series of itineraries that take you from place to place. The itineraries are organized by time (Auckland in 1 Day), by region (Driving the Surf Highway), by town (Napier), and by special interest (Maori Northland). You can follow these itineraries to the letter, or customize your own based on the information we provide. Within the tours, we suggest cafes, bars, or restaurants where you can take a break. Each of these stops is marked with a coffee-cup icon ☕. In each chapter, we provide detailed hotel and restaurant reviews so you can select the places that are right for you.

The hotels, restaurants, and attractions listed in this guide have been ranked for quality, value, service, amenities, and special features using a **star-rating system.** Hotels, restaurants, attractions, shopping, and nightlife are rated on a scale of zero stars (recommended) to three stars (exceptional). In addition to the star-rating system, we also use a kids icon **kids** to point out the best bets for families.

The following **abbreviations** are used for credit cards:

AE American Express	**MC** MasterCard
DC Diners Club	**V** Visa
DISC Discover	

A Note on Prices

Frommer's lists exact prices in local currency. Currency conversions fluctuate, so before departing consult a currency exchange website such as **www.oanda.com/currency/converter** to check up-to-the-minute conversion rates.

How to Contact Us

In researching this book, we discovered many wonderful places—hotels, restaurants, shops, and more. We're sure you'll find others. Please tell us about them, so we can share the information with your fellow travelers in upcoming editions. If you were disappointed with a recommendation, we'd love to know that, too. Please email us at frommersfeed back@wiley.com or write to:

Frommer's New Zealand Day by Day, 1st Edition
John Wiley & Sons, Inc.
111 River Street
Hoboken, NJ 07030-5774

Travel Resources at Frommers.com

Frommer's travel resources don't end with this guide. **Frommers.com** has travel information on more than 4,000 destinations. We update features regularly, giving you access to the most current trip-planning information and the best airfare, lodging, and car-rental bargains. You can also listen to podcasts, connect with other Frommers.com members through our active reader forums, share your travel photos, read blogs from guidebook editors and fellow travelers, and much more.

An Additional Note

Travel information can change quickly and unexpectedly, and we strongly advise you to confirm important details locally before traveling, including information on visas, health and safety, traffic and transport, accommodation, shopping and eating out. We also encourage you to stay alert while traveling and to remain aware of your surroundings. Avoid civil disturbances, and keep a close eye on cameras, purses, wallets, and other valuables.

About the Author

Photojournalist **Adrienne Rewi**'s passion for words and writing has taken her throughout Asia and into almost every writing genre and every subject. When not organizing her next overseas trip, taking photographs, or writing her next book, she is based in Christchurch writing for numerous New Zealand and international magazines. She is the author of seven editions of the bestselling travel guide *Frommer's New Zealand,* and has published three other non-fiction titles and assorted short stories.

About the Photographers

Born in Leeds, England, **Tim Clayton** learned his profession on the *Yorkshire Evening Post* and *The Yorkshire Post* in Leeds. He emigrated to Australia in 1990 to work for *The Sydney Morning Herald,* where he became full time Sports Photographer for the SMH in 1992. His many assignments have included seven Olympic Games, four Rugby World Cups, Coverage of the Australian Soccer team around the globe, as well as daily life stories in Australia, Uganda, Romania, France, Italy, Vanuatu, The Philippines, and Bolivia. He has won eight World Press Awards (including three first place awards) and in 2003, *The Observer* chose four of Tim's pictures for a feature showing the 50 best sports pictures ever. He is a keen campaigner on ethics in photo-journalism. He left the *Sydney Morning Herald* in 2008 to pursue a freelance career and has travelled extensively through South America, Europe, and New Zealand covering sport and travel photography.

Lisa Wiltse was born in Weston, Connecticut, and graduated from the Art Institute of Boston with a BFA in photography. In 2004 she moved to Sydney, Australia where she worked as a staff photographer for *The Sydney Morning Herald.* In 2008, she decided to pursue her freelance career. She has traveled extensively, focusing on documenting everyday life in marginalized communities in places such as Bangladesh, Uganda, Philippines, and the USA. Her work has been recognized by Photo District News, the National Press Photographers Association, the Sony awards, and Magenta: Flash Forward. She is the recipient of two Walkley awards in Australia, The One Life award (2011), and was selected as one of eight photographers for Pour L'Instant in Niort, France in 2009. She is currently a contributor with Getty Reportage. Her publications and clients include *TIME, New York Times, Geo, Marie Claire, The Fader, PDN, The Walrus, Virginia Review Quarterly, International Herald Tribune,* and *Frommer's Rio de Janeiro Day by Day, 1st Edition.*

1
The Best of
New Zealand

My Favorite Moments

> PREVIOUS PAGE *Indulge in a helicopter flight for incredible views of Northland's islands, bays, and beaches.* THIS PAGE *Test your mettle walking around the top of Sky Tower, high above Auckland city.*

Watching walkers on top of Auckland's Sky Tower. I get a shiver down my spine just thinking about the adventurous types who see walking around a thin metal circle 192m (630 ft.) in the air as some sort of thrill. But I have a fear of heights, which is why, perhaps, I am completely in awe of this astonishing spectacle. See "Auckland for Adrenaline Junkies," p. 45.

Sailing an America's Cup yacht. Experience the power and speed of a superyacht when you step onto either *NZL 40* or *NZL 41,* which were built for New Zealand's 1995 America's Cup challenge in San Diego. Roll up your sleeves and get into the crewing action on a match race in Viaduct Harbour, or sit back and enjoy the wind in your hair, leaving the hard work to the experts. See p. 44, ❹.

Sitting alone on a Far North beach. Pick any one of the stunning beaches on the Far North's Karikari Peninsula and you'll as good as have

the place to yourself. For me, there's nothing better than sitting thinking on a grassy knoll overlooking the double golden horseshoe of remote Matai Bay. When I first visited here thirty years ago, there wasn't another person for miles. The roads have been developed since then, so you may have some company—but not much. See p. 100, ⓯.

Flying over Mount Tarawera. There are many amazing geothermal sights in the central North Island but flying over the giant volcanic rift of Mount Tarawera gives you some idea of the phenomenal power of its 1886 eruption—an eruption that buried an entire village and one of New Zealand's most famous tourist attractions, the Pink and White Terraces. Following the 15km (9⅓-mile) rift in a helicopter is an unforgettable experience. See p. 184.

Visiting Hawke's Bay vineyards. This region is home to some of our oldest winemaking establishments and over 80% of New Zealand's red wine grape plantings. There are at least 70 vineyards, many of them sporting stunning, architecturally interesting wineries and restaurants, not to mention plenty of chances to relax in one of the prettiest, most abundant provinces in the country. See "Hawke's Bay & Eastland for Wine Lovers," p. 203.

Wandering Wellington's Cuba Mall. There's a sloppy, bohemian charm to this central Wellington shopping zone that never gets tired. From grungy tattoo and piercing parlors to upmarket fashion boutiques to trendy cafes and restaurants, it's a vital, egalitarian part of the capital you shouldn't miss. Sit awhile. You won't be disappointed. See p. 275.

Flying over Doubtful Sound. No matter how much you read about Doubtful Sound beforehand, nothing quite prepares you for the majesty of this stunning World Heritage wilderness region. It's ten times bigger than more famous Milford Sound and it's filled with ancient rainforests, cascading waterfalls, towering peaks, pods of dolphins, fur seals, and an all-encompassing, mysterious silence. See "A Sound Decision," p. 372.

My Favorite Small Towns

> *Arrowtown's quaint early settler architecture, boutique stores, and magnificent displays of autumn foliage make it a favorite side trip for Queenstown visitors.*

Russell, Bay of Islands. When you stand on the shore of this quiet, pretty village, it's hard to believe it was once the lawless whaling and trading center described as "the Hell Hole of the Pacific." That was back in the early 19th century. By 1840 it had become New Zealand's first permanent European settlement and, for a short time, our first capital city. Today it is a benign, charming, warm place that somehow avoids the summer holiday chaos. It's filled with important history, good fishing, beaches, and lovely stays. See p. 94, ❸–❼.

Greytown, Wairarapa. Founded in 1890 as the country's first planned inland town and named after Governor Sir George Grey, Greytown's cute Victorian main street now bulges with boutique stores and cafes. It's a popular weekend base for those exploring the many wineries that cling to the skirts of nearby Martinborough, and it's well set up with many

delightful, private, self-contained guest cottages. I love wandering its leafy streets—our first Arbor Day celebrations were held here and the town has a register of all its important trees—and then relaxing over coffee and pastries at the French bakery. See p. 291, ❶–❹.

Hanmer Springs, Canterbury. Located 136km (85 miles) north of Christchurch, Hanmer has been built around the famous hot springs that were discovered here in the mid-19th century. It's come a long way since then and today the pools are a sophisticated attraction with a classy day spa. But there's more to this beautiful alpine spot than hot pools—bungy jumping, jet-boating, horseback riding, and walking in its sublime heritage forest are all popular activities. Or you can simply while away hours in a B&B or cafe. See p. 338, ⓬.

Akaroa, Canterbury. Dramatic peninsula landscapes, big skies, and pretty seashore walks are the defining characteristics of this idyllic village an hour from Christchurch—that and the French connection of course. After French explorer Jean Langlois took word of this heavenly spot back to France, two French ships and a handful of settlers arrived to colonize the site in 1840. They were too late; the British had beaten them to it but the French settlers stayed on, giving rise to the area's original French names. Today the 1,000 residents happily continue the French theme but if you can see past that overt marketing ploy, you'll find plenty to please. See p. 335, ❻.

Arrowtown, near Queenstown. Pretty at any time of year, Arrowtown is especially famous for its autumn splendor. That's when the town's many huge trees burst into a fiery parade of reds, yellows, oranges, and browns, and cameras from all round the world click in a delighted frenzy. Arrowtown kept a keen eye on its fascinating gold-mining origins and you'll find plenty of evidence of that in local buildings and attractions. The rural lanes between Arrowtown and Queenstown are home to some of the most expensive real estate in New Zealand. See p. 374, ❾.

The Best of New Zealand Outdoors

> The multi-colored Champagne Pool at Waiotapu Thermal Wonderland in central North Island is one of the most photographed volcanic attractions in the country.

The Far North. The balmy climate, the beaches, the marine reserves, the kauri forests, and the laidback northern lifestyle all lend themselves to a summer outdoors. Pack up your campervans and tents, your buckets and spades, your walking shoes and fishing gear, and set the compass to guide you north. Most international visitors seem to come to our shores to ski or to hike in the rugged southern landscapes, forgetting that we have some of the funkiest camping grounds and summer activities in the north. See chapter 4.

Central North Island. To get an idea of the grandeur of the central North Island, you need to visit the steamy, volcanic regions of Rotorua, where mud pools bubble up in unexpected places and whole valleys present a myriad of volcanic colors and action. Drive on to the vast expanse of Lake Taupo, which sits in an ancient volcanic crater, and finish with a drive through the desert-like center to see our oldest national park, Tongariro, which was designated a World Heritage Area in 1990 for its outstanding natural and cultural features. See chapter 6.

Abel Tasman National Park, Nelson. As marvelous as all our national parks are, this one is the jewel in the crown, a small, perfect place of just 23,000 hectares (57,000 acres). Its easily accessible coastline, forested headlands, and unbeatable golden-sand beaches can all be experienced firsthand on the famous Abel Tasman Track, one of the Department of Conservation's Great Walks. But you don't have to be a serious hiker to enjoy it. If you love kayaking, there is no better place in all of New Zealand for it than on these mirror-like ocean waters. See chapter 10.

Te Waipounamu, the South West New Zealand World Heritage Area. Over 2.6 million hectares (6.4 million acres)—that's 10% of New Zealand's total landmass—make up this exquisite, untamed wilderness region at the bottom of the South Island. It's readily subdivided into Mount Aspiring National Park, near Wanaka, Westland National Park, on the West Coast, and Fiordland National Park, near Te Anau. At its heart are some of the grandest beauties of all—rugged mountains, native bush, waterfalls, glaciers, rivers, rare wildlife, and some of the best multi-day walks in the world. It's as treacherous and mercurial as it is beautiful but that doesn't stop millions of visitors seeking out their own tiny piece of paradise every year. See p. 378, ❹.

The Best of Maori New Zealand

Auckland Museum. There is something haunting and deeply moving about standing in front of ancient Maori carvings. They seem to have a life and a presence of their own and you'll certainly feel that in Auckland Museum, which has the largest collection of Maori and Polynesian artifacts in the world. From enormous carved *waka* (war canoes) to the artistry of meetinghouses, finely woven baskets, intricately finished feather cloaks, and exquisite hand-carved jewelry and weapons, you'll be entranced. See p. 42, .

Te Puia, Rotorua. This may seem like a pricey attraction but it's worth every cent if you want to get a feel for Maori history, culture, and contemporary life. Based around a stunning replica Maori village with genuine historic buildings and carvings, it features major geothermal activity (including the famous Pohutu geyser), interactive galleries, and contemporary weaving and carving schools training the next generation of craftspeople. You can also enjoy traditional song and dance performances, a *hangi* (feast), and the chance to shop for top quality Maori crafts. It's a must-do activity in my opinion. See p. 168, .

Whakarewarewa Thermal Village, Rotorua. Unlike Te Puia, Whakarewarewa is a real-life, lived-in Maori village. It is home to the Ngati Wahiao *hapu* (sub-tribe), who have occupied and harnessed the power of this pretty geothermal valley for the last 300 years. It's probably the only place in the world, in fact, where people still use natural geothermal energy as part of their everyday cooking and washing practices, so it's worth a visit on that basis alone. It's a very different, much more low-key experience than Te Puia and will give you a privileged glimpse into modern marae life. See p. 170, .

East Cape, Eastland. I'm in two minds about singing the praises of remote beauties like East Cape because an influx of visitors invariably changes things. But if you want to see the richness of Maori life untouched by tourism, this is the place to do it. Forty-five percent of Gisborne's population is Maori but around East

> The haka *is a traditional Maori war dance now used as a dramatic welcome for visitors, for rejoicing in victories, and for protesting injustices. You can see one performed at Te Puia, among other places.*

Cape, the percentage is much higher. Te Reo Maori (language) is used in everyday life and in some places you'll see few Pakeha (Europeans). The long journey around the cape will take you past hundreds of marae but you must not enter them without permission—they are after all, someone's private homeland. See p. 209, .

Museum of New Zealand–Te Papa Tongarewa, Wellington. Te Papa is a partnership between Pakeha and Maori culture and it includes a range of magnificent exhibitions featuring some of the country's most significant Maori treasures. It also features a unique 21st century carved meetinghouse, where visitors can share in formal Maori welcomes and *hui* (tribal) ceremonies. There are also some beautiful historic marae buildings here that you can enter (without shoes and without cameras). Although the interior of every marae is different, it will give you an idea of basic marae style and architecture. See p. 256, .

The Best Beaches

> *There's no better place than the sprawling white sands of Mount Maunganui for getting an insight into New Zealand summer holiday culture.*

Matai Bay, Karikari Peninsula. The farther north you go the better the beaches get—at least in terms of isolation and smaller crowds of people. Those on skinny Karikari Peninsula, particularly the intimate twin horseshoes of Matai Bay, are close to perfect. These lonely seascapes will quickly lull you into a sense of paradise lost. See p. 110.

90 Mile Beach, Far North. Closer to 90 kilometers than 90 miles, this vast sweep of beach is not so much a swimming and sunbathing destination as a geographic attraction. Every February it hosts a surf-casting contest offering big prize money and thousands come along to watch. The crowds are also attracted to its massive sand dunes, especially at Te Paki at the northern end. As tempting as it seems, don't drive on the beach; as rusted wrecks in the sand will attest, this is a hazardous business that always ends in tears. See p. 110.

Mount Maunganui, Bay of Plenty. This was the beach I visited during summer holidays as a child. Not a lot has changed. The population still almost triples in summer, it's still a major surfie hangout, the beach babes are still gorgeous, and the nearby Mount (Mauao), formerly a Maori fortress, is still a popular walking spot. See p. 128, ⑬.

Coromandel beaches. The eastern side of this peninsula is famous for its many beautiful beaches and you'll have to beat your way through crowds of New Zealanders, who have made this their summer holiday destination for generations. Waihi, Whangamata, Cooks, New Chums, Hot Water, and Hahei beaches are the top favorites. You'll find the beach camping grounds overflowing with people who've settled in their tents, sometimes for months on end. See p. 142.

Abel Tasman National Park beaches. Kaiteriteri Beach has become a little gentrified lately with paved walkways and such, but it's still the most accessible and most popular of the stunning Abel Tasman beaches, favored for its golden sand, good swimming, boating, fishing, and its pretty-as-a-picture seascapes. See p. 300, ⑥.

The Best Dining Experiences

> *Savoring wild game at Wellington's classy Logan Brown is a culinary highpoint in the capital city.*

The French Café, Auckland. This multi-award-winning restaurant is formal, polished, and sophisticated, yet not so stuffy you can't relax and enjoy yourself. Chef-owner Simon Wright and his wife, Creghan Molloy Wright, are a strong partnership. Sugar-coated salmon, roasted French goat cheese, seared duck breast, and a crème caramel are all classic examples of the divine modern French food served. See p. 74.

The Grove, Auckland. There's a string of awards associated with this formal joint, including Supreme Winner of Auckland's 2010 Restaurant of the Year Awards. Owners Michael and Annette Dearth run a tight ship, ensuring service is impeccable, the meals outstanding, and wine choices plentiful. Although formal, the restaurant has a relaxed bistro feel to it. Sink into deep brown leather seats and savor terrine of rabbit and duck served with white raisin puree and truffle brioche, followed by butter poached crayfish served with roasted poussin, young carrots, and edamame. See p. 74.

Matterhorn, Wellington. The original Matterhorn was started back in 1963. It's a Wellington icon and now, fresh from a contemporary makeover and new ownership, it's back on the "hot list." It's open all hours, morphing from café to lunch spot to cocktail bar, night restaurant, and late-night hangout. Clever design, moody lighting, and tucked away rooms give it oodles of character, and the food is always sublime. See p. 281.

Logan Brown, Wellington. Al Brown and Steve Logan are known for their love of honest simple cooking—that's the emphasis of their television cooking shows and books too—and local fish and game dishes are their signature successes. It's an elegant restaurant in a former bank vault, all white starched cloths, leather booths, and Corinthian columns. See p. 280.

The Bunker, Queenstown. Don't start celebrating until you've actually found the discreet door that leads to this culinary gem in the back lanes of Queenstown. Notoriously hard to find (all part of the marketing charm) and expensive when you get there, this moody, leather-filled den deserves all the superlatives it gets. Expect lots of local game, a big wine list, and an enviable collection of single malt whiskeys. After dinner, you can sit by the fire with the hip bar crowd. See p. 402.

The Best Luxury Stays

> *A top golf course, first class cuisine and prime rural views are all draw cards at The Farm at Cape Kidnappers.*

Kauri Cliffs, Matauri Bay, Northland. When you're snuggled into your luxurious villa, with native bush brushing against side windows and big picture windows opening out to breathtaking views of a perfect par-72 David Harman-designed golf course, life doesn't seem bad. Set on 2,630 hectares (6,500 acres) of rolling coastal farmland, this world-class lodge commands its cliff-top location with dignity and style. Outstanding cuisine, massages on a private beach, and a divine day spa are top indulgences. **See p. 114.**

Huka Lodge, Taupo. It's hard to surpass the luxuries provided by Huka Lodge. There's a number of New Zealand properties nipping at its heels, but none have quite the same indefinable quality that keeps royalty, celebrities, and world leaders coming back decade after decade. As the menacing bulk of the Waikato River sidles by at the bottom of the lawn, you can be tucked away in the glamorous wine cellar, feasting on award-winning cuisine. **See p. 189.**

The Farm at Cape Kidnappers, Hawke's Bay. This is a sister property to Kauri Cliffs and Matakauri Lodge in Queenstown; like its siblings, it delivers the best of everything, including a spectacular, cliff-top, par-72 golf course designed by Tom Doak. Sublime is a word that springs to mind. Everything about it is chic and sumptuous, with rurally inspired rooms looking about over a green tablecloth of farmland to the sea beyond. Lying back in the heated pool, cocktail in hand, you're a world away from noise and distraction. **See p. 225.**

Otahuna Lodge, Christchurch. This huge country mansion, built in 1895, is one of the finest examples of Queen Anne architecture in Australasia and it still has some period elements. Built for Canterbury gentleman Sir Heaton Rhodes, it has hosted royalty and been party to all the luxury that came with the Victorian landed gentry. Now it delivers a new kind of luxury—the kind that comes with large suites and award-winning cuisine served at a huge antique dining room table. **See p. 359.**

My Favorite Boutique Hotels

Hotel de Brett, Auckland. High style and modern technology meet old hospitality in this gorgeous hotel, with plush rooms individually decorated in mid-20th-century modern style. It has come a long way since its days as the Commercial Hotel, Auckland's first hotel, established in this building in 1841. See p. 81.

Ohtel, Wellington. Architect Alan Blundell indulges his passion for mid-20th-century modern design and furnishings in this small hotel in a prime waterfront location. Every room is cool and contemporary, embellished with collectible German ceramics. Alan has also put a strong emphasis on sustainability, with solar-powered showers and recycling facilities. This place has the courage to be different and I love it. See p. 285.

The George, Christchurch. This multi-award-winning member of the Small Luxury Hotels of the World group focuses its attention on individual guest needs and providing an experience they'll remember long after—and that includes a take-home teddy bear called George. They've annexed an old adjacent homestead, which has two luxury suites and one studio apartment, plus a formal dining room, lounge and kitchen for those looking to book the whole property. The hotel itself has a quiet, understated glamour. See p. 359.

Eichardt's Private Hotel, Queenstown. This hotel delivers first-class service to guests lucky enough to snare one of the five glamorous in-house rooms. Demand has been such that they've opened up an equally exclusive cluster of four modern two-bedroom suites a short distance away, on the lakefront. Rooms here are lavish and elegant—classic Virginia Fisher, the designer responsible for the interiors of several of New Zealand's top exclusive lodges. See p.398.

> Enjoy the classy 1960s-style surroundings at Ohtel.

2 The Best All-New Zealand Itineraries

New Zealand Highlights

I hear it all the time: "This is such a small country but we never realized there would be so much to see; we wish we'd allowed more time." Seeing New Zealand in one week is possible but it will require early starts and long days. Personally, I'd ditch the car idea and fly between four major stops—Auckland, Wellington, Christchurch, and Queenstown—to save time. There are regular internal flights between all major cities and if you shop around some of the smaller airlines, you can get good deals. I've planned this as a flying itinerary; otherwise, you'll spend 90% of your time in a vehicle suffering from jet lag, with little energy left over for the sights.

> PREVIOUS PAGE *Another brave customer leaps off the Kawarau River suspension bridge with AJ Hackett Bungy.* THIS PAGE *Relive the elegance of turn-of-the-century travel on Queenstown's iconic vintage steamship TSS Earnslaw.*

START **Fly into Auckland.**

❶ Arrive in Auckland. Try to arrive early and focus your attention on **Viaduct Harbour** (p. 44, **❹**), a great introduction to New Zealand's passion for boats. This is where the America's Cup yacht race was staged between October 1999 and March 2000 and again between 2002 and 2003. Go for a sail on *NZL 40* yacht, which is moored here. The **Voyager New Zealand National Maritime Museum** (p. 51, **❿**) is also here and gives a great overview of our maritime history and short cruises on the

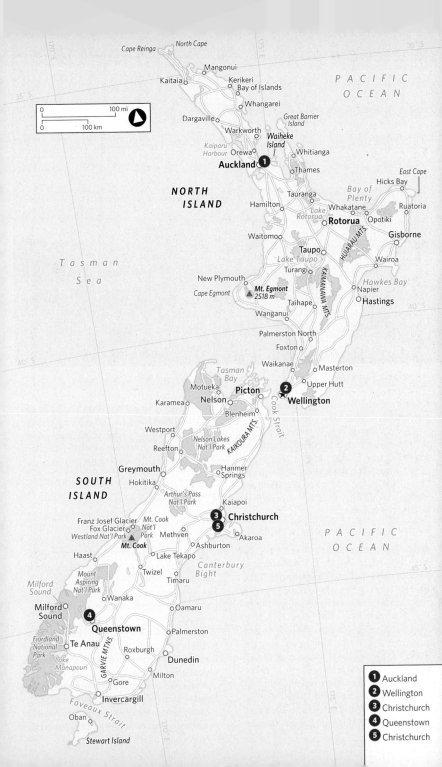

> *Auckland's Viaduct Harbour is home to multi-million dollar yachts and fabulous restaurants.*

historic scow *Ted Ashby*. In between, join the crowds lazing about over good coffee and fine food, or perhaps take a jaunt across the water on Devonport ferry to browse around **Devonport village** (p. 51, ⓲). On your second day, visit the **Auckland Art Gallery** in the morning (p. 46, ❶) and embark on an **Auckland art walk** (p. 54, ❸). ⏲ 2 days. For more on Auckland, see chapter 3.

On day 3, get up early and fly to Wellington.

❷ **Wellington.** For the definitive overview of New Zealand, go straight to the **Museum of New Zealand–Te Papa Tongarewa** (p. 256, ❶). This is a big museum and you should allow a minimum of two hours to get the most from your visit. Also, don't forget to check out the fabulous museum store for high-quality souvenirs. Follow that with a walk along the waterfront and call in at **Museum of Wellington City & Sea** (p. 265, ❽) to get an understanding of the capital's maritime history. Walk down to the **Lambton Quay** shopping precinct (p. 275) and catch the **cable car** (p. 258, ❷) up to **Wellington Botanic Garden**

(p. 260, ❻). This is also where you'll find the **Carter Observatory** (p. 260, ❹), which will introduce you to the astonishing beauties of the Southern Hemisphere skies. ⏲ 1 day. For more on Wellington, see chapter 9.

On day 4, take an early flight to Christchurch.

❸ **Christchurch.** On February 22, 2011, central Christchurch was devastated by a 6.3-magnitude earthquake that killed an estimated 180 people and condemned some 775 buildings, many of them historic treasures, to demolition. Recovery and rebuilding efforts will go on in the city for years after the life of this guidebook. However, the Christchurch Airport is open and still acting as a gateway to the south island; many attractions in greater Christchurch and Canterbury were unaffected by the quake; and by the time you hold this book in your hands, it's likely that a number of central Christchurch attractions, hotels, and restaurants will be open that we were unable to report on in these pages. Regardless of the pace of recovery, Christchurch's central location, proximity to a host of activities, and status as the primary south island

> *Around 1.5 million visitors a year flock to the Museum of New Zealand – Te Papa Tongarewa in Wellington.*

airport hub make it well worth a spending a day in the area. ⏱ 1 day. For more on Christchurch, see chapter 11.

Take a morning flight to Queenstown. Hire a car at the airport.

④ Queenstown. Ease into relaxed Queenstown life with morning coffee at one of the many local cafes. Find your way to Brecon Street and take a ride on the **Skyline Queenstown gondola** (p. 372, ❸) to the top of Bob's Peak. Enjoy a late lunch at the **Skyline restaurant** (p. 403), overlooking the spectacular landscape. Back at street level, call into the **Kiwi Birdlife Park** (p. 372, ❹) to meet some of our native creatures and explore a replica Maori village. Then drive down to Steamer Wharf and set off on a cruise on **TSS *Earnslaw*** (p. 391). This gives you a wonderful lake perspective, the chance to take terrific photographs, and an insight into New Zealand farming when you arrive on the opposite shore.

On your second day in Queenstown, rise early, meet the locals for breakfast at **Joe's Garage** (p. 403), and then have the quintessential adventure experience on **Shotover Jet** (p. 373,

❽). Drive on to the impossibly cute, historic village of **Arrowtown** (p. 374, ❾), explore the former Chinese Miners' Camp, and do a spot of shopping. If you're ready for more action, head to **Gibbston Valley** (p. 374, ❿) and **AJ Hackett Bungy Centre,** the original bungy jump. If leaping off bridges isn't your thing, at least do the very good Secrets of Bungy Tour and watch others taking the leap. The architecture of the bungy center is well worth seeing. While you're here, visit **GVW Winery** for a spot of wine tasting and perhaps a visit into their underground barrel hall. Alternatively, use this day to enjoy a **scenic flight to Milford Sound** (p. 370, ❶). ⏱ 2 days. For more on Queenstown, see chapter 12.

Fly back to Christchurch to connect with your international flight.

❺ Christchurch. If you have time between flights, visit the nearby **Orana Wildlife Park** (p. 345, ❼), or **Willowbank Wildlife Reserve** (p. 345, ❾), where you're sure to see a kiwi. Alternatively, unwind with a round of golf at **Clearwater Resort Golf Club** (p. 354).

The Best of New Zealand in 2 Weeks

Two weeks in New Zealand gives you more opportunities to drive between destinations and take in the color of the provinces. Still, don't underestimate the time your journey will take. New Zealand has good roads, but 20km (12 miles) in some parts of the country could involve narrow, steep, and winding routes—which means it might take you twice as long to negotiate them as you might expect. In general, roads are well maintained and all major roads are paved. Drive with care on narrow, unpaved roads if you venture into remote areas. What I've suggested here gives you a taste of both main islands, sticking to centers with the greatest concentration of activities.

> *Rotorua Museum of Art & History began life as a Bath House in 1908; people from all over the world visited to soak in therapeutic waters.*

START Fly into Auckland.

1 Auckland. Spend your first 2 days as described in "New Zealand Highlights," above. The morning of the third day, do some shopping (p. 62), or spend a morning relaxing at **Mission Bay Beach** (p. 50, **4**). ⏲ 2½ days.

Take a midday flight to Rotorua. Hire a car at the airport and drive to your hotel. Have dinner (p. 70) and spend the night.

2 Rotorua. If you want a day of complete rest and solitude in unabashed luxury, head for **Treetops Lodge & Estate** (p. 189). If you want to see the sights, go straight to **Rotorua Museum of Art & History** (p. 158, **1**) for an excellent overview of geothermal, Maori, and volcanic history. Remember to wander **Government Gardens,** surrounding the museum, exploring Maori carvings and mud pools for free. Spend

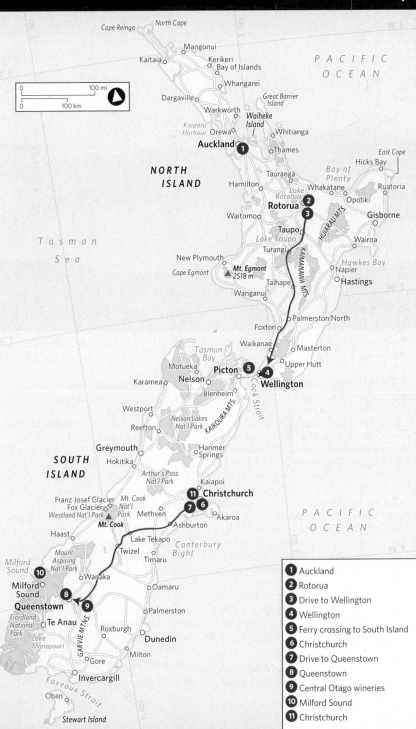

1. Auckland
2. Rotorua
3. Drive to Wellington
4. Wellington
5. Ferry crossing to South Island
6. Christchurch
7. Drive to Queenstown
8. Queenstown
9. Central Otago wineries
10. Milford Sound
11. Christchurch

> *Stop to enjoy picture-postcard views of Lake Tekapo as you drive from Christchurch to Queenstown.*

the rest of the afternoon at **Te Puia** (p. 168, ❸) to see bubbling mud, the famous Pohutu Geyser, a superb replica Maori village, weaving and carving schools, and Maori cultural performances. Watch the sun set over the lake and relax in a hot rock pool at **Polynesian Spa** (p. 161, ⓫), before heading out for dinner and turning in. On your second day, leave Rotorua and drive south on St. Hwy. 5 to take in some of the thermal attractions. My pick is **Waiotapu Thermal Wonderland** (p. 161, ⓬), which has plenty of colorful, intensive geothermal activity within a relatively small area. If you're back in town by early afternoon you could take a free wander around **Ohinemutu Village** (p. 171, ❻), the original Maori village on the lakefront, followed by a walk along the **Redwood Memorial Grove Track** (p. 167, ⓯). Finish the night with a tour and cultural performance at **Tamaki Maori Village** (p. 172, ❽). ⏱ 2 days. For more on Rotorua, see chapter 6.

On day 6, rise early for a day of driving to Wellington. The trip is 460km (286 miles) and will take about 6½ hr.

❸ **Drive to Wellington.** Allow a full day for this trip so that you can stop along the way to take photographs, enjoy snacks, and visit any sites of interest. But be careful, as roads in the Rotorua region are often busy with huge logging trucks. The journey will take you around Lake Taupo, where there are plenty of lake-edge stops for photographs, through the stark beauty of Tongariro National Park, and through heartland farming provinces. Your most direct route to Wellington is via St. Hwy. 1 along the Kapiti Coast, but if you're up for a slightly longer journey, you could go via the **Wairarapa** (p. 290) and stop for coffee and snacks in **Greytown** (p. 291, ❸) before driving the last taxing, winding, uphill leg over the Rimutaka Hills to Wellington. To take the Wairarapa route, follow signs from Palmerston North to St. Hwy. 2. Drive through the Manawatu Gorge and follow signs to Masterton/Greytown. The 131km (81-mile) drive takes about 1 hour and 45 minutes. ⏱ 1 day.

❹ **Wellington.** ⏱ 1 day. For more on Wellington, see p. 14, ❷.

Rise early on day 8 and catch one of the first ferries to Picton.

5 **Ferry crossing to South Island.** Catch the **Interislander Ferry** (☎ 0800/802-802; www.interislander.co.nz). The 3-hour trip is an experience in its own right and if the weather's good you'll have a picturesque passage through Queen Charlotte Sound to Picton. Catch the 1:40pm **TranzCoastal** (p. 306). This rail journey is a scenic feast through vineyards and along a rugged coastline hugged by steep mountains. You might want to get out for some whale-watching at **Kaikoura** (p. 339, **14**), or continue on to Christchurch, arriving around 7pm. ◷1 day.

6 **Christchurch.** ◷1 day. For more on Christchurch, see p. 14, **3** and chapter 11.

On day 10, leave Christchurch early on St. Hwy. 1, following signs south to Queenstown. It's 486km (302 miles), about a 7-hr. drive.

7 **Drive to Queenstown.** Prepare to be impressed by the landscapes on this wonderful road trip. Allow a full day so you can stop along the way and enjoy the small villages you pass through. You'll pass by the unbelievably turquoise Lake Tekapo—look out for the stop at the south end of the lake, which affords picture-perfect views of Aoraki/Mount Cook—and through the grand beauty of Lindis Pass. Stop on the Queenstown side of Cromwell to take photographs of some of the region's vineyards and wineries. Don't miss stops at the fresh summer fruit stalls along the way. Apricots are near perfect here. ◷1 day.

8 **Queenstown.** Sleep in and eat breakfast late at **Joe's Garage** (p. 403) before taking an early cruise across Lake Wakatipu on the vintage steamship **TSS *Earnslaw*** (p. 391). When you get back to town, take the **Skyline Queenstown gondola** (p. 372, **3**) up to Bob's Peak for breathtaking views over Queenstown. Leap off the **bungy** (p. 388) if you dare, or descend on the gondola and wander into the **Kiwi Birdlife Park** (p. 372, **4**) to see some of our native creatures and a replica Maori village. ◷1 day. For more on Queenstown, see chapter 12.

9 **Central Otago wineries.** Visit **Queenstown i-SITE Visitor Centre** (p. 405), to pick up a copy of the Central Otago wine map and drive yourself around the wineries, sampling wines that

> *The Interntaional Antarctic Centre, near the Christchurch Airport, makes a great final stop before you head home.*

are making this region famous. Closest to Queenstown are **GVW Winery** and **Chard Farm** in the **Gibbston Valley** (see p. 374, **10**). Don't miss GVW's wine cave, the adjacent cheesery, and the winery's excellent lunches under a canopy of vines. Alternatively, wander around central Queenstown stores for excellent duty-free shopping or take in a round of golf at **Millbrook Resort Arrowtown** (p. 393), then finish off with a soothing massage in the splendid spa. ◷1 day.

10 **Fly to Milford Sound.** Be up early on day 13 for a memorable scenic flight or helicopter ride to **Milford Sound** (p. 370, **1**). Flying is by far the best option if you're short on time, although it is weather dependent. Bus tours can take around 12 hours round-trip. When you're back in Queenstown at the end of the day, take a walk along the lakefront and watch the sun set over the water. ◷1 day.

11 **Return to Christchurch.** Enjoy a lazy morning in Queenstown before flying to Christchurch to connect with your international flight. If you have time between the two flights, go to the **International Antarctic Centre** (p. 336, **8**) near the airport, or, if you've yet to see a live kiwi, check out the nearby **Willowbank Wildlife Reserve** (p. 345, **9**). If you fancy big cats, visit the cheetahs at **Orana Wildlife Park** (p. 345, **7**).

New Zealand with Kids

Kids will love New Zealand. There are enough weird, wonderful, curious, funny, and interesting things on these islands to amuse the most inquiring child's mind. This two-week tour centers on Auckland, Rotorua, and Nelson, which have the best concentration of kid-related activities. Another option would be to pitch a tent at a northern beach camping ground and let the kids run wild and free for a week. Much of the gut-busting excitement of Queenstown has age limits but if your kids are old enough, also check out the 10 Action-Packed Days in the South Island tour, outlined later in this chapter.

> They make 3 tons of snow every day at Kelly Tarlton's Antarctic Encounter & Underwater World, to keep the penguins happy.

START Fly into Auckland.

❶ Auckland. Pick up a rental car at the airport when you arrive and start slowly with an easy day, checking out combo deals and family passes at the **Auckland i-SITE Visitor Centre** (p. 87) at **Viaduct Harbour** (p. 44, ❹). Kids can watch the boats and visit the **Voyager New Zealand Maritime Museum** (p. 51, ❿). Boys, especially, seem to get a real kick out of a ride on the historic scow, *Ted Ashby*. From Viaduct Harbour it's a short walk uphill to **Sky Tower** (p. 42, ❶), where they'll get a thrill

out of whizzing up the side of the tower in the exterior glass lift. Let them walk over the glass floor and make sure everyone takes in the bird's-eye view of the city. Spend the rest of the afternoon enjoying a leisurely wander around the city shops. On your second day, impress the kids right from the start with **Kelly Tarlton's Antarctic Encounter & Underwater World** (p. 48, ❸). Where else can they see an underground colony of penguins or hand-feed a giant sting ray? Spend at least two hours here as there's plenty for kids to do. From

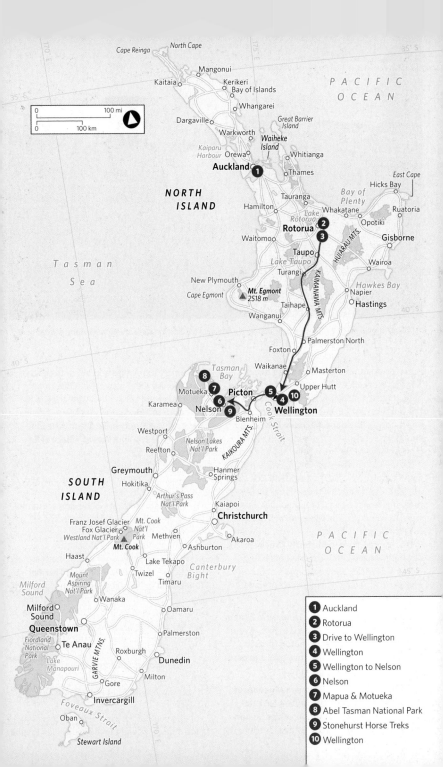

Cape Reinga
North Cape
Mangonui
Kaitaia
Kerikeri
Bay of Islands
Whangarei

PACIFIC
OCEAN

Dargaville
Great Barrier
Island
Warkworth
Kaiparu
Harbour
Waiheke
Island
Orewa
Whitianga
Auckland ❶
Thames

East Cape
Hicks Bay

NORTH
ISLAND

Tauranga
Bay of
Plenty
Whakatane
Ruatoria
Hamilton
Lake
Rotorua
Opotiki
Gisborne
Rotorua ❷
Waitomo
❸
Wairoa
Taupo
HUIARAU MTS.
Lake Taupo
Turangi
Hawkes Bay
New Plymouth
KAIMANAWA MTS.
Napier
Cape Egmont
▲ **Mt. Egmont**
2518 m
Hastings
Taihape
Wanganui

Tasman
Sea

Palmerston North
Foxton
Waikanae
Masterton
Tasman
Bay
❽
Upper Hutt
Motueka
❼ **Picton**
❺ ❿
❻
❹
Nelson
❾
Wellington
Karamea
Blenheim

Westport
KAIKOURA MTS.
Cook Strait

SOUTH
ISLAND

Reefton
Nelson Lakes
Nat'l Park
Hanmer
Springs
Greymouth
Hokitika
Arthur's Pass
Nat'l Park
Kaiapoi
Franz Josef Glacier
Mt. Cook
Nat'l Park
Christchurch
Fox Glacier
Westland Nat'l Park ▲ **Mt. Cook**
Methven
Akaroa

PACIFIC
OCEAN

Haast
Ashburton
Lake Tekapo
Canterbury
Bight
Mount
Aspiring
Nat'l Park
Twizel
Timaru
Milford
Sound
Wanaka
Oamaru
Milford
Sound
Queenstown
Palmerston
Fiordland
National
Park
Te Anau
Roxburgh
Dunedin
GARVIE MTS.
Lake
Manapouri
Milton
Gore
Invercargill
Foveaux Strait
Oban
Stewart Island

❶ Auckland
❷ Rotorua
❸ Drive to Wellington
❹ Wellington
❺ Wellington to Nelson
❻ Nelson
❼ Mapua & Motueka
❽ Abel Tasman National Park
❾ Stonehurst Horse Treks
❿ Wellington

> *Rolling down a hill in the Zorb's plastic bubble is just one of the thrills in store at Rotorua's Agroventures park.*

there, drive around to **Mission Bay Beach** (p. 50, ④), rent roller blades, swim at the beach, have a picnic lunch, buy ice creams, and feed the seagulls. Back in central city, spend the afternoon at **Auckland Museum** (p. 42, ②) and make sure you let them loose in the superb Discovery Centre, where they can open drawers and touch exhibits. On your third day, get off to an early start at **Auckland Zoo** (p. 50, ⑦). Check out the daily animal encounters and view sea lions through underwater viewing windows. The **Museum of Transport & Technology** (p. 50, ⑧) is nearby and from there, you can drive to **Butterfly Creek** (p. 51), flirt with winged beauties, ride on the Red Admiral Express, and see animals at Buttermilk Farm. ⏱ 3 days. For more on Auckland, see chapter 3.

Leave Auckland on St. Hwy. 1 and drive 234km (145 miles) to Rotorua. Allow 2 to 3 hr. If you feel like a break, stop at Hamilton (p. 138) and feed the ducks at Hamilton Lake and burn some energy at the playground.

② **Rotorua.** Start off at **Rotorua Museum of Art & History** (p. 158, ①) and experience a simulated volcanic eruption in the theater there. Kids will love climbing the stairs into the

museum's attic spaces and out onto the museum roof for great views over Government Gardens. Spend some time wandering in the gardens to see mud pools and Maori carvings. Next, take a leisurely drive around the Blue and Green lakes to the **Buried Village of Te Wairoa** (p. 172, ⑨), which was destroyed by the eruption of Mount Tarawera in 1886. Walk the fern-clad paths to the waterfall and see who can be first to see fat trout in the stream that follows the pathway. Have a snack in the village cafe or head back into town and let the kids play on the lakefront, where there's a playground and takeaway snack cart.

The next day, check out one of the thermal attractions—my pick is **Waiotapu Thermal Wonderland** (p. 161, ⑫). Back in town, feed the kids from one of the takeaway stands at the lakefront and then let them loose at **Skyline Skyrides** (p. 165, ⑥), where they can plummet downhill on a luge or, better still, have an adventure in the **Zorb,** one of many activities at the **Agrodome and Agroventures** (p. 162, ①)—I'd plan to spend the afternoon here. Finish with a relaxing dip at **Polynesian Spa** (p. 161, ⑪).

Spend your last day in the region exploring Maori culture. Spend the morning investigating the wonders of **Te Puia** (p. 168, ❸), which includes a thermal reserve with mud pools and the national Maori carving and weaving schools. Stay and watch Pohutu Geyser blow its top and let kids watch the carvers and weavers at work at the institute. In the afternoon take a guided tour of **Whakarewarewa Thermal Village** (p. 170, ❺), which is a real Maori village as opposed to the replica that is Te Puia. Let the kids buy a corn cob, which will be cooked for them in one of the steaming geothermal pools. If the Maori kids are diving from the bridge, give your kids a handful of coins to throw to the divers. Set the evening aside for a hangi meal and a Maori experience at **Tamaki Maori Village** (p. 172, ❽). ⏱ 3 days. For more on Rotorua, see chapter 6.

Rise early for a day of driving to Wellington. It's 460km (286 miles) and about 6½ hr. away.

❸ **Drive to Wellington.** The drive south normally takes about 5 to 6 hours but allow a day. Stop at **Huka Falls** (p. 179, ❻), just off the main highway north of Taupo, then have a go at the **Lake Taupo Hole in One Challenge** (p. 178, ❸). Have a picnic at one of the little

beaches around the lake. Continue to Tongariro National Park and enjoy the beautiful mountain landscapes. Continue south via the Kapiti Coast, stopping at your leisure. Settle into your accommodation and have a wander around some of the city shops or go for a walk along the capital's waterfront. ⏱ 1 day.

❹ **Wellington.** Spend your first 3 hours exploring the **Museum of New Zealand–Te Papa Tongarewa** (p. 256, ❶) and allow extra time for the kids to experience the interactive displays on the ground floor. Let them run free along the waterfront after that—there'll be boats and people aplenty for them to watch, and ice creams to be eaten. Head up the **Wellington Cable Car** (p. 258, ❷) next to **Wellington Botanic Garden** (p. 260, ❻), where you should take them to the **Carter Observatory** (p. 260, ❹). This is a marvelous interactive experience where they will see and learn plenty. If you never got to the zoo in Auckland, don't miss the **Wellington Zoo** (p. 264, ❹) and its interactive animal experiences. Wander down **Cuba Mall** (p. 275) in the late afternoon and let the kids get wet in the Bucket Fountain. ⏱ 1 day. For more on Wellington, see chapter 9.

> *People of all ages love using the interactive displays in Our Space at Wellington's Te Papa museum.*

> *Over 50 classic cars and hundreds of inspiring costumes are on display at Nelson's World of WearableArt™ & Classic Cars Museum.*

Get up early to catch a ferry to Picton.

❺ Wellington to Nelson. The Interislander Ferry (☎ 0800/802-802; www.interslander. co.nz) has movie theaters and play areas for kids; there are snack bars and plenty of deck levels for them to explore. When you arrive in Picton, hire a car and drive to Nelson, a journey that normally takes about 2 hours. Stop 10 minutes short of Nelson at **Happy Valley Adventures** (p. 310, ❺). In Nelson, wander about the shops to get a feel for this friendly little town and then buy fish and chips or pizza for dinner. ⏱ 1 day.

❻ Nelson. Start day 10 at the **World of WearableArt™ & Classic Cars Museum** (p. 314, ❼) where everyone's eyes will pop out on stalks. Allow a good 2 hours to check out the crazy costumes and the vintage cars before heading back to **Nelson Fun Park** (p. 308, ❶) and **Natureland Zoo** (p. 308, ❷). For lunch, take a picnic to nearby **Tahunanui Beach** (p. 310, ❹). Spend the afternoon swimming, making sandcastles, and relaxing on one of the most popular beaches in the area. ⏱ 1 day.

Leave Nelson on St. Hwy. 6, heading to Richmond and on to Mapua via the Coastal Highway (St. Hwy. 60); it's about 19km (12 miles), a 20 min. drive.

❼ Exploring Mapua and Motueka. On your way out of Nelson, stop just out of Richmond to watch glass blowing at **Höglund Art Glass** (p. 314, ❽), then drive to **Mapua** (p. 300, ❹), visiting pottery studios along the way and stopping at orchards stalls for a crisp apple snack. At Mapua Wharf, kids can dabble fingers in open displays at Touch the Sea Aquarium and have a yummy late lunch at the **Naked Bun Patisserie** (p. 300, ❺). Drive on through Motueka, following signs to **Kaiteriteri Beach** (p. 300, ❻), one of the prettiest golden-sand beaches you'll ever see. Spend the afternoon playing and swimming. Stay at Kaiteriteri or Motueka for the night. ⏱ 1 day.

Drive through Kaiteriteri on the Sandy Bay-Marahau Rd. and around to Marahau (4km/2½ miles).

❽ Abel Tasman National Park. Hook up with **Abel Tasman Wilson's Experiences** (p. 318) at Kaiteriteri and take a half-day cruise up this

> *Nelson's golden sand beaches are a major holiday draw for hundreds of New Zealand families every summer.*

beautiful coast. They also offer kayaks and combination cruise/kayak tours. Get back to Nelson in time for dinner—perhaps fish and chips on the beach as the sun sets. ⏱ **1 day.**

9 Outdoor adventures. Get a feel for Nelson's big open spaces on a 4-hour outing with **Stonehurst Farm Horse Treks** (p. ###). They'll take you over hill-country farming land, down valleys, along rivers, and over plains. Don't forget to take your camera and a picnic to have in the country afterwards. In the afternoon, hire bikes (p. 316), go swimming at the beach, or fish off the end of the Nelson wharves. If you'd rather have a less active afternoon, you'll find plenty to amuse kids at **Founders Heritage Park** (p. 300, **7**), where they can see how New Zealand life used to be in colonial times. ⏱ **1 day. For more on the Nelson region, see chapter 10.**

10 Return to Wellington. Rise early for the 2-hour drive to Picton. Allow time to wander along the foreshore to watch boats coming and going, before getting back on the ferry to Wellington. Connect with your international flight home in the afternoon or early evening.

> *You haven't lived until you've been kayaking in the crystal clear waters of Abel Tasman National Park.*

A Wine Lover's Tour

New Zealand has come of age as a producer of internationally acclaimed wines and the great thing about the country's six major grape-growing regions is that they're packed into some of the most stunning landscapes. They're often close to outstanding food producers and many wineries have terrific restaurants. Some winemakers offer boutique lodgings and impressive architecture is to the fore. You could easily spend 2 to 3 weeks on a New Zealand wine tour because it offers so much more than just wine and vineyards, but the following itinerary—a mix of driving and flying—outlines a 10-day tour of highlights.

> Waiheke Island, just 35 minutes from Auckland city, is home to numerous boutique wineries and vineyards.

START **Fly into Auckland.**

1 Arrive in Auckland. The greater Auckland region (including Waiheke Island) has over 100 vineyards and wineries. Head for **Glengarry Wines,** corner of Sale and Wellesley sts. (☎ 09/308-8345; www.glengarry.co.nz), in center city to sample your first New Zealand wines and to pick up information on New Zealand wine tourism. Have dinner at **Vinnies** (p. 77). Opt for the wine-matched degustation menu for a special treat. ⏱ 1 day.

From inner city, get onto Northwestern Motorway. Take Te Atatu Rd. exit and at second roundabout, exit onto Edmonton Rd., then turn right into Great North Rd. Follow signs to Henderson Valley. The drive is about 20km (12 miles) and 25 minutes.

2 Henderson Valley. This is New Zealand's oldest grape-growing region and there is a bundle of wineries along Henderson Valley Road and Lincoln Road. Seek out **Soljans Estate's Winery and Cafe,** (☎ 09/412-5858; www.soljans.co.nz), for lunch from a

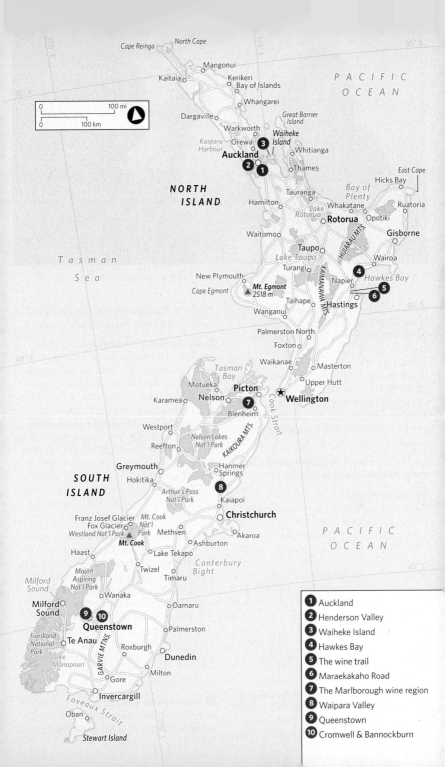

PACIFIC OCEAN

Cape Reinga
North Cape
Mangonui
Kaitaia
Kerikeri
Bay of Islands
Whangarei
Dargaville
Great Barrier Island
Warkworth
Kaipara Harbour
Orewa
Auckland
Waiheke Island
Whitianga
Thames

NORTH ISLAND

Tauranga
Hamilton
Lake Rotorua
Rotorua
Bay of Plenty
Whakatane
Opotiki
Ruatoria
Hicks Bay
East Cape

Waitomo
Taupo
Lake Taupo
Turangi

Gisborne

Wairoa

New Plymouth
Cape Egmont
▲ **Mt. Egmont** 2518 m
Taihape
Wanganui
Napier
Hawkes Bay
Hastings

HUIARAU MTS.
KAIMANAWA MTS.

Tasman Sea

Palmerston North
Foxton
Waikanae
Masterton
Upper Hutt

Motueka
Tasman Bay
Nelson
Picton
Blenheim
Karamea

Cook Strait

Wellington ★

Westport
Nelson Lakes Nat'l Park
KAIKOURA MTS.

Reefton
Greymouth
Hanmer Springs
Hokitika
Arthur's Pass Nat'l Park

SOUTH ISLAND

Kaiapoi
Christchurch

Franz Josef Glacier
Fox Glacier
Westland Nat'l Park
Mt. Cook Nat'l Park
▲ **Mt. Cook**
Methven
Ashburton
Akaroa

Haast
Lake Tekapo
Canterbury Bight

Mount Aspiring Nat'l Park
Twizel
Timaru

Milford Sound
Wanaka
Oamaru

Milford Sound
Queenstown
Palmerston

Fiordland National Park
Te Anau
GARVIE MTS.
Roxburgh
Dunedin

Lake Manapouri
Gore
Milton

Invercargill

Foveaux Strait
Oban

Stewart Island

PACIFIC OCEAN

Scale: 0 — 100 mi / 0 — 100 km

① Auckland
② Henderson Valley
③ Waiheke Island
④ Hawkes Bay
⑤ The wine trail
⑥ Maraekakaho Road
⑦ The Marlborough wine region
⑧ Waipara Valley
⑨ Queenstown
⑩ Cromwell & Bannockburn

> *Sample award-winning wines at family-owned Soljans Estate's Winery and Cafe near Kumeu.*

Mediterranean-inspired menu, then drive on to **Nobilo Wines,** 45 Station Rd., Huapai (☎ 09/412-6666; www.nobilowinegroup. com), especially known for its sauvignon blancs. The safest and most practical way of touring is with Phil Parker's **Fine Wine Tours** (☎ 09/849-4519; www.finewinetours.co.nz), as you don't have to worry about getting lost, and you won't risk drinking and driving. Return to the city to dine at **The French Café** (p. 74). ⏱1 day.

On day 2, catch the ferry to Waiheke Island at the Ferry Terminal on Quay St.

❸ **Waiheke Island.** Pick up a rental car and some maps from the Waiheke Island Visitor Centre, 2 Korora Rd., Oneroa (☎ 09/372-1234; www.waihekenz.com), and set off to visit some of the 45 vineyards on the island. You can't really get lost on this little paradise, and if you did, would you care? **Fullers** (☎ 09/367-9111; www. fullers.co.nz) and **Ananda Tours** (☎ 09/372-7530; www.ananda.co.nz) both offer wine tours if you'd rather leave the driving to someone else. If you do strike out on your own, make sure you visit **Te Whau Vineyard & Café,** 218 Te Whau Dr. (☎ 09/372-7191; www.tewhau.com), which has more than 500 cellared wines. It's highly rated by *Wine Spectator* and has an impressive menu. Splurge on a stay at **Te Whau Lodge,** 36 Vintage Lane, Te Whau Point (☎ 09/362-2288; www.tewhaulodge.co.nz), where you'll wine and dine in style overlooking vineyards. ⏱1 day.

Return to Auckland on a morning ferry and head for Auckland International Airport.

❹ **Hawkes Bay.** Fly to **Napier** (p. 220) and hire a car at the airport, so you can explore this bountiful province filled with endless grapes, oh-so-pretty Art Deco architecture, gorgeous boutique vineyard accommodations, and some of the best wines in the country. Spend the afternoon at **The National Aquarium of New Zealand** (p. 220, ❶) for a change of pace. After exploring the Art Deco buildings of Tennyson Street, drink afternoon champagne at the bar of **The County Hotel** (p. 225) before settling into an evening meal at one of the restaurants recommended on p. 226. ⏱1 day. For more on Napier and Hawke's Bay, see chapter 7.

❺ **Exploring the wine trail.** On day 5, do a fun bicycle tour of a handful of vineyards with **On Yer Bike Winery Tours** (p. 203), passing olive groves, orchards, wineries, and ostrich farms. Take your camera, as well as bottled water, a hat, sunscreen, and sunglasses. Splash out on dinner at the unforgettable **Terroir** (p. 227) at Craggy Range Winery in the Havelock North area. Get there in daylight so you can look through the fabulous winery and tasting gallery. ⏱1 day. For more on Hawke's Bay wineries, see chapter 7.

❻ **Maraekakaho Road.** Head for the vineyards in the Maraekakaho Road area, finishing up at **Sileni Estates,** 2016 Maraekakaho Rd.

(☎ 06/879-8768; www.sileni.co.nz), in time for lunch. Head back into Napier for a 2-hour, self-guided afternoon **Art Deco walk** (p. 220, ❺). Make sure you stop at **Ujazi** (p. 227) for coffee and cake. ⏱1 day.

Rise early for the 4-hour, 325km (202-mile) journey to Wellington via the Wairarapa. Go straight to the Interislander ferry terminal for the crossing to Picton.

❼ **The Marlborough wine region.** If you'd like to spend time in the **Wairarapa region** (p. 290) exploring the **Martinborough wineries** (p. 291, ❺), cut your Hawke's Bay stay by a day and head south a day earlier. Otherwise, continue on to the Interislander ferry and cross to **Picton** (p. 302). Hire a car when you land (it's a good idea to book in advance). You'll find world-class vineyards as far as the eye can see throughout Marlborough. Take plenty of film and stamina, along with a wine map from the **Picton i-SITE Visitor Centre** (p. 323). Splurge on dinner at **Herzog** (p. 322), an Epicurean heaven with top European chefs. ⏱1 day. For more on the Marlborough region, see chapter 10.

Drive the 3½ hr. south on St. Hwy. 1 to Waipara Valley. It's about 200km (124 miles).

❽ **Waipara Valley.** Call in at **Waipara Springs Winery,** St. Hwy. 1, Waipara (☎ 03/314-6777; www.waiparasprings.co.nz) for coffee and save your appetite for lunch at award-winning **Pegasus Bay Winery & Restaurant,** just down the road. Visit other local wineries, including **The Mud House Winery & Café**—you can't miss its huge brick building that comes before your turnoff to Pegasus Bay Winery. Mud House also does a very good lunch with wine tasting if you'd rather dine there. Pegasus has a more formal (and more expensive) restaurant. ⏱1 day. See p. 336, ❿.

Drive 50 min. south on St. Hwy. 1 to Christchurch. As you enter the outer suburb of Belfast, look out for airport signposts, turn right into Johns Rd., and follow signs to the airport. Catch an early evening flight to Queenstown. It's about 58km (36 miles).

❾ **Queenstown.** Assuming you hired a car when you landed at Queenstown airport, start day 9 by picking up a Central Otago wine map

> You'll find award-winning cuisine and over 500 cellared wines at Te Whau Vineyard & Café on Waiheke Island.

from the **Queenstown i-SITE Visitor Centre** (p. 405) and head out to **Amisfield Winery** (p. 375, ⑪) overlooking Lake Hayes. Enjoy wine tasting and morning coffee before moving on to the wineries of **Gibbston Valley,** (p. 374, ❿), including Chard Farm and Peregrine Wines. Make an extended stop at GVW Winery to have lunch and explore their wine tunnel, the great gift shop, and the adjacent cheesery. When you get back into Queenstown, make it your mission to find the secretive wine and foodies' paradise, **The Bunker** (p. 402), for dinner with perfectly matched wines. ⏱1 day.

Leave Queenstown on the Gibbston Highway, driving through Kawarau Gorge. Carry straight on to Cromwell or turn right into Pearson Rd. after the gorge to get to the Bannockburn wine region. Both Cromwell and Bannockburn are well signposted. It's about 60km (37 miles) and 1 hr. away.

❿ **Cromwell and Bannockburn.** Take a scenic drive through Kawarau Gorge. Near Cromwell stop at fruit stalls and **The Big Picture,** corner of Sandflat Rd. and St. Hwy. 6 (☎ 03/445-4052; www.bigpicturewine.com) for an excellent film, a tasting auditorium, a selection of wines and gourmet foods, and a cafe. If you'd rather take a tour of this area, contact **Queenstown Wine Trail** (☎ 0800/827-8464; www.queenstownwinetrail.co.nz) or **Appellation Central Wine Tours** (☎ 03/442-0246; www.apellationcentral.co.nz). The wineries in this region are especially known for their pinot noirs. Catch a late flight to Christchurch to meet your international connection.

10 Action-Packed Days on South Island

The title of this itinerary assumes you're a fun-loving, adventure-seeking, fear-proof adrenaline addict with tons of stamina. If that's the case, you might want to head straight for Queenstown and stay there. It has more crazy, pulse-quickening activities per square inch than anywhere else and most are easily accessed without a vehicle. There's also an active hotel pick-up plan at work. I haven't listed late-night fun here because that's a whole other story; chapter 12 gives you the pointers you'll need to ensure your nights are as vigorous as your days.

> Get a great Queenstown view from AJ Hackett's Bungy.

START **Fly into Queenstown.**

❶ Arrive in Queenstown. Spend the day regaining preflight energy with a leisurely amble around the town's adventure suppliers. Get social at **Joe's Garage** (p. 403), the preferred hangout of local adventure types, and soak up the energetic hum of hundreds of fellow international thrillseekers. Do some research at the **Queenstown i-SITE Visitor Centre** (p. 405) and have a few drinks at **Tatler** (p. 403), where local bar staff will fill you in on all the best nightspots. ⏱ 1 day.

❷ Up and about. Start day 2 with a gobsmackingly daring burst of speed through high rock canyons on the **Shotover Jet** (p. 373, ❽). Pick up your stomach and head back into town and take the **Skyline Queenstown gondola** (p. 372, ❸) to the top of Bob's Peak. Pick up speed with a few luge rides and scare yourself with a **bungy** (p. 388) overlooking the town. If you still have money and energy to burn, float back down to Queenstown park via a **tandem parapente** (p. 397). ⏱ 1 day.

❸ The ultimate jump. Be the ultimate daredevil and tackle the full **AJ Hackett Bungy** (p. 388) package—yes, that means all four of them! Start with 43m (141 ft.) at the **Kawarau Suspension Bridge,** site of the first commercial bungy

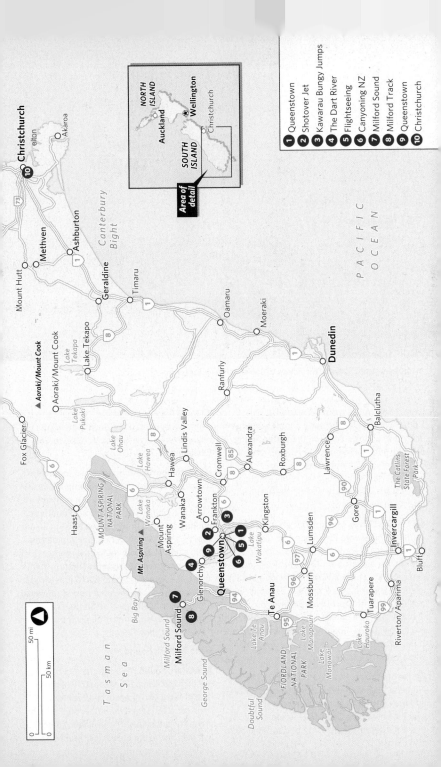

1. Queenstown
2. Shotover Jet
3. Kawarau Bungy Jumps
4. The Dart River
5. Flightseeing
6. Canyoning NZ
7. Milford Sound
8. Milford Track
9. Queenstown
10. Christchurch

> *You'll get terrific views on the ride up to Bob's Peak in Queenstown.*

jumps, and work your way up (and down) from there. If you've already done **The Ledge** at the top of Bob's Peak, do the **Ledge Swing** instead—or try the bungy here again at night. Forget being squeamish and take your camera because all four bungys are in stunning landscapes. Make sure you get the T-shirt that attests to your courage! ⏱1 day.

4 The Dart River. Imagine rivers wild and calm overhung with lush ferns, the sound of native birdcalls—and the excited squeals of your fellow adventurers. The Dart River deserves all the superlatives. Start with a 5-hour jet-boat ride and a walk through unspoiled native bush with **Dart River Safaris** (p. 396). If you're short on daredevil confidence after all the bungy jumps, float the river with Funyaks. A day to remember in an amazing unspoiled wilderness. ⏱1 day.

5 Take to the air. Push your budget to the limits with a helicopter ride into the mountains and have the highest altitude picnic you're ever likely to enjoy. See p. 391 for descriptions of the numerous flightseeing options available.

This is a once-in-a-lifetime experience that's worth every cent. Calm down afterwards by taking a leisurely afternoon cruise on **The Earnslaw** (p. 391). ⏱1 day.

6 Watersports. Fast-paced watersports are today's test. Start with **Canyoning NZ** (p. 391) and you'll be slipping down river canyons in a wet suit and a helmet. **Serious Fun River Surfing** (p. 397) brings a new twist to an old sport—it's all washing-machine rapids and rapid slithering down rocky river gorges. In the afternoon, go **white-water rafting** (p. 397). There are several operators to choose from and river grades to suit your nerves, physical prowess, and stamina. The Shotover River is generally viewed as more challenging than the Kawarau. ⏱1 day.

Fly to Milford Sound.

7 Milford Sound. Your toughest choice will be fixed-wing or helicopter. Whichever kind of flight you choose, be prepared to be impressed by jagged mountain peaks, lush greenery, unbelievably blue lakes, golden tussock, and azure blue skies. Team up with

> *Floating down the Dart River in a Funyak.*

Rosco's Milford Kayaks (p. 396) for a surreal paddling adventure on Milford Sound. Take your camera and stay overnight at one of the Te Anau accommodations I've suggested on p. 398. ⏱ 1 day.

⑧ Milford Track. Join a 1-day guided walk on Milford Track with **Trips 'n' Tramps** (☎ 03/249-7081; www.milfordtourswalks. co.nz), just 12 people getting a taste of this world-famous mountain route. Enjoy total silence, majestic mountain landscapes, remote passes, a wilderness tea break, photography stops, waterfalls, and rainforest glades. This may be the quietest of your adventures but it may be the *pièce de résistance.* ⏱ 1 day.

⑨ Back to Queenstown. Return to Queenstown by helicopter or plane (the 5- to 6-hour bus trip is dead time) and spend the afternoon chilling out by the lake. There are several bars on Steamer Wharf that will be only too happy to help you relax. Or go shopping for New Zealand-made outdoor clothing in the small, easily negotiated shopping zone. ⏱ 1 day.

⑩ Back to Christchurch. Rise before dawn and join **Sunrise Balloons** (p. 394) for a last magical overview of the Queenstown area, where mountains and lakes rise out of the early morning mists. It's the perfect memory to take away before you drive back to Christchurch and fly home.

1 Week in the Subtropical North

It always astounds me that so many overseas visitors arrive in Auckland and immediately drive or fly south—or that they avoid the North Island altogether in favor of the South. Sure, the South Island landscapes are more dramatic but the top of the North Island, especially in summer, is a quintessential Kiwi experience: white-sand beaches, warm oceans, endless days of swimming and sunbathing, barbecues at the beach, campfires, parties, boats, surf, and sun. I've mapped out a week that will have you quickly relaxing into a New Zealand summer, leaving it up to you as to whether you spend one, two, or more nights in any one place.

> Sail the sparkling waters of Waitemata Harbour aboard the Voyager New Zealand National Maritime Museum's historic scow, Ted Ashby.

START Fly into Auckland.

1 Auckland. Rest for a while before heading off to **Viaduct Harbour** (p. 44, **4**), which will give you an instant appreciation of New Zealanders' obsessions with boats. Sit in one of the stylish cafes and watch the boats come and go. Visit the **Voyager New Zealand National Maritime Museum** (p. 51, **10**) for an insight into what the ocean really means to New Zealanders. In the afternoon, visit **Auckland Museum** (p. 42, **2**). Drive around to the seaside promenade at **Mission Bay Beach** (p. 50, **4**) and have a picnic dinner as you watch people swim at sunset.

It's straight into the water on day 2 for a rare sailing experience on an America's Cup yacht, **NZL 40** (p. 44, **4**). It's all sea spray, sunshine, and flapping sails out there, plus you'll have great views of the city skyline. Enjoy lunch wharf-side and then go up the **Sky Tower** (p. 42, **1**) to enjoy the view. ⊕ **2 days.**

Take St. Hwy. 1 north to Whangarei. It's about 158km (98 miles) and about 2 hr.

2 Whangarei. This pretty northern city is the gateway to some of the loveliest beaches in the country. Spend one or two nights in the area if you're a beach lover; I've listed my favorite beaches starting on p. 108. The **Poor Knights Island Marine Reserve** (p. 110) is bathed in tropical currents and has some

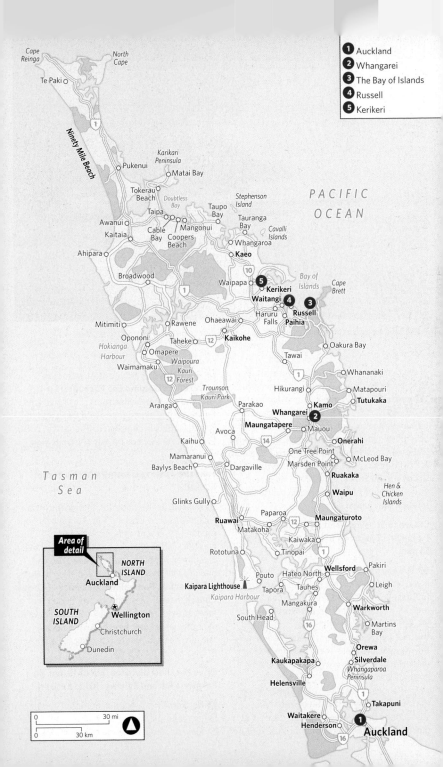

> *The Northland coast unfolds in an endless series of pristine, near-empty white sand beaches.*

of the richest marine life in the world, making it a diver's paradise. In the city itself, the **Whangarei Town Basin** is a fun place to start (p. 96, ❶). That's where you'll find international yachts moored, along with a cluster of boutiques, cafes, and the intriguing Clapham's National Clock Museum. **Whangarei Museum & Kiwi House** (p. 98, ❷) and the **Native Bird Recovery Centre** (p. 98, ❸) are also worth a visit. ☺ At least 1 day. For more on the Whangarei area, see chapter 4.

Return to St. Hwy. 1 and follow signs north to Paihia. It's 70km (44 miles) and about 1 hr. 15 min.

❸ **The Bay of Islands.** Stay in Paihia (p. 114) if you want to try all the attractions, or go to **Russell** (p. 114) if you're after a peaceful retreat. Visit **Waitangi Treaty Grounds** (p. 92, ❶) for an insight into Maori culture and the makings of our nation. Wander some of the lovely boardwalks there that run through native bush and mangrove swamps. On the grounds you'll also find the massive Maori *waka* (canoe) on display by the beach. Sit on the beach and enjoy the sun before trying some of the best water-based activities. **Explore NZ's On the Edge** catamaran adventure

(p. 94, ❽) is a beauty to start with. Don't miss **Fullers Dolphin Eco Encounter** (p. 113). **Gungha's Super Cruise** (p. 113) will give you a terrific sailing experience—and no visit to the Bay of Islands is complete without that. ☺ 2 days. For more on the Bay of Islands area, see chapter 4.

Take the water taxi from Paihia across to Russell.

❹ **Russell.** Believe it or not, this sleepy little village was New Zealand's first organized European settlement and our first capital. That was back in the wild days of the 1800s; things are somewhat more peaceful now. You can find out all about this key early history at **Russell Museum, Pompallier Mission,** and **Christ Church,** as well as simply by wandering the quiet streets. Finish your day here with a walk over the hill to **Long Beach.** Take a dip and relax in the sand before returning to Paihia. ☺ 1 day. See p. 94, ❸–❼.

Drive the short distance (about 15 min. via Puketona Rd. and St. Hwy. 10) to Kerikeri.

❺ **Kerikeri.** This is our northern fruit capital. Enjoy citrus, persimmons, kiwifruit, and macadamia nuts. Stop at **Makana Confections** (p.

> *Te Whare Runanga on the Waitangi Treaty Grounds is one of the few traditionally carved Maori meeting houses that allows photographs.*

95, ⑫) for mouthwatering chocolates and at **Kerikeri Bakehouse Café** (p. 106, ⑦) for picture-perfect picnic food. Take your bounty down to the Kerikeri Basin and eat by the river before exploring local sights like the **Kerikeri Mission Station** (p. 95, ⑨), **Rewa's Village** (p. 106, ⑧), and **Wharepuke Subtropical Garden** (p. 95, ⑩). Spend the afternoon at **Marsden Estate Winery** (p. 117) or drive to a local beach and swim until the sun goes down. ⊕ 1 day.

Return to Auckland the way you came, via St. Hwy. 1. There's flexibility in this itinerary to spend more than one or two days at any of the listed stops. If you wish to explore further north from the Bay of Islands—and I strongly recommend it if you have the time—you could drive straight to the Bay of Islands on your first day (about 4–5 hours driving), spend a day or two there and then head farther north, following suggestions I've made for attractions and accommodations in the chapter 4. The farther north you go, the warmer and less crowded it gets.

> *Northland's warm, subtropical climate gives rise to lush vegetation and flowers that you won't find growing freely elsewhere in New Zealand.*

3
Auckland

My Favorite Moments

Auckland is known as the City of Sails—people here own more boats per capita than anywhere else in the world. It's our biggest, flashiest city and I don't know why so many travelers bypass it as little more than an entry point. It's leafy, luscious, and beautiful, and having the world's largest Polynesian population gives it a unique character. It's a place to enjoy daring adventures, superb New Zealand wine, white-sand beaches, and world-class art. You can explore offshore islands and dead volcanoes, and nowhere else in the world can you sail on superyachts at such a reasonable price.

> *PREVIOUS PAGE Auckland's Sky Tower is designed to withstand wind gusts up to 200kmph (124mph). THIS PAGE New Zealanders love boats and Auckland's Viaduct Harbour is a yachtie's paradise.*

❶ Taking photos from the top of Sky Tower. Even with a fear of heights, I ritually make my way to the top of this, one of the tallest structures in the Southern Hemisphere, to take photographs of the amazing panoramic views of the city and harbor. See p. 42, ❶.

❷ Browsing shops in Ponsonby. I love strolling along one of Auckland's hippest streets (especially on Saturday, when everyone is out to be seen) and browsing the boutiques and cafes. See p. 69.

❸ Eating ice cream on Mission Bay Beach. Just 20 minutes from the center of downtown Auckland, this great little beach is hugely popular on summer weekends. Come along and be part of the action. See p. 50, ❹.

❹ Watching penguins at Kelly Tarlton's Antarctic Encounter & Underwater World. You'll

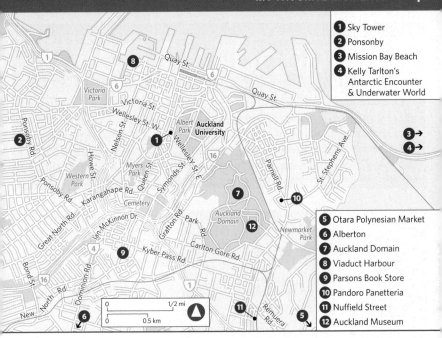

1 Sky Tower
2 Ponsonby
3 Mission Bay Beach
4 Kelly Tarlton's Antarctic Encounter & Underwater World

5 Otara Polynesian Market
6 Alberton
7 Auckland Domain
8 Viaduct Harbour
9 Parsons Book Store
10 Pandoro Panetteria
11 Nuffield Street
12 Auckland Museum

be bewitched by this, the only underground, self-sustaining population of Gentoo and King penguins in the world. They live happily in a simulated Antarctic environment, complete with saltwater pools. See p. 48, 3.

5 **Visiting Otara Polynesian Market.** Come here to get a feel for Auckland's Polynesian core. It's the largest Polynesian market in the world and is filled with larger-than-life characters, exotic foods and smells, and a good selection of crafts. See p. 68.

6 **Exploring the old rooms at Alberton.** This fine old mansion offers an intimate peek into how Victorians colonialists passed their days. See p. 59, 21.

7 **Walking in Auckland Domain.** This is Auckland's oldest park, and it offers a network of lovely walks.

8 **Drinking coffee and people-watching at Viaduct Harbour.** Walk the marinas to see beautiful superyachts or just sit in one of the bars or cafes to while away a lazy summer afternoon. If you're a night owl, come back after dark to browse the hip bar scene. See p. 44, 4.

9 **Looking at art books at Parsons Bookshop.** Close to Auckland Art Gallery, this little den is an art and booklover's heaven. Step inside and leaf through a zillion glossy titles—I rarely manage to leave without buying something. See p. 63.

10 **Eating cake and pastries at Pandoro Panetteria.** I can't think of a better place for a special vacation indulgence than right here among cream-filled pastries at this Italian bakery. See p. 44, 3.

11 **Checking out the latest fashions in Nuffield Street.** This recent addition to the Newmarket shopping-scape is all about expensive designer labels from home and abroad; it's a fun place to window-shop. Finish off with coffee in one of the cafes. See p. 69.

12 **Looking at Maori treasures at Auckland Museum.** The museum's extensive Maori culture and natural history galleries present the largest collection of Maori and Polynesian artifacts in the world. The giant *waka* (war canoe) is one of the most impressive you'll see anywhere. See p. 42, 2.

Auckland in 1 Day

If you've decided to rush through Auckland in one day, I can help. I've put together a plan that introduces you to the most quintessentially Auckland attractions, plus a yachting adventure. I've allowed at least 30 to 40 minutes between stops because of Auckland's nightmare traffic infrastructure and parking shortages. If you'd rather ditch your car altogether, consider a day hopping on and off the Auckland Explorer Bus, which is detailed below.

> *If you lose your way in central Auckland, you only have to scan the horizon for the Sky Tower, the preeminent landmark.*

START SKYCITY on the corner of Federal and Victoria sts., downtown Auckland.

1 ★★★ kids **Sky Tower.** A glass lift whisks you to the top of this 328m (1,076 ft) tower in just 40 seconds. There are three observation decks. On the Lower Deck you'll find Orbit, the revolving restaurant and Observatory, the brasserie-style restaurant. The Main Observation Level features live weather feeds and touch computer screens giving geographical information. The Outdoor Observatory on this level has high-powered binoculars and is open to the elements. The Sky Deck is the highest public viewing area, with 360-degree views through seamless glass. If you're looking for an adrenaline rush check out Sky-Jump and SkyWalk. (See "Auckland for Adrenaline Junkies," p. 45). ⏰ 1 hr. SKYCITY (corner of Victoria and Federal sts.). ☎ 0800/759-2489 or 09/363-6355. www.skytower.co.nz. Admission to observation decks NZ$30 adults, NZ$14 kids 6–14, NZ$65 family. Admission to Sky Deck NZ$5 extra. Daily 8:30am–late.

2 ★★★ kids **Auckland Museum.** The huge classical form of this museum, perched on a hill in Auckland Domain, is impossible to miss. Inside, the Maori galleries house the world's largest collection of Maori and Polynesian artifacts, including

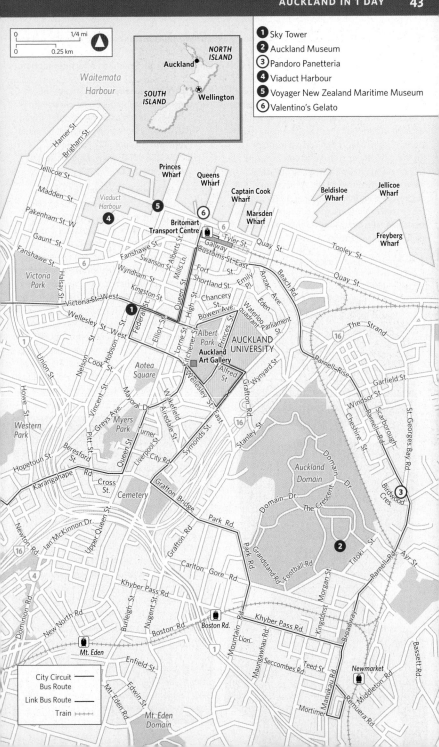

1 Sky Tower
2 Auckland Museum
3 Pandoro Panetteria
4 Viaduct Harbour
5 Voyager New Zealand Maritime Museum
6 Valentino's Gelato

the heavily carved Hotunui meetinghouse (1878) and the huge *waka* (war canoe), Te Toki-a-Tapiri (1836). The Natural History Gallery showcases everything from skeletons of dinosaurs and moa (a flightless bird) to shell collections. The Discovery Centre is aimed at kids but there's a lot that will interest adults as well. In addition, there are changing exhibitions, regular Maori cultural performances, and two excellent shops and cafes on site. ⏱ 2 hr. Auckland Domain. ☎ 09/309-0443. www.aucklandmuseum.com. Admission NZ$10, suggested donation. Additional charges apply for special exhibitions, guided tours, and Maori performances. Daily 10am–5pm; guided tours daily 11:30am and 2pm.

> *Ancient carvings at Auckland Museum give you an insight to the ancient Maori practice of facial* Ta moko—*tattoo.*

Drive a short distance on Domain Dr. to Parnell Rd. and turn left to get to the next stop, opposite the St. Stephens Ave. intersection.

③ 🍞 **Pandoro Panetteria.** Stop at this authentic Italian bakery to choose from a host of delicious picnic goodies. Head back to the Domain and have a picnic at your chosen spot. **427 Parnell Rd.** ☎ 09/358-1962. www.pandoro.co.nz. Most items NZ$4–NZ$10.

④ ★★★ kids **Viaduct Harbour.** This whole area—encompassing restaurants, bars, cafes, hotels, and apartments—was created in the late 1990s as the venue for the America's Cup yacht race. It was the first time in the history of the Cup that a special village had been created to support syndicates, corporations, superyachts, and the public together in one venue. Between October 1999 and March 2000, and again from October 2002 to March 2003, more than 2,000 competitors and millions of visitors crammed in to soak up the excitement of the America's Cup challenge. The harbor has also been a stop-over on the epic Volvo Ocean Race. The village changed the face of Auckland forever, providing first-rate entertainment and accommodation

Forget Driving

Avoid the nightmare that is Auckland traffic by buying a ticket for the Auckland Explorer Bus (☎ 0800/439-756; www.explorerbus.co.nz). It departs from the Ferry Terminal on Quay Street every 30 min from 9am to 4pm daily in summer and 10am to 4pm in winter. Other central city departure points are Civic Theatre (from 9:40am) and Sky Tower (from 9:45am). The bus visits 14 major Auckland attractions and you can hop on and off as many times as you like in a day, stopping at the attractions that appeal to you most. Some of the key attractions it visits are the Auckland Museum, SKYCITY, Parnell Village, Viaduct Harbour, Kelly Tarlton's Antarctic Encounter & Underwater World, and Auckland Zoo. An all-day pass costs NZ$35 adults, NZ$15 children, NZ$80 family. There is a free pick-up service from city hotels if you phone before 8:30am.

venues, including some of Auckland's best eateries. Get a taste of America's Cup yacht racing by taking a 2-hour sail on the *NZL 40* or *NZL 41*, built for the 1995 America's Cup challenge in San Diego and now moored here (book with Explore NZ, ☎ 09/359-5987; www.explorenz.com; NZ$150 adults, NZ$110 kids 10–15). 🕐 3 hrs (1 hr if you skip the sail).

❺ ★★★ kids **Voyager New Zealand Maritime Museum.** If you have time, squeeze in a visit to this excellent museum, which continues the yachting and maritime theme. 🕐 At least 1 hr. See p. 51, ❿.

From Viaduct Harbour, wander along the waterfront to the Harbour Board Building and Ferry Terminal.

⑥   🍦 **Valentino's Gelato.** Buy a big cone and sit outside, watching the ferries coming and going. Later, enjoy dinner at one of the restaurants I've suggested on p. 71. 99 Quay St. ☎ 09/358-0091. Gelato NZ$5–NZ$7.

Auckland for Adrenaline Junkies

My feet start tingling just thinking about walking around the upper rims of **Sky Tower,** much less jumping off it. But you can do both here: The 75-minute stroll around the 1.2m (4-ft.) rim 192m (630 ft.) above ground (wearing a body harness, of course) costs NZ$145 adults, NZ$115 kids 10–15. You can also opt to do a "base jump" off the tower; you fall, attached to a wire, for about 11 seconds then come to a landing in the plaza below (NZ$225 adults; NZ$175 kids). For details, see www.skywalk.co.nz or www.skyjump.co.nz (☎ 09/368-1835).

The **Sky Screamer,** at the corner of Albert and Victoria streets (☎ 09/377-1328; www.skyscreamer.co.nz) does the reverse of a normal bungy jump—it throws you skyward at a rate of 200kmph (124 mph). Prices start around NZ$50.

★★★ **Auckland Bridge Climb and Bungy** (☎ 09/360-7748; www.aucklandbridgeclimb.co.nz or www.bungy.co.nz) lets you choose between jumping off the Auckland Harbour Bridge and walking over the top of it. You get amazing views of Auckland on the 1½-hour guided Bridge Climb (pictured). By comparison, the 40m (131-ft.) bungy sounds easy—you just jump! Bridge Climb NZ$120 adults, NZ$65 kids 8–15; bungy NZ$120 per person.

Auckland in 2 Days

On your second day in Auckland, I recommend getting out to some of the more far-flung attractions. Auckland is the most spread-out city in the country and it has a confusing network of traffic-clogged motorways leading to the outer suburbs. Rather than sitting in your car studying maps for half the day, I've suggested a half-day tour in the afternoon that will enable you to see much more of the city. If you'd rather skip the morning's two inner city attractions, you could opt for two half-day tours or one full-day tour.

> Get a feel for New Zealand's cultural heritage at Auckland Art Gallery, which houses the country's largest art collection.

START Auckland Art Gallery is in the heart of the city just up from Queen St., on the corner of Wellesley and Kitchener sts.

1 ★★★ kids **Auckland Art Gallery (Toi o Tamaki).** This is New Zealand's premier art gallery. It's home to one of the most important collections of European Old Masters in the South Pacific. At press time, its early French-Renaissance-style buildings (1888) were closed for restoration and a new NZ$121-million extension. They should be open by the time you read this, but call first to check. The new extension's design (by Australia's Richard

Francis-Jones with Auckland architects Archimedia, and Auckland City Council) will make it one of the most exciting new buildings in the city. The gallery holds over 14,000 New Zealand and European works dating from the 14th century to present-day, including a superb collection of works by expatriate New Zealander Frances Hodgkins (1869–1947); early works by colonial artist Petrus Van der Velden (1837-1913); and a remarkable collection of 20th-century works by New Zealand's greatest modernist painter, Colin McCahon (1919–1987), which are shown in a dedicated

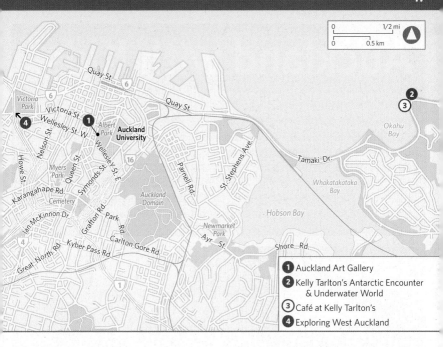

1 Auckland Art Gallery
2 Kelly Tarlton's Antarctic Encounter & Underwater World
3 Café at Kelly Tarlton's
4 Exploring West Auckland

room in the New Gallery across the street, home to the gallery's contemporary collections. ⏱ At least 1 hr. Main Gallery, corner of Kitchener St. and Wellesley St. E. ☎ 09/307-7700. Free admission; fees for some shows. New Gallery, corner of Lorne St. and Wellesley St. E. ☎ 09/307-4540. Free admission to downstairs galleries; NZ$12–NZ$25 for touring shows. www.aucklandartgallery.com. Both galleries open daily 10am–5pm.

Head east on Quay Street, which becomes Tamaki Drive. Kelly Tarlton's is well signposted on the right.

2 ★★★ kids **Kelly Tarlton's Antarctic Encounter & Underwater World.** The penguins in the Antarctic Encounter here are the must-see attraction, especially if you're traveling with kids. Underwater World and Stingray Bay are equally interesting. ⏱ At least 1½ hr. See p. 48, **3**.

③ 🐟 **Café at Kelly Tarlton's.** Grab a quick snack from the food kiosk here and head back into the city to meet your tour. 23 Tamaki Dr., Orakei. ☎ 0800/805-050. NZ$3–NZ$12.

4 ★★ **Exploring West Auckland.** Spend the rest of your day being driven in comfort on a small exclusive tour. **NZWinePro Auckland Wine Tours** (☎ 09/575-1958; www.nzwinepro. co.nz), offers two afternoon tours, both with free city pick-ups. One takes in food and wine producers in the Kumeu area, plus rugged black sand beaches and a gannet colony (NZ$165 per person); the other visits Henderson wine producers and the coastal settlement of Piha (NZ$180 per person). **Absolute Tours** (☎ 09/486-5212; www.absolutetours. co.nz), offers a 4-hour afternoon tour (with free pick-up) that takes you out into the countryside to boutique brewers and then back into the city to try cask-conditioned ales (NZ$170 per person). **Bush & Beach** (☎ 09/837-4130; www.bushandbeach.co.nz) has afternoon tours to west coast beaches and rainforest areas (NZ$140 per person). Alternatively, you could skip the first two stops on this itinerary and do a Maori-focused full-day tour with **Potiki Tours** (☎ 0800/692-3836; www.potikitours. com) that includes an urban marae visit, shellfish gathering at the beach, and much more (NZ$200 per person). ⏱ Half-day.

Auckland with Kids

Most of Auckland's major attractions are well suited to children, although some of the more adventure-focused activities (such as bungy jumping and walking the Harbour Bridge) have weight and height limits that will preclude younger children participating. But to compensate, there are numerous free activities that will appeal—dozens of parks, beaches, extinct volcano craters, and bush walks. This itinerary focuses on the key inner city attractions so you won't have to grapple with traffic too much. An all-day ticket on the Auckland Explorer Bus (see "Forget Driving," p. 44) is an economical, fun, and practical solution to getting around—and an adventure in its own right from a kid's perspective.

> This snarling big cat may look uncomfortably close, but there's solid plate glass between you and the animals at Auckland Zoo.

START Auckland Museum is in Auckland Domain, which can be accessed off Stanley St., Grafton Rd., Park Rd., Carlton Gore Rd., and Parnell Rd. in the suburb of Parnell. **TRIP LENGTH** About 60km (37 miles) and 3 days.

① ★★★ **Auckland Museum.** ⏱ 2 hr. See p. 42, **②**.

② 🍴 **Auckland Museum's Atrium Café.** In the interests of time-saving, have a snack before heading off to your next stop. Auckland Domain. ☎ 09/309-0443. Drink and sandwich about NZ$10.

Head east on Domain Drive, then turn left to drive down Parnell Rd., veering left onto Parnell Rise then right onto The Strand, then right onto Tamaki Dr. It's 7km (4⅓ miles) to the next stop, about a 15-minute drive depending on traffic. Or take the free shuttle departing opposite Ferry Terminal on Quay St.

❸ ★★★ **Kelly Tarlton's Antarctic Encounter & Underwater World.** Kids will love the 8-minute snowcat rides that take you through the colony of over 80 King and Gentoo penguins here. Phoebe, the giant short-tailed stingray,

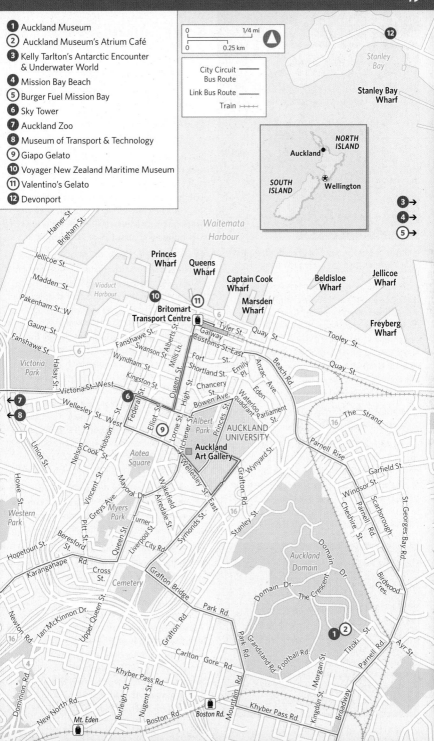

1 Auckland Museum
2 Auckland Museum's Atrium Café
3 Kelly Tarlton's Antarctic Encounter
   & Underwater World
4 Mission Bay Beach
5 Burger Fuel Mission Bay
6 Sky Tower
7 Auckland Zoo
8 Museum of Transport & Technology
9 Giapo Gelato
10 Voyager New Zealand Maritime Museum
11 Valentino's Gelato
12 Devonport

> No trip to Mission Bay Beach is complete without an ice cream from one of the promenade shops.

is also a big favorite. There is an excellent kids' interactive room and some exciting Animal Adventures, which include taking a plunge in a shark cage, snorkeling through thousands of fish, and scuba diving (all at extra cost). ⏱ 2 hr. 23 Tamaki Dr., Orakei. ☎ 0800/805-050 or 09/531-5065. www.kellytarltons.co.nz. Admission NZ$34 adults, NZ$10 kids 4–14. Daily 9:30am–5:30pm (last entry 4:30pm).

Continue around Tamaki Dr. to Mission Bay, 2km (1¼ miles).

❹ ★★ **Mission Bay Beach.** Spend the rest of the afternoon swimming and playing at this popular and safe beach. There's a big fountain and heaps of grassy play areas between the beach and the shopping/restaurant zone. The promenade is a favorite spot for rollerblading, bicycling, and walking. ⏱ Half-day.

Saving Money

Buy an Auckland Multipass to get four leading attractions—Sky Tower, Kelly Tarlton's, Fullers Auckland (ferries), and Rainbow's End—for one unbelievable price, at over 25% discount. It can be used over a 2-week period and includes a pass to revisit the attraction you liked the best. Purchase the pass at any one of the attractions, at an i-SITE Visitor Centre, or book online at www.aucklandmultipass.com. It costs NZ$99 for adults and NZ$59 for kids age 5–15.

❺ 🍔 **Burger Fuel Mission Bay.** You're probably starving by now, so indulge in a big healthy burger. 61 Tamaki Dr. ☎ 09/521-0400. Most burgers around NZ$10.

Day 2 starts at the Sky Tower, at the corner of Victoria and Federal sts.

❻ ★★★ **Sky Tower.** ⏱ 1 hr. See p. 42, ❶.

From Sky Tower, head west on Victoria St. W. and turn left into Hobson St. Take the ramp to the North Western Motorway and keeping right, merge onto the motorway. Take the exit onto St. Lukes Rd. Turn right at South Rd., then left into Great North Rd. Take the first right onto Motions Rd. The drive is 6km (3¾ miles) and about 15 or 20 minutes.

❼ ★★★ **Auckland Zoo.** While lions, tigers, and elephants are all bound to appeal, small children will get just as much fun out of the free-range hens and roosters that scuttle in and out of bushes and across walkways. The zoo covers a wide area so take your time. The South American Rainforest area, filled with all manner of monkeys, is always a hit; and Pridelands is home to the giraffe, zebra, ostrich, and rhinos. Stop halfway through for refreshments at one of the two zoo cafes, then continue on to see kiwi, tuatara (endemic reptiles that resemble lizards), parrots, lions, tigers, and sea lions. ⏱ At least 2 hr. Motions Rd., Western Springs. ☎ 09/360-3800. www.aucklandzoo.co.nz. Admission NZ$20 adults, NZ$10 kids 4–15, NZ$36–NZ$55 family.. Daily 9:30am–5:30pm (last admission 4:15pm).

It's a short drive back down Motions Rd. and left onto Great North Rd. to the next stop; or you can catch the tram that runs between the zoo and museum for a minimal fee.

❽ ★★ **Museum of Transport & Technology.** Kids will get a real thrill out of rides on old steam trains, traction engines, and numerous other vehicles. Free vintage tram rides, a mirror maze, flight simulators, and educational trails should keep everyone plenty busy for an hour or two. Young children might not have the stamina for both this museum and the zoo; consider picking one or the other depending on your kids' interests. ⏱ 2 hr. 805 Great North Rd., Western Springs. ☎ 0800/668-286 or 09/815-5800. www.motat.org.nz. Admission NZ$14 adults, NZ$8 kids 5–16, NZ$35 family. Daily 10am–5pm.

Follow Great North Rd. back to the city and continue onto Karangahape Rd., then turn left onto Queen St. Try to park as close as possible to Aotea Sq. and walk to the next stop.

⑨ 🍴 **Giapo Gelato.** Even if the kids are tired, they should perk up when you take them here for delicious Italian gelato made from 100% natural products. They also sell coffee and cake—you probably all deserve a treat after a busy day. **279 Queen St., next to Civic Theatre.** ☎ 09/550-3677. Gelato NZ$7.

Start day 3 at Viaduct Harbour.

⑩ ★★★ **Voyager New Zealand Maritime Museum.** The giant, white form of *KZ1* marks the entrance to some excellent maritime exhibitions. The museum covers Polynesian migrations and the arrival of European settlers, plus an excellent look at the place of boats in modern New Zealand culture. The stunning "Blue Water, Black Magic—A Tribute to Sir Peter Blake" exhibit highlights the work of Sir Peter before he was gunned down in the Amazon in 2002. Take a cruise aboard one of the museum's three historic vessels: *Ted Ashby,* a traditional ketch-rigged deck scow; *Breeze,* a traditional square-rigged brigantine sailing ship; and SS *Puke,* New Zealand's oldest working steamboat. ⏱ **2 hr. Viaduct Harbour.** ☎ 0800/725-897 or 09/373-0800. www. maritimemuseum.co.nz. Admission NZ$20 adults, NZ$10 kids 5–15, NZ$42 family. The 15-min trips on SS *Puke* are included in price of museum entry; additional charge for Ted Ashby and Breeze sailings. Daily 9am–5pm.

From Viaduct Harbour, wander along the Waterfront to the Fullers Ferry Terminal on Quay St.

⑪ 🍴 **Valentino's Gelato.** See p. 45, ⑥.

⑫ ★★★ **Devonport.** The 12-minute ferry to Devonport (Fullers Ferry; ☎ 09/367-9111; www.fullers.co.nz) departs every half-hour daily from 7:15am to 8pm, then every hour from 8pm to 11pm ($10 adult, $5 kids round trip). The ferry ride will give you wonderful views of Auckland city from the water and of the North Shore as you approach Devonport. Once there, you'll find it small and easy to negotiate. Just a short walk from the wharf on your way to the main street, the visitor center (p. 87) will help you get your bearings quickly and offer advice and timing for any local tours you find interesting. I suggest you browse the shops and cafes, taking particular note of **Devonport Chocolates**, 17 Wynyard St. (☎ 09/445-6001; www.devonportchocolates. co.nz), and then buy picnic supplies and head to the beach. Devonport Beach is the closest—just down from the village, across from the wharf—and it has safe swimming and a playground; or walk for about 20 minutes to get to pretty Cheltenham Beach, which occupies the stretch of coast on the other side of North Head. Just walk along King Edward parade, across the head on Cheltenham Rd., and you're there. Spend the afternoon picnicking, swimming, and lazing about. ⏱ **Half-day.**

At the End of the Rainbow

If you have more time to spend in Auckland, I have two more attractions to suggest. **Rainbow's End Theme Park,** Great South and Wiri Station Rds., Manukau City (☎ 0800/438-672; www.rainbowsend. co.nz), has 9 hectares (22 acres) devoted to crazy rides and attractions like roller coasters, Ferris wheels, bumper boats, and more. An All-Day Super Pass (NZ$50 adults, NZ$35 kids 4–13) gives you unlimited rides. Near the airport, **Butterfly Creek,** Tom Pearce Drive (☎ 09/275-8880; www. butterflycreek.co.nz) has everything from exotic birds and over 800 butterflies to a small farm, train rides, and crocodile encounters. Combo prices start around NZ$20 adults and NZ$10 kids.

Auckland Art & Architecture

More than any other New Zealand city, Auckland is a sprawling, sometimes unruly spread of suburbs that seems to get bigger every year. At its core is a battle between old and new, as modern high-rises replace smaller, older structures. For all that, it's still home to some grand old buildings and some inspiring examples of contemporary architecture. It has a host of art galleries and, if you know where to look, plenty of public sculpture. Step out on this 3-day itinerary to discover the best.

> *"Blue Water, Black Magic" is an architectural tribute to the late New Zealand humanitarian, Sir Peter Blake.*

START Auckland Art Gallery is in the heart of the city just up from Queen Street, on the corner of Wellesley and Kitchener streets.
TRIP LENGTH About 20km (12 miles) and 3 days (much can be done on foot).

① ★★★ **Auckland Art Gallery.** By the time you visit, the Main Gallery of New Zealand's finest art gallery should be open after a NZ$121-million upgrade and extension. ⏱ 1 hr. See p. 46 **①**.

② 🍴 **Café Reuben.** Enjoy a light lunch at this light, airy spot at treetop level in the New Gallery, across the street from the main Auckland Art Gallery building. The wonton soup here is divine, but the menu delivers everything from pasta to sandwiches, plus coffee and cake. ☎ 09/302-0226. NZ$8–NZ$18.

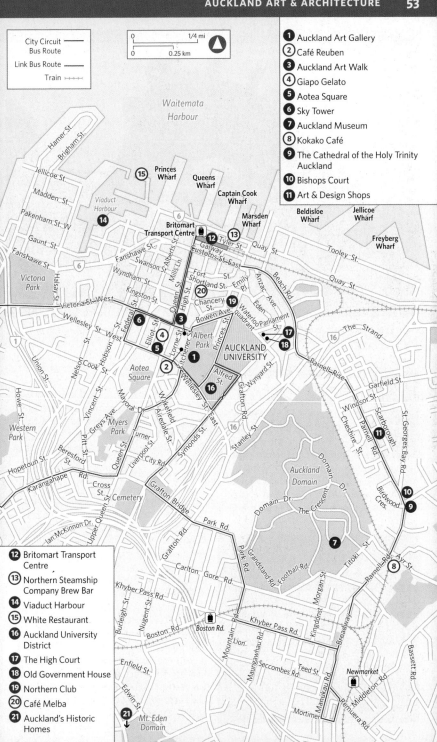

City Circuit Bus Route
Link Bus Route
Train

0   1/4 mi
0   0.25 km

1 Auckland Art Gallery
2 Café Reuben
3 Auckland Art Walk
4 Giapo Gelato
5 Aotea Square
6 Sky Tower
7 Auckland Museum
8 Kokako Café
9 The Cathedral of the Holy Trinity Auckland
10 Bishops Court
11 Art & Design Shops

12 Britomart Transport Centre
13 Northern Steamship Company Brew Bar
14 Viaduct Harbour
15 White Restaurant
16 Auckland University District
17 The High Court
18 Old Government House
19 Northern Club
20 Café Melba
21 Auckland's Historic Homes

Waitemata Harbour

Hamer St.
Brigham St.
Jellicoe St.
Madden St.
Pakenham St. W
Gaunt St.
Fanshawe St.
Halsall St.
Hobson St.
Nelson St.
Cook St.
Union St.
Howe St.
Western Park
Hopetoun St.
Karangahape Rd.
Cross St.
Ian McKinnon Dr.
Upper Queen St.

Princes Wharf
Queens Wharf
Captain Cook Wharf
Marsden Wharf
Beldisloe Wharf
Jellicoe Wharf
Freyberg Wharf

Viaduct Harbour

Britomart Transport Centre
Galway St.
Customs St. East
Tyler St.
Quay St.
Tooley St.
Beach Rd.
Anzac Ave.
Eden
Emily Pl.
Fort St.
Shortland St.
Chancery St.
Bowen Ave.
Waterloo Quadrant
Parliament St.

Victoria Park
Fanshawe St.
Swanson St.
Wyndham St.
Kingston St.
Victoria St. West
Wellesley St. West
Elliot St.
Federal St.
Lorne St.
High St.
Queen St.
Albert St.
Mills Ln.
Kitchener St.
Albert Park

AUCKLAND UNIVERSITY

Aotea Square
Wakefield St.
Airedale St.
Wellesley St. East
Wynyard St.
Alfred St.
Grafton Rd.
Vincent St.
Greys Ave.
Mayoral Dr.
Myers Park
Turner
Pitt St.
Beresford St.
Liverpool St.
City Rd.
Symonds St.
Stanley St.
Cheshire St.

The Strand
Parnell Rise
Garfield St.
Windsor St.
Scarborough St.
St. Georges Bay Rd.
Parnell Rd.
Birdwood Cres.

Auckland Domain
Domain Dr.
The Crescent
Grafton Bridge
Park Rd.
Grafton Rd.
Carlton Gore Rd.
Grandstand Rd.
Football Rd.
Titoki St.
Morgan St.
Kingdon St.
Ayr St.

Khyber Pass Rd.
Burleigh St.
Nugent St.
Boston Rd.
Mountain Rd.
Khyber Pass Rd.
Lion
Maungawhau Rd.
Seccombes Rd.
Teed St.
Manukau Rd.
Broadway
Middleton Rd.
Remuera Rd.
Mortimer
Bassett Rd.
Newmarket

Edwin St.
Enfield St.
Mt. Eden Domain

> *This large* waharoa *(gateway) in Auckland's Aotea Square was carved by Maori artist Selwyn Muru in 1990.*

SITE GUIDE
PAGE 55

❸ ★★ **Auckland Art Walk.** There are several dealer art galleries in this area (most open Tuesday through Saturday) but before you check those, walk across the road and up to Albert Park to view public sculptures by Chris Booth (above the steps on Kitchener Street), Reg Nichol, Andrea Lucchesi, Walter MacFarlane, Francis J. Williamson, and W. Parkinson. Back at street level, check out some of the city's top art stops.

Paper Treasures

Just across the road from Auckland Art Gallery, there is a treasure trove of rare manuscripts—some as early as the 10th and 11th centuries—along with early books, early Maori documents, and the largest collection of Alexandre Dumas manuscripts outside France. All of this is tucked away at **Auckland Central City Library,** 44-46 Lorne St. (☎ 09/377-0209; www.aucklandcity libraries.co.nz). Admission is free. It's open Monday to Friday from 9am to 8pm, Saturday and Sunday from 10am-4pm.

❹ 🍦 **Giapo Gelato.** See p. 51, ⑨.

❺ **Aotea Square.** Giapo's is right beside the city's main performing arts venue, the ★★ **Civic Theatre.** Originally designed by architects Charles Bohringer and William Leighton and built in 1929 in the style of an Indian temple, it was extensively refurbished in 1999. Inside, it has an amazing replica of the southern sky on the auditorium ceiling saved from the original building. On the western edge of Aotea Square, off Queen Street, is the **Aotea Centre** (☎ 09/307-5060), opened in 1990 by famed New Zealand soprano Dame Kiri Te Kanawa. Just across the square—remodeled in 2010— is the **Auckland Town Hall,** one of the city's best known buildings. The Great Hall seats over 1,600 and is modeled after the Gewandhaus Concert Hall in Leipzig, Germany. It is regarded as one of the finest acoustically tuned concert halls in the world. It hosts regular performances by the Auckland Philharmonia and the New Zealand Symphony Orchestra. To check current events, call The Edge at ☎ 09/307-5060 or go to www.akcity. govt.nz. ⏱ 1 hr.

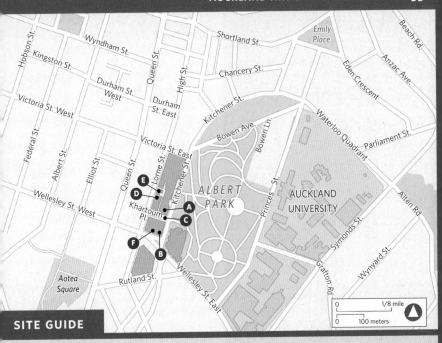

SITE GUIDE

③ Auckland Art Walk

There are several dealer art galleries in this area (most open Tuesday through Saturday) but before you check those out, walk across the road and up to Albert Park (when open, the gallery extension will include a landscaped link from Kitchener Street to the park), to view public sculptures by Chris Booth (above the steps on Kitchener St.), Reg Nichol, Andrea Lucchesi, Walter MacFarlane, Francis J. Williamson and W. Parkinson. Back at street level, check out New Zealand treasures at ⓐ **Fingers,** 2 Kitchener St. (☎ 09/373-3974; www.fingers.co.nz), a contemporary jewelry store. You'll find established artists at ⓑ **John Leech Gallery,** at the corner of Kitchener St. and Wellesley St. E. (☎ 09/303-9395). Look for new talent at ⓒ **Oedipus Rex Gallery,** opposite the New Gallery entrance on Khartoum Place (☎ 09/379-0588; www.orexgallery.co.nz). Next, check out what the influential dealers at ⓓ **Gow Langsford Gallery,** 26 Lorne St. (☎ 09/303-4290; www.gowlangsfordgallery.co.nz) have on display. You'll generally see some challenging new art projects at ⓔ **City Art Rooms,** Level 1, 28 Lorne St. (☎ 09/308-9855; www.cityartrooms.co.nz).

Just around the corner, you can round off your tour at the very fine ⓕ **Parsons Bookshop,** 26 Wellesley St. E. (☎ 09/303-1557; www.parsons.co.nz), which has a superb range of art and architecture books. ⏱ At least 3 hr.

> Be amazed by the stained glass windows created by leading contemporary artists at The Cathedral of the Holy Trinity in Parnell.

From here, walk back down Queen St., turn left into Victoria St. and head for the Sky Tower.

6 ★★★ **Sky Tower.** Designed by Craig Craig Moller Architects, Sky Tower is one of the tallest structures in the Southern Hemisphere. See p. 42, **1**.

7 ★★★ **Auckland Museum.** Start day two at this huge, neoclassical building (1929) designed by Auckland architects Grierson Aimer & Draffin. The towering seven-story Grand Atrium, designed by Auckland architect Noel

Art in the Park

If you have about an hour to spare, ask at the Auckland War Memorial Museum reception for the map and guide to the Auckland Domain Sculpture Walk, which features eight large public works scattered through the Domain not too far from the Museum.

Lane, opened in 2006. Inside, the museum presents a wealth of cultural treasures; from an art and architectural perspective, the Maori and Polynesian galleries will be of particular interest. ⏲ 2 hr. See p. 42, **2**.

Head east on Domain Dr. to Parnell Rd.

8 🍵 ★ **Kokako Café.** Stop for some superb coffee or choose from a good range of organic products and lovely salads. See if you can get a pavement table so you can watch the world go by. 492 Parnell Rd. ☎ 09/366-4464. NZ$14-NZ$16.

9 ★★★ **The Cathedral of the Holy Trinity Auckland.** It's worth a stop here just to see the breathtaking stained glass windows in the nave—the western side designed by Maori artist Shane Cotton, the eastern side by artist Robert Ellis. The window above the great doors was designed by artist Nigel Brown. The Cathedral itself was completed in two parts. The Gothic chancel, designed by Charles Towle, was built between 1959 and 1972; then from 1990 to 1996, the nave, designed by Richard H. Toy, Professor of Architecture at the University of Auckland, was added. It was Toy who also conceived the idea of shifting the original Auckland Cathedral, St. Mary's (1887), in one piece across Parnell Road to be part of the new cathedral complex. A wooden church of considerable beauty, St. Mary's was designed by Christchurch architect Benjamin Mountfort and constructed of native kauri. The stained glass windows on the north wall were designed by Auckland artist Claudia Pond Eyley. ⏲ At least 1 hr. Parnell Rd., Parnell. ☎ 09/303-9500. Free admission. Open to visitors Mon 10am-3pm, Tues-Fri 9am-3pm

10 ★★★ **Bishops Court.** Across the road from the cathedral complex, peek through the gate at the private residence of the Bishop of Auckland. The house was designed by architect/cleric Frederick Thatcher (1814-90) and completed in 1865. The library and bell tower fronting St. Stephens Avenue were built in 1863. ⏲ 10 min. St. Stephens Ave., Parnell.

11 ★★ **Art and Design Shops.** Two particularly good galleries on Parnell Road are **Essenze,** 223 Parnell Rd. (☎ 09/300-6238; www.essenze.co.nz), which stocks an excellent

> *It's all shimmering steel and glass at Britomart Transport Centre at the bottom of Queen Street.*

range of New Zealand design objects. A few doors down you'll find **Sanderson Contemporary Art,** 251 Parnell Rd. (☎ 09/374-4476; www.sanderson.co.nz), which exhibits some fascinating New Zealand contemporary works. ⏲ 30 min.

Drive down Parnell Rd. onto Parnell Rise, then veer right onto Beach Rd. Turn right into Britomart Place and park in the main carpark.

⑫ ★★★ **Britomart Transport Centre.** The Britomart Transport Centre, completed in 2003 at a cost of NZ$211 million, was designed to help reduce Auckland's traffic congestion. On the Queen Street side, the new center took over the old English baroque-style Chief Post Office (1910–1912), which ceased operating in 1993. To its rear, opening onto Britomart Place, is the "blue glass box" which leads to the underground rail system. Take the escalators down to train level to see massive steel sculptures by Maori artist Michael Parakowhai. The center was designed by Californian architect

Mario Madayag. The Transport Centre was the first phase in a long-term project that will bring shops, bars, restaurants, and office space to the area. ⏲ 1 hr. Access off Quay St., Britomart Pl., and Customs St. www.britomart. co.nz and www.britomart.org.

⑬ 🍺 ★★ **Northern Steamship Company Brew Bar.** This bar on the wharf-side edge of Britomart is in the 130-year-old headquarters of the Northern Steamship Company. Sit down and enjoy a quiet afternoon ale with some chips and marvel at the funky lighting on the ceiling—dozens of old table lamps in a myriad of styles have been cleverly inverted to spectacular effect. 122 Quay St. ☎ 09374-3952; www.northernsteamship.co.nz. Snacks and small plates NZ$7–NZ$20.

It's a short walk west, along Quay St. to Viaduct Harbour. Look out for public sculptures on both sides of the road as you go.

⑭ ★★★ **Viaduct Harbour.** Architectural highlights here include the "Blue Water, Black Magic—A Tribute to Sir Peter Blake" addition to the **Voyager New Zealand Maritime Museum** (p. 51, ⑩), which debuted in 2009. Also of note on Princes Wharf is the **Hilton Auckland** (p. 81), which dominates the ocean end of the wharf. The hotel takes its inspiration from the cruise ships that berth alongside it. It was designed by the local Leuschke Group and opened in 2001. ⏰ At least 1 hr. See p. 44, ④.

⑮   🍽 ★★★ **White Restaurant.** Make this divine, serene space inside Hilton Auckland your dinner stop—it was designed by architect and interior designer Dan Kwan, who also designed the hotel's Bellini Bar. **See p. 81.**

Start day 3 at the upper section of Symonds St. (at the intersection of Karangahape Rd.) and amble down into the busy Auckland University district.

⑯ ★★ **Auckland University District.** Symonds Street epitomizes much of Auckland's architectural fabric—old buildings and new nudging up against each other to create a material and stylistic overlay that I always find interesting. Look out for the Auckland University Marae on your left (always a startling discovery in an urban environment); St. Andrew's Church on your right; and the School of Engineering, also on the right, with its sleek, glass, modern addition that houses a red neon artwork by Auckland artist Paul Hartigan. Keep an eye out for the business school's new landmark Owen G. Glenn Building on your right, designed by the Auckland Art Gallery team: Archimedia and FJMT of Sydney. You get great views of it from Stanley Street down in Grafton Valley if you happen to be driving down that way. ⏰ 1 hr.

Turn left into Waterloo Quadrant, an area rich in old buildings.

> *The foundation stone of The High Court was laid in 1865, with a military band and 200 guests in attendance.*

> Get an insight into the indulgent lifestyles of the colonial elite at the historic homes of Alberton, Highwic and Ewelme.

17 ★★ **The High Court.** Opened in 1868, this Gothic Revival building was designed by Edward Rumsey. The richly decorated brick building features turrets and gargoyles and is said to have been modeled after Warwick Castle in England. A less charming foyer and extension were more recently added. ⏱ 15 min. Corner of Waterloo Quadrant and Parliament St. ☎ 09/916-9600. www.courtsofnz.govt.nz.

18 **Old Government House.** Designed by architect William Mason and built in 1856, this grand old Georgian-style building is now a senior common room for Auckland University and its grounds are open to the public. ⏱ 15 min. Waterloo Quadrant.

19 ★★ **Northern Club.** This hefty, creeper-covered Italianate giant is one of my favorite Auckland buildings. It's a private club, but you can view the fabulous old-world interior on its website. ⏱ 15 min. 19 Princes St. ☎ 09/379-4755. www.northernclub.co.nz.

Go down Kitchener St. to the Chancery Lane retail area.

20 🍴 **Café Melba.** This small cafe is very popular for its excellent coffee and good food. 33 Vulcan Lane (off the O'Connell St. end). ☎ 09/377-0091. NZ$6–NZ$20.

21 **Auckland's Historic Homes.** Pick up the brochure for the self-guided *Historic Auckland House and Garden Tour* from the Auckland i-SITE Visitor Information Centre (p. 87) and explore three gorgeous homes: Alberton, Highwic, and Ewelme. The brochure comes with a map and you will have to pay an admission fee of NZ$8 for adults at each of the houses, or one discounted fee for all three. The *Ponsonby Heritage Walks* brochure is another good way to spend the afternoon, combining historic buildings and public art with boutique shopping, cafes, and art galleries in Auckland's trendiest suburb. ⏱ Half-day. For historic home details see www.historic.org.nz, www.alberton.co.nz, www.highwic.co.nz, and for Ponsonby Historic Walk details and information on free guided tours see www.ponsonby.org.nz.

RUGBY MAD

New Zealand's National Obsession   BY ADRIENNE REWI

YOU DON'T HAVE TO BE IN NEW ZEALAND long to realize that rugby is an integral part of the culture. People's passion for the game borders on frenzied. Husbands risk the wrath of wives to attend matches and the all-important after-match parties. Whole towns can virtually come to a standstill as everyone traipses off to watch the Saturday games.

A National Love Affair

Charles Monro, who was introduced to rugby while studying in England, organized New Zealand's first rugby game in Nelson's Botanical Reserve in 1870. Today it's our most viewed, most played sport, with over 145,500 players of all ages taking to the field every Saturday. Most of our rugby heroes can trace their first games back to the cold mornings when they headed off to the local rugby field to play, with their parents cheering from the sidelines. The national side, the All Blacks, are now known throughout the world, both for their skilled play and their rousing performance of a Maori haka before each game. New Zealand hosted and won the first Rugby World Cup in 1987; and in 2011 the country turned itself inside out to once again stage this prestigious international event.

Rugby Heroes

GEORGE NEPIA (1907–1989)
One of New Zealand's most famous Maori players, Nepia was the only player to play all

32 games of the 1924 All Blacks' tour of the United Kingdom. He was inducted into the NZ Sports Hall of Fame in 1990.

COLIN 'PINETREE' MEADS (1936–)
Named the New Zealand Rugby Football Union's Player of the Century in 1999, Meads is a living rugby legend and regarded by many as the greatest player to ever take the field. Notoriously tough, he once played against South Africa with a broken arm. He is a member of both the International Rugby Hall of Fame and the New Zealand Sports Hall of Fame.

WAYNE 'BUCK' SHELFORD (1957–)
The All Blacks never lost a game under Shelford's captaincy from 1987 to 1990. The fearless No. 8 is famous for continuing play with a torn scrotum during a test match against France in 1986. His fans were shocked when he was dropped from the team in 1990 and they began appearing at games with signs saying "Bring Back Buck."

JONAH LOMU (1975–)
The giant of New Zealand rugby, Lomu burst onto the international scene in 1994. He was acknowledged as the top player at the 1995 World Cup in South

Africa and from there, became a hero and one of the game's biggest drawcards. He was inducted into the International Rugby hall of Fame in 2007.

CHRISTIAN CULLEN (1976–)
Cullen is one of the top try scorers in rugby history. His 46 tries in 58 tests has earned him the repu-

tation as a force to be reckoned with and he is widely regarded as one of the greatest All Blacks of his generation. In 2003 he moved to Ireland to play for Munster, and he retired from rugby in 2007.

RICHARD 'RICHIE' McCAW (1980–)
McCaw has been named IRB (International Rugby Board) International Player of the Year a record three times. In 2010 he

played his 100th Super Rugby game. He led the All Blacks in the 2007 World Cup.

Where to Catch a Game

ON THE FIELD AND AT THE STADIUM
During the rugby season (Mar–Oct) you can catch a rugby match at almost any rugby club in town in New Zealand. School and club matches are often held on public grounds and it's free to watch from the sidelines. The major matches in the big cities are always well publicized, and tickets sell fast.

AT A BAR
Many bars, pubs, and cafes all around the country have big-screen televisions relaying the current matches to a large, noisy, boisterous crowd of fans. A visit to one of these will give you an insight into the social side of New Zealand rugby culture.

FOR THE HISTORY
The New Zealand Rugby Museum features over 30,000 items of rugby memorabilia and by 2011, it will be housed in a dedicated wing of the revamped Te Manawa, the museum of Palmerston North. Check www.rugbymuseum.co.nz for updated location details and opening times, or call ☎ 06/358-6947.

Auckland Shopping Best Bets

Best Bohemian Shopping Zone
Karangahape Road (K'Rd.) (p. 69).

Best Bookstore
Unity Books, 19 High St. (p. 66).

Best Contemporary Maori Design
Native Agent, 507B New North Rd., Kingsland
(p. 68).

Best Department Store
Smith & Caughey, 261 Queen St. (p. 66).

Best Edibles
Nosh Metro, 254 Ponsonby Rd., Ponsonby
(p. 66).

Best Fashion District
Broadway and Nuffield Street, Newmarket
(p. 69).

Best Market
Otara Market, Otara Shopping Centre, Newbury
St. (p. 68).

Best New Zealand Art
Gow Langsford Gallery, 26 Lorne Street. (p. 63).

Best New Zealand Design Store
Essenze, 223 Parnell Rd. (p. 66).

Best New Zealand Jewelry
Fingers, 2 Kitchener St. (p. 68).

Best Shopping Street
Parnell Road (p. 69).

Best Stationery Store
kikki.K, 22 Nuffield St. (p. 69).

> *Otara's Polynesian market brims with vendors selling everything from fresh fruit and vegetables to pretty leis.*

Auckland Shopping A to Z

Antiques

★★★ Baran de Bordeaux PARNELL

An exquisite store featuring imported 17th- and 19th-century French antiques and decorative pieces including eye-popping crystal chandeliers, sourced in France by Bordeaux native Chrystelle Baran. **367 Parnell Rd.** ☎ 09/307-1201. www.frenchantiques.co.nz. AE, DC, MC, V.

★★ Murdoch McLennan PARNELL

I love this store for its wide range of English antiques—everything from beautiful tea sets and paintings to chairs, elaborate sideboards, elegant tables, and quirky collectibles. **377 Parnell Rd.** ☎ 09/309-4757. AE, DC, MC, V.

Art

★★★ Gow Langsford Gallery CITY

This should be your first stop for the big-name New Zealand artists. One of the most influential contemporary art dealers in the country. **26 Lorne St.** ☎ 09/303-4290. www.gowlangsfordgallery.co.nz. AE, DC, MC, V.

★★ Masterworks PONSONBY

Come here for high quality New Zealand and Australian applied arts, especially ceramics, glass art, and jewelry. **77 Ponsonby Rd.** ☎ 09/378-1256. www.masterworksgallery.com. AE, DC, MC, V.

★ Sanderson Contemporary Art PARNELL

This gallery focuses on supporting new and emerging New Zealand artists and you'll find some highly creative works (paintings, prints, sculptures, mixed media, photography) at incredibly good prices. **251 Parnell Rd.** ☎ 09/374-4476. www.sanderson.co.nz. AE, MC, V.

Book Stores

★★★ Parsons Bookshop CITY

This great independent bookstore was started in 1975 by Roger and Helen Parsons, who still stock the shelves with an incredible range of art, fashion, architecture, and art theory titles. They also have a very good selection of New Zealand, Maori, and Pacific books, and beautiful coffee table tomes. **26 Wellesley St. E.** ☎ 09/303-1557; www.parsons.co.nz. AE, MC, V.

> *Take home a unique piece of handcrafted glass or ceramic from Ponsonby's stylish Masterworks store.*

Auckland Shopping

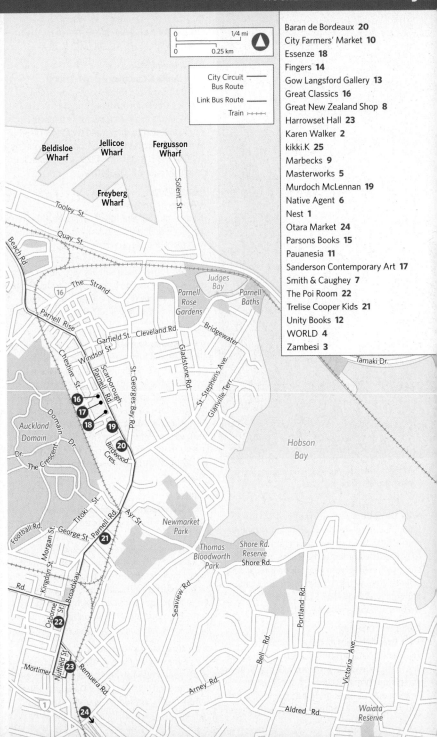

Baran de Bordeaux **20**
City Farmers' Market **10**
Essenze **18**
Fingers **14**
Gow Langsford Gallery **13**
Great Classics **16**
Great New Zealand Shop **8**
Harrowset Hall **23**
Karen Walker **2**
kikki.K **25**
Marbecks **9**
Masterworks **5**
Murdoch McLennan **19**
Native Agent **6**
Nest **1**
Otara Market **24**
Parsons Books **15**
Pauanesia **11**
Sanderson Contemporary Art **17**
Smith & Caughey **7**
The Poi Room **22**
Trelise Cooper Kids **21**
Unity Books **12**
WORLD **4**
Zambesi **3**

> *Nuffield Street, Newmarket is a shopping hub for classy fashionistas.*

★★★ **Unity Books** HIGH STREET

If you're struggling to find some unusual title, come to Unity—they're known for their ability to source the unique and the obscure. They stock everything from gay, philosophical, and scientific nonfiction to a wonderland of international fiction. 19 High St. ☎ 09/307-0731. www.unitybooks.co.nz. AE, DC, MC, V.

Children's Clothing

★★★ **Great Classics** PARNELL

This little boutique store bulges with the best international kids' brands, from Bengh & Borz of Holland to Jean Bourget, Rare Tom Boy, Bellerose, Fred Bare, and Ben Sherman. Boys and girls alike will come out looking classy yet casual. 219 Parnell Rd. ☎ 09/377-0120. www.greatclassics.co.nz. AE, DC, MC, V.

Department Stores

★★★ **Smith & Caughey** QUEEN STREET

This 130-year-old retail icon is one of the country's best-loved department stores. In addition to a top-notch perfume department you'll find quality men's and women's fashion, home ware, accessories, and duty-free goods. 261 Queen St. ☎ 09/377-4770. www.smithandcaughey.co.nz. AE, DC, MC, V.

Design Stores

★ **Askew** BROADWAY

Bright, colorful, and full of surprises, this is the place to find the perfect gift for someone who has almost everything—except perhaps a Mont Blanc pen, some Mandarina Duck luggage, or some Alessi salt and pepper shakers. International design brands shuffle shelf space with fun, quirky gift possibilities. 178 Broadway, Newmarket. ☎ 09/522-8444. www.askew.co.nz. MC, V.

★★★ **Essenze** PARNELL

New Zealand furniture designer David Trubridge exhibits with the best designers in the world in Milan—and at this bright, crisp, colorful store that specializes in top New Zealand design. I love Garry Nash's exquisite glass pieces and the delicate ceramics of Susannah Bridges and Peter Collis; I'm sure you'll find plenty that takes your eye as well. 285 Parnell Rd. ☎ 09/300-6238. www.essenze.co.nz. AE, DC, MC, V.

Edibles

★★★ **Devonport Chocolates** PONSONBY

Biting through crisp chocolate and sinking your teeth into decadent truffle fillings is one of life's great pleasures, and you'll have plenty of flavor choices in this sweet heaven. Truffle logs, luxury handcrafted chocolates, and boxed gourmet gifts, all made across the water in Devonport, are all guaranteed to bring a smile to your face. 177b Ponsonby Rd. ☎ 09/361-6952. www.devonportchocolates.co.nz. MC, V.

★★★ **Nosh Metro** PONSONBY

Don't come here if you're feeling peckish or you'll spend way too much money. Temptations abound—fresh cheeses, pastas, coffee, bread, meats, seafood, vegetables, and a

> *You'll find the very best of New Zealand hand-crafted contemporary jewelry at Fingers.*

> *Our distinctive pukeko is a bird that finds its way onto all manner of gift items at Pauanesia.*

host of imported ingredients from around the globe. A great place to load up your basket for a picnic. 254 Ponsonby Rd. ☎ 09/360-5557. www.noshfoodmarket.com. AE, DC, MC, V.

Fashion—New Zealand Designers
★★★ Karen Walker NUFFIELD STREET

Karen Walker shops are decorated in a simple, 1950s-chic style that perfectly suits her tailored, unpretentious designs—designs that slip easily from stylish street wear to business ensembles to sexy evening wear. Now a regular on runways at London, New York, Sydney, and Tokyo fashion weeks, Walker also has stores in the city (15 O'Connell St; ☎ 09/309-6299) and Ponsonby (2/171 Ponsonby Rd.; ☎ 09/361-6723). Corner of Nuffield and Balm sts., Newmarket. ☎ 09/522-4286. www.karen walker.com. AE, DC, MC, V.

★★★ WORLD PONSONBY

I adore the startling surprises you get with WORLD clothes—unexpected fabric combinations, a burst of color in a jacket lining, a clash of vibrant shades. Established in 1989 by Denise L'Estrange-Corbet and Francis Hooper, they're all about flouting expectations and making you think again about the potential of fashion as art. In addition to this store, there

is another in the city (57 High St.; ☎ 09/373-3034). 97 Ponsonby Rd. ☎ 09/378-0897. www.worldbrand.co.nz. AE, DC, MC, V.

★★ Zambesi PONSONBY

Zambesi founder Elisabeth Findlay takes an intellectual approach to fashion, creating sculptured garments that reek of style. Knitwear plays an important part in her collections, which have been enthusiastically received in Paris and other leading world fashion centers. There are four Zambesi stores in Auckland but I like this one the best. 169 Ponsonby Rd. ☎ 09/360-7391. www.zambesi.co.nz. AE, DC, MC, V.

Homeware
★★ Harrowset Hall NUFFIELD STREET

This is one of New Zealand's leading bed linen and designer accessory stores. You'll find top quality sheets and beautiful floral quilts, plus exquisite nightwear and soft dressing gowns for good measure. 7 Nuffield St. ☎ 09/524-4452. www.harrowsethall.com. AE, MC, V.

★ Nest NUFFIELD STREET

I love coming to Nest. It always has a wonderful range of color-coordinated tableware to drool over. They have glassware at great prices too, along with all the kitchen essentials like wooden chopping boards, tea towels, and cooking gadgets. They also have a store in Ponsonby (239 Ponsonby Rd.; ☎ 09/361-5555). 2 Nuffield St. ☎ 09/522-1448. www.nest.co.nz. AE, MC, V.

> *Britomart Place comes alive every Saturday when vendors come together to sell fresh fruit and vegetables at the City Farmers' Market.*

Jewelry

★★★ Fingers CITY

Lovers of contemporary, handcrafted, art-inspired jewelry will be dazzled by the cabinets and drawers at Fingers. You may find pieces inspired by a seed pod, a seashell, a native tree, some strange domestic item, a postage stamp, even a twig. The results are always startling and beautiful. 2 Kitchener St. ☎ 09/373-3974. www.fingers.co.nz. AE, MC, V.

Maori Design & Gifts

★★★ Native Agent KINGSLAND

Native Agent has embraced New Zealand's bicultural foundation to create a unique range of household items—stunning cushions, clothing for men and women, ceramics, jewelry, lighting, furniture, and a host of decorative items that pool the talents of New Zealand's upcoming designers. Wonderfully Maori-themed products. 507B New North Rd., Kingsland. ☎ 09/845-3289. www.nativeagent.co.nz. AE, MC, V.

★ Pauanesia HIGH STREET

I especially love the huge range of colorful Kiwiana tea towels available here. There's also a massive range of jewelry, cushions, toys, and ornaments, all taking their color cues from our gorgeous coastal landscapes. 35 High St. ☎ 09/366-7282. www.pauanesia.co.nz. AE, MC, V.

★★ The Poi Room NEWMARKET

This shop is proof that the traditional Maori *tiki* has undergone a huge renaissance as a design symbol. It's incorporated into everything from money boxes and paintings to tea towels. If you're looking for a unique New Zealand-made item to take home, this is the place. 17 Osborne St., Newmarket. ☎ 09/520-0399. www.thepoiroom.co.nz. AE, MC, V.

Markets

★ City Farmers' Market BRITOMART

This popular market showcases a wide range of fresh fruit and vegetables, plants, and food items. Corner of Galway and Gore Sts. Sat 8:30am-12:30pm.

★★★ Otara Market OTARA

A market like no other in New Zealand, this one showcases Auckland's Polynesian and, increasingly, Asian cultures. Stalls bulge with tapa cloth, weaving, flax baskets, exotic island foods, fruits, vegetables, and much more. Well worth visiting. Otara Shopping Centre, Newbury St. Sat 6am-noon.

Music

★★ Marbecks QUEEN STREET

A very knowledgeable staff forms the backbone of this big store that stocks everything from the classics and Christian music to

The Main Shopping Districts

Auckland has endless shopping choices but the best are found in some key zones. Britomart (www.britomart.org) is still being constructed but there are already a number of designer boutiques and bars tucked away in the side lanes. **Newmarket** (www.new market.co.nz), is the mainstream fashion capital, where everyone shops on a Saturday. The lanes west of **Broadway** are home to a host of fashionable boutique stores. Expensive international labels congregate in Newmarket's classy **Nuffield Street; High Street** is another top fashion zone that spills into Chancery Lane and O'Connell Street east of Queen Street. **Karangahape Road** (www.kroad.com) runs across Upper Queen Street and is home to funky stores, tattoo parlors, sex shops, strip clubs, and excellent vintage clothing stores. **Kingsland** is an old suburb southeast of Ponsonby that has become trendy. **Parnell Road** has always been a favorite because it has so many galleries and fashion boutiques in a short stretch. Many prefer **Ponsonby Road,** but it's much longer and the shops more spread out. Still, this is where you'll find top fashion labels and boutique stores of all kinds—not to mention cafes and top restaurants galore. **Queen Street** is often called The Golden Mile but in terms of quality shopping it has, apart from a few exceptions, been outclassed by many of the smaller areas outlined above.

> *Samoan tapa cloth bags are just some of the Polynesian wares on sale at Otara's weekend market.*

hip-hop, jazz, blues, New Zealand music, and everything in between. Queens Arcade, 34–40 Queen St. ☎ 0800/113-344; www.marbecks. co.nz. AE, DC, MC, V.

New Zealand Gift Stores

★ Great New Zealand Shop CITY
This big souvenir shop stocks all the usual take-home favorites from mass-produced jade and bone pendants, paua jewelry, and T-shirts to an extensive selection of New Zealand-made beauty products and chocolates. If you've left souvenir hunting to the last minute this is a good standby for reasonably priced items. Westfield Downtown, 31 Queen St. ☎ 09/377-3009; www.tgnzs.co.nz. AE, DC, MC, V.

★★ Texan Art Schools PONSONBY
Despite the unlikely name, this colorful store stocks predominantly New Zealand-made jewelry, ceramics, toys, photography, art, paintings, and small sculptures. Friendly, helpful staff are happy to gift-wrap your purchase and make sure it's safe for overseas travel. 95 Ponsonby Rd. ☎ 09/376-6064. www.texan artschools.co.nz. AE, DC, MC, V.

Stationery

★★ kikki.K NUFFIELD STREET
Swedish designers have had a field day creating this colorful, beautifully coordinated, and ever-growing range of classy stationery. Everything from folders and photo albums to file boxes, diaries, notebooks, and a host of other goodies that stationery freaks like me swarm over. 22 Nuffield St. ☎ 09/524-0156. www. kikki-k.com. AE, DC, MC, V.

Auckland Restaurant Best Bets

Best Asian Noodles
Wagamama, Level 2, 1 Courthouse Lane (p. 77).

Best Breakfasts
Bambina, 268 Ponsonby Rd. (p. 71).

Best Family Restaurant
Portofino, 156 Parnell Rd. (p. 76).

Best Fish and Chips
Fish Kitchen, 363 Parnell Rd. (p. 74).

Best Formal Restaurant
The Grove, St. Patrick's Sq., Wyndham St. (p. 74).

Most Glamorous
Barolo, Langham Hotel, 83 Symonds St. (p. 71).

Best for Meat Lovers
Jervois Steakhouse & Saloon, 70 Jervois Rd. (p. 76).

Best People Watching
Soul, Viaduct Harbour (p. 77).

Best Seafood
Harbourside Seafood Bar & Grill, 1st floor, Ferry Terminal, Quay St. (p. 75).

Best Splurge
Vinnies, 166 Jervois Rd. (p. 77).

Best Wine List
Clooney, 33 Sale St. (p. 74).

Best Yakitori
Tanuki's Cave, 319B Upper Queen St. (p. 77).

> *The glamorous and famous—including Beyonce and Jay Z—lunch at Soul in Viaduct Harbour.*

Auckland Restaurants A to Z

★★★ **Antoine's** PARNELL *FRENCH*
Chef-owner Tony Astle has been serving award-winning meals in this iconic restaurant since 1973. Everyone from royalty to rock stars has sampled his fresh New Zealand produce woven into French-inspired dishes like roasted quail with wild mushroom and truffle risotto with truffle jus. It's a formal, silver-service night out. 333 Parnell Rd. ☎ 09/379-8756. www.antoinesrestaurant.co.nz. Main courses NZ$46–NZ$50. AE, DC, MC, V. Dinner Mon–Sat, lunch Wed–Fri.

★ kids **Bambina** PONSONBY *CAFE*
A big, all-day blackboard menu announces such breakfast favorites as eggs any way you want them, ricotta hot cakes, muesli, and fruit. Lunch fare runs to Turkish sandwiches, bruschetta and rare grilled tuna with coriander and lime. Lemon muffins and coffee are also tasty and there's always a lively atmosphere. 268 Ponsonby Rd. ☎ 09/360-4000. Main courses NZ$14–NZ$24. AE, DC, MC, V. Breakfast and lunch daily.

★★★ **Barolo** CITY *ITALIAN*
Luscious fabrics and gilt mirrors lend a quiet glamour to this restaurant that I love. The Piedmontese chef from Turin is a big fan of slow food so expect rabbit and duck to be cooked to perfection and pasta dishes that go beyond the ordinary. Service is first rate. Langham Hotel, 83 Symonds St. ☎ 09/379-5132. www.langhamhotels.com. Main courses NZ$35–NZ$42, pasta dishes NZ$22. AE, DC, MC, V. Dinner daily.

★★ **Cin Cin** CITY *SEAFOOD/INTERNATIONAL*
Fresh fish always has a starring role on this menu—appropriate given that this popular spot overlooks the water at the ferry terminal. You can never go wrong with the ever-popular Cin Cin bouillabaisse or Hawke's Bay lamb cutlets. Make sure you save space for white chocolate sorbet with orange sauce. Ferry Term., 99 Quay St. ☎ 09/307-6966. www.cincin.co.nz. Main courses NZ$36–NZ$42. AE, DC, MC, V. Lunch and dinner daily.

> Savor slow-cooked rabbit or duck at the elegant Piedmontese restaurant, Barolo, at the Langham Auckland.

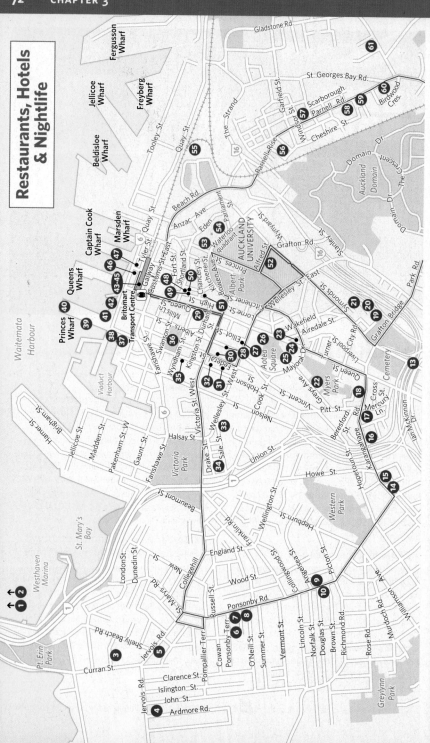

Restaurants, Hotels & Nightlife

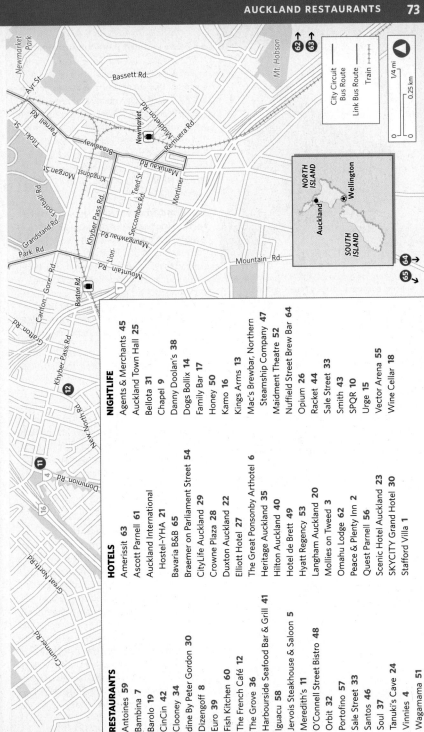

RESTAURANTS

Antoines **59**
Bambina **7**
Barolo **19**
CinCin **42**
Clooney **34**
dine By Peter Gordon **30**
Dizengoff **8**
Euro **39**
Fish Kitchen **60**
The French Café **12**
The Grove **36**
Harbourside Seafood Bar & Grill **41**
Iguacu **58**
Jervois Steakhouse & Saloon **5**
Meredith's **11**
O'Connell Street Bistro **48**
Orbit **32**
Portofino **57**
Sale Street **33**
Santos **46**
Soul **37**
Tanuki's Cave **24**
Vinnies **4**
Wagamama **51**

HOTELS

Amerissit **63**
Ascott Parnell **61**
Auckland International
  Hostel-YHA **21**
Bavaria B&B **65**
Braemer on Parliament Street **54**
CityLife Auckland **29**
Crowne Plaza **28**
Duxton Auckland **22**
Elliott Hotel **27**
The Great Ponsonby Arthotel **6**
Heritage Auckland **35**
Hilton Auckland **40**
Hotel de Brett **49**
Hyatt Regency **53**
Langham Auckland **20**
Mollies on Tweed **3**
Omahu Lodge **62**
Peace & Plenty Inn **2**
Quest Parnell **56**
Scenic Hotel Auckland **23**
SKYCITY Grand Hotel **30**
Stafford Villa **1**

NIGHTLIFE

Agents & Merchants **45**
Auckland Town Hall **25**
Bellota **31**
Chapel **9**
Danny Doolan's **38**
Dogs Bollix **14**
Family Bar **17**
Honey **50**
Kamo **16**
Kings Arms **13**
Mac's Brewbar, Northern
  Steamship Company **47**
Maidment Theatre **52**
Nuffield Street Brew Bar **64**
Opium **26**
Racket **44**
Sale Street **33**
Smith **43**
SPQR **10**
Urge **15**
Vector Arena **55**
Wine Cellar **18**

> Splurge on fine cuisine at SKYCITY Grand's award-winning restaurant, dine by Peter Gordon.

★★★ Clooney CITY INTERNATIONAL

Venison with preserved cherries, cocoa *mille-feuille*, black pudding, and licorice is a typically creative dish at this top city restaurant—a place of seductive dark leather and sophistication favored by Auckland's who's who. One of the best wine lists in the city. 33 Sale St., City. ☎ 09/358-1702. www.clooney.co.nz. Main courses NZ$32–NZ$44. AE, DC, MC, V. Lunch Friday, dinner Mon–Sat.

★★★ dine by Peter Gordon CITY INTERNATIONAL

Founder of London's legendary Sugar Club restaurant, top New Zealand chef Peter Gordon designs the menu at this chic eatery. The menu that zig-zags through Asian and European flavors and is complimented by a superb New Zealand wine list. SKYCITY Grand Hotel, 90 Federal St. ☎ 09/363-7030. www.skycity auckland.co.nz. Main courses NZ$35–NZ$48. AE, DC, MC, V. Lunch Friday, dinner daily.

★ kids Dizengoff PONSONBY CAFE

Having eggs Benedict Dizengoff on the weekend is almost a Ponsonby ritual, but expect a crowd any day of the week. They cover all the healthy bases here too, so if chicken pasta is off-limits you can sip one of those strange health shakes that are all the rage. 256 Ponsonby Rd. ☎ 09/360-0108. Main courses NZ$16–NZ$26. AE, DC, MC, V. Breakfast and lunch daily.

★★★ Euro VIADUCT HARBOUR MODERN NZ

Home to celebrity chef Simon Gault, this is one of Auckland's hot spots. It's a bit of a legend of its own making but that aside, you will be served divine meals that draw on Pacific produce and flavors. Cajun kingfish on wood-roasted Provençal vegetables with miso ginger butter is a tasty example. Shed 22, Princes Wharf, Viaduct Harbour. ☎ 09/309-9866. www.eurobar.co.nz. Main courses NZ$38–NZ$42. AE, DC, MC, V. Lunch and dinner daily.

★ kids Fish Kitchen PARNELL FISH AND CHIPS

This is a cool, chic take on the old Kiwi favorite, fish and chips. It's all white tiles and freshness here. Choose the fish you would like and they'll cook it on the spot. The Moet & Chandon champagne-battered snapper is a winner but it's much pricier of course (NZ$35). 363 Parnell Rd. ☎ 09/379-8042. Chips NZ$4 per scoop, most fish NZ$6–NZ$8 per piece. AE, MC, V. Lunch and dinner daily.

★★ The French Café CITY CONTEMPORARY EUROPEAN

This sophisticated, formal, multi-award winning restaurant has won the hearts and minds of thousands. It's silver service minus the pretensions. Come here to savor foie gras, roast duckling, and raspberry soufflé tart with white chocolate sorbet and pistachio praline. It's in a scruffy part of town, but don't let that fool you—this place is a class act matched by few. 210 Symonds St. ☎ 09/377-1911. www.thefrenchcafe.co.nz. Main courses NZ$30–NZ$44. AE, DC, MC, V. Lunch Fri, dinner Tues–Sat.

★★★ The Grove CITY EUROPEAN

Named Supreme Winner in Auckland's Best Restaurant Awards in 2010, The Grove is a formal restaurant where plates reach the level of high art (I wanted to photograph every dish). Butter-poached crayfish tail with roasted baby poussin, Parma ham, and rosemary is a taste sensation; the vanilla and Medjool date crème brûlée tart with spiced ice cream and rhubarb confit was definitely worth saving space for. St Patrick's Sq., off Wyndham St. ☎ 09/368-4129. www.thegroverestaurant.co.nz. Main courses NZ$38–NZ$48. AE, DC, MC, V. Lunch and dinner Mon–Sat.

> *The French Café offers sophisticated, award-winning cuisine with friendly service.*

★★ **Harbourside Seafood Bar & Grill** CITY
SEAFOOD   Superb fish dishes dominate the
menu at this chic spot with great views over
the ferry terminal. The seafood platters are
amazing, but meats, pasta dishes, vegetarian
and gluten-free options, and yummy desserts
are all available. 1st floor, Ferry Term., Quay St.
☎ 09/307-0556. www.harboursiderestaurant.
co.nz. Main courses NZ$34–NZ$38. AE, DC,
MC, V. Lunch and dinner daily.

★ kids **Iguaçu** PARNELL *MODERN NZ/
INTERNATIONAL*   Giant silver-framed mirrors
lend a grandiose note to a restaurant made
light and airy by a glazed ceiling, earthy colors,
and big windows that keep you in touch with
the street. A favorite with lunching businessmen and the good-time crowd, it has an extensive wine list and a big kids' menu. Despite the
South American name, the menu shows global
influences, with such tasty menu choices, as
shredded duck and mandarin salad with chili
lime dressing, prawn risotto, and Hawke's Bay
lamb rump. 269 Parnell Rd. ☎ 09/358-4804.
www.iguacu.co.nz. Main courses NZ$28–
NZ$44. AE, DC, MC, V. Lunch and dinner daily.

> *What could be nicer than dining on fine seafood
at Harbourside, while looking out over boats
and water?*

> At Tanuki's Cave, a moody little underground yakitori bar, people squeeze in to sample tasty morsels on skewers.

★ kids **Jervois Steakhouse & Saloon** HERNE BAY *STEAKHOUSE* If you don't know the difference between grass-fed and grain-fed beef, this is the place to find out. It's all about premium cuts of lamb and beef, which such menu items as lamb Wellington, steak tartare, or black Angus filet. 70 Jervois Rd., Herne Bay. ☎ 09/376-2049. www.jervoissteakhouse.co.nz. Main courses NZ$28–NZ$32. AE, DC, MC, V. Dinner daily.

★★★ **Meredith's** MT. EDEN *MODERN NZ* Owner-chef Michael Meredith creates a menu at this formal restaurant with dishes that are mesmerizing—for the eye and the palate. If you dine on Friday or Saturday night, it's entirely degustation—a great way to experience the magic. 365 Dominion Rd., Mt. Eden. ☎ 09/623-3140. www.merediths.co.nz. Main courses NZ$38–NZ$48. AE, DC, MC, V. Lunch Thurs–Fri, Dinner Tues–Sat.

★★★ **O'Connell Street Bistro** CITY *INTERNATIONAL* Veuve Clicquot bottles lined up along the window sills hint at the good times that have gone on before (as well as the impressive wine list). Service here is impeccable and it's long been a favorite with the lunching business crowd. Corner of O'Connell and Shortland sts. ☎ 09/377-1884. www.oconnell stbistro.com. Main courses NZ$36–NZ$46. AE, DC, MC, V. Lunch Mon–Fri, dinner Mon–Sat.

★ **Orbit** CITY *MODERN NZ* New Zealand's only revolving restaurant delivers remarkable views and an a la carte menu with such treats as harissa-roasted salmon fillet with saffron risotto cake and wilted spinach, or baked goat cheese wrapped in filo pastry with thyme-roasted beetroot and reduced balsamic vinegar. Sky Tower, Victoria St. W. ☎ 09/363-6240. www.skycityauckland.co.nz. Main courses NZ$34–NZ$40. AE, DC, MC, V. Lunch Mon–Fri, dinner daily.

★ kids **Portofino** PARNELL *ITALIAN* When you're exhausted and just want to eat quickly and well, Portofino obliges with delicious pastas, pizzas, and chicken and veal dishes that will please all the family. It's small, cozy, and very popular, so get in early for a guaranteed spot. Watch the chefs at work and chat with the friendly Italian staff. 156 Parnell Rd. ☎ 09/373-3740. www.portofino.co.nz. Main courses NZ$22–NZ$30. AE, MC, V. Lunch and dinner daily.

★★ **Sale Street** CITY *MODERN NZ/FRENCH* Part of a larger complex that includes everything from a yakitori grill and a huge dining deck to a microbrewery and a smart dining room, this is one of the hippest spots in the city. Come here for a fun night out and taste treats like duck confit served with roast yam puree or aged eye fillet steak with oxtail ravioli

> *O'Connell Street Bistro is one of those iconic little restaurants where service, fine food, and wine never disappoint.*

and red onion jam. 7 Sale St., Freemans Bay. ☎ 09/307-8148. www.salest.co.nz. Main courses NZ$30-NZ$34. AE, MC, V. Lunch Tues-Sun, dinner daily.

★ kids Santos CITY CAFE

This is an excellent stop for a light lunch or coffee and a snack. The lunch menu roams across pasta, big tasting platters, salads, and delicious soups that come with chunky homemade bread. This busy, relaxed spot, with views across the wharves, attracts everyone from lunching businessmen to hungry travelers. 130 Quay St., Britomart. ☎ 09/337-0088. www.santoscoffee.co.nz. Main courses NZ$15-NZ$22. AE, MC, V. Breakfast and lunch Mon-Sat.

★★★ Soul VIADUCT HARBOUR MODERN NZ

This iconic restaurant is one of the most popular eateries by the water. As you tuck into succulent whitebait fritters and the freshest fish dishes, you can watch the Viaduct nightlife heat up, the businessmen loosening their ties, and the crowds ambling past moored yachts. Viaduct Harbour. ☎ 09/7249. www.soulbar.co.nz. Main courses NZ$32-NZ$44. AE, DC, MC, V. Lunch and dinner daily.

★ Tanuki's Cave CITY JAPANESE TEPPANYAKI

I fell love with this place the minute I stepped underground. It's a huge, popular den that pulses most nights of the week and you have to get in early (6pm) to get a spot. People line up all the way back up the stairs to the street but don't let their hungry looks make you rush. Choose from a selection of skewers (chargrilled yakitori and deep-fried, breaded *kushiage*), or the delicious tofu salad. 319B Upper Queen St. ☎ 09/379-5151. Main courses NZ$6-NZ$14. MC, V. Dinner Wed-Sat.

★★★ Vinnies HERNE BAY MODERN NZ

Vinnies has endured as one of the premium special-occasion restaurants. Its plush, moody, formal interior, complete with a lovely art collection and an award-winning wine selection, is the perfect setting for a tasty menu that adds a twist to old favorites. Wild rabbit is served with fig and blue cheese; spiced quail with papaya; and goose egg with asparagus. 166 Jervois Rd., Herne Bay. ☎ 09/376-5597. www.vinnies.co.nz. Main courses NZ$38-NZ$42. AE, DC, MC, V. Dinner Tues-Sat.

★ kids Wagamama CITY JAPANESE NOODLE BAR

Wagamama has the snazzy noodle bar concept down to a fine art—all around the world. Here in Auckland, their long, communal tables are always filled with hungry, happily slurping diners, filling up for a great price. Level 2, 1 Courthouse Lane, off High St. ☎ 09/359-9266. www.wagamama.co.nz. Main courses NZ$12-NZ$16. AE, MC, V. Lunch and dinner daily.

Auckland Hotel Best Bets

Best Art Collection
SKYCITY Grand Hotel, Victoria St. W. and Federal St. (p. 83).

Best Budget Stay
Auckland International Hostel – YHA, 1-35 Turner St. (p. 79).

Most Central B&B
Braemar on Parliament Street, 7 Parliament St. (p. 80).

Most Charming B&B
Peace and Plenty Inn, 6 Flagstaff Terrace (p. 82).

Funkiest Decor
Hotel de Brett, 2 High St. (p. 81).

Best for Kids
Heritage Auckland, 35 Hobson St. (p. 81).

Most Luxurious
The Langham Hotel Auckland, 83 Symonds St. (p. 82).

Most Romantic
Mollies on Tweed, 6 Tweed St. (p. 82).

Best Sea Views
Hilton Auckland, Princes Wharf, 137-147 Quay St. (p. 81).

Best Shopping Location
CityLife Auckland, 171 Queen St. (p. 80).

Best Spa and Pool
Hyatt Regency, Waterloo Quadrant at Princes St. (p. 82).

Travel Tip

For locations of the hotels in this section, see the map on p.72-73.

> *You can't help but feel special when you spend a night in one of the elegant Hilton Auckland suites.*

Auckland Hotels A to Z

★ **Amerissit** REMUERA
Barbara McKain's quiet cul-de-sac address in an affluent suburb quickly lulls you into a state of bliss. She's an amazing host who goes out of her way to exceed guests' expectations and her modern rooms are very well priced. Each has its own bathroom. 20 Buttle St., Remuera. ☎ 09/522-9297. www.amerissit.co.nz. 3 units. Doubles NZ$240–NZ$295 w/breakfast. AE, DC, MC, V. Map p. 72.

★ kids **Ascot Parnell** PARNELL
Bart and Therese Blommaert have hosted over 63,000 guests in 17 years as accommodation providers and you'll be very comfortable in their modern, meticulously maintained town-house complex that provides individual suites for separate parties (including kids over 10 years old). St.Stephens Ave., Parnell. ☎ 09/309-9012. www.ascotparnell.com. 3 units- Doubles NZ$265–NZ$365 w/breakfast. MC, V. Map p. 72.

Auckland International Hostel–YHA CITY
When all you want is a comfortable bed to fall into at night, this exceptionally well maintained hostel delivers. Formerly an office block, it's one of the best hostels in the country and hosts over 50,000 guests a year. Security is tight and it's just a 5-minute walk to downtown Auckland. 1-35 Turner St. ☎ 0800/278-299 or 09/302-8200. www.yha.co.nz. 170 beds. NZ$20–NZ$28 multi-share, NZ$75–NZ$125 private room. AE, MC, V. Map p. 72.

kids **Bavaria B&B** MT. EDEN
Rudi and Ulricke Stephan run a cosmopolitan establishment in a quiet, leafy, suburban street not far from the city. Three upstairs rooms are the sunniest and all rooms have ensuite bathrooms. The big, old villa is close to Mt. Eden Village where there are several restaurants and cafes; nearby bus stops will deliver you into the city. 83 Valley Rd., Mt. Eden. ☎ 09/638-9641. www.bavariabandbhotel.co.nz. 11 units. Doubles NZ$140–NZ$155 w/breakfast. AE, MC, V. Map p. 72.

> *You'll have all the comforts of home in a roomy suite at Ascot Parnell.*

> *A room at the plush, posh Langham Auckland.*

★ kids Braemar on Parliament Street CITY

This stunning three-story property is the only Edwardian townhouse in the central business district that is still a private family home. I adore it and its vast, shabby-chic interior, filled with antiques and Asian rugs. John and Susan Sweetman leave you to do your own thing and then provide a delicious big breakfast in the morning. 7 Parliament St. ☎ 0800/155-463 or 09/377-5463. www.aucklandbedandbreakfast.com. 4 units. Doubles NZ$225–NZ$375 w/ breakfast. AE, DC, MC, V. Map p. 72.

★★ kids CityLife Auckland CITY

I love these spacious, serviced apartments right in the heart of Queen Street. You can shop all day and you're back in your quiet retreat in no time at all. The one-, two-, and three-bedroom suites have everything you need and are ideal for families and couples traveling together. 171 Queen St. ☎ 09/379-9222; www.heritagehotels.co.nz. 210 units. Doubles NZ$185–NZ$600. AE, DC, MC, V. Map p. 72.

★★ kids Crowne Plaza CITY

I always enjoy the big, friendly Crowne Plaza for a lively atmosphere that somehow encapsulates what Auckland's all about. You get spacious and well-appointed rooms in a central location. 128 Albert St. ☎ 0800/801-111 or 09/302-1111. www.crowneplazaauckland.co.nz. 352 units. Doubles NZ$185–NZ$500. AE, DC, MC, V. Map p. 72.

★★ kids Duxton Auckland CITY

The Duxton is much smaller than many of the city's inner city hotels and with that comes a serene calm and a friendly intimacy. It's tucked away on a leafy street overlooking Myers Park. Apartments with full kitchen and laundry facilities are also a big plus. 100 Greys Ave. ☎ 0800/655-555 or 09/375-1800; www.duxton.com. 149 units. Doubles NZ$155–NZ$550. AE, DC, MC, V. Map p. 72.

★★ kids Elliott Hotel CITY

There's old-world charm in this restored building and the self-contained one- and two-bedroom apartments are spacious and smart. It's ideally located above the Elliott Stables, an epicurean "village" filled with cafes and restaurants, and just a few steps off Queen Street. 15-31 Wellesley St. ☎ 0800/565-665. www.theelliotthotel.com. 60 units. Doubles NZ$135–NZ$325. AE, DC, MC, V. Map p. 72.

★ The Great Ponsonby Arthotel PONSONBY

This big B&B run by Gerry Hill and Sally James

> *Work off some of your holiday excesses in this gorgeous pool at SKYCITY Grand Hotel.*

has a colorful Pacific feel to it. The upstairs penthouse has its own balcony and lounge and all rooms have ensuite bathrooms. Palm Garden studios apart from the house have a bit more space and privacy—some of these have their own kitchenette. **30 Ponsonby Terrace.** ☎ 0800/766-792 or 09/376-5989. www.great-pons.co.nz. 11 units. Doubles NZ$245–NZ$400 w/breakfast. AE, MC, V. Map p. 72.

★★ kids **Heritage Auckland** CITY
Fresh from a big makeover, the centrally located Heritage is looking glamorous and inviting. Two separate hotel wings give it two of everything so it's very well set up with gyms, pools, and rooftop tennis courts. The apartment-style suites here are fabulous— perfect for families and longer stays. **Hotel Wing, 35 Hobson St.; Tower Wing, 22 Nelson St.** ☎ 0800/368-888 or 09/379-8553. www. heritagehotels.co.nz. 327 units. Doubles NZ$205–NZ$575. AE, DC, MC, V. Map p. 72.

★★★ kids **Hilton Auckland** VIADUCT HARBOUR
Perched on the end of a wharf, completely surrounded by water, this modern, sophisticated hotel isn't big, but it's beautifully appointed. If you want the best views, ask for one of the 12 deluxe corner rooms that have two fully glazed walls looking over the harbor. **Princes Wharf, 137-147 Quay St.** ☎ 0800/448-002 or 09/978-2000. www.hilton.com. 165 units. Doubles NZ$645–NZ$815. AE, DC, MC, V. Map p. 72.

★★ kids **Hotel de Brett** CITY
Rooms at this gorgeous little boutique hotel

> *Stafford Villa's antique furnishings hint at its former life as a Victorian homestead.*

are individually decorated in mid-20th century modern style, showcasing New Zealand arts and crafts. It's colorful and classy and the glass-roofed brick atrium and courtyard give it a unique edge. It's located in the city's most stylish, upmarket shopping neighborhood. 2 High St. ☎ 09/925-9000. www.hoteldebrett.com. 25 units. Doubles NZ$290–NZ$590. AE, DC, MC, V. Map p. 72.

★★★ kids **Hyatt Regency** CITY

This old favorite has both stylish, classic hotel rooms and modern, chic apartments—not to mention a gym, pool, and spa facility to die for. The apartment suites—many interconnecting—are especially good for families or couples traveling together and all have kitchenettes and balconies. Residence suites have full kitchens. Waterloo Quadrant and Princes St. ☎ 0800/441-234 or 09/355-1234. www.auckland.regency.hyatt.com. 358 units. Doubles NZ$430–NZ$655. AE, DC, MC, V. Map p. 72.

★★★ kids **The Langham Hotel Auckland** CITY

I love the Langham. It's Auckland's plushest hotel and the service is impeccable. Staff thinks of everything. All rooms are opulent and Club Level takes that up a notch further. It's traditional style at its best and the new rooftop Chuan Spa and pool is a little heaven on earth. 83 Symonds St. ☎ 0800/616-261 or 09/379-5132. www.langhamhotels.co.nz. 411 units. Doubles NZ$200–NZ$700. AE, DC, MC, V. Map p. 72.

★★★ **Mollies on Tweed** ST.MARY'S BAY

Between the grand 1870s home and the contemporary addition, you won't find a single fault here. Mollies is about romance and beauty—a feast for all the senses. Rooms are filled with art and antiques and the restaurant is a singular pleasure. It's handy to Ponsonby shops but I doubt you'll want to leave. 6 Tweed St., St. Mary's Bay. ☎ 09/376-3489. www.mollies.co.nz. 13 units. Doubles NZ$630–NZ$1,005. AE, DC, MC, V. Map p. 72.

★ **Omahu Lodge** REMUERA

Retreat to a beautiful room overlooking a swimming pool in one of the city's best suburbs. Fine bed linens, ensuite bathrooms, a sauna, and delicious breakfasts served in the conservatory overlooking the pool are all part of the deal at Ken and Robyn Booth's place. 33 Omahu Rd., Remuera. ☎ 09/524-5648. www.omahulodge.co.nz. 4 units. Doubles NZ$195–NZ$325 w/breakfast. V. Map p. 72.

★ **Peace and Plenty Inn** DEVONPORT

Romantics will love this sumptuous, floral-themed haven in a gracious old home set in sub-tropical gardens. All rooms are beautifully decorated and have ensuite bathrooms. The sunny upstairs rooms have views and balconies but the downstairs spaces are intimate and cool. Shops are around the corner. **6 Flagstaff Terrace, Devonport. ☎ 09/445-2925. www.peaceandplenty.co.nz. 7 units. Doubles NZ$350–NZ$375 w/breakfast. MC, V. Map p. 72.**

★ kids **Quest Parnell** PARNELL
You always get a good price deal at Quest and here, you'll be close to Parnell's shops and restaurants. The serviced studio, one-bedroom, and two-bedroom apartments are modern, roomy, and smartly furnished. There's a fabulous heated lap pool and gym. **8 Heather St., Parnell. ☎ 0800/804-808 or 09/337-0804. www.questparnell.co.nz. 36 units. Doubles NZ$140–NZ$300. AE, DC, MC, V. Map p. 72.**

★ kids **Scenic Hotel Auckland** CITY
You'll get great rates at this hotel, which occupies a beautiful historic building across the road from the Town Hall. It's not as flash as some but it has a terrific city atmosphere and it's always buzzing with activity. Try to get one of the northwest-facing rooms for views straight down Queen Street. **380 Queen St. ☎ 09/374-1741. www.scenicgroup.co.nz.**

100 units. Doubles NZ$230–NZ$530. AE, DC, MC, V. Map p. 72.

★★★ kids **SKYCITY Grand Hotel** CITY
Linked to the casino complex by a bridge, SKYCITY Grand offers the best of everything and New Zealand art makes a big statement. It's home to a top restaurant and a beautiful spa and pool complex. All rooms are bright and beautiful. It's bigger than the Hilton and less formal than the Langham. **90 Federal St. ☎ 0800/759-2489 or 09/363-7000; www.skycitygrand.co.nz. 316 units. Doubles NZ$635–NZ$675. AE, DC, MC, V. Map p. 72.**

★★ **Stafford Villa** BIRKENHEAD POINT
Mark and Chris Windram are superb hosts and their beautiful Victorian villa, filled with antiques and art, couldn't be in a nicer, quieter spot, just a 5-minute walk from the ferry. A leafy garden curls around the elegant home and both beautifully appointed upstairs rooms open onto a wide verandah. **2 Awanui St., Birkenhead Point. ☎ 09/418-3022. www.staffordvilla.co.nz. 2 units. Doubles NZ$468 w/breakfast and evening port. AE, DC, MC, V. Map p. 72.**

> *Enjoy fine examples of New Zealand contemporary art throughout SKYCITY Grand Hotel.*

Auckland Nightlife Best Bets

Best Beer Bar
Mac's Brewbar, Northern Steamship Company, 122 Quay St. (p. 85).

Celebrity Favorite
Sale Street, 7 Sale St. (p. 86).

Best Cocktails
Racket, 6-10 Roukai Lane (p. 86).

Funkiest Decor
Smith, Corner of Commerce and Galway sts. (p. 86).

Best Gay Bar
Family Bar, 270 Karangahape Rd. (p. 86).

Best Irish Bar
Danny Doolan's, Viaduct Harbour (p. 86).

Best Kiwi Music
Kings Arms, 59 France St. (p. 87).

Best Tapas Bar
Bellota, 91 Federal St. (p. 85).

Best Theater
Maidment Theatre, Auckland University, 8 Alfred St. (p. 87).

Best Wine Bar
Honey, 5 O'Connell St. (p. 85).

Travel Tip

For locations of the establishments in this section, see the map on p. 72–73.

> *Unwind with the cool crowd at Bellota, a moody Spanish tapas bar.*

Auckland Nightlife A to Z

Bars & Cocktail Lounges

★★ Agents & Merchants BRITOMART

Inspired by Britomart's 19th-century trading roots, this sophisticated little tapas bar is located in the city's only private licensed lane, where it serves up great cocktails and your choice of over 200 wines. They double as a lunch spot during the week. Roukai Lane, Britomart. ☎ 09/5854. www.agentsandmerchants. co.nz. Map p. 72.

★★★ Bellota CITY

This is a beautiful, dark, super-cool, expensive, sensuously modern take on a Spanish tapas bar. Long wooden tables are the perfect surface to welcome the culinary skills of Peter Gordon and the divine tapas he has devised for you to enjoy with Spanish sangria—and anything else that takes your fancy. Sophisticated, elegant, and a great way to start any night. SKYCITY, 91 Federal St. ☎ 09/363-6000. Map p. 72.

★ Chapel PONSONBY

Excellent bar snacks—especially thin-crust pizzas—and live music attract crowds that overflow onto the pavements at this neighborhood institution. 147 Ponsonby Rd. ☎ 09/360-4528. www.chapel.co.nz. Map p. 72.

★★★ Honey CITY

This upmarket champagne and cocktail bar is classy and super-sexy, with purple sofas, gold velvet drapes, and a dim, moody atmosphere. Flit between The Moth Room, with its sunken dance floor, the sexy Honey Bar, or walk up marble stairs to the Breeze Bar, Auckland's only outdoor roof bar. 5 O'Connell St. ☎ 09/369-5639. www.honeybar.co.nz. Map p. 72.

★★ Mac's Brewbar, Northern Steamship Company BRITOMART

This Mac's Brewbar inhabits the 130-year-old headquarters of the Northern Steamship Company and attracts a mixed group of beer lovers. House and soul DJs play Thursday through Saturday nights. 122 Quay St., Britomart. ☎ 09/374-3952. www.northernsteamship.co.nz. Map p. 72.

★★ Opium CITY

This luxurious Asian-themed spot (deep chestnut red and hot pink with wooden floors, gilded Buddhas, and Chinese calligraphy) is a favorite of the A-list crowd, who slink in here

> *Mac's Brewbar Northern Steamship Company has turned interior decoration on its head—or at least the lamps.*

> *You'll get a real feel for Auckland's grass roots music culture at one of its many live music venues.*

when the pressure of being famous becomes too much. SKYCITY Metro Bldg, Aotea Sq., 291-297 Queen St. ☎ 09/378-0888. www.relish group.com. Map p. 72.

★★★ Racket BRITOMART
Start your night relaxing at this laid-back bar, maybe on one of the old sofas beside the outdoor fireplace. Known for their superb cocktails and the country's biggest selection of premium rums, they also host live music most nights of the week. 6-10 Roukai Lane, Britomart ☎ 09/309-5852. Map p. 72.

★★★ Sale Street FREEMAN'S BAY
There's something for everyone at this popular mega-nightspot, from a restaurant and yakitori bar to live music stages, a microbrewery, private bars, and huge outdoor decks. The merriment overflows into the wee small hours. Expect anything from comedy nights to themed parties. 7 Sale St., Freemans Bay. ☎ 09/307-8148. www.salest.co.nz. Map p. 72.

★★★ Smith BRITOMART
Modeled after an ornate Victorian sitting room complete with gilt mirrors, flocked armchairs, and stags' heads, this is just the place to enjoy fine wine and delicious cocktails. The service is suave, the music mellow and well chosen. Corner of Commerce and Galway sts., Britomart. ☎ 09/309-5529. www.smith-bar. co.nz. Map p. 72.

★★ SPQR PONSONBY
This Ponsonby institution is favored by the gay and the straight—and the television crowd. Such cocktails as the Slapper and the Horny Monkey have set the tone for some wild nights

and good times. 150 Ponsonby Rd. ☎ 09/360-1710. www.spqrnz.co.nz. Map p. 72.

Gay Bars & Clubs

★★★ Family Bar NEWTON
Auckland's most popular drag club and DJ bar always attracts a colorful gay, lesbian, and transgender crowd. Miss Ribena, the resident drag queen, makes appearances on stage on Wednesday and Saturday nights. 270 Karangahape Rd. ☎ 09/309-0213. www.familybar. co.nz. Map p. 72.

★ Kamo NEWTON
A popular spot for drag queen shows and karaoke. Eat, drink, chat, and dance. 382 Karangahape Rd. ☎ 09/377-2313. Map p. 72.

Urge NEWTON
I'm told Urge is a good bar for "the bear, rugged, masculine crowd." Be sure to wear leather. It's been an iconic part of the Auckland gay scene since 1997. 490 Karangahape Rd. ☎ 09/307-2155. www.urgebar.co.nz. Map p. 72.

Live Music Bars & Pubs

★ Danny Doolan's VIADUCT HARBOUR
Live music is staged here Thursday through Saturday nights and the place pulsates with activity as the night wears on. Definitely popular with the rowdy, beer-drinking crowd. Viaduct Harbour. ☎ 09/358-2554. www.danny doolans.co.nz. Map p. 72.

★★★ Dogs Bollix NEWTON
This is one of the city's premium music venues; it showcases the best homegrown talent along with international rock, pop, Celtic, folk, and blues talent. There's outstanding pub food and good ale to boot. Corner of Karangahape

and Newton Rds. ☎ 09/376-4600. www.dogs
bollix.co.nz. Map p. 72.

★★★ Kings Arms NEWTON
Another of the country's top live rock-n'-roll
venues, this one also features international
and local favorites. They have live shows several nights a week and in the large garden bar
on Sunday afternoons. 59 France St. ☎ 09/373-
3240. www.kingsarms.co.nz. Map p. 72.

★★ Nuffield Street Brewbar NUFFIELD STREET
Chandeliers suspended over wooden floors
create a stylish interior that focuses on Macs'
brew beers. It's incredibly popular with the
after-work crowd so get in before 5pm if you
want a seat—and don't expect a big wine list.
23 Nuffield St. ☎ 09/523-4554; www.nuffield
stbrewbar.co.nz. Map p. 72.

★★★ Wine Cellar NEWTON
This bohemian, slightly underground, student
grunge type of place is enormously popular.
You'll get indie rock, live or recorded, with a bit
of blues, jazz, country, and pop thrown in for
good measure. St Kevin's Arcade, 183 Karangahape Rd. Map p. 72.

Performing Arts

★★★ Auckland Town Hall CITY
This is one of Auckland's best-known historic
buildings. They regularly host a wide range of
performances from symphony orchestras to
blues, funk, jazz, and soul gigs. The Auckland
Philharmonia and the New Zealand Symphony
Orchestra are regular performers. 50 Mayoral
Dr. For performance information contact The
Edge Booking Office ☎ 09/307-5060. www.
buytickets.co.nz. Map p. 72.

★★★ Maidment Theatre CITY
Auckland University's 448-seat Maidment
Theatre is well known for its New Zealand
drama shows and theatersports (improv). The
associated Musgrove studio seats another 104
for second shows. 8 Alfred St. ☎ 09/308-2383.
www.maidment.auckland.ac.nz. Map p. 72.

★★★ Vector Arena PARNELL
Come here for the big-name music shows,
along with major sporting events, theater, and
exhibitions. It's Auckland's newest, world-
class, multiple purpose arena. Mahuhu Cres.,
Parnell. ☎ 09/358-1250. www.vectorarena.
co.nz. Map p. 72.

Auckland Fast Facts

Arriving
BY PLANE Auckland International Airport
(☎ 0800/247-767; www.auckland-airport.
co.nz) is 21km (13 miles) south of the city,
about a 35–45 minute car trip. More than
25 airlines serve the airport. **BY BUS** Both
Intercity (☎ 09/623-1503) and **Newmans**
(☎09/623-1504) arrive and depart from
Auckland to all major North Island centers.

Emergencies & Medical Care
Dial **111** for all police, fire, and ambulance
emergencies. **Auckland City Hospital,** 2
Park Rd., Grafton (☎ **09/367-7000**) includes
National Women's Hospital and Starship
Children's Hospital. For dental care try **Emer-
gency Dental Service,** Corner of Greenlane E.
Rd. and Peach Parade, Remuera (☎ **09/523-
3030**). For emergency medical care visit
CityMed Medical Centre, Corner of Mills
Lane and Albert St., City (☎ **09/377-5525**;
www.citymed.co.nz); or try **Auckland Metro**

Doctors & Travelcare, 17 Emily Place
☎ **0508/306-306**; www.aucklandmetro
doctors.co.nz).

Internet
Get online at **Cyber Max,** 291 Queen St.
(☎ 09/979-2468) or **Net Central Cyber Café,**
5 Lorne St. (☎ 09/373-5408).

Taxis
Try **Auckland Co-Op Taxis** (☎ 09/300-3000;
www.cooptaxi.co.nz) or **Corporate Cabs**
(☎ 09/377-0773). You can also find cab
stands throughout the city and at major hotels, or hail cabs on the street.

Visitor Information Centers
AUCKLAND I-SITE VISITOR INFORMATION
CENTRE Princes Wharf, Corner of Quay
and Hobson sts.; ☎ 09/307-0615; www.
aucklandnz.com. DEVONPORT I-SITE VISITOR
CENTRE 3 Victoria Rd., Devonport; ☎ 09/446-
0677; www.northshorenz.com.

4
Northland

My Favorite Moments

This skinny finger of land is one of nature's best playgrounds but surprisingly, many visitors overlook it. The ocean has nibbled out hundreds of pretty bays, the weather is warm and balmy, the scenery unforgettable, the beaches sublime, and the history intriguing—but you need to venture beyond the comforts of the Bay of Islands to find the best treasures. Northland, known to Maori as Te Tai Tokerau (Birthplace of a Nation), has much to offer, with two contrasting coastlines: white scenic beaches that curve around sheltered coves to the east and long stretches of wild, dune-backed beaches and kauri forests pounded by the Tasman Sea to the west.

> **PREVIOUS PAGE** *Experience the adrenaline rush of kayaking right up to the foot of Waitangi's Haruru Falls.* **THIS PAGE** *Cape Reinga's Te Paki sand dunes bring out the kid in people of all ages.*

1 Picnicking at Matai Bay. This exquisite little horseshoe of golden sand and crystal-clear turquoise water is one of my favorite places in all of New Zealand. Last year I celebrated my birthday with a picnic on the grassy hill above the beach. I couldn't have chosen a better place. See p. 110.

2 Standing on Cape Reinga. It's a rare day in summer when you're the only person visiting this narrow wisp of land that marks the northern end of New Zealand, but when you are, there's something almost mystical about it. The Maori think so too: Cape Reinga is believed to be the leaping-off point for their spirits after death. See p. 101, **17**.

3 Eating fish and chips at Mangonui. This cute-as-a-button little fishing village is just the place to hang a fishing line with the kids. If you don't catch anything it doesn't really matter because they have one of the best fish and chip shops in Northland. Eat them from the newspaper on the waterfront. See p. 100, **14**.

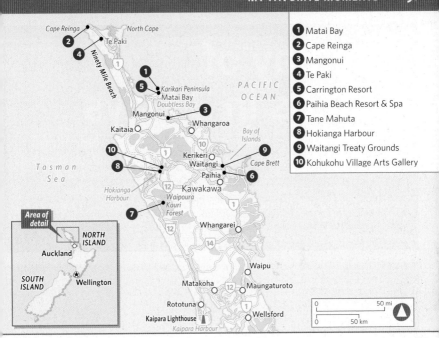

1. Matai Bay
2. Cape Reinga
3. Mangonui
4. Te Paki
5. Carrington Resort
6. Paihia Beach Resort & Spa
7. Tane Mahuta
8. Hokianga Harbour
9. Waitangi Treaty Grounds
10. Kohukohu Village Arts Gallery

④ Racing down giant sand dunes at Te Paki.
Youngsters (and the young at heart) will get
a kick out of racing down the face of these
gigantic sand dunes at the top end of 90 Mile
Beach. There are usually boarding operators in
business here too if you feel like accelerating
the pace. See p. 110.

⑤ Lounging by the pool at Carrington Resort.
We all deserve a treat from time to time, and
basking in the sun like a lizard on the edge of
the pool at Carrington, being handed drinks
and tasty edibles, goes a long way to the sort of
personal indulgence I aspire to. See p. 115.

**⑥ Having spa treatments at Paihia Beach
Resort & Spa.** I don't think there's a part of you
that can't be primped, pummeled, preened,
and perfected in this beautifully presented spa
facility. It gives a whole new meaning to the
term makeover. See p. 114.

**⑦ Gazing up into the towering branches of
kauri giant, Tane Mahuta.** No matter how
many times I stand under this magnificent giant
kauri tree, I am still filled with awe. It's one of
New Zealand's treasures and thousands of us
still grin at childhood photos of ourselves posed
beneath its massive trunk. See p. 103, ⑲.

⑧ Crossing Hokianga Harbour on a fine day.
Many call it the haunted Hokianga—a moody,
remote, shadowy place that early Maori
claimed was formed by a *taniwha* (sea mon-
ster). It is still a Maori stronghold and you'll
see dozens of cute little red-roofed churches
that invariably mark a Maori community. If the
weather is fine when you make the ferry crossing, have your camera ready to capture the
water's perfect reflections. See p. 107, ⑫.

⑨ Exploring the Waitangi Treaty Grounds.
Taking a personalized tour of Waitangi Treaty
Grounds with one of their informed local
guides is a highlight of any Northland trip.
You'll learn all about the native plants Maori
used, how waka are carved, and what the
carvings in the elaborate Maori meetinghouse
mean. See p. 92, ①.

**⑩ Discovering the Kohukohu Village Arts Gal-
lery.** I was as surprised as anyone when I came
upon a couple of very good art galleries in this
tiny Hokianga town just up from the Kohukohu
ferry terminal. It's not what you expect of a
minute village that's home to just 150 people.
See p. 102, ⑱.

The Bay of Islands in 3 Days

Rather than having you race around the entire Northland province, spending most of your time in a car, I've designed this 3-day itinerary to focus on the Bay of Islands area—a place that is central to New Zealand history. It's where the Treaty of Waitangi was signed; Russell was New Zealand's first European settlement and (briefly) our first capital. It's also where American author Zane Grey spent his days hauling in huge catches during his deep sea fishing exploits in the 1920s.

> Sunrise or sunset, all is quiet in the little seaside village of Russell, across the water from Paihia.

START Paihia is the main town of the Bay of Islands, 233km (145 miles) north of Auckland. From Pahia's main shopping area, head northwest on Marsden Rd. Follow this as it becomes Te Karuwha Parade and then Tau Henare Dr., about 2.4km (1½ miles) to the Waitangi Treaty Grounds. **TRIP LENGTH** About 55km (34 miles).

1 ★★★ kids **Waitangi Treaty Grounds.** The Confederation of Maori chiefs signed the first treaty here in 1840, granting Maori the rights of British subjects in exchange for recognition of British sovereignty. Many of the chiefs did not fully understand what they had signed, in part because the Maori version of the treaty included some inadequate or imprecise

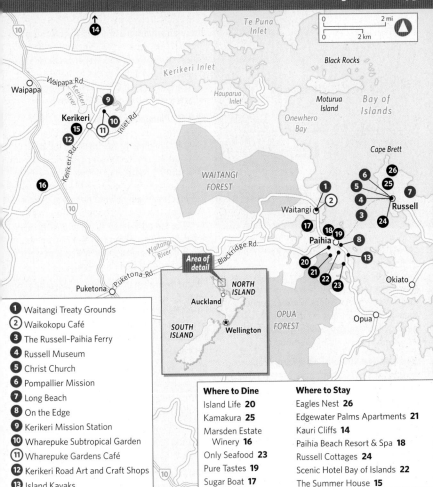

1 Waitangi Treaty Grounds
2 Waikokopu Café
3 The Russell–Paihia Ferry
4 Russell Museum
5 Christ Church
6 Pompallier Mission
7 Long Beach
8 On the Edge
9 Kerikeri Mission Station
10 Wharepuke Subtropical Garden
11 Wharepuke Gardens Café
12 Kerikeri Road Art and Craft Shops
13 Island Kayaks

Where to Dine
Island Life 20
Kamakura 25
Marsden Estate Winery 16
Only Seafood 23
Pure Tastes 19
Sugar Boat 17

Where to Stay
Eagles Nest 26
Edgewater Palms Apartments 21
Kauri Cliffs 14
Paihia Beach Resort & Spa 18
Russell Cottages 24
Scenic Hotel Bay of Islands 22
The Summer House 15

translations of important concepts like "sovereignty." These misunderstandings sparked conflict that continues to this day; a special tribunal was convened in 1975 to investigate claims of the Crown's alleged breaches of treaty and issue reparations. You'll see a copy of the treaty written in Maori. The 506-hectare (1,250-acre) reserve is home to the magnificent *whare runanga* (meetinghouse), completed in 1940 under the direction of master carver Pine Taiapa to mark the treaty centenary, and the impressive 35m (115-ft.) Maori *waka* (canoe) *Ngatokimatawhaorua*. Start off with the film in the main pavilion, then take one of the 1-hour guided tours. This gives you a more detailed overview from a Maori perspective. During the February 6 Waitangi Day celebrations, thousands of Maori from all over the country descend on the Treaty Grounds. ⏱ Half-day. Tau Henare Dr., Waitangi. ☎ 09/402-7437. www.waitangi.net.nz. Admission NZ$25 adults, NZ$12 for kids 13 and under. Ask about value packages that include tours and activities. Oct–April daily 8:30am–7:30pm; May–Sept daily 9am–5pm.

② 🍴 ★ 🅺🅸🅳🆂 **Waikokopu Café.** This cafe is tucked away in the bush on the Treaty Grounds. Stop in for a tasty salad or coffee and sandwiches. Waitangi Treaty Grounds, Tau Henare Dr., Waitangi. ☎ 09/402-6275. Most meals around NZ$16.

> Whenever you enter a Maori meeting house, you must remove your shoes and place them neatly outside the main door.

Drive back into Paihia the way you came and park in the wharf carpark. Catch a ferry to Russell. When you get off the ferry you'll be in the center of town and the next four stops are within close walking distance.

3 ★★ kids **The Russell-Paihia Ferry.** You can drive to Russell (via the Opua car ferry) but there's really no need—everything in Russell is within walking distance and the passenger ferry from Paihia is much more convenient. Kids will love it and you'll get a different perspective of both settlements from the water. Paihia Wharf/Russell Wharf. Round-trip fare NZ$11 adults, NZ$5.50 kids 5–15. Hourly 7am–7:30pm daily with extended summer sailings until 10:30pm.

4 ★ kids **Russell Museum.** Start by watching the 10-minute video about the town's history and then explore an interesting Maori section, a 1/5 scale model of Captain James Cook's HMS *Endeavour*, early whaling artifacts, and Zane Grey fishing memorabilia. ⏱ 40 min. 2 York St., Russell. ☎ 09/403-7701; www.russell museum.org.nz. Admission NZ$7.50 adults, NZ$2 kids 5–15. Feb–Dec daily 10am–4pm, Jan daily 10am–5pm.

5 ★ **Christ Church.** This little gem—Te Whare Karakia o Kororareka—is the oldest wooden church in New Zealand. Built in 1836, it still bears old musket and cannonball holes from an 1845 battle. The cemetery contains interesting memorials; the largest is to Tamati Waka Nene, a prominent Ngapuhi chief, who colluded with European settlers against Hone Heke in the Northland wars of the 1840s. ⏱ 30 min. Corner of Church St. and Robertson Rd. www.oldchurch.org.nz. Free admission.

6 ★ kids **Pompallier Mission.** Built in 1841, this is New Zealand's oldest surviving Roman Catholic building. It was the French Catholic headquarters to the Western Pacific and from 1842–1849 it housed a printing press, used to print religious documents in Maori language (*te reo*). Today, along with the press, there's a working tannery and book-bindery. ⏱ 40 min. The Strand, Russell. ☎ 09/403-9015. www. pompallier.co.nz. Admission NZ$7.50 adults, free kids; pre-booked tours NZ$5 per person. Daily 10am-4pm (5pm Nov–Apr).

Pick up some edible treats in town and then, from the north end of The Strand, turn right into Cass St., right into York St., then left into Chapel St. This veers left and becomes Oneroa Rd. Walk 1.2km (¾ mile) over the hill to Oneroa Bay and Long Beach.

7 ★★ kids **Long Beach.** Spend the rest of your afternoon lounging about on the sand, taking a swim, eating snacks, and letting local life glide by. ⏱ At least 2 hr.

Walk back over the hill to catch the ferry back to Paihia. On day 2, start early and head to Paihia Wharf.

8 ★★★ kids **On the Edge.** You can't come to this region and not get out on the water. You have multiple choices, of course, and a trip to the Bay of Islands i-SITE Visitor Centre (p. 119) will give you all the options. I recommend Explore NZ's adrenaline-pumping On the Edge day sail on New Zealand's largest and fastest commercial catamaran. You'll get to snorkel, swim, kayak, or enjoy a nature walk on a deserted island. These waters are also home to numerous dolphins, so have your camera ready. ⏱ 1 day. Explore NZ, Paihia Waterfront. ☎ 0800/365-744 or 09/402-8234. www.explorenz.co.nz. Admission NZ$125 adults, NZ$90 kids 5–15. Daily departures Oct–April from Paihia and Russell wharves.

On day 3, leave Paihia village heading northwest on Marsden Rd. Turn left onto Puketona Rd., then right into St. Hwy.

10, which becomes Bulls Rd. At the main roundabout, take the 3rd exit onto Kerikeri Rd. Drive straight through the town following signs to Kerikeri Basin. It's 24km (15 miles) and takes about 25 min.

⑨ ★★ kids Kerikeri Mission Station. This tiny settlement beside the Kerikeri River was once the site of a blacksmith's shop, school, chapel, houses, and shops. The old Stone Store has been operating since 1836 and Kemp House (1821), originally built for the Reverend John Butler, is now the oldest surviving building in New Zealand. Entry to the ground floor of the shop is free. ⏱ 1 hr. 246 Kerikeri Rd. ☎ 0800/802-010 or 09/407-9236. www.historic.org.nz; www.stonestore.co.nz. The full Mission Experience, which includes an overview of the area's early history and the Stone Store, costs NZ$10. A visit to the upper levels of the store costs an additional NZ$5 per person. Open daily, Nov–April 10am–5pm, May–Oct 10am–4pm.

Drive back up Kerikeri Rd. a short distance to Wharepuke Subtropical Garden.

⑩ ★★ Wharepuke Subtropical Garden. You don't have to be a dedicated gardener to enjoy this lush creation. Wander through sub-tropical fruiting plants, bromeliads, dragon trees, palms, and more. It's a great place to take close-ups if you're into plant photography, and you can take a guided tour with the owner. ⏱ 1 hr. 190 Kerikeri Rd., Kerikeri. ☎ 09/407-8933. www.sub-tropicalgarden.co.nz. Free admission to garden; guided tours by appointment NZ$25 per person. Daily 8:30am–6pm.

⑪   🍽 **Wharepuke Gardens Café.** There's a very nice cafe serving lunch and dinner at Wharepuke Gardens in summer, so stop awhile and enjoy a light lunch among the leafy scenery. 190 Kerikeri Rd., Kerikeri. ☎ 09/407-8933. Meals about NZ$16.

⑫ ★ Kerikeri Road Art and Craft Shops. Kerikeri is home to a thriving arts and crafts community and you can spend an afternoon following *The Kerikeri Art & Craft Trail*, a brochure available from visitor centers, which details around 20 excellent outlets and artisans located within a few kilometers of the town. Even if you're heading back to Paihia, there are a number of excellent shopping opportunities along Kerikeri Road, including Makana Confections (504 Kerikeri Rd., www.makana.co.nz), which sells delicious handmade chocolates. ⏱ At least 1 hr.

⑬ ★★★ kids Island Kayaks. The professional team at Island Kayaks will show you the basics, then you'll take to the water with a guide on a custom-made tour that includes offshore islands, rock pools, mangrove swamps, historical landmarks, and wildlife. Bottlenose dolphins are frequent visitors to these waters. There's an afternoon tea stop along the way and you'll get the chance to trying snorkeling and fishing too. ⏱ Half-day. Beachfront, Paihia. ☎ 0800/611-440 or 021/121-8720. www.baybeachhire.co.nz. Half-day tour NZ$65 per person. Daily morning and afternoon; call for times.

> *Plant photographers will have plenty of chances to exercise their skills in the lush environs of Wharepuke Subtropical Garden.*

Northland in 1 Week

This week-long road trip covers a lot of ground and gives you a chance to go beyond the norm—to experience a little of the underrated Whangarei region and to move north from the Bay of Islands to discover remote beaches and rich cultural and pioneer history. Take your swimsuit and plenty of sunscreen.

> According to Maori legend, the land beyond the Cape Reinga lighthouse is the leaping-off point for the souls of the dead returning to Hawaiki.

START Whangarei is 169km (105 miles) north of Auckland and 66km (41 miles) south of the Bay of Islands. **TRIP LENGTH** 730km (454 miles).

❶ ★★ kids Whangarei Town Basin. Also known as Quayside, the paved promenade stretching along the marina is the prettiest part of Whangarei city. I suggest you stop in the Quayside Information Centre (☎ 09/438-3993), then investigate Clapham's Clock Museum, Dent St. (☎ 09/438-3993; www.claphamsclocks.com), where you can see over 1,500 clocks, the largest collection in the Southern Hemisphere, including one that travels backwards. Admission is NZ$10 adults, NZ$5 kids and the museum is open daily 9am to 5pm. The basin is also home to shops and galleries with handcrafted jewelry, kauri woodwork, crafts, fine art, glass, and ceramics. ⏲ 1½ hr.

From the Whangarei Town Basin, turn onto Walton St., then left onto Maunu St., which becomes St. Hwy. 14 after you've crossed over St. Hwy. 1. The museum is about a 10 min. drive from the Town Basin.

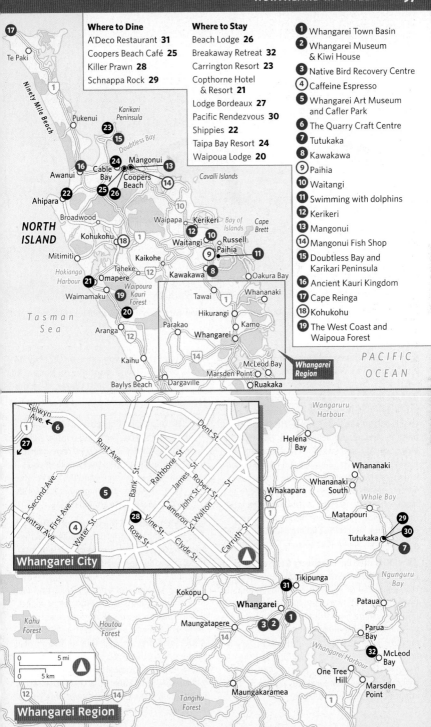

Where to Dine

A'Deco Restaurant **31**
Coopers Beach Café **25**
Killer Prawn **28**
Schnappa Rock **29**

Where to Stay

Beach Lodge **26**
Breakaway Retreat **32**
Carrington Resort **23**
Copthorne Hotel & Resort **21**
Lodge Bordeaux **27**
Pacific Rendezvous **30**
Shippies **22**
Taipa Bay Resort **24**
Waipoua Lodge **20**

1 Whangarei Town Basin
2 Whangarei Museum & Kiwi House
3 Native Bird Recovery Centre
4 Caffeine Espresso
5 Whangarei Art Museum and Cafler Park
6 The Quarry Craft Centre
7 Tutukaka
8 Kawakawa
9 Paihia
10 Waitangi
11 Swimming with dolphins
12 Kerikeri
13 Mangonui
14 Mangonui Fish Shop
15 Doubtless Bay and Karikari Peninsula
16 Ancient Kauri Kingdom
17 Cape Reinga
18 Kohukohu
19 The West Coast and Waipoua Forest

Whangarei City

Whangarei Region

> *Exquisite beaches along the Tutukaka Coast, near Whangarei, are a beacon for holidaymakers and surfers alike.*

② ★★★ kids **Whangarei Museum & Kiwi House.** Highlights of this excellent little museum, set in a 25-hectare (62-acre) heritage park, include its collection of Northland Maori artifacts—beautiful old *korowai* (cloaks), *kete* (baskets), and carvings—and the Fairburn beetle collection, which displays 20,000 New Zealand specimens. The adjacent Kiwi House features the endangered North Island brown kiwi in a nocturnal house; you can catch up with our native lizards in the Gecko House. ⏱ 1½ hr. St.Hwy. 14, Maunu, Whangarei. ☎ 09/438-9630. www.whangareimuseum. co.nz. Admission NZ$12 adults, NZ$6 kids 3–16, NZ$28 family. Daily 10am–4pm.

③ ★ kids **Native Bird Recovery Centre.** Located next door to the Whangarei Museum & Kiwi House, this avian refuge center helps rehabilitate injured and distressed native birds. You'll find everything here from the talking tui (a permanent resident) to recovering owls, recuperating kiwi, tiny fantails, and perhaps even an exhausted albatross. ⏱ 30 min. St. Hwy. 14, next to Whangarei Museum. ☎ 09/438-1457. www.whangareinativebirdrecovery.org.nz. Free admission. Mon–Fri 9am–5pm.

Drive back the way you came on St. Hwy. 14, cross over St. Hwy. 1, continue on Maunu Rd. and go straight ahead onto Water St. at the roundabout.

④ 🍴 ★ **Caffeine Espresso.** This is one of the city's most lively and popular places to stop for a bite to eat. They have delicious vegetarian burgers that will keep you going all afternoon—and the best coffee in town. 4 Water St., Whangarei. ☎ 09/438-6925. Most meals around NZ$16.

⑤ ★ **Whangarei Art Museum and Cafler Park.** This is Northland's only public gallery and as such, you can expect very worthwhile shows of national and Northland art, both contemporary and heritage. It's situated among the rose gardens of Cafler Park and you'll also find sculptures in the gardens. If you enjoy plant collections, cross the nearby footbridge over the river and visit Botanica, on First Avenue (☎ 09/430-4200; www.wdc.govt.nz; free admission; daily 10am–4pm), where you can immerse yourself in native ferns, subtropical plants, and a large cacti garden. ⏱ 1½ hr. Water St. ☎ 09/430-4240. www.whangareiartmuseum.co.nz. Free admission. Tues–Fri 10am–4pm, Sat–Sun noon–4pm.

From Water St., turn left into Bank St., then left again into Rust Ave., which becomes Selwyn Ave. Cross over St. Hwy. 1 and follow signs to the Quarry Craft Centre.

6 ★ kids **The Quarry Craft Centre.** End your day wandering around this bush-clad quarry site where working artists and craftspeople belonging to the Northland Arts Trust work. There's a large shop filled with a wide range of arts and crafts. Spend the night in Whangarei. ⏱ 1 hr. 21 Selwyn Rd., Whangarei. ☎ 09/438-1215. www.quarryarts.org. Free admission. Daily 9:30am–4:30pm.

On day 2, from Dent St. at the Town Basin, head east and turn left into Hatea Dr., left at Nixon St., then right into Mill Rd. Veer left onto Waiatawa Rd. and continue onto Kiripaka Rd. Go through the roundabout and onto Ngunguru Rd., following signs to Tutukaka. It's 29km (18 miles) and takes about 35 min.

7 ★★★ kids **Tutukaka.** Start early and spend your day exploring this gorgeous beach area. From the small settlement of Kiripaka on, the road winds past numerous beaches, harbors, and estuaries, and you can stop at your leisure. Tutukaka is the takeoff point for exploration of the **Poor Knights Islands Marine Reserve,** 24km (15 miles) off the coast. It's world renowned as a prime diving spot but sightseeing tours also depart daily (p. 112, "Cruising"). Spend the night in Tutukaka. ⏱ 1 day.

Leave Tutukaka traveling south on Marina Rd. Turn right onto Matapouri Rd., which you follow around the coast and then inland via Waipaipai and Marua. Continue on, following signs to Hikurangi and St. Hwy. 1. Turn right and head north, following signs to Kawakawa. It's 73km (45 miles) and will take about 1½ hr.

8 ★★ kids **Kawakawa.** You'll only need to make a brief stop here to see the local public toilets—and yes, it is worth it. Brightly colored tiles, columns, and arches make this a public toilet like no other. Designed by renowned Austrian-born artist and architect Friedensreich Hundertwasser, the grass-roofed toilets have put the otherwise unremarkable town of Kawakawa on the map. ⏱ 15 min.

> At Waitangi Treaty Grounds meeting house, Te Whare Runanga, you'll have the chance to take excellent photos of detailed Maori carvings.

Back in the car, veer right out of Kawakawa following signs to Paihia/Bay of Islands, about 18km (11 miles) and 25 min. away.

9 🍽 **Paihia.** There are numerous small cafes and takeaway bars along Marsden Road and down Williams Road in central Paihia. Take your pick and stop for lunch.

It's just a few minutes to the next stop; drive through Paihia on Marsden Rd. and follow it around the coast, veering right onto Tau Henare Dr.

10 ★★★ kids **Waitangi.** Spend the rest of day three here, exploring the Waitangi Treaty Grounds (p. 92, **1**); followed by a snack at Waikokopu Café (p. 93, **2**) and some late afternoon kayaking (p. 95, **13**). Spend the night in Paihia.

> *Bottlenose dolphins are plentiful in the warm Bay of Islands' waters, and several operators can get you up close and personal.*

⑪ ★★★ kids Swimming with dolphins. There are estimated to be around 450 bottlenose dolphins living in the Bay of Islands area and a number of operators will take you to see them. See p. 112, "Dolphin Watching," for more information. If you opt for a half-day dolphin experience, spend the rest of the afternoon catching the passenger ferry to Russell and exploring the town (p. 94, ❸–❼). Spend the night in Paihia. ⏱ 1 day.

On day 4, leave Paihia heading northwest on Marsden Rd. Turn left onto Puketona Rd., then right into St. Hwy. 10, which becomes Bulls Rd. At the main roundabout, take the third exit onto Kerikeri Rd. Drive straight through the town following signs to Kerikeri Basin. It's 24km (15 miles) and takes about 25 min.

⑫ ★★ kids Kerikeri. Kerikeri is all about history, orchards, arts and crafts, good food, and wine. Start at the Kerikeri Mission Station (p. 95, ❾) and Wharepuke Subtropical Garden (p. 95, ❿) before going on to explore the galleries, craft outlets, orchards, and chocolate-makers along Kerikeri Road. Spend the night in Kerikeri or splurge on a fancy night at Kauri Cliffs (p. 114) in nearby Matauri Bay. ⏱ 1 day.

Hit the road early on day 5, driving north from Kerikeri on St. Hwy. 10, following the signs to Mangonui. It's 60km (37 miles) and about 1 hr. away.

⑬ ★★★ kids Mangonui. This little fishing village marks the beginning of Doubtless Bay. Take a stroll along the Mangonui Boardwalk, checking out local shops and commercial fishing boats. ⏱ 1 hr.

⑭ 🍽 ★★★ Mangonui Fish Shop. If you're going to eat fish and chips in New Zealand, this legendary spot, with fish straight off the wharves and a quaint shop hanging over the water, is the very best place to do it. Beach Rd., Mangonui. ☎ 09/406-0478. NZ$10–NZ$15.

Drive north on Beach Rd. to rejoin St. Hwy. 10, turn right and head north, following signs to Karikari Peninsula. Once you've explored the beaches of Doubtless Bay, turn right on Inland Rd.

⑮ ★★★ kids Doubtless Bay and Karikari Peninsula. Although it's not far to your next bed on Karikari Peninsula, I suggest you take the rest of the day to get there, stopping along the way at some of the amazing beaches and spots of interest in Doubtless Bay. After lunch spend an hour at pretty, 2.5km (1½-mile) Coopers Beach, which is fringed by flowering *pohutu-kawa* (otherwise known as the New Zealand Christmas tree for its red blooms), and take a swim in the safe waters. It's just a few kilometers from Mangaonui and Cable Bay is just a few more kilometers away. I love its unique pinkish-white sand and kids can play safely

> *Cable Bay is just one of numerous pristine beaches in the Far North, where you'll have acres of sand all to yourself.*

where the creek meets the sea. You'll come to Taipa next, yet another picturesque beach spot, popular for swimming, boating, and fishing. Five kilometers (3 miles) north of that, stop at the well-signposted **Matthews Vintage Collection** (St. Hwy. 10, Taipa; ☎ 09/406-0203; www.matthewsvintage.com) and browse through an astonishing collection of classic farm equipment, machinery, musical instruments, moa bones, and more (admission NZ$10 adults, NZ$5 kids; open daily 9am–5pm). Continue on to Karikari Peninsula and follow signs to Matai Bay on Matai Bay Rd. It's 34km (21 miles) and about 35 minutes to Matai Bay from the St. Hwy. 10 turnoff. Laze away the last hours of the day on one of Matai Bay's pretty beaches, before retracing your steps to Carrington Resort on Matai Bay Road. (p. 115). ⏱ Half-day.

Leave Carrington early on day 6 and return the way you came to rejoin St. Hwy. 10. Drive 33km (21 miles) and about 30 min. to Awanui.

🔟 ★★ 𝗸𝗶𝗱𝘀 **Ancient Kauri Kingdom.** It's worth a quick stop at this factory and showroom to learn about the retrieval of massive 30,000- to 50,000-year-old kauri logs from Northland's peat swamps. The logs are then crafted into fine household products. The staircase carved into the largest kauri log ever found is something to see. ⏱ 30 min. 229 St. Hwy. 10, Awanui. ☎ 406-7172. www.ancientkauri.co.nz. Free admission. Daily 8:30am–5:30pm.

At Awanui, turn right and drive north on St. Hwy. 11, following signs 104km (65 miles) to Cape Reinga (about 1 hr. and 20 min.). Grab some picnic food and make sure you have a full tank of gas.

🔢 ★★★ 𝗸𝗶𝗱𝘀 **Cape Reinga.** This narrow, remote stretch will reward you with dramatic scenery and fabulous photos. Stop often to stretch your legs—perhaps on the silica sand beaches at Henderson's Bay or Rawarawa Beach—and when you reach the spectacular Parengarenga Harbour, make sure you're wearing sunglasses because the pure white quartz sand is truly

> *Tauteihiihi Marae at Kohukohu in the Hokianga is one of many marae belonging to New Zealand's largest Maori tribe, Ngapuhi.*

dazzling. Turn off Far North Road just north of Waitiki Landing onto Te Hapua Rd. to detour 12km (7½ miles, about 15 min.) to the Maori community of Te Hapua, New Zealand's northernmost settlement, and look out for the unique Ratana Church. Return the way you came and continue north to the lighthouse at Cape Reinga, which has been operating since 1941. The Maori believe that Cape Reinga is the departure point for the spirits of the recently deceased. Check out the nearby Te Paki sand dunes—a towering, sandy landscape that is heaven for kids (turn left off Cape Reinga Rd. onto Te Paki Stream Rd.). Note that private cars are not allowed on 90 Mile Beach because of hazardous tidal sweeps, quick sand, and sand holes. If you want to travel the beach take a tour; I recommend Sand Safaris Cape Reinga Tours (☎ 0800/869-090; www.sand safaris.co.nz) which cost around $65 for adults and $35 for kids 14 and under. ⏲ 1 day.

At the end of the day, return to Awanui and drive south to Kaitaia. Spend the night here, or at nearby Ahipara at the base of 90 Mile Beach. It's 111 km (69 miles) from Cape Reinga to Kaitaia (1 hr 25 min.) and another 14km (8⅔ miles) to Ahipara (15 min.). On day 7, leave Ahipara and soon after the township, turn right onto St. Hwy. 10 and follow signs to Broadwood and the Hokianga. Soon after Broadwood, turn right into St. Hwy. 12 and follow signs to the Kohukohu vehicle ferry. It takes about 1 hr (62km/39 miles) to reach the ferry.

⑱ 🛳 **Kohukohu.** Before you board the ferry, take a peek into Kohukohu Village Arts Gallery and enjoy pizza, burgers, cake, and coffee overlooking the water at **Waterline Café** (☎ 09/405-5557) or get a coffee from the mobile **Ferry Stop Espresso Truck** that parks by the ferry ramp (Tues-Sun 8am-7pm; NZ$5-NZ$12).

The Hokianga Vehicle Ferry makes its 15-minute crossing to Rawene every hour on the hour daily from 7:30am to 8pm. The journey to Waipoua Forest is 53km (33 miles) and takes 1 hr.

⑲ ★★★ kids The West Coast and Waipoua Forest. Take a quick look around Rawene's cute historic buildings before heading southwest to Opononi. This tiny beach town (with huge sand dunes across the harbor) was the center of national attention in 1955, when a friendly dolphin (named Opo after the town) spent a summer here, playing with swimmers. There's a statue of Opo overlooking the harbor, and the Hokianga i-SITE Visitor Centre in nearby Omapere shows a video of the dolphin. To get close up to the Hokianga Harbour sand dunes, the *Hokianga Express* boat departs Opononi Wharf on the hour (NZ$25 adults, NZ$15 kids). Further south, stop at Waipoua Forest. A colossal kauri called Tane Mahuta is well

signposted and is just a short walk from the carpark. The largest trees here are over 1,000 years old; Tane Mahuta (God of the Forest) and Te Matua Ngahere (Father of the Forest) are the two largest known in the country. If you prefer, save your forest visit until after dark and join Footprints Waipoua (29 St. Hwy. 12, Opononi ☎ 0800/687-836; www.foot printswaipoua.com) on a fascinating 4-hour night walk through the forests with Maori guides (NZ$90 adults, NZ$30 kids). Shorter tours are available as well. ☉ **1 day.**

> *Tane Mahuta (God of the Forest) is the largest known kauri tree in New Zealand.*

A Final Northland Stop

If you have time as you're leaving Waipoua, head south through Dargaville to Matakohe Kauri Museum, 5 Church Rd., Matakohe (☎ 09/431-7417; www.kauri-museum. com). It's 91km (57 miles) from Waipoua, about an hour and 20 minute drive. It's well sign-posted and is a memorable way to end your Northland adventures. The museum is open daily from 8:30am to 5:30pm; admission is NZ$12 adults, NZ$5 kids 5–15, or NZ$35 family.

Maori Northland

It was here in Northland that the great Polynesian navigator Kupe first set foot in New Zealand. Archeological evidence suggests that Polynesians first adapted to life here around the year A.D. 1000 before moving south into other areas, and the resident *iwi* (tribe), Ngapuhi, is still the largest tribe in New Zealand. Northland, though, is not so much about Maori tourism attractions as it is about an intrinsic presence, about myths, legends, and an interweaving with European history that has set the foundations for life in New Zealand today. This itinerary therefore focuses on several attractions already mentioned, but from a Maori perspective.

> *This giant waka (war canoe), Ngatokimatawhaorua, was built by the Ngapuhi tribe for the 1940 Treaty of Waitangi centenary.*

START Paihia is the main town of the Bay of Islands, 233km (145 miles) north of Auckland. From Pahia's main shopping area, head northwest on Marsden Rd. Follow this as it becomes Te Karuwha Parade and then Tau Henare Dr., about 2.4km (1½ miles) to the Waitangi Treaty Grounds. **TRIP LENGTH** About 125km (78 miles) and 3 days.

① ★★★ **kids** **Waitangi Treaty Grounds.** ⏱ Half-day. See p. 92, **①**.

② ★★ **kids** **Te Tii Marae.** Te Tii is located at the Waitangi River mouth just before you enter the Treaty Grounds. The *wharenui* (meeting-house) was built by members of the Maori Women's League after World War I and the influenza epidemic had a severe impact on

the male members of Northland *iwi* (tribe). As with all marae, do not enter without permission. Note the huge carvings in the adjacent field too—this is where much of the Waitangi Day celebrations on February 6 are centered. ⏱ 20 min. Tau Henare Dr., Paihia.

③ 🍴 **Café over the Bay.** This spot has excellent food for a light lunch and great views over the harbor. The beach opposite Te Tii Marae is a lovely spot for a picnic lunch as well. Upstairs, The Mall, Marsden Rd., Paihia. ☎ 09/402-8147. NZ$10–NZ$15.

Take the ferry (p. 94, **③**) to Russell from Paihia Wharf.

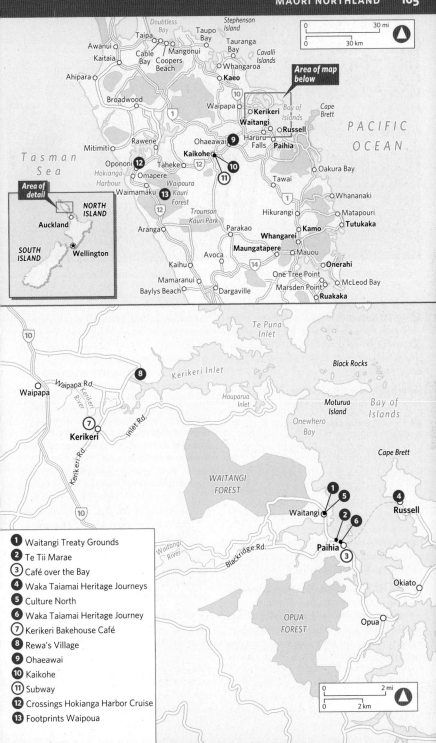

1 Waitangi Treaty Grounds
2 Te Tii Marae
3 Café over the Bay
4 Waka Taiamai Heritage Journeys
5 Culture North
6 Waka Taiamai Heritage Journey
7 Kerikeri Bakehouse Café
8 Rewa's Village
9 Ohaeawai
10 Kaikohe
11 Subway
12 Crossings Hokianga Harbor Cruise
13 Footprints Waipoua

> *Treat yourself to an authentic Maori experience with the tattooed Ngapuhi people of Taiamai Heritage Tours.*

④ ★★ kids Russell. It was in Russell that Maori chief Hone Heke felled the British flagpole on Flagstaff Hill four times in 1844–1845, in protest at the undermining of his authority. ⏲ 2 hr. See p. 94, ③–⑦.

Return to Paihia at your leisure after exploring greater Russell township.

⑤ ★★★ kids Culture North. This terrific show combines Maori and European settlement history in the Bay of Islands with contemporary drama, light, and sound, alongside traditional song and dance—all within the beautifully carved interior of the Waitangi Treaty Grounds meetinghouse. ⏲ 2 hr. Waitangi Meeting House, Treaty Grounds. ☎ 09/402-5990. www.culturenorth.co.nz. Admission NZ$65 per person, including free pick-up from accommodation. Shows 7:30pm Oct–Jan Mon–Thurs & Sat; Feb–Mar Mon–Sat.

⑥ ★★★ kids Waka Taiamai Heritage Journeys. Start day 2 with a unique, award-winning cultural experience with Hone Mihaka and his *whanau* (family). Climb into a 16m-long (52-ft.) traditional *waka* (war canoe) at Horotutu Beach and await your paddling instructions. As you move up the tidal estuary you'll learn about ancient customs, rituals, and traditions, and then, at the family marae, you'll meet local Ngapuhi, who will relate family histories. Various tour options

can include a marae welcome, traditional *hangi* (meal), and a soak in mineral hot springs with Ngapuhi elders. ⏲ 3 hr. Taiamai Heritage Tours. ☎ 09/405-9990. www.taiamaitours.co.nz. Admission NZ$140 adults, NZ$85 kids 6–12. Tours depart 10am and 1pm Oct–Apr.

From Waitangi Bridge, return along Tau Henare Dr. and turn right into Puketona Rd., then right into St. Hwy. 10, which becomes Bulls Rd. At the main roundabout, take the 3rd exit onto Kerikeri Rd.

⑦ **🍴 Kerikeri Bakehouse Café.** Stop here for lunch, and a selection from the racks and racks of sweet treats. 324 Kerikeri Rd. (on your left as you head toward Kerikeri township). ☎ 09/407-7266. NZ$4–NZ$12..

Drive straight through the town on Kerikeri Rd., over the bypass, right on Waipapa Rd., then right again on Landing Rd.

⑧ ★★ kids Rewa's Village. This full-scale reconstruction of a *kainga* (fortified pre-European Maori fishing village) gives you a good understanding of how early Maori lived. Across the valley you can see the site of the well-preserved ancient Kororipo Pa, the fortified village occupied by chief Hongi Hika, who famously sailed to England on board the *New Zealander* in 1820, intent upon buying weapons. On his return he initiated a series of campaigns against Maori further south—the first of the musket wars—and Kororipo became the base for numerous cannibalistic feasts. ⊙ 1 hr. Landing Rd., Kerikeri. ☎ 09/407-6454. Admission NZ$6 adults, NZ$2 kids 5–15. Daily 9am–5pm Nov–Apr; daily 10am–4pm May–Oct.

Spend the rest of your day relaxing in Kerikeri or Paihia. On day 3, leave Paihia early on Puketona Rd. (St. Hwy. 11). Turn left onto St. Hwy. 10 and drive to Pakaraka, veering right on St./Hwy. 1 to get to Ohaeawai. It's 29km (18 miles), about a 25 min. drive.

⑨ ★ kids Ohaeawai. Traditionally known as Taiamai, this unassuming little settlement is near the site of the bloody Battle of Ohaeawai, fought in 1845 between British troops and a Ngapuhi contingent led by Ngati Hine chief Te Roki Kawiti. The significantly outnumbered Maori won the battle. In Ngawha, about 4km (2½ miles) southwest of Ohaeawai, you'll find St. Michael's Anglican Church, often called Ohaeawai Maori Church, which sits on the site of the original *pa* and battleground. ⊙ 20 min.

From Ohaeawai, follow signs to Kaikohe on St. Hwy. 12. It's 14km (8⅔ miles) and 15 min away.

⑩ ★ ★ kids Kaikohe. Originally a Maori village called Opango, Kaikohe is the recognized heartland of the Ngapuhi iwi. Around 69% of its population of 4,000 identifies as Maori. The area around Kaikohe is home to several old *pa* sites and many little white Maori churches with red roofs. ⊙ 30 min.

⑪ 🚇 Subway. Kaikohe is not exactly overflowing with cafes but the town is a good chance to stretch your legs a little nonetheless. If you're hungry, Subway might be your best bet. **73 Broadway, Kaikohe.** ☎ 09/405-3375. NZ$8–NZ$15.

From Kaikohe, continue on St. Hwy. 12 for 45 min., following signs 52km (32 miles) to Opononi.

⑫ ★ ★ ★ kids Crossings Hokianga Harbour Cruise. Make sure you've timed your road trip to arrive in Opononi for the 11:45am scenic Crossings Hokianga harbor cruise. Kupe, the first great Maori navigator, is said to have settled here and the area is still important to modern Maori. They'll be guiding you on this trip and will point out all the important historical and cultural landmarks around the harbor. You'll also get a chance to disembark on the giant Hokianga Harbor sand dunes. ⊙ 3½ hr. 29 St. Hwy. 12, Opononi. ☎ 0800/687-836 or 09/405-8207. www.crossingshokianga.co.nz. Admission NZ$70 adults, NZ$40 kids 5–15. Bookings essential and minimum numbers required. Tours daily 8:30–11:30am and 11:45am–3:15pm.

From Opononi, drive 2.5km (1½ miles) to Omapere.

⑬ ★ ★ ★ kids Footprints Waipoua. This fantastic, award-winning Maori experience takes you deep into the nearby kauri forests after dark. Accomplished local Maori guides relate traditional stories and legends, telling you about forest gods, spiritual inhabitants, and the plants that Maori have traditionally used as medicines. And naturally you'll get to meet Tane Mahuta, God of the Forest, the largest kauri tree in New Zealand. Note that this tour is not suitable for children under 5. ⊙ 4 hr. 29 St. Hwy. 12, Opononi. ☎ 0800/687-836 or 09/405-8207. www.footprintswaipoua.com. Admission NZ$90 adults, NZ$30 kids 5–12. Tours daily starting at 6pm Oct–May; 5pm June–Sept.

A Remote Marae Visit

★ ★ ★ **Motuti Marae** is located 25km (16 miles) west of Kohukohu in the heart of the remote Hokianga region. An hour-long visit includes a traditional *powhiri* (greeting) and morning or afternoon tea with Motuti locals. Spend the whole day and you also get to visit the cute little Hata Maria Church, where the remains of Bishop Jean Baptiste Pompallier (b. 1802, in Lyon), the first Bishop of Auckland, are interred beneath the altar. 318 Motuti Rd., Motuti, Kohukohu. ☎ 09/405-2660. www.motuti.co.nz. Admission for 1-hr visits NZ$25 adults, NZ$10 students 13–17, free for kids 12 and under; for full-day visits, NZ$50 adults, NZ$25 students 13–17, NZ$10 kids 12 and under. Mon–Fri, 1-hour visits at 11am and 2pm, full-day visits at 10am. Bookings for all visits essential.

Northland Beaches A to Z

★★★ kids **Baylys Beach** WEST COAST/DARGAVILLE Baylys is a small part of the vast Ripiro Beach, which stretches 107km (66 miles) and is New Zealand's longest drivable beach. It's a popular spot for horseback riding, kite surfing, fishing, trail bikes, and 4WD vehicles. The long coastline has a history of over 150 shipwrecks and you'll still find parts of some embedded in the sand. **Well signposted off St. Hwy. 12, 13km (8 miles) north of Dargaville.**

★★ kids **Cable Bay** DOUBTLESS BAY/FAR NORTH A perfect little horseshoe of pinkish sand that gets its color from crushed shells. A little stream runs into the ocean at one end, forming shallow rivulets that are ideal for small children to play in. There are also rock pools at one end and, occasionally, a seal or two. It has a playground, general store, plenty of accommodations, and is good for surf casting. **Right beside St. Hwy. 10 a few kilometers north of Coopers Beach.**

★★★ kids **Coopers Beach** DOUBTLESS BAY/FAR NORTH Famous for the shady, red-flowering pohutukawa trees that overhang a safe, 2.5km (1½ miles) white-sand beach, Coopers is a popular summer holiday destination for families. There's now a shopping center, cafes, playground, tennis, and bowling, and plenty of accommodations. It's bordered on one side by a conservation reserve that includes three ancient defended Maori pa sites. **On St. Hwy. 10 85km (53 miles) north of Paihia and 2km (1¼ miles) north of Mangonui.**

★★ kids **Langs Beach** MANGAWHAI HEADS/WHANGAREI A lovely white-sand beach with views of offshore islands and craggy headlands framed by ancient coastal trees, where walking, surfing, swimming, and body-surfing are all popular. It's a favorite haunt for Aucklanders and expensive houses line the shores. The population explodes in summer so expect crowds. **Signposted off St. Hwy. 1 at Waipu; 90km (56 miles) north of Auckland and 52km (32 miles) south of Whangarei.**

> *Don't be surprised to find yourselves the only people walking some of Northland's beautiful, remote beaches.*

Beaches
Baylys Beach **1**
Cable Bay **7**
Coopers Beach **8**
Langs Beach **17**
Matai Bay **4**
90 Mile Beach **3**
Ocean Beach **15**
Taipa **6**
Taupo Bay **10**
Waipu Cove **16**

Boating & Cruising
The Bay of Islands **11**

Diving
The Poor Knights
Marine Reserve **14**

Fishing
Bay of Islands **11**
Mangonui area **9**

Ocean Kayaking
Paihia **13**

Surfing
Ahipara **2**
Ocean Beach **15**
Taupo Bay **10**
Tokerau Beach **5**

Wildlife Viewing
Dolphins in the Bay
of Islands **12**

Yachting
Bay of Islands **11**

Northland Beaches & Ocean Adventures

> *Matai Bay, on the Karikari Peninsula, is made up of pretty twin horsehoes—it's one of my favorite places in all of New Zealand.*

★★★ kids **Matai Bay** KARIKARI PENINSULA/FAR NORTH This remote, uncrowded spot has two perfect, golden horseshoes of sand separated by a grassy headland. Once completely isolated (there are still no shops), it's now popular with fishermen and campers, who stay in the large DOC camping ground. It's ideal for a day picnic, has safe swimming, and is home to a small Maori settlement. Do not venture onto Maori land without permission. **34km (21 miles) to Matai Bay on Karikari Peninsula from the St. Hwy. 10 turnoff.**

★★★ kids **90 Mile Beach** FAR NORTH WEST COAST This famous surf-casting beach is not actually 90 miles long at all. It is just 55 miles (89km) and although commonly thought to be New Zealand's longest beach it is surpassed by Ripiro (above), which lies farther south. Huge sand dunes—some up to 147m (482 ft.) above sea level—give this place an almost desert-like feeling. Do not drive cars on the beach. A photographer's paradise. **Can be accessed at Te Paki near Cape Reinga in the north, or at Ahipara, near Kaitaia, in the south.**

★★ **Ocean Beach** WHANGAREI HEADS
This is yet another beautiful spot, but away from the sheltered coves, the surf pounds in and strong rips and deceptively quick side currents make it less desirable for young or weak swimmers. It is patrolled in summer, though, and the 5km (3-mile) stretch of white sand is ideal for long walks and beachcombing. Popular with surfers and body-boarders. **Located 40 minutes east of Whangarei on the east coast of Whangarei Heads.**

The Perfect Dive

The Poor Knights Island Marine Reserve, off the Tutukaka Coast, was rated one of the top 10 diving spots in the world by Jacques Yves Cousteau. Its crystal-clear waters near the edge of the continental shelf are bathed in sub-tropical currents from the Coral Sea. Sheer cliff faces, sea caves, tunnels, and archways are teeming with fish, including many subtropical species not usually found in New Zealand waters. The area is strictly controlled by the Department of Conservation with regard to fishing zones and restricted areas, so make sure you go diving with a licensed operator (p. 112). Two decommissioned navy ships have also been sunk here to create a rich marine environment for divers to explore.

> *From the giant Te Paki sand dunes to the vast expanse of 90 Mile Beach, the Far North delivers many unexpected sights.*

★★ kids **Taipa** DOUBTLESS BAY/FAR NORTH
Here you have the best of an open ocean beach—sometimes with excellent surf—and a calm, sheltered estuary that's good for boat launching, swimming, fishing, and sailing. The community includes cafes, accommodation, shops, and a cinema. Taipa is where the ancient Maori navigator, Kupe, is said to have landed and there is a memorial in the town commemorating this. Located on St. Hwy. 10, 7km (4⅓ miles) northeast of Mangonui in Doubtless Bay.

★★★ kids **Taupo Bay** WHANGAROA HARBOUR/
FAR NORTH This is another of the remote beauties that is worth the extra drive. It's the most popular surf beach on the far North's east coast but because of its location, it is far less crowded than many lesser spots. A river forms an estuary at the east end of the beach and the crystal blue waters and white sands make it a family favorite. There are holiday homes and a camping ground here. Turn right off St. Hwy. 10 onto Taupo Bay Rd. 8km (5 miles) south of Mangonui, then travel another 13km (8 miles).

★★ kids **Waipu Cove** MANGAWHAI HEADS/
BREAM BAY There's a real village feel to Waipu Cove that makes it a popular summer destination. Factor in good surfing, swimming, bird-watching, horseback riding, and fishing; a vibrant camping ground; a store and cafes; and a safe estuary for small children, and you can see why the population skyrockets in summer. Located 47km (29 miles) south of Whangarei and 4km (2½ miles) north of Langs Beach. Signposted off St. Hwy. 1 at Waipu.

Safe Shellfish

Every summer the Northland Regional Council (www.nrc.govt.nz) tests water quality at all popular Northland beaches popular for shellfish gathering. Always check for signs warning of contaminated water and avoid collecting shellfish in these areas to avoid possible poisoning. Be aware too that there are rigidly enforced limits on all shellfish gathering to ensure species survival. Note limits posted on signs and know that you will face steep fines if you are caught exceeding limits. The **Ministry of Fisheries** (☎ 0800/478-537; www.fish.govt.nz) enforces limits and can advise if you are unsure. If you see other people poaching large quantities of fish or shellfish call ☎ 0800/476-224 immediately.

Northland Ocean Adventures A to Z

Boating

In the far north you have the choice of almost any sort of boat from simple kayaks to leisure and wildlife cruises (see below). For a high-speed water adventure, ★★ **Excitor** (☎ 0800/653-339; www.awesomenz.com) will rev up its two 800hp engines and race you over the waves to explore some of the Bay of Islands highlights. The 1½-hour ride departs both Paihia and Russell wharves several times a day and costs around NZ$95 adults and NZ$50 kids 14 and under. ★★ **Mack Attack** (☎ 0800/622-528) is a similarly priced high speed adventure.

Cruising

A cruise with ★★★ **Crossings Hokianga** (p. 107, ⑫) will give you a far deeper insight into this intriguing, myth-ridden harbor. Meanwhile, over in the Bay of Islands on the east coast, ★★★ **Fullers Bay of Islands,** Maritime Building, Waterfront, Paihia (☎ 0800/653-339; www.fboi.co.nz) offers several cruises. The most popular is the Cream Trip-Day in the Bay, which includes swimming with dolphins and a trip to the Hole in the Rock (a large, natural, island rock formation that boats pass through). It costs around NZ$105

adults and NZ$55 kids age 5–15, plus NZ$30 extra to swim with dolphins. Farther south, in Tutukaka, ★★★ **A Perfect Day,** Poor Knights Dive Centre, Marina Rd. (☎ 0800/288-882 or 09/434-3867; www.aperfectday.co.nz) has a brilliant outing in the world-renowned Poor Knights Islands Marine Reserve that will take you into some of the richest marine waters you'll ever see. There are kayaks and snorkeling gear on board and lunch is included (NZ$135 adults, NZ$65 kids 12 and under, NZ$375 family).

Diving

The **Poor Knights Islands Marine Reserve** offers some of the best subtropical diving conditions in the world (see "The Perfect Dive," p. 110), and **Dive! Tutukaka,** Poor Knights Dive Centre, Marina Rd., Tutukaka (☎ 0800/288-882 or 09/434-3867; www.diving.co.nz) is New Zealand's premier full-service dive charter operator. There are over 100 dive spots to choose from and they know them all.

Dolphin Watching

Dolphins love the warm Bay of Islands waters. A number of different vessels are licensed for dolphin viewing and swimming. The main

> *Fly across the waves in a high-speed, adrenalin-packed marine adventure on Paihia's Excitor.*

operators are **Fullers Dolphin Eco Encounter,** Maritime Bldg, Waterfront, Paihia (☎ 0800/653-339; www.fboi.co.nz) and **Explore NZ Dolphin Discoveries,** corner of Marsden and Williams Rds., Paihia (☎ 0800/365-744; www.explorenz.co.nz), which both charge around NZ$95 for a 4-hour trip. There's also **Carino Sailing & Dolphin Adventures,** 67 School Rd., Paihia (☎ 09/402-8040; www.sailingdolphins.co.nz), a terrific all-day sailing adventure on a catamaran for around NZ$110 adults, NZ$75 kids that includes a barbecue lunch.

Fishing

No Northland holiday is complete without a spot of leisurely fishing off a wharf with the kids; a day of serious sport fishing with local experts; or surf-casting off an idyllic sandy beach with hardly anyone in sight. Light-line fishing is very affordable here and most information centers have lists of charters; most supply bait and rods and run 3- to 5-hour trips. Snapper fishing is especially popular and ranges from NZ$65 to NZ$165 for a 4-hour boat trip. For game fishing, contact **Earl Grey Fishing Charters,** Paihia and Russell Wharf (☎ 09/407-7165; www.earlgreyfishing.co.nz). In the Far North, Peter Wright of **Snapa Slapa Fishing Charters** (☎ 027/453-5258; www.fishingnz.net.nz) will take you to prime snapper and kahawai fishing grounds in Doubtless Bay and Whangaroa and Rangaunu harbors. A 2-hour charter starts at NZ$155. For superb surf-casting, head for 90 Mile Beach (p. 110) in the Far North or Tokerau Beach (p. 109) on Karikari Peninsula.

Ocean Kayaking

Northland has are a myriad of waterways, estuaries, islands, and ocean sweeps to explore. Every one of them will take you close to birds and wildlife—don't forget your camera. In the Bay of Islands, **Coastal Kayakers** in Paihia (☎ 09/402-8105; www.coastalkayakers.co.nz) can take you to explore waterfalls, mangrove swamps, and deserted islands. No experience is necessary. A 4-hour trip costs around NZ$70 and a full-day around NZ$95. **Island Kayaks** in Pahia are also good operators (p. 95, ⑬). Farther north, **Northland Sea Kayaking,** Tauranga Bay Rd., Northland (☎ 09/405-0381; www.northlandseakayaking.co.nz), is more of a wilderness experience with

accommodation provided on private beaches. Full and half-day tours start around NZ$95.

Surfing

There are numerous good surfing beaches in Northland. Among the best are Taupo Bay, Tokerau Beach, Ocean Beach, and 90 Mile Beach at Ahipara (see Northland Beaches A–Z, p. 108). In Tutukaka, the **Tutukaka Surf Company Shop,** Shop 2, Oceans Resort, Marina Rd. (☎ 09/434-4135; www.tutukakasurf.co.nz) offers lessons with qualified Surf New Zealand instructors on all the prime surf beaches along the Tutukaka Coast. They also have boards for hire and can advise on the best beaches to suit your skills and preferences.

Yachting

Over 100 islands, quiet coves, dolphins, and open waters all make for great sailing. **Great Escape,** 4 Richardson St., Opua (☎ 09/402-2143; www.greatescape.co.nz), has 14 yachts for charter from NZ$160 a day. They also offer sailing lessons and skippered charters, if you want fun without responsibility, **Gungha's Super Cruise** (☎ 0800/478-900 in NZ, or 09/407-7930; www.bayofislandssailing.co.nz) puts you in the safe hands of Max and Debbie Carere, who have sailed throughout the Pacific. A day-sail on their 20m (66-ft.) maxi yacht *Gungha II* includes at least one island stopover and lunch. You can get as involved in the sailing action as you want—all for around NZ$95 per person (Oct–May). *She's A Lady* **Island Sailing Adventures** (☎ 0800/724-584 or 09/402-8119; www.bay-of-islands.com) is favored by the backpacker crowd and includes knee-boarding, fishing, and a full-day outing with two island stops for about NZ$100 per person. The *R. Tucker Thompson,* Maritime Bldg, Paihia (☎ 0800/882-537; www.tucker.co.nz), is a wonderful tall-ship sailing experience. The 26m (85-ft.) gaff-rigged schooner is as pretty as a picture and offers day-sails for 45 passengers for around NZ$140 adults, NZ$70 kids, lunch included (Oct–April).

Travel Tip

For locations of the activities in this section, see the map on p. 109.

Where to Stay

> You'll think you've landed in heaven when you wake up to views like this at Beach Lodge, Coopers Beach.

Bay of Islands

★★★ Eagles Nest RUSSELL
Spoil yourself in a sublime, eco-friendly, world-class sanctuary where no expense has been spared to create something you'll remember forever. The core philosophy here is relax, regenerate, rejuvenate, and there are several sumptuous villas where you can do just that. It's an experience to relish but it doesn't come cheap. 60 Tapeka Rd., Russell. ☎ 09/403-8333. www.eaglesnest.co.nz. 19 rooms in 6 self-contained units. NZ$2,075–NZ$5,250 per villa, with breakfast and airport transfer; from NZ$18,500 for Rahimoana (Presidential Villa) which includes Porsche Cayenne Turbo and personal concierge. AE, DC, MC, V. Map p. 93.

★★ kids Edgewater Palms Apartments PAIHIA
These new, one- and two-bedroom apartments are located right on the waterfront opposite the main Paihia beach, putting you right in the center of activities, shops, and restaurants. All apartments have their own balconies with sea views. In addition to safe swimming at the beach, there's also a swimming pool and Jacuzzi on site. 10 Marsden Rd., Paihia. ☎ 09/402-0090. www.edgewaterapartments. co.nz. 34 units. Doubles NZ$300–NZ$550. AE, DC, MC, V. Map p. 93.

★★★ Kauri Cliffs MATAURI BAY
You don't have to be a golfer to fall in love with this world-class lodge complete with top-rated golf course, luxury day spa, and villas to die for—all set on 2,630 hectares (6,500 acres) of rolling coastal farmland overlooking the ocean. Rooms are spacious, bathrooms luxurious, and you can have just about anything you want. Matauri Bay, 25 min. northeast of Kerikeri. ☎ 09/407-0010. www.kauricliffs.com. 22 units, 1 2-bedroom cottage. Suites NZ$1,500–NZ$3,000; cottage NZ$6,500–NZ$10,500 w/ breakfast, pre-dinner drinks, and dinner. AE, DC, MC, V. Map p. 93.

★★ kids Paihia Beach Resort & Spa PAIHIA
Fresh from a NZ$6-million revamp, this prime spot on the Paihia waterfront close to town has large apartments that are bound to please. Ideal for families or groups traveling together, the complex has a lovely swimming pool,

Pure Tastes Restaurant (p. 117), and one of the biggest and best day spas in Northland. 116 Marsden Rd., Paihia. ☎ 09/402-0111. www.paihiabeach.co.nz. 21 units. Doubles NZ$575–NZ$850. AE, DC, MC, V. Map p. 93.

★ kids **Russell Cottages** RUSSELL
This is my pick for the independent traveler who likes a modern, self-contained stay. You have a choice of one- to four-bedroom, two-level cottages set in park-like gardens with a heated pool and Jacuzzi. The cottages are modeled after historic Russell buildings and are as cute as buttons, but are modern, comfortable, and spacious inside. 16 Chapel St., Russell. ☎ 09/403-7737. www.russellcottages.co.nz. 16 units. Doubles NZ$495–NZ$900. AE, MC, V. Map p. 93.

★ kids **Scenic Hotel Bay of Islands** PAIHIA
This large complex has recently been completely renovated and now offers good-sized, reasonably priced rooms. I like the new deluxe rooms the best. They open onto private sub-tropical gardens and are farther away from the main reception complex. They're close to the beach and also have their own solar-heated swimming pool. Corner of Seaview and Mac-Murray roads, Paihia. ☎ 09/402-7826. www.scenicgroup.co.nz. 114 units. Doubles NZ$255–NZ$315. AE, DC, MC, V. Map p. 93.

★ **The Summer House** KERIKERI
If you're a garden lover, you'll be right at home here among the citrus orchards and subtropical gardens that Rod and Christine Brown have developed. Both upstairs bedrooms have their own bathrooms and views over the pond and lush greenery. The semi-detached downstairs suite is much bigger and has a Pacific theme. 424 Kerikeri Rd., Kerikeri. ☎ 09/407-4294. www.thesummerhouse.co.nz. 3 units. Doubles NZ$275–NZ$355. MC, V. Map p. 93.

Far North

★ **Beach Lodge** COOPERS BEACH/DOUBTLESS BAY You only have to walk down a few steps to hit the sand here. The two-bedroom, self-contained apartments have private decks with lovely sea views and a relaxed style that fits well with the beach location. 121 St. Hwy. 10, Coopers Beach. ☎ 09/406-0068. www.beachlodge.co.nz. 5 units. Doubles NZ$300–NZ$475. V. Map p. 97.

★★★ kids **Carrington Resort** KARIKARI PENINSULA Set amid 3,000 hectares (7,410 acres) of coastal land, this beautiful property combines spacious lodge rooms with clusters of villas set well away from the main buildings, across the rolling golf course. A point of difference there are the tee markers, which have all been carved by local Maori carvers. I love this spot. It's remote, stylish, and close to some of the best beaches in the country. Matai Bay Rd., Karikari Peninsula. ☎ 09/408-7222. www.heritagehotels.co.nz. 24 units. Doubles NZ$465–NZ$650. AE, DC, MC, V. Map p. 97.

★ kids **Copthorne Hotel & Resort Hokianga** OMAPERE/HOKIANGA My picks here are the superior rooms in the front wing, overlooking the harbor, the huge sand dunes, and the pretty jetty. It's all water's edge and the simple, uncluttered rooms make an ideal, reasonably priced base for your Hokianga adventures. St. Hwy. 12, Omapere, Hokianga. ☎ 09/405-8737. www.copthornehokianga.co.nz. 33 units. Doubles NZ$130–NZ$315. AE, DC, MC, V. Map p. 97.

Happy Camping

First a word on freedom camping (or camping outside a designated campground): Don't do it! There are plenty of official camping grounds across New Zealand and freedom camping is only permitted in a few restricted areas. Regional agencies check that regulations are not being breached. Here are a few more camping tips:

- If you're towing a caravan or driving a camper van, pull over to let other traffic pass.

- If you intend to camp over summer, book well in advance. Many Kiwis book from one year to the next.

- If you're camping with kids, take books, toys, cards, and similar distractions in case it rains.

- Always travel with a cell phone, a first aid kit, a pocketknife, matches, and coins for shower and laundry facilities on camping sites.

- NEVER leave litter and NEVER use the open spaces as your toilet.

> *The comfortable, modern Lodge Bordeaux.*

★ **Shippies** AHIPARA/KAITAIA
There's a 2-night minimum stay here but once you're inside these contemporary two-bedroom apartments with sweeping views over Shipwreck Bay and 90 Mile Beach, you won't want to move. Each is fully self-contained and there are balconies where you can enjoy views and watch the spectacular sunsets. Reef View Rd., Shipwreck Bay, Ahipara. ☎ 09/409-4729. www.shippies.co.nz. 3 units. Doubles NZ$200–NZ$275. MC, V. Map p. 97.

★★ kids **Taipa Bay Resort** TAIPA/DOUBTLESS BAY Mediterranean style meets Pacifica in this beachfront resort complex that is eternally popular with holidaying Kiwi families. With a restaurant, cafe, swimming pool, spa, bar, and kayaks and boats for hire, you'll have everything you need. All you need to do is step out of your room and onto the beach—all for a great value price. What could be better? 22 Taipa Point Rd., Taipa. ☎ 09/406-0656. www. taipabay.co.nz. 32 units. Doubles NZ$120–NZ$350. AE, MC, V. Map p. 97.

★★ **Waipoua Lodge** WAIPOUA FOREST
Set in the grounds of a historic 120-year-old villa, these smartly appointed apartments—each different—are private, cozy, and very comfortable. They have views over the lush garden and forest beyond, and you'll enjoy social interactions and meals in the homestead itself. It's close to the kauri forest and deserted golden sand beaches. St. Hwy. 12, Waipoua. ☎ 09/439-0422. www.waipoualodge.co.nz. 4 units. Doubles NZ$570–NZ$650 w/breakfast; NZ$850 w/ breakfast & dinner. MC, V. Map p. 97.

In & Around Whangarei

★ kids **Breakaway Retreat** WHANGAREI HEADS
This purpose-built, two-bedroom, self-contained beachfront guesthouse is an idyllic hideout for one couple, two couples, or a small family. It's a modern take on the simple, traditional holiday bach (holiday home) and it's just meters away from a small beach, complete with kayaks, a dingy, and life jackets. It has all the makings of a charming family holiday. 1856 Whangarei Heads Rd., McLeod Bay, Whangarei Heads. ☎ 09/434-0711. www.breakawayretreat.co.nz. 1 cottage. Doubles NZ$290–NZ$325 w/breakfast; NZ$50 each extra person. V. Map p. 97.

★★ kids **Lodge Bordeaux** WHANGAREI
This modern motel complex (with swimming pool), is maintained to an especially high standard and you won't find much wrong with their large, spotlessly clean rooms. Big bathrooms are delightful and have double Jacuzzis to soak away your traveler's aches and pains. 361 Western Hills Dr., St. Hwy. 1, Whangarei. ☎ 09/438-0404. www.lodgebordeaux.co.nz. 15 units. Doubles NZ$190–NZ$340. AE, MC, V. Map p. 97.

★★ kids **Pacific Rendezvous** TUTUKAKA
You'll be hard-pressed to find a better location anywhere. Perched on the top of a peninsula with breathtaking 360-degree views of the ocean, this property is an ideal family stay. The one-, two- and three-bedroom, self-contained units all have balconies or patios. There's a playground, pool, barbecue, spa, tennis courts, putting golf, and a short walk down the hill to a secluded beach. 73 Motel Rd., Tutukaka. ☎ 0800/999-800 or 09/434-3847. www. pacificrendezvous.co.nz. 30 units. Doubles NZ$145–NZ$250. AE, MC, V. Map p. 97.

Where to Dine

> *It's well worth catching the water taxi from Paihia to dine alfresco at Kamakura on the Russell waterfront.*

Bay of Islands

★★ kids **Island Life** PAIHIA *NZ/EUROPEAN*
This casual restaurant offers a reasonably priced a la carte menu showcasing local produce with a hint of classic Europe—aged beef served with béarnaise sauce, fries, and salad is just one example. A fixed-price menu is also available. During the day the deli serves big breakfasts and lunches. You can also order picnic hampers here and take-home evening meals. Marsden Rd., Paihia. ☎ 09/402-6199. www.islandlifepaihia.co.nz. Main courses NZ$25–NZ$34. MC, V. Daily breakfast, lunch, and dinner. Map p. 93.

★★★ **Kamakura** RUSSELL *INTERNATIONAL*
Pacific Rim meets Mediterranean with a hint of Japanese in this sophisticated dining spot. You'll get the freshest local produce and seafood, including New Zealand crayfish, blended into first-class meals. The crab ravioli is a must-have delicacy. 29 The Strand, Russell. ☎ 09/403-7771. www.kamakura.co.nz. Main courses NZ$30–NZ$40. MC, V. Daily lunch and dinner. Map p. 93.

★★ kids **Marsden Estate Winery** KERIKERI *MODERN NZ* This is a delightful vineyard setting for a tasty lunch that focuses on generous antipasto platters with estate-grown wine—all served in a grapevine-covered courtyard overlooking lakes and vineyards. A small menu focuses on light, tasty dishes like chargrilled lamb on flat bread, Thai red curry, and slow-roasted beef fillet. Wiroa Rd., Kerikeri ☎ 09/407-9398. www.marsdenestate.co.nz. Main courses NZ$18–NZ$24. MC, V. Lunch daily. Map p. 93.

★★ **Only Seafood** PAIHIA *SEAFOOD*
Seafood takes center stage in a smart, white-walled, timber-floored interior that is as relaxed as it is comfortable. Sushi, calamari, raw fish salad, salmon fillet with oysters, and oven-baked, grilled, and marinated fresh fish are all on the menu. 40 Marsden Rd., Paihia. ☎ 09/402-7085. Main courses NZ$22–NZ$32. AE, DC, MC, V. Dinner daily. Map p. 93.

★★ kids **Pure Tastes** PAIHIA *MODERN NZ*
The tantalizing mix of fresh seafood and Pacific Rim culinary style is a winner for me. Dishes like cured salmon with horseradish panna cotta and smoked eel salad, or poached rabbit, are but a hint of the tastes you can savor in this modern restaurant. Don't miss the homemade ice creams for dessert! You can choose a four- or five-course set menu, with or without wine matches; there's also a kids' menu. Paihia Beach Resort & Spa, 116 Marsden Rd., Paihia. ☎ 09/402-0003. www.puretastes.

> *Brothers Michael and Gerard Venner have established a little gem of a stop at Coopers Beach Café.*

co.nz. Main courses NZ$32–NZ$36; four-course set menu NZ$75, with wine NZ$115; five-course set menu NZ$90, with wine NZ$135. AE, MC, V. Breakfast, lunch, and dinner daily. Map p. 93.

★ **kids** **Sugar Boat** PAIHIA *NZ/MEDITERRANEAN* One of six lighters to be built by Auckland's Chelsea Sugar Refinery in 1890, this gorgeous old boat is now a near-perfect place to enjoy an early evening cocktail at the on-deck bar, watching the sun go down before descending to the smart little restaurant in the hold. Blackened chicken with local chorizo or grilled lamb loin with capsicum (pepper) and seaweed dumplings are two selections from an interesting menu. **Waitangi Bridge, Paihia.** ☎ 09/402-7018. www.sugarboat.co.nz. Main courses NZ$34–NZ$40. MC, V. Dinner daily Nov–April. Map p. 93.

Far North

★★ **kids** **Coopers Beach Café** COOPERS BEACH CAFE Chef/owner Michael Venner is passionate about food and his local community. You get a sense of that as soon as you arrive at this cute, contemporary cafe with big decks for alfresco dining. Choose open sandwiches or

quiche for lunch; or fish, steaks, lamb racks, or linguini for dinner. This place is a real gem. 157 St. Hwy. 10, Coopers Beach. ☎ 09/406-0860. www.cooperscafe.co.nz. Main courses NZ$28–NZ$36. MC, V. Lunch and dinner daily. Map p. 97.

In & Around Whangarei

★★★ **kids** **A'Deco Restaurant** WHANGAREI *MODERN NZ* Set in an elegantly furnished, 1939 Art Deco house, this eatery has been voted Northland's top restaurant for the last eight years. It may not match big city equivalents but it's the best in this region. Chefs work closely with local producers to source top raw ingredients and their attention to detail is reflected in a comprehensive, creative menu. 70 Kamo Rd., Whangarei. ☎ 09/459-4957. www.a-deco.co.nz. Main courses NZ$25–NZ$38. AE, DC, MC, V. Dinner Tues–Sat, lunch Friday. Map p. 97.

★ **kids** **Killer Prawn** WHANGAREI *SEAFOOD/PIZZA* Deep red walls and bricks combine to give this old standby a warm atmosphere that keeps drawing in the crowds. Expect a casual night out that serves up big steaks, a range of very tasty signature prawn dishes (including tempura prawns and prawn kebabs), sizzling lamb dishes, and hearty wood-fired pizzas. 26–28 Bank St., Whangarei. ☎ 09/430-3333. www.killerprawn.co.nz. Main courses NZ$32–NZ$38. AE, MC, V. Lunch and dinner Mon–Sat. Map p. 97.

★ kids **Schnappa Rock** TUTUKAKA *MODERN NZ* It's one big beach party here in the summer, as surfers, Kiwi holidaymakers, and international tourists come together for casual light meals for lunch (prawn and mussel curry, calamari rings) and traditional Kiwi favorites by night (crispy pork belly, venison medallions, lamb rack, and fresh fish). Corner of Marina Rd. and Martin Pl. ☎ 09/434-3774. www.schnapparock. co.nz. Main courses NZ$26–NZ$37. AE, MC, V. Breakfast, lunch, and dinner daily. Map p. 97.

> *Whangarei's A'Deco has been judged Northland's top restaurant for the last eight years.*

Northland Fast Facts

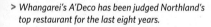

Arriving
BY PLANE Whangarei Airport (☎ 09/436-0047), Kerikeri Airpot (also known as Bay of Islands Airport, ☎ 09/407-6133), and Kaitaia Airport (☎ 09/407-6133) serve Northland. **Air New Zealand Link** has a daily service from Auckland to Kerikeri (with shuttle bus to Paihia) and Kaitaia. BY BUS Both **Intercity** (☎ 09/623-1503; www.intercity.co.nz) and **Northliner Express** (☎ 09/583-5780; www. northliner.co.nz) have daily service across Northland.

Emergencies & Medical Care
Dial ☎ **111** for all police, fire, and ambulance emergencies. **Whangarei Hospital,** Maunu Rd., Whangarei (☎ **09/430-4100**) is the main hospital servicing all of Northland. There's also **Kaitaia Hospital,** 29 Redan Rd., Kaitaia (☎ **09/408-9180**). If you need a doctor, try **Bayview Medical Centre,** 7 Bayview Rd.,

Paihia (☎ **09/402-7132**). For a dentist, options include **Kerikeri Dental Centre,** Clocktower Bldg., Cobham Rd., Kerikeri (☎ **09/407-8338**) and **Bay of Islands Dental Centre,** corner of Williams and Selwyn roads, Paihia (☎ **09/402-5577**).

Internet
Get online at **Easinet,** 46 John St., Whangarei (☎ 430-0930) or **s'wich Café,** John Butler Centre, 60 Kerikeri Rd., Kerikeri (☎ 09/407-3941).

Visitor Information Centers
BAY OF ISLANDS I-SITE VISITOR CENTRE The Wharf, Marsden Rd., Paihia; ☎ 09/402-7345; www.visitfarnorthnz.com. THE FAR NORTH I-SITE VISITOR CENTRE Jaycee Park, South Rd., Kaitaia; ☎ 09/408-0879. WHANGAREI I-SITE VISITOR CENTRE Tarewa Park, 92 Otaika Rd., Whangarei; ☎ 09/438-1079; www. whangareinz.com.

My Favorite Moments

These are two of the prettiest, sunniest provinces in the North Island—a beach lover's paradise, where the coastline dishes up dozens of beautiful white sand beaches. Both are favorite summer holiday destinations for New Zealand families, so book well ahead if you plan on visiting. Coromandel is the more rugged of the two and still boasts large tracts of untouched native bush. Bay of Plenty, as the name suggests, is a productive horticultural region famous for its subtropical fruits, especially kiwifruit.

> PREVIOUS PAGE *Take your camera on Discovery Tours' Coromandel Coastal Walkway outing to capture beautiful vistas in every direction.* THIS PAGE *Relax in naturally hot water at The Lost Spring.*

❶ Hunting for gemstones at Tapu Beach. Arm yourself with optimism and a fossicker's spirit and you may well be rewarded with small gemstones on Tapu Beach. Once famous for its nearby alluvial goldfield, it is now more famous as a popular holiday destination. See p. 146.

❷ Riding the miniature railway at Driving Creek. One of the best decisions accomplished potter Barry Brickell ever made was to build New Zealand's only narrow-gauge mountain railway, which passes through replanted native forest. It's a hit with people of all ages and when you're done with the train you can visit the pottery. See p. 126, ❻.

❸ Eating freshly smoked fish in Coromandel. Stopping for freshly smoked fish and shellfish at Coromandel Smoking Company is the perfect introduction to this quaint little town. See p. 126, ❺.

❹ Stargazing from a bathtub. Few pleasures are more sublime than a stay at Ridge Country Retreat in the rural hills above Tauranga's Welcome Bay, with a private soak in your own outdoor bath on your own balcony, under the star-filled Bay of Plenty sky. See p. 151.

❺ Sea kayaking at Cathedral Cove. The crystal-clear, turquoise waters and the tortured sea cliffs of Cathedral Cove make it a favorite with kayakers. See p. 148.

❻ Walking around The Mount. Once a heavily fortified Maori fortress at the end of a long peninsula, Mauao, commonly called The Mount, is the most recognized landmark in Bay of Plenty. Take an hour and walk around its base before sprawling out on the beach. See p. 128, ⓭.

❼ Discovering The Lost Spring. This remarkable, hand-built spa facility is the perfect place to while away a hour or two here before hitting the road again. See p. 127, ❿.

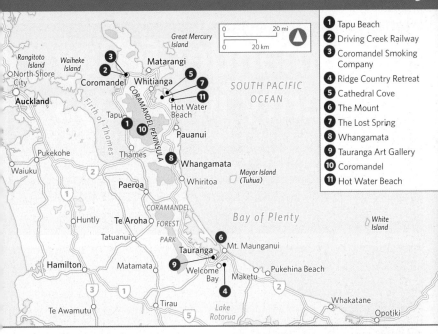

1 Tapu Beach
2 Driving Creek Railway
3 Coromandel Smoking Company
4 Ridge Country Retreat
5 Cathedral Cove
6 The Mount
7 The Lost Spring
8 Whangamata
9 Tauranga Art Gallery
10 Coromandel
11 Hot Water Beach

8 **Watching surfers at Whangamata.** Surf culture is alive and well here–every summer the usual population of about 4,000 multiplies several times over as boarders come to town to hang out, catch the waves, and party on the beach. See p. 128, 11.

9 **Checking out the latest shows at Tauranga Art Gallery.** Like a little cultural oasis in a desert of sand, beaches, and surf boards, the Tauranga Art Gallery does a marvelous job of showing off both traditional and contemporary New Zealand art. See p. 134, 17.

10 **Hiking in Coromandel's native bush.** It's sometimes a cool, refreshing relief to get away from the Coromandel's hot sand and head into the leafy, untouched bush. Join a professional hiking tour to get the best from the bush, or simply go for a leisurely wander along one of the many well-used, short bush walks. You can get information on these at any of the local visitor information centers. See p. 132, 7.

11 **Soaking in hot, wet sand at Hot Water Beach.** There's nothing else like this anywhere in New Zealand—dig a hole in the sand at low tide and it fills with bubbling thermal water from a natural spring deep below the earth's crust. See p. 144.

> *Some of New Zealand's best surf beaches lie around the Coromandel and Bay of Plenty coastlines.*

Coromandel & Bay of Plenty in 3 Days

This is a lot of ground to cover in three days but even a fleeting, drive-through visit will give you a feel for why these two beach-riddled regions are among the top holiday destinations for New Zealand families. Because Coromandel coastal roads are narrow, winding, and crowded with travelers, you'll need to drive very carefully. But don't let that dissuade you; you'll love this part of New Zealand.

> *Stand on the top of Mauao (The Mount) for breathtaking views of the Mount Maunganui beaches.*

START Thames is 113km (70 miles) southeast of Auckland (about 1½ hr. drive). **TRIP LENGTH** 268km (167 miles).

❶ Thames. Thames is the gateway to the Coromandel Peninsula and although it has declined from its former glory as a gold-rush town, its quaint streets and old shop facades are still worth a look. It was once home to over 80 hotels; the Brian Boru (1860s), on Pollen Street, is the best known of the survivors. You'll also find interesting historic buildings on Queen Street—look for yellow signs that explain their significance. It's in this area that you'll also find the very interesting **Thames School of Mines,** on the corner of Brown and Cochrane streets (☎ 07/868-6227; admission NZ$5 adults, kids free). ⏱ At least 1 hr.

Leave Thames on Queen St. and travel north on St. Hwy. 25 for 3km (1¾ miles) to Tararu. Turn right into Victoria St. and follow the signs to the next stop.

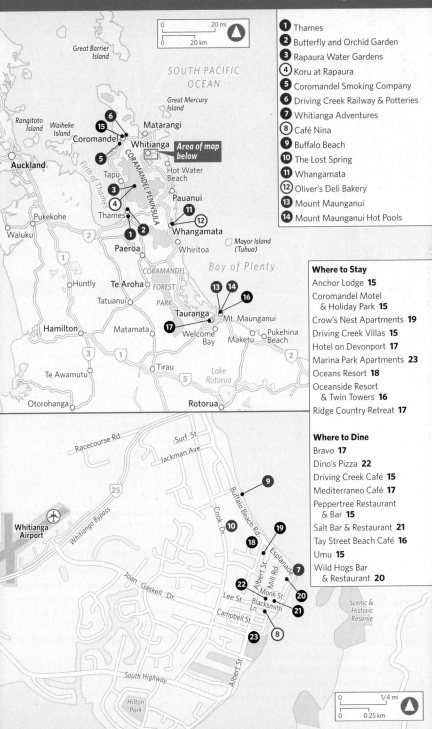

1. Thames
2. Butterfly and Orchid Garden
3. Rapaura Water Gardens
4. Koru at Rapaura
5. Coromandel Smoking Company
6. Driving Creek Railway & Potteries
7. Whitianga Adventures
8. Café Nina
9. Buffalo Beach
10. The Lost Spring
11. Whangamata
12. Oliver's Deli Bakery
13. Mount Maunganui
14. Mount Maunganui Hot Pools

Where to Stay

Anchor Lodge **15**
Coromandel Motel & Holiday Park **15**
Crow's Nest Apartments **19**
Driving Creek Villas **15**
Hotel on Devonport **17**
Marina Park Apartments **23**
Oceans Resort **18**
Oceanside Resort & Twin Towers **16**
Ridge Country Retreat **17**

Where to Dine

Bravo **17**
Dino's Pizza **22**
Driving Creek Café **15**
Mediterraneo Café **17**
Peppertree Restaurant & Bar **15**
Salt Bar & Restaurant **21**
Tay Street Beach Café **16**
Umu **15**
Wild Hogs Bar & Restaurant **20**

> If you've driven up the Coromandel coast from Thames, you deserve a stop at Coromandel Smoking Company for tasty smoked seafood treats.

2 ★ kids **Butterfly and Orchid Garden.** This enclosed, heated glass house is home to hundreds of butterflies, moths, and birds. Pathways drip with flowering orchids and subtropical plants. ⏱ 30 min. Dickson Holiday Park, Victoria St., Tararu. ☎ 07/868-8080; www.butterfly.co.nz. Admission NZ$12. Summer (beginning of daylight savings time–Easter) daily 10am–4pm, winter daily 10am–3pm; closed mid-July to end of August.

Rejoin St. Hwy. 25 and drive north for 14km (8⅔ miles) to Tapu. Turn right onto Coroglen Rd. and drive another 6.5km (4 miles).

3 ★ kids **Rapaura Water Gardens.** Numerous paths meander through this 26-hectare (64-acre) garden, which features 14 water lily ponds, a beautiful cascading waterfall, native bush stands, ferneries, bog gardens, and much more. ⏱ 1 hr. 586 Tapu-Coroglen Rd., Tapu. ☎ 07/868-4821. www.rapaura.com. Admission NZ$12 adults, NZ$5 kids 5–15. Daily 9am–5pm.

④   🍴 **Koru at Rapaura.** This is the perfect place for a quick lunch. The cafe within the gardens serves seasonal salads, soups, sandwiches, and very good coffee. Rapaura Water Gardens (see above). Most items NZ$12–NZ$15.

Return the way you came on Tapu-Coroglen Rd., and rejoin St. Hwy. 25. Drive north 38km (24 miles); Coromandel Smoking Company is on the left-hand side of the highway next to the BP station as you head into Coromandel town.

5 ★★ **Coromandel Smoking Company.** A wide range of smoked fishes, mussels, and other shellfish provide the makings of a wonderful evening meal or a barbecue or picnic on the beach. The habanero-smoked mussels here are divine. ⏱ 15 min. 70 Tiki Rd. ☎ 07/866-8793. www.corosmoke.co.nz. Daily 9am–5pm.

Continue the last kilometer (½-mile) into Coromandel township. Turn right into Kapanga Rd., drive through the village, over the bridge, and onto Rings Rd. Follow this and turn right into Driving Creek Rd. (about 3km/1¾ miles).

6 ★★★ kids **Driving Creek Railway & Potteries.** Barry Brickell, artist, potter, engineer, conservationist, and generally clever fellow, spent 32 years building this gem: New Zealand's only narrow gauge mountain railway. Kids and adults alike will love the 1-hour train ride through native bush. You'll see assorted art features and superb views along the way. After your ride climb the Eyefull Tower Terminus to get an overview of your beautiful location. A glass blowing studio (in summer) and an ecology bookshop round out the experience. ⊕ 2 hr. 380 Driving Creek Rd., Coromandel. ☎ 07/866-8703. www.drivingcreekrailway.co.nz. Train rides NZ$25 adults, NZ$55 families. Advance booking recommended. Train departures daily 10:15am and 2pm.

End your first day with a relaxed evening picnic down on the beach or at your accommodation. Rise early on day 2 and drive 45km (28 miles) to Whitianga on St. Hwy. 25. The trip should take about 45 min.

❼ ★★★ kids **Whitianga Adventures.** The small seaside town of Witianga comes alive in summer, when it becomes the main base for deep sea fishing, diving, and holiday activities. On Whitianga Adventures' sea cave adventure you get a terrific overview of over 25km (16 miles) of gorgeous beach and cave coastline; view fish and stingrays in the marine reserve; idle beneath towering cliffs; and visit the famous Cathedral Cove, an area used as part of *The Lion, the Witch and the Wardrobe* film set. ⊕ 2 hr. Whitianga Wharf. ☎ 0800/806-060. www.whitianga-adventures.co.nz. Admission NZ$75 adults, NZ$50 kids 4–12, family discounts available. Tours daily 10:30am and 1:30pm (also 8am and 3:30pm on demand).

⑧ 🍴 kids **Café Nina.** This cafe, tucked away down a sliver of a side street in a tiny, 100-year-old miner's cottage, is a lovely spot to tuck into a light lunch. 20 Victoria St., Whitianga. ☎ 07/866-5440. Lunch items NZ$10–NZ$16.

❾ ★★★ kids **Buffalo Beach.** Spend the afternoon enjoying the long, white stretch of Buffalo Beach. It's ideal for swimming and sunbathing, and it's just a short walk from shops and cafes if you feel the need for further refreshments. ⊕ At least 2 hr. Buffalo Beach Road, Whitianga.

From Buffalo Beach Rd., turn into Halligan Rd. and then left into Cook Dr.

❿ ★★★ **The Lost Spring.** Old stories about a lost volcanic spring in the Coromandel inspired Alan Hopping to start digging in 1988. Twenty years and two failed attempts later, he finally hit the spring and set about creating this remarkable "back yard" spa facility, tucked away in a residential suburb. The crystal-clear thermal water is drawn from 644m (2,113 ft.) beneath the earth's surface. Its high concentration of minerals (and a 7.4 pH level) leaves your skin feeling wonderful. ⊕ 2 hr. 121A Cook Drive, Whitianga. ☎ 07/866-0456.

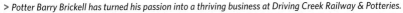

> *Potter Barry Brickell has turned his passion into a thriving business at Driving Creek Railway & Potteries.*

> *Thousands of Kiwis flock to the Mount Maunganui area for their summer holidays.*

www.thelostspring.co.nz. Admission NZ$25 per hour, NZ$50 all-day pass. Sun–Thurs 11am–7pm, Fri–Sat 11am–8pm. Kids over 14 only.

Leave Whitianga early on day 3 on St. Hwy. 25 and follow signs to Whangamata, a drive of 79km (49 miles) and about 1 hr 15 min. without stops.

⓫ ★★ 🅺🅸🅳🆂 **Whangamata.** I frequented this beach when I was a child growing up in the Waikato and it's still one of the most popular beaches of the Coromandel–Bay of Plenty region. Its natural assets—one of the best surf spots, a terrific beach with safe swimming, and a calm harbor and river estuary ideal for kayaking—make it a preferred holiday choice for many. Take a drive around the settlement, explore the marina and harbor, watch the surfers at the north end of Ocean Beach, and take a swim. ⏱ Half-day.

⓬ 🍽 ★★ **Oliver's Deli Bakery.** This is the place to buy a fabulous range of picnic foods, which you can enjoy overlooking Ocean Beach or the harbor. 1002 Port Rd., Whangamata. ☎ 07/865-6979. NZ$4–NZ$12.

From Whangamata, rejoin St. Hwy. 25 and follow the signs to Waihi, where you'll turn left into St. Hwy. 2 and follow signs to Tauranga. It's 89km (55 miles) and will take about 1 hr 20 min. If you choose to go straight to Mount Maunganui, follow the signs on the Tauranga Motorway. Once you're across the harbor, turn left into Totara St., right into Rata St. and then left into Maunganui Rd. at the first roundabout. Follow this straight ahead.

⓭ ★★★ 🅺🅸🅳🆂 **Mount Maunganui.** Wander along the town's main cafe strip to get yourself into the holiday mood and then turn onto Marine Parade to catch the beach action. This is an internationally regarded surf beach, and you'll probably spot beach volleyball players too. The Mount has lots of festivals in January and February—factor in thousands of Kiwi holidaymakers and you're bound to have a good time. If you feel like stretching your legs, take a walk around the iconic cone-shaped mountain, Mount Maunganui (or Mauao in Maori), which takes about an hour. Walking to the summit (252m/827 ft.) takes about 2 hours. The walking track is well signed at the end of the beach. ⏱ Half-day.

⓮ ★★ 🅺🅸🅳🆂 **Mount Maunganui Hot Pools.** I can't think of a nicer way to end your three-day jaunt than lying back in one of these five hot pools that range in temperature from 90°–102°F (32°–39°C). There are two outdoor pools, private spas, a toddlers' pool, and a large activity pool suitable for all ages. ⏱ At least 1 hr. 9 Adams Ave., Mount Maunganui. ☎ 07/575-0868. Admission NZ$15 adults, NZ$9 kids 5–15; private pools from NZ$12 per person for 30 min. Mon–Sat 6am–10pm, Sun 8am–10pm.

> *Surf culture thrives at Whangamata, Waihi, and Mount Maunganui Ocean Beaches.*

Coromandel & Bay of Plenty in 1 Week

By extending your time in this prime summer holiday location, you'll be able to explore some of the more off-the-beaten track attractions and spend some time relaxing on gorgeous beaches. Just to reiterate though, you'll need to book accommodations well ahead to beat the Kiwi holidaymakers and take care on the crowded, narrow, winding roads. That said, when I talk about crowds, remember that it's relative—our crowds aren't much compared to Northern Hemisphere crowds. You'll still find plenty of beautiful beaches with hardly anyone on them.

> White Island is a mecca for volcanologists, who come from all over the world to study its lava flows and ash eruptions.

START Thames is 113km (70 miles) southeast of Auckland (about 1½ hr. drive). **TRIP LENGTH** 310km (193 miles).

①–⑥ Follow the first day of "Coromandel & Bay of Plenty in 3 Days." See p. 124.

On day 2, your tour bus will pick you up at your hotel in Coromandel town for the Coastal Walkway Tour. If you'd rather spend the day discovering Coromandel town, go to the Coromandel i-SITE Visitor Centre, 355 Kapanga Rd. (☎ 07/866-8598; www.coromandeltown.co.nz) and pick up the Historic Places Trust brochure, Coromandel Town, then set out on foot to explore the architectural heritage of this early gold mining settlement.

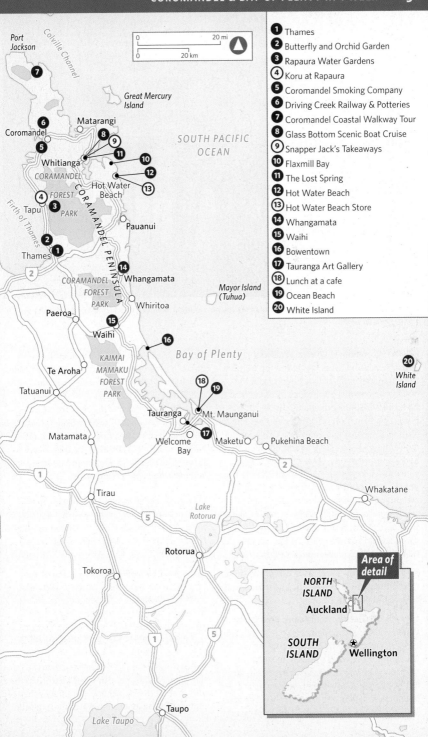

1 Thames
2 Butterfly and Orchid Garden
3 Rapaura Water Gardens
4 Koru at Rapaura
5 Coromandel Smoking Company
6 Driving Creek Railway & Potteries
7 Coromandel Coastal Walkway Tour
8 Glass Bottom Scenic Boat Cruise
9 Snapper Jack's Takeaways
10 Flaxmill Bay
11 The Lost Spring
12 Hot Water Beach
13 Hot Water Beach Store
14 Whangamata
15 Waihi
16 Bowentown
17 Tauranga Art Gallery
18 Lunch at a cafe
19 Ocean Beach
20 White Island

> *The Coromandel Coastal Walkway Tour takes you on a journey along the coast, over farmland, and through fern-covered valleys.*

7 ★★★ **Coromandel Coastal Walkway Tour.** This outing takes you to the top of the Coromandel Peninsula, well away from the holidaying crowds. Your tour bus drives you up a coastline flushed red with flowering pohutukawa. You then walk from Fletcher Bay to Stony Bay—an easy, 2- to 4-hour walk for the moderately fit, across farmland, through bush, and along coastlines. (Make sure you wear sensible walking shoes.) There are plenty of photo stops and all you need to take is your swimming gear, camera, and lunch. The bus returns to Coromandel via Port Charles and Colville. ⏱ 1 day. ☎ 0800/668-175. www.coromandeldiscovery.co.nz. NZ$95 adults, NZ$55 kids. Daily departures at 8:30am.

Rise early on day 3 and drive 45km (28 miles) to Whitianga on St. Hwy. 25. The trip should take about 45 min.

8 ★★★ **kids Glass Bottom Scenic Boat Cruise.** When you're surrounded by some of the clearest ocean water in the country, why wouldn't you want to see what's under the surface? And this way, you don't even have to get wet. But of course, you wouldn't want to miss a brilliant snorkeling opportunity either, so take your swimsuits and prepare to be impressed.

You may see everything from seals and dolphins to penguins, cormorants, and multitudes of fish—not to mention the spectacular Cathedral Cove, which was part of the film set for *The Lion, the Witch and the Wardrobe.* ⏱ 2 hr. Whitianga Wharf. ☎ 07/867-1962 or 021/478-291; www.glassbottomboatwhitianga.co.nz. NZ$95 adults, NZ$60 kids 3–15. Daily departures at 10:30am and 1pm (more frequently in summer). Bookings essential.

9 🍽 **Snapper Jack's Takeaways.** Stop here for some takeaway fish and chips to eat on Buffalo Beach. Corner of Albert and Monk sts. ☎ 07/866-5482. NZ$10-NZ$15.

10 ★★★ **kids Flaxmill Bay.** In the spirit of continuing exploration, head down to Whitianga Wharf and catch the passenger ferry across to Ferry Landing (Whitianga Water Transport; ☎ 07/866-5472; www.whitiangaferry.co.nz; round-trip tickets NZ$4 adults, NZ$2 kids). You'll alight on the oldest stone wharf in Australasia (1837). Buy an ice cream at the Ferry Landing shop and walk 5 to 10 minutes around to Flaxmill Bay. It's smaller than many of the beaches in this area—just a little

> *Dig in the sand at Hot Water Beach in the two hours either side of low tide to make your own hot spa.*

horseshoe—but it's sheltered and has good swimming. If you feel like an energetic stretch, carry on past Flaxmill to Shakespeare Reserve. You can take the track (or road) to the top for wonderful views of Mercury Bay and the near-by coastline. If you'd like, you can take a steep, 10-minute walk down to Lonely Bay, which has a pretty white-sand beach that awaits. ⏱ 3 hr.

Catch the ferry back to Whitianga. From the wharf, turn right and then turn left onto The Esplanade, which becomes Buffalo Beach Rd. Turn left on Halligan Rd. then left again on Cook Dr.

⑪ ★★★ **The Lost Spring.** Ease your tired muscles at this wonderful thermal pool and spa facility, unexpectedly tucked away in the middle of Whitianga suburbia. ⏱ 2 hr. See p. 127, ⑩.

Leave Whitianga early on day 4 on the Tairua-Whitianga Road (St. Hwy. 25), driving by Mill Creek and through Coroglen. At Whenuakite, turn left into Hot Water Beach Rd. and follow the signs to the beach. The trip is 34km (21 miles) and will take about 40 min.

⑫ ★★★ **kids Hot Water Beach.** ⏱ Half-day. See p. 144.

⑬ 🍴 **Hot Water Beach Store.** I had one of the best vegetarian panini of my travels at the little store. Buy some coffee and snacks here and have a picnic on the beach before continuing your travels. **Beside the Hot Water Beach carpark.** ☎ 07/866-3006. Most food items NZ$4–NZ$12.

Go back the way you came on Hot Water Beach Rd. to rejoin St. Hwy. 25. Turn left and follow the signs to Whangamata. It's 61km (38 miles) and will take a little over an hour.

⑭ **Whangamata.** Start at the i-SITE Visitor Centre, 616 Port Rd. (☎ 07/865-8340; www.whangamatainfo.co.nz) and inquire about their kayaking options on the harbor, or per-haps take to the water on a fishing charter for the afternoon. Another good choice is to park your car and walk from the marina, around the harbor, and along the beachfront to the river estuary. That way you'll get to see all the best spots and you can decide which one to settle into for the afternoon. ⏱ Half-day.

Rejoin St. Hwy. 25 on day 5 and follow the signs 30km (19 miles) to Waihi town—about 35 min.

⓯ ★ kids Waihi. Like Thames, Waihi was founded on gold mining—Martha Hill, above the town, was the site of one of the richest gold strikes in history. You can still see the huge, eerie ruin of the Martha pump house, directly across the road from the Waihi Visitor Centre, Seddon St. (☎ 07/863-6715; www.waihi.org.nz). The mine still produces significant amounts of gold and silver each year, and has been the seed of much controversy, which you'll understand when you look down into the huge crater mining has created. You can either walk up the paths near the old ruin and on to the 4km (2½ mile) Pit Rim Walkway, or drive around to the Dewmont Mines lookout on Moresby Avenue. The information center also has a good mining display downstairs. Ask at the information center about mine tours. ⏱ At least 2 hr.

> The eerie ruin of the old Martha Hill pump house looms above the small, historic gold mining town of Waihi.

From Waihi, take Tauranga Rd. (St. Hwy. 2) off Rosemont Rd. and follow signs to Waihi Beach, veering left on Waihi Beach Rd. Turn right on Seaforth Rd. and travel all the way to the end to Bowentown. It's 18km (11 miles) in total and should take about 20 min.

⓰ ★★★ kids Bowentown. Round out the afternoon exploring this charming area. It's at the southern end of Waihi Beach, so you get a choice of ocean waves or a quiet harbor perfect for kayaking, a short walk across the headland. The 128-hectare (316-acre) headland is home to three old Maori *pa* (hill fort) sites and you can see the ancient terraces that formed Te Kura a Maia Pa running down to the sea at the southern end of the headland. You can also drop down into three perfect little headland beaches. Anzac Bay offers safe swimming for kids and is a popular picnic spot. Shelly Bay, a half-hour walk from there or via a steep track over the hill, also has safe swimming and no crowds. Cave Bay, accessed via a steep track from the headland carpark, has a tiny beach and lovely harbor views. You won't be short of good picnic spots here, so unpack your hamper and relax for a lazy afternoon. ⏱ Half day.

From Bowentown, drive back along Seaforth Rd. to Island View and turn left onto Athenree Rd. Follow the signs to St. Hwy. 2 and Tauranga, where you'll spend the night. The drive to Tauranga is 57km (35 miles) and will take about 1 hr.

⓱ ★★ kids Tauranga Art Gallery. Start your day with a peek into the cultural side of this thriving port city. This small gallery always impresses me with its diverse and interesting range of exhibitions, showcasing local, national, traditional, and contemporary works in at least half a dozen different exhibition spaces. If you need a change from New Zealand beach culture, this is just the place to find it. ⏱ 1 hr. 108 Willow St., corner of Wharf St. ☎ 07/578-7933. www.artgallery.org.nz. Donations appreciated. Daily 10am-4:30pm.

In central Tauranga, get onto The Strand and turn right over the railway line into Dive Crescent. At the next roundabout veer right and cross the harbor bridge. Following the signs to Mount Maunganui, turn left

> *The Mount Maunganui's Ocean Beach is one of New Zealand's surfing hot spots but is equally popular with holidaying families.*

on Totara St., right on Rata St., and left on Maunganui Rd., which takes you to shops and beach areas.

⑱   🍽 **Lunch at a cafe.** There are numerous cafes along the busy strip of Maunganui Rd. and further down, on the corner of Adams Avenue and Marine Parade, which faces onto Ocean Beach. I suggest you try the latter. Find a carpark for the afternoon and walk to your preferred cafe for lunch.

⑲ ★★★ kids **Ocean Beach.** Sprawling out on Mount Maunganui's Ocean Beach is a must-do. It's a prime surf hangout and thousands of New Zealand families also make an annual pilgrimage here for safe swimming and a host of holiday activities. There are several festivals throughout the summer too. When you get tired of the beach, you can walk around, or climb Mauao (p. 128, ⑬) or soak in the hot saltwater pools (p. 128, ⑭). Alternatively, you might want to spend the afternoon swimming with dolphins or hiring a fishing charter for some of the region's legendary game or sport fishing. 🕑 Rest of the day.

Leave Tauranga early on day 7 via The Strand. Turn right into Dive Crescent and at

the next roundabout take the 2nd exit onto Te Awanui Dr. Continue on Hewletts Rd. to St. Hwy. 2 and follow signs to Whakatane. The 90km trip (56 miles) takes about 1½ hr.

⑳ ★★★ kids **White Island.** I can't think of a more spectacular way to end your time in the Bay of Plenty than to take to the air in a helicopter and fly over New Zealand's only active marine volcano, White Island. The helicopter will land and you'll have an hour on the ground to explore this barren, beautiful place located 48km (30 miles) offshore. Trips with **Vulcan Helicopters** (☎ 0800/804-354 or 07/308-4188; www.vulcanheli.co.nz) start at NZ$475 per person and booking is essential. If a helicopter ride is out of your price range, book a cruise and 1½-hour guided walking tour of the volcanic crater with **Pee Jay White Island Tours,** 15 The Strand, Whakatane (☎ 0800/733-529 or 07/308-9588; www.whiteisland.co.nz; NZ$195 adults, NZ$125 kids under 13). The tour also includes an exploration of the historic sulfur mining factory. On the way back to shore (via boat or helicopter), you'll pass a large gannet colony and in summer, you'll often see pods of dolphins, whales, and sharks. 🕑 Half-day.

NOW SHOWING
New Zealand Filmmaking BY ADRIENNE REWI

THE FIRST FILMS WERE SHOWN IN NEW ZEALAND in 1896 and the first short films based on Maori stories were produced in 1913. But it was not until the establishment of the New Zealand Film Commission—set up to encourage filmmaking—that the industry found its feet. *Sleeping Dogs,* directed by Roger Donaldson in 1977, got the ball rolling and since then, more than 350 films have been made in New Zealand. The growth of the industry has been an unparalleled success story and the number of New Zealand filmmakers hitting international headlines is far in excess of what would be expected of a small country so far from major world film centers. And then came the huge success of Sir Peter Jackson's *Lord of the Rings* trilogy, which changed the face of the New Zealand film industry forever.

The Directors

ROGER DONALDSON
(1945–)
Known for films like *Sleeping Dogs* (1977) and *Smash Palace* (1982) that celebrate quirky Kiwi life—often with a dark undercurrent—Donaldson got his first American break with *The Bounty* (1984), a re-make of *The Mutiny of the Bounty.*

JANE CAMPION
(1954–)
One of New Zealand's most successful international directors, Campion now lives in Australia. She shot to prominence with *The Piano* (1993), which won an Academy Award for Best Original Screenplay in 1994. She is the second of only four women ever nominated for the Academy Award for Best Director.

VINCENT WARD
(1956–)
Ward's films, which include *Vigil* (1984),

New Zealand Stars

SAM NEILL
(1947–)
The dashing and eloquent Sam Neill has played both hero and villain in numerous international films. He is probably best known for his role as palaeontologist Dr Alan Grant in *Jurassic Park* and *Jurassic Park II*, although he also distinguished himself in *Omen II, The Hunt for Red October,* and, more recently, the television series *The Tudors.*

ANNA PAQUIN
(1982–)
Paquin, who was born in Canada but grew up in New Zealand, was just 11 when she won an Academy Award for Best Supporting Actress for her role in *The Piano* (1993)— the second-youngest winner in history. She won the 2008 Golden Globe Award for Best Actress in a Television Series Drama for her role in *True Blood;* and in between she has starred in *She's All That, Almost Famous* and the *X-Men* series.

MELANIE LYNSKEY
(1977–)
Best known for her role as Charlie Harper's neighbor/stalker Rose in the U.S. television series *Two and a Half Men,* the enigmatic Lynskey has played a range of memorable characters in *Heavenly Creatures, The Informant, Up in the Air,* and *Coyote Ugly.* She lives in Los Angeles with her American actor husband, Jimmi Simpson.

The Navigator: A Medieval Odyssey (1988), *Map of the Human Heart* (1993), and *River Queen* (2005), are known for their originality, atmosphere and often brooding enigmatic imagery. He was also executive producer of *The Last Samurai* (2003), starring Tom Cruise.

SIR PETER JACKSON
(1961–)
Jackson won early acclaim for a series of "splatstick" horror comedies before going mainstream with *Heavenly Creatures* (1994), the *Lord of the Rings* trilogy (2001, 2002, and 2003), *King Kong* (2005), and *The Lovely Bones* (2009). He was a co-founder of Weta Workshops (p. 254, ⑪) and has won three Academy Awards, including Best Director in 2003.

NIKI CARO (1967–)
Caro's most significant film to date was the portrayal of the moving Maori legend *Whale Rider* (2002), which won worldwide praise at numerous international film festivals. She later directed Charlize Theron in the Oscar nominated *North Country* (2005). Her most recent film was *The Vintner's Luck* (2008).

On Location in New Zealand

In addition to a growing number of successful New Zealand films, the country has also hosted many international productions that have capitalised on New Zealand's spectacular natural beauty. Chief among them have been *The Last Samurai* (2004), *Dororo* (2007), *The Chronicles of Narnia* movies (2004-05), *10,000BC* (2008) *30 Days of Night* (2007), *Bridge to Terabithia* (2007) and the 2000 Bollywood super-hit *Kaho Naa....Pyaar Hai* (2000). Major productions such as James Cameron's *Avatar* (2009) and *The Water Horse: Legend of the Deep* (2007), in addition to shooting in New Zealand, also made use of the highly-skilled special effects team at Weta Digital Studios in Wellington.

A Side Trip to Hamilton

It always seems a pity to me that travelers so often overlook Hamilton and its neighboring areas. I can see why—it is only an hour from Auckland after all, and most people want to get further south on their first day—but there are quiet charms here that will give you an insight into rural life in the more populated half of the North Island. If you have some extra time on your way to or from the Coromandel–Bay of Plenty region, consider spending a day or two to see why so many people have settled here.

> Take time out from the city at Hamilton Lake, where you can wander leafy paths, sail small boats, or ride bikes.

START Hamilton is 127km (79 miles) south of Auckland on St. Hwy. 1. Garden Place is the central plaza on Victoria St., the city's main shopping street.

1 Hamilton i-SITE Visitor Centre. Make a quick stop here to pick up brochures for attractions and activities that interest you. The staff is always keen to help with bookings, directions, and transport suggestions. ⊕ 30 min. 5 Garden Place (opposite Skycity Casino), Victoria St. ☎ 07/958-5960. www.visithamilton.co.nz. Daily Mon–Fri 9am–5pm, Sat–Sun 9:30am–3:30pm.

2 ★★ kids Waikato Museum. One of the highlights here is the Te Winika Gallery, which features the giant *waka taua* (Maori war canoe), *Te Winika*. Now 200 years old, it was gifted to the museum by Maori Queen Te Arikinui Dame Te Atairangikaahu in 1973. The gallery walls are decorated with a magnificent carved history of the Tainui people. *The Mighty River Waikato* details the historical, ecological, and social importance of the river to its community, and *Never a Dull Moment* showcases Hamilton's social history from 1864-1945. In addition there are changing displays of

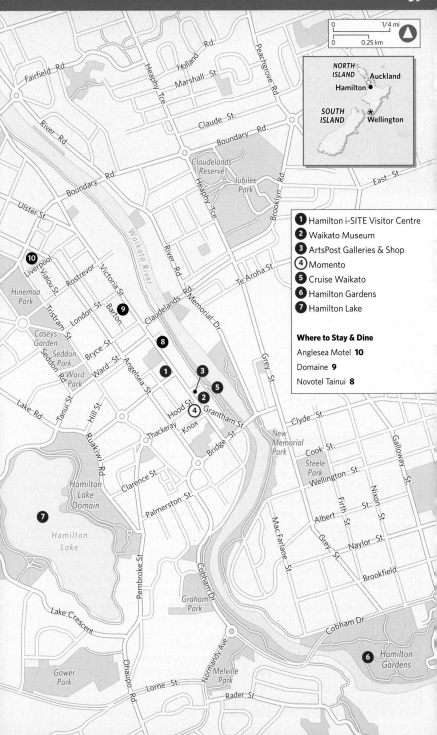

1 Hamilton i-SITE Visitor Centre
2 Waikato Museum
3 ArtsPost Galleries & Shop
4 Momento
5 Cruise Waikato
6 Hamilton Gardens
7 Hamilton Lake

Where to Stay & Dine

Anglesea Motel **10**
Domaine **9**
Novotel Tainui **8**

> *Splurge on unique, handcrafted, take-home gifts at Hamilton's ArtsPost Galleries & Shop.*

contemporary New Zealand art. ⏱ 1 hr. 1 Grantham St., Hamilton. ☎ 07/838-6606. www.waikatomuseum.co.nz. Free admission; charges on some touring shows. Daily 10am–4:30pm.

❸ ★ **ArtsPost Galleries & Shop.** In a historic building beside the Waikato Museum, ArtsPost features changing exhibitions of quality local art and a retail outlet that stocks a wide range of ceramics, glassware, jewelry, prints, and textiles. ⏱ 30 min. 120 Victoria St., Hamilton. ☎ 07/838-6928. www.artspost.co.nz. Free admission. Daily 10am–4:30pm.

Where to Stay & Dine in Hamilton

★ **Anglesea Motel,** 36 Liverpool St. (☎ 07/834-0010; www.angleseamotel.com), is always my first choice for a convenient inner city motel. It's directly across the street from a supermarket, has kitchen facilities, spacious rooms, a swimming pool and playground, and free high speed Internet access (doubles NZ$155–NZ$220).

★★ **Novotel Tainui,** 7 Alma St. (☎ 0800/450-050 or 07/838-1366; www.novotel.com), is a lively, fresh, great value hotel with large rooms and excellent amenities for the price (doubles NZ$165–NZ$375).

★★ **Domaine,** 575 Victoria St. (☎ 07/839-2100) is the local favorite for best restaurant. New Zealand salmon, beef, and lamb feature prominently on the menu (lunch and dinner Tues-Sat; main courses NZ$24–NZ$34).

> *The Indian Char Bagh Garden is one of several stunning international displays at Hamilton Gardens.*

④ 🍽 **Momento.** This popular, sunny meeting place for locals has bright '60s decor. It makes for a fun coffee break. 109 Victoria St., Hamilton. ☎ 07/834-4365. www.momentoespresso.co.nz. Coffee and cake about NZ$12.

❺ ★★ **kids** **Cruise Waikato.** For centuries, the Waikato River has served as both highway and food source to Maori, who built many villages along its course. Its full name, *Waikato-taniwha-rau,* means "the flowing water of a hundred water monsters." You'll find out much more about Hamilton and the river's history as you glide on *Te Awa Kuiri, The River Queen.* You'll see Hamilton from a completely different perspective, gliding under the city bridges, passing canoeists and rowers, all the while getting wonderful views of the city and private homes clinging to the leafy banks. ⏱ 1½ hr. Memorial Park Jetty, Memorial Ave., Hamilton. ☎ 0508/426-458; www.cruise-waikato.co.nz. Prices start at NZ$25 adult and NZ$10 kids 15 and under. Cruises depart Memorial Park Jetty daily at 2pm and from Hamilton Gardens jetty off carpark A daily at 2:30pm.

6 ★★★ kids **Hamilton Gardens.** This verdant core began life as a rose garden in the 1960s. Today the 58-hectare (143-acre) gardens attract over 1.3 million visitors a year. You'll find themed gardens (such as the Italian Renaissance Garden), begonia collections, a cactus house, camellia walks, the rhododendron lawn, an herb and kitchen garden, and the Te Parapara Garden, which features a *pataka* (Maori storehouse) carved following traditional lines. ⏱ At least 1 hr. Cobham Drive, Hamilton. ☎ 07/838-6782; www.hamiltongardens.co.nz. Free admission. Central theme gardens daily 7:30am–5:30pm (8pm in summer); information center daily 10am–4pm; Victorian Flower Garden Display Houses daily 10am–4pm (5pm in summer).

7 ★ kids **Hamilton Lake.** Lake Rotoroa, commonly called Hamilton Lake, and its 56-hectare (138-acre) reserve is a pleasant place for a late afternoon wander or an early evening dinner picnic. A pretty, circular walking track winds around the edge of the water, plus playgrounds and picnic spots aplenty. The Verandah Café near the main entrance to the lake is a lovely place to sit and watch the sun set over the lake. ⏱ At least 1 hr. Hamilton Lake Domain, off Ruakiwi Rd. ☎ 07/838-9975. Free admission. Daily dawn–dusk.

The Waitomo Caves

Waitomo, a tiny village about 70km (43 miles) south of Hamilton, is home to a labyrinth of roughly 500 caves and deep, well-like holes that Maori call *tomo*. A number of excellent tourism operators offer cave adventures to suit families and daredevils alike. I've described my personal favorites below but there are so many options that the best place to start is the **Waitomo Caves Discovery Centre & i-SITE Visitor Centre,** 21 Waitomo Caves Rd. (☎ 0800/474-839 or 07/878-7640. www.waitomodiscovery. org). Staff here can help you make sense of the complex range of caves and activities available in the town. They can also do the booking for you and provide you with all the brochures and maps you might need.

The ★★★ **Waitomo Glowworm Caves and Waitomo Aranui Cave** tour takes you through 250m (820 ft.) of stunning underground scenery, culminating in the glowworm caves. Floating through the cave in a boat is a silent, surreal experience. It's a good idea to buy a combo ticket (NZ$65 adults, NZ$28 kids 4–14) that also gets you into Aranui Cave, nearby. Aranui's magnificent formations are among the most spectacular in the area. Tickets for both caves are sold at the Waitomo Glowworm Cave Centre, 39 Waitomo Caves Rd. (☎ 0800/456-922 or 07/878-8227; www.waitomo.com).

If you're looking for more of an adrenaline rush, book a tour of Ruakuri Cave with ★★★ **The Legendary Blackwater Rafting Company,** 585 Waitomo Caves Rd. (☎ 0800/228-464; www.waitomo.co.nz). Depending on which option you choose, you may float beneath glowworm clusters, rush through underground waterfalls, abseil into the depths of the cave, and do a zip line in the dark. Adventure tours start at NZ$115.

Coromandel & Bay of Plenty Beaches A to Z

★★ kids **Bowentown** WAIHI/BAY OF PLENTY
At the southern end of Waihi Beach, Bowentown offers a broader choice of landscape and activities than many beaches and it's a great family spot. You get a choice of ocean waves or, a short walk across the headland, a quiet harbor perfect for kayaking. The 128-hectare (316-acre) headland is home to three old Maori *pa* (hill fort) sites (p. 134, ⑯) and it also gives access to three perfect little beaches tucked away from the crowds. Anzac Bay offers safe swimming for kids and is a popular picnic spot. Shelly Bay, a half-hour walk from there, also has safe swimming. Cave Bay, accessed via a steep track from the headland carpark, has a tiny beach and lovely harbor views. You won't be short of good picnic spots here and there is a good camping ground.
From Waihi Town take Tauranga Rd. (St. Hwy. 2) off Rosemont Rd. and follow signs to Waihi Beach, veering left into Waihi Beach Rd., then right into Seaforth Rd. and travel all the way to the end.

★★★ kids **Cathedral Cove.** See p. 148.

★★ kids **Cooks Beach.** MERCURY BAY/EAST COAST COROMANDEL Named after Captain James Cook, who discovered it in 1769, this pretty crescent of white sand stretches 3km (1¾ miles), giving everyone plenty of room to spread their towels and soak up the sun. It's popular with boaties and has excellent swimming and fishing. There's a tire swing in the pine trees just up from the central part of the beach near the main carpark that kids will love. At the east end of the beach, sheltered Purangi Estuary is popular for picnics and canoeing. The west end of the beach rises to Shakespeare Cliff and there are a number of walking tracks to the summit that give wonderful views of Mercury Bay. The beach is backed by a growing, modern residential settlement and there are accommodations, a general store, and camping facilities. You can catch a ferry from Whitianga to Ferry Landing and walk 20–30 min. to Cooks Beach; or drive in via Tairua-Whitianga Rd. (St. Hwy. 25), turning onto Hot Water Beach Rd. at Whenuakite and following signs to Cooks Beach.

> Kids will adore Mount Maunganui with its vast expanses of sand and safe swimming beaches.

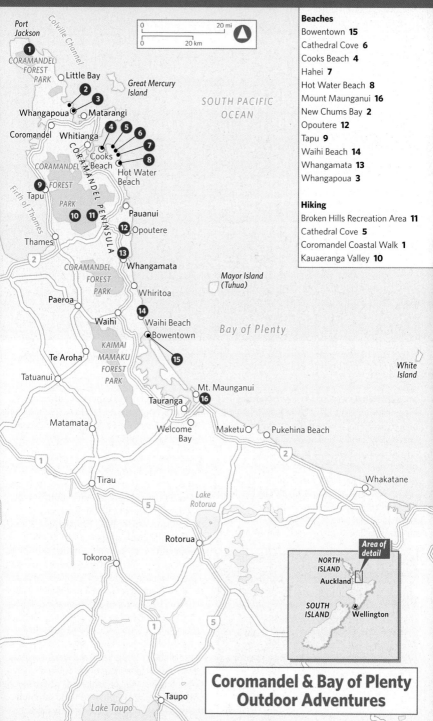

Beaches

Bowentown **15**
Cathedral Cove **6**
Cooks Beach **4**
Hahei **7**
Hot Water Beach **8**
Mount Maunganui **16**
New Chums Bay **2**
Opoutere **12**
Tapu **9**
Waihi Beach **14**
Whangamata **13**
Whangapoua **3**

Hiking

Broken Hills Recreation Area **11**
Cathedral Cove **5**
Coromandel Coastal Walk **1**
Kauaeranga Valley **10**

**Coromandel & Bay of Plenty
Outdoor Adventures**

> *The entire coastline from Coromandel, through Bay of Plenty and around Eastland, offers a never-ending string of beautiful beaches, including Waihi, pictured here.*

★★★ kids **Hahei** EAST COAST COROMANDEL
It's small, with just 1.5km (1 mile) of white-sand beach, but Hahei is nonetheless one of the prettiest beaches in the region. It has a quiet charm and is not as modernized as some of the larger, more populated beaches. It offers excellent swimming, boating, and surfcasting, and there is a small cluster of shops and cafes just up from the beach. A creek runs into the sea here, making an ideal play area for small children. There are pretty islands offshore and plenty of coastal nooks and crannies to explore. Road access is via Tairua-Whitianga Rd. (St. Hwy. 25); turn onto Hot Water Beach Rd. at Whenuakite and follow signs to Hahei Beach.

★★ kids **Hot Water Beach.** EAST COAST COROMANDEL People from all over the world have dug holes in the sand here (2 hours either side of low tide), and soaked in the naturally occurring thermal water that bubbles up through the sand at a rate of 10 to 15 liters per minute. Water in the north spring is 147°F (64°C); the second spring, about 20m (66 ft) south is slightly cooler. All this comes about as a result of activity more than 2km (1¼ miles) beneath the earth's surface, where a reservoir of water is heated by a remnant of Coromandel's volcanic activity of 5 to 9 million years ago. The hot surface water is rich in minerals and it's fun to lie here and chat with people from all parts of the globe. It's otherwise a popular surfing beach but extreme caution is required when swimming because of dangerous ocean rips; only very strong swimmers should attempt the waves and only between safety flags.

Get in First

Accommodation and camping grounds at almost all the Coromandel and Bay of Plenty beaches fills up fast—some is booked ahead from one year to the next, so make sure you book well in advance of your visit to avoid disappointment. A useful reference is www.nzcamping.co.nz, which details contact points for many major camping grounds around the country. Local visitor information centers also have camping information.

> *Little ones will enjoy splashing around in the thermal water at Hot Water Beach.*

There's an excellent little beach store here, a camping ground, and kids will enjoy playing in the shallow waters where a calm creek meets the ocean, just below the parking area. **Road access is via Tairua-Whitianga Rd. (St. Hwy. 25).** Turn onto Hot Water Beach Rd. at Whenuakite and follow signs to Hot Water Beach.

★★ **kids Mount Maunganui.** TAURANGA/BAY OF PLENTY   This is one of New Zealand's surf capitals and every year the population swells with holidaying families who have called this their summer escape for decades. It's home to New Zealand's first purpose-built artificial surf reef and there's never a dull moment as one summer event quickly succeeds another—everything from world-class surf and lifesaving competitions to volleyball, windsurfing, water skiing, parasailing, and assorted festivals.

Beach Safety

If you're planning a day at the beach, be sure to wear sunhats and plenty of sunscreen. Ultra-violet rays are much stronger in New Zealand then in the Northern Hemisphere and you'll burn quickly. Around 200 people a year drown on New Zealand beaches and children under 14 make up 40% of all beach rescues. Here are some tips to help keep you safe in the water:

• Swim only at lifeguard-patrolled beaches and only between red and yellow safety flags.

• Never swim alone and never leave children unattended.

• Never swim in street clothes or while drinking alcohol.

• Be aware of dangerous rips and currents.

• Check water depth before diving in.

• Regularly check your position against a static on-shore landmark to make sure you're not drifting in a dangerous current.

• If you get into trouble, raise your arm above your head.

• Shark attacks do happen in New Zealand. Always keep an eye on your environment.

• If you're not sure of anything, stay out of the water.

> Mount Manganui beach is a popular spot for vacationing families.

A large shopping area filled with cafes and holiday resorts backs onto the beach. You can enjoy the quieter waters of Pilot Bay on the harbor side of the mountain. Signposted walks up and around The Mount (Mauao) and a soak in the Mount Maunganui Hot Pools (p. 128, **14**) are also popular. **Drive across the Tauranga Harbour Bridge and follow the signs to Mount Maunganui.**

★★★ kids **New Chums Bay.** WAINUIOTOTO BAY/ NORTHEAST COROMANDEL This gem is one of the last undeveloped beaches of the Coromandel—a small, remote horseshoe of white sand that has several times been voted among the world's top 20 beaches. Backed by native bush, nikau palms, and flowering pohutukawa, it offers good fishing and shellfish digging in the surf and is often deserted. You'll have to make a special effort, as it's a 40- to 50-minute walk to reach it. **Access is by foot only.** At the north end of Whangapoua Beach (see below), wade through the estuary and follow the shoreline to a track that crosses the low part of the headland and takes you to New Chums.

★★★ kids **Opoutere.** WHAREKAWA HARBOUR/ EAST COAST COROMANDEL This is one of the most sought-after undeveloped beaches with road access on the whole peninsula. You walk through bush to 5km (3 miles) of white sand with clear water that provides good surfing, surfcasting, and swimming (safest for kids at low tide). It is protected by a huge forested reserve that means it won't be developed into a resort, and there are lovely forest and harbor walks when you're tired of the beach. At the south end, the narrow entrance into Wharekawa Harbour is dominated by a spectacular sand spit, which is a breeding ground for a number of endangered birds. Department of Conservation rangers are on duty here from November to February to make sure the birds are not disturbed. You'll find the Ohui rock pools at the north end of the beach. There is also a YHA hostel and camping ground. **Turn off St. Hwy. 25 26km (16 miles) south of Tairua onto Opoutere Rd. and drive 4km (2½ miles) to the beach carpark.**

★★ kids **Tapu.** THAMES/WEST COAST COROMANDEL As you drive up the west coast of the Coromandel Peninsula, you'll pass dozens of tiny bays and beaches, but Tapu is the most developed. This is relative; it's just a tiny cluster of old baches (holiday homes), a hotel, and a large camping ground, which has a well-stocked store. The camping ground is the center of summer life here. It's well equipped with caravan site and small cabins, all of which have easy access to a fine little beach. The fishing and bird life are great on this side of the peninsula too. Kids will love playing in the shallow waters where the Tapu River runs into the sea. **19km (12 miles) north of Thames and 35km (22 miles) south of Coromandel town on St. Hwy. 25.**

★★ kids **Waihi Beach.** NORTHERN BAY OF PLENTY With 9km (5⅔ miles) of white sand, Waihi is

> *The re's great surfing all along the Coromandel & Bay of Plenty coastline.*

one of the longest and most popular beaches in the region. Like Whangamata (below), it has an almost cult-like following among surfers and you'll often find them gathered in friendly groups along the beachfront. You'll find plenty of New Zealand families here too, who come because of the variety and lively holiday mood on offer. In addition to plenty of spots for swimming, surfing, walking, surfcasting, and rock fishing, the beach is backed by a small town with plenty of shops, accommodation, and cafes. **Turn onto Waihi Beach Road off SH2.**

★★★ kids **Whangamata.** SOUTHEAST CORO-MANDEL Once a small seaside village with a cluster of old baches (holiday homes), Whangamata is now filled with expensive houses and permanent residents, who have flocked in for the relaxed lifestyle. That aside, it is still a Mecca for surfers, who come for the legendary "Whanga bar" at the north end of the beach, and for holidaying families who enjoy the variety

here. There's safe swimming among ocean waves, in the calm harbor, and the pretty river estuary. The annual Beach Hop in March draws over 70,000 people. The town has expanded in proportion to the resident population and you'll find plenty of cafe, shopping, and accommodation choices. **Well signposted from St. Hwy. 25.**

★★★ kids **Whangapoua.** WHANGAPOUA HAR-BOUR/NORTHEAST COROMANDEL This is another of the more out-of-the-way northern Coromandel beaches that really is worth the extra drive. It has excellent swimming, surfing, and boogie boarding conditions and far fewer people. You'll also find good fishing, plenty of walking trails, and rich birdlife. A lagoon at one end is popular with families. There are baches (holiday homes) to rent, a holiday park, and a general store. **Turn off St. Hwy. 25 east of Coromandel town, heading toward Matarangi Peninsula, and then follow signs to Whangapoua.**

Coromandel Hiking A to Z

★★ **Broken Hills Recreation Area.** There are walks for all ages and stages within this popular part of Puketui Valley. The area was a major mining area, so make sure you stick to marked tracks to avoid dangerous mine shafts hidden by vegetation. Along with good swimming and fishing spots on the Tairua River, the track network also features impressive rock formations and old mining relics. The Puketui Track connects the two road ends and a number of shorter circular tracks loop off it. Tracks, from 5 minutes to 10 hours, are marked by orange triangles and signs indicate where easy walking tracks change to more testing hiking trails. 19km (12 miles) south of Tairua, turn off St. Hwy. 25 into Morrison's Rd. (opposite the Pauanui turnoff), then onto Puketui Valley Rd. It is 6km (3¾ miles) to the carpark. Alternative access from the west side of the peninsula is off the Kopu-Hikuai Rd. (St. Hwy. 25A), 26km (16 miles) south of Thames. Turn onto Puketui Rd., just before the Tairua River and Fourth Branch Scenic Reserve. Travel 4km (2½ miles) on a gravel road to the carpark and the southern end of the track system.

★★★ kids **Cathedral Cove.** When you first lay eyes on the pristine, crystal-clear waters and golden sands of Cathedral Cove, you'll understand why this is one of the most visited spots on the peninsula—and why it was chosen as a major film set in the movie *The Lion, the Witch and the Wardrobe*. This popular walk starts at the Cathedral Cove carpark above Hahei Beach. The carpark is often full during summer, in which case you'll need to park at Hahei Beach and add another 25 minutes each way onto the 2-hour (round-trip) walk. The 2.5km (1½ mile) track drops down from there and leads you to the breathtakingly lovely Gemstone and Stingray bays, which are separated by the famous cathedral-like land mass and are perfect for swimming and snorkeling. This is also a magic place to go sea-kayaking—you can organize that with one of the tour operators in Whitianga. Make sure you take your swimsuit, camera, and sensible walking shoes. Cathedral Cove is signposted near the Hahei Beach shops. Drive to the top, park your car, and walk from there.

> *The distinctive rock formations at Cathedral Cove make it a winner with walkers, swimmers, and photographers.*

★★★ **Coromandel Coastal Walk.** This 8km (5-mile) walk takes about 7 to 8 hours round-trip, between Fletcher Bay and Stony Bay at the top of Coromandel Peninsula. You'll walk across farmland, through coastal forest, and along the coastline, catching good views of a number of offshore islands. You can do this return walk independently or join the Coromandel Coastal Walkway Tour (p. 132, ❼) and walk from Fletcher Bay to Stony Bay, with transportation to and from Coromandel town at either end. Fletcher Bay is at the end of the Peninsula road, 36km (22 miles) from Colville and 7km (4⅓ miles) past Port Jackson. The gravel road is narrow and winding, and some rental car companies do not cover it in their insurance policies. The trip from Coromandel town is 56km (35 miles) in total and will take over an hour.

★★★ **Kauaeranga Valley.** Located 13km (8 miles) from Thames, this beautiful valley was once filled with huge kauri trees. Sadly, early logging depleted the area, but thick native bush, streams, rocky outcrops, and gorges make it an attractive hiking proposition. In addition to eight camping grounds and an 80-bed tramping hut there are many remote camping opportunities and numerous short and long walks. Pick up the *Kauaeranga Valley Recreation* brochure—available at the main visitor information centers around the peninsula—for full details and descriptions of them all to make your pick. The Pinnacles (1½ hr.),

the Wainora Kauri Walk (3–4 hr.), Catleys Track (1½ hr.) and Billygoat Landing Walk (20 min.) are all popular choices. From St. Hwy. 25 at the southern entrance to Thames, turn right on Banks St. beside the BP petrol station. Veer right on Parawai Rd., which becomes Kauaeranga Valley Rd. The road becomes gravel after 10km (6 miles). The Kauaerenga i-SITE Visitor Centre is located 13km (8 miles) up the valley and has detailed information about huts, camping, and safe hiking in the area.

Going with the Experts

There are two superb guided walk and hiking companies offering a wide range of multi-day nature treks and personalized tours on Coromandel Peninsula. **Johansen & Wincorp Adventures** (☎ 07/864-8731; www.coromandel.co.nz; www.remote nzjourneys.co.nz) have a number of options, including a Night Glow Worm Experience. Their walks always include history and information about plants, Maori medicines, and foods of the forest. Prices start at NZ$100 per person. **Kiwi Dundee Adventures** (☎ 07/865-8809; www.kiwidundee.co.nz) is the brainchild of passionate outdoors enthusiast Doug Johansen and his partner, Jan Poole. They offer a number of full-day and multi-day tours beginning around NZ$250 per person.

The Full Story

Pick up Department of Conservation walking and hiking brochures for the Coromandel region from local i-SITE visitor information centers (see "Fast Facts" at the end of this chapter). *Coromandel Recreation* gives the best overview. They usually cost NZ$1 to NZ$3 dollars and with their detailed descriptions and maps, they're a must on any long walk. In a number of areas, the Department of Conservation (DOC) has also provided good information boards detailing walks, huts, and campsites. Note that walks are free but the huts and campsites carry fees and camping outside designated areas is not permitted. Make sure you're well equipped for long hikes and carry a flashlight and cell phone.

Where to Stay

> *Stay in one of the roomy, modern suites at Tauranga's stylish Hotel on Devonport in the heart of the city.*

Coromandel Town

★ kids Anchor Lodge CENTRAL

Centrally located a short walk from the township, this motel has a lovely setting in native bush, overlooking Coromandel Harbour. The self-contained units all have private balconies and when you're not at the beach or exploring, you can enjoy a barbecue by the heated swimming pool or borrow one of the free mountain bikes. 448 Wharf Rd. ☎ 07/866-7992. www.anchorlodgecoromandel.co.nz. 22 units. Doubles NZ$85–NZ$310. MC, V. Map p. 125.

kids Coromandel Motel & Holiday Park CENTRAL

Come here for a relaxed holiday park atmosphere at a good price. Set on 1.4 hectares (3½ acres) of park-like grounds in the historic part of the town, it has a mix of modest self-contained motel units, small cottages with bunk rooms, and powered and non-powered camping sites. There are bikes for hire, a swimming pool, playground, and a games room to keep the kids happy. 636 Rings Rd. ☎ 07/866-8830. www.coromandelholidaypark.co.nz. Doubles NZ$24–NZ$175. MC. V. Map p. 125.

★★ Driving Creek Villas CENTRAL

These gorgeous boutique villas are located in a private bush setting and fitted out with all the modern goodies. Each villa has two bedrooms, one bathroom, a full kitchen, a big lounge, and a private garden. Egyptian cotton bed linens and a Japanese hot tub complete the picture. 21a Colville Rd. ☎ 07/866-7755. www.drivingcreekvillas.com. 3 units. Doubles NZ$305. MC, V. Map p. 125.

Tauranga & Mount Maunganui

★★ Hotel on Devonport CENTRAL TAURANGA

This is a great-value, stylish stay in the heart of Tauranga. The large rooms all have balconies and large bathrooms and many interconnect. This boutique property has a strong corporate emphasis and while not ideal for families, it's perfect for couples traveling together. 72 Devonport Rd., Tauranga. ☎ 0800/322-856 or 07/578-2668. www.hotelondevonport.co.nz. 38 units. Doubles NZ$250–NZ$320. AE, DC, MC, V. Map p. 125.

★★★ kids Oceanside Resort & Twin Towers MOUNT MAUNGANUI

You can choose between beach, mountain, or garden views in this modern apartment complex. In a prime spot, just across the road from the ocean beach and a few steps from cafes, bars, restaurants, and shops, it has one- and two-bedroom suites and two-bedroom apartments. The property also has its own heated swimming pools, gym, and sauna. 1

Maunganui Rd., Mt. Maunganui. ☎ 0800/466-868 or 07/575-5371. www.oceanside.co.nz. 40 units. Doubles NZ$180–NZ$600. AE, DC, MC, V. Map p. 125.

★★★ **Ridge Country Retreat** WELCOME BAY
When you're perched high in the hills overlooking the Bay of Plenty coastline, lounging about in giant suites, soaking in an outdoor bath under the stars, and dining on gourmet meals, you'll wish you came here sooner and stayed longer. Factor in a geothermal heated pool, fabulous hosts, and spa treatments, and you have a winner. 300 Rocky Cutting Rd., Welcome Bay, Tauranga. ☎ 07/542-1301. www.rcr.co.nz. 11 units. Doubles NZ$650 w/breakfast. AE, MC, V. Map p. 125.

Whitianga

★★ kids **Crows Nest Apartments** CENTRAL
These large one-, two-, three- and four-bedroom apartments, directly across the street from Whitianga's Buffalo Beach, set you up with such comforts and conveniences as your own private, furnished balcony overlooking the beach, a heated Jacuzzi, and outdoor furniture on the roof. They're close to cafes, shops, and the ferry. 18–20 Mill Rd. ☎ 07/869-5979. www.crowsnestwhitianga.co.nz. 27 units. Doubles NZ$200–NZ$600. V. Map p. 125.

★ kids **Marina Park Apartments** CENTRAL
The bright, roomy one-, two- and three-bedroom apartments with harbor views are perfect for families and friends traveling together. Amenities include two heated Jacuzzis, a swimming pool, and gym. 84 Albert St. ☎ 0800/743-784; www.marinapark.co.nz. 59 units. Doubles NZ$175–NZ$475. AE, DC, MC, V. Map p. 125.

★★★ kids **Oceans Resort** CENTRAL
You'll sleep well here, tucked away in a quiet side street, a short walk from Buffalo Beach and shopping areas. I could happily have moved into my two-bedroom, self-contained apartment permanently. With all the practical concerns covered, you can come home to comfort and peace. There are tennis courts, a heated pool, and a children's play area too. 18 Eyre St. ☎ 07/869-5222. www.oceansresort.co.nz. 20 units. Doubles NZ$150–NZ$350. MC, V. Map p. 125.

Where to Dine

Coromandel Town

★★ kids **Driving Creek Café** DRIVING CREEK ROAD CAFE Located in an old villa, this cafe has a great range of home baking, good coffee, and light meals. They use local organic produce whenever possible and they cater to gluten-free, vegan, and vegetarian dietary needs. Relax on the verandah in summer, or curl up on a couch by the fire in winter. 180 Driving Creek Rd. ☎ 07/866-7066. Main courses NZ$10–NZ$16. V. Daily breakfast and lunch in summer; closed Wed in winter. Map p. 125.

★★ kids **Peppertree Restaurant & Bar** CENTRAL SEAFOOD The Peppertree has been around for years and can still be relied upon to serve up tasty fresh meals based on the wealth of local seafood on their doorstep. You can also order local beef and fresh vegetables. Eat inside, in the sunny courtyard, or on shaded verandahs. They offer a kids' menu. 31 Kapanga Rd. ☎ 07/866-8211. www.peppertreerestaurant.co.nz. Main courses NZ$25–NZ$35). AE, DC, MC, V. Daily breakfast, lunch, and dinner from 11am. Map p. 125.

★★ kids **Umu** CENTRAL CAFE
By day, this relaxed cafe serves divine breakfasts, light lunches, and tasty goodies from a well-stocked cabinet (perfect for picnic supplies). At night, choose from a menu that features local seafood, pizzas, salads, lamb, big steaks, and vegetarian meals. You can also order pizzas as takeaways and eat them on the beach. 22 Wharf Rd. ☎ 07/866-8618. Main courses NZ$25–NZ$32. MC, V. Daily breakfast, lunch, and dinner. Map p. 125.

Tauranga & Mount Maunganui

★★ kids **Bravo** TAURANGA CAFE/MODERN NZ
I've been here at all times of the day and I've never been disappointed. From brunch through to dinner it's always lively but I especially like late afternoon at the end of a busy day, unwinding with a glass of wine and a light snack. By night it converts to a restaurant with a menu that features award-winning beef and

> *Start the day with a hearty breakfast at Tay Street Café, overlooking Mount Maunganui Beach.*

lamb dishes. Red Sq., Downtown Tauranga. ☎ 07/578-4700. Main courses NZ$28–NZ$32. AE, DC, MC, V. Daily breakfast and lunch, Tues-Sat breakfast, lunch, and dinner. Map p. 125.

★★ kids **Mediterraneo Café** TAURANGA CAFE I always think it's a good sign when staff knows the locals by name, and the friendly service and tasty food I enjoyed here certainly back that up. Expect hearty breakfasts and tempting lunch dishes like salads, soups, pasta, curries, or beer-battered fish and chips. Laid-back and delightful. 62 Devonport Rd., Tauranga. ☎ 07/577-0487. Main courses NZ$13–NZ$22. MC, V. Breakfast and lunch daily. Map p. 125.

★★ kids **Tay Street Beach Café** MOUNT MAUN-GANUI MODERN NZ Relaxing on the street-front, overlooking one of our busiest beaches with a glass of New Zealand wine and a plate of grilled salmon, is my idea of heaven. This bright, popular spot attracts everyone from families and businessmen to surfers and beach-goers, who come for curries, lamb salad, soft-shell crab, battered fish and chips, and much more. Corner of Tay St. and Marine Parade, Mt. Maunganui. ☎ 07/572-0691. www.taystreetbeachcafe.co.nz. Main courses NZ$18–NZ$28. AE, MC, V. Daily breakfast, lunch, and dinner. Map p. 125.

Whitianga

★ kids **Dino's Pizza** CENTRAL PIZZERIA At this great-value choice, you can eat your fill of delicious pizzas, salads, and pasta dishes without breaking the bank. The pizza menu is also available for takeaway, which is an excellent option for an early evening beach picnic. Shop 3, 1 Blacksmith Ln. ☎ 07/867-1010. Main courses NZ$15–NZ$25. MC, V. Daily lunch and dinner. Map p. 125.

★★★ kids **Salt Bar & Restaurant** CENTRAL IN-TERNATIONAL This is my pick for the restaurant with the best views—right on the edge of the water overlooking Whitianga Marina. Savor beautifully presented local seafood, duck, lamb, or beef tenderloin out on the deck or inside in a modern dining room. Whitianga Marina hotel, 1 Blacksmith Ln. ☎ 07/866-5818. www.whitiangahotel.co.nz. Main courses NZ$25–NZ$35. DC, MC, V. Daily lunch and dinner. Map p. 125.

★ kids **Wild Hogs Bar & Restaurant** CENTRAL MODERN NZ This one also overlooks the marina but it's more relaxed and casual than Salt. The menu swings across beef tenderloin steaks, salads, pizza, steak sandwiches, pork ribs, and beer-battered local fish. 9 Esplanade. ☎ 07/866-4828. Main courses NZ$15–NZ$26. AE, DC, MC, V. Daily breakfast, lunch, and dinner. Map p. 125.

Coromandel & Bay of Plenty Fast Facts

> Cruising into Coromandel by ferry.

Arriving

BY AIR Air New Zealand (☎ 0800/737-000; www.airnewzealand.co.nz) operates daily flights from Tauranga and Whakatane to Auckland, Wellington, and Christchurch. The airport is in Mt. Maunganui, 5km (3 miles) from Tauranga City. **Air Coromandel/ Great Barrier Airlines** (☎ 0800/900-600; www.greatbarrierairlines.co.nz) runs daily service between Whitianga, Auckland, and Tauranga. **BY BUS Intercity** (☎ 09/623-1503) runs regular services to Whitianga, Coromandel, Thames, and Tauranga. **BY FERRY 360 Discovery Cruises** (☎ 0800/360-3472; www.360discovery.co.nz) operates between Auckland and Coromandel town.

Emergencies & Medical Care

Dial ☎ **111** for all emergencies. The local hospitals are **Thames Hospital,** Mackay St.,Thames (☎ **07/868-6550**) and **Tauranga Hospital,** Cameron Rd., Tauranga (☎ **07/579-8000**). Other options for medical care include **Mercury Bay Medical Centre,** 87 Albert St., Whitianga (☎ **07/866-5911**) and **CentralMed,** corner of Devonport Rd. and 14th Ave., Tauranga (☎ **07/928-8000**). For a dentist, try **Whitianga Dental Centre,** 42 Albert St., Whitianga (☎ **07/866-4019**) or **Taylor, Burley, Kleiman Dental,** 8 Willow St., Tauranga (☎ **07/578-9849** or A/H 07/579-3132).

Internet

Get online at **Interearth Internet Café,** 14/1 Blacksmith Lane, Whitianga (☎ 07/866-5991) or **Flash Internet,** 391 Maunganui Rd., Mt. Maunganui (☎ 07/572-0668).

Visitor Information Centers

COROMANDEL I-SITE VISITOR CENTRE 355 Kapanga Rd., Coromandel; ☎ 07/866-8598; www.thecoromandel.com. **MOUNT MAUNGANUI I-SITE VISITOR CENTRE** Salisbury Ave., Mt Maunganui; ☎ 07/578-8103. **TAURANGA I-SITE VISITOR CENTRE** 95 Willow St., Tauranga; ☎ 07/578-8103; www.bayofplentynz.com. **THAMES I-SITE VISITOR CENTRE** 206 Pollen St., Thames; ☎ 07/868-7284; www.thamesinfo.co.nz. **WAIHI INFORMATION CENTRE** Seddon St., Waihi; ☎ 07/863-6715; www.waihi.org.nz. **WHANGAMATA I-SITE VISITOR CENTRE** 616 Port Rd., Whangamata; ☎ 07/865-8340; www.whangamatainfo.co.nz. **WHITIANGA I-SITE VISITOR CENTRE** 66 Albert St., Whitianga; ☎ 07/866-5555; www.whitianga.co.nz.

My Favorite Moments

Rotorua and Taupo sit on the edge of one of the most concentrated volcanic areas in the world. There is tangible evidence of their explosive history in every direction. Lake Taupo is, in fact, a vast volcanic crater lake—all that remains of a mountain that blew its top in A.D. 135, in one of the most devastating eruptions to ever take place on earth. Today, these two hissing, steaming provinces rival Queenstown as the adventure capital of New Zealand. With dozens of lakes, mountains, forests, and geothermal attractions, they offer unlimited opportunities for a holiday of a lifetime.

> PREVIOUS PAGE *The city of Rotorua spreads out around the shores of Lake Rotorua.* THIS PAGE *St. Faith's Maori church, in the shoreline Maori village of Ohinemutu, is a distinctive city landmark.*

1 Soaking in hot pools at Polynesian Spa. Sink into one of the outdoor Japanese-style thermal pools close to the edge of Lake Rotorua and feel all your aches and pains melt away. See p. 161, **11**.

2 Exploring the tiny streets at Ohinemutu Village. This small Maori village, located among steaming vents and bubbling mud pools on the Lake Rotorua foreshore, is home to two marae and the beautiful St. Faith's Maori church. See p. 171, **6**.

3 Eating whitebait fritters at Rotorua Farmers' Market. Buy a freshly made whitebait fritter for breakfast and wander about enormous fresh vegetable stands and Maori craft stalls. This is one of the best farmers' markets I've been to. See "To Market, To Market," p. 171.

4 Walking among giant redwoods. If you feel the urge to hug a tree, Whakarewarewa Redwood Forest is the place to do it. Take a walk along the Redwood Memorial Grove Track to view these stately, 60m (197-ft) giants. See p. 167, **15**.

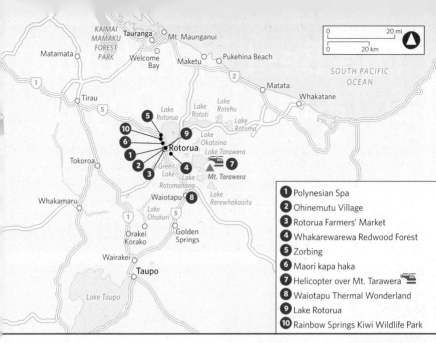

Legend:
1. Polynesian Spa
2. Ohinemutu Village
3. Rotorua Farmers' Market
4. Whakarewarewa Redwood Forest
5. Zorbing
6. Maori kapa haka
7. Helicopter over Mt. Tarawera
8. Waiotapu Thermal Wonderland
9. Lake Rotorua
10. Rainbow Springs Kiwi Wildlife Park

5 Careening down a hill in a giant bubble. Whoever invented the Zorb™ needs a medal. Rolling downhill inside this giant, clear plastic bubble has got to be one of the craziest things anyone has ever done. But don't miss it! See p. 162, 1.

6 The spine-tingling chill of a Maori kapa haka. No matter how many times I watch a kapa haka performance, I always get a spine-tingly thrill as *piupiu* (skirts) click together, *poi* swirl, melodies ring out, and warriors advance threateningly toward the crowd. See p. 170, 5.

7 Hovering over the Mt. Tarawera crater in a helicopter. Try your utmost to stretch your budget to include this adventure of a lifetime—it's worth every single cent. See p. 184.

8 Photographing the geothermal beauties at Waiotapu Thermal Wonderland. I never tire of the exquisite colored pools and steaming pools at Waiotapu. Try to get there early before the crowds and just as the sun is casting magical shafts of light through the steam. It's a photographer's paradise. See p. 161, 12.

9 Walking around the edge of Lake Rotorua to Sulphur Flat. Visit in spring and summer to see the huge flocks of red-billed gulls, sacred

> *The meeting house at Ohinemutu Village.*

to the Te Arawa people. See "Where the Birds Are," p. 170.

10 Watching a baby kiwi hatch. Watching a baby kiwi pecking its way out of its egg to emerge into the world wet and scruffy is a moving experience. You can watch it on video at Rainbow Springs Kiwi Wildlife Park, where you learn all the Operation Nest Egg Project and see the live kiwi babies. See p. 160, 7.

The Best of Rotorua & Taupo in 3 Days

There are enough attractions and unique activities in these two areas to keep you busy for a fortnight, so condensing things into a three-day trip is going to mean compromise. You can however, get a good feel for the area's unique aspects: the geothermal and volcanic activity, and the concentration of Maori culture. Throw in some fun (jet-boats and thermal spas) and a cultural appraisal at the magnificent Rotorua Museum of Art & History and you'll leave the richer for it.

> The Champagne Pool at Waiotapu Thermal Wonderland is New Zealand's largest bubbling mud pool.

START Rotorua is 221km (137 miles) southeast of Auckland on St. Hwy. 5. Rotorua Museum is in Government Gardens off Hinemaru Street.
TRIP LENGTH 112km (70 miles).

1 ★★★ kids **Rotorua Museum of Art & History.** Spend your first morning exploring this excellent museum located in one of New Zealand's most spectacular buildings (a former bath house) to get a feel for the region's geological and cultural history. Of key importance here is the amazing collection of Te Arawa *taonga* (treasures). Check out the Te Arawa War Memorial near the museum, the contemporary Maori sculpture on the south side of the museum, and the assorted Maori carvings along the front fence of the gardens. It's in this area too, that you'll see the Te Runanga Tea House, built in 1903. ⊙ Half-day. Government Gardens. ☎ 07/349-4350. www.rotoruamuseum.co.nz. Admission NZ$18 adults, NZ$7 kids, NZ$29-NZ$40 family. Daily 9am-8pm summer; 9am-5pm winter. Free tours daily on the hour starting at 10am.

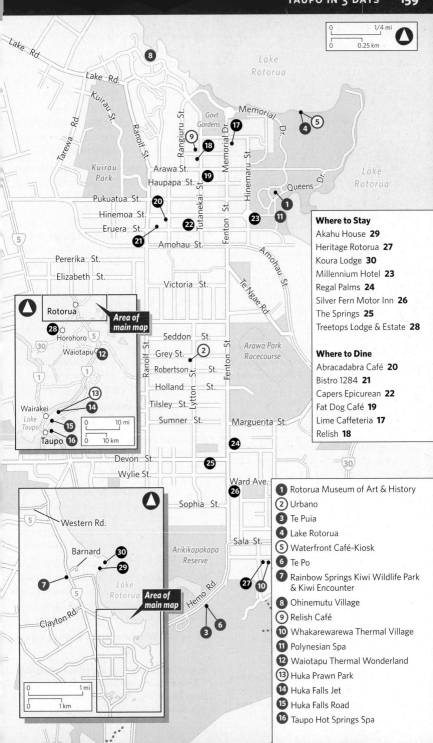

Where to Stay

Akahu House **29**
Heritage Rotorua **27**
Koura Lodge **30**
Millennium Hotel **23**
Regal Palms **24**
Silver Fern Motor Inn **26**
The Springs **25**
Treetops Lodge & Estate **28**

Where to Dine

Abracadabra Café **20**
Bistro 1284 **21**
Capers Epicurean **22**
Fat Dog Café **19**
Lime Caffeteria **17**
Relish **18**

1 Rotorua Museum of Art & History
2 Urbano
3 Te Puia
4 Lake Rotorua
5 Waterfront Café-Kiosk
6 Te Po
7 Rainbow Springs Kiwi Wildlife Park & Kiwi Encounter
8 Ohinemutu Village
9 Relish Café
10 Whakarewarewa Thermal Village
11 Polynesian Spa
12 Waiotapu Thermal Wonderland
13 Huka Prawn Park
14 Huka Falls Jet
15 Huka Falls Road
16 Taupo Hot Springs Spa

> *Native to America, Rainbow Trout were introduced to New Zealand in 1883 and are now one of our most popular sport fish.*

Head back onto Fenton St. and head south. Turn right on Grey St.

② 🍽 ★★ **Urbano.** The soups and salads at this smart little bistro are worth the stop. They also serve fair-trade coffee with sweet treats. 289 Fenton St., corner of Grey St. ☎ 07/349-3770. www.urbano bistro.co.nz. About NZ$20 for a full lunch; NZ$10–NZ$12 coffee and cake.

Continue south on Fenton St., veering right as it becomes Hemo Rd. Te Puia is 4km (2½ miles) and about 10 min. from the museum.

③ ★★★ **kids** **Te Puia.** ⏱ 2 hr. See p. 168, ③.

Head back into town on Fenton St. and park near the lakefront.

④ ★★ **kids** **Lake Rotorua.** Spend the rest of the afternoon relaxing on the lakefront. If you're traveling with kids it's an especially good place for them to let off steam. They can feed ducks, enjoy the Volcanic Playground, and watch the boats, planes, and helicopters coming and going from the jetty. ⏱ At least 1 hr.

⑤ 🍽 ★ **Waterfront Café-Kiosk.** Hundreds of peckish visitors stop here for cold drinks, milkshakes, ice cream, hamburgers, hot dogs, chips, and waffles. Beside the Volcanic Playground on the waterfront. NZ$5–NZ$10.

⑥ ★★★ **kids** **Te Po.** Locals give the Te Po Maori Performance at Te Puia the nod for best in the region and I agree. Another good option is the performance at Tamaki Maori Village (p. 172, ⑧). ⏱ 3 hr. See Te Puia, p. 168, ③.

On day 2, get onto Lake Rd. and head northwest. Veer right on Fairy Springs Rd (St. Hwy. 5) and follow signs to Rainbow Springs. It's about 4km (2½ miles) and about 10 min.

⑦ ★★ **kids** **Rainbow Springs Kiwi Wildlife Park and Kiwi Encounter.** This large park is the only purpose-built Operation Nest Egg Project (a conservation effort that removes kiwi eggs from the wild so they can hatch in a predator-free environment) that is open to the public and a tour is well worthwhile. You can also watch kiwi chicks hatching on video. ⏱ 2 hr. Fairy Springs Rd. ☎ 0800/724-626 or 07/350-0440. www.rainbowsprings.co.nz or www.kiwiencounter.co.nz. Admission NZ$28 adults, NZ$17 kids 5–15; Kiwi Encounter tour NZ$32 adults, NZ$20 kids. Combo tickets available. Daily 8am–10pm (9pm in winter).

Head back into the city, veering off St. Hwy. 5 to rejoin Lake Rd. Turn left into Ariariterangi St., then right along the lakefront to the carpark in front of the church.

⑧ ★★ **kids** **Ohinemutu Village.** ⏱ 2 hr. See p. 171, ⑥.

Backtrack to Ariariterangi St., then turn left on Haukotuko St. and left again on Lake Rd. Veer right on Tutanekai St.

⑨ 🍽 ★ **Relish Café.** Good coffee and delicious wood-fired pizzas make this a great lunch stop. There are plenty of other cafes at this end of Tutanekai Street as well. 1149 Tutanekai St. ☎ 07/343-9195. NZ$15–NZ$25.

Head one block east to Fenton St. and travel south, turning left at the roundabout into Sala St. (St. Hwy. 30), then right into Tryon St., about 5km (3 miles) and 12 min. away.

⑩ ★★★ **kids** **Whakarewarewa Thermal Village.** ⏱ 2 hr. See p. 170, ⑤.

Return to the city via Fenton Rd. Turn right on Amohau St., left on Hinemaru St, and right on Hinemoa St. It's 3km (1¾ miles) and about 10 min. away.

> *End your day of adventuring with a luxurious soak under the stars in the hot pools at Polynesian Spa.*

11 ★★★ kids **Polynesian Spa.** There are some things you just *have* to do when you're in Rotorua and sinking beneath the hot, soothing waters of this wonderful spa complex is one of them. The jewel in the watery crown is the Lake Spa complex, with four Japanese rotem-buro (open-air) pools set in rocks beside the lake. Those with kids can head to the Family Spa. ⏱ At least 2 hr. Government Gardens, lakefront end of Hinemoa St. ☎ 0508-765-977 or 07/348-1328. www.polynesianspa.co.nz. Admission NZ$20 for adults-only and Priest Spa; NZ$42 adults, NZ$15 kids 5–14 for Lake Spa; Family Spa NZ$15 adults, NZ$8 kids. Daily 8am–11pm.

Leave Rotorua on day 3, heading south on Fenton St., which becomes St. Hwy. 5. Continue south, following signs to Waimangu and/or Waiotapu (4km/2½ miles further south). Turn left off St. Hwy. 5 to reach both and follow signs. It's 29km (18 miles) to Waiotapu (30 min.).

12 ★★★ kids **Waiotapu Thermal Wonderland.** Waimangu Volcanic Valley is also nearby, but I recommend Waiotapu because it has a much more intensive and colorful geothermal selection. The bulk of the best attractions are on the shorter (40 min.) walk—for instance, the Champagne Pool (New Zealand's largest bubbling mud pool) and the vivid green Devil's Bath. Lady Knox Geyser, which performs around 10:15am daily, is in a separate nearby park but you get in on the same ticket price. ⏱ At least 1 hr. Waiotapu Thermal Wonderland. ☎ 07/366-6333. www.waiotapu.co.nz. Admission NZ$34 adults, NZ$11 kids 5–15, NZ$76 family. Daily 8:30am–5pm (last admission 3:45pm).

Go back to St. Hwy. 5, turn left, and head south, following signs to Taupo. Soon after passing Bayview Wairakei Resort, turn left, following signs to Huka Falls Rd. Turn left and drive to the Prawn Farm at the end of the road. It's 49km (30 miles) and 30 min. from Waiotapu.

13 🦐 ★★ kids **Huka Prawn Park.** At this unique spot, the world's only geothermally heated prawn farm, you can catch your own lunch, and the prawns will be cooked for you. If you'd rather not work for your lunch, head to the restaurant, where prawns naturally feature on the already-cooked menu. Wairakei Tourist Park, Huka Falls Rd. ☎ 07/374-8474. www.prawnpark.co.nz. Admission NZ$24 for adult full-day pass; NZ$14 kids 5–15; NZ$42–NZ$70 family full-day pass. Restaurant meals NZ$15–NZ$30.

14 ★★★ kids **Huka Falls Jet.** This thrilling ride takes you within a few meters of thundering Huka Falls. Make sure you have your camera ready. ⏱ 1 hr. See p. 179, **8**.

Drive 4km (2½ miles) to Taupo via Huka Falls Rd., which rejoins St. Hwy. 5 just before Taupo township.

15 ★★ kids **Huka Falls Road.** After your boat ride, drive straight ahead on Huka Falls Road and spend the rest of the afternoon stopping at the Volcanic Activity Centre (p. 179, **7**) and the Honey Hive (p. 180, **10**). ⏱ At least 2 hr.

16 ★ kids **Taupo Hot Springs Spa.** End your trip soaking in the waters of a spa that has been a favorite for over 120 years. See p. 181, **14**.

Rotorua with Kids

You won't have any trouble getting the kids out of bed
once you start talking about jetboats, high-speed swings, rolling down hillsides,
swimming, and boat rides. There's enough in Rotorua to keep you going for at least
a week but I've prepared a concise 3-day itinerary that takes in the highlights.

> Squeezing into a giant plastic bubble may not sound like fun, but most kids love rolling downhill in a Zorb.

START Agrodome is 4km (2½ miles) northwest of central Rotorua, just off St. Hwy. 5. **TRIP LENGTH** About 50km (31 miles) over 3 days.

❶ ★★★ Agrodome and Agroventures. This hotbed of adventure activity has everything from helicopters, jet-boating, bungy jumping, Zorb™, and Freefall Xtreme (a huge outdoor windtunnel that suspends you in midair as if you're flying). Agrodome introduces you to over 19 different sheep breeds and sheep-dog demonstrations, and you get a tour of the 160-hectare (395-acre) farm. Nearby (on the Agrodome grounds), Agroventures focuses on the adrenalin-pumping activities, which

you pay for individually, although be sure to ask about their good-value combo packages. Western Rd. ☎ 0800/339-400 or 07/357-1050. www.agrodome.co.nz. Admission for Agrodome show NZ$28 adults, NZ$15 kids 5–15, NZ$76 family; Agrodome show and farm tour combo NZ$55 adults, NZ$30 kids 5–15, NZ$115 family. Daily 8:30am–5pm. Shows daily at 9:30am, 11am, and 2:30pm.

② 🍴 **Agrodome's Farmview Café.** Enjoy coffee and a sandwich at this cafe overlooking the trout stream before you head for your next destination. **Agrodome, Western Rd.** NZ$10–NZ$12.

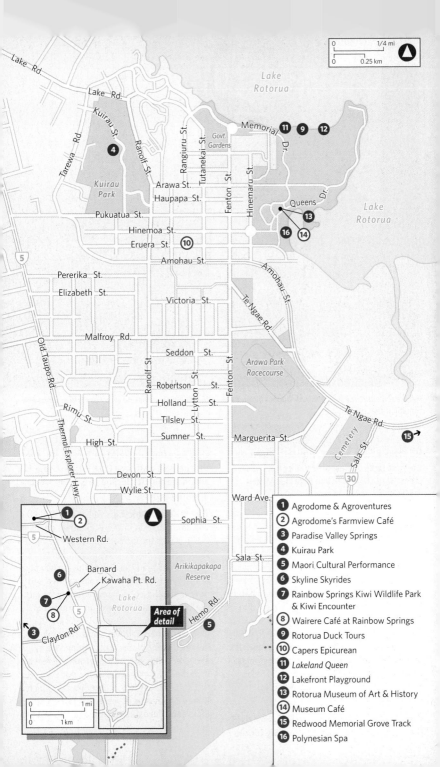

1	Agrodome & Agroventures
2	Agrodome's Farmview Café
3	Paradise Valley Springs
4	Kuirau Park
5	Maori Cultural Performance
6	Skyline Skyrides
7	Rainbow Springs Kiwi Wildlife Park & Kiwi Encounter
8	Wairere Café at Rainbow Springs
9	Rotorua Duck Tours
10	Capers Epicurean
11	*Lakeland Queen*
12	Lakefront Playground
13	Rotorua Museum of Art & History
14	Museum Café
15	Redwood Memorial Grove Track
16	Polynesian Spa

0   1/4 mi
0   0.25 km

Lake Rotorua

Lake Rd.
Lake Rd.
Kuirau St.
Tarewa Rd.
Ranolf St.
Rangiuru St.
Rangitekei St.
Tutanekai St.
Fenton St.
Hinemaru St.
Memorial Dr.
Govt. Gardens
Kuirau Park
Arawa St.
Haupapa St.
Pukuatua St.
Hinemoa St.
Eruera St.
Amohau St.
Pererika St.
Elizabeth St.
Victoria St.
Malfroy Rd.
Seddon St.
Robertson St.
Holland St.
Tilsley St.
Sumner St.
High St.
Devon St.
Wylie St.
Ranolf St.
Lytton St.
Fenton St.
Te Ngae Rd.
Arawa Park Racecourse
Queens Dr.
Lake Rotorua
Amohau St.
Te Ngae Rd.
Cemetery
Sala St.
Marguerita St.
Ward Ave.
Sophia St.
Sala St.
Arikikapakapa Reserve
Hemo Rd.
30
Old Taupo Rd.
Thermal Explorer Hwy.
Rimu St.

Western Rd.
Barnard
Kawaha Pt. Rd.
Clayton Rd.
Lake Rotorua
Area of detail

0   1 mi
0   1 km

> *Take the easy way to the top of Mount Ngongotaha with Skyline Skyrides and enjoy expansive views and a meal at the top.*

Head back to St. Hwy. 5, turn left, then take the first right on Paradise Valley Rd. Follow signs 11km (6¾ miles) to Paradise Valley Springs. It's about 15 min.

❸ ★★ **Paradise Valley Springs.** From sheep to lions in one short trip. Try to get here in time for the 2:30pm lion feeding and then let the kids run free around the tracks between trout-filled streams and friendly animals (in enclosures). There's an underwater viewing cave and a spawning stream where you can hand-feed the trout. When there are lion cubs in-house, you can pet them. Wetland areas and bush walks are nice areas to wander in when it's hot. ⏱ At least 1 hr. 467 Paradise Valley Rd. ☎ 07/348-9667. www.paradisevalleysprings. co.nz. Admission NZ$30 adults, NZ$17 kids 5-15, NZ$75 family. Daily 8am–dark (last ticket sales 5pm).

Go back the way you came to SH5, turn right, then veer left onto Lake Rd., heading for the city. Take the third right on Tarewa Rd., then the first left on Kuirau Park Rd. Park your car and make sure it's locked; break-ins are not uncommon here.

❹ ★★ **Kuirau Park.** This was the site of a big volcanic eruption in 2000 and then again in 2001. Rocks the size of footballs were hurled 200 meters (656 ft.) into the air and you can still see the dead trees and white ash in some areas. The area is geothermally active and new vents and pools open regularly. There are several steaming vents and mud pools that you can see for free but it is vital that you stay on formed pathways and don't ever cross fences to get a closer look. Young kids will also enjoy the colorful playground here—and if you're in town on a Saturday, you can catch the Rotorua Farmers' market (p. 171). ⏱ 1 hr. Kuirau Park can be accessed off Tarewa Rd. and Ranolf and Pukuatua sts. It is unsafe to wander here at night.

> *Take home one of our favorite, furry, flightless birds—the iconic kiwi.*

⑤ ★★★ Maori Cultural Performance. See p. 170, **④**.

On day 2, head down to the lakefront, and veer left to get onto Lake Rd. Travel to the intersection with Fairy Springs Rd. (St. Hwy. 5) and veer right. It's 5km (3 miles) to the next stop.

⑥ ★★★ Skyline Skyrides. This is one of Rotorua's most popular attractions and the views at the top definitely make the ride up Mount Ngongotaha worth it. There are a number of ways to descend—by the regular scenic luge, intermediate and advanced luge tracks, or via the chairlift. The scenic track has viewing bays where you can pull over to take photos of the great views. If you feel like living on the wild side, try the Sky Swing. It hoists passengers over 36m (118 ft.) before swinging them out over Mount Ngongotaha at speeds up to 140kmph (87 mph). ⊙ **2 hr.** 185 Fairy Springs Rd. ☎ 07/347-0027. www.skylineskyrides.co.nz. Admission for gondola NZ$25 adults, NZ$13 kids 5–14; luge rides from NZ$10. Gondola and luge packages are available. Daily 9am–late.

Head north a short distance (less than a mile) on Fairy Springs Rd. to the Rainbow Springs Kiwi Wildlife Park.

⑦ ★★ Rainbow Springs Kiwi Wildlife Park and Kiwi Encounter. This is a great spot for kids to get an insight into how major conservation projects work and how our rare national bird, the kiwi, is being looked after and reared to prevent the extinction of the species. There's plenty of room for them to run about to discover animals and fish, and a shop brimming over with cuddling souvenirs is bound to win them over. ⊙ **At least 1 hr.** See p. 160, **⑦**.

---

⑧ 🍴 Wairere Café at Rainbow Springs. Sit outside under the trees to enjoy sandwiches, savories, and cakes with a drink. Or spread out a picnic away from the crowds. Free-range chickens may come in search of crumbs. At Rainbow Springs Kiwi Wildlife Park, Fairy Springs Rd. ☎ 07/347-0443. Around NZ$12.

Head back into the city on Lake Rd. At the second roundabout, turn left on Whakaue St., then right on Memorial Dr., which becomes Fenton St. Find a park close to the visitor center on the corner of Fenton and Arawa sts.

❾ ★★★ Rotorua Duck Tours. I can't imagine any kid not loving this adventure. You'll climb aboard an amphibious WWII vehicle at the Rotorua i-SITE Visitor Centre and ride to one of Rotorua's 16 lakes, where you'll splash into the water. The "duck" then becomes a boat (of sorts) and you get to see beautiful scenery and hear local stories and legends. The shorter 90-minute tour is a popular option but the 2-hour tour includes Lake Tarawera and views of the mountain that erupted so fiercely in 1886. ⏱ 2 hr. Rotorua Duck Tours. ☎ 07/345-6522. www.rotoruaducktours.co.nz. Admission City & Lakes Tour NZ$65 adults, NZ$36 kids, NZ$150 family; Tarawera & Lakes Tour NZ$75 adults, NZ$42 kids, NZ$170 family. Booking at Rotorua i-SITE Visitor Centre. City & Lakes Tour departs 11am, 1pm, and 3:30pm Oct–April, 11am and 2:15pm May-Sept; Tarawera & Lakes Tour departs 3:30pm Oct–April. Tours depart daily.

⑩ 🍴 Capers Epicurean. Choose from a range of delicious goodies from the deli-cabinet selections for an early picnic dinner down by the lake. After they've eaten, let the kids feed the ducks, romp in the playground, and run about to burn off the last of their energy before bed. 1181 Eruera St., Rotorua. ☎ 07/348-8818; www.capers.co.nz. Allow about NZ$15 per person.

Start day 3 down at the lakefront. Park your car and head for the jetty.

⓫ ★★ *Lakeland Queen*. Treat the family to a breakfast cruise on this grand old vessel and see Rotorua from the water while you enjoy cereals and fruit, fruit juices, bacon, eggs, and a range of other choices. Built locally in 1986, the *Lakeland Queen* is modeled after shallow draft, stern-driven Mississippi River boats and is ideal for the sometimes shallow parts of Lake Rotorua. Your cruise will take you around to Sulphur Bay, across to Mokoia Island, and then to Kawaha Point. Note that it does not make stops during the cruise. Memorial Dr., lakefront ☎ 07/348-0265. www.lakelandqueen.com.

> You'll keep toddlers happy for hours by letting them feed the swans, ducks, and geese that swim close to the lake edge.

Admission NZ$42 adults, NZ$21 kids 5–12. Ship departs daily 7am and 8am. Lunch and dinner cruises also available.

⑫ Lakefront Playground. Back on shore, let the kids have an early run about at the lakefront playground. If you're all feeling fit, you can walk around the lakefront (following the road) to the museum (below), which will take about 15 minutes. There's usually lots of birdlife about and thermal activity at various points around the walkway. ⏱ 1 hr.

⑬ ★★★ Rotorua Museum of Art & History. Kids will enjoy rummaging around the basement, climbing up to the rooftop viewing platform, and keeping an eye out for the friendly resident ghost. ⏱ At least 1 hr. See p. 158, ❶.

---

⑭ 🍴 Museum Café. Buy some goodies and take them out into the gardens for an impromptu picnic. If you'd rather, pull up a seat in the cafe and enjoy your coffee at leisure. **Government Gardens.** NZ$10–NZ$12.

From the lakefront, turn right onto Memorial Ave., which becomes Fenton St. at the intersection with Arawa St. Continue south on Fenton St. Turn left onto Amohau St., which becomes Te Ngae Rd. (St. Hwy. 30A). Turn right into Sala St., left into Long Mile Rd., and follow signs to the Redwoods visitor center. 4km (2½ miles).

⑮ ★★★ Redwood Memorial Grove Track. There are numerous free strolls through Whakarewarewa Forest but this is by far the most impressive and one that kids will remember for its awe-inspiring 60m (200-ft.) Californian coastal redwoods. Check into the visitor center first to see what other trails they recommend for kids. ⏱ 1 hr. Redwoods Gift Shop & Visitor Centre, Long Mile Rd. ☎ 07/350-0110. www.redwoods.co.nz. Free admission. Visitor Centre open daily, Oct–March Mon–Fri 8:30am–5:30pm, Sat–Sun 10am–5pm; April–Sept Mon–Fri 8:30am–4:30pm, Sat–Sun 10am–4pm.

⑯ ★★★ Polynesian Spa. Finish your day here. The Family Spa area has a warm freshwater pool with a toddlers' pool and a mini water slide. ⏱ At least 1 hr. See p. 161, ⑪.

> *The bronze sculpture Wai Tu Kei by Maori artist/ carver Lyonel Grant was presented to the people of Rotorua in 2001 to mark the new millennium.*

Saving on the Sights

A number of offers represent significant savings on the leading attractions. Packages with **Rotorua Hot Deals** (www.rotoruahotdeals.com); **Rotorua Adventure Combos** (☎ 0800/338-786 in NZ, or 07/357-2236; www.rotoruacombos.com); and Rotorua 5 Star Super Pass (☎ 07/348-5179; www.rotorua5star.co.nz) combine many of the city's star attractions and activities (such as Polynesian Spa, Agrodome, and Skyline Skyrides) in well-priced packages.

Maori Rotorua

New Zealand tourism has its origins in the early activities of Rotorua Maori, many of whom acted as guides for 19th-century European visitors coming to see the famous Pink and White Terraces—then billed as the eighth natural wonder of the world. Though the terraces were destroyed by the Mount Tarawera eruption, many of the guides went on to become household names. Guide Sophia (Sophia Hinerangi), Guide Maggie (Makereti Papakura), and Guide Rangi (Rangitiara Dennan) were among the most famous. In the late 20th century, Tamaki Maori Village and an updated Te Puia joined Whakarewarewa in a new era of Maori tourism in the region. Maori have lived here for centuries and the Te Arawa people are integral not only to the city's tourism economy but to its very character.

> Take your camera to Rotorua's Government Gardens to get superb close-up photographs of detailed Maori carvings.

START Rotorua Museum is in Government Gardens off Hinemaru St. **TRIP LENGTH** About 50km (31 miles) over 3 days.

① ★★★ **kids Rotorua Museum of Art & History.** ① At least 2 hr. See p. 158, **①**.

② 🍽 **Museum Café.** See p. 167, ⑭.

From the Government Gardens, turn left on Hinerau St., right on Amohau St., then take your first left on Fenton St. Head south and soon after Fenton St. becomes Hemo Rd. (St. Hwy. 30), you'll find Te Puia on your left. It's about 4km (2½ miles).

③ ★★★ **kids Te Puia.** Te Puia includes a geothermal valley—complete with the famous Pohutu geyser—and the New Zealand Maori Arts & Crafts Institute. The main entrance, Te Heketanga a Rangi, is made up of 12 monumental contemporary carvings reaching skywards, each representing a celestial guardian in Te Arawa culture. There are modern, interactive galleries, traditional *wharenui* (meeting houses), a kiwi house, and the replica pre-European Pikirangi Village. In addition, at Te Wananga Whakairo Rakau, the National Carving School, you can watch trainee carvers working on projects in their workshop. Across the courtyard, women prepare fibers and weave at Te Rito, the National Weaving School. Guided tours of Te Puia run hourly from 9am and daytime cultural performances are staged at 10:15am, 12:15pm, and 3:15pm. I think the

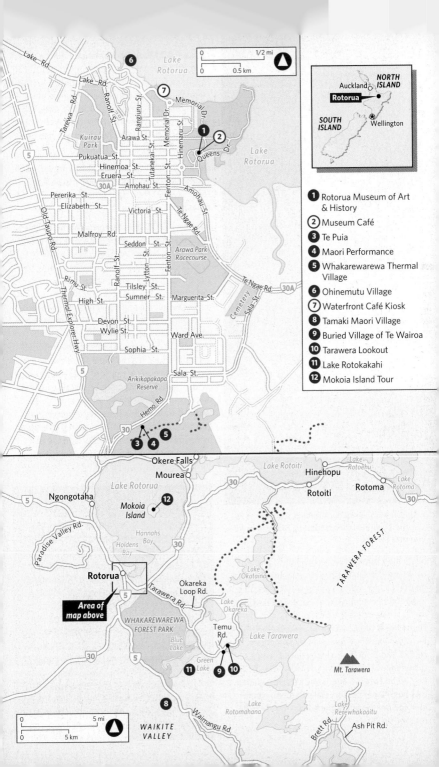

Map Legend

Scale: 1/2 mi / 0.5 km

North Island — Auckland, Rotorua, Wellington
South Island

1. Rotorua Museum of Art & History
2. Museum Café
3. Te Puia
4. Maori Performance
5. Whakarewarewa Thermal Village
6. Ohinemutu Village
7. Waterfront Café Kiosk
8. Tamaki Maori Village
9. Buried Village of Te Wairoa
10. Tarawera Lookout
11. Lake Rotokakahi
12. Mokoia Island Tour

Streets and places (upper map):
Lake Rd., Memorial Dr., Queens Dr., Lake Rotorua, Kuirau Park, Tarewa Rd., Ranolf St., Rangiuru St., Arawa St., Memorial Dr., Hinemaru St., Pukuatua St., Hinemoa St., Eruera St., Tutaneka St., Fenton St., Amohau St., Amohau St., Pererika St., Elizabeth St., Te Ngae Rd., Victoria St., Malfroy Rd., Seddon St., Lytton St., Arawa Park Racecourse, Old Taupo Rd., Rimu St., Tilsley St., Sumner St., Marguerita St., Te Ngae Rd., Cemetery, Sala St., High St., Devon St., Wylie St., Ward Ave., Sophia St., Thermal Explorer Hwy., Sala St., Arikikapakapa Reserve, Hemo Rd.

Streets and places (lower map):
Okere Falls, Mourea, Lake Rotorua, Lake Rotoiti, Lake Rotoehu, Hinehopu, Rotoma, Lake Rotoma, Ngongotaha, Mokoia Island, Paradise Valley Rd., Hannahs Bay, Holdens Bay, Rotorua, Area of map above, Tarawera Rd., Okareka Loop Rd., Lake Okataina, Lake Okareka, Tarawera Forest, Whakarewarewa Forest Park, Temu Rd., Lake Tarawera, Blue Lake, Green Lake, Mt. Tarawera, Waikite Valley, Waimangu Rd., Lake Rotomahana, Lake Rerewhakaaitu, Brett Rd., Ash Pit Rd.

Scale: 5 mi / 5 km

④ ★★★ **kids** **Maori Performance.** End the day with a traditional Maori performance. Choose the Te Po Combo (above) and stay on for the evening song and dance performance and traditional hangi meal, or choose a different evening performance option, such as the one at Tamaki (p. 172, ⑧). Many hotels also offer evening Maori performances.

On day 2, get onto Fenton St. and travel south, turning left at the roundabout into Sala St., (St. Hwy. 30) then right into Tryon St. 5km (3 miles) and 12 min. to:

⑤ ★★★ **kids** **Whakarewarewa Thermal Village.** The people of the Te Arawa *hapu* (sub-tribe) Tuhourangi/Ngati Wahiao have lived here for over 300 years and they've been guiding tourists through their village since the early 1800s. It is probably the only place in the world where you'll see people still using natural geothermal energy as part of their everyday cooking, washing, and bathing activities. This is an entirely different experience to government-owned Te Puia; it's more personalized and you are seeing a slice of real life. The resident *kapa haka* (traditional dance) group performs and on the guided tour you'll see bathing areas, two community churches and *urupa* (burial grounds), and assorted craft stores operated by residents. You can cook corn on the cob in the scalding hot geothermal pools and in summer, you can watch the local kids diving

> *Students at the National Carving School at Te Puia spend 3 years learning traditional Maori skills from master carvers.*

best value though, lies in the Te Po Combo (4:30pm–9pm), which gives you an exclusive guided tour of Te Puia along with the excellent Indigenous Evening Experience, Te Po, which many locals say is the best of the night shows. Hemo Rd. ☎ 0800/837-842 or 07/348-9047. www.tepuia.com. Admission NZ$44 adults, NZ$22 kids 5–15; Te Po Indigenous Evening Experience NZ$109 adults, NZ$54.50 kids; Te Po Combo NZ$140 adults, NZ$70 kids; guided tour NZ$72 per person. Daily 8am–6pm summer, to 5pm winter; Night Admission for Te Po 6:15pm–9:15pm.

Where the Birds Are

A short walk from the museum, just south of Polynesian Spa, is Sulphur Flat, or Te Arikiroa, where centuries ago, a Maori battle raged on the sandy beach. The dead and dying were said to be so thickly strewn that they resembled *inanga* (whitebait, a tiny fish) cast on the shore. The area is also important because of the red-billed gulls (*Tarapunga*) that breed and roost here. In 1823, the northern Māori tribe, Ngapuhi, led by Hongi Hika, attacked a Te Arawa tribe on Mokoia Island. Te Arawa were warned of the attack coming out of the mist by the flight and squawking of the gulls, thus enabling them to prepare for battle. Ever since then, the gulls have been *tapu* (sacred) to Te Arawa people.

> *Look out for the traditional* Ta Moko (tattoo) *on the Maori performers at Rotorua's Te Puia.*

for coins in the river below the bridge. Plan on having lunch or a snack here; you can book the Hangi Experience when you purchase your tickets, or just snack on corn and one of the specialties of Whakarewarewa, hangi pies (meat and vegetable pies), which can be purchased at their little onsite cafe. ⏱ At least 2 hr. 17 Tryon St., Rotorua. ☎ 07/349-3463. www.whakarewarewa.com. Tour and cultural show NZ$30 adults, NZ$13 kids 5-12; tour, cultural show and Hangi Experience NZ$62 adults, NZ$31 kids 5-12. Daily 8:30am-5pm.

Head back into the city on Fenton St., turn left into Amohau St., then take the third right on Ranolf St. Go through 2 roundabouts and at the traffic lights veer left on Lake Rd. Turn right on Ariariterangi St. (take care, it's very narrow). Go straight ahead to the lakefront, then right to get to the carpark in front of the church.

6 ★★★ kids **Ohinemutu Village.** This small Maori settlement is not a paying tourist attraction, so do not, under any circumstances, enter the marae buildings or the private gardens of the homes here. It is all private property and must be respected. You can, however, enter the very beautiful St. Faith's Church (please remove your shoes and do not take photographs), which is filled with Maori carvings and a stained glass window that shows Christ as a Maori walking over the lake. You can also take photographs of the exterior of the magnificent Tamatekapua meetinghouse and its surrounding carvings. Follow the sign between buildings to the left of the meetinghouse, to Ohinemutu Maori Handcrafts on Mataiawhea St. (☎ 07/350-3378), where you can watch a local carver working in his studio. Also check out the lakeside memorial to Maori soldiers killed at war. You'll see lots of steaming, hissing geothermal activity in this area. ⏱ At least 1 hr.

To Market, To Market

If you're in town on a Saturday, get up early and make your way down to the Rotorua Farmers' Market in Kuirau Park (p. 164, **4**). It's a quintessential Rotorua experience, and many Maori set up stalls selling *rewena* (Maori bread), *puha* and watercress, whitebait and mussel fritters, fresh *kina* (sea eggs), *kumera* (sweet potato), carvings, *kete* (baskets), *pounamu* (greenstone), and *korowai* (cloaks). The crowds start arriving around 8am and it's usually all over by around 1pm, so get there early for some terrific photographs and tasty treats. It's located next to the playground.

> *St. Faith's Anglican Church at Ohinemutu has a Tudor-style exterior and is elaborately decorated with traditional Maori arts and crafts inside.*

⑦ 🍽 **Waterfront Café-Kiosk.** See p. 159, ⑤.

❽ ★★★ **kids Tamaki Maori Village.** The winner of numerous national tourism awards, this family-owned enterprise introduces you to a recreated pre-European Maori village. It's a night experience 20 minutes from the city (you're collected from your hotel), which lends an air of intrigue to the whole business. Carving, weaving, *moko* (tattoo), singing, dancing, chanting, and cooking are all on display, and you can wander beneath lit trees, talking with the Maori performers. Afterwards, you join several hundred people for a hangi dinner and then a chance to browse the craft shops. It's fun for kids but can be a late night, so if you're taking young children, give them an easy afternoon or a nap. ⏱ 5 hr. 1220 Hinemaru St., Rotorua. ☎ 0508/826-254. www.globalstory tellers.com. NZ$110 adults, NZ$65 kids 5–15, NZ$325 family. Daily 5:30pm.

On day 3, leave town heading east on Amohau St., which becomes Te Ngae Rd. and then St. Hwy. 30A after the traffic lights. At the first roundabout turn right on Tarawera Rd. and continue 25km (16 miles) past the Green and Blue lakes.

❾ ★★ **kids Buried Village of Te Wairoa.** It's a little creepy to wander around this now-pretty village setting imaging the devastation and terror that reigned here in 1886 when Mount Tarawera erupted. Meandering pathways set among trees, meadows, and a fern-clad stream teeming with fat trout lead you around the excavated remains of Maori *whare* (houses), a flour mill, stores, and the Rotomahana Hotel. If you're fit, climb the steps and steep path to view the waterfall, and take time to look through the small but excellent museum that details the eruption and displays objects unearthed during the excavation of the buried village. ⏱ 1 hr. Tarawera Rd. ☎ 07/362-8287. www.buriedvillage.co.nz. NZ$31 adults, NZ$8 kids under 15, NZ$70 families. Daily 9am–5pm (to 4:30pm in winter).

Drive a few hundred meters past the Buried Village of Te Wairoa on Tarawera Road.

❿ ★ **Tarawera Lookout.** Stand here and look across Lake Tarawera to Mount Tarawera. There's an interesting information board here that considers the eruption, along with a beautiful *pouwairua*, a carved totem honoring the Te Arawa leader, Tuhourangi, whose people occupied these lands and the buried village of Te Wairoa.

> *Rotorua's Green and Blue lakes sit side by side a few kilometers from the city on the road to Lake Tarawera.*

Return to the city the way you came, pausing briefly after few kilometers at the lookout signposted on the left to view **Lake Rotokakahi.**

⓫ ★ **Lake Rotokakahi.** More commonly known as the Green Lake, Lake Rotokakahi takes its name from the fresh shellfish (called *kakahi*) that were once abundant in its waters (*roto* means lake). It is privately owned by the Te Arawa hapu, Tuhourangi, and because it is considered *tapu* (sacred/forbidden), no one ventures upon it. There are many myths and legends surrounding the lake and prior to the Tarawera eruption (which killed the shellfish), it was heavily populated. The Tuhourangi people lived on the island on the lake and many of their ancestors are buried there.

⓬ ★★★ kids **Mokoia Island Tour.** Finish your Maori itinerary with an afternoon tour to this island wildlife sanctuary, sacred to Maori. You'll learn all about the legendary love story between Tutanekai, who lived on the island, and Hinemoa, the daughter of a famous chief, who despite being forbidden to see Tutanekai, swam to the island at night to be with him. Today the island is a conservation reserve dedicated to the preservation and breeding of native species of flora and fauna. The birdlife is amazing and a tour will expose you to that, along with indigenous food tasting, geothermal pools, and Maori legends. If you want to skip the visit to Te Wairoa (p. 172, ❾), you can take a full-day tour to both Mokoia Island and the geothermal attraction, Hell's Gate. This option includes a traditional hangi lunch. ☺ **At least 3 hr.** Tours depart from the lakefront, Memorial Dr., Rotorua. ☎ 0800/665-642 or 07/345-7456. www.mokoiaisland.co.nz. NZ$125 adults, NZ$65 kids 5–12. Daily tours at 9:30am and 2pm.

Out of the Mists

According to legend, one day in 1886, both Maori and Pakeha reported seeing a phantom war canoe emerging from the mists on Lake Tarawera. A Maori *tohunga* (priest) declared this an omen of disaster. A few days later, Mount Tarawera erupted, burying the landscape—and the three Maori villages of Te Wairoa, Te Ariki, and Moura—in mud and ash. More than 150 died and the famous Pink and White Terraces, where Maori acted as guides, were destroyed.

MAORI TRADITIONS

Arts, Crafts, and Cultural Protocols

BY ADRIENNE REWI

WHEN YOU ARRIVE IN NEW ZEALAND you'll be surrounded by things Maori—words, place names, the people, the politics, and traditional arts and crafts. Over the last twenty years, New Zealand has become a bicultural nation and the inclusion of Maori words and phrases in everyday life has become increasingly common. Here's an introduction to some of the key terms related to Maori art and crafts.

POUNAMU

Jade, greenstone, and pounamu are all names for the same thing—the highly prized green stone found on the South Island's West Coast and used by Maori for centuries to make tools, weapons and adornments. Genuine New Zealand pounamu is usually certified as such.

TA MOKO

Regarded purely as adornment, traditional tattoo was based on designs similar to those used in wood carving and even today, it tells the story of a person's whakapapa, or family heritage. You'll see elegant ta moko on arms, legs, necks, backs, and sometimes faces and chins.

HEI TIKI

Tiki was the first man according to Maori legend, and carved human forms are usually called tiki. The hei tiki (hanging human form) is a neck pendant traditionally made of bone or pounamu. Today you'll find contem-

porary tiki in every material from plastic and resin to wood, silver, or gold.

TUKUTUKU

This ornamental lattice work inside meeting houses has a long tradition. Vertical rods with horizontal battens are lashed together with colored fibers into intricate patterns that served as both decoration and insulation against the cold.

KETE

A kete is a woven basket made from the leaves of flax or cabbage tree. Today weavers also use synthetic or dyed materials to create decorative kete that can be both useful and ornamental.

WHAKAIRO

Wood carving has always been a key means of artistic expression for Maori. Used to decorate everything from domestic implements to adze handles and waka (canoes), it reached its highest form in the carvings of large meeting houses and food storehouses.

On the Marae

The word marae literally means an expanse of anything but it usually refers to a large open space or village green, where special social and business activities are conducted in Maori communities. Most often it is in front of a large wharenui (meeting house). It is private property and must not be entered without permission or invitation. Guests must be welcomed onto a marae and you must never eat, chew gum, or take food onto the premises. Shoes must be removed before entering the wharenui and cell phones turned off. And never take photographs inside a meeting house. Behavior on a marae is strictly governed by protocol and you will be challenged if you ignore the rules.

Taupo with Kids

Taupo is a favorite summer holiday destination for many New Zealanders, many of whom come close to worshipping the place for its ideal boating and fishing possibilities. The vast, sparkling waters of Lake Taupo—the largest freshwater lake in Australasia—are certainly attractive, and have spawned many additional activities and attractions that are particularly suitable for families. You can bungy, waterski, swim, play golf, go mountain biking and horse riding, fly in planes, or take to the water in kayaks, jetboats, and cruise vessels.

> Evaluate your golf swing by trying to score a hole-in-one on Taupo's floating pontoon.

START Taupo is 84km (52 miles) south of Rotorua. Taupo Boat Harbour is accessed via Redoubt Rd., the first turn left after crossing the Waikato River Bridge at the north entrance to Taupo. **TRIP LENGTH** About 75km (47 miles) and 3 days.

1 ★★★ **Taupo Lake Cruise.** Get a feel for this great big lake out on the water. There are three excellent cruise choices and while each follows a similar path—passing by the remarkable Maori rock drawings at Okuta Bay—they are all very different. Ernest Kemp Cruises (☎ 07/378-3444) operates a 2-hour cruise on a vintage steamer (NZ$42 adults, NZ$12 kids;

daily 10:30am, 2pm, and 5pm). The Cruise Cat Experience (☎ 07/378-0623; www.chrisjolly. co.nz) offers a 1½-hour scenic cruise on a luxury vessel (NZ$42 adults, NZ$16 kids; daily 10:30am and 1:30pm). The *Barbary* Carvings Cruise (07/378-3444; www.barbary. co.nz) takes you aboard a vintage 1926 yacht for a 2½-hour scenic sailing adventure with swimming stops (NZ$42 adults, NZ$12 kids; 10:30am, 2pm, and 5pm). As you can see, they're all a similar price and duration, so you may have to have a family vote to choose your vessel type. ⏱ 3 hr. All vessels depart from the Taupo Boat Harbour off Redoubt St.

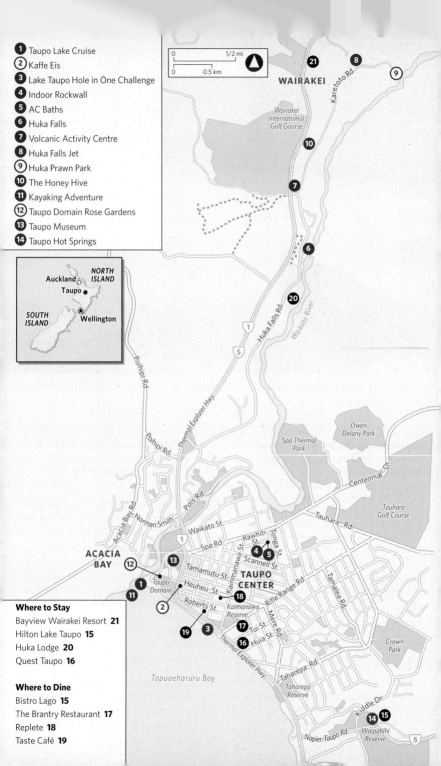

1. Taupo Lake Cruise
2. Kaffe Eis
3. Lake Taupo Hole in One Challenge
4. Indoor Rockwall
5. AC Baths
6. Huka Falls
7. Volcanic Activity Centre
8. Huka Falls Jet
9. Huka Prawn Park
10. The Honey Hive
11. Kayaking Adventure
12. Taupo Domain Rose Gardens
13. Taupo Museum
14. Taupo Hot Springs

Where to Stay
Bayview Wairakei Resort **21**
Hilton Lake Taupo **15**
Huka Lodge **20**
Quest Taupo **16**

Where to Dine
Bistro Lago **15**
The Brantry Restaurant **17**
Replete **18**
Taste Café **19**

> *The volume of water flowing through Huka Falls often approaches 220,000 liters (58,000 gal.) per second.*

Drive back up Redoubt Rd. and turn right into Tongariro St. Go straight ahead through the roundabout and park your car as close to the lake end as you can.

② 🍴 ★★★ **Kaffe Eis.** Once you've tasted the creamy gelato here you won't be able to stay away. They do have a range of other food options if you insist on something healthier, but don't leave without giving in to temptation at least once. 13 Tongariro St.,Taupo ☎ 07/378-8535; www.kaffeeeis.co.nz. Cones start around NZ$4.

Wander south along the lakefront on Lake Tce. to the first carpark.

❸ ★★ **Lake Taupo Hole in One Challenge.** Challenge each other to whacking a golf ball 102 meters (335 ft.) across water to a golf tee on a floating pontoon in the hope of scoring a hole-in-one. It's not as impossible as it sounds—they get at least one winner every two weeks. You could walk away with a great prize like a bungy jump, luxury accommodation, free

dinner, or even NZ$10,000. ⏱ 1 hr. Lakefront Car Park, 61 Lake Terrace, Taupo. ☎ 07/378-8117. www.holein1.co.nz. Balls cost NZ$1 each, NZ$15 for 18, and NZ$20 for 25. Daily 9am–9pm.

Drive north on Tongariro St. and at the roundabout turn right on Spa Rd. Take the first right onto AC Baths Ave. It's about 3km (1¾ miles).

❹ ★★ **Indoor Rockwall.** I've never met a kid that doesn't leap at the chance to climb to the scariest height possible. They can do just that here—safely harnessed and under the supervision of qualified instructors. Everyone from rank beginners to experienced climbers can give it a go and all the gear you'll need is available for hire at very reasonable prices. ⏱ At least 1 hr. Taupo Event Centre, AC Baths Ave., Taupo. ☎ 07/376-0350. www.taupovenues.co.nz. NZ$12 adults, NZ$6 kids under 17; harness, rope, and shoe hire NZ$3, chalk bags NZ$2. Call or check the website first to check their timetable of open climb hours and classes.

5 ★★★ **AC Baths.** While away the rest of your first day here, where you have a choice of warm, geothermally heated pools, hot pools, hydro slides, a toddler area, sauna, private pools, and lap pools for the serious swimmers. ⏱ 2 hr. AC Baths Ave., Taupo. ☎ 07/376-0350. www.taupovenues.co.nz. Admission NZ$7 adults, NZ$3 kids 5–15, NZ$16 family, NZ$4 unlimited hydro-slide rides, NZ$7 per person for private mineral pools. Daily 6am–9pm.

On day 2, drive north from Taupo and soon after you leave the town, turn right into Huka Falls Rd. and follow signs to Huka Falls. It's about 3km (1¾ miles).

6 ★★★ **Huka Falls.** There are plenty of taller waterfalls around than Huka, but this famous thundering 24m (79 ft.) drop is impressive nonetheless. The blue-green waters of the Waikato River surge through a narrow canyon before plummeting over the drop at a rate of around 220,000 liters (58,000 gal.) of water per second. There's a very safe walk bridge across the river and a fenced pathway to the lookout. It's great to stand up here and watch the cruise and jetboats come all the way up to the base of the falls. ⏱ 40 min. Huka Falls Rd. Free admission.

Continue north a short distance along Huka Falls Rd., then turn right on Karetoto Rd.

7 ★★★ **Volcanic Activity Centre.** If you've ever wondered about what causes earthquakes and volcanoes, you've come to the right place. The Taupo volcanic region is one of the world's largest, and this is the best place to get an understanding of what's bubbling underfoot. Along with 3D maps of the area, there are touch-screen computers, a working model of a geyser, a tornado machine, an earthquake simulator, interactive volcanoes, and excellent short films on all aspects of volcanic and geothermal activity. ⏱ 1 hr. Huka Falls Rd. ☎ 07/374-8375. www.volcanoes.co.nz. Admission NZ$10 adults, NZ$6 kids, NZ$26 family. Mon–Fri 9am–5pm, Sat–Sun 10am–4pm.

Travel a few minutes farther along Karetoto Rd. to the Wairakei Tourist Park.

8 ★★★ **Huka Falls Jet.** Just in case there are any sensitive digestive systems among you, it might pay to do your jet-boat ride before

> *Huka Prawn Park raises tropical prawns using waste geothermal heat from the geothermal power station next door.*

lunch. This is not the only jet-boating company operating but it's the one that specializes in 360-degree river spins and close-ups of Huka Falls—an adrenaline-pumping adventure that you'll certainly be talking about long afterwards. ⏱ Ride is about 35 min. Wairakei Tourist Park. ☎ 0800/485-253 or 07/375-8572. www.hukafallsjet.com. NZ$105 adults, NZ$65 kids 15 and under. Kids must be a minimum of 1m (3 ft. 4in.) tall. Daily 9am–5pm.

9 🦐 **Huka Prawn Park.** You have two choices here: you can take the easy way out and buy lunch at Huka Prawn Park Restaurant (non-prawn dishes and kids' menus are available), or the whole family can fish for prawns and have them cooked for lunch. There are also walks, tours and mini-golf available here, so plan to stay and unwind for a bit—I'd allow a couple hours, at least. Wairakei Tourist Park. ☎ 07/374-8474. www.prawnpark.co.nz. Full day pass NZ$24 adults, NZ$14 kids 5–15. Daily, summer 9:30am–4:30pm (to 3:30pm in winter).

Head back on Karetoto Rd. toward Huka Falls Rd.

> *Burn off some of your excess holiday calories with a brisk kayak trip across Lake Taupo.*

⑩ ★★ kids The Honey Hive. Who would have thought the humble honeybee could give rise to such a diverse array of produce? More than a retail outlet, this is a homage to bees and their industriousness. And might I say right from the start, you'd be silly to miss the Kapiti honey ice cream sold here. The honey fudge isn't bad either and kids can busy themselves inspecting the bee-related toys while Mum and Dad sample the honey-based liqueurs. There's a short bee movie and glazed live bee displays too. ⏱ 40 min. 65 Karetoto Rd. ☎ 07/374-8553. www.honeyhivetaupo.com. Free admission. Daily 9am–5pm.

Drive back into Taupo for the night.

⑪ ★★★ kids Kayaking Adventure. Start your last day with a kayaking adventure. There are a number of different operators offering guided kayaking expeditions and your choice will depend on the age of your children, you fitness levels, the time you have available, and whether you want a lake or river outing. Regardless of choice, you will be treated to some spectacular scenery so don't forget your camera and a waterproof bag to put it in. ⏱ Half-day. See p. 186.

Back in town, buy picnic treats at Replete (p. 192). Take Heu Heu St. west to Tongariro St. and head for the Taupo Domain, on the lake side of the visitor information center.

⑫ ☛ Taupo Domain Rose Gardens. Spread yourselves out on the grass under the trees and tuck into a picnic lunch. All that paddling you've done deserves a rest and a few indulgences. Story Place.

Walk through the Taupo Domain trees to the rear of the carpark.

⑬ ★★★ kids Taupo Museum. As small as it is, Taupo Museum has a few real gems. I especially love their caravan display filled with 1950s camping memorabilia and their documentation on the classic Kiwi summer camping ground holiday. There's also an excellent fishing display, an old timber mill, and some exquisite Maori *taonga* (treasures). Don't forget to explore beyond the main gallery, where you'll find an astonishing collection of model airplanes and military paraphernalia. ⏱ 1 hr. Story Place, Taupo. ☎ 07/376-0414. www.taupomuseum.co.nz. Admission NZ$5 adults, students NZ$3, kids free. Daily 10am-4:30pm.

> *Taupo Hot Springs has the best of both worlds—large play pools for the kids and therapeutic mineral pools for the adults.*

From central Taupo, drive south on Lake Terrace (St. Hwy. 1), around the lake. Turn left onto Napier-Taupo Highway (St. Hwy. 5) and drive about 1km (½ mile) before turning left into the road that leads to Taupo Hilton (4km/2½ miles total). Veer left at the top and go to the carpark.

⑭ ★★★ 🄺🄸🄳🅂 **Taupo Hot Springs.** Soak away your aches and pains in mineral-rich geothermal waters that have been attracting visitors for over 120 years. There are several pools and water temperatures to choose from—the main pool, spa pools, private pools, and a kids' area with a huge hydroslide. It's not as big and glamorous as Rotorua's Polynesian Spa but it's cheaper, and there's no sulfur in the water here. At the end of your swim plan dinner out (see p. 191 for recommendations), or buy fish and chips or pizza and eat them by the lake as the sun goes down. ⏱ At least 1 hr. St. Hwy. 5, Taupo. ☎ 07/377-6502. www.taupohotsprings.com. NZ$15 adults (NZ$18 private pools), NZ$6 kids 13-17, NZ$4 kids 3-12 and non-swimmers; NZ$5 hydroslide. Daily 7:30am-9:30pm.

DO Feed the Animals

Lilliput Farm, 136 Link Rd. (☎ 07/378-2114; www.lilliput-farm-park.co.nz), is a 4-hectare (10-acre) treat for kids who like animals. They can hand-feed 20 different species and enjoy pony and donkey rides. The farm is open Monday to Friday 10am to 2pm, weekends 10am to 4pm. Admission is NZ$12 adults, NZ$6 children 5-12, NZ$30 families. Follow SH1 to Hamilton. Link Road is the first left, 4.5km (2 miles) from the Wairakei turnoff. Watch for signs.

Rotorua & Taupo Outdoor Adventures A to Z

Biking

Rotorua and Taupo both lend themselves to leisure biking and they also have some of New Zealand's best mountain trails. In Rotorua, Whakarewarewa Forest has an extensive network of tracks for all levels of ability. There are over 70km (43 miles) of off-road tracks in the Taupo area. **Planet Bike,** Waipa State Mill Rd., off St. Hwy. 5 south of Te Puia, Whakarewarewa (☎ 07/346-1717; www.planetbike.co.nz), is the most experienced mountain bike outfitter in Rotorua. They hire bikes (NZ$35 for 2 hr.) and offer mountain bike tours. In Taupo, serious bikers should head to **Avanti Plus Corner Shop,** 47 Horomatangi St., (☎ 07/378-7381; www.cornershop.co.nz), for mountain and road bike rentals. Families looking for a fun day of easy cycling should check out **Tri Trikes Taupo** (☎ 07/377-1498 or 027/428-6110), which rents bikes of all sizes. They bring the bikes to your accommodation and pick them up when you're done.

Bungy Jumping

You can leap from a 43m (141-ft.) tower at **Rotorua Bungy,** Agrodome (☎ 07/357-4747; www.rotoruabungy.co.nz), for around NZ$100, but they offer assorted combo deals that can include a jet-boat ride or other on-site activities. In Taupo, the bungy platform is cantilevered 47m (154 ft.) above the Waikato River. The scenery is impressive—but you probably won't have time to see that. **Taupo Bungy,** Spa Rd., Taupo (☎ 0800/888-408; www.taupobungy.com), charges around NZ$125 for a solo jump and NZ$275 for a tandem jump. In both cases, the minimum age is 10 years.

Fishing

Rotorua, Taupo, and Tongariro National Park (about 99km/61 miles southwest of Taupo) combined make up one of the best fishing grounds in the world. Famous for the size and quality of trout, they attract fishermen from all over the world. The Tongariro River is Lake Taupo's main spawning river and the

> *Mountain tracks for all abilities weave through giant Redwood trees at Rotorua's Whakarewarewa Forest.*

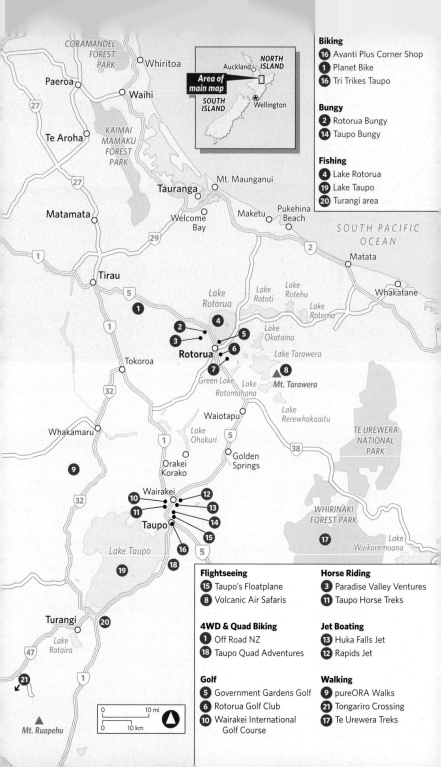

Biking
- 16 Avanti Plus Corner Shop
- 1 Planet Bike
- 16 Tri Trikes Taupo

Bungy
- 2 Rotorua Bungy
- 14 Taupo Bungy

Fishing
- 4 Lake Rotorua
- 19 Lake Taupo
- 20 Turangi area

Flightseeing
- 15 Taupo's Floatplane
- 8 Volcanic Air Safaris

4WD & Quad Biking
- 1 Off Road NZ
- 18 Taupo Quad Adventures

Golf
- 5 Government Gardens Golf
- 6 Rotorua Golf Club
- 10 Wairakei International Golf Course

Horse Riding
- 3 Paradise Valley Ventures
- 11 Taupo Horse Treks

Jet Boating
- 13 Huka Falls Jet
- 12 Rapids Jet

Walking
- 9 pureORA Walks
- 21 Tongariro Crossing
- 17 Te Urewera Treks

> *Taupo locals like to joke that their trout are so big, the lake level drops when you pull one out.*

best time for river fly-fishing is during winter spawning, June to September. Lake fishing is excellent year-round but you'll need a special Taupo-issued license and there are daily limits on what you can catch. Fifteen of Rotorua's sixteen lakes are fishable but Tarawera, Okataina, and Rotoiti offer the best chance of catching a trophy fish. They're open for fishing from October to the end of June and hold both wild and stocked trout. You need a Rotorua fishing license and as the lakes have variable seasons and regulations, make sure you check first. Visitor centers in all three areas (p. 193) can point you to one of the many professional fishing guides and charters operating in the region, most of whom will organize your license. Prices start around NZ$275 for a half-day guided fishing experience.

Flightseeing/Helicopter Rides

The rugged volcanic nature of the central North Island makes for some spectacular scenic flying.

★★ **Taupo's Floatplane.** This is a great-value chance to get some wind in your wings. Apart from their very well priced short flight options around Taupo, they have a wonderful flight over Mount Ruapehu and Mountt Tongariro, which gives you breathtaking views into crater lakes before gently splashing down on the Lake Taupo lakefront. Ferry Rd., Taupo Boat Harbour. ☎ 07/378-7500. www.tauposfloatplane.co.nz. 10-min flights NZ$80 adults, NZ$40 kids 5–15; 60-min Ruapehu Vista NZ$325 adults, NZ$160 kids. Family rates available. Flights daily, weather permitting.

★★★ **Volcanic Air Safaris.** This outfitter offers a range of helicopter and floatplane tours, from an 6-minute floatplane or helicopter spin over the city to unforgettable 1- to 3-hour flights over the huge volcanic rifts of Mount Tarawera and the steaming vents of New Zealand's only active marine volcano, White Island in the Bay of Plenty. You can soar over Rotorua's lakes, or over the geothermal regions as far south as Orakei Korako. A number of their flights include landings, so make sure you take your camera. They offer free Rotorua hotel pick-ups. Lakefront, Rotorua. ☎ 0800/800-848; www.volcanicair.co.nz. 6-min flight NZ$77–NZ$85; Mount Tarawera flights

NZ$195–NZ$350; White Island flights NZ$750–NZ$850. Kids 2–11 pay 75% of adult fare. Fights daily, weather permitting.

4WD Driving & Quad Biking

Test your nerve at **Off Road NZ,** Amoore Rd., Rotorua (☎ 07/332-5748; www.offroadnz.co.nz), where, 20 minutes north of the city, a 4WD bush safari takes you through ferny glades, over a waterfall, down the luge, and through muddy streams. It's all about testing your speed, skill, and accuracy—and your bravery—for the very reasonable sum of NZ$90 per adult and NZ$15 kids 5 to 16 years old. In Taupo, the whole family can take to the mud (min. age 12) at **Taupo Quad Adventures,** 23km (14 miles) north of Taupo on St. Hwy. 1 (☎ 07/377-6404; www.taupoquads.co.nz). Their 30-minute introductory ride over farmland, through bush, and across streams (NZ$40 per person), is a great way to start if you've never tried it before.

Golf

Beautiful **Wairakei International Golf Course,** St. Hwy. 1., Taupo (☎ 07/374-8152; www.wairakeigolfcourse.co.nz), sprawls out over 182 hectares (450 acres) to create a course that was voted by *Golf Digest* magazine as among the top 100 in the world outside the US. Green fees for visitors are NZ$225. **Rotorua Golf Club,** 399 Fenton St.(☎ 07/348-4051; www.rotoruagolfclub.co.nz), is a gently undulating, all-weather course with an international reputation. Here you'll pay NZ$70 for a round. **Government Gardens Golf,** Government Gardens, Rotorua (☎ 07/348-9126; www.governmentgardensgolf.co.nz), features a 21-bay driving range where you can polish up your swing. NZ$30 will get you 18 balls.

Horseback Riding

Horse trekking through forests, across farms, through ferny valleys, around lakes and geothermal action is a brilliant summer activity suitable for all the family and for riders of all levels.

★★★ **Paradise Valley Ventures,** 679 Paradise Valley Rd., Rotorua (☎ 07/348-3300; www.paradisetreks.co.nz), offers a free lesson before every ride and their treks range from 45 minutes (NZ$45) to 2½ hours (NZ$175). **Taupo Horse Treks,** Karapiti Rd., Taupo (☎ 0800/244-3987; www.taupohorsetreks.co.nz), covers lovely

> Splurge on a flight to see the true scale of the rugged, lake-spotted central North Island landscape.

> Off Road NZ's 4WD drive outing through rugged, fern-covered terrain will leave you breathless.

> *Explore farmlands and forests on horseback with Paradise Valley Ventures.*

countryside that includes thermal areas and the Wairakei Forest. Their treks are NZ$60 to NZ$125 for 1- or 2-hour rides.

Jet-Boating

Two operators in Taupo work different areas of the Waikato River. **Huka Falls Jet** (p. 179, ⑧) gets you up close and personal with Huka Falls. **Rapids Jet,** Nga Awa Purua Rd., Aratiatia (☎ 0800/727-437; www.rapidsjet.com), runs farther upstream in the fast waters of Aratiatia Rapids at the base of the Aratiatia Dam. They pass through the narrowest canyon on the river too—just to complete your adrenaline rush. Riders must be 5 years and older and taller than 1m (3ft. 4in.) and it costs NZ$95 adults and NZ$55 for kids.

Kayaking

There are several kayaking operations in Rotorua and Taupo, offering both rentals and tours on different parts of Lake Taupo and the Waikato River. **Canoe & Kayak,** corner of Tani-wha and Spa rds., Taupo (☎ 0800/529-256; www.canoeandkayak.co.nz), has a half-day outing to the Maori carvings on Lake Taupo for

NZ$90 per person and a 2-hour guided family trip on the Waikato River with a soak in natural hot pools for NZ$50 adults and NZ$30 kids. **Kiwi River Safaris** (☎ 0800/723-8577; www.krs.co.nz), has a similar trip (similarly priced). **Kayaking Kiwi** (☎ 0800/353-435; www.kayakingkiwi.com) offers guided tours on both the Waikato River and Lake Taupo (1½ hrs to 4 hrs), priced from NZ$95 per person.

Walking & Hiking

Keen walkers are blessed with endless possibilities in these regions. Both information centers have details on popular walks. In Taupo, ask for *Taupo Walks*, available for NZ$1 from the information center.

In Taupo, ★★★ **pureORAwalks** (☎ 021/619-075; www.pureorawalks.com) offers guided walks with a Maori focus throughout the region. Their popular 3- to 6-hour Nature-Culture Walk can lead off from Whirinaki Forest Park, Pureora Forest Park, or Tongariro National Park and costs around NZ$90 for adults and NZ$65 for kids 5 to 15. They also take guided walks to what has been described as New Zealand's most spectacular one-day walk, the **Tongariro Crossing.** This 17km (11-mile), 7-hour walk is challenging and regardless of fine summer weather, requiring warm clothing to combat rapidly changing alpine conditions. You'll be rewarded with spectacular views, a colorful volcanic landscape, and jewel-like crater lakes. Although you can undertake this walk alone, I strongly advise joining the pureORAwalks team, who know the landscape and the conditions. They charge around NZ$300 for adults and NZ$200 for kids 8 to 15 years old. The price includes transport and lunch. The tour operates between November and April.

★★★ **Te Urewera Treks** is another Maori-owned company, this time taking treks into parts of the remote Te Urewera and Whirinaki rainforests and to Lake Waikaremoana. The Maori guides know these remote regions well and can take you places to which you would never otherwise have access. They'll point out native birds and plants and tell Maori myths and legends along the way. Their easy 1-day Whirinaki Loop Trek takes you through towering native podocarp forests. It operates daily from late October to April and costs around NZ$195 adults and NZ$165 kids 8 to 12. The Te Urewera Ridgeline walk requires moderate fitness and takes you through dense beech forest. Children need to be over 10 and it costs the same as the loop trek.

Whitewater Rafting

The Rangitaiki, Wairoa, Kaituna, Mokau, Motu, Mohaka, and Tongariro rivers can all be accessed for white-water rafting by several Taupo- and Rotorua-based companies, who all know their stuff. The rivers, from grade 2 to grade 5, each take you into beautiful, unspoiled backcountry and even the most laidback outing will get your heart racing. If you're keen to give it a try, compare brochures at i-SITE visitor centers in both places to gauge which will suit you best. Prices usually start at about NZ$90 per person.

Zorbing

Rolling down a hill in a giant plastic bubble—now known as Zorbing—all started in Rotorua. You climb inside an inflatable ZORB™ and roll down a specially designed hill course—with or without water thrown inside with you. This is one of many activities available at the **Agrodome** (p. 162, ❶), Western Rd., Ngongotaha, Rotorua (☎ 0800/227-474; www.zorb.co.nz). Rides start at NZ$50 per person.

> *Hurtle down central North Island backcountry rivers with professional guides, who know every turn in every river.*

Where to Stay

> *The Hilton Lake Taupo offers large, sylish suites and apartments.*

Rotorua

★★ Akahu House KAWAHA POINT

Treat yourself to contemporary Maori hospitality at this gorgeous, modern, lakeside home. The sumptuous ensuite bedrooms are at ground level, set apart from the main living areas, and all feature contemporary Maori art. It's a big-hearted family experience and rooms are superb value. 155 Kawaha Point Rd. ☎ 07/347-4148. www.akahu.co.nz. 4 units. Doubles NZ$380–NZ$390 w/breakfast. DC, MC, V. Map p. 159.

★★ kids Heritage Rotorua WHAKAREWAREWA

Throw open the curtains here and you'll be greeted by the rising geothermal steam of nearby Whakarewarewa Thermal Village, just across the road. The Heritage is a peaceful retreat with everything you'll need at your fingertips. They have an excellent cultural performance each night, a lovely heated swimming pool, and big rooms with comfortable beds. It's always busy and lively. Corner of Froude and Tryon sts. ☎ 0800/108-114. www.heritagehotels.co.nz. 203 units. Doubles NZ$175–NZ$410. AE, DC, MC, V. Map p. 159.

★★ kids Koura Lodge KAWAHA POINT

You won't believe your luck when you arrive at this peaceful, lakeside location and find big, classy rooms spread over two buildings. Four rooms are close to the lake, the others, located in the upper building, are larger and have private patios. All are beautifully appointed and the upper 2-bedroom apartment is perfect for families or couples traveling together. It even has its own billiard table. 209 Kawaha Point Rd. ☎ 07/348-5868. www.kouralodge.co.nz. 10 units. Doubles NZ$345–NZ$1,040 w/breakfast. Discounts for multiple nights. MC, V. Map p. 159.

★★ kids Millennium Hotel LAKESIDE GOVERNMENT GARDENS

This is a friendly hotel, perfectly located just across from the Polynesian Spa, a short walk from town. They have excellent facilities—full day spa, heated pool, gymnasium, restaurant, bars. The hotel is geothermally heated and has a lovely leafy central courtyard. Corner of Eruera and Hinemaru sts. ☎ 0800/654-685 or 07/347-1234; www.millenniumrotorua.co.nz. 227 units. Doubles NZ$190–NZ$550. AE, DC, MC, V. Map p. 159.

★★ kids **Regal Palms** FENTON ST. AREA

This is the best motel in Rotorua. Its large, well-appointed rooms are of a higher standard than some hotels and its wide range of facilities—heated outdoor pool, mini-golf, tennis court, gymnasium, barbecue areas, sauna, day spa, and kids' playgrounds—make it an ideal stop for families. 350 Fenton St. ☎ 07/350-3232; www.regalpalms.co.nz. 44 units. Doubles NZ$190–NZ$400. AE, DC, MC, V. Map p. 159.

★ kids **Silver Fern Motor Inn** FENTON ROAD AREA

This motel complex is a great-value stay, made all the more pleasant by the high level of hospitality extended by owners, Allan and Shirley, who go out of their way to make sure you're comfortable. All rooms have either hot tubs (in ground-floor rooms) or Jacuzzi baths and all upstairs rooms have balconies. Two-bedroom and interconnecting suites are ideal for families. 326 Fenton St. ☎ 0800/118-808 or 07/346-3849. www.silverfernmotorinn.co.nz. 25 units. Doubles NZ$150–NZ$300. AE, DC, MC, V. Map p. 159.

★★ **The Springs** FENTON ST. AREA

Step behind the tall hedge that shelters this modern home and you enter a world of first-rate hospitality and comfort. Murray and Colleen Ward have been hosting international guests for several years and they're skilled at anticipating your needs. Everything is finished with class and style, all rooms have ensuite bathrooms, and the breakfasts are divine. 16 Devon St. ☎ 07/348-9922. www.thesprings.co.nz. 4 units. Doubles NZ$385 w/breakfast. DC, MC, V. Map p. 159.

★★★ **Treetops Lodge & Estate** HOROHORO

This exclusive lodge is tucked away on a vast wilderness game reserve about 30 minutes south of the city. Big villas are appointed with top-quality fittings and have huge bathrooms. It's one of the most renowned lodges in New Zealand. A sublime stay. 351 Kearoa Rd., Horohoro. ☎ 07/333-2066. www.treetops.co.nz. 12 units and The Pheasant House. Doubles NZ$1,666–NZ$2,454 lodge and villa suites. AE, DC, MC, V. Map p. 159.

Taupo

★ kids **Bayview Wairakei Resort** WAIRAKEI

If you're traveling with a family, this would be an ideal base. They have accommodation to suit all tastes and budgets. Recreational facilities include heated pools, tennis courts, Jacuzzis, a 9-hole golf course, and a fitness center—all spread over a large, landscaped site close to town. 640 St. Hwy. 1, Wairakei. ☎ 0800/737-678 or 07/374-8021. www.wairakei.co.nz. 187 units. Doubles NZ$125–NZ$300. AE, DC, MC, V. Map p. 177.

★★★ kids **Hilton Lake Taupo** STATE HIGHWAY 5

Rooms in this stylish complex have either lake or thermal valley views. The suites and apartments are large with private terraces or balconies. Apartments with full kitchen and laundry facilities are great value for families or couples traveling together. A heated pool, sauna, gym, steam room, and an excellent restaurant complete the picture. 80-100 Napier-Taupo Hwy., St. Hwy. 5. ☎ 07/378-7080. www.laketaupo.hilton.com. 113 units. Doubles from NZ$320. AE, DC, MC, V. Map p. 177.

★★★ kids **Huka Lodge** HUKA FALLS ROAD

This iconic luxury retreat, sought out by world leaders, royalty, and celebrities, sits beside the moody Waikato River. Your wallet will be considerably lighter after you've left but you'll take away memories of first-class service, beautifully furnished suites, divine food, and the chance to lounge about in one of the best lodges in the world. Huka Falls Rd. ☎ 07/378-5791. www.hukalodge.co.nz. 19 units, 2 cottages. Doubles NZ$1,685–NZ$5,885 lodge, NZ$3,550–NZ$9,750 cottage rooms, w/breakfast, cocktails, 5-course dinner, airport transfers, and use of all facilities. AE, DC, MC, V. Map p. 177.

★ kids **Quest Taupo** CENTRAL TAUPO

This is a very good option for families who want space without blowing the budget, within walking distance of the lake and town. The 2- and 3-bedroom apartments are the best value, or you can pay a little less for motel-style, self-contained studios. There's a heated outdoor pool and spa, too. 9 Tui St. ☎ 0800/350-005. www.questtaupo.co.nz. 32 units. Doubles NZ$125–NZ$425. AE, MC, V. Map p. 177.

Shopping in Rotorua

Art lovers should stop by ★ **Red Spot Gallery,** 1239 Haupapa St. (☎ 07/347-3110; www.redspotgallery.co.nz), for New Zealand pottery, glass art, contemporary sculpture, and original paintings. They also foster the work of emerging artists so this could be a chance to spot a bargain. Stock up on holiday reading material at ★★ **Mcleod's Bookseller,** 1269 Tutanekai St. (☎ 07/348-5388; www.mcleodsbooks.co.nz). Head to **Jade Factory,** 1288 Fenton St. (☎ 07/349-1828; www.jadefactory.com), for a wide range of gifts and moderately priced souvenirs. Their second store across the road offers jewelry in jade, bone, and paua and some larger jade sculptures. Personally, I think ★★★ **Te Puia Store,** Hemo Rd. (☎ 0800/837-842; www.tepuia.com), is the best shop in town for all New Zealand- and Maori-related

souvenirs. The quality is exceptional and the Maori carving and weaving has often been produced on-site in the carving and weaving schools. You'll find **Simply New Zealand** stores throughout the country and they're always a good bet for quality New Zealand products—everything from sports clothing and woolen accessories to toys, books, jewelry, and chocolates. They're at the Tourism Rotorua Centre, 1161 Fenton St. (☎ 07/348-8273; www.simplynewzealand.co.nz), and they also have a second store in Rotorua at Skyline Skyrides. Head to the **Agrodome,** Western Rd., Ngongotaha (☎ 0800/339-400; www.agrodome.co.nz) for all things woolly. They have cushions, rugs, beautiful wool knitted jackets, leather coats, and much more; they ship items worldwide.

Where to Dine

> Bistro 1284 has been voted Rotorua's top restaurant numerous times for its fine food, service, and charming cottage atmosphere.

Rotorua

★★ kids **Abracadabra Café** CENTRAL CITY *CAFE/ MOROCCAN* Luscious color-themed Moroccan rooms off the main cafe give this place a creative edge. The menu includes North African chicken kebabs, couscous salad, and star anise vegetable tagine. There's a delicious selection of tapas if you just want a light meal with a glass of wine. 1263 Amohia St. ☎ 07/ 348-3883. www.abracadabracafe.com. Main courses NZ$22–NZ$30. MC, V. Breakfast, lunch, and dinner Tues–Sat, breakfast and lunch Sunday. Map p. 159.

★★★ **Bistro 1284** CENTRAL CITY *MODERN NZ* I only have to write "fresh market fish on lemon and scallop risotto" for my heart to skip a few hungry beats. Mention espresso and Kahlua crème brûlée with mascarpone and I wonder why I'm not actually at this award-winning restaurant right now. Consistently voted Rotorua's top restaurant. 1284 Eruera St. ☎ 07/346-1284. www.bistro1284.co.nz. Main courses NZ$32–NZ$38. MC, V. Dinner Tues–Sat. Reservations required. Map p. 159.

★★ kids **Capers Epicurean** CENTRAL CITY *CAFE/ DELI* Come here for an impressive array of salads, pies, and cakes. That's just the cabinet food. The menu also comes up trumps—crispy skin salmon fillet and stuffed aubergine roulade are just two examples. They also have a kids' menu. 1181 Eruera St. ☎ 07/348-8818. www.capers.co.nz. Main courses dinner NZ$24–NZ$30. AE, MC, V. Breakfast, lunch, and dinner daily. Map p. 159.

★★ kids **Fat Dog Café** CENTRAL CITY *CAFE* It's bright, colorful, cheerful, and it attracts everyone from businessmen to truck drivers, tourists, and grannies. Food is cheap and tasty, the portions big, and kids will love old favorites like nachos, pies, and big sticky cakes. There are toys to keep kids amused too. No trip to Rotorua is complete until I've called in here for espresso and something scrumptious. 1161 Arawa St. ☎ 07/347-7586. www. fatdogcafe.co.nz. Main courses NZ$12–NZ$26. AE, DC, MC, V. Breakfast, lunch, and dinner daily. Map p. 159.

> *Service at Lime Caffeteria is always smiling and friendly and delicious food is an added bonus.*

★★★ kids **Lime Caffeteria** CENTRAL CITY *CAFE*
I come here for the blueberry and custard brioche—but that's usually just the beginning. As fresh and bright as a squeezed lime, this modern cafe consistently turns out delicious breakfasts and lunches. Beef bourguignon with potato mash and ciabatta is a filling lunch; the soups are excellent; and cabinet foods all tempting. 1096 Whakaue St. ☎ 07/350-2033. Main courses NZ$19–NZ$24. MC, V. Breakfast and lunch daily. Map p. 159.

★ kids **Relish** CENTRAL CITY *CAFE/PIZZERIA*
The menu here dances all over the place, from pizzas and pasta dishes to slow-roasted beef casseroles, salt and pepper squid, lamb shanks, and chicken on Turkish bread. It's a pleasant enough spot for a casual meal in an uncluttered interior with wooden tables and friendly service. 1149 Tutanekai Rd. ☎ 07/343-9195. www.relishcafe.co.nz. Main courses NZ$16–NZ$34 AE, MC, V. Breakfast and lunch daily, dinner Wed–Sat. Map p. 159.

Taupo

★★★ **Bistro Lago** HILTON LAKE TAUPO *MODERN NZ* Created by master chef Simon Gault, this is Taupo's leading restaurant. Wood-roasted market fish with carrot and ginger butter followed by quince and chestnut clafoutis with goat cheese ice cream and caramelized quince are just two examples from the innovative menu. Hilton Lake Taupo, 80-100 Napier-Taupo

> *Visitors are often surprised to discover that many New Zealand restaurants serve world class meals (a dish from Bistro Lago is pictured here).*

Hwy. ☎ 07/376-2310. www.bistrolago.co.nz. Main courses NZ$33–NZ$38. AE, DC, MC, V. Breakfast, lunch, and dinner daily. Map p. 177.

★★★ **The Brantry Restaurant** RIFLE RANGE ROAD *MODERN NZ*
This excellent restaurant is located in a two-story 1950s house in suburban Taupo, just up from the lake. The moody interior makes a change from the rest of Taupo's casual eateries. Meals like slow-cooked lamb shoulder, marinated prawn tails, and twice-cooked pork belly will make you glad you came. Try and get an outdoor garden table in summer. 45 Rifle Range Rd. ☎ 07/378-0484. www.thebrantry.co.nz. Main courses NZ$32–NZ$38. AE, MC, V. Dinner daily. Map p. 177.

★★ kids **Replete** CENTRAL TAUPO *DELI/CAFE*
It seems Replete is always busy, but it's worth hanging around for a table because the food is just so delicious. They have excellent salads and pies, tasty soups, and divine sweet treats. They also have a kitchen store next door.

> *You may have to queue at Taupo's Replete cafe but the wait will be worth it.*

45 Heu Heu St. ☎ 07/377-3011. www.replete. co.nz. Main courses NZ$15–NZ$25. AE, DC, MC, V. Breakfast and lunch daily. Map p. 177.

★ kids **Taste Café** CENTRAL TAUPO *DELI/CAFE* Field mushrooms with bacon, eggs Benedict, or French toast with bacon and maple syrup are just some of the big breakfast choices at this lakefront cafe. There's a tempting array of cabinet food and a menu that scoots across soups and salads, antipasto platters, and burgers. Outdoor tables are the best spot in summer. 10 Roberts Rd. ☎ 07/377-0086. Main courses NZ$12–NZ$22. MC, V. Breakfast and lunch daily. Map p. 177.

Rotorua & Taupo Fast Facts

Arriving
BY PLANE Rotorua and Taupo are both serviced by **Air New Zealand** (☎ 0800/767-767; www. airnewzealand.com) to and from all major New Zealand centers. BY BUS **InterCity** (☎ 09/623-1503) and **Newmans** (☎ 09/623-1504) provide service to and from Rotorua and Taupo.

Emergencies & Medical Care
Always dial **111** in any emergency. Hospitals serving the region include **Taupo Hospital,** Kotare St., Taupo (☎ **07/376-1000**) and **Lakeland Health Rotorua,** Pukeroa St. (☎ 07/**348-1199**). For a doctor you can try **Taupo Medical Centre,** corner of Kaimanawa and Heuheu sts., Taupo (☎ **07/378-4080**). For dental care, visit **Dentist Taupo,** 127 Spa Rd., Taupo (☎ **07/378-8005**).

Internet
You can get online at **E-Funz,** corner of Tutanekai and Amohau sts., Rotorua (☎ 07/349-3789); **Cyber World,** 1174 Haupapa St., Rotorua (☎ 07/348-0088); or **CyberGate Internet Café,** 12 Gasgoine St., Taupo (☎ 07/377-8118).

Visitor Information Centers
ROTORUA I-SITE VISITOR CENTRE 1167 Fenton St., Rotorua (☎ 0800/768-678; www. rotoruanz.com). TAUPO I-SITE VISITOR CENTRE Tongariro St., Taupo (☎ 07/376-0027; www. laketauponz.com).

7
Hawke's Bay
& Eastland

My Favorite Moments

Hawke's Bay is one of the prettiest provinces in the country. It's also one of our top wine regions and a foodie's paradise. It has a balmy climate, great beaches, fabulous Art Deco architecture, and some of the best boutique hotels in the country. Eastland, however, is one of the last areas of the country largely untouched by encroaching tourism. Wine production is a mainstay of the economy here—many call the town of Gisborne the chardonnay Capital—and 45% of the population is Maori. It's that thriving Maori culture and the common use of Maori language in everyday life that sets Eastland apart.

> *PREVIOUS PAGE Catch the last sun on top of Te Mata Peak, near Hastings. THIS PAGE The Australasian gannet has been nesting at Cape Kidnappers since the 1870s.*

❶ Drinking coffee and people-watching at Ujazi. Everyone loves this funky cafe. There's a bohemian edge to the place that somehow typifies Napier. See p 227.

❷ Photographing Art Deco architecture. Napier is virtually a museum of Art Deco and Spanish Mission architecture built after the 1931 earthquake. Dust off your camera and get snapping. See p. 200, ❺.

❸ Exploring remote Eastland beaches. When you drive the East Cape Road, you'll be awe-struck by the beautiful, empty beaches that loop around this pristine coastline. See p. 209, ⓬.

❹ Sitting and thinking in Tikitiki's St. Mary's Church. This small, historic church in the remote Maori settlement of Tikitiki is a true work of art. See p. 211, ❽.

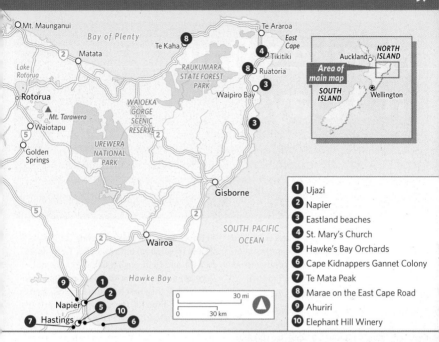

Map legend:

1. Ujazi
2. Napier
3. Eastland beaches
4. St. Mary's Church
5. Hawke's Bay Orchards
6. Cape Kidnappers Gannet Colony
7. Te Mata Peak
8. Marae on the East Cape Road
9. Ahuriri
10. Elephant Hill Winery

5 Eating freshly picked fruit from Hawke's Bay orchards. It's hard to beat the crunch of a fresh Hawke's Bay apple, the succulent ooze of juice from a just-bitten peach, or lips stained fresh, strawberry red. See p. 215, **12**.

6 Gazing at gannets. Since the 1870s, Australian gannets have been nesting on the cliffs of Cape Kidnappers—the largest, most accessible mainland gannet colony in the world. It's a spectacular sight. See p. 219.

7 Soaking up the view from Te Mata Peak. On a cloudless day, the cobalt sky slips into the azure blue ocean and the rolling green landscape catches the late afternoon sun. Unforgettable. See p. 202, **11**.

8 Discovering Maori marae on the East Cape Road. If you stop to peep over the fence at every marae you see on this road, you'll never get to where you're going. There are dozens of them—all magnificent—so do stop at those you can see easily. See p. 209, **12**.

9 Wandering around the port village of Ahuriri. I love this little portside village, tucked over the other side of Napier's Bluff Hill. Check out the marina, restaurants, boutiques, and the famous Art Deco jewel, the

> Ahuriri was Napier's main port until major shipping facilities were relocated after the 1931 earthquake.

National Tobacco Company Building. See p. 200, **9**.

10 A romantic dinner at Elephant Hill Winery. Treat yourself to the succulent dishes that are spun together in the kitchens of this gorgeous winery restaurant. See p. 226.

11 Wine tasting. No matter where you go in these two eastern provinces, you're never far from a delicious chardonnay—and that's only one wine style on offer. Numerous vineyards offer tastings. See p. 203.

Hawke's Bay in 3 Days

If there's one thing experience has taught me, it's that it's self-defeating to spend half your holiday rushing about in a car. If you only have three days to spare for this side of the country, you're much better off focusing on the bounty of Napier and its near environs. The wineries, beaches, wildlife, orchards, and the art in this area can easily fill 3 days.

START Napier is 423km (263 miles) southeast of Auckland; 228km (142 miles) southeast of Rotorua; and 216km (134 miles) southwest of Gisborne. **TRIP LENGTH** 109km (68 miles).

1 ★★★ kids **Napier.** Start at the i-SITE Visitor Centre (p. 227) and then spend the morning wandering along Marine Parade, a lovely beachfront promenade. Choices here include the **National Aquarium of New Zealand** and **Opossum World.** ☺ Half-day. See p. 220.

2 🍽 ★ kids **Soak.** This restaurant overlooks the swimming pools and has a delicious cafe menu well-suited to a light lunch. Ocean Spa, Marine Parade. ☎ 06/835-7888. NZ$10–NZ$15.

In Napier, get onto Marine Parade (St. Hwy. 2) and travel south onto Main Rd. Turn left at Mill Rd. and go through the first roundabout. Turn left at Haumoana Rd. Take first right onto Parkhill Rd., then first left onto East Rd., then right into Clifton Rd. Drive to Clifton Beach. It's 22km (14 miles) and will take about 25 min.

3 ★★★ kids **Cape Kidnappers Gannet Colony.** You have three choices here: either go it alone or (my advice), choose between two excellent tours (p. 219). The largest mainland colony of gannets in the world is open to the public from September to May, but the best time to view the birds is from early November to mid-December. If you go alone, it's a 2½-hour walk along 8km (5 miles) of sandy beach which *must* be done at low tide only. Check with the

> Wine lovers can enjoy the vast expanses of vines and fine wineries in the Hawke's Bay area.

1. Napier
2. Soak
3. Cape Kidnappers Gannet Colony
4. Ocean Spa
5. Art Deco Walk
6. Groove Kitchen Espresso
7. New Zealand Wine Centre
8. A wine tour
9. Ahuriri
10. Ahuriri Corner Store
11. Te Mata Peak
12. Te Mata Cheese Café
13. Hastings
14. Bay Espresso
15. Marine Parade

> Napier's Ocean Spa is a great place to let off steam—in the gym or in the pools.

visitor center or the Department of Conservation (☎ 06/834-3111) for tide times. ⏱ 4 hr for a tour; longer if you go it alone.

Return to Napier the way you came, heading for Marine Parade.

❹ ★★★ kids Ocean Spa. While away the last hours of daylight here, soaking sore muscles and perhaps a sauna and massage. If you're traveling with kids, let them loose on the beach for a bit to tire them out for an early night. ⏱ At least 2 hr. See p. 220, ❹.

SITE GUIDE PAGE 201

❺ ★★★ Art Deco Walk. Start day 2 with an appraisal of Napier city's beautiful Art Deco buildings. Hastings and Napier together form the largest concentration of Art Deco and Spanish Mission architecture in the Southern Hemisphere. Art Deco here is unique for the fact that it often includes Maori motifs. Born out of the tragedy of the 1931 earthquake, which razed the central business district in Napier and damaged over 200 buildings in Hastings, the period buildings form an impressive, cohesive architectural body of work. Napier has embraced this architectural heritage and has come into its own. Every year the Art Deco festival in mid-February attracts thousands of visitors who come to party in 1930s style. This self-guided tour covers Napier highlights; in both Napier and Hastings the i-SITE visitor centers (p. 227) can furnish you with information and walking guides. There

are also independent tour operators who can take you on a dedicated tour of the two towns. ⏱ At least 1 hr.

❻ 🍴 Groove Kitchen Espresso. You'll pass a number of cafes when you're on your Art Deco walk, so you can take your pick. But Groove Kitchen has delicious food for a morning tea snack. **112 Tennyson St.** ☎ 06/835-8530. NZ$10–NZ$12.

❼ ★★ New Zealand Wine Centre. ⏱ 1 hr. See p. 220, ❸.

❽ ★★★ A wine tour. You can pick up a comprehensive guide to Hawke's Bay wineries from the visitor center (or see "Hawke's Bay & Eastland for Wine Lovers," p. 203 for my favorites) but to get the most from your visit in a short time, I suggest you take a wine tour. The visitor center can show you the options but I recommend Grape Escape, On Yer Bike Winery Tours, and Grant Petherick Exclusive Wine Tours. At the end of the day, treat yourself to a world-class meal at Elephant Hill Winery restaurant (p. 226) or Terroir at Craggy Range (p. 227). ⏱ Half-day and evening.

On day 3, in Napier, get onto Marine Parade and travel north, then west onto Breakwater Rd. This becomes the Ahuriri Bypass. At the second roundabout, turn right into Custom Quay. Turn left into West Quay and park your car. It's 4km (2½ miles) from town.

❾ ★★ kids Ahuriri. Drive around the port side of town to explore the little village of Ahuriri. The ★★★ **National Tobacco Company,** on the corner of Coronation and Mahia streets, is the jewel in Napier's Art Deco crown and probably the most photographed building in the region. Designed by Louis Hay and built in 1933, it's one of the most elaborately decorated post-1931 buildings and is seen by many as Hay's tour de force for the way it combines Art Nouveau, Art Deco, and Chicago School styles. Check out the *raupo* (bulrush) and roses on either side of the main door, and make sure you enter the foyer to see the exquisite glass dome. Explore the waterfront, around the marina, and the boutiques, antique stores, and galleries there. If you have kids with you, let them loose on the Kiwi Adventure Trust climbing wall (p. 214, ❿). ⏱ 2 hr.

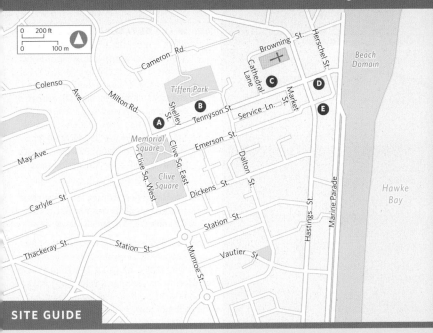

⑤ Art Deco Walk

The **Ⓐ** ★★★ **Art Deco Trust & Shop,** 163 Tennyson St. (☎ 06/835-0022; www.art deconapier.com), should be your first port of call. Not only do they stock a wide range of Art Deco-style gifts and books but it's also the booking point for a number of guided Art Deco walks and tours. The hefty **Ⓑ** ★★ **Municipal Theatre**, 1119 Tennyson St., was built in 1938. It was refurbished in the 1990s and has a superb interior featuring decorative plaster work, neon lighting, and chrome detailing. Once home to the city's newspaper, the solid, symmetrical, **Ⓒ** ★★ **Daily Telegraph Building,** 47 Tennyson St., was designed by architect E.A. Williams and was built in 1932. It features elegant detailing in ziggurat motifs and decorated window columns. The long, two-story **Ⓓ** ★★ **Masonic Hotel,** at the corner of Tennyson Street and Marine Parade, was designed by Wellington architect W.J. Prouse. Its most striking feature is its grand entrance foyer and the stained-glass windows on its street frontage. You need to step inside the **Ⓔ** ★★★ **ASB Building,** at the corner of Emerson and Hastings streets, to see this best of its Art Deco beauty. Designed by Wellington

architect Vivian Haughton, it caused quite a stir when it first opened because it was painted apple green. Today, the beautifully restored interior showcases the 6m-high (20-ft.) banking chamber with its elaborate plaster ceiling and friezes complete with Maori *kowhaiwhai* patterns in traditional red, black, and white. The exterior and bronze grilles also feature Maori designs symbolizing Raumano, the whale.

> Ecliptic, *a sculpture by artist/designer David Trubridge, was installed on the Napier foreshore to mark the new millennium.*

⑩ 🍴 kids **Ahuriri Corner Store.** All that walking and climbing definitely deserves a treat so stop here for some divine fruit ice cream. 83 Bridge St., Ahuriri, Napier. ☎ 06/835-3255. Ice creams from NZ$5.

From Ahuriri, go back the way you came to Marine Parade and continue south through Clive, following signs to Havelock North. At the first roundabout, turn left on Te Mata Rd. Go through one roundabout and at the second, turn right on Simla Rd., veering left on Te Mata Peak Rd. It's 27km (17 miles) and about 45 min. away.

⑪ ★★★ kids **Te Mata Peak.** This is one of the best known landmarks in Hawke's Bay and at 399m (1,309 ft.), it's a great spot to get a 360-degree view of the whole lush, green province. On a clear day you can see for miles and you'll get some terrific photographs, especially if there are people parasailing. ⏱ 30 min.

Drive back to Te Mata Rd., turn right at the roundabout and travel 3km (1¾ miles) to the next stop.

⑫ 🍴 ★★★ kids **Te Mata Cheese Café.** Sit down to a delicious cheese platter at this award-winning artisan cheese-making factory. They specialize in goat, cow, and sheep cheeses, and in addition to the cheeses themselves, they sell a range of tasty cheese-based treats. You can also watch through large windows see how the cheese is made. 393 Te Mata Rd., Havelock North. ☎ 06/875-8282. www.tematacheese.co.nz. Cheese platters NZ$20-NZ$25.

Return to Havelock North and follow the signs to Hastings; the route is well-marked. It's about 12km (7½ miles) and about 25 min. away.

⑬ ★★ kids **Hastings.** If you're art lovers, pick up a brochure at the visitor center detailing Hastings's public artworks. There are at least a dozen major sculptures by leading local and national artists within walking distance in the center of town. Hastings City Art Gallery, 201 Eastbourne St. (☎ 06/871-5095; www.hastingscityartgallery.co.nz), is also worth a visit and admission is free. The Hastings i-SITE Visitor Centre (p. 227) is in one of the city's most famous Spanish Mission buildings, the Westerman's Building. You'll see many other fine Art Deco and Spanish Mission buildings in the central area. ⏱ At least 2 hr.

Leave Hastings on Karamu Rd. N. (St. Hwy. 2). It's less than a mile to the next stop.

⑭ 🍴 **Bay Espresso.** This is the perfect place for a late afternoon snack. It's a colorful spot and they sell organic and fair-trade coffees, as well as full breakfasts and cabinet food. 141 Karamu Rd., Hastings. ☎ 06/876-5682; www.bayespresso.co.nz. NZ$10-NZ$12.

Continue north on on St. Hwy. 2 to Napier, about 22km (14 miles) and 25 min.

⑮ kids **Marine Parade.** Spend the rest of your afternoon wandering along Marine Parade. If you have kids, play a round at Par 2 MiniGolf (p. 214, ❹) or give them another few hours playing, either on the beach or at Ocean Spa (p. 220, ❹). Catch an early night before continuing your travels.

Hawke's Bay & Eastland for Wine Lovers

Hawke's Bay has over 80% of the country's red wine grape plantings and over 70 wineries. Gisborne is called the chardonnay capital of New Zealand and has around 20 wineries. By far the best way to get an overview of the these regions is to take a tour with a local expert. I recommend **Grape Escape** (☎ 0800/100-489; www.grapeescape.net.nz; NZ $100); **On Yer Bike Winery Tours** (☎ 06/879-8735; www.onyerbikehb.co.nz; NZ$55); **Grant Petherick Exclusive Wine Tours** (☎ 06/876-7467; www.flyfishingwinetours.co.nz; NZ$110); and in Gisborne, **Grant's Wine Tours** (☎ 06/868-6139; NZ$60).

My personal favorites are below, but no matter which wineries I list here, dozens of other worthy candidates have to be left out. If wine is your passion, make sure you pick up free winery guides from local visitor centers to give your trip the oenological color it deserves.

★★★ **Black Barn Vineyard,** Black Barn Rd., Havelock North (☎ 06/877-7985; www.blackbarn.com) is blessed with not only a choice range of limited-release wines available exclusively on site, but also a classy bistro, an art gallery, picturesque vineyards, an amphitheater for live performances, and some of the best accommodation in Hawke's Bay (p. 225).

★★★ **Craggy Range,** 253 Waimarama Rd., Havelock North (☎ 06/873-7126; www.craggyrange.co.nz) is a specialist producer of single-vineyard wines from New Zealand's prime winegrowing regions. It's also home to award-winning restaurant Terroir (p. 227). The buildings themselves, designed by Queenstown architect John Blair, are an architectural triumph.

Another John Blair-designed winery, ★★★ **Elephant Hill,** 86 Clifton Rd., Te Awanga, Hastings (☎ 06/873-0400; www.elephanthill.co.nz), produces outstanding sauvignon blanc, viognier, chardonnay, syrah, and pinot noir. Their restaurant is a must.

Certified both organic and biodynamic, ★★★ **Millton Vineyard,** 119 Papatu Rd., Manutuke, Gisborne (☎ 06/862-8680; www.millton.co.nz) produces chenin blanc, viognier, chardonnay, pinot noir, and more—a good number of them internationally awarded.

With a cellar door, restaurant ,and gallery in a huge seminary building dating back to 1880, ★★★ **Mission Estate Winery,** 198 Church Rd., Taradale, Napier (☎ 06/845-9350; www.missionestate.co.nz), offers something a little different. Having started in 1851, it's New Zealand's oldest winery and offers excellent historical tours twice daily.

★★★ **Te Awa Winery**, 2375 St. Hwy. 50, Hastings (☎ 06/879-7602; www.teawa.com), produces exquisite wines with subtle characteristics, especially the pinotage, merlot, and chardonnay. The winery restaurant has a legendary reputation.

State-of-the-art technology and traditional winemaking techniques combine at ★★★ **Vidal Wines,** 913 St. Aubyn St., Hastings (☎ 06/872-7441; www.vidal.co.nz). Quality chardonnays, syrah, and rieslings are the order of the day and you can savor them in what was New Zealand's first vineyard restaurant when it was opened back in 1979.

GRAPE GUIDE

New Zeland's Wine Regions   BY ADRIENNE REWI

NEW ZEALAND PRODUCES AWARD-WINNING WINES in ten main regions. A decade ago our wine exports totalled around $100 million; today they are over $800 million. That's a rapid growth by anyone's standards and with over 500 winemakers operating mostly small, boutique operations across a diverse climatic range, New Zealand is able to produce a wide variety of wine types. Best known internationally for sauvignon blanc, we also have a growing reputation for pinot noir, chardonnay, pinot gris, riesling, merlot, cabernet sauvignon, and methode traditionnalle sparkling wines. Here's a brief guide to the six main wine regions and their specialities.

MARTINBOROUGH

This charming area has over 50 boutique vineyards and food producers, many of them family-owned.

The region specializes in pinot noir, riesling, syrah, and pinot gris. The best time to visit is from late October to early March, when new wine stocks have been released.

HAWKE'S BAY & GISBORNE

Gisborne is known as the Chardonnay Capital of New Zealand. It also produces significant quantities of award-winning riesling and gewurztraminer. Hawke's Bay is home to New Zealand's oldest vineyard, Mission Estate, which was established by the Roman Catholic Church in 1851.

AUCKLAND & WAIHEKE ISLAND

Greater Auckland is home to over 110 vineyards. Henderson Valley is the country's oldest grape-growing region thanks to the

arrival of Croatian immigrants in the early 1900s. Today the western suburbs produce cabernet sauvignon, merlot, pinot noir, chardonnay and sauvignon blanc. Nearby Waiheke Island, home to over 40 vineyards, produces some of the best red wines in the country.

MARLBOROUGH

Long, sunny days and cool nights during the ripening season give the wines of Marlborough-Wairau Valley an extraordinary depth and intensity of flavor and aroma. It's the largest grape growing region in the country and architecturally-designed vineyards,

cellar doors, and restaurants make for happy exploring.

WAIPARA/ CANTERBURY

Located 40 minutes north of Christchurch, Waipara is set in beautiful, rolling, limestone country. The small, boutique wineries here tend to focus on

pinot noir, chardonnay, sauvignon blanc, and riesling.

CENTRAL OTAGO

This southern-most wine producing region in the world is famous for its full-bodied red

wines, and it's one of the fastest growing wine regions in New Zealand. Pinot noir makes up 85% of plantings. A drive to Cromwell and Bannockburn (40 minutes from Queenstown), sheds light on this vast spread of vines.

Sustainable Wine-Growing in New Zealand

Growers in many New Zealand grape regions have introduced sustainable wine-producing programs. Sustainable Winegrowing New Zealand was established by volunteer grape growers in 1995 as an industry initiative, directed through the New Zealand Winegrowers Association, which has funded research into sustainable production methods. It was also a key player in the development of a BioGro organic grape and wine standard. For more information on SWNZ, see www.nzwine.com/swnz/.

Hawke's Bay & Eastland in 1 Week

You won't regret devoting a week to these two beautiful provinces. In addition to the activities outlined in the 3-day itinerary, you'll be able to spend more time getting to know the boutique food and wine producers that have made Hawke's Bay famous, and you'll be able to go on to discover the charming small-town atmosphere of Gisborne with its strong underpinning of Maori culture. You'll find remarkable beaches here, some of the best surf in the country, a chance to come face-to-face with live sharks, and more "living" Maori marae in close proximity than anywhere else in the country.

> *Historic Raukokore Anglican Church on State Highway 35 sometimes has an odd smell—don't worry, it's just penguins nesting underneath.*

START Napier is 423km (263 miles) southeast of Auckland; 228km (141 miles) southeast of Rotorua; and 216km (142 miles) southwest of Gisborne. **TRIP LENGTH** 650km (404 miles) over 7 days.

❶-❹ See day 1 of "The Best of Hawke's Bay in 3 Days."

Start day 2 in Napier.

❺ ★★★ **New Zealand Wine Centre.** Before your day's wine tour, slip in here for a solid grounding in the region's specialties. ⏱ 1 hr. See p. 220, ❸.

❻ ★★★ **A wine tour.** Spend the rest of day 2 exploring this impressive wine region. If you're going under your own steam, pick up a free copy of the *Hawke's Bay Winery Guide* and the *Classic New Zealand Wine Trail Guide* from the Napier i-SITE Visitor Centre, and see the box "Hawke's Bay & Eastland for Wine Lovers," p. 203, for a list of my favorites. Have lunch at one of the winery restaurants. To save on

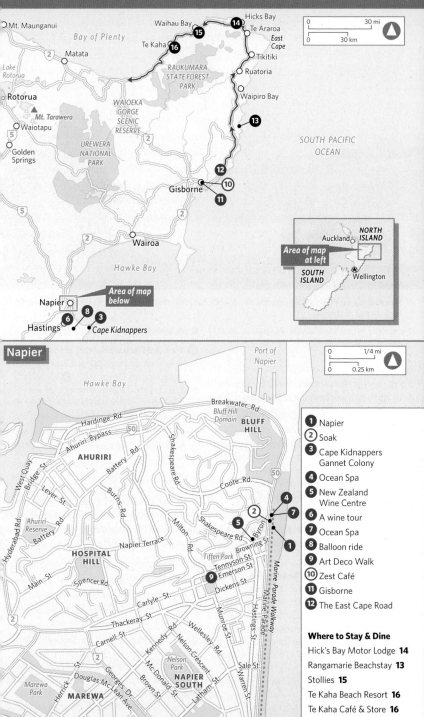

0 ____ 30 mi
0 ____ 30 km

Hicks Bay
Waihau Bay
15
14 Te Araroa
*East
Cape*
Te Kaha **16**
Tikitiki
RAUKUMARA
STATE FOREST
PARK
Ruatoria

Mt. Maunganui
Bay of Plenty
Matata
*Lake
Rotorua*
Rotorua
▲ *Mt. Tarawera*
Waiotapu
Golden
Springs

WAIOEKA
GORGE
SCENIC
RESERVE

UREWERA
NATIONAL
PARK

Waipiro Bay

13

*SOUTH PACIFIC
OCEAN*

12
10
Gisborne
11

Wairoa

Hawke Bay

Napier
**Area of map
below**

Napier
6 **8** **3**
Hastings
Cape Kidnappers

**Area of map
at left**

*NORTH
ISLAND*
Auckland

*SOUTH
ISLAND*

✱ Wellington

Napier

*Port of
Napier*

0 ____ 1/4 mi
0 ____ 0.25 km

Hawke Bay

Breakwater Rd.
*Bluff Hill
Domain*
**BLUFF
HILL**

Hardinge Rd.
Ahuriri Bypass
50
AHURIRI
West Quay
Bridge St.
Lever St.
Battery Rd.
Shakespeare Rd.
Burns Rd.
Coote Rd.
50
Ahuriri
Reserve
Battery Rd.
Hyderabad Rd.
Milton Rd.
Napier Terrace
Shakespeare Rd.
2
5
Browning St.
Byron St.
4
7
1
**HOSPITAL
HILL**
Main St.
Spencer Rd.
Tiffen Park
Tennyson St.
Emerson St.
9
Dickens St.
Carlyle St.
Thackeray St.
Carnell St.
Kennedy Rd.
Wellesley Rd.
Munroe St.
Hastings St.
*Nelson
Park*
**NAPIER
SOUTH**
Nelson Crescent
Mc-Donald St.
Brown St.
Sale St.
Latham St.
Warren St.
Marine Parade Walkway
Marine Parade
*Marewa
Park*
Herrick St.
Douglas McLean Ave.
Georges Dr.
MAREWA

1 Napier
2 Soak
3 Cape Kidnappers
   Gannet Colony
4 Ocean Spa
5 New Zealand
   Wine Centre
6 A wine tour
7 Ocean Spa
8 Balloon ride
9 Art Deco Walk
10 Zest Café
11 Gisborne
12 The East Cape Road

Where to Stay & Dine

Hick's Bay Motor Lodge **14**
Rangamarie Beachstay **13**
Stollies **15**
Te Kaha Beach Resort **16**
Te Kaha Café & Store **16**

> *You certainly won't regret getting up at dawn when Early Morning Balloons whisks you over the beautiful Hawke's Bay landscape.*

time, take your pick of available wine tours at the visitor center. If you choose the splendid On Yer Bike Winery Tours (p. 203) you will have to miss the New Zealand Wine Centre so you can get on your bike early. Some other tour operators will tailor a tour to suit (including lunch), while others offer fixed half- and full-day tours. ⏲ 1 day.

❼ ★★★ kids Ocean Spa. Unwind at the end of your wine adventures with a relaxing soak in the hot pools before dinner out (see p. 226 for recommendations), but remember it's an early start tomorrow. ⏲ 1 hr. See p. 220, ❹.

Drive south via St. Hwy 2 to Hastings to meet your tour operator at the assigned meeting place. It's about 20km (12 miles) and will take about 25 min.

❽ ★★★ kids Early morning balloon ride. Nothing compares to floating over any landscape at dawn but here you're blessed with one of the prettiest aerial views you'll get anywhere. Soar over a patchwork of vines, orchards, fields, and towns. Take your camera and warm clothes. ⏲ 4 hr. ☎ 06/879-4229. www.hotair.co.nz. Admission NZ$355 per person, w/ breakfast. Hastings meeting place arranged on booking.

Drive back to Napier the way you came.

❾ ★★★ Art Deco walk. Start at the Art Deco Trust & Shop and sign up for a tour, or head out on your own (see p. 200, ❺). You can browse any shops and galleries that appeal at the same time. Since you were up before dawn this morning, take it easy for the rest of the afternoon, pottering about at your leisure. It's an early start on day 4 too, so get to bed early. ⏲ Half-day.

On day 4, leave Napier on St. Hwy. 2 (follow signs to Napier Airport and you'll be on the right road) and drive 216km (134 miles) to Gisborne. In the center of town heading north, turn left off the main street, Gladstone Rd., into Peel St. Allow 3 hr.

❿ 🍽 Zest Café. Ease into Gisborne life slowly with a leisurely lunch. They serve a wide range of tasty food (including gluten-free and organic options). 22 Peel St. Gisborne ☎ 06/867-5787. NZ$12–NZ$15.

⓫ ★★ kids Gisborne. Start at **Tairawhiti Museum** for changing exhibitions and a wealth of Maori treasures. Ring ahead to make an appointment to see inside **Te Poho-o-Rawiri Marae,** one of the largest carved meeting houses in New Zealand. Then drive up to

> *This statue of Captain James Cook, on Gisborne's Kaiti Hill, commemorates Cook's first sighting of Poverty Bay in 1769.*

Kaiti Hill Lookout for picturesque views of Gisborne city and the coastline. In the early evening, join **Waka Toa** for a Maori experience that will give you a good understanding of Maori culture before you embark on the journey around East Cape. Stay overnight (see my hotel recommendations on p. 224). ⊙ Halfday. See p. 222.

Make sure you have a full tank of gas before you leave Gisborne, heading north on the Pacific Coast Hwy. (St. Hwy. 35). Start early and travel 4km (2½ miles) to Wainui Beach.

SITE GUIDE PAGE 210

⓬ ★★★ The East Cape Road.
Spend the last 3 days of your trip exploring the winding East Cape Road (St. Hwy. 35, also called the Pacific Coast Road), with overnight stops at Anaura Bay, Hicks Bay, and Opotiki. This is my favorite road trip in all of New Zealand. The population is thin, the landscapes astonishingly beautiful, the Maori culture rich and always evident. Tourism hasn't taken off here, so don't expect luxury accommodation or classy restaurants. The often-narrow, winding roads

have only just been sealed in many places. But if you kick back and take life as it comes, you'll be rewarded with a special time in a remote region that even most New Zealanders haven't visited. Take your time and stop often. Make sure you travel with a copy of the *Pacific Coast Highway* brochure, free from visitor centers.

Learning the Legends

If you want to get a deeper insight into Maori culture, **Tipuna Tours** (☎ 06/862-6118; www.tipunatours.com) will lead the way. Annie McGuire knows the region like the back of her hand and she can take you to places you would not otherwise have access to—places like beautiful Whangara Bay, where the award-winning movie *Whale Rider* was filmed. This 2-hour tour (NZ$75) takes you to meet the descendants of Paikea (the people of Ngati Konohi and Te Atianga Hauiti), who will tell you the story and welcome you into their carved meeting house. Annie also customizes half- and full-day tours that include marae visits, ancient *pa* sites, and beautiful bays.

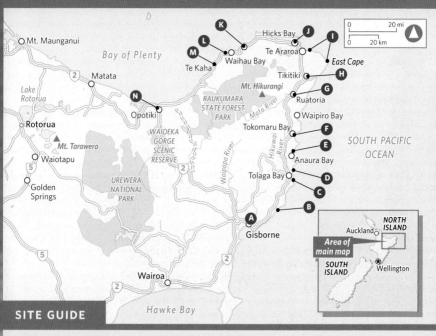

⑫ The East Cape Road

I know you've only just left town but pop in at Ⓐ ★★★ kids **Wainui Beach** (www.wainuibeach.co.nz) for a few minutes to watch early surfers hitting the waves. About 9km (5⅔ miles) on, the brave can stop at Ⓑ ★★★ **Tatapouri** for a chance to swim with the sharks (see p. 216). From Tatapouri travel 41km (25 miles) and turn right into Wharf Rd. to follow the signs 2km (1¼ miles) to Cook's Cove ★★ kids **Tolaga Bay Wharf.** Built between 1926 and 1929, this now decommissioned wharf is the longest pier in New Zealand at 660m (2,165 ft). Consider taking the Cook's Cove Walkway, a 5km/3-mile walk over farmland and through bush to Cook's Cove, where Captain James Cook anchored the HMS *Endeavour* for 6 days in October 1769. The walk takes about 2½ hours round-trip. From the wharf, continue about 5km (3 miles) to Ⓓ ★★ **Tolaga Bay** (Uawa to Maori), distinguished by its beautiful curve of sandy beach. Stop at a shop or cafe and take your grub to Tolaga Bay Beach for a picnic. Captain Cook sailed into this harbor over 240 years ago. Rejoin St. Hwy. 35 and drive about 3km (1¾ miles) to Ⓔ ★★★ kids **Anaura Bay,** a popular

family holiday spot where you'll spend the night. The 2km (1¼-mile) curve of sandy beach is backed by the 225-hectare (556-acre) Anaura Scenic Reserve. The delightful 3.5km (2¼-mile) Anaura Bay Walkway is an easy, 2-hour round-trip outing for all the family.

On day 2, start early and rejoin St. Hwy. 35 turning north (right) and drive 24km (15 miles) to Ⓕ ★ kids **Tokomaru Bay.** Ignore the shabby buildings and stretch your legs on the stunning 8km (5-mile) golden sand beach. It's a Maori stronghold for the Te Whanau-a-Ruataupere people and there are four marae here (which are private property). Head north on St. Hwy. 35 for 37km/23 miles (35 min.), then veer right into Waiomatatini Rd., following signs 3km (1¾ miles) to Ⓖ ★★ kids **Ruatoria.** This rugged, remote town is the core of Ngati Porou—New Zealand's second-largest Maori tribe—who have their headquarters here. Ngati Porou Tourism (☎ 06/864-8660; www.ngatiporou.com) offers a range of Maori tours, including a 4WD tour to see nine huge, carved sculptures depicting Maui-Tikitiki-a-Taranga. Book ahead and budget extra time if you're interested. Be sure to try one of the

town's famous meaty Ruatoria pies before you leave; Sunburst Café (157 Waiomatatini Rd.) is a good spot to tuck in. Leave Ruatoria on Waiomatatini Rd. and turn right into St. Hwy. 35. Drive 19km/12 miles (25 min.) for a quick stop in Tikitiki at **H** ★★★ **St. Mary's Church.** Built as a memorial to Ngati Porou soldiers who died in WWI, it is one of New Zealand's most ornate Maori churches. If I had to name one place on this entire drive that shouldn't be missed, this would be it. Continue on St. Hwy. 35 for 24km/15 miles (25 min.), following signs to **I** ★★ kids **Te Araroa and the East Cape Lighthouse.** In Te Araroa, you'll turn onto the unsealed East Cape Road, which takes you along the coastline, past numerous sandy coves, to New Zealand's most eastern point and the lighthouse standing 154m (505 ft.) above sea level (44km/27 miles round trip). Once there, you'll need to climb 700 steps to the lighthouse itself (which is not open to the public). Back on St. Hwy. 35, it's just 10km (6¼ miles) to **J** ★★★ kids **Hicks Bay,** where you'll spend the night.

Set off early on day 3, heading south on St. Hwy. 35. Travel 52km (32 miles),

stopping at any beaches you like on the way, to **K** ★★ kids **Raukokore.** It's just the place for a picnic. Drive 6km (3¾ miles) to **L** **Pacific Coast Macadamias** (☎ 07/325-2960). Travel another 18km (11 miles) on St. Hwy. 35 to **M** ★★★ kids **Te Kaha.** Check into your accommodation and then spend the rest of day 3 exploring this popular beach. Find a private cove, splash about in the crystal clear water, and fish off the rocks before falling into your bed for the night.

From Te Kaha, it's 70km (43 miles) south on St. Hwy. 35 to **N** **Opotiki,** which completes your journey around the cape. If you have time to spare, I recommend a few stops along the way—these are all along the main road and well signposted. Omaio is a long shingle beach good for walking. Past there, opposite the Omaio Store on your left, you can swing right to find a small, sheltered harbor. There's another huge sweep of beach at Hawai—and you must stop at Torere Primary School to see the amazing carved gateway. If you continue through Opotiki, make sure you stop at lovely Waiotahi Beach with its carved *poupou* (totems).

Hawke's Bay with Kids

Most kids tire of long car journeys very quickly, so I've restricted this itinerary to the Hawke's Bay, which is a dream family location. Everything is close: huge swimming pool complexes, beaches, miniature golf, kayaking, wildlife, ice cream parlors, and sharks, lizards, and crocodiles at the National Aquarium of New Zealand. I've kept it simple so you can mix-and-match a little yourself if the kids start getting too tired.

> Your kids will love you forever if you let them loose for the day at Splash Planet in Hastings.

START To get to the Gannet Beach Adventures launch point from Napier, get onto Marine Parade (St. Hwy. 2) and travel south onto Main Rd. Turn left at Mill Rd. and go through one roundabout. Turn left at Haumoana Rd. Take the first right onto Parkhill Rd., then the first left onto East Rd., then right on Clifton Rd. Drive to Clifton Beach. It's 22km (14 miles) and will take about 25 min. **TRIP LENGTH** 100km (62 miles) and 3 days.

1 ★★★ **Gannet Beach Adventures.** Setting off on a vintage tractor and trailer journey along the beach to see the world's largest mainland gannet colony is the sort of adventure most kids will remember forever. ⏱ 4 hr. See p. 219.

2 🍽 ★★ **Clearview Estate Winery.** This place is a treat for the whole family. There's a kids' menu and the play area gives parents time to relax with a well-earned glass of wine and a light lunch. 194 Clifton Rd., Te Awanga. ☎ 06/875-0150. www.clearviewestate.co.nz. Lunch menu NZ$18–NZ$20.

The next stop is just a few minutes away. From Clearview Estate, turn left and drive north on Clifton Rd. Turn left on East Rd.

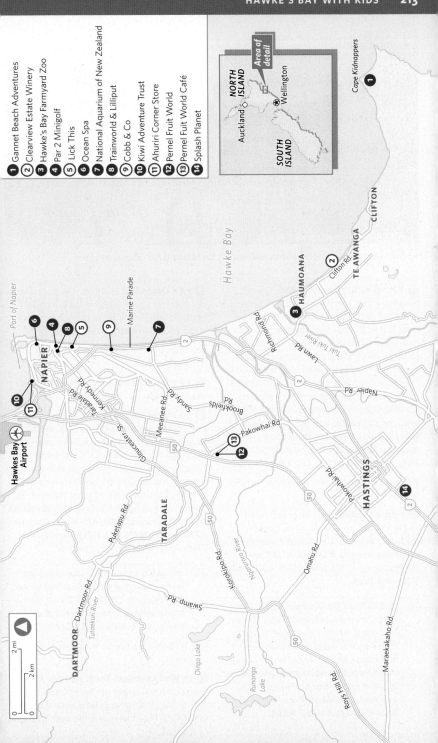

1. Gannet Beach Adventures
2. Clearview Estate Winery
3. Hawke's Bay Farmyard Zoo
4. Par 2 Minigolf
5. Lick This
6. Ocean Spa
7. National Aquarium of New Zealand
8. Trainworld & Lilliput
9. Cobb & Co
10. Kiwi Adventure Trust
11. Ahuriri Corner Store
12. Pernel Fruit World
13. Pernel Fuit World Café
14. Splash Planet

NORTH ISLAND
Auckland
Wellington
Area of detail
SOUTH ISLAND

Cape Kidnappers

CLIFTON

TE AWANGA

HAUMOANA
Clifton Rd

Hawke Bay

Tuki Tuki River

Richmond Rd
Lawn Rd
Napier Rd

Port of Napier

NAPIER
Marine Parade

Taradale Rd
Kennedy Rd
Meeanee Rd
Sandy Rd
Brookfields Rd
Pakowhai Rd

Hawkes Bay Airport

Gloucester St

TARADALE

Puketapu Rd

Pakowhai Rd

HASTINGS

DARTMOOR
Dartmoor Rd

Tutaekuri River

Korokipo Rd

Ngaruroro River

Swamp Rd

Omahu Rd

Ongo Lake

Runanga Lake

Maraekakaho Rd

Ross Hill Rd

2 mi
2 km

> Pony rides are a big hit on any holiday and Hawke's Bay Farmyard Zoo caters to all ages.

③ ★ Hawke's Bay Farmyard Zoo. You don't have to be a kid to enjoy contact with tame animals. Buy some pet food from the onsite store and let the kids feed sheep, goats, llama, and alpacas. Kids as young as two can be led on pony rides and there are horseback riding lessons with a qualified instructor Wednesday, Thursday, and Friday afternoons and weekend mornings. If you're all competent riders, ask about their group horse rides and treks. ⏲ At least 1 hr. 32 East Rd., Haumoana, Hastings. ☎ 06/875-0244. www.farmyardzoo.co.nz. Admission NZ$10 adults, NZ$7 kids, NZ$35 family. Daily, weather permitting, Oct–Feb 10am–5pm.

Return to Napier the way you came. Park on Marine Parade.

④ ★ Par 2 MiniGolf. Challenge each other to a round and try and add your names to the leader board. ⏲ 1 hr. Marine Parade, next to the visitor center. ☎ 06/834-0248. www.par2golf.co.nz. NZ$10 adults, NZ$6 kids. Daily 9:30am–4:30pm.

⑤ 🍴 Lick This. Choose from over 30 flavors of unbelievably good Rush Munro ice cream, which is produced in nearby Hastings. They also serve Italian gelato and sorbet which you can watch being made through a viewing window. Dairy-, fat-, and gluten-free options are also available. 290 Marine Parade, Napier. ☎ 06/835-9427. NZ$5–NZ$8.

⑥ ★★★ Ocean Spa. Wind up your day here. A last carefree splash about in these excellent heated pools is sure to tire the kids out so they sleep well. ⏲ At least 1 hr. See p. 220, ❹.

Start day 2 at the National Aquarium on Marine Parade.

⑦ ★★★ National Aquarium of New Zealand. See p. 220, ❶.

⑧ ★★ Trainworld and Lilliput. Every small boy's dream (and possibly some of the big boys too), this is one of the world's largest 00 gauge model railways. It's also home to Lilliput, where small trains zoom through tiny tunnels, and through miniature towns and forests. Kids can also take a turn at the controls. There's a small ride-on train, too. ⏲ 45 min. 88 Dickens St., Napier. ☎ 06/935-8045. Admission NZ$10 adults, NZ$5 kids, NZ$25 family. Daily 10am–4pm (Wed–Sun only in winter).

⑨ 🍴 Cobb & Co. Kids will love the chips and burgers, the special kids' menu, and the playroom, DVDs, and toys at this unpretentious spot. 311 Marine Parade, Napier. ☎ 06/835-6567. NZ$8–NZ$15.

Follow Marine Parade north around the port to Ahuriri.

⑩ ★★ Kiwi Adventure Trust. Kids love something to climb and they can burn off some energy on the climbing walls here while stretching their limits. They'll be safe in this well-organized

> You can't visit Hawke's Bay and not sample at least one of the 30 flavors of Rush Munro ice cream.

environment—wearing full harness gear—that caters for climbers of all levels, from beginners as young as 4 to experts. ⏲ At least 2 hr. 58 West Quay, Ahuriri, Napier. ☎ 06/834-3500. www.kiwi-adventure.co.nz. Admission (all-day pass) NZ$15 adults, NZ$14 kids 6–12; NZ$6 kids 5 and under. Equipment: climbing shoes NZ$5, chalk bags NZ$3. Summer daily 10am–6pm; winter Tues and Thurs 3pm–6pm, Sat–Sun 10am–6pm.

⑪   🍴 **Ahuriri Corner Store.** See p. 202, ⑩.

Spend the rest of day 2 relaxing, walking along the Ahuriri beachfront, or browsing Napier shops. On day 3, leave Napier heading south on Tennyson St. Turn right into Carlyle St. and continue on Hyderabad Rd. At the roundabout take the first exit onto Taradale Rd. At the second roundabout take the first exit onto Hawke's Bay Expressway. Veer slight left onto Pakowhai Rd. It's 18km (11 miles) and 25 min. to Pernel Fruit World.

⑫ ★ **Pernel Fruit World.** Leap aboard the small apple wagon and tour through this 33-hectare (82-acre) family orchard where they grow 85 different varieties of fruit commercially. Apples and stone fruit are the biggest focus. Harvest season is December through May. There is also a small animal farm, where kids can get to know goats, sheep, pigs, and donkeys. Buy some fresh fruit to take away for your lunch. ⏲ At least 1 hr. 1412 Pakowhai Rd., Hastings.

☎ 06/878-3383. www.pernel.nzliving.co.nz. Tour NZ$16 adults, NZ$8 kids 11 and under. Bookings advised. Daily 9am–4pm.

⑬   🍴 **Pernel Fruit World Café.** Grab a take-away coffee and a fresh fruit ice cream for the kids before heading for your next adventure. 1412 Pakowhai Rd., Hastings. NZ$6–NZ$12.

Head southwest on Pakowhai Rd., following signs 4.5km (2¾ miles) to Hastings and Splash Planet.

⑭ ★★★ **Splash Planet.** You'll have everything you need and more here, so settle in for the rest of the day. The park has everything from go-karts, bumper boats, a pirate ship, a train, castles, a continuous river raft ride, an activity pool, a safe toddler area, miniature golf, tunnels, and indoor pools. Your pass covers all activities, rides, and pools throughout your stay. There's a cafe on site, plus the Fuel Shed for ice cream, drinks, and snacks. It's a great way to unwind on the last day of your Hawke's Bay family holiday. ⏲ At least a half-day. Grove Rd., Hastings. ☎ 06/876-9856. www.splashplanet.co.nz. Super Pass NZ$30 adults, NZ$20 kids 4–13, NZ$5 spectators. Daily 10am–5:30pm.

> Kids will get a great sense of accomplishment out of reaching the top of the Kiwi Adventure Trist climbing wall.

Hawke's Bay & Eastland Outdoor Adventures A to Z

Bicycling

★★ **Bike About Tours,** 47 Gloucester St., Greenmeadows, Napier (☎ 06/845-4836; www.bikeabouttours.co.nz), offers bikes and maps for a number of organized routes starting from NZ$45 per person.

★★★ **Eskdale Mountain Bike Park** is located within 356 hectares (880 acres) of forest and has over 80km (50 miles) of dedicated mountain bike tracks suited to all levels of ability. Contact the Hawke's Bay Mountain Bike Club (☎ 06/873-8793; www.hawkesbaymtb.co.nz) for maps and permit information.

Diving

★★★ **Arlidge Adventures Dive Center,** 87 Carlyle St., Napier (☎ 06/835-3005; www.aadivecenter.co.nz) offers dive courses for all abilities, guided underwater tours, and organized dive trips to colorful underwater locations like Cape Kidnappers that include reefs, trenches, and lots of sea mammals.

Tours are tailor-made to ability and priced on application.

★★★ **Dive Tatapouri,** Tatapouri Beach, St. Hwy. 35 (☎ 06/868-5153; www.tatapouri. co.nz), is run by Dean Savage, who has worked as a commercial diver for over 20 years. He'll take you into nearby Te Tapuwae O Rongokako Marine Reserve or to his favorite spot, Ariel Reef.

Fishing

You can do anything from freshwater fly-fishing for brown trout to game fishing for marlin in the Pacific here. For the independent angler, the Pacific Coast Highway (St. Hwy. 35) is the ultimate route for surf-casting and game fishing. There's good surf-casting at Hawai and Torere beaches, while fishing from the rocks is best at Whitianga, Omaio, Te Kaha, and Lottin Point beaches. Local knowledge is plentiful so ask about the best fishing spots or use guides and charter services. Saltwater fishing does

> *Fishermen rejoice—there are good fishing rivers aplenty in Hawke's Bay and Eastland.*

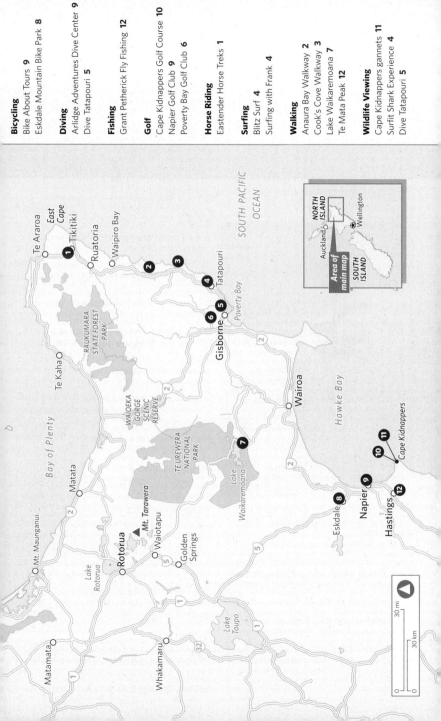

Bicycling
Bike About Tours **9**
Eskdale Mountain Bike Park **8**

Diving
Arlidge Adventures Dive Center **9**
Dive Tatapouri **5**

Fishing
Grant Petherick Fly Fishing **12**

Golf
Cape Kidnappers Golf Course **10**
Napier Golf Club **9**
Poverty Bay Golf Club **6**

Horse Riding
Eastender Horse Treks **1**

Surfing
Blitz Surf **4**
Surfing with Frank **4**

Walking
Anaura Bay Walkway **2**
Cook's Cove Walkway **3**
Lake Waikaremoana **7**
Te Mata Peak **12**

Wildlife Viewing
Cape Kidnappers gannets **11**
Surfit Shark Experience **4**
Dive Tatapouri **5**

> *Teeing off at Cape Kidnappers, one of the world's best golf courses.*

> *With large swells from the east and south, the Gisborne coastline has been attracting surfers since the 1960s.*

not require a license but freshwater fishing does. Call **Fish & Game New Zealand's Trout Line** (☎ 0800/876-885; www.fishandgame. org.nz) to get the details.

★★★ **Grant Petherick Fly Fishing,** 805 Fitz-roy Ave., Hastings (☎ 06/876-7467; www. flyfishingwinetours.co.nz), caters to anglers of all abilities and offers full- and half-day trips for nymph and dry fly-fishing for NZ$110 per person per hour.

Golf

★★★ **Cape Kidnappers Golf Course,** 446 Clifton Rd., Te Awanga, Hastings (☎ 06/873-1018; www.capekidnappers.com), is one of the finest golf courses in the world. Its spectacular cliff-top setting is part of the luxury property The Farm at Cape Kidnappers (p. 225) and you'll pay around NZ$450 for a round of golf here. If your wallet won't stretch to that sort of indulgence, **Napier Golf Club,** Waiohiki, St. Hwy. 50, Taradale, Napier (☎ 06/844-7913; www.napiergolf.co.nz), iscan excellent 18-hole course where you'll pay NZ$65 to NZ$70 for a round. In Gisborne, **Poverty Bay Golf Club,** corner of Awapuni and Lytton rds., Gisborne (☎ 06/867-4402; www.gisbornegolf.co.nz), is one of the top 18-hole courses in the country. You'll pay NZ$45 for a round.

Horseback Riding

Horseback is still a popular means of transport in the wilderness reaches of Eastland. **East-ender Horse Treks,** Rangitukia Rd., Tikitiki (☎ 06/868-3033; www.eastenderhorsetreks. co.nz), will take you along beaches, over hills, through forests, all the while exposing you to the Ngati Porou culture that makes this area famous. Treks start at NZ$130 for 2 hours and there are overnight treks for experienced riders who can cope with very steep country. Backpacker accommodation is also available.

Surfing

The Gisborne coastline has a legendary repu-tation when it comes to surfing and there are at least 20 good breaks within an hour's drive of the city. Close to Gisborne, Makorori Point,

> *Walkers enjoying the views from Te Mata Peak.*

Pouawa, Sponge Bay, and Kaiaua are all popular and have a variety of beach and reef breaks. You can get the surfing lowdown from **Blitz Surf,** 34 Wainui Rd., Gisborne (☎ 06/868-4428; www.blitzsurf.co.nz), as well as rent boards and take a lesson (group lesson NZ$50, private lesson NZ$75). **Surfing with Frank,** Wainui Beach, Gisborne (☎ 06/867-0823; www.surfingwithfrank.com), will give you a great time whether you're 8 or 80. Surf lessons (NZ$75 per hour), tours, and surf guiding are all on the books and you can hire surfboards.

Walking

Both provinces have walks for all levels of ability and interest from a leisurely beach amble to taxing multi-day guided walks in the remote **Te Urewera National Park,** which lies between Hawke's Bay and the Bay of Plenty. You need to be a serious and competent tramper to take this latter area on and it pays to contact the **Department of Conservation,** Aniwaniwa Visitor Centre, Private bag, Wairoa (☎ 06/837-3803; www.doc.govt.nz), for details. The 3- to 4-day, 46km/29-mile hike around **Lake Waikaremoana** is the most popular of at least 15 walks in this area. **Cook's Cove Walkway** and **Anaura Bay Walkway** (p. 209, ⑫) are two lovely, short beach walks. In Hastings, give yourself a decent workout by climbing to the top of **Te Mata Peak** (p. 202, ⑪).

Wildlife Viewing

Cape Kidnappers is home to the largest mainland colony of Australian gannets in the world (Sept–May; best viewing is early Nov–mid-Dec) and you get great chances to photograph at close quarters. Join ★★★ **Gannet Safaris Overland** (☎ 0800/427-232; www.gannetsafaris.co.nz) if you prefer the comfort of an air-conditioned coach and no walking. Their 3½-hour trip costs NZ$70 per person. ★★★ **Gannet Beach Adventures** (☎ 0800/426-638; www.gannets.com) has more of a sense of adventure, as you ride 8km (5 miles) of beach to the cliffs in a trailer towed by an old-fashioned tractor. You have to walk 20 to 30 minutes but that's a small price to pay. It costs NZ$40 adults, NZ$25 kids 2–14, and there are several departures daily from Clifton Beach, about a 25-minute drive from Hastings or Napier.

The brave among you might like to head north to ★★★ **Surfit Shark Cage Experience,** 48 Awapuni Rd., Gisborne (☎ 06/867-2970; www.surfit.co.nz), an outfitter who will take you to reef waters teeming with sharks, slip you into a wetsuit and a wire cage, and lower you into the predator-infested waters. All this for just NZ$350! The trips run from November to April. ★★★ **Dive Tatapouri** (see Diving, above) also offers a shark cage experience (NZ$300) and a wild stingray feeding adventure (NZ$50 adults, NZ$25 kids).

Napier

I never tire of this pretty, enthusiastic little city (pop. 67,500) bursting at the seams with award-winning wine, fabulous local food producers, all that Art Deco architecture, and a thriving arts community. That's before we even get to the beaches, the marvelous array of up-market boutique accommodations, and the superb climate. Often overlooked in favor of the bigger cities, I always recommend it as a gem worth making time for.

> On February 3, 1931, 256 people died when Napier was struck by an earthquake measuring 7.9 on the Richter Scale.

START Napier is 423km (263 miles) southeast of Auckland; 228km (141 miles) southeast of Rotorua; and 216km (142 miles) southwest of Gisborne.

① ★★★ kids **National Aquarium of New Zealand.** Walking through the middle of a huge ocean tank via a giant acrylic tunnel with a moving walkway always leaves me with a sense of awe and wonder. Numerous fish species, stingrays, and sharks all swim around you. If you're here at 10am, you'll be able to watch divers feed the fish and sharks. Other highlights include a lovely seahorse display, Izzy the crocodile, the Kiwi House, and the largest coral display in New Zealand. The behind-the-scenes tours are also fascinating if you have extra time. ⏲ 2 hr. Marine Parade. ☎ 06/834-1404. www.nationalaquarium.co.nz. Admission NZ$18 adults, NZ$10 kids, NZ$45 family. Open daily 9am–5pm.

② ★ kids **Opossum World.** The brushtail opossum may look cute and cuddly but this is one of New Zealand's worst introduced pests. It is estimated that 70 million possums eat 21,000 tons of foliage each night, making them an ecological nightmare. They also eat the eggs of many of our cherished native birds. You'll get an insight into all that—and more—at this "retail attraction" that couples education with the chance to indulge in beautiful possum fur garments, rugs, and cushions at factory prices. ⏲ 45 min. 157 Marine Parade. ☎ 06/835-7697. www.opossumworld.co.nz. Daily 9am–5pm.

③ ★★★ **New Zealand Wine Centre.** If wine is your passion, you should make this your first stop before you go exploring the vineyards. Their red and white aroma awareness rooms, the cellar door wine sales, and the Big Picture Wine Theatre will give you a good introduction to what the Hawke's Bay wine region is all about. ⏲ At least 1 hr. AMP Building, 1 Shakespeare Rd. ☎ 06/835-5326. www.newzealandwinecentre.co.nz. Full wine experience with tasting NZ$35 per person, NZ$20 non-drinkers. Daily 10am–8pm.

④ ★★★ kids **Ocean Spa.** It goes without saying that this is a terrific place to keep the kids amused for hours, but it's more than that—it's also a wonderful place for adults to unwind at the end of a long day of exploring. Forget the toddlers' pool for a moment and think about sinking into heated pools, taking a sauna, and enjoying a massage or a range of indulgent body treatments. ⏲ At least 1 hr. 42 Marine Parade. ☎ 06/835-8553. www.oceanspa.co.nz. Admission NZ$10 adults, NZ$8 kids 2–14, NZ$26 family; massages NZ$40–NZ$64. Mon-Sat 6am–10pm, Sun 8am–10pm.

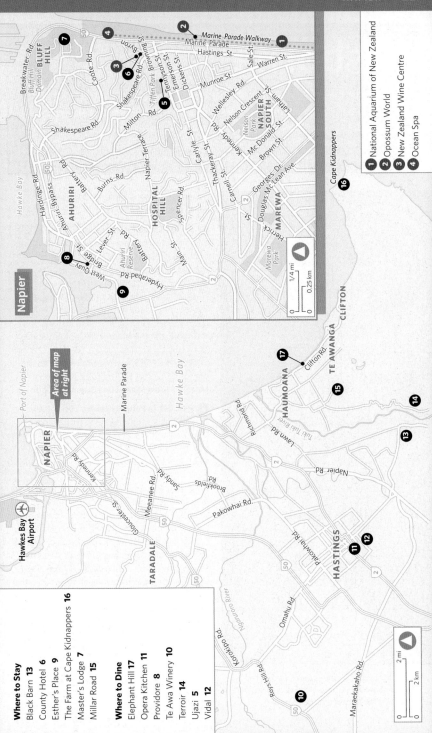

Napier

1/4 mi
0.25 km

2 km
2 mi

Where to Stay
Black Barn **13**
County Hotel **6**
Esther's Place **9**
The Farm at Cape Kidnappers **16**
Master's Lodge **7**
Millar Road **15**

Where to Dine
Elephant Hill **17**
Opera Kitchen **11**
Providore **8**
Te Awa Winery **10**
Terroir **14**
Ujazi **5**
Vidal **12**

1 National Aquarium of New Zealand
2 Opossum World
3 New Zealand Wine Centre
4 Ocean Spa

Hawkes Bay Airport

Port of Napier

Area of map at right

NAPIER

Hawke Bay

Marine Parade

TARADALE

HASTINGS

HAUMOANA

TE AWANGA

CLIFTON

Cape Kidnappers

Gisborne

Gisborne (pop. 44,500) is the most isolated city in New Zealand, separated by mountain ranges from both Bay of Plenty and Hawke's Bay. It is a bastion of Maori culture and language with over 45% of the population identifying as Maori, who call the city Turanganui-a-Kiwi. This, along with the wine and the unspoiled beaches that lie to the north, are key attractions.

> Designed by Maori carvers Derek Lardelli and Te Aturangi Nepia Clamp, this Gisborne sculpture takes the form of a canoe prow.

START Gisborne is 216km (134 miles) northwest of Napier.

1 ★★ kids **Tairawhiti Museum.** This small but vital museum contains a fabulous collection of Maori artifacts in the semi-permanent exhibition *Watersheds Nga Waipupu*, a display that provides a snapshot of Gisborne and East Coast history. This is beautifully balanced by the Star of Canada Maritime Gallery, which covers 1,000 years of maritime history, from the coming of the Maori and Captain James Cook to local surfing culture. ⏱ 1 hr. 18–22 Stout St. ☎ 06/867-3832. www.tairawhitimuseum. org.nz. Admission NZ$6 adults, NZ$3 kids. Mon–Sat 10am–4pm, Sun 1:30pm–4:30pm.

2 ★★★ kids **Te Poho-o-Rawiti.** The heavily carved *waharoa* (gateway) to this, one of New Zealand's largest marae, is a clue to the traditional beauties that lie within. Home to Ngati Oneone, one of the Ngati Porou *hapu* (sub-tribes), it features an internal stage framed by carvings and fine examples of *tuku-tuku* (woven) paneling. You are not permitted to take photographs here and you must not enter without permission. There is also a very cute Maori church, Toko Toro Tapu, on the hill behind the marae. ⏱ 1 hr. Corner of Ranfurly St. and Queens Dr., Kaiti Hill. ☎ 06/868-5364. Visits can be arranged by appointment or at the Gisborne i-SITE Visitor Centre, ☎ 06/868-6139. Admission by donation.

3 ★ kids **Kaiti Hill Lookout.** Titirangi Hill, more commonly known as Kaiti Hill, is the ancestral site of the Ngati Oneone people, who occupy Te Poho-o-Rawiri marae at its base. Drive up here for the best views in town—right across the city and Poverty Bay, where Captain James Cook visited in 1769. At the top you'll find the

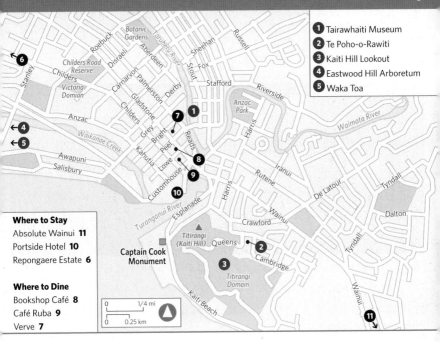

1 Tairawhaiti Museum
2 Te Poho-o-Rawiti
3 Kaiti Hill Lookout
4 Eastwood Hill Arboretum
5 Waka Toa

Where to Stay
Absolute Wainui **11**
Portside Hotel **10**
Repongaere Estate **6**

Where to Dine
Bookshop Café **8**
Café Ruba **9**
Verve **7**

James Cook Observatory, a park, four lookouts, a World War II gun emplacement, and numerous walks and nature trails through the reserve, should you feel like stretching your legs. ⏱ 1 hr.

Leave central Gisborne (with picnic food) heading south on Gladstone Rd. Turn left at Customhouse St., go through one roundabout, then veer right on Awapuni Rd. Turn left at Wharerata Rd. and continue onto Tiniroto Rd. Turn right at Brunton Rd., then left at Wharekopae Rd. Travel another 18km (11 miles). It's 38km (24 miles) total, a 1-hr. drive, to reach the Eastwood Hill Arboretum.

4 ★★★ kids **Eastwood Hill Arboretum.** This magnificent 70-hectare (173-acre) woodland park is a testament to one man's passion for trees. It's also a beautiful place to while away the rest of your day. The work of William Douglas Cook, who began planting the bare site in 1910, is the loveliest and largest arboretum in New Zealand, boasting more than 3,500 species of trees. It's a haven for scientists, photographers, garden enthusiasts, and picnickers. There are over 25km (16 miles) of walking tracks and plenty to see; guided tours are available at additional cost. Plan a picnic under the maples. ⏱ At least 2 hr. 2392 Wharekopae Rd., Ngatapa. ☎ 06/863-9003. www.eastwoodhill.org.nz. Admission NZ$12 adults, free for kids under 14. Daily 9am–5pm.

Drive back into Gisborne the way you came.

5 ★★★ kids **Waka Toa.** Imagine sitting high on a hill overlooking Gisborne valley and the sunset as a spine-tingling traditional Maori welcome rings through the early evening. That's the setting for an evening with professional performing arts group Waka Toa, which combines traditional Maori dance, stories, and legends with modern drama, music, and humor. Located on the remnants of their historic *whanau* (family) Whaitiripapa Pa site, in the hills of Knapdale Forest, the performance is all about cross-cultural conversation and entertainment. If you're heading north from Gisborne around the East Cape, this is an ideal introduction to Maori culture. ⏱ 3 hr. ☎ 06/868-5425. www.wakatoa. com. Adults NZ$265, kids NZ$185, family NZ$375; includes transportation to performance site. Bookings can also be made at Gisborne i-SITE Visitor Centre, ☎ 06/868-6139. Performances 6pm year-round.

Where to Stay

> *Families or couples alike can enjoy every comfort at Millar Road's Haumoana House, which overlooks a vineyard.*

East Cape Road

Hicks Bay Motor Lodge HICKS BAY

This very modest, 1960s-style B&B has a dramatic location on the hill above Hicks Bay just a few minutes from the beach below, which helps make up for the dated rooms. There's a modest restaurant here where you'll have a chance to meet some of the friendly locals. St. Hwy. 35. ☎ 06/864-4880. www.hicksbaymotel. co.nz. Doubles NZ$110–NZ$175. V. Map p. 207.

★★★ **Rangamarie Beachstay** ANAURA BAY

David and Judy Newell's B&B rooms and self-contained cottage are a little slice of East Coast heaven. Situated above one of the coast's loveliest golden sand beaches, all rooms have sensational views of the bay and private decks. 930 Anaura Rd. ☎ 021-633-372. www.anaura-stay.co.nz. 4 units. Cottage double NZ$205; B&B rooms NZ$165–NZ$205. No cards. Dinner provided by arrangement. Map p. 207.

★ **Stollies** WAIHAU BAY

This modern, 2-bedroom seaside unit is an excellent spot for families as it's self-contained and with bunks in one room, it can sleep seven. There's a large timber deck and it's just a 2-minute trek to the safe-swimming beach across the road. St. Hwy. 35. ☎ 07/325-3603. www.holidayhomes.co.nz. 1 unit. Double NZ$135–NZ$300. AE, MC, V. Meals by arrangement. Map p. 207.

★★★ kids **Te Kaha Beach Resort** TE KAHA

This hotel complex has studios and 1- or 2-bedroom apartments on a spectacular hilltop site overlooking the bay. All have balconies and come with everything you'll need, including modern bathrooms and comfortable bedding. The property has a restaurant and swimming pool, too. St. Hwy. 35. ☎ 07/325-2830. www. tekahabeachresort.co.nz. 24 units. Doubles NZ$160–NZ$375. AE, MC, V. Map p. 207.

Gisborne

★ **Absolute Wainui** WAINUI BEACH/GISBORNE

If you're a beach fan, then bed and breakfast rooms in this modern, beachside home will suit you perfectly. Sit out on the big decks as the sun goes down, sip a local chardonnay, and listen to the waves. 69 Wairere Rd. ☎ 06/867-0386. www.absolutewainui.com. 2 units. Doubles NZ$260–NZ$400 w/breakfast. AE, DC, MC, V. Map p. 223.

★★ kids **Portside Hotel** GISBORNE CITY

Portside offers large, modern apartments in a quiet setting with a beautiful pool. Two-bedroom suites, connecting rooms, and full kitchens make it an ideal choice for families and couples traveling together. 2 Reads Quay. ☎ 06/869-1000. www.portsidegisborne.co.nz. 64 units. Doubles NZ$175–NZ$450. AE, DC, MC, V. Map p. 223.

★★★ Repongaere Estate PATUTAHI/GISBORNE

This quiet, rural site offers three modern, 2-bedroom villas with views of grape vines and olive trees cascading down the hill. The villas are self-contained but breakfast provisions are provided and evening meals can be arranged. 30 Repongaere Rd., Patutahi. ☎ 06/862-7515. 3 units. NZ$325–NZ$450. No credit cards. Map p. 223.

Napier and Environs

★★★ Black Barn HAVELOCK NORTH

Black Barn Vineyards offer more than a dozen of the most beautiful stays in Hawke's Bay in a range of styles and locations. Rush Cottage (NZ$375) and Black Barn (NZ$575) are both on the vineyard property. The River Houses (NZ$450–NZ$600) are stylish, contemporary apartments in the Tuki Tuki River valley. Black Barn Rd. ☎ 06/877-7985. www.blackbarn.com. At least 12 properties priced individually. AE, DC, MC, V. Map p. 221.

kids The County Hotel NAPIER

This traditional English-style boutique hotel is in one of only two major historic buildings that survived the 1931 earthquake. Large rooms, friendly service, and a great location. 12 Browning St. ☎ 06/835-7800. www.countyhotel.co.nz. 18 units. Doubles NZ$275–NZ$900. AE, DC, MC, V. Map p. 221.

★★ kids Esther's Place AHURIRI/NAPIER

This modern, 2-bedroom apartment, filled with works by leading New Zealand artists and designers, has a quiet location with broad views over the Ahuriri district and marina. Apt. 504, the Waterfront, 7 Humber St. ☎ 06/875-1977. www.esthersplace.co.nz. 1 self-contained apartment. Double NZ$500 w/breakfast provisions. Two night min. Map p. 221.

★★★ The Farm at Cape Kidnappers

TE AWANGA/CAPE KIDNAPPERS This gorgeous cliff-top retreat leaves no stone unturned when it comes to comfort, service, and luxury. Every suite opens onto a private porch with panoramic views. Choose from lodge suites in the main building, one of the separate ridge suites, or the

> You'll be well away from the madding crowds at The Farm at Cape Kidnappers.

luxurious 2- or 4-bedroom Owner's Cottage. 446–448 Clifton Rd. ☎ 06/875-1900. www.capekidnappers.com. 22 suites, 1 cottage. Suites NZ$2,075–NZ$2,750; 4-bedrm Owner's Cottage NZ$14,500 w/breakfast, pre-dinner drinks, and dinner. AE, DC, MC, V. Map p. 224.

★★ Master's Lodge NAPIER

Once owned by tobacco baron Gerhard Husheer, this gracious home on the hill contains two large suites. Colorful and filled with stylish antiques of the day, it's a gem not to be missed. 10 Elizabeth Rd., Bluff Hill. ☎ 06/834-1946. www.masterslodge.co.nz. 2 units. Doubles NZ$889 w/breakfast. Also includes afternoon tea, pre-dinner hors d'oeuvres, and access to Ocean Spa. AE, MC, V. Map p. 221.

★★ Millar Road HASTINGS

Perched high above a small vineyard with postcard views of the vines and ocean, the two modern 2-bedroom villas are filled to overflowing with fine contemporary New Zealand design and art. Take advantage of the heated pool. Nearby 3-bedroom Haumoana House is also available. 83 Millar Rd., Hastings. ☎ 06/875-1977. www.millarroad.co.nz. 3 units. Villas NZ$600; house NZ$1,200, w/breakfast provisions. AE, MC, V. Two night min. Map p. 221.

Where to Dine

> *Relax with a good magazine, good food, and good coffee at Gisborne's Café Ruba.*

East Cape Road

Te Kaha Café & Store TE KAHA *CAFE*
Sit here for longer than five minutes drinking surprisingly good coffee and half the local community will probably have passed through. Don't expect too much culinary finesse but cabinet selections are adequate for a quick snack. St. Hwy. 35. ☎ 07/325-2894. www.tekahaholidaypark.co.nz. MC, V. Daily breakfast, lunch, and takeaway. Map p. 207.

Gisborne

★★ kids **Bookshop Café** CITY *CAFE*
Upstairs from an excellent book store, this roomy cafe attracts a diverse crowd, who come for the reliably good food and coffee. Enjoy salads, soups, sandwiches, and pastries on the little balcony overlooking Gisborne's main street. 62 Gladstone Rd. ☎ 06/869-0653. Main courses NZ$12–NZ$20. AE, MC, V. Breakfast and lunch daily. Map p. 223.

★ kids **Café Ruba** CITY *CAFE*
In the grand old Union Steamship Company building close to the river, this hidden-away treat is worth seeking out. The light lunch menu includes soups, salads, and fish dishes; breakfast is very good too. They have a kids' menu and vegetarians are always well looked after. 14 Childers Rd. ☎ 06/868-6516. Main courses NZ$15–NZ$22. AE, DC, MC, V. Breakfast and lunch daily. Map p. 223.

★ kids **Verve** CITY *CAFE*
This slightly scruffy local haunt is one of my favorites. They always have great coffee, their breakfasts are hearty, the seafood is excellent, and the live music on Friday nights is an added bonus. The antipasto platter, curries, and salads are all good value—and there's a kids' menu. 121 Gladstone Rd. ☎ 06/868-9095. Main courses NZ$12–NZ$28. AE, MC, V. Breakfast and lunch daily, dinner Mon-Sat. Map p. 223.

Napier

★★★ **Elephant Hill** TE AWANGA/HASTINGS *MODERN NZ/EUROPEAN* Wall-to-wall windows and beautiful views over vines provide the perfect backdrop for exquisite wine-matched meals. Lamb shanks, sesame-crusted tuna, tenderloin steak, and duck confit all feature on an exciting menu. 86 Clifton Rd. ☎ 06/873-0400. www.elephanthill.co.nz. Main courses NZ$32–NZ$38. AE, DC, MC, V. Sept-April lunch and dinner daily; May–Aug lunch daily, dinner Wed-Sat. Map p. 221.

★ **Opera Kitchen** HASTINGS *CAFE*
Taking its name from the nearby Opera House, this slick, contemporary joint is one of

Hawke's Bay's most popular eateries. Prawn and sweet potato fritters, green pea risotto, and steak sandwiches are typical of tasty dishes made with fresh local ingredients. 312 Eastbourne St. ☎ 06/870-6020. www.operakitchen.co.nz. Main courses NZ$15–NZ$25. MC, V. Breakfast and lunch Mon–Sat. Map p. 221.

★★ **Providore** AHURIRI/NAPIER *MODERN NZ* The daily fish dish is a reliable choice at this ever-popular, marina-side eatery. Tapas choices such as lamb skewers and tempura artichokes are a great way to start any evening. 60 West Quay. ☎ 06/834-0189. Main courses NZ$26–NZ$36. AE, DC, MC, V. Dinner Tues–Sun, Brunch and lunch Sat–Sun. Map p. 221.

★★★ **Te Awa** HASTINGS *MODERN NZ/EURO-PEAN* Executive chef Francky Godinho (who has accrued over 50 medals over 15 years) brings true international flair and standards to this exquisite restaurant. Sit down at big wooden tables and savor European-influenced cuisine featuring local ingredients whenever possible (such as roasted lamb rump with locally-grown vegetables and feta cheese from a Hawke's Bay cheesery). Te Awa Winery, 2375 St. Hwy. 50. ☎ 06/879-7602. www.teawa.com. Main courses NZ$34–NZ$40. AE, MC, V. Lunch daily, dinner Fri–Sat. Map p. 221.

★★★ **Terroir** HAVELOCK NORTH *COUNTRY FRENCH* This lovely, rustic restaurant overlooking the Craggy Range lake and winery has a first-rate reputation and a string of awards to prove it. Hawke's Bay lamb served three ways is a popular menu choice, along with ostrich and the delectable chocolate soufflé. Craggy Range Winery, 253 Waimarama Rd. ☎ 06/873-7126. www.craggyrange.com. Main courses NZ$28–NZ$38. MC, V. Lunch daily, dinner Mon–Sat. Map p. 221.

★ **Ujazi** NAPIER *CAFE* A colorful, funky environment with friendly service, good coffee, outstanding cabinet food, and diverse salad choices. 28 Tennyson St. ☎ 06/835-1490. Main courses NZ$12–NZ$26. MC, V. Breakfast and lunch daily. Map p. 221.

★★ **Vidal** HASTINGS *EUROPEAN* This iconic, top-rated winery restaurant is always worth the pilgrimage—especially when roast poussin, duck breast, or wild pork are waiting. Save room for the coffee and chocolate-layered torte with mochaccino ice cream, Kahlúa anglaise, and coffee crisp. 913 St. Aubyn St. E. www.vidal.co.nz. NZ$33–NZ$40. AE, DC, MC, V. Lunch and dinner daily. Map p. 221.

Hawke's Bay & Eastland Fast Facts

Arriving
BY PLANE **Air New Zealand** (☎ 06/867-1608 in Gisborne and 06/833-5400 in Napier) provides daily service to and from most major New Zealand centers. BY BUS **Intercity** (☎ 09/623-1503) provides daily service between Gisborne, Napier, Auckland, Wellington, and Rotorua.

Emergencies & Medical Care
Always **dial 111** for all emergencies. Local hospitals include **Hawke's Bay Hospital,** Omahu Rd., Hastings (☎ 06/878-8109) and **Gisborne Hospital,** 421 Ormond Rd., Gisborne (☎ 06/869-0500). For non-emergency medical care, try **Napier Health Centre,** Wellesley Rd., Napier (☎ 06/878-8109). For dental care, contact **Clive Square Dental Associates,** 27 Clive Sq. E., Napier (☎ 06/835-8169) or **Grey Street Surgery,** 20 Grey St., Gisborne (☎ 06/867-4879).

Internet
Get online at **Cybers Internet Café,** 98 Dickens St., Napier (☎ 06/835-0125).

Visitor Information Centers
GISBORNE I-SITE VISITOR CENTRE 209 Grey St. (☎ 06/834-1911; www.gisbornenz.com). HASTINGS I-SITE VISITOR CENTRE Corner of Russell and Heretaunga sts. (☎ 06/873-0080; www.hastings.co.nz). NAPIER I-SITE VISITOR CENTRE Marine Parade (☎ 06/834-1911; www.visitus.co.nz). OPOTIKI I-SITE VISITOR CENTRE Corner of St. John and Elliott sts. (☎ 07/315-3031; www.odc.govt.nz).

8

Taranaki & Whanganui

My Favorite Moments

These western North Island provinces are two of the greenest places in the country. Taranaki is dominated by iconic Mount Taranaki, a perfect Fuji-like dome that springs out of fertile dairy pastures and offers beautiful native bush walks, lush gardens, and adventure opportunities. Its beaches are a huge hit with surfers and the main city, New Plymouth (pop. 73,000), is prosperous and energetic. The biggest draw to Whanganui is its moody river—the longest navigable waterway in the country.

> PREVIOUS PAGE *Mount Taranaki rises above grass that is always greener.* THIS PAGE *The moody Whanganui River introduces you to some of the North Island's most remote areas.*

❶ **Taking the Surf Highway from Hawera to New Plymouth.** This back road gives you a peek into small-town New Zealand, weaving through tiny coastal settlements from Hawera in the south to New Plymouth in the north. See p. 242.

❷ **Watching Len Lye's *Wind Wand* sway in the breeze.** The late Len Lye, a world-renowned kinetic artist, is one of New Zealand's most

famous creative exports. I always spend some time watching Lye's captivating *Wind Wand* swaying in the wind outside Puke Ariki. See p. 236, ❸.

❸ **Cruising up the Whanganui River.** You haven't really experienced the little river city of Whanganui until you've taken to the water. The *Waimarie* paddle steamer will take you 13km (8 miles) upriver to Upokongaro and

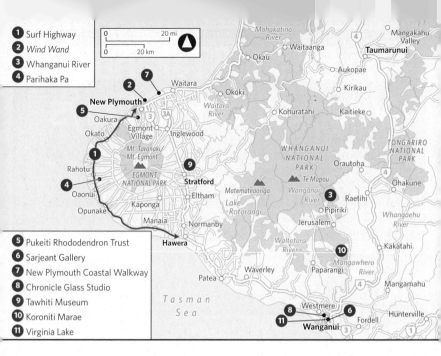

you'll hear stories about the history and significance of the river along the way. It's the best option if you're short of time. See p. 238.

4 Contemplating pacifist actions at Parihaka Pa. In 1881, Parihaka was the scene of an appalling breach of civil and human rights when 1,500 armed militia invaded. The people stood fast in non-violent protest and the event is now celebrated annually with the colorful Parihaka Peace Festival. See p. 244, 8.

5 Admiring the scented beauties at Pukeiti Rhododendron Trust. This jewel in the Taranaki gardening crown is a world-class showcase of rhododendrons and azaleas set against centuries-old rainforest. See p. 249.

6 Checking out the latest exhibitions at Whanganui's Sarjeant Gallery. This is one of the finest provincial art galleries in New Zealand—the architecture alone is worth the visit, as are the thought-provoking works by leading contemporary New Zealand artists. See p. 232, 2.

7 Walking the New Plymouth Coastal Walkway. This terrific boardwalk stretches over 7km (4⅓ miles) along the New Plymouth coastline, taking you past world-class surf breaks, fabulous family beaches, art works, and residential suburbs. See p. 237, 17.

8 Watching glass artists at Whanganui's Chronicle Glass Studio. Come to this creative collective hangout for beautiful handcrafted glass art and at the same time, watch the glass blowers at work. See p. 234, 4.

9 Reviving childhood wonder at Stratford's amazing Tawhiti Museum. You won't believe your eyes when you walk into Nigel Ogle's masterpiece. His incredibly realistic scale-model and life-size figures are arranged in fascinating displays that depict Taranaki's rich history. Don't miss it. See p. 236, 10.

10 Visiting Koroniti Marae. This is one Maori marae you can enter, and a visit to this serene little settlement above the Whanganui River is well worth your time. See p. 240, 8.

11 Watching the fountain at Whanganui's Virginia Lake. I used to live just across the road from Virginia Lake and enjoyed many a wander around its leafy perimeter. Arrive early evening for a picnic and stay on until dusk to watch the fountain go through its colorful paces. See p. 235, 9.

The Best of Taranaki & Whanganui in 3 Days

This itinerary assumes you are driving north from Whanganui but it's just as easily adapted to a start from New Plymouth. I've kept it to the basics but you might want to linger in some places or explore the many small towns you'll pass along the way more fully. It's an easy, quiet slice of the North Island characterized by fertile farmlands, sandy beaches, Maori communities, and, for the most part, good roads.

> Take the pedestrian tunnel and historic elevator from Victoria Avenue to reach the base of Whanganui's Durie Hill Tower.

START Whanganui is 164km (102 miles) south east of New Plymouth and 193km (120 miles) north of Wellington. Queens Park is in the middle of the town center off Victoria St. **TRIP LENGTH** 400km (249 miles).

1 ★★ kids **Whanganui Regional Museum.** This museum gives a terrific overview of the Whanganui River, the Whanganui National Park, and the significance of both throughout history. You'll see some rare Maori artifacts and a handsome 23-meter (75-ft.) war canoe that is still embedded with bullets from 1860s battles. *Te Puna Whakaari–Voices from Whanganui River* is a fascinating film that will give you an insight into river life. Kids will love the beautiful Bug Room. ⏱ At least 1 hr. Watt St., Queens Park. ☎ 06/349-1110. www.wanganui-museum.org.nz. Admission NZ$10 adults, free for kids 15 and under. Daily 10am–4:30pm.

2 ★★★ kids **Sarjeant Gallery.** With its prominent location, its striking neoclassical architecture, a 13-meter (43-ft). glass dome,

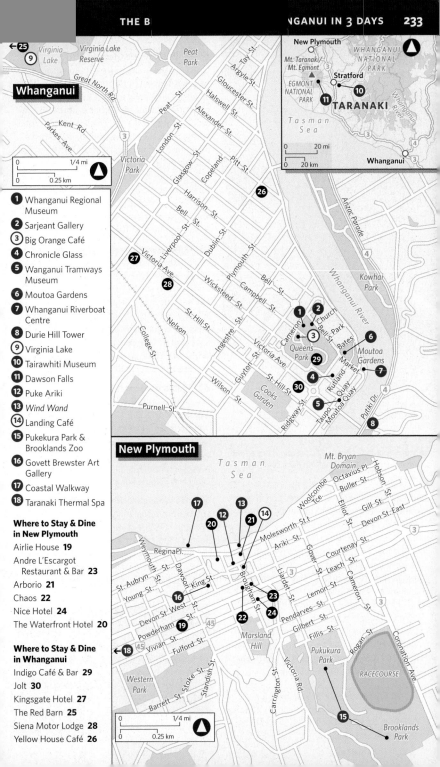

Whanganui

1 Whanganui Regional Museum
2 Sarjeant Gallery
3 Big Orange Café
4 Chronicle Glass
5 Wanganui Tramways Museum
6 Moutoa Gardens
7 Whanganui Riverboat Centre
8 Durie Hill Tower
9 Virginia Lake
10 Tairawhiti Museum
11 Dawson Falls
12 Puke Ariki
13 *Wind Wand*
14 Landing Café
15 Pukekura Park & Brooklands Zoo
16 Govett Brewster Art Gallery
17 Coastal Walkway
18 Taranaki Thermal Spa

Where to Stay & Dine in New Plymouth

Airlie House **19**
Andre L'Escargot Restaurant & Bar **23**
Arborio **21**
Chaos **22**
Nice Hotel **24**
The Waterfront Hotel **20**

Where to Stay & Dine in Whanganui

Indigo Café & Bar **29**
Jolt **30**
Kingsgate Hotel **27**
The Red Barn **25**
Siena Motor Lodge **28**
Yellow House Café **26**

> Whanganui's Chronicle Glass studio is one of my favorite places—bursting with heat, color, and action.

superb natural light, and a collection of over 6,000 artworks ranging from 16th-century European paintings to contemporary New Zealand works, it's easy to see why the Sarjeant is highly regarded. Numbered among the New Zealand greats are works by Charles Goldie, Gottfried Lindauer, Petrus van der Velden, Colin McCahon, and Ralph Hotere. It also has a wonderful collection of New Zealand photography including works by my personal favorites Lawrence Aberhart, Ans Westra, and Anne Noble. ⏱ 1 hr. Queens Park. ☎ 06/349-0506. www.sarjeant.org.nz. Free admission. Daily 10:30am–4:30pm.

③ 🍽 **Big Orange Café.** Stop here for a tasty, quick snack on the run. **31 Victoria St. ☎ 06/348-4449. NZ$10–NZ$12 for coffee and a sandwich.**

④ ★★ kids **Chronicle Glass.** In 2005, a collective of Whanganui glass artists colonized a 1912 print house used by the local newspaper (*Wanganui Chronicle*) and today it's a thriving creative enterprise. Watch molten glass ooze and curl around a steel rod as it's shaped into a beautiful glass object, then browse finished works in a beautiful mezzanine gallery. During the city's Festival of Glass (www.wanganuiglass.co.nz) in September, the main street comes alive with glass artists, workshops, and hot glass displays. ⏱ 30 min. 2 Rutland St. ☎ 06/347-1921. www. chronicleglass.co.nz. Free admission. Mon–Fri 9am–5pm, Sat–Sun 10am–3pm.

⑤ kids **Wanganui Tramways Museum.** While you're down in the historic riverfront area, check out the 1912 Boon tram, which is being restored in a shed by the riverbank. When the city's trams first started running in 1912, it was the first provincial tramway system in New Zealand. It continued until 1950 when buses took over. ⏱ 30 min. Red Shed, Taupo Quay. ☎ 06/345-7034. www.tramwayswanganui.org. nz. Free admission. Mon–Sat 9am–5pm.

⑥ **Moutoa Gardens (Pakaitore).** Once the site of a Maori fishing *pa* (settlement), this small park on a bend in the river is set with mature trees and war memorials. It was the scene of the 1995 Maori protest against land ownership issues and now provides a focus for Maori celebrations. ⏱ 15min. Corner or Taupo Quay and Somme Parade.

⑦ ★ kids **Whanganui Riverboat Centre.** When you see New Zealand's last paddle steamer, *Waimarie* (1890), gliding upriver, it's hard to believe that it spent 41 years submerged in the river after it sank in 1952. Salvaged in 1993, it has been painstakingly restored —a labor of love detailed in the museum's exhibits—and

Whanganui or Wanganui?

You'll notice the city's name spelled two ways: Whanganui and Wanganui. There's a long history of disagreement over the difference between Pakeha and Maori spelling and pronunciation. All government organizations use the name Whanganui (in Maori, *whanga* = bay, *nui* = big) but either spelling is considered acceptable.

> *Have an early evening picnic at Virginia Lake and wait for the Higginbottom Fountain to light up the night.*

now you can travel 13km (8 miles) upstream on it to Upokorongo. The journey is a slow one but it's a lovely way to end the afternoon. There's a good commentary about the boat and the river's history. You can also enjoy old-fashioned tea and scones as you go. Get a feel for the old days by visiting the engine room and volunteering as a coal-fire stoker. ⏱ 2 hr. 1A Taupo Quay. ☎ 06/347-1863. www.river boats.co.nz. Admission NZ$45 adults, NZ$15 kids 5–15, NZ$105 family. Museum Mon–Sat 9am–4pm, Sun and public holidays 10am–4pm; cruises Oct 21–May 1, daily 2pm.

Spend the night in Whanganui (see p. 250).

8 ★ kids **Durie Hill Tower.** This gigantic memorial to local soldiers killed during WWI overlooks the city from the top of Durie Hill. If you climb the narrow, spiral, tower stairway, you'll get wonderful views of Mount Taranaki and possibly Mount Ruapehu in Tongariro National Park. Park your car near the pedestrian tunnel at the bottom of Victoria Ave. The tunnel takes you 205m (673 ft.) underground to the historic elevator (1919), which rises 66m (217 ft.) through the hill to the base of the tower. Alternatively, you can walk up the 191 steps of the adjacent walkway to the base

of the tower. ⏱ 1 hr. Opposite the Wanganui City Bridge at the bottom of Victoria Ave.

Travel back through the city on Victoria Ave., cross the railway line, and turn right onto Great North Rd. At the top of the hill on your right, you'll find the park surrounding Virginia Lake.

9 🐦 kids **Virginia Lake.** This is the perfect place for last snacks, toilet stops, and a 25-minute woodland walk around the lake before you leave town for Taranaki. There are pretty formal gardens filled with flowering annuals, plant displays in the Winter Gardens, and birds swooping through the open-flight aviary. The Higginbottom fountain always puts on a good show, especially at night when it's illuminated with changing colored lights.

Turn right on Great North Rd., which now becomes St. Hwy. 3. Travel about 90km (56 miles) to Hawera. The drive should be about 1 hr. 15 min. As you come into Hawera, turn right into Princes St. and travel 4km (2½ miles) straight ahead onto Tawhiti Rd., then turn right on Ohangai Rd.

⑩ ★★★ kids Tairawhiti Museum. This extraordinary museum is the work of Nigel Ogle, a former school art teacher, and his wife, Teresa. You'll be amazed at the accuracy and life-like qualities of the scale models and life-size exhibits that depict Taranaki's history. The life-size figures are all created from moulds cast from real Taranaki people and are designed and built on the premises. You can see inside the Nigel's working studio as part of your visit. ⏱1 hr. 401 Ohangai Rd., Hawera. ☎0800/921-921 or 06/278-6837. www.tairawhitimuseum.co.nz. Admission NZ$12 adults, NZ$5 kids 5–15. Dec 26–Jan 31, daily 10am–4pm; June–Aug, Sun 10am–4pm; Sept–Dec 24 Fri–Mon 10am–4pm.

From the museum travel west along Ohangai Rd. to rejoin St. Hwy. 3. Continue on to Eltham (about 20km/12 miles). Turn left on Eltham Rd. and drive about 12km (7½ miles) to the town of Kaponga. Turn right into Manaia Rd., which leads you into Egmont National Park, and travel about another 15km (9⅓ miles), which takes about 50 min. on this narrow, winding road. Follow signs to Dawson Falls.

⑪ ★★ kids Dawson Falls. The 20-minute walk from the car park to the 17m (56-ft.) Dawson Falls is the perfect introduction to the beauty of Mount Taranaki and Egmont National Park. The Dawson Falls Visitor Centre (☎027/

443-0248) has information about the history of the mountain and its flora and fauna. ⏱1 hr. Egmont National Park; Manaia Rd.

Leave the falls on Manaia Rd. Turn left on Opunake Rd. and travel to the town of Stratford to rejoin St. Hwy. 3. At Inglewood veer left on St. Hwy. 3 and continue to New Plymouth, where you'll spend the night (see p. 250 for hotel recommendations). The 50km (31-mile) drive is about an hour.

⑫ ★★★ kids Puke Ariki. Begin day 3 at this impressive complex that houses a museum, library, and the i-SITE Visitor Centre. The museum showcases a vast repository of Taranaki history. Make sure you check out *Taranaki Life*, which details turbulent Maori land wars, pioneer history, and current life in this lush, green province. ⏱1 hr. 1 Ariki St. ☎06/758-4544. www.pukeariki.com. Free admission. Mon–Fri 9am–6pm, Sat–Sun 9am–5pm.

⑬ ★★ kids Wind Wand. World-renowned New Zealand-born kinetic artist Len Lye (who spent most of his life in New York) died in 1980 but is still an active cultural force. Born in Christchurch in 1901, Lye moved to New York in 1944, where he established himself as an innovative filmmaker and sculptor. The Len Lye Foundation, established shortly before his death, houses his archives, sculptures,

> *Pack a picnic and walk scenic native forest tracks to the 16-meter, twin-streamed Dawson Falls.*

paintings, textiles, and photography at the Govett-Brewster Art Gallery (**16**). The foundation also develops reconstructions of his works—*Wind Wand* is one of those. It's a thin red fiberglass tube 45m (148 ft.) high that can bend at least 20m (66 ft.). At night the light at the top glows soft red. ⏲ 15 min. Foreshore, Molesworth St.

---

⑭ ☕ **Landing Café.** Grab a quick cup of coffee or a delicious Kapiti ice cream. Corner of Ariki and Brougham sts., across from Puke Ariki. ☎ 06/769-9121. NZ$10–$15.

15 ★★ kids **Pukekura Park and Brooklands Zoo.** This is a terrific stop if you're traveling with children. Enjoy three playgrounds and visit the small collection of animals, including a cute farmyard and a free-flight bird aviary. The entire area of Pukekura Park (52 hectares/128 acres) has something for everyone, from lily ponds and waterfalls to a lush fernery (see "Taranaki's Parks & Gardens," p. 249) and a magnificent lighted fountain. If you're in town between mid-December and early February, try to visit the park at night to see the stunning TSB Bank Festival of Lights (www.festivaloflights.co.nz). ⏲ 2 hr. Main entrances off Rogan St., Fillis St., Victoria Rd., and Brooklands Rd. ☎ 06/759-6060. www.newplymouthnz.com. Free admission. Park daily dawn to dusk; fernery and display houses daily 8:30am–4pm; Brooklands Zoo daily 9am–5pm.

16 ★★★ kids **Govett-Brewster Art Gallery.** Established in 1970, this is the one of the most exciting contemporary art spaces in the country, known for its innovative exhibition program and its willingness to feature experimental artists and new media. It is also home to the collection and archive of New Zealand filmmaker and kinetic artist, Len Lye (1901–1980). The gallery has a small but well-stocked design store too. ⏲ 1 hr. Queen St. ☎ 06/759-6060. www.govettbrewster.com. Free admission. Daily 10am–5pm.

17 ★★★ kids **Coastal Walkway.** This beautiful boardwalk runs 7km (4⅓ miles) along the city's waterfront, from the mouth of the Waiwhakaiho River in the east to Port Taranaki in the west. It leads you past pounding surf,

> *New Plymouth's Govett-Brewster Art Gallery is home to a large collection of kinetic works by the late Len Lye.*

beaches, suburban homes, and city buildings. The easiest place to start is opposite Puke Ariki. ⏲ 1 hr. Park in the Molesworth St. car park, opposite Puke Ariki.

18 ★ kids **Taranaki Thermal Spa.** End your day with a relaxing soak in mineral waters that were discovered in 1909 when the Bonithon Freehold Petroleum Company drilled a 940m (3,084-ft.) hole in search of oil. What they found instead was hot mineral water. The first baths were built in 1914 and today the alkaline waters are sought out for their curative powers. ⏲ At least 1 hr. 8 Bonithon Ave. ☎ 06/759-1666 or 06/759-1642. Admission from NZ$6. Mon–Tues 9am–5pm, Wed–Fri 9am–9pm, Sat noon–9pm, Sun 2pm–8pm. Kids 10 and under welcome before 5:30pm only.

The Whanganui River Journey

The Whanganui River Road gives partial access to one of the last wilderness areas of the North Island—a vast, bush-clad tract that is both awe-inspiring and somehow melancholy and forbidding. To early Maori the region was an important food source and the river was believed to be home to powerful *taniwha* or water monsters. The narrow, winding road took 30 years to complete and is one-way in some places so drive carefully and take your time. You can drive to Pipiriki and back comfortably in a day—or do the full (195km/121-mile) loop back to Whanganui via Raetihi and the scenic Parapara Highway. I've included an overnight stop so you can delve further into the remote reaches of the river and Whanganui National Park.

> *The Whanganui River curls through the city like a broad, brown, moody snake.*

START Whanganui is 164km (102 miles) southeast of New Plymouth and 193km (120 miles) north of Wellington. The i-SITE center is on Taupo Quay, near Drews Ave. **TRIP LENGTH** 76km (47 miles) and 2 days.

❶ Whanganui i-SITE Visitor Centre. Start here to look at a model of the region and get a feel for where you're headed. They have free Wi-Fi and have 2 computers with Internet access you can use free for up to 30 minutes. Make sure you also pick up their excellent brochure, *Whanganui River Road & The Scenic Parapara Highway*, which gives you a brief introduction

to the many sites along the journey. It's also important to have a full tank of gas and some food for a picnic along the way. 31 Taupo Quay, Whanganui. ☎ 0800/926-426 or 06/349-0508. www.wanganui.com. January Mon–Fri 8:30am–6pm, Sat–Sun 9am–4pm; Feb–Dec Mon–Fri 8:30am–5pm, Sat–Sun 9am–4pm.

To head upriver, get onto Dublin St., cross the Dublin Street Bridge, and turn left into Anzac Parade. This becomes Riverbank Rd./ St. Hwy. 4 as it leaves town. Travel 4km (2½ miles) upriver to the signposted location of the Waitaha Pa Site.

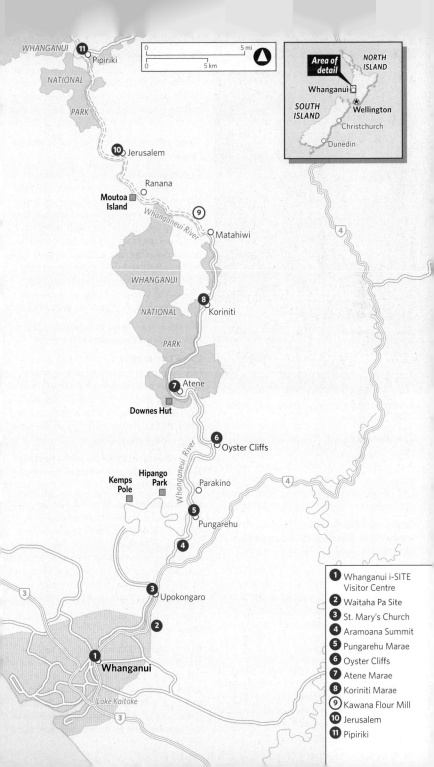

WHANGANUI
NATIONAL
PARK

11 Pipiriki

0 ——————— 5 mi
0 ——————— 5 km

Area of detail
NORTH ISLAND
Whanganui
Wellington
SOUTH ISLAND
Christchurch
Dunedin

10 Jerusalem

Ranana
Moutoa Island

Whanganui River

9
Matahiwi

4

WHANGANUI
NATIONAL
PARK

8 Koriniti

7 Atene
Downes Hut

Whanganui River

6 Oyster Cliffs

Kemps Pole **Hipango Park**
Parakino
4
5 Pungarehu

4

3 Upokongaro

2

3

1 **Whanganui**

Lake Kaitoke

3

1 Whanganui i-SITE Visitor Centre
2 Waitaha Pa Site
3 St. Mary's Church
4 Aramoana Summit
5 Pungarehu Marae
6 Oyster Cliffs
7 Atene Marae
8 Koriniti Marae
9 Kawana Flour Mill
10 Jerusalem
11 Pipiriki

> Native tree ferns, or ponga, line the banks of the Whanganui River.

2 ★ **Waitaha Pa Site.** This ancient *pa* site is believed to be around 200 years old. It was once heavily fortified and would have had an excellent strategic viewpoint of the river below. You can take a quick walk to the top of the site for great views over the river. ⏱ 15 min.

Continue on Riverbank Rd./St. Hwy. 4 for another 7km (4⅓ miles) to the small town of Upokongaro.

3 **St. Mary's Church.** Built in 1877, this cute little church in the settlement of Upokongaro is the oldest church in Whanganui still on its original site. It was consecrated in 1879 and is well known for its unusual three-sided spire. ⏱ 15 min. Open weekends when the Waimarie steamer docks at the landing.

When you reach a fork in the road 2.5km (1½ miles) farther on, veer left onto Whanganui River Rd. There's an information board here if you want to stop for a quick read about the sights ahead. Then proceed another 3.7km (2⅓ miles) to the summit.

4 ★★ **Aramoana Summit.** When you reach the top of the hill, pull over onto the wide parking area and get out your camera. There are terrific views of the Whanganui River looking upstream from here. On a clear day, you might see all the way to Mount Ruapehu. ⏱ 15 min.

About 2.6km (1⅗ miles) on, you'll come to Pungarehu Marae.

5 **Pungarehu Marae.** This is the take-off point of one of the jet-boat operators on the river and also the site of Pungarehu Marae, which is dominated by the restored *wharenui* (meeting house), Maranganui II, which can be seen from the road. Another 2.1km (1⅓ miles) farther down the road is Parikino Pa, the sister marae to Pungarehu. Both are home to the Ngati Tuera and Ngati Hinearo *hapu* (sub-tribes). You should not enter either marae without permission. ⏱ 20 min. ☎ 06/342-5871.

From Parikino Marae, travel another 5.1km (3¼ miles) to the Oyster Cliffs turnoff.

6 ★★ **Oyster Cliffs.** It can be difficult to stop here because of the limited parking space, but if you glance at the cliffs on your right, you'll see they're thickly embedded with seashells—proof that this whole area was once a seabed. If you do stop, please don't remove the fossilized oyster shells. ⏱ 5 min.

Drive on another 7km (4⅓ miles) keeping an eye out for the yellow marae sign on your right, under the trees.

7 ★★ **Atene Marae.** From this point on you'll find many places with Maori versions of the names of some of the great cities in the world, Atene or Athens is one of them. There's a cute little marae on the brow of the hill just above the road. Maori legend has it that the stretch of water beyond Atene was home to fair-haired fairy Maori known as Children of the Night. ⏱ 5 min.

Travel another 11km (6¾ miles) to Koroniti Marae.

8 ★★★ **Koriniti Marae.** This is my favorite marae in the area and it's one you can visit—just be sure to ask permission from any locals you might see, to make sure there are no marae gatherings or *tangi* (funerals) taking place. Turn left off Whanganui River Road at the large sign and you'll find the marae at the

> *Turn off Whanganui River Road to discover the beautiful trio of Maori meeting houses at Koroniti Marae.*

end of the road. Named after Corinth, the little settlement includes a cute church built by Maori in 1920 and the special little Hikurangi Museum, which sits between the 19th-century meeting houses, Waiherehere and Poutama. The carvings are worth the sidetrack alone. ⏱ 40 min. ☎ 06/342-8198. www.koriniti.com. Admission free; donations appreciated.

Drive another 9.2km (5¾ miles) to Kawana Flour Mill.

⑨ 🏭 **Kawana Flour Mill.** Break your journey here with a picnic beside this old water-powered mill complete with its original water wheel. Built in 1854 to grind wheat grown by local Maori farmers, it stopped operating in 1913. It was restored in 1980 by the New Zealand Historic Places Trust and now sits beside the old miller's cottage.

Continue for another 9.5km (6 miles) to the village of Jerusalem.

⑩ ★★★ **Jerusalem.** Also known as Hiruharama, Jerusalem has a colorful history. It is dominated by the Catholic mission and convent (established in 1883) and is most famous for a commune founded here in the 1970s by New Zealand poet James K. Baxter. ⏱ 30 min.

About 12km (7½ miles) on you'll come to the last stop on this tour.

⑪ ★ **Pipiriki.** Once a busy tourist resort, Pipiriki is now little more than a launching pad for your jet-boat or canoe ride upstream. Join **Bridge to Nowhere Lodge & Jetboat Tours** (☎ 0800/480-308 or 06/385-4622; www.bridgetonowheretours.co.nz) and travel 30km (19 miles) upstream through deep, fern-clad gorges to Mangapurua Landing. You'll then walk 40 minutes through native bush to the Bridge to Nowhere (1935), learning about the last (and failed) pioneering settlement of the New Zealand Government that was abandoned in 1942. At the end of your adventures, you'll be taken deep into the Whanganui National Park wilderness area to spend a night at Bridge to Nowhere Lodge (doubles around NZ$300 w/breakfast and dinner). The next morning you can jet-boat or canoe back to your vehicle at Pipiriki. The tour costs NZ$110 per person. Alternatively, you can travel the Whanagnui River Road with **Whanganui River Road Mail Tour** (☎ 06/347-7534; www.whanganuitours.co.nz;), delivering mail to remote farms and marae, and they'll return you to Whanganui after your stay at the lodge. This tour costs NZ$70. ⏱ 1½ days.

Driving the Surf Highway

The Surf Highway is named for its numerous world-class surf breaks. Almost every coastal side road leads to a beach and while they're not all patrolled, there's plenty of safe swimming. You'll pass through some of the greenest farmland in New Zealand along the way. I've mapped this State Highway 45 itinerary as an alternative to State Highway 3 to or from Whanganui, but you could also do a complete 190km (118 miles) loop, leaving New Plymouth on State Highway 45 and then traveling from Hawera back to New Plymouth on State Highway 3. You can do the drive in about one and a half hours but I suggest you pack a picnic and make a day of it. Take a copy of the brochure *Surf Highway 45*, available at i-SITE visitor centers.

> *It's worth taking a whole day to drive the Surf Highway, pulling off to admire the wild beaches loved by surfers worldwide.*

START Hawera is about 80km (50 miles) south of New Plymouth at the junction of St. Hwy. 3 and St. Hwy. 45. As you come into Hawera, turn right into Princes St. and travel 4km (2½ miles) straight ahead onto Tawhiti Rd., then turn right on Ohangai Rd. **TRIP LENGTH** 120km (75 miles) over 1 day.

1 ★★★ **kids Tawhiti Museum.** See p. 236, **10**.

From Hawera, take the Surf Highway (St. Hwy. 45) and drive about 5km (3 miles). Turn left on Ohawe Rd. and travel down to the beach, 7km (4⅓ miles) in total.

2 ★★ **kids Ohawe Beach.** Your biggest challenge today will be deciding which beach you want to spend the most time at. This is southern Taranaki's most popular choice—a good swimming and fishing spot at the mouth of the Waingongoro River. It has excellent surf breaks for expert surfers. ⏱ 45 min.

Drive back the way you came on Ohawe Rd. and rejoin St. Hwy. 45. Travel about 6km (3¾ miles) to the small town of Manaia.

3 **Manaia.** The first thing you'll see in this village will probably be Yarrow's Bakery, which

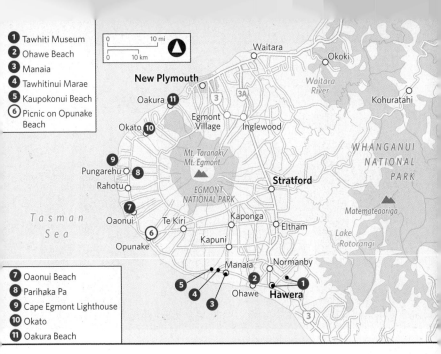

1 Tawhiti Museum
2 Ohawe Beach
3 Manaia
4 Tawhitinui Marae
5 Kaupokonui Beach
6 Picnic on Opunake Beach

7 Oaonui Beach
8 Parihaka Pa
9 Cape Egmont Lighthouse
10 Okato
11 Oakura Beach

is the largest privately owned bakery in New Zealand and has been operating since 1923. It is one of the largest employers in the area, hence the town's welcome sign, describing it as the Bread Capital. Manaia, named after former Maori chief of the area, Hukunui Manaia, was built on the site of an old Maori *pa* in 1880. The central band rotunda is a WWI memorial. ⏱ 30 min.

Continue on St. Hwy. 45 from Manaia a few kilometers until you see the buildings of Tawhitinui Marae behind a big hedge on your left. (There's plenty of room to pull over.)

4 Tawhitinui Marae. Take a quick look through the gate (do not enter) to see a good example of marae layout, with the large courtyard areas in front of the *wharenui* (meeting house), where people gather. The marae is home to the Ngati Mutunga *hapu* (sub-tribe) Aotea and Tai Hauauru. ⏱ 5 min.

Travel north on St. Hwy. 45 a few more kilometers, then turn left on Lower Glen Rd. Turn right on Kaupokonui Heads Rd. and continue on to Kaupokonui Beach.

5 ★ kids Kaupokonui Beach. In addition to being a rugged surfing spot, there is a long, broad sand beach here, where the Kaupokonui River meets the sea. There was a Maori settlement here once and many archaeological treasures have been found in the area. It's a popular fishing spot and in summer the camping ground fills up as families move in for their holidays. ⏱ 45 min.

Go back the way you came and rejoin St. Hwy. 45. Travel on to the town of Opunake. It's 28km (17 miles) and should take you about 30 min. to reach.

6 🍴 Picnic on Opunake Beach. Follow the signs from Opunake's main street down to the beach a few minutes away. This is a popular spot in summer. If you haven't brought food with you, pick up some fish and chips in the fish shop on the main street. While you're there, take a quick look at the murals painted on the town buildings.

From Opunake, drive 9km (5⅔ miles) to Oaonui. Turn left into Lower Kina Rd. to get to the beach.

> *The grave of Maori spiritual leader Te Whiti, at Parihaka Pa.*

7 ★★ kids **Oaonui Beach.** This beach is known for its big waves—wind and kite surfers come from all around the world to make the most of the perfect conditions. Oaonui is also home to the Maui Production Station and you can stop by the visitor center on Tai Road. (☎ 06/757-7071) to get an insight into this NZ$2-billion energy industry. It's the largest gas processing plant in New Zealand and can be visited Monday to Friday, 9am to 5pm. ⏱ 1 hr.

Return the way you came to rejoin St. Hwy. 45. Drive 13.5km (8⅓ miles) and turn right on Mid-Parihaka Rd. Travel 2km (1¼ miles) to the next stop.

8 ★★★ **Parihaka Pa.** In 1870, Parihaka was the largest Maori village in New Zealand. Then, in 1879, the government decided to open up nearby land to British settlement. The people of Parihaka protested and under the leadership of Te Whiti o Rongomai and Tohu Kakahi, they sought to resolve land issues without physical violence. Their pacifist movement took on legendary proportions when government troops invaded in 1881, arresting 1,500 men, women, and children. The rape, pillage, burning, and resettlement of 1,556 people without money, food, or shelter is still a blot on New Zealand's history. Every January the community hosts the multi-day Parihaka Peace Festival, which attracts top musicians from all over the country. You can drive into the small settlement and visit the large memorial to Te Whiti o Rongomai, which stands on the small hillock overlooking the village, but please respect the privacy of village residents. ⏱ 30 min.

Go back the way you came, turn right on St. Hwy. 45, then take the first left onto Cape Rd. Travel 5km (3 miles) to the Cape Egmont Lighthouse.

9 ★★ kids **Cape Egmont Lighthouse.** This much-travelled lighthouse was originally built in London in the mid-1800s and shipped to New Zealand in pieces. It was reconstructed on Mana Island, near Wellington, in 1865 and then dismantled in 1881 and carried in sections to Cape Egmont. It sits 33m (108 ft.) above sea level, marking the westernmost point of the Taranaki coastline, and can be seen for 19 nautical miles. ⏱ 30 min.

> *The Cape Egmont Lighthouse is almost as well travelled as the ships it protects from the rocky coastline.*

Rejoin St. Hwy. 45 and turn left. Follow the signs to Okato—it's about 20km (12 miles), which should take around 30 min.

⑩ ★ kids Okato. This little community has a population of under 600 people, but that swells every summer as holidaymakers come visiting. Most coastal roads along this stretch of the highway lead to beaches and the village itself has cafes, craft stores, and a gas station. ⏲ 15 min.

Continue on St. Hwy. 45 for another 12km (7½ miles) to:

⑪ ★★★ kids Oakura Beach. Given its proximity to New Plymouth (14km/8⅔ miles), Oakura is probably the city's most popular beach. The surf rolls in and there are plenty of safe areas for swimming, good nature walks, fishing, and good paddling spots for kids. Mellow out for the rest of the afternoon, soaking up the last of the sun, or perhaps take a leisurely short walk south on the sand to Ahu Ahu Beach. You could also get a copy of the *Oakura Arts Trail* brochure, available at visitor centers, and visit some of the local painters, jewelers, or sculptors. ⏲ At least 1 hr.

The last leg of your journey is a short 14km (8⅔-mile) drive into New Plymouth city.

> *Oakura Beach on the Surf Highway is a popular beach within an easy drive of New Plymouth.*

Taranaki & Whanganui Outdoor Adventures A to Z

Canoeing & Kayaking

One of the best ways of exploring any river is at water level and outfitters along the Whanganui River offer several options. I recommend **Whanganui Tours,** 12A Cambridge St., Whanganui (☎ 06/345-3475 or 027/201-2472; www.whanganuitours.co.nz), which charges NZ$75 per day for a 2-person canoe, NZ$40 per day for a single kayak, NZ$55 per person for road transport and NZ$120 per day for a group river guide. **Whanganui Kayak Hire,** 67A Anzac Parade, Whanganui (☎ 021/133-6938; www.kayakhire.co.nz), has assorted trip options starting at NZ$35 per kayak.

In New Plymouth you have the choice of sea, surf, or river kayaking. One of the nicest options is a paddle around the Sugar Loaf Islands, where you can get up close to a seal colony. You can do this 3-hour outing with **Canoe & Kayak Taranaki,** Unit 6, 631 Devon Rd., Waiwhakaiho, New Plymouth (☎ 06/769-5506; www.canoeandkayak.co.nz) for around NZ$75 per person. **Taranaki Outdoor Adventures,** based in the seaside village of Oakura on SH45 (☎ 0800/200-625; www.toa.co.nz) has expert guides to take you out on surf-and river-kayaking expeditions. Surf kayaking costs around NZ$55 per person and river kayaking NZ$65 per person.

Golf

Taranaki has 20 golf courses (www.golftaranaki.co.nz) but the best of the bunch is **New Plymouth Golf Club,** Ngamotu Links, Devon Rd., Bell Block, New Plymouth (☎ 06/755-1349; www.taranakigolf.co.nz). Their 18-hole, par 72 championship course is on magnificent park-like grounds and is consistently rated among New Zealand's top five courses. Green fees start at NZ$70 for non-affiliated players.

Helicopter Touring

I can think of no better way to experience the near-perfect peak of Mount Taranaki than to hover over its icy pinnacle in a helicopter.

> *The Bridge to Nowhere was built in 1936 to give access to remote lands opened up for returning WWI soldiers.*

Canoeing & Kayaking
Whanganui River **1**

Golf
New Plymouth Golf Club **2**

Helicopter Touring
Precision Helicopters **5**

Hiking
Matemateaonga Track **3**
Mangapurua Valley Walk **4**
New Plymouth Coastal Walkway **6**

Jet Boating
Bridge to Nowhere Tours **8**
Spirit of the River Jetboat Tours **7**

Mountain Biking
Wanganui Pro-Cycle Center **11**

Surfing
Oakura & the Surf Highway beaches **9**

Swimming
Todd Energy Aquatic Centre **10**

> Take a jet boat ride up Whanganui River to see parts of the National Park that are otherwise inaccessible.

I suggest you join **Precision Helicopters,** 450 Kaipikari Road Upper, Urenui (☎ 0800/246-359; www.precisionhelicopters.com). Its pilots will whisk you over the Stratford Plateau to Fathams Peak and, weather permitting, spiral you around the volcano to the summit. It's a 1-hour trip that is worth every penny of the NZ$300 per person you'll pay.

Hiking & Walking

Contact the **Department of Conservation,** Whanganui Area Office, 74 Ingestre St. (☎ 06/345-2402; www.doc.govt.nz), for information on a range of walks. In brief, the **Skyline Walk** requires 6 to 8 hours and affords views of Mount Ruapehu and Mount Taranaki. The **Matemateaonga Track** takes 3 to 4 days; the 3-day **Mangapurua Valley Walk** includes the Bridge to Nowhere. **Whanganui River Jet,** Wades Landing Outdoors, RD2, Owhango (☎ 07/895-5995; www.whanganui.co.nz), offers a complete charter service for trampers. It will drop you off and pick you up at prearranged times on the riverbanks. Costs vary depending on which track you choose. Bridge to Nowhere Jet-Boat Tours (see below) also offers a track transport service.

See also the **New Plymouth Coastal Walkway,** p. 237, **17.**

Jet-Boating

There are a number of operators in Whanganui, all offering something a little bit different. Since the river has special meaning to Maori, I recommend you try **Spirit of the River Jetboat Tours** (☎ 0800/538-8687; www.spiritoftheriverjet.co.nz), which is based about 20 minutes from Whanganui at 1018 Para Para Rd. (St. Hwy. 4), north of Upokongaro. **Bridge to Nowhere Tours** (☎ 0800/480-308; www.bridgetonowhere.co.nz) has a number of different options that can include a link to major hiking tracks (see above). Prices vary for all but generally start around NZ$75–NZ$100 per person for short tours.

Mountain Biking

Mountain bikers will be in their element in Whanganui given the access they have to Lismore Forest, 20km (12 miles) north of Whanganui on St. Hwy. 4 toward Raetihi. It is a working forest, however, and bikers should beware of trucks and logging action. There are numerous trails behind the car park bounded by Mangaone Road and Airstrip Road. These are well signposted. Close to Whanganui, bikers can also let loose on recreational bike trails at Hylton Park, 4km (2½ miles) from the city on Brunswick Road. **Wanganui Pro-Cycle Centre,** 199 Victoria Ave. (☎ 06/368-5459), rents bikes for around NZ$55–NZ$65 per day.

Surfing

If you've always had a hankering to get out in the surf, **Tara Wave Surf School,** Oakura Beach (☎ 06/752-7474), can make it happen. All gear is provided and the instructors have 35 years of surfing experience to help you get up on those boards.

Swimming

New Plymouth's excellent **Todd Energy Aquatic Centre,** Kawaroa Park (☎ 06/759-6060), has a large wave pool, lane swimming areas, ropes, play areas, hydroslides, outdoor pools, inflatables, and an air-conditioned fitness center.

Taranaki's Parks & Gardens

This is a region known for its perfect growing conditions: high sunshine, plentiful rain, rich, volcanic soils, and plenty of gardeners keen to get the most out of the land. The Taranaki Rhododendron and Garden Festival, held every year in early November, is a good time to see gardens not otherwise open to the public. There are more Gardens of National Significance in Taranaki than in any other region, so no matter when you visit, you'll find plenty to whet your green-fingered appetites.

Pukekura Park (p. 237, ⓯), a 52-hectare (128-acre) verdant core in the heart of New Plymouth (entrances off Rogan St., Fillis St., Victoria Rd., and Brooklands Rd.; free admission), features dense native bush walks, native and exotic tree collections, lush fern gullies, and formal flowerbeds. There's also a large lily pond and the pride and joy, the Fernery, which has around 2,340 New Zealand ferns covering 145 species. Pick up a map and explanatory pamphlet from the i-SITE Visitor Centre (p. 251).

Also in New Plymouth, **Te Kainga Marire,** 15 Spencer Place (☎ 06/758-8693; www.tekaingamarire.co.nz; admission NZ$10), is a Garden of National Significance and was one of the gardens to feature in the prestigious BBC documentary *Around the World in 80 Gardens.* You'll find everything here from forest plants to sub-alpine plants, ponds, grasses, walkways and dense ferns all set within rustic fences. It's open daily from September to April, 9am to 5pm.

The magnificent, 360-hectare (890-acre) ★★ **Pukeiti Rhododendron Trust,** 2290 Carrington Rd., New Plymouth (☎ 06/752-4141; www.pukeiti.org.nz), features over 20km (12 miles) of walking tracks winding through world-class collections of rhododendrons (which flower Oct–Nov) and azalea, along with thousands of beautiful specimen trees and shrubs. The garden is open daily September through March, 9am to 5pm, and April through August, 10am to 3pm. Adult admission costs NZ$12, while kids 15 and under are free.

Tupare, 487 Mangorei Rd., New Plymouth (☎ 0800/736-222; www.tupare.info), is one of the finest gardens in New Zealand. The 3.6-hectare (9-acre) garden spreads out from a gorgeous Chapman-Taylor-designed homestead overlooking the Waiwhakaiho River and includes ponds, walks, beautiful trees, glasshouses, an old orchard, glasshouses, and a cliff cascade. Admission is free and the grounds are open daily from 9am to 5pm.

About an hour's drive from New Plymouth, the 4-hectare (10-acre) **Hollard Gardens,** 1686 Upper Manaia Rd., Kaponga (☎ 0800/736-222; www.hollardgardens. info), grow over 500 varieties of rhododendrons, azaleas, and camellias. The property is at its best in October and November. The gardens are open daily from 9am to 5pm and admission is free.

Where to Stay & Dine

> *When you've finished exploring New Plymouth's Puke Ariki, enjoy a delicious meal at Arborio.*

New Plymouth

★ Airlie House CENTRAL CITY
This beautifully restored 115-year-old villa is tucked into an inner city garden and has roomy bedrooms full of character and charm with modern conveniences. 161 Powderham St. ☎ 06/757-8866. www.airliehouse.co.nz. 3 units. Doubles NZ$160. MC, V. Map p. 233.

★★ André L'Escargot Restaurant & Bar CENTRAL CITY *FRENCH* This elegant restaurant is an institution. Reliably excellent meals include such classics as filet mignon, duck confit, and venison rump. 37–43 Brougham St. ☎ 06/758-4812. www.andres.co.nz. Main courses NZ$35–NZ$42. AE, DC, MC, V. Lunch and dinner Mon–Sat. Map p. 233.

★★ kids Arborio CENTRAL CITY *MODERN NZ* Arborio is always my first port of call when I hit town. I love its bright, contemporary interior and the ocean views. There's a hint of pizzeria about it by day, although the menu is far from limited to pizza. Fresh fish is always a good bet. 1st floor, North Wing, Puke Ariki, 1 Ariki St. ☎ 06/758-4544. Main courses NZ$15–NZ$22. AE, MC, V. Breakfast, lunch, and dinner daily. Map p. 233.

★ kids Chaos CENTRAL CITY *CAFE*
This is another of my favorite New Plymouth spots, a terrific, laidback cafe that's also popular with locals. Everyone, from businessmen to ladies fresh from the gym, comes here for good coffee, friendly service, and excellent food that includes pies, quiche, soups, and salads. 36 Brougham St. ☎ 06/759-8080. Main courses NZ$10–NZ$16. AE, MC, V. Breakfast and lunch daily. Map p. 233.

★★★ Nice Hotel CENTRAL CITY
This small, luxurious boutique hotel delivers on style and character. Rooms have quality bedding, generous bathrooms, and lots of contemporary artwork. The large suite with its own lounge, fireplace, and grand piano is very good value. 71 Brougham St. ☎ 06/758-6423. www.nicehotel.co.nz. 7 units. Doubles NZ$255–NZ$310. AE, MC, V. Map p. 233.

★★ kids The Waterfront Hotel CENTRAL CITY
Smart, modern, uncluttered design and one of the best locations in town come together here. You'll get roomy bathrooms, modern kitchens, laundry facilities, and sea views. Connecting rooms are available. 1 Egmont St. ☎ 0508/843-928. www.waterfront.co.nz. 42 units. Doubles NZ$165–NZ$525. MC, V. Map p. 233.

Whanganui

★★ kids Indigo Café & Bar CENTRAL CITY *MODERN NZ* The doors are thrown open to the courtyard and museum views in summer; in the winter there's a roaring fire. The day menu favors light meals (salads, pasta, soup). Veal, lamb, pork, and salmon take the evening limelight. Majestic Square. ☎ 06/348-7459. www. indigocafe.co.nz. Main courses NZ$29–NZ$32 dinner. MC, V. Lunch Sun–Mon, breakfast, lunch, and dinner Wed–Sat. Map p. 233.

★ kids **Jolt** CENTRAL CITY *CAFE*
I like the laidback, friendly neighborhood mood at this small cafe. Sit back on red leather sofas or at tables and join the locals reading newspapers and chatting. Coffee and light lunches are the focus here. 19 Victoria St. ☎ 06/345-8840. Coffee and sandwich NZ$10–NZ$12. V. Breakfast and lunch daily. Map p. 233.

kids **Kingsgate Hotel** CENTRAL CITY
Two-bedroom family units with full kitchens and large standard rooms make this modest but comfortable hotel a good family choice. Kids can also enjoy a large outdoor pool. 379 Victoria Ave. ☎ 0800/808-228 or 06/349-0044. www.millenniumhotels.com. 61 units. Doubles NZ$145–NZ$275. AE, DC, MC, V. Map p. 233.

★★★ kids **The Red Barn** NORTH OF WHANGANUI
Set amid an olive grove, just off St. Hwy. 3 on the way to New Plymouth (a few minutes from Whanganui), this 3-bedroom, self-contained accommodation in a new, replica red barn is a charmer. Westmere Station Rd., RD1. ☎ 06/348-4979. www.havoccoffee.co.nz. 1 self-contained unit. Doubles NZ$190 w/breakfast. MC V. Map p. 233.

★ kids **Siena Motor Lodge** CENTRAL CITY
I often stay here because it's central, within walking distance of the main shops and restaurants and it's always meticulously clean and tidy. Service is friendly too and you'll get premium quality beds, CD/DVD players, and air-conditioned rooms. 335 Victoria Ave. ☎ 0800/888-802 or 06/345-9009; www. siena.co.nz. 10 units. Doubles NZ$125–NZ$155. DC, MC, V. Map p. 233.

★★ kids **Yellow House Café** DUBLIN STREET BRIDGE AREA *CAFE* You'll get a delicious daytime menu here—brilliant corn fritters and lovely cabinet food—and dinner three nights a week. It's the perfect place to stop for River Road snacks or a refreshing coffee on your way back into town. Corner of Pitt and Dublin sts. ☎ 06/345-0083. Main courses NZ$10–NZ$30. MC, V. Breakfast and lunch daily; dinner Thurs–Sun. Map p. 233.

Taranaki & Whanganui Fast Facts

Arriving
BY PLANE Whanganui Airport is 10 minutes (about 7km/4⅓ miles) southwest of the town center; New Plymouth Airport is 8km (5 miles) north of the city. Both are serviced daily by **Air New Zealand** (☎ 0800/737-000; www.airnz.co.nz). BY BUS **Intercity** (☎ 09/623-1503) and **Newmans** (☎ 09/623-1504) both provide service between Whanganui and New Plymouth, Auckland, National Park Village (a small town on the edge of Tongariro National Park), and Wellington.

Emergencies & Medical Care
Always **dial 111** in an emergency. Hospitals serving the area include **Whanganui Hospital,** 100 Heads Rd. (☎ **06/348-1300**), and **Taranaki Base Hospital,** corner of Tukupa and David streets, New Plymouth (☎ **06/753-6139**). Other options for medical care include **Phoenix Urgent Doctors,** 95 Vivian St., New Plymouth (☎ **06/759-4295**) and **Wanganui City Doctors' Clinic** (☎ **06/348-8333**).

Visitor Information Centers
WHANGANUI I-SITE VISITOR INFORMATION CENTRE 31 Taupo Quay (☎ 0800/926-426 or 06/349-0508; www.wanganui.com). NEW PLYMOUTH I-SITE VISITOR CENTRE Puke Ariki, 65 St. Aubyn St. (☎ 0800/639-759 or 06/759-6060; http://www.i-site.org.nz/taranaki).

9
Wellington

My Favorite Moments

Wellington has come of age. Once seen as a stuffy, bureaucrat-filled political capital, it has reinvented itself to become a compact entertainment and cultural Mecca, with a cosmopolitan vibrancy that you don't get in other New Zealand cities. Come here and savor a little sophistication.

> PREVIOUS PAGE *Parliament House and The Beehive sit in the center of the capital city, Wellington.* THIS PAGE *The Wellington Waterfront promenade is a great place for people-watching.*

❶ Walking along the Waterfront. Major redevelopment of the Waterfront in recent years has created a wonderful boulevard teeming with activity and interest. Harbor views, contemporary art and architecture, fun kids' activities, cafes, museums, parks—they're all there.

❷ Exploring Te Papa. This national museum is an exciting, dynamic storehouse of treasures and interactive activities that truly reinforces the fact that learning can be fun. See p. 256, ❶.

❸ Eating and drinking in Wairarapa vineyards. Big skies, wide, vineyard-filled valleys, olive groves, boutique hotels, vineyard cafes—they're all just an hour away from the big city. See p. 291, ❺.

❹ Browsing antiques stores in Greytown. Once a plain little country village, Greytown is now a super-hip retreat for Wellingtonians. Its quaint old buildings, fruit orchards, nearby vineyards, and cafes are a perfect foil for designer boutiques and antique stores. See p. 291, ❸.

❺ Check the latest shows at TheNewDowse. It's worth driving to Lower Hutt just to view some of New Zealand's best contemporary art and craft in this stylish gallery. See p. 269.

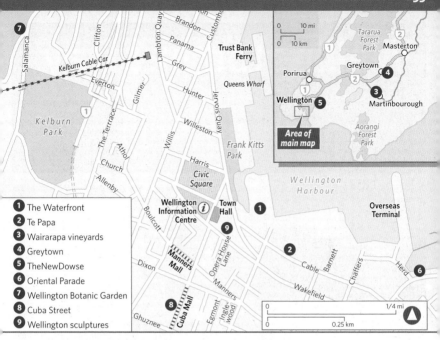

Map Legend

1. The Waterfront
2. Te Papa
3. Wairarapa vineyards
4. Greytown
5. TheNewDowse
6. Oriental Parade
7. Wellington Botanic Garden
8. Cuba Street
9. Wellington sculptures

6 People-watching on Oriental Parade.
I always think of this as one of the prettiest stretches in Wellington—old wooden houses, giant palm trees, bike paths, walkways, a pretty little beach—all looping around the harbor. Set up in a cafe and let the hours roll by.

7 Taking the cable car up to the Wellington Botanic Garden. On a fine day, this is one of the prettiest (and cheapest) thrills you can get in the capital and it's a quintessentially Wellington experience. See p. 258, 2.

8 Browsing Cuba Street shops and cafes. It's bohemia all the way in this part of town. Expect everything from tattoo parlors and street art to boutique design and fashion stores, plus loads of cafes and cheap eateries. See p. 275.

9 Discovering Wellington's inner city sculptures. I love roaming the inner city discovering the many sculptures permanently installed in the urban landscape. It's a brilliant initiative that gives Wellington an artistic edge. See "Art Smart," p. 270.

> Just an hour over the Rimutaka Hills from Wellington, a giant tablecloth of grapevines spreads out across the Wairarapa region.

Wellington in 1 Day

If you can only spare a day for the capital, the compact nature of the city is in your favor. Most of the major attractions are within the main business district and if you're a keen walker you'll get to see more of the cityscape as you wander between sights. So leave your car behind and enjoy the lively pedestrian activity.

> Wharf posts beside the Museum of New Zealand–Te Papa Tongarewa are popular diving and swimming spots in summer.

START Museum of New Zealand–Te Papa Tongarewa on Cable Street, which runs along the Waterfront.

① ★★★ kids **Museum of New Zealand–Te Papa Tongarewa.** This is essential viewing for anyone coming to New Zealand. Opened in 1998, it is one of the largest museums in the world and it's redefining the word *museum*. It combines interactive technology with world-class displays that tell the whole New Zealand story—the history, art, the people, and natural environment. You'll be entranced by advanced motion simulators that take you back in time to the explosive, volcanic formation of the prehistoric landscape. You'll squeal with fright

at the 3D animated squid movie and you'll be fascinated by the huge, preserved colossal squid that was caught in New Zealand waters. Go inside a traditionally carved Maori *wharenui* (meeting house); fossick in drawers in the kids' Discovery Centre; and play on The Wall, a fabulous interactive space that allows you to upload your holiday snaps to the Te Papa database and create works of art that merge with everyone else's. Go early to beat the crowds. ◷ At least 3 hr. Cable St., on the Waterfront. ☎ 04/381-7000; www.tepapa. govt.nz. Free admission; fees for some activities and short-term exhibitions. Fri–Wed 10am–6pm, Thurs 10am–9pm.

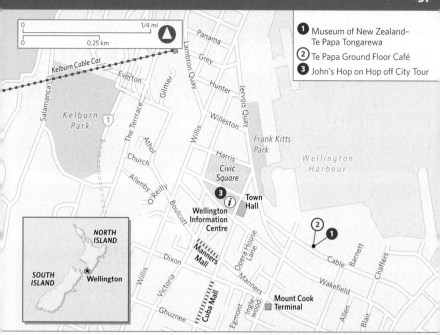

1 Museum of New Zealand–
Te Papa Tongarewa

2 Te Papa Ground Floor Café

3 John's Hop on Hop off City Tour

---

② 🔊 **kids Te Papa Ground Floor Café.** Stop in this big, bright, family-friendly place for a sandwich or a reviving snack. You may have to queue but there's heaps of choice so be patient; and in summer, you can eat outside in the amphitheater by *Bush City*, a concentrated planting of native trees and shrubs. Te Papa. ☎ 04/381-7000. Most items NZ$6–NZ$13.

Turn right as you come out of Te Papa and join the Waterfront walkway to the Civic Bridge Crossing and Civic Square. This walk will take you past some beautifully restored buildings and several major sculptures. Allow 30 min. for a leisurely walk with photo stops to the Wellington i-SITE Visitor Centre.

③ ★★ **kids John's Hop on Hop off City Tour.**
This is the most flexible of a number of different sightseeing tours you could take this afternoon. It leaves the visitor center on the hour every hour, visits 18 attractions, and allows you to get on and off the bus at any time. You can of course choose to stay on the bus (in which case the ride takes about 1½ hours) but you can also explore any of the following: Wellington Zoo (p. 264, **4**), Weta Cave (p. 265, **11**), Museum of Wellington City & Sea

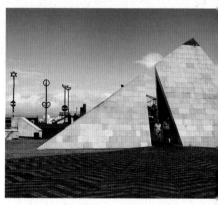

> *Wellington's Civic Square is home to several large sculptures by some of New Zealand's leading artists.*

(p. 265, **8**), Parliament Buildings (p. 261), Wellington Botanic Garden (p. 260, **6**), Wellington Cable Car (see p. 258, **2**), Carter Observatory (p. 260, **4**), and Te Papa (see above). For a full list of stops, see the website. Use your afternoon to visit the places that appeal to you most. ⏱ Half-day. www.hopon hopoff.co.nz. Admission NZ$40 adults, NZ$20 kids 14 and under. Daily on the hour every hour, 10am–2pm.

Wellington in 2 Days

This is a day for striding out a little and including some of Wellington's iconic outdoor attractions like the Wellington Botanic Garden, Carter Observatory, and ZEALANDIA, which will give you an insight to the natural side of the capital. If you're traveling with kids, it will be a good chance for them to enjoy some exploring and running around time.

> Jump on the Wellington Cable Car just off Lambton Quay and take a ride up to the Botanic Gardens and Carter Observatory.

START The intersection of Lambton Quay and Willis St. marks the division between Wellington's two main shopping streets.

1 ★ **Old Bank Shopping Arcade.** You can't miss this grand edifice—the former Bank of New Zealand—at the intersection of Wellington's two main shopping districts. Enter at street level off Lambton Quay and find **Smith the Grocer** (☎ 04/473-8591; www.smiththe grocer.co.nz), where you can pick up delicious picnic supplies for your lunch in the Botanic Garden. ⏱ 30 min.

Head down Lambton Quay to Cable Car Lane—easily spotted by the mini-cable car on top of the sign post.

2 ★★ kids **Wellington Cable Car.** You can't come to Wellington and not take this brilliant little 4½-minute trip, which climbs a 1 in 5 gradient up to the Botanic Garden. If it's a fine day you'll get marvelous views across the city

and harbor and it's by far the easiest way to access the gardens (p. 260, **6**) and Carter Observatory (p. 260, **4**). ⏱ 5 min. Round-trip fares NZ$5 adults, NZ$3 kids, NZ$14 families. Mon–Fri 7am–10pm, Sat 8:30am–10pm, Sun and holidays 9am–10pm. Car runs every 10 min.

3 ★★ kids **Wellington Cable Car Museum.** This small, award-winning museum pays homage to the residents of this hilly city and the cable cars they use to make their lives easier. You'll be able to see the antiquated machinery that was once used to haul cars up the cable car incline. Make sure you watch the 20-minute free movie about the 400 cable cars in private use around the city—I like the story about the man who built one because his dog could no longer manage the steps to their home. ⏱ 1 hr. Beside the upper Cable Car terminus. ☎ 04/ 475-3578. www.cablecarmuseum.co.nz. Free admission. Daily 9:30am–5:30pm summer, 9:30am–5pm winter.

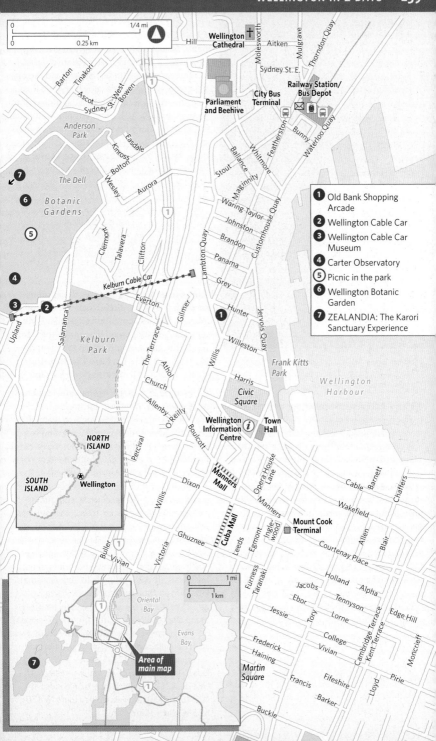

1 Old Bank Shopping Arcade
2 Wellington Cable Car
3 Wellington Cable Car Museum
4 Carter Observatory
5 Picnic in the park
6 Wellington Botanic Garden
7 ZEALANDIA: The Karori Sanctuary Experience

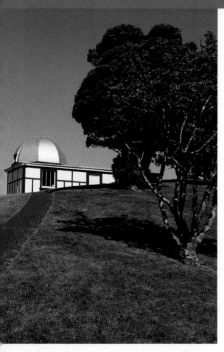

> *It's not every day you get the chance to explore black holes, so head to Carter Observatory for a state-of-the-art experience.*

4 ★★★ kids **Carter Observatory.** Thanks to a major redevelopment, New Zealand's longest-serving national observatory can now send you on a virtual tour through space in its new planetarium. The state-of-the-art, full-dome digital theater and interactive multi-media space experiences are a must-visit attraction. You'll see Southern Hemisphere skies at their starry best and learn about Matariki (Maori New Year), as well as Polynesian voyaging and celestial navigation. There are also heritage telescopes and a space-themed gift shop the kids will love. ⏱ 1½ hr. A 2-min. sign-posted walk from top of cable car line. ☎ 04/472-8167. www.carterobservatory.org. NZ$18 adults, NZ$8 kids 4–16, NZ$36–NZ$54 families. Daily 10am–5pm, late night star-gazing Sat until 9pm.

⑤ 🍴 **Picnic in the park.** Head to the Botanic Garden (see next stop) and spread out under a big tree—preferably with a harbor view. Spare a thought for all those homeowners carrying their shopping up steep paths.

6 ★ kids **Wellington Botanic Garden.** This verdant 25-hectare (62-acre) spread is a calm retreat with protected native bush, conifer varieties, seasonal floral displays, and the biggest show-off of all, the Lady Norwood Rose Garden, with 106 formal beds that flower from November to May. The orchids and water lilies in the Begonia House are always lovely—look out for the amazing giant water lily, *Victoria amazonica.* The Treehouse Visitor Centre is the information hub and there's a playground area for children. I recommend taking the Cable Car to get here, but if you drive, you'll find public parking next to the Lady Norwood Rose Garden ⏱ 1 hr. Access is via the cable car or the Centennial Entrance on Glenmore St., Thorndon. ☎ 04/499-1400. www.wellington.govt.nz. Free admission. Daily sunrise–sunset. The Treehouse is open Mon–Fri 9am–4pm. Bus: 12.

Take Glenmore St. west from the gardens through the traffic circle, then turn left on Waiapu Rd. It's about 4km (2½ miles) and about a 7-minute drive. If you took the Cable Car to the gardens and are on foot, you can take bus 3 or 21 to the Karori Tunnel stop then walk about 5 minutes down Waiapu Rd.

7 ★★★ kids **ZEALANDIA: The Karori Sanctuary Experience.** If you want to see our legendary tuatara reptiles you've come to the right place. They're in their natural habitat here and they recently bred successfully outdoors for the first time. Start at the new visitor center, which gives a detailed overview of New Zealand's geographic evolution and the conservation practices now in place to protect our most treasured flora and fauna. Interactive displays will capture kids' imaginations before you venture out into the world's first fully fenced urban wildlife sanctuary. You can wander alone but you'll learn more by taking a 1½-hour guided bush walk. The 2½-hour Night Tour is also a lot of fun and you may spot a kiwi foraging for food. Wear sensible shoes—several tracks are steep and require moderate fitness. ⏱ At least 2 hr. 31 Waiapu Rd., Karori. ☎ 04/920-9200; www.visitzealandia.com. Admission (exhibition and sanctuary) NZ$28–NZ$35 adults, NZ$14–NZ$18 kids 5–14, NZ$70–NZ$75 families; valley only NZ$18–NZ$23 adults, NZ$9–NZ$14 kids 5–14, NZ$45–NZ$50 families. Guided tours NZ$30–NZ$80. Daily 10am–5pm.

Wellington for Architecture Lovers

Like many New Zealand cities, Wellington faced its fair share of demolition and destruction in the name of progress but a number of old beauties remain. Most of the city's finest buildings date from the 1850s and many are made of wood. The suburb of Thorndon has several perfect examples. Here's a round-up of Wellington's greatest architectural hits.

New Zealand's ★★★ **Parliament Buildings**, on Molesworth Street (tour desk ☎ 04/817-9503; www.parliament.nz), are of three distinct architectural styles. The central Edwardian neo-classical Parliament House (1922) was designed by architects John Campbell and Claude Paton. The beautiful Victorian Gothic Parliamentary Library was designed by Thomas Turnbull and was built in two parts: the west wing in 1883 and the front section in 1899. (Peek into the highly embellished foyer.) The Executive Wing, nicknamed the Beehive, was designed by British architect Sir Basil Spence in 1964. Free tours are available daily.

★★★ **The Old Government Buildings,** 15 Lambton Quay, were designed by pioneer architect W.H. Clayton and built in 1876. This magnificent structure is the world's second-largest wooden building (after Todai-ji in Nara, Japan). You can look around the ground floor and the Cabinet Room on the first floor (Mon–Fri 9am–5pm).

Just a short walk down to the seafront, off Waterloo Quay, you'll find a number of interesting historic buildings, including warehouses, boatsheds, and the old **Bond Store** (1892), which now houses the Museum of Wellington City & Sea (p. 265, ❽). On the way, you'll pass by the bulk of ★★ **Wellington Railway Station,** designed by W. Gray Young. When it was completed in 1937, it was one of the largest buildings in New Zealand, using up 1.75 million bricks and 1,500 tons of decorative marble and granite.

★★★ **Old St Paul's,** 34 Mulgrave St. (☎ 04/473-6722; www.oldstpauls.co.nz), is an exquisite Gothic Revival church designed by English architect and cleric Reverend Frederick Thatcher and built in 1866. It boasts beautiful stained glass windows and an impressive native timber ceiling.

Tinakori Road is at the center of the suburb of Thorndon, tucked under Tinakori Hill and home to many of Wellington's loveliest old homes. From cute workers' cottages to larger, grander dwellings, it is one of the most photographed streets in Wellington—especially the "painted ladies" at numbers 296 to 306, built in 1906 and just one room wide.

Wellington with Kids

You don't have to be in the Museum of New Zealand–Te Papa Tongarewa long to know it's a real hit with children of all ages. They squeal, they run, they laugh; so of course it's where we'll kick of this 3-day itinerary. I've interspersed attraction visits with parks, playgrounds, or beaches so the kids can let off a bit of steam or just sit quietly after the more intense and stimulating learning environments.

> *Upload some of your own photos to Te Papa's interactive Wall and have them recorded for posterity in the museum archives.*

START Te Papa on Cable Street. **TRIP LENGTH** 3 days.

❶ ★★★ **Museum of New Zealand–Te Papa Tongarewa.** See p. 256, **❶**.

② 🍽 **Te Papa Ground Floor Café.** This is the best place to fill small tummies in a hurry. See p. 257, **②**.

❸ ★★★ **The Waterfront.** Let the kids loose along the Waterfront. There's plenty here to keep them amused for the rest of the day. Take your pick from the largest indoor real rock wall in the country at Ferg's Kayaks (see

❾, below); the playground and open green spaces of Frank Kitts Park; or pedal-boating on the lagoon at Wet & Wild (☎ 027/450-5515). Or stop by the Enormous Crocodile Company by the entrance to the overseas passenger terminal (☎ 04/298-6680) and get the whole family onto a Crocodile Quadricycle for a ride around the waterfront promenade. For more information, pick up the *Go the Distance* Waterfront brochure from the i-SITE Visitor Centre (p. 293). It has a fold-out map and details of all the Waterfront attractions. ⏱ 2 hr. www.wellingtonwaterfront.co.nz.

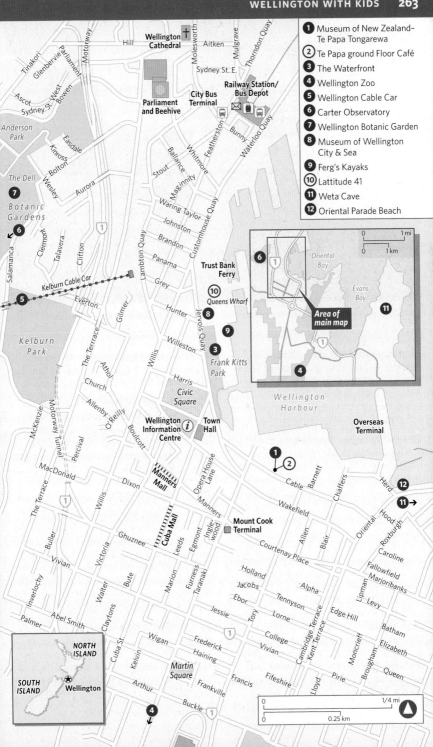

1 Museum of New Zealand–
   Te Papa Tongarewa

2 Te Papa ground Floor Café

3 The Waterfront

4 Wellington Zoo

5 Wellington Cable Car

6 Carter Observatory

7 Wellington Botanic Garden

8 Museum of Wellington
   City & Sea

9 Ferg's Kayaks

10 Lattitude 41

11 Weta Cave

12 Oriental Parade Beach

> *Our largest native parrot, the kea, is a real trickster. You can see him perform at Wellington Zoo.*

From the Waterfront on day 2, head south on Cable St. and turn right into Kent Terrace. Veer around the roundabout and turn left on Adelaide Rd. Veer left on Riddiford St., then left on Daniel St. The zoo is well signposted. Allow 10–15 min. driving time.

❹ ★★★ **Wellington Zoo.** Start the day off with some animal encounters. You can meet Tahi the one-legged kiwi every day in the Wild Theatre at 1:15pm and you can watch veterinary surgeons operating on animals and listen to them talk about wildlife care at the zoo's new animal hospital, The Nest. "Close Encounters" available for those over 6 include hand-feeding a red panda or climbing a ladder to feed a giraffe. Kids over 14 can meet the cheetahs and their keepers, or help with big cat training (lions and tigers) for medical purposes. There are over 500 animals to see but don't forget a visit to the Kiwi House (open daily 9:30–5pm). There are several food outlets at the zoo for lunch or bring a picnic to enjoy on the grounds. ⊕ 3 hr. 200 Daniell St., Newtown. ☎ 04/389-3692. www.wellingtonzoo.com. Admission NZ$19 adults, NZ$10 kids 3–16, NZ$37–NZ$55 families; NZ$76–NZ$125 for Close Encounters—bookings required. Daily 9:30am–5pm. Bus: 10 or 23 to Newton Park.

Drive or catch a bus back into the city and make your way to Cable Car Lane on Lambton Quay. Allow 30 min. driving time.

❺ ★★ **Wellington Cable Car.** This cute little red cable car has been transporting Wellington citizens and visitors from all over the world, for more years than most of us can remember. No trip to Wellington is complete without a ride on it—and don't forget to check out the free Cable Car Museum at the top. ⊕ 15 min. See p. 258, ❷.

❻ ★★★ **Carter Observatory.** Just 2 minutes from the top of the cable car line, you can take a virtual trip into space, explore black holes and the solar system, and learn how the early Maori negotiated the oceans with ancient celestial navigation techniques. Kids will remember these remarkable "journeys" long after the event. ⊕ 1½ hr. See p. 260, ❹.

❼ ★ **Wellington Botanic Garden.** When the kids are done seeing stars, take them down through the botanic gardens to the children's playground, where they can burn off the last of their energy before collapsing into bed later for a sound night's sleep. See p. 260, ❻.

Start day 3 on Queens Wharf.

8 ★★ **Museum of Wellington City & Sea.** You'll find this compact museum in the stunning, historic Bond Store (1892). It's full of great sound effects and audio-visual presentations. A 12-minute special effects show that introduces Maori creation legends and exhibits detailing 800 years of Wellington's maritime history, including the sinking of the inter-island ferry the *Wahine*, will be of particular interest to kids. ⏱ 1 hr. Queens Wharf, 8 min. north of Te Papa on Waterfront. ☎ 04/472-8904. www. museumofwellington.co.nz. Free admission. Daily 10am–5pm.

9 ★ **Ferg's Kayaks.** If you never got to Ferg's climbing wall on your first day, now would be a good time for the kids to test their skills on the 13m (43-ft.) wall. They have all the safety gear and the kids will love it. If you've already done that, inquire about kayaking or hire inline skates or one of their bikes and roll along the Waterfront. ⏱ 2 hr. Shed 6, Queens Wharf. ☎ 04/499-8898. www.fergskayaks.co.nz. Climbing NZ$16 adult, NZ$10 kids 14 and under, NZ$6 bouldering only, NZ$4 harness hire, NZ$4 shoe hire. Kayaking NZ$16–NZ$26 per hour. Inline skating NZ$8 , NZ$11 1 hr. Cycling NZ$22 1 hr. Daily summer 9am–8pm, winter Mon–Fri 10am–8pm, Sat–Sun 9am–6pm.

10 🍴 **Latitude 41.** Opposite Ferg's, this cafe has small snacks and light meals. Afterwards give the kids a gelato treat at Kaffee Eis, Boatshed 8, by the lagoon (☎ 04/472-9155). 19 Jervois Quay. ☎ 04/473-8776. NZ$10–NZ$16.

To reach the next stop, Weta Cave, you can take bus route 2 toward Miramar and get off at Camperdown Rd. If you've got your own car, drive around Oriental Parade, turn left at the intersection, and follow the signs past the airport turnoff to Miramar and Weta Cave. Allow 30 min. driving time by car.

11 ★★ **Weta Cave.** Long after the release of the trilogy *Lord of the Rings,* the mystique lingers on. That's why Weta Workshop, which created the Academy Award-winning special effects for the movies, set up Weta Cave. It's a cave-like mini-museum with close encounters with movie characters, props, and displays from Middle Earth and other well-known

> *Come face-to-face with characters from the* Lord of the Rings *trilogy at Weta Cave.*

movies like *King Kong* and *The Lion, the Witch, and the Wardrobe.* You'll also want to check out the concept store, where you can buy a range of pop culture and collectible items from around the world and watch free film screenings. ⏱ 2 hr. Corner of Camperdown Rd. and Weka St., Miramar. ☎ 04/380-9361. www.wetanz.com. Free admission. Daily 9am–5:30pm.

Retrace your route back to Oriental Parade.

12 ★★ **Oriental Parade Beach.** After all the movie fun, stop at the beach on your way back into town and build sand castles and swim. (Make sure you swim between the flags when the lifeguards are on duty over the summer holidays.) And let the kids make a wish in the Wellington Jaycee's wishing well, which is across the street opposite the beach, beside the toilets. Make sure you cross with them as this is a very busy road. ⏱ 2 hrs.

The Best Museums & Art Galleries

Wellington, more than any other New Zealand city, is immersed in the arts. It has a wealth of contemporary public sculptures easily discovered in the inner city area, a host of museums big and small, the best live theater in the country, excellent dealer galleries, and thought-provoking gallery collections and exhibitions. I've included a lot in this 2-day itinerary so you can make choices based on your own preferences. I've also clustered the attractions based on location and proximity to each other.

> *The large, sculptural pedestrian bridge from Civic Square to the Waterfront was designed by leading Maori artist Para Matchitt.*

START Te Papa, Cable St., on the Waterfront.

1 ★★★ kids **Museum of New Zealand–Te Papa Tongarewa.** The cultural starting point to any Wellington visit, Te Papa presents a wealth of history, culture, and art. ⏱ 3 hr. p. 256, **1**.

2 🍴 **Te Papa Level 4 Espresso.** Relax in soft armchairs and enjoy a snack before setting off on foot. Te Papa. ☎ 04/381-7000. NZ$10–NZ$15.

3 ★ kids **Waterfront walk.** As you turn right out of Te Papa's main doors, you'll be looking

directly at the sculpture *Mimetic Brotherhood,* by Peter Trevelyan, and the very lively and innovative **Circa Theatre,** (☎ 04/801-7992; www.circa.co.nz), housed in an historic building. Wander north along the waterfront to the lagoon to see Tanya Ashken's *Albatross,* installed by the Wellington Sculpture Trust in 1985-86, and the *Water Whirler,* a major work by world renowned New Zealand sculptor/film maker Len Lye (1901–1980). At the entrance to Queens Wharf, you'll find **The Academy Galleries** (☎ 04/499-8807; www.nzafa.com),

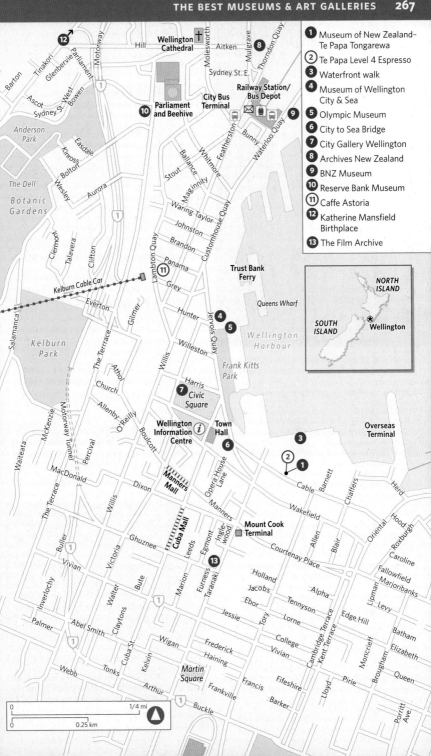

1 Museum of New Zealand–Te Papa Tongarewa
2 Te Papa Level 4 Espresso
3 Waterfront walk
4 Museum of Wellington City & Sea
5 Olympic Museum
6 City to Sea Bridge
7 City Gallery Wellington
8 Archives New Zealand
9 BNZ Museum
10 Reserve Bank Museum
11 Caffe Astoria
12 Katherine Mansfield Birthplace
13 The Film Archive

NORTH ISLAND
SOUTH ISLAND
Wellington

> You'll feel like you've stepped into a Victorian novel when you visit the Katherine Mansfield Birthplace.

home to the New Zealand Academy of Fine Arts and exhibitions by New Zealand artists. It has free admission and is open daily from 10am to 5pm. ⏱ At least 1 hr.

④ ★★ kids Museum of Wellington City & Sea. ⏱ 1 hr. See p. 265, **⑧**.

⑤ kids Olympic Museum. This small museum, operated by the New Zealand Olympic Committee, celebrates over 100 years of New Zealand's participation at the Olympic Games and features treasures donated by our Olympic heroes. ⏱ 30 min. TSB Arena Building, 4 Queens Wharf. ☎ 04/385-0070. www.olympic.org.nz. Free admission. Mon–Fri 10am–4pm.

⑥ ★★ kids City to Sea Bridge. Walk back to the lagoon and cross the City to Sea Bridge, a striking architectural addition to the cityscape built in 1994. Two huge timber whales form the bridge and at the top there's a set of totem sculptures by leading Maori artist Para Matchitt that tell the story of the creation of Wellington Harbour. If you look down into Civic Square from here, you'll get a great view of the marvelous aerial sculpture *Ferns*, by Christchurch-based sculptor Neil Dawson. You'll see another of Dawson's large works hanging outside the Bank of New Zealand on Lambton Quay. ⏱ 30 min.

⑦ ★★★ kids City Gallery Wellington. If you want to find out what's happening at the leading edge of New Zealand contemporary art, this is the place to begin. It has a reputation for challenging viewers with the very best—everything from painting, sculpture, film, and video to industrial and graphic design and architecture. ⏱ 1 hr. Civic Sq., 101 Wakefield St. ☎ 04/801-3021. www.citygallery.org.nz. Admission by donation; some international exhibitions may carry an entry fee. Daily 10am–5pm.

Have dinner (see p. 276 for recommendations) and return to your hotel for the night.

⑧ ★ Archives New Zealand. This repository is where you'll find the original 1840 Treaty of Waitangi, a group of nine documents—all in Maori except for the Waikato sheet in English—which was the agreement drawn up between the British Crown and a group of Maori chiefs. The Constitution Room also holds the 1893 Women's Suffrage Petition. ⏱ 1hr. 10 Mulgrave St., Thorndon. ☎ 04/499-5595. www.archives.govt.nz. Free admission. Mon–Fri 9am–5pm.

⑨ BNZ Museum. The Bank of New Zealand has played a key role in this country's development since 1861 and the static and interactive displays here provide an insight into the way the country has evolved financially and

The Writer's Walk

As you move around the Waterfront and Civic Square areas, see how many concrete text sculptures in The Writers' Walk you can find. There are 11 altogether—quotes from poems and texts by some of New Zealand's best-known authors who have called Wellington home. You'll find one by poet James K. Baxter "floating" in one of the ponds at Te Papa and a quote by author Lauris Edmond on the wall as you come up the steps to the City to Sea Bridge. There's another on the grassy knoll to one side of the bridge. The i-SITE Visitor Centre in Civic Square has a map and brochure detailing their location.

socially. You'll see early bank notes, coins, advertising, and displays that reference the Gold Rush days, bank architecture, and modern technology. ⏱ 45 min. Level 1, Harbour Quays, 60 Waterloo Quay (opposite the railway station). ☎ 04/474-6933. www.bnz.co.nz. Free admission. Mon–Fri 9:30am–4pm.

⑩ ★ Reserve Bank Museum. Check out 1844 promissory notes, wax sealing machines, the first check ever issued in New Zealand, and this country's only working example of the MONIAC hydro-mechanical econometric computer—all displayed along with New Zealand's economic and banking heritage. ⏱ 45 min. 2 The Terrace. ☎ 04/471-3682. www.rbnzmuseum.govt.nz. Free admission. Mon–Fri 9:30am–4pm.

⑪ 🍽 **Caffe Astoria.** Sit back and watch Wellington cafe life at its best in this busy central eatery, where you can choose grilled panini, risotto, soup, or just coffee and cake. 159 Lambton Quay. ☎ 04/473-8500. NZ$12–NZ$18.

⑫ ★ Katherine Mansfield Birthplace. Anyone with a literary bent will get a great deal of pleasure out of this tranquil old home, where New Zealand's most distinguished short story writer, Katherine Mansfield, was born into the Beauchamp family in 1888. She left for Europe when she was 19 and kept company with the likes of Virginia Woolf, T. S. Eliot, and D. H. Lawrence. If you know her stories, you'll get a sense of what inspired some of them here, in this beautifully restored family home. ⏱ 45 min. 25 Tinakori Rd., Thorndon. ☎ 04/473-7268. www.katherinemansfield.com. Admission NZ$7

adults, NZ$5 seniors/students, NZ$3 kids. Tues–Sun 10am–4pm.

⑬ ★★ The Film Archive. Movie buffs can spend the rest of the afternoon winding down here, learning about the history of New Zealand's film and television industry. You can watch old newsreels, television commercials, documentaries, and New Zealand feature films—all free to view in the media library. ⏱ At least 1 hr. Corner of Ghuznee and Taranaki sts. ☎ 04/384-7647. www.filmarchive.org.nz. Free admission. Mon–Fri 9am–5pm.

TheNewDowse

TheNewDowse is one of my favorite Wellington art experiences. Although it is out in Lower Hutt city, a 15-minute drive along St. Hwy. 2, it's well worth the trip if you're an art fan. Its ever-changing exhibitions of the best of New Zealand contemporary art and craft—ceramics, jewelry, glass, textiles, wood, sculpture, photography—are shown to their best advantage in a light, colorful, contemporary building. They're usually a little less intellectual than the shows at City Gallery Wellington. Make sure you give your coin purse a shake-up in their excellent store too. 45 Laings Rd., Lower Hutt. ☎ 04/570-6500; www.newdowse.org.nz. Free admission; fees for some special exhibitions. Mon–Fri 10am–4:30pm, Sat–Sun 10am–5pm. Located 20km (12 miles) from central Wellington. Take the train to Waterloo Station and walk down Knights Rd. to the museum, or catch the Eastbourne/Big Red bus, which departs hourly from Courtenay Place to Queensgate.

Sculpture City

The Wellington Sculpture Trust (www.sculpture.org.nz) was established in 1982 to raise funds for the Tanya Ashken sculpture *Albatross* in Frank Kitts Park. Since then the trust, in partnership with Wellington City Council, has installed 13 sculptures around the city, including four on the NZ$750,000 Meridian Wind Sculpture Walkway on Cobham Drive. There are six further sculptures in the Botanic Garden and three on Lambton Quay and Woodward Street.

ART SMART
New Zealand Artists Past and Present   BY ADRIENNE REWI

NEW ZEALAND'S ARTISTIC ROOTS are firmly embedded in a mix of European tradition and Maori/Pacific island influences. Early European tradition favored an emblematic and literary pairing of image and poetic allusion with subject matter leaning toward the land and self-questioning. The Maori tradition of figurative imagery (traditionally expressed in carving) asserted a strong genealogical identity. In contemporary New Zealand art, Maori artists still tend to create works that focus on what it means to be Maori, often with strong reference to heritage, myths, and legends; while Pakeha (European New Zealanders) are often heavily inspired by nature, the land, and social issues.

The Best Places to See New Zealand Art Collections

Auckland Art Gallery (p. 46, ❶); Waikato Museum, Hamilton (p. 138, ❷); Rotorua Museum of Art & History (p. 158, ❶); Govett-Brewster Art Gallery, New Plymouth (p. 237, ⑯); Sarjeant Gallery, Whanganui (p. 232, ❷); Museum of New Zealand–Te Papa Tongarewa, Wellington (p. 256, ❶); Suter Art Gallery–Te Aratoi o Whakatu, Nelson (p. 301, ❾); Christchurch Art Gallery (closed due to the earthquake at press time; check www.christchurchartgallery.org.nz for updates); Dunedin Public Art Gallery (p. 422, ❶); Southland Museum & Art Gallery, Invercargill (p. 428, ❶).

New Zealand Public Art & the Sculpture Walks

WELLINGTON SCULPTURE TRUST

The Wellington Sculpture Trust (www. sculpture.org.nz) has published an excellent guide, Art & About, available from city bookstores, that leads you around the capital city's outstanding collection of public sculptures. Established in 1982, the trust works in partnership with Wellington City Council to raise funds and install works by leading New Zealand sculptors. You'll find wonderful works scattered around the city streets, along the waterfront, and in the Botanic Gardens.

AUCKLAND WATERFRONT SCULPTURE TRAIL

Art fans will find at least seven major sculptures in and around the Britomart precinct, in Viaduct Harbour, and along the city foreshore on Quay Street. Dramatic sculptures also form part of the landscape around Auckland Museum, who can provide you with a map of their growing outdoor collection. For a map and location of the Auckland city sculptures visit www. aucklandcity.govt.nz/ whatson/arts/public art/waterfront.asp.

CONNELLS BAY SCULPTURE PARK, WAIHEKE ISLAND

This private sculpture park showcases works by New Zealand sculptors in a dramatic island location. It's a great family day out (take a picnic lunch) and well worth a trip to Waiheke. Guided tours (which must be pre-booked) will lead you around at least 28 works by leading artists. The park also hosts an annual Temporary Sculpture Installation project and a biannual photographic project in its gallery. For details and tour prices see www. connellsbay.co.nz.

ZEALANDIA SCULPTURE GARDEN

This private sculpture garden gives you an insight into the life and work of leading New Zealand sculptor Terry Stringer. Located 45 minutes north of Auckland, it presents a survey of his and his colleagues' work both in the garden and within an architecturally-designed gallery. You can either enjoy the experience on your own or take a guided tour. For further details and bookings check www.zealandia sculpturegarden.co.nz

Collectible New Zealand Artists

Among the most collectible of our contemporary artists are Colin McCahon (1919–1987), Len Lye (1901–1980), who spent much of his artistic life in New York, Toss Wollaston (1910–1998), Rita Angus (1908–1970) and Philip Clairmont (1949–1984). Among those still practicing, seek out Bill Hammond, Philip Trusttum, Barry Cleavin, Andrew Drummond, Neil Dawson, Serephine Pick, Richard Killeen, Dick Frizzell, and Gretchen Albrecht. Top Maori artists include Ralph Hotere, Peter Robinson, Shane Cotton, Michael Parekowhai, and Robyn Kahukiwa to name just a few.

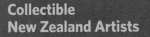

Wellington Shopping Best Bets

Best Art
Hamish McKay Gallery, 1st floor, 39 Ghuznee St. (p. 273).

Best Bohemian Shopping Area
Cuba Street and Cuba Mall (p. 275).

Best Books
Unity Books, 57 Willis St. (p. 273).

Best Department Store
Kirkcaldie & Stains, 165–177 Lambton Quay (p. 275).

Best Mainstream Shopping Area
Lambton Quay (p. 275).

Best Maori Arts & Crafts
Iwi Art, 19 Tory St. (p. 275).

Best New Zealand High Fashion
WORLD, 98 Victoria St. (p. 275).

Best New Zealand Leisure Clothing
Untouched World, 147 Featherston St. (p. 273).

The Shopping Scene

Wellington is such a compact city that it's easy for visitors to find their way around and to wander at ease. You can pick up the free guides, *The Fashion Map* and *The Arts Map*, at the visitor center. From the department and designer stores of Lambton Quay (nicknamed the Golden Mile) up Willis Street to the funkier side of town on Cuba Street, you'll find markets, alternative boutiques, secondhand stores, and great cafes. It's all easy and shopper-friendly. Store hours are usually Monday through Friday from 9am to 5:30pm, Saturday from 9am to 4:30pm, and Sunday from 10am to 2pm.

> *Expect all kinds of colorful store interiors in the funky Cuba Street shopping zone.*

Wellington Shopping A to Z

Art

★★★ Hamish McKay Gallery CENTRAL CITY

If you're after works by some of the hippest young artists in Australasia, this is the pace to come. Hamish McKay's upstairs gallery is the best in the capital and he stocks leading contemporary artists like Ronnie van Hout, Billy Apple, and Shane Cotton. 1st floor, 39 Ghuznee St. ☎ 04/384-7140. www.hamishmckaygallery.com. MC, V.

★★★ Peter McLeavey Gallery CUBA STREET AREA

Peter McLeavey has been dealing art from two small, upstairs rooms since 1966. He is an institution, a fine storyteller, and a stockist of the undisputed champions of New Zealand art like Toss Woollaston, John Reynolds, Peter Robinson, Laurence Aberhart, and Richard Killeen. 147 Cuba St. ☎ 04/384-7356. www.petermcleaveygallery.com. MC, V.

Books

★★★ Unity Books CENTRAL CITY

Unity is an oasis of excellent titles, exciting local publishing, and informed, book-crazy staff. Willbank House, 57 Willis St. ☎ 04/499-4245. www.unitybooks.co.nz. AE, MC, V.

Clothing

★★★ Karen Walker CENTRAL CITY

Once you get over the surprise of giant crocodiles on the ceiling, you'll find racks filled with the high-casual, clean-cut garments that have made New Zealand fashion icon Karen Walker a popular regular at both New York and London fashion weeks. 126 Wakefield St. ☎ 04/499-558. www.karenwalker.com. AE, DC, MC, V.

★★★ Untouched World LAMBTON QUAY AREA

When you pick up a luxuriously soft, featherweight, pure merino-and-possum garment by Untouched World, you'll never want to put it down. Shop here for natural, sustainable fashion and sportswear in a classic, enduring style. 147 Featherston St. ☎ 04/473-2596. www.untouchedworld.com. AE, DC, MC, V.

> *Lambton Quay is the place to shop if you're a shoe fan.*

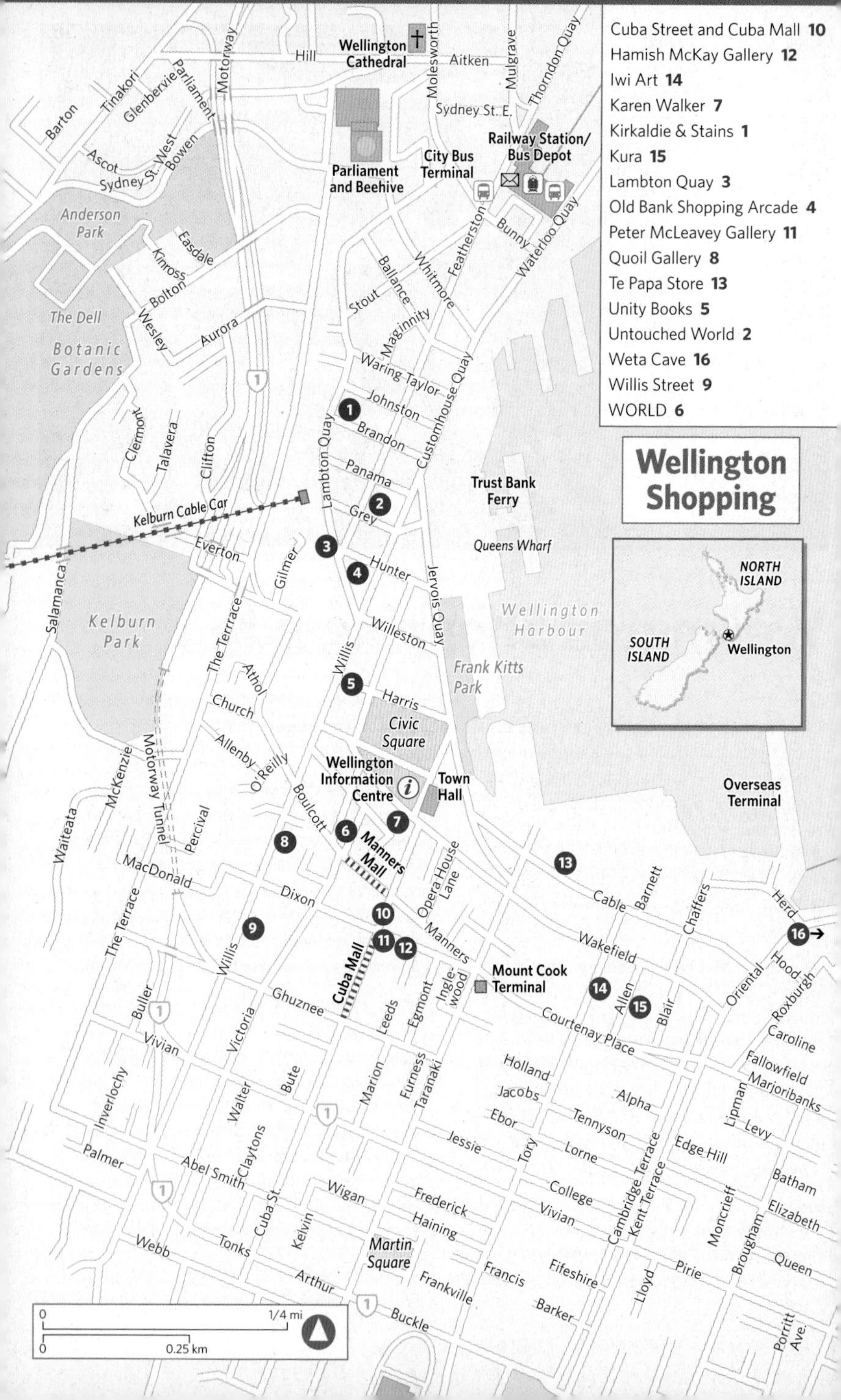
Wellington Shopping
Cuba Street and Cuba Mall 10
Hamish McKay Gallery 12
Iwi Art 14
Karen Walker 7
Kirkaldie & Stains 1
Kura 15
Lambton Quay 3
Old Bank Shopping Arcade 4
Peter McLeavey Gallery 11
Quoil Gallery 8
Te Papa Store 13
Unity Books 5
Untouched World 2
Weta Cave 16
Willis Street 9
WORLD 6
NORTH ISLAND
SOUTH ISLAND
Wellington
Wellington Cathedral
Parliament and Beehive
City Bus Terminal
Railway Station/ Bus Depot
Anderson Park
The Dell
Botanic Gardens
Kelburn Cable Car
Kelburn Park
Trust Bank Ferry
Queens Wharf
Wellington Harbour
Frank Kitts Park
Civic Square
Wellington Information Centre
Town Hall
Overseas Terminal
Manners Mall
Cuba Mall
Mount Cook Terminal
Martin Square
Motorway Tunnel
Hill
Aitken
Molesworth
Mulgrave
Thorndon Quay
Sydney St. E.
Motorway
Parliament
Glenbervie
Tinakori
Barton
Ascot
Sydney St. West
Bowen
Easdale
Kinross
Bolton
Wesley
Aurora
Bunny
Waterloo Quay
Featherston
Whitmore
Ballance
Stout
Maginnity
Waring Taylor
Johnston
Brandon
Panama
Grey
Customhouse Quay
Lambton Quay
Hunter
Willeston
Jervois Quay
Harris
Willis
Gilmer
Everton
Salamanca
The Terrace
Athol
Church
Allenby
O'Reilly
Boulcott
Clermont
Talavera
Clifton
McKenzie
Waiteata
Percival
MacDonald
Dixon
Opera House Lane
Manners
Cable
Barnett
Chaffers
Herd
Wakefield
Oriental
Hood
Roxburgh
Ingle-wood
Allen
Blair
Ghuznee
Leeds
Egmont
Courtenay Place
Caroline
Fallowfield
Marjoribanks
Buller
Vivian
Victoria
Bute
Marion
Furness
Taranaki
Holland
Jacobs
Ebor
Alpha
Tennyson
Lipman
Levy
Edge Hill
Inverlochy
Walter
Jessie
Tory
Lorne
Cambridge Terrace
Kent Terrace
Batham
Palmer
Abel Smith
Claytons
College
Wigan
Frederick
Haining
Elizabeth
Moncrieff
Brougham
Webb
Tonks
Cuba St.
Kelvin
Francis
Fifeshire
Lloyd
Pirie
Queen
Arthur
Frankville
Barker
Buckle
Porritt Ave.
0
1/4 mi
0
0.25 km

★★★ WORLD CENTRAL CITY

WORLD founders Denise L'Estrange-Corbet and Francis Hooper create high-fashion, avant-garde garments that continually flout expectations. 98 Victoria St. ☎ 04/472-1595. www.worldbrand.co.nz. AE, DC, MC, V.

Department Store

Kirkcaldie & Stains LAMBTON QUAY

From top cosmetic lines and silk scarves to fine furnishings, accessories, housewares, and fashion, Kirkcaldies has been offering quality merchandise and traditional service since 1863. They also have an excellent overseas packing and postal service. 165–177 Lambton Quay. ☎ 04/472-5899. www.kirkcaldies.co.nz. AE, DC, MC, V.

Jewelry

★★ Quoil Gallery CENTRAL CITY/WILLIS

You'll find Wellington's largest selection of contemporary New Zealand jewelry here—beautiful, innovative pieces in gold, silver, gemstones, and contemporary materials that will surprise and delight. 149 Willis St. ☎ 04/384-1499. www.quoil.co.nz. AE, MC, V.

Maori Arts

★★ Iwi Art NEAR COURTENAY PLACE

This classy little gallery shows the best of contemporary Maori adornment, sculpture, textiles, and paintings. 19 Tory St. ☎ 04/803-3253. www.iwiart.co.nz. AE, MC, V.

★ Kura NEAR COURTENAY PLACE

Kura has a wide range of contemporary arts and crafts created in New Zealand by Maori artists, from wood, bone, and *pounamu* (greenstone) carving to woven works, jewelry, and household objects. 19 Allen St. ☎ 04/802-4934. www.kuragallery.co.nz. AE, DC, MC, V.

★★★ Te Papa Store WATERFRONT

This is my pick for the very best of New Zealand handcrafted jewelry, contemporary Maori carvings and jewelry, New Zealand books, toys, and clothing. Museum of New Zealand–Te Papa Tongarewa. ☎ 04/381-7013. www.tepapastore.co.nz. AE, DC, MC, V.

Main Shopping Zones

★★★ Cuba Street and Cuba Mall. Well-known and loved for its bohemian air, this long street and mall is packed with high-quality second-hand boutiques, trendy fashion, and urban

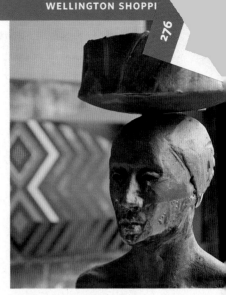

> *Kura is a great place to shop for Maori art.*

design stores, tattoo parlors, street-wear shops, cafes, and restaurants.

★★★ Lambton Quay. Known locally as 'the Golden Mile,' Lambton Quay is a must if you're after fashion, accessories and shoes. It's much more mainstream than the Cuba Street area and generally a little less pricey than the Old Bank boutiques.

★★ Old Bank Shopping Arcade. The big, creamy yellow former Bank of New Zealand building at the intersection of Willis Street and Lambton Quay is home to three levels of top boutiques and specialty stores.

★ Willis Street. Along with Featherston and Victoria streets, Willis is home to a wide range of mainstream shops selling everything from fashion and shoes to books and music.

Movie & Designer Collectibles

★★★ Weta Cave MIRAMAR

The brainchild of multi-Academy Award-winning company Weta Studios, who brought *The Lord of the Rings, King Kong,* and *The Chronicles of Narnia* to life, this place is a dream come true for collectors of movie memorabilia, books, and DVDs. Corner of Camperdown Rd. and Weka St. ☎ 04/380-9361; www.wetanz.co.nz. AE, DC, MC, V.

Wellington Restaurant Best Bets

Best Ambiance
Matterhorn, 106 Cuba St. (p. 281).

Best Asian Food
Chow, 45 Tory St. and 11 Woodward St. (p. 277).

Best for Families
One Red Dog, 9–11 Blair St. (p. 281).

Best People-Watching
Ernesto, 132 Cuba St. (p. 277).

Best Pizza
Scopa, 141 Cuba St. (p. 281).

Most Romantic
Logan Brown, corner of Cuba and Vivian sts. (p. 280).

Best Seafood
Martin Bosley's Yacht Club Restaurant, 103 Oriental Parade. (p. 280).

Best Splurge
Boulcott Street Bistro, 99 Boulcott St. (p. 277).

Best Sunday Brunch
Floriditas, 161 Cuba St. (p. 280).

Best Views
The White House, 232 Oriental Parade. (p. 281).

Deli Fixings

Whether you want to stock up on picnic food or just sit and enjoy coffee with a fine range of edibles, don't miss these inner city delis and bakeries. **Dixon Street Gourmet Deli,** 45 Dixon St. (☎ 04/384-2436), has a glowing reputation as long as my arm; and **Smith the Grocer,** in the Old Bank Arcade, Lambton Quay (☎ 04/473-8591), is a surprise tucked in between leading fashion stores. Both have a wide range of specialty items to take home, plus delicious ready-to-eat treats for the moment. **Bordeaux Bakery,** 220 Thorndon Quay (☎ 04/499-8334), and **Le Moulin,** 248 Willis St. (☎ 04/382-8118), are two superlative French bakeries; and for Italian-style breads, try **Pandoro,** 2 Allen St. (☎ 04/385-4478 www.pandoro.co.nz).

> Outside dining at hip, European Matterhorn.

Wellington Restaurants A to Z

★ kids **Arabica** CENTRAL CITY *CAFE*
This is one of my favorite Wellington stops. It's always packed with an interesting crowd of businesspeople, the service is slick, and the coffee and cabinet food are excellent. 1 Grey St. ☎ 04/473-7697. NZ$5–NZ$15. MC, V. Breakfast and lunch daily.

★★★ **Boulcott Street Bistro** CENTRAL CITY *MODERN NZ* Inside this little Victorian Plimmer House is an intimate restaurant with a giant reputation. It's fine dining without the snobbery. The menu presents the best of New Zealand with such classic dishes as lamb shanks, cured duck, and aged sirloin. 99 Boulcott St. ☎ 04/499-4199. www.boulcottstbistro. co.nz. Main courses NZ$35–NZ$40. AE, DC, MC, V. Lunch Mon–Fri, dinner Mon–Sat.

kids **Burger Fuel** COURTENAY PLACE *BURGERS* This New Zealand burger chain was founded in Auckland in 1995 and now dispatches their wholesome, great-value burgers (including vegetarian and vegan options) right around the country. Prepared and cooked while you wait and served with sauces made in-house, they're a great meal in a moment. 101 Courtenay Place. ☎ 04/801-9222. www.burgerfuel. co.nz. Main courses NZ$8–NZ$14. MC, V. Lunch and dinner daily.

★★ kids **Chow** CENTRAL CITY *SOUTHEAST ASIAN* I adore Chow and the way you can nibble your way through tapas-style dishes that include noodles, dumplings, stir-fried vegetables, and salads along with wine, sake, cocktails, or tea. There's another location at 11 Woodward St. 45 Tory St. ☎ 04/382-8585. www.chow.co.nz. Main courses NZ$16–NZ$26. AE, MC, V. Lunch and dinner daily.

★ kids **Ernesto** CUBA STREET *CAFE* If you want a great people-watching spot and a sunny, relaxed, friendly cafe in which to read your morning paper, this is the place. They do great breakfasts and have muffins as big as houses. 132 Cuba St. ☎ 04/801-6878. Main courses NZ$12–NZ$25. AE, MC, V. Breakfast, lunch, and dinner daily.

> *Martin Bosley's Yacht Club serves up innovative cuisine amid striking harbor views.*

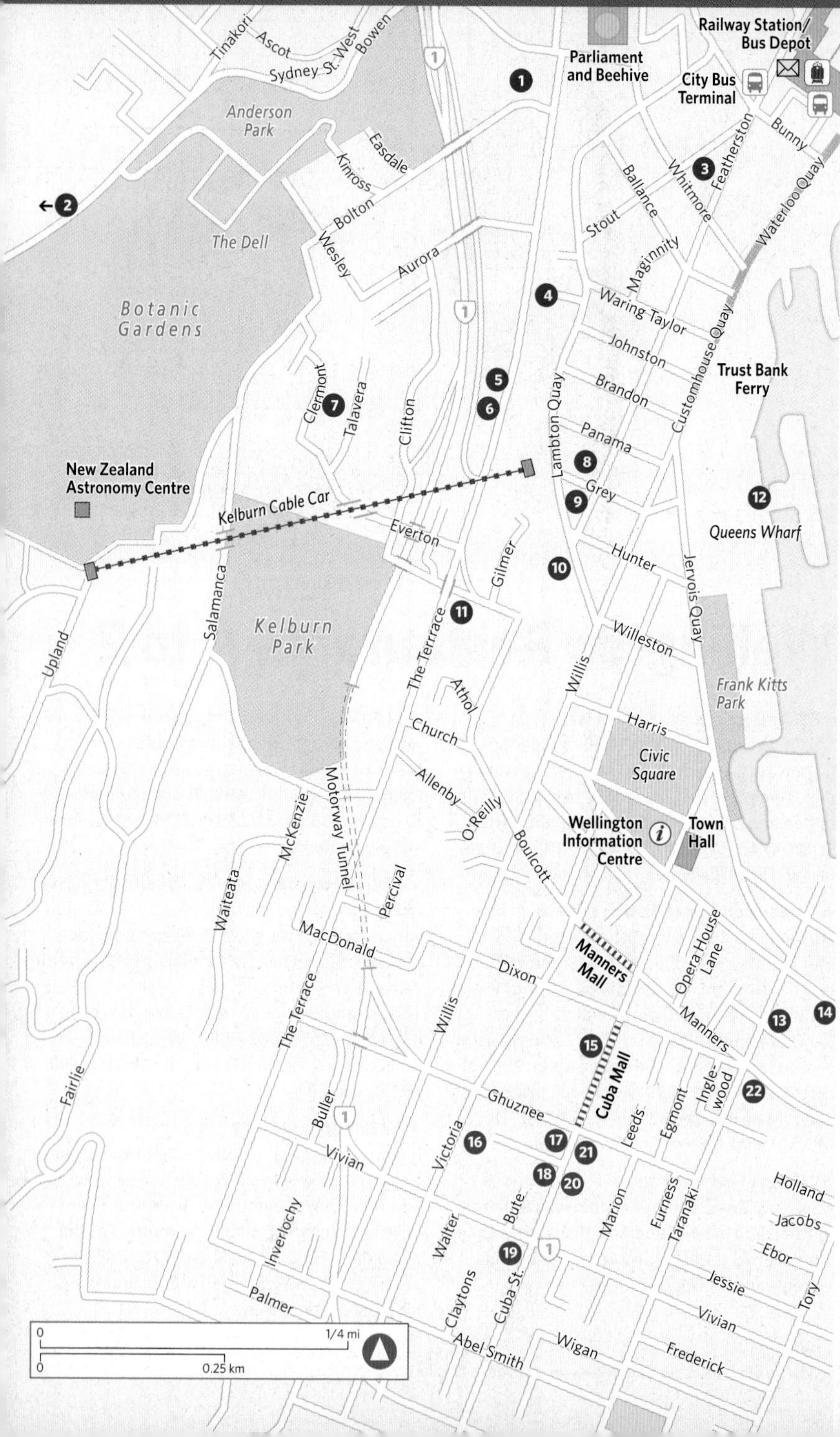

Tinakori

Ascot

Sydney St. West

Bowen

Parliament
and Beehive

Railway Station/
Bus Depot

City Bus
Terminal

1

Anderson
Park

Easdale

Kinross

Bolton

Wesley

Aurora

The Dell

← **2**

Botanic
Gardens

Stout

Ballance

Whitmore

Featherston

Bunny

Waterloo Quay

3

Maginnity

Waring Taylor

Johnston

Brandon

Customhouse Quay

Trust Bank
Ferry

4

Clermont

Talavera

Clifton

7

5

6

Lambton Quay

Panama

8

Grey

9

12

Queens Wharf

New Zealand
Astronomy Centre

Kelburn Cable Car

Everton

Gilmer

Hunter

Jervois Quay

Upland

Salamanca

Kelburn
Park

The Terrace

Athol

Church

Allenby

O'Reilly

Boulcott

Willis

Willeston

Harris

10

11

Frank Kitts
Park

Civic
Square

Wellington
Information
Centre

ⓘ

Town
Hall

Fairlie

Waiteata

McKenzie

Motorway Tunnel

Percival

MacDonald

Dixon

Manners
Mall

Opera House
Lane

The Terrace

Willis

Buller

Vivian

Ghuznee

Victoria

16

Leeds

Cuba Mall

15

17

21

18

20

Manners

13

14

Ingle-
wood

22

Egmont

Taranaki

Furness

Marion

Holland

Jacobs

Ebor

Inverlochy

Walter

Bute

Cuba St.

19

Claytons

Palmer

Abel Smith

Wigan

Jessie

Vivian

Frederick

Tory

0   1/4 mi

0   0.25 km

Wellington Restaurants & Hotels

NORTH ISLAND

SOUTH ISLAND

⊛ Wellington

RESTAURANTS

Arabica **9**
Boulcott Street Bistro **11**
Burger Fuel **22**
Chow **4**, **24**
Ernesto **17**
Floriditas **20**
Hummingbird **25**
Le Metropolitain **18**
Lido Café **13**
Logan Brown **19**
Martin Bosley's Yacht Club Restaurant **33**
Matterhorn **15**
Monsoon Poon **27**
One Red Dog **28**
Scopa **21**
Shed 5 **12**
The White House **34**
Zico Cucina **26**

HOTELS

Bolton Hotel **1**
Booklovers B&B **31**
City Life Wellington **10**
Duxton Hotel **14**
Gardens Homestay **2**
Holiday Inn Wellington **3**
InterContinental Wellington **8**
James Cook Hotel Grand Chancellor **6**
Lambton Heights **7**
Mount Victoria Homestay **30**
Museum Hotel **23**
Novotel Wellington **5**
Ohtel **32**
Victoria Court Motor Lodge **16**
Wellington City YHA **29**

Wellington Harbour

Overseas Terminal

> *Fish and game are the stars of the menu at Logan Brown.*

★★ kids **Floriditas** CUBA STREET *EUROPEAN/ CAFE* This paisley-embellished corner retreat is one of the most popular brunch spots in the city. I like the atmosphere, even when service standards occasionally waver under pressure. Eggs Benedict and scrambled eggs are always good brunch bets and a range of European-inspired dishes make a lovely light dinner. 161 Cuba St. ☎ 04/381-2212. www.floriditas.co.nz. Main courses NZ$16–NZ$26. AE, DC, MC, V. Breakfast, lunch, and dinner daily.

★ **Hummingbird** COURTENAY PLACE *PACIFIC RIM* It's all dark brown timber and leather here—a moody interior that starts off quietly around lunch time and gets louder as evening and the bar crowd descends. Small plates are the order of the day here, so you can indulge in a number of lovely flavors without breaking the bank. 22 Courtenay Place. ☎ 04/801-6336. www.hummingbird.net.nz. Main courses NZ$20–NZ$38. AE, DC, MC, V. Brunch, lunch, dinner, and late night suppers daily.

★ **Le Metropolitain** CUBA STREET *BISTRO* The tasty menu at this little corner bistro presents French classics like coq au vin using the best New Zealand ingredients. I loved the cauliflower and lemon risotto. 146 Cuba St. ☎ 04/801-8007. www.lemetropolitain.co.nz. Main courses NZ$22–NZ$35. MC, V. Lunch and dinner Tues–Sun.

★ kids **Lido Café** CENTRAL CITY *CAFE* The Lido is a Wellington icon. No matter what time of the day you visit, you'll find a relaxed crowd of locals picking their plates clean of light meals like scrambled eggs and corn fritters, chosen from an all-day menu. It's a trusty option for a quick, good-value meal and an interesting crowd. **Corner of Wakefield and Victoria sts.** ☎ 04/499-6666. Main courses NZ$16–NZ$22. MC, V. Breakfast, lunch, and dinner daily.

★★★ **Logan Brown** CUBA STREET *MODERN NZ* This multi-award-winning, romantic restaurant is among the country's best. The menu focuses on fish and game coupled with top French and New Zealand wines. Service is impeccable. **Corner Cuba and Vivian sts.** ☎ 04/801-5114. www.loganbrown.co.nz. Main courses NZ$40–NZ$50. AE, DC, MC, V. Lunch Mon–Fri, dinner daily.

★★★ **Martin Bosley's Yacht Club Restaurant** ORIENTAL PARADE *MODERN NZ/SEAFOOD* The beautiful panoramic views aside, you'll surely fall in love with this restaurant. The menu is based around what the chefs gather from the fish market each day and you can expect innovative treatment and presentation. You might choose a smoked eel mousse, for instance, or perhaps an oyster broth. **Royal Port Nicholson Yact Club, 103 Oriental Parade.** ☎ 04/385-6963. www.martin-bosley.com. Main

> *The Seafood is the specialty at Shed 5.*

courses NZ$32–NZ$48. AE, MC, V. Lunch Mon–Fri, dinner Tues–Sat.

★★ **Matterhorn** CUBA STREET *EUROPEAN* Mellow, moody, modernist, and mouthwatering—all the M words that sum up the Matterhorn. This is the cool, stylish den of the hip crowd who, once they've finished dinner, party into the night at the bar. But the food alone—locally-sourced ingredients (when possible) in preparations influenced by the chef's classical French training—is the worth the visit. 106 Cuba St ☎ 04/384-3359. www.matterhorn. co.nz. NZ$34–NZ$38. MC, V. Breakfast, lunch, and dinner daily.

★★ kids **Monsoon Poon** COURTENAY PLACE AREA *SOUTHEAST ASIAN* Monsoon Poon has most of Southeast Asia covered in a menu that delivers Vietnamese summer rolls, Bangkok street noodles, Thai beef salad, Indian curries, Thai jumbo prawns, and much more. It's mouthwatering all the way and the restaurant has a lively atmosphere as well. 12 Blair St. ☎ 04/803-3555. www.monsoonpoon.co.nz. Main courses NZ$16–NZ$24. MC, V. Dinner daily, lunch Mon–Fri.

★ kids **One Red Dog** COURTENAY PLACE AREA *PIZZA* This is a great spot for hungry families. There's a wide range of tasty, wood-fired pizzas, plus a kids' menu and delicious salads and pasta dishes. 9–11 Blair St. ☎ 04/384-9777. www.onereddog.co.nz. Main courses NZ$18–NZ$30. AE, DC, MC, V. Lunch and dinner daily.

★ kids **Scopa** CUBA STREET *PIZZA/CAFE* I love sitting in the window at Scopa, munching on delicious thin-crust pizza, a tasty risotto, or some handmade gnocchi, watching the crowds go by on Cuba Street. 141 Cuba St. ☎ 04/384-6020. www.scopa.co.nz. Main courses NZ$16–NZ$28. AE, DC, MC, V. Breakfast, lunch and dinner daily.

★★ kids **Shed 5** WATERFRONT *MODERN NZ/ SEAFOOD* Occupying one of the oldest wharf sheds on the waterfront, this restaurant serves excellent seafood—they have an in-house fishmonger who shops daily for produce. There are also lamb, beef, venison, and chicken options. Shed 5, Queens Wharf. ☎ 04/499-9069. www. shed5.co.nz. Main courses NZ$34–NZ$40. AE, DC, MC, V. Lunch and dinner daily.

★★★ **The White House** ORIENTAL PARADE *MODERN NZ* This preeminent restaurant attracts both corporate types and die-hard romantics. Expect lovely sea views, flavors mixed to perfection, and dishes of edible art that are bound to impress. 232 Oriental Parade (upstairs). ☎ 04/385-8555. www.whr.co.nz. Main courses NZ$42–NZ$50. AE, DC, MC, V. Dinner daily, lunch Wed–Sun.

★★ kids **Zico Cucina** COURTENAY PLACE *ITALIAN* This is one of my favorite Italian restaurants in the capital. It's informal, lively, and great for families, who can pick from a vast menu that covers pizzas, seafood, veal dishes, and numerous pastas. 8 Courtenay Place. ☎ 04/802-5585. Main courses NZ$24–NZ$34. AE, DC, MC, V. Dinner daily, lunch Mon–Fri.

Wellington Hotel Best Bets

Best Apartments
CityLife Wellington, 300 Lambton Quay (p. 283).

Best Budget Stay
Wellington City YHA, Corner of Cambridge Terrace and Wakefield St. (p. 285).

Most Charming B&B
Booklovers Bed & Breakfast, 123 Pirie St. (p. 283).

Best Club Level Amenities
InterContinental Wellington, 2 Grey St. (p. 284).

Most Interesting Interior
Museum Hotel, 90 Cable St. (p. 284).

Best for Kids
Holiday Inn Wellington, 75 Featherston St. (p. 284).

Best Moderately Priced
Novotel Wellington, 133-137 The Terrace (p. 285).

Best Motel
Victoria Court Motor Lodge, 201 Victoria St. (p. 285).

Most Original Decor
Ohtel, 66 Oriental Parade (p. 285).

Best Shopping Location
James Cook Hotel Grand Chancellor, 147 The Terrace (p. 284).

> SkyBlues, *by ex-pat New Zealand artist Bill Culbert, stands outside the InterContinental Wellington.*

Wellington Hotels A to Z

★★ kids Bolton Hotel CENTRAL CITY
This crisp, modern, classy hotel has great views of the Thorndon hills. An enviable central location just across the street from the Beehive (part of the Parliament Buildings) means it's popular with business visitors. The fully equipped 2-bedroom suites are ideal for families. **Corner of Bolton and Mowbray sts. ☎ 0800/996-622 or 04/472-9966. www. boltonhotel.co.nz. 142 units. Doubles NZ$285– NZ$525. AE, DC, MC, V. Map p. 279.**

★ Booklovers B&B MT. VICTORIA
Journalist and author Jane Tolerton has four large rooms in her two-story Victorian home and she's a knowledgeable hostess who knows just when to leave you alone. The whole house heaves with New Zealand books, you get a delicious breakfast, and it's about a 15-minute walk to Courtenay Place. **123 Pirie St., Mt. Victoria. ☎ 04/384-2714. www.book- lovers.co.nz. 4 units. Doubles NZ$250–NZ$275. MC, V. Map p. 279.**

★★ kids CityLife Wellington LAMBTON QUAY
These stylish apartments—fully equipped with kitchens and laundry facilities—have size and location on their side. The 1- or 2-bedroom suites are ideal for families. Best of all, it's just a lift ride down to one of the best shopping precincts in the capital. **300 Lambton Quay; entrance and reception on Gilmer Terrace off Boulcott St. ☎ 0800/368-888 or 04/922-2800. www.heritagehotels.co.nz. 70 units. Doubles NZ$260–NZ$475. AE, DC, MC, V. Map p. 279.**

★★ kids Duxton Hotel WATERFRONT
Just a block away from the Te Papa museum, the Duxton is known for its elegant, classic style and large rooms with sweeping harbor views. The club-level rooms take service and amenities up a notch and they're well worth the extra dollars. **170 Wakefield St. ☎ 0800/655-555 or 04/473-3900. www. duxtonhotels.com. 192 units. Doubles NZ$195– NZ$750. AE, DC, MC, V. Map p. 279.**

kids Gardens Homestay THORNDON
Neil Harrap and Sally Guiness are enthusiastic hosts who welcome guests into their grand, two-story, 1892 Victorian home perched in the Thorndon hills just above Tinakori Village. Neil

> *Keen readers will love the book-filled Victorian Booklovers B&B, where tomes are piled high.*

> *There are wide views over Tinakori Road and the city beyond from the Gardens Homestay balconies.*

has worked in tourism for years and he loves to share his knowledge. It's quiet and private with lovely views. **11 St. Mary St., Thorndon.** ☎ 04/499-1212. www.gardenshomestay.co.nz. 1 2-bedroom suite, NZ$285. MC, V. Map p. 279.

★★ kids **Holiday Inn Wellington** CENTRAL CITY This is one of the best value stays in the capital—for a start, kids stay and eat free! It has a prime location on fashionable Featherston Street, within walking distance of most major attractions, restaurants, and shopping areas. Factor in kitchenettes in every room, a heated lap pool, spa, and sauna and there are plenty of reasons to give it a tick of approval. **75 Featherston St.** ☎ 0800/801-111 or 04/499-8686; www.holidayinn.co.nz. 280 units. Doubles from NZ$215. AE, DC, MC, V. Map p. 279.

★★★ kids **InterContinental Wellington** CENTRAL CITY This is Wellington's only internationally branded five-star hotel and my pick for the best service and the most style. It may be over 20 years old but continual refurbishment keeps it at the top of the game. Club-level rooms are the best. Lying in the swimming pool looking out on high rises is quite something. **2 Grey St.** ☎ 0800/801-111 or 04/472-2722. www.intercontinental.com/wellington. 232 units. Doubles NZ$200–NZ$575. AE, DC, MC, V. Map p. 279.

★ kids **James Cook Hotel Grand Chancellor** CENTRAL CITY I have a soft spot for the liveliness, the prime location, and the great value that this hotel offers. It has endured for almost 30 years and the 17 club-level rooms here are the pick of the bunch. Jump in the lift and you're down on Lambton Quay in minutes. **147 The Terrace.** ☎ 0800/699-500 or 04/499-9500. www.ghihotels.com. 260 units. Doubles NZ$185–NZ$450. AE, DC, MC, V. Map p. 279.

Lambton Heights KELBURN
Lovers of heritage homes and great views will enjoy a stay here, in the privacy of suburban Kelburn, just a short stroll from the Wellington Botanic Garden. There are two generous king-size rooms and one double, all with their own ensuite bathrooms. Guests share a charming lounge. **20 Talavera Terrace, Kelburn.** ☎ 04/472-4710. www.lambtonheights.co.nz. Doubles NZ$195–NZ$300. MC, V. Map p. 279.

Mount Victoria Homestay MT. VICTORIA
The visitors' book at Bill and Coral Aitchison's central city bed and breakfast is filled with glowing reports about their hospitality and generosity. Their 1920s restored villa offers two private, upstairs guest rooms, and guests have the use of the lounge and pretty outdoor courtyard. **11 Lipman St., Mt. Victoria.** ☎ 04/802-4886. www.mountvictoria.co.nz. 2 units. NZ$325 with breakfast, canapés, and pre-dinner drinks. MC, V. Map p. 279.

★★ kids **Museum Hotel** WATERFRONT
There are some delightfully opulent touches here—and an eccentric art collection that, along with its prime waterfront location across the road from the Te Papa museum, make it a consistently popular choice. There are modern apartments in one wing, hotel rooms in

> The bar at the opulent Museum Hotel.

another. The former are ideal for families. 90 Cable St. ☎ 0800/994-335. www.museumhotel. co.nz. 160 units. NZ$190–NZ$450. AE, DC, MC, V. Map p. 279.

★ kids **Novotel Wellington** CENTRAL CITY Just a few doors away from the James Cook hotel (see above), the Novotel shares the same convenient closeness to downtown shopping and attractions. It's an excellent, moderately priced option where new, well-appointed rooms are complemented by very good amenities. 133–137 The Terrace. ☎ 04/918-1900. www.novotel.com. 139 units. Doubles NZ$115–NZ$175. AE, DC, MC, V. Map p. 279.

★★★ **Ohtel** ORIENTAL PARADE I love this chic boutique hotel for its great location, its striking individuality, and its total commitment to sustainability. It also happens to be incredibly stylish and is furnished throughout with mid-20th-century modern furniture and German ceramics. All rooms are large but the six front-facing are best for harbor views. 66 Oriental Parade, Mt. Victoria. ☎ 04/803-0600. www.ohtel.com. 10 units. Doubles NZ$550–NZ$725. AE, MC, V. Map p. 279.

★ kids **Victoria Court Motor Lodge** CENTRAL CITY The tidy, spacious, reasonably priced units here back onto a short street that runs off Cuba Street, the busy shopping and restaurant area. Two-bedroom units are perfect for families and couples traveling together. 201 Victoria St. ☎ 04/472-4297. www.victoriacourt. co.nz. 25 units. Doubles NZ$150–NZ$250. AE, DC, MC, V. Map p. 279.

★ **Wellington City YHA** COURTENAY PLACE/ WATERFRONT This is the best backpacker facility in Wellington and it's always abuzz as people of all ages settle into crisp, colorful rooms (private or bunk-style). Its location near the waterfront and Courtenay Place is a prime attraction. It comes with large cooking facilities and lots of quiet areas. Corner of Cambridge Terrace and Wakefield St. ☎ 04/801-7280. www.yha.co.nz. 320 beds. NZ$30–NZ$115. MC, V. Map p. 279.

Wellington Nightlife Best Bets

Best Beer Bar
The Malthouse, 48 Courtenay Place (p. 289).

Best Cocktails
Matterhorn, 106 Cuba St. (p. 287).

Best Gay Bar
S & M's, 176 Cuba St. (p. 289).

Best Irish Bar
Molly Malone's, corner of Taranaki St. and Courtenay Place (p. 289).

Best Live Theatre
Downstage Theatre, corner of Courtenay Place and Cambridge Terrace (p. 289).

Best Movie Theatre
Embassy Theatre, 10 Kent Terrace (p. 289).

Most Romantic Bar
Hawthorn Lounge, 82 Tory St. (p. 287).

Best Wine Bar
Arbitrageur, 125 Featherston St. (p. 287).

A Night at the Movies

All Wellington cinemas offer discounted tickets for daytime and Tuesday-night screenings. Students and seniors also get a discount. Look in the newspapers for schedules. Try the Embassy Theatre, 10 Kent Terrace (☎ 04/384-7657), with a giant screen and a new sound system; Hoyts Cinemas, which has two multiscreen complexes in Manners Mall and Manners Street; or Rialto Cinemas, Cable Street and Jervois Quay (☎ 04/385-1864), a three-theater complex. Penthouse Cinema & Café, 205 Ohiro Rd., Brooklyn (☎ 04/384-3157), is the city's only suburban theater and draws a loyal local crowd.

> *Wellington has a wealth of specialized brew bars for the beer connoisseur, including The Malthouse, pictured here.*

Wellington Nightlife A to Z

Bars & Cocktail Lounges

★★★ Arbitrageur CENTRAL CITY

Wine purists will love this sophisticated, club-style wine bar/restaurant in the heart of the city. There are over 600 of the best wines to sample and regular tastings of vintage cellar wines not normally available by the glass. 125 Featherston St. ☎ 04/499-5530. www.arbitrageur.co.nz.

★★★ Hawthorn Lounge COURTENAY PLACE

AREA Based on a 1920s gentleman's club, this beautiful, intimate, tucked-away bar is a real find. Lounge back in leather armchairs and sip cocktails under green shaded lamps. Staff members wear waistcoats and natty caps. 82 Tory St. ☎ 04/890-3724. www.hawthornlounge.co.nz.

★★★ Matterhorn CUBA STREET

This saucy hangout has been an institution since the 1960s. It's for expensive tastes—everyone from trendy young things to monied bankers, artists, and musicians winds up here. It's classy without pretension and you'll be won over by some of the best cocktail makers in the country. 106 Cuba St. ☎ 04/384-3359. www.matterhorn.co.nz.

DJ Bars

★★★ Mighty Mighty CUBA STREET

This quirky little place is one you either love or hate. It's totally kitschy—wacky colors, old pink lamps, pink drapes, crafts, vintage clothing, and old-fashioned nibbles. They serve beer by the jug, menus are on old record covers, there's a great dance floor, and it's a favorite with the locals. Upstairs, 104 Cuba St. ☎ 04/385-2890.

★★ Red Square COURTENAY PLACE AREA

Seductive, sexy, and stylish, Red Square is a favorite with well-heeled clientele, who linger among blood-red velvet curtains, leather booths, and a Versace-styled pool table–that is, when they're not dancing to DJ beats. There is a head-spinning vodka list and outdoor smoking lounges. 28 Blair St. ☎ 04/802-4244. www.redsquare.co.nz.

> You can catch touring shows as well as local productions at Downstage Theatre.

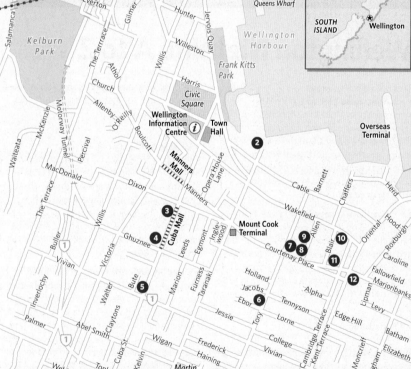

Wellington Nightlife

NORTH ISLAND

SOUTH ISLAND

★ Wellington

> *The streets around Courtenay Place come alive with party-goers from Thursday through Saturday nights.*

Gay Bar

S & M's CUBA STREET AREA

Scotty & Mal's is an intimate, two-level gay cocktail lounge that offers coffee in the afternoons and cocktails in the evenings. Downstairs there's a B&D (that's Basement and Dance) bar that revs up every Friday and Saturday from 10pm to 3am. 176 Cuba St. ☎ 04/802-5335. www.scottyandmals.co.nz.

Performing Arts & Film

★ Circa Theatre WATERFRONT

Inside a cute historic building, Circa puts on innovative productions—everything from comedies and dramas to musicals and pantomines. With 30 years of professional experience and 20 different shows a year, it's a busy, buzzing place. 1 Taranaki St. ☎ 04/801-7992. www.circa.co.nz. Ticket prices $46 adult, $38 students/seniors, $25 for under 25s.

★★★ Downstage Theatre COURTENAY PLACE

AREA Located within Hannah Playhouse, Downstage's season presents its own productions and some of the best touring shows, including classics, contemporary drama, comedy, and dance, with an emphasis on top New Zealand works. Tickets are NZ$35 to NZ$45 for most shows. 12 Cambridge Terrace. ☎ 04/801-6946. www.downstage.co.nz.

★★★ Embassy Theatre MT. VICTORIA

Built in 1924, the Embassy was New Zealand's grandest picture place. Now owned by Wellington City Council, it got a huge makeover in the early 2000s for the premieres of Peter Jackson's *Lord of the Rings* and *King Kong*. It now shows a mix of current and classic films. Blondini's jazz lounge and cafe is in the foyer. 10 Kent Terrace, Mt. Victoria. ☎ 04/384-7657. www.deluxe.co.nz.

Pubs & Breweries

Courtenay Arms COURTENAY PLACE AREA

This is Wellington's top English pub—a place where you'll find English tap beers and many imported beers, pool tables, dart boards, big screen sports, a gaming lounge, dance floor with DJ and juke box, and an open fire. It's popular with young and old. 26–32 Allen St. ☎ 04/385-6908.

★★★ The Malthouse COURTENAY PLACE

They're a little bit potty about beer here. There are over 150 New Zealand and international beers, ranging from beer made by Belgian Trappist monks to a brew made by a Canterbury university professor, all on tap or kept in carefully temperature-controlled fridges. 48 Courtenay Place. ☎ 04/802-5484. www.themalthouse.co.nz.

★ Molly Malone's COURTENAY PLACE AREA

This is the biggest and busiest Irish bar in town with live music every weekend. It serves classic Irish bar food like beef and Guinness stew and bangers and mash. Upstairs, Corner of Taranaki St. and Courtenay Place. ☎ 04/384-2896. www.mollymalones.co.nz.

A Day in Wairarapa

The Wairarapa may seem like a sleepy cluster of rural villages but there's a lot happening behind that facade. Just over an hour's drive from Wellington, the region is home to some of the world's finest boutique vineyards. If you decide to stay over, there is a host of fine small hotels and B&Bs. It's a popular weekend destination for Wellingtonians, who come to browse Martinborough's wineries and Greytown's shops and cafes.

> The Martinborough wine region is known for the quality and character of its pinot noir.

START Greytown is 61km (38 miles) north of Wellington over the Rimutaka Hills. From central Wellington, take St. Hwy. 2, driving around the harbor toward Lower Hutt, and follow the signs to Wairarapa. This route takes you over the Rimutaka Hills to Featherston. Greytown is a further 10 min. drive north. If you prefer to go straight to the wineries, veer right at Featherston and follow the signs to Martinborough. It's a 15- or 20-min. drive.

1 ★ **kids** **Cobblestones Museum.** This is a perfect introduction to Greytown the way it used to be. It's a laid-back little country museum with historic displays, old farm machinery, and a blacksmith's shop that the kids will love. It's located on the site of the old Cobb & Co.

coaching depot and has stables dating back to the 1850s, an 1858 woolshed, and an 1862 cottage. ⏱ 45 min. 169 Main St., Greytown. ☎ 06/304-9687. Admission NZ$6 adults, NZ$4 kids under 14. Daily 9am-4:30pm.

2 ★ **kids** **Schoc Chocolates.** Kids will love this sweet diversion and I suspect the adults will be just as enamored. Set your taste buds to work on over 50 different handmade chocolate flavors—wasabi, lime, chili, and sea salt for instance—and explore your personality traits through your chocolate flavor preferences. ⏱ 30 min. 177 Main St., Greytown. ☎ 06/304-8960. www.schoc.co.nz. Free admission. Mon-Fri 10am-5pm, Sat-Sun 10:30am-5pm.

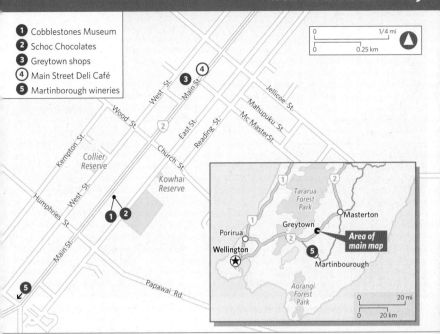

1. Cobblestones Museum
2. Schoc Chocolates
3. Greytown shops
4. Main Street Deli Café
5. Martinborough wineries

❸ ★★ kids **Greytown shops.** Greytown's delightful main street is filled with little Victorian wooden stores selling everything from antiques to clothing and jewelry. Settled in 1854, this was New Zealand's first planned inland town, intended to be the region's provincial capital. Eventually, though, the railway bypassed the town and it became better known for its orchards and market gardens. ⏱ 1½ hr. Main St., Greytown.

④ 🍽 ★ **Main Street Deli Café.** I always stop at this friendly village cafe. It's laid-back and attracts a happy stream of regulars who come for tasty lunches and delicious cakes. 88 Main St. ☎ 06/304-9022. NZ$10–NZ$16.

Head to the south end of Greytown and where the road veers left past the high school, follow the signs to Martinborough and the main wine region. It's a 15–20 min. drive.

❺ ★★★ **Martinborough wineries.** If you're a keen wine buff, you can bypass the morning in Greytown and spend the whole day exploring vineyards and wineries around the village of Martinborough. Stop at the Martinborough

> Greytown's Cobblestones Museum highlights early pioneer life in the district.

> *The main street of Greytown is filled with old shops that now house cafes and chic boutique stores.*

i-SITE Visitor Centre (p. 293) for a copy of the *Classic New Zealand Wine Trail Guide* (www.classicwinetrail.co.nz), which details wineries, sights, shopping, and dining opportunities in the area. The visitor center can also supply details of various local wine tours, which is a good way to get the most out of your limited time in the area. There are 40 vineyards in the area and while choosing the best is a subjective matter, local opinion consistently swings in the direction of **Ata Rangi,** Puruatanga Rd. (☎ 06/306-9750; www.atarangi.co.nz); **Palliser,** Kitchener St. (☎ 06/306-9019; www.palliser.co.nz); **Martinborough Vineyard,** Princess St. (☎ 06/306-9955; www.martinborough-vineyard.co.nz); and **Te Kairanga,** Martins Rd. (☎ 06/306-9122; www.tekairanga.co.nz). Make sure you also stop at **Martinborough Wine Centre,** in the center of the village (☎ 06/306-9040; www.martinboroughwinecentre.co.nz), which represents 30 of the region's 40 vineyards. If you're short on time, or visiting out of the main wine season, this is the perfect place to get a comprehensive overview. Tastings cost NZ$12 to NZ$16 per person. ⏱ At least a half-day.

Where to Stay & Dine Near the Wairarapa Vineyards

The Wairarapa is blessed with over 100 lovely self-contained cottages and a number of very good bed and breakfasts. The visitor center can help you with bookings. If you want to spoil yourself, though, go straight to the remote beauties of ★★★ **Wharekauhau Country Estate,** Western Lake Rd., Palliser Bay (☎ 06/307-7581; www.wharekauhau.co.nz), which is one of New Zealand's outstanding high-end luxury lodges. It stands regally on the top of cliffs overlooking the rugged southern coast. You'll pay top dollar for sublime comforts in cottage suites with all the best trimmings. The 18 units start at NZ$2,250. In Martinborough itself, ★★ **Peppers Martinborough Hotel,** The Square (☎ 06/306-9350; www.peppers.co.nz), has 16 lovely, large guest rooms for NZ$350 to NZ$425. Your best restaurant bet is award-winning ★★ **Wendy Campbell's French Bistro,** 3 Kitchener St., Martinborough (☎ 06/306-8863), which offers lunch and dinner in a small, charming country restaurant. ★ **Est Wine Bar,** 8 Memorial Sq. (☎ 06/306-9665; www.est.org.nz) is another good local choice.

Wellington Fast Facts

Arriving

BY PLANE **Wellington International Airport** (www.wellingtonairport.co.nz), is 8km (5 miles) southeast of the city. The quickest route passes through Mount Victoria via a two-lane tunnel. A more circuitous, but more scenic, route travels via Oriental Parade. The trip usually takes 15 to 20 minutes.

The **Wellington Airport Visitor Information Centre** (☎ 04/385-5123; www.wellington airport.co.nz) is on level one of the main terminal building. It's open daily from 7am to 8pm.

Super Shuttle (☎ 0800/748-885 in NZ or 04/472-9552; www.supershuttle.co.nz), operates between the airport, the city, and the railway station Monday through Friday. It costs NZ$15 per person. **The Airport Flyer** express bus (☎ 0800/801-700 in NZ; www.airportflyer.co.nz), goes right into the city center and then on to Waterloo Interchange in Lower Hutt. It operates daily with departures every 20 minutes from 5:30am to 8:20pm. An All Day Star Pass costs NZ$12 per person and gives unlimited all-day travel on all Flyer, GO Wellington, and Valley Flyer bus services. It's available from bus drivers. The trip from the airport to central-city stops takes about 45 minutes. A **taxi** between the city center and the airport costs NZ$25 to NZ$50. Taxi stands are directly outside the main terminal.

BY TRAIN Most long-distance trains depart from the **Wellington Railway Station,** on Waterloo Quay. For long-distance rail information, call ☎ 0800/802-802 in New Zealand or 04/495-0775, or visit www.tranzscenic.co.nz.

BY BUS For bus information, call **InterCity** (☎ 04/385-0520; www.intercity.co.nz) or **Newmans** (☎ 09/913-6200; www.newmanscoach.co.nz). Both of these coach lines operate out of the railway station. **Kiwi Experience** (p. 474) and **Magic Travellers Network** (p. 474) bus tours also stop in Wellington. BY CAR Wellington is reached via St. Hwys. 1 and 2. It's 195km (121 miles) from Whanganui (approximately 2 hr.); 460km (286 miles) from Rotorua (approximately 5 hr.); and 655km (407 miles) from Auckland (approximately 8 hr.). BY FERRY For information on the

Interislander Wellington-Picton ferry, call ☎ 0800/802-802 (or 04/498-3302) or check www.interislander.co.nz. The three Interislander ferries operate all year and take three hours to cross the strait. **Strait Shipping Ltd.,** Waterloo Quay (☎ 0800/844-844 or 04/471-6188 ; www.bluebridge.co.nz), operates **Bluebridge Cook Strait Ferry.** The Bluebridge trip is cheapest but it takes 3 hours 20 minutes. If you book either online you get the best fares. Cook Strait can be notoriously rough in bad weather so if you get seasick, take some medication.

Embassies & Consulates

The **U.S. Embassy** is at 29 Fitzherbert Terrace, Thorndon (☎ 04/462-6000); the **Canadian High Commission** is at Level 11, 125 The Terrace. (☎ 04/473-9577; www.gc.ca); and the **British High Commission** is at 44 Hill St. (☎ 04/924-2888).

Emergencies & Medical Care

Dial ☎ **111** to call the police, report a fire, or request an ambulance. **Wellington Hospital** is on Riddiford Street, Newtown (☎ **04/385-5999**). For emergency doctor referrals, call ☎ **04/472-2999**. For a dentist, call ☎ **04/801-5551** (available 24 hours).

Internet Access

The **Email Shop,** 175 Cuba St. (☎ 04/384-1534), has a full range of Internet and computer services; it's open daily from 9am to 10pm. It also has outlets at the Wellington i-SITE Visitor Information Centre. For other options, try **Cybernomad,** 43 Courtenay Place (☎ 04/801-5964), which offers high-speed Internet service, or **Cyber Spot Internet,** 180 Lambton Quay (☎ 04/473-0098).

Visitor Information Centers

WELLINGTON I-SITE VISITOR CENTRE 101 Wakefield St., Civic Square (☎ 04/802-4860; www.wellingtonnz.com). HUTT CITY I-SITE VISITOR CENTRE 25 Laings Rd., Lower Hutt (☎ 04/560-4715; www.huttvalleynz.com) or UPPER HUTT I-SITE VISITOR CENTRE 84–90 Main St., Upper Hutt (☎ 04/527-2141; www.upperhuttcity.com) MARTINBOROUGH I-SITE VISITOR CENTRE 18 Kitchener St. (☎ 06/306-5010).

My Favorite Moments

In addition to having the highest sunshine hours in New Zealand, Nelson is also famous for its beautiful national parks, arts and crafts, beaches, and laidback lifestyle. The combined population of Nelson city and nearby Richmond is about 45,000. The jewel in the crown of the Nelson–Tasman region is the Abel Tasman National Park—a place of crystal waters and golden-sand beaches. In Marlborough, the Marlborough Sounds, boating adventures, and Queen Charlotte Walkway are key attractions. The Marlborough wine region is known throughout the world and is responsible for over 50% of New Zealand's total wine production.

> PREVIOUS PAGE *Take a kayak paddle on one of the region's pristine rivers.* THIS PAGE *Wine tasting is a must in the Marlborough Wine Region.*

① **Kayaking in Abel Tasman National Park.** The Abel Tasman is a kayaker's Nirvana—once you've paddled across these impossibly clear ocean waters, pulling into remote, empty, golden-sand beaches, any other kayaking adventure will seem mediocre by comparison. See p. 319.

② **Wine tasting at Cloudy Bay Winery.** When you're talking wine, there's no bay like Cloudy Bay. It's known the world over for its premium sauvignon blanc, 75% of which is exported. See "Marlborough Vineyards," p. 307.

③ **Eating green-lipped mussels in Marlborough Sounds.** Nothing compares to eating freshly barbecued green-lipped mussels plucked straight from the deep green waters of Marlborough Sounds, on the back of a boat. See p. 302, **①**.

④ **Swimming at Kaiteriteri Beach.** Every summer, thousands of South Islanders

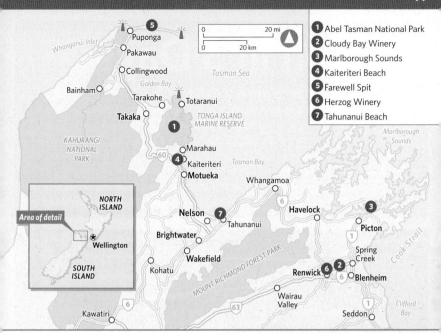

Abel Tasman National Park
Cloudy Bay Winery
Marlborough Sounds
Kaiteriteri Beach
Farewell Spit
Herzog Winery
Tahunanui Beach

descend on this golden crescent of sand to swim and soak up the sun. It's the classic Kiwi summer holiday scene with an overflowing camping ground, boats everywhere, and everyone having fun. See p. 300, ⑥.

⑤ **Bird-watching on Farewell Spit.** I could spend days here with my camera photographing the enormous sand dunes and the incredible birdlife. The longest sand spit in New Zealand, it is home to several migratory species. See p. 316.

⑥ **Having lunch at luxurious Herzog Winery.** After my first visit to this culinary heaven, I decided it had to be a regular event. It combines one of the best wine lists in the country with Michelin-rated chefs, beautiful alfresco lunches, and views of the pretty vineyard. See p. 322.

⑦ **Walking Tahunanui Beach at sunset.** Stretching my legs on this dreamy stretch of white sand is one of my favorite things to do as the sun closes on another sun-baked Nelson day. You're never alone but that doesn't matter a bit. It's great to watch families at play, or to stop and chat with fellow holiday-goers. See p. 301, ⑪.

> *The beaches of the greater Nelson province offer a vast playground for kids and adventurers.*

Nelson in 3 Days

Nelson is a very large province that subdivides into five distinct areas, each with its own character: Nelson-Richmond, the urban heart; Motueka, the horticultural heartland; Abel Tasman National Park, a paradise of bush-wrapped beaches and crystal-clear waters; Golden Bay, a fertile valley between two giant, bush-covered national parks; and St. Arnaud-Murchison, an alpine lakes area in the heart of Nelson Lakes National Park. It's impossible to experience all of this in 3 days but I've included some strategically planned tours in this itinerary so you can see as many highlights as possible in a short time.

> *There's a chance to get to know New Zealand's sea creatures at Mapua's Touch the Sea Aquarium.*

START Nelson sits at the top of the South Island, 146km (91 miles) west of Picton, where the North Island ferries land. The Nelson i-SITE Visitor Centre is at the north end of Nelson's main shopping center on Tafalgar St. **TRIP LENGTH** About 100km (62 miles) over 3 days.

1 Nelson i-SITE Visitor Centre. Make a brief stop here to familiarize yourself with the lay of the land. There are excellent displays and loads of brochures, and you should watch the short non-stop video that plays on the big screen. Make sure you pick up a copy of the *Nelson Art Guide* brochure. ⏱ 30 min. 77 Trafalgar St. ☎ 03/548-2304. www.NelsonNZ.com/isite. Mon–Fri 8:30am–5:30pm, Sat–Sun 9am–5pm.

2 ★★★ kids Nelson Provincial Museum. This is a small museum that will give you a sense of how this thriving little city has flourished from first indigenous settlement to present day. ⏱ 1 hr. See p. 312, **1**.

3 ★★★ Explore the Plains tour. Join Roy Thompson of Bay Tours for this half-day tour, which includes visits to four wineries on the Waimea Plains. Breweries can also be included

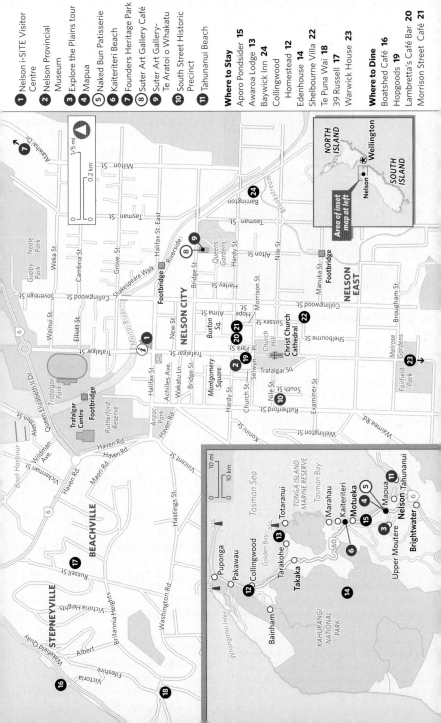

1 Nelson i-SITE Visitor Centre
2 Nelson Provincial Museum
3 Explore the Plains tour
4 Mapua
5 Naked Bun Patisserie
6 Kaiteriteri Beach
7 Founders Heritage Park
8 Suter Art Gallery Café
9 Suter Art Gallery-Te Aratoi o Whakatu
10 South Street Historic Precinct
11 Tahunanui Beach

Where to Stay
Aporo Pondsider 15
Awaroa Lodge 13
Baywick Inn 24
Collingwood Homestead 12
Edenhouse 14
Shelbourne Villa 22
Te Puna Wai 18
39 Russell 17
Warwick House 23

Where to Dine
Boatshed Café 16
Hopgoods 19
Lambretta's Café Bar 20
Morrison Street Café 21

> *Mobile coffee carts are one of the best features of Nelson's Trafalgar Street.*

if you're a beer fan. Bay Tours will arrange for pickup when you book, and there will be a stop for lunch (at your own cost) at a vineyard or seaside restaurant. The tour is a good way to get a feel for the landscapes between Nelson and Moutere Hills and to meet some of the enterprising locals working in the wine industry. ⏱ At least 5 hr. Bay Tours. ☎ 0800/229-868 or 03/548-6486. www.baytoursnelson.co.nz. NZ$80 per person. Tour departs at 12:30; call the check the schedule and reserve a spot.

On day 2 leave Nelson, heading west on Wakefield Quay and Rocks Rd. (St. Hwy. 6). At Tahunanui, veer left onto Tahunanui Dr., then right at the main roundabout onto Whakatu Dr. Continue on Richmond Deviation, following signs to Motueka/Mapua. Turn right at the roundabout, then go over the bridge and onto Appleby Hwy. This becomes the Coastal Hwy. (St. Hwy. 60). Follow the Mapua signs, turning right on Higgs Rd., and go through village to wharf. It's 33km (21 miles) and about 40 min. without stops.

❹ ★★ kids **Mapua.** The little seaside village of Mapua comes into its own in summer. It's a lovely place to stop for morning tea or lunch and to visit galleries and craftspeople. Cool Store Gallery, Laughing Fish Studio, and Serious Straws are all easy-to-find, fun stops. If you're traveling with kids, pop into **Touch the Sea Aquarium** at Mapua Wharf (☎ 03/540-3557; NZ$10 adult, NZ$8 kids), where they can discover the mysteries of sea urchins and starfish. Otherwise, buy some bait and have a shot at fishing off the wharf. ⏱ At least 1 hr.

⑤ 🍴 ★★ **Naked Bun Patisserie.** This is one of my favorite stops in this area. Settle in for delicious seafood chowder or choose from their freshly baked pies and cakes. You could also buy picnic goodies to eat at your next beach stop. 66-68 Aranui Rd., Mapua Village ☎ 03/540-3656. NZ$10-NZ$15.

Return to Coastal Hwy. (St. Hwy. 60) and follow signs to Motueka. Drive through the township, following signs to Riwaka and Kaiteriteri. Soon after you've driven through Riwaka, turn right onto Riwaka-Kaiteriteri Rd. and drive to beach. It's 32km (20 miles) and about 40 min.

❻ ★★★ kids **Kaiteriteri Beach.** There are three small but perfectly formed beaches at Kaiteriteri but once you hit the main beach opposite the camping ground, you probably won't want to move an inch. Unfurl your picnic, swim, and play as the whim takes you for the rest of the afternoon. I suggest taking the Split Apple Classic tour with **Kaiteriteri Kayak** (☎ 0800/252-925; www.seakayak.co.nz; NZ$100 adults, NZ$75 kids). This is a 2-hour kayak tour in the most sheltered part of the Abel Tasman coastline. It's suitable for kids over 8 and takes you by beautiful beaches, islands, and caves; you'll probably see seals along the way. After your kayak adventure, buy an ice cream or coffee at the campground store and head back to the beach for some more swimming and lazing about. ⏱ Half-day.

Return to Nelson the way you came and spend the night.

❼ ★★ kids **Founders Heritage Park.** There's more to see at this replica historic village than you might imagine—a boutique organic brewery, artists, bakers, and a very good cafe for starters. You'll be surrounded by elements from the 1800s to the 1930s, including a windmill, a working railway, an old plane, and vintage horse-drawn vehicles and fire engines. In summer there's also a Friday market from 3pm to 6pm. The Founders Brewery was the first in Australasia to be certified organic and the brewery cafe is a popular spot to relax. ⏱ 2 hr. 87 Atawhai Dr. ☎ 03/548-2649. www.founderspark.co.nz. Admission NZ$5 adults, NZ$2 kids, NZ$15 family. Daily 10am–4:30pm.

⑧ 🍽 **Suter Art Gallery Café.** This cafe has divine food served in a conservatory–like setting to one side of the gallery, looking out over leafy Queen's Gardens (a Victorian-style park). 208 Bridge St. ☎ 03/548-4040. NZ$12–NZ$18.

❾ ★★ **Suter Art Gallery–Te Aratoi o Whakatu.** The region's public art museum collections include some wonderful works by some of New Zealand's greatest 19th-century artists, such as John Gully, Petrus van der Velden, and Gottfried Lindauer. There is also a superb collection of works by the late Toss Woollaston (1919–1988), a local artist and one of the champions of modern art in New Zealand. Regularly changing national and international temporary exhibitions rotate through as well. ⏱ 1 hr. 208 Bridge St. ☎ 03/548-4699. www.thesuter.org.nz. Admission NZ$3 adults, NZ$1 students, 50¢ kids; free admission on Sat. Daily 10:30am–4:30pm.

❿ ★★ **South Street Historic Precinct.** Park your car and wander up South Street to see the cute-as-a-button cottages that characterize this part of town. The 16 working-class dwellings were built between 1863 and 1867 and families still live in them. Check out South Street Gallery, which shows works by 25 Nelson potters; Flame Daisy Glass Design, to watch glass-blowers at work; and Jens Hansen Gold and Silversmith, to see superb jewelry craftsmanship in action. The late Jens Hansen was the man who made the rings for the blockbuster *Lord of the Rings* movie trilogy. Nelson's **Christ Church Cathedral,** Trafalgar Square (☎ 03/548-1008) is on the hill just above this part of town. It's built of local Takaka marble and is known for its striking stained glass, carvings, and unique free-standing organ. It's open daily from 8am to 6pm and admission is free. ⏱ At least 2 hr.

> *Nelson's Christ Church Anglican Cathedral features beautiful stained glass, including this colorful Rose Window.*

⓫ ★★★ 🧒 **Tahunanui Beach.** As you drive around Wakefield Quay toward Tahunanui Beach, stop at Haven Fish and Chips, 268 Wakefield Quay (☎ 03/548-7969) for takeaway. To get to the beach, turn right at the end of Wakefield Quay just as you enter the Tahunanui shopping area. Enjoy your feast as the late afternoon sun creeps lower in the sky. There is an excellent kids' playground just above the beach. Go for a walk along this gorgeous stretch of sand and watch the sky turn pink. If it's still warm, you could even have a late dip. ⏱ At least 1 hr.

The Center of New Zealand

Botanical Hill, a short walk from downtown Nelson, is commonly known as the Centre of New Zealand. However, the actual center of the country is a point in the Spooners Range in the Golden Downs Forest to the south of Nelson. Botanical Hill, which can be climbed in about 25 or 30 minutes if you're fit, owes its name to the actions of the chief Nelson surveyor, John Spence Browning back in the 1870s. He decided to connect all the independent surveys that had been carried out by early European settlers and he began in Nelson. He climbed the hill and, using the triangulation method of surveying, he pinpointed the top as the starting point for his first set of triangles. Thus it became known as the Centre of New Zealand.

Blenheim & Picton in 3 Days

Blenheim is at the heart of Marlborough's famous wine-making province. It's an easygoing place and apart from various wine-based activities, not a lot happens. Picton is smaller still but it has the advantage of being the southern hub of the inter-island ferry system. It is also the gateway to the Marlborough Sounds, with over 1,500km (932 miles) of unspoiled coastline. Within the Marlborough Sounds, the Queen Charlotte, Kenepuru, and Pelorus sounds are especially good for fishing, sailing, kayaking, and bush walking, while the Queen Charlotte Walkway is one of the most popular treks in the country.

> To experience the true beauty of Marlborough Sounds, take a cruise to see pretty, pristine, and peaceful bays and private beaches.

START Picton, 146km (91 miles) east of Nelson, is the landing point for the Interislander ferry from Wellington. It is 28km (17 miles) from Blenheim and 336km (209 miles) from Christchurch.

❶ ★★★ kids **Marlborough Icons Tour.** Kick off your first day with this superb all-day tour that will give you a taste of the Marlborough wine region at internationally famous Cloudy Bay Winery before whisking you off to pretty Havelock for lunch at Slip Inn Café (at your own cost). You'll then depart on the Greenshell Mussel Cruise, which takes you out into the beautiful sounds to learn about the multimillion-dollar mussel industry. You'll get to taste mussels fresh from the sea (cooked on the boat) before heading back to shore. A great day out that highlights the best features of the region. Tour includes pick-ups; bookings essential. ⏱1 day. Marlborough Travel. ☎ 0800/990-800 or 03/577-9997; www.marlboroughtravel.co.nz or www.greenshellmusselcruise.co.nz. NZ$199 adults, NZ$99 kids 5–15. Daily Sept–Apr.

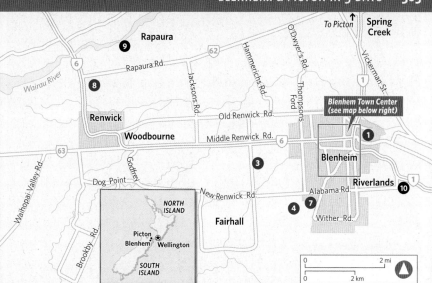

1. Marlborough Icons Tour
2. Dolphin Watch Ecotours
3. Wine Tours by Bike
4. Omaka Aviation Heritage Centre
5. Millennium Art Gallery
6. CPR HQ
7. Marlborough Museum
8. Wineries and vineyards

Where to Stay

Escape to Picton **13**
McCormick House **12**
Peppertree Lodge **10**

Where to Dine

Herzog **9**
Le Café **11**
Raupo **14**

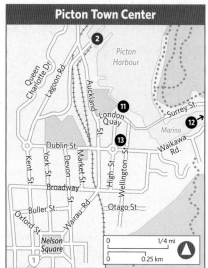

Picton Town Center

Blenheim Town Center

> *Several species of dolphins come out to play in Marlborough Sounds, so your chances of a sighting are excellent.*

2 ★★★ kids **Dolphin Watch Ecotours.** On day 2, head out onto the water with this group of marine biologists. They have a Department of Conservation permit that allows their boat and passengers to interact with the dusky, common, bottlenose, and Hector's dolphins that frequent the pristine Marlborough Sounds. Pull on a wet suit to watch these beautiful creatures speed through the water, leaping and nosing up to you. Throughout the journey, you'll get great views of the Sounds scenery. Make sure you take your camera. ⊙ **Half-day.** Booking office at Picton Foreshore. ☎ 03/573-8040. www.dolphinswimming.co.nz. Tours depart from Picton Wharf. NZ$150 per person (NZ$100 for boat ride/dolphin-watching only). Tours depart 8am Dec–March; 9am Apr–Nov.

3 ★★★ **Wine Tours by Bike.** This has got to be one of the loveliest summer activities in the country—a slow pedal from winery to winery, stopping off to visit artists, craftsmen, vineyards, and food producers at your leisure. Along with your cycling gear, you'll get a map with self-guiding instructions and hints on all the best places to visit. Make sure you take a camera, sunscreen, and bottled water. If you decided to miss the dolphin swimming earlier, you could do the full-day winery tour. Wine

> *Join Wine Tours by Bike for a leisurely pedal around some of the region's top wineries.*

Tours By Bike, 191 Bells Rd., Blenheim. ☎ 03/577-6954; www.winetoursbybike.co.nz. NZ$42 for 4 hr, NZ$58 for 8 hr. Free transport to and from Blenheim accommodation. Oct–April 9am–6pm; May & Sept 9am–5pm; closed Jun–Aug.

> *Aviation buffs will love seeing rare aircraft on display at Omaka Aviation Heritage Centre, near Blenheim.*

④ ★★★ Omaka Aviation Heritage Centre.
Start here on day 3. Even if you think you're not interested in aircraft or war history, you'll find this unique museum a fascinating experience. The *Knights of the Sky* exhibit incorporates a mix of static displays and flyable planes and is one of the world's largest collections of World War I aircraft and memorabilia. It includes a 1913 Caproni CA 22, the only known aircraft of its type left in existence. Extensive dioramas, created in meticulous detail with special effects lighting (made by the special effects gurus at Weta Workshop, p. 265, ⑪), make for an amazing multi-sensory experience. The center's trust is chaired by renowned New Zealand cinematic genius, Sir Peter Jackson. ⏱ At least 1 hr. 79 Aerodrome Rd., Omaka, beside Omaka Airfield. ☎ 03/579-1305. www.omaka.org.nz. Admission NZ$20 adults, NZ$8 kids 5–14, NZ$32–NZ$48 family. Guided tours NZ$25 per person, 10:30am and 2pm during summer. Daily 10am-4pm.

⑤ ★★ kids Millennium Art Gallery. Marlborough's public art gallery opened in December 1999 and since then, it has staged many excellent exhibitions of painting, sculpture, photography, and weaving by local and New Zealand-wide artists. They stage around 23 exhibitions a year, often in conjunction with a program of curator and artist talks. ⏱ 45 min. Seymour St., Blenheim. ☎ 03/579-2001. www.marlboroughart.org.nz. Admission by donation. Mon-Fri 10:30am-4:30pm, Sat-Sun 1pm-4pm.

Queen Charlotte Walkway

Renowned for its stunning views, historical landmarks, and contrasting landscapes, this 71km (44-mile) walk passes through lush coastal forest, around coves and inlets, and along ridges, offering unforgettable views of Queen Charlotte and Kenepuru sounds. Stretching from historic Ship Cove to Anakiwa, it can be walked in 3 to 5 days depending on your fitness and preferences—kayaking, mountain biking, diving, swimming, and fishing can all be added to make it a richer and longer experience. If you take a guided walk, you'll stay in cabins, rustic lodges, and homestays, while your pack will be carried by boat, meeting you at each overnight stop. The track is open all year but guided walks only operate November through May. In addition to camping costs (NZ$10–NZ$12 per night) and any other variously priced lodgings, unguided walkers are also asked to contribute NZ$5 to the Queen Charlotte Track Tribute Fund, which helps maintain the track as a place of rare beauty. Ticket dispensing machines for the fund are located at Picton Town Wharf, or you can pay your contribution to your water transport operator prior to departure. Independent walkers should contact the Department of Conservation, Picton Field Centre (☎ 03/575-7582; www.qctrack.co.nz) for track and booking details.

> *Marlborough is acclaimed as the producer of the best sauvignon blanc wines in the world.*

⑥ ☕ **CPR HQ.** This place roasts their own coffee beans and serves up tasty snacks to go with your favorite brew. 18–20 Wynen St. ☎ 03/579-5030; www.cprcoffee.com. NZ$5–NZ$12.

❼ ★★ **kids Marlborough Museum.** Like most small-town New Zealand museums, this one has some unexpected surprises—a replica village called Beavertown, for instance, which reflects how Blenheim looked in the 1900s. Created in the 1960s, the village takes its name from Blenheim's early names, "The Beaver" and "Beaver Station," which came about because of the town's propensity to flood. In addition, there are excellent collections of historical photographs, film and video collections, textiles, and, outside, vintage cars and machinery. ⏱ 1 hr. 26 Arthur Baker Place, Blenheim. ☎ 03/578-1712. www.marlboroughmuseum.org.nz. Admission NZ$10 adults, NZ$5 kids 5–15. Daily 10am–4pm.

❽ ★★★ **Wineries and vineyards.** I suggest you spend the rest of your afternoon visiting more wineries. I've listed my top choices in the "Marlborough Vineyards" box below but you should also pick up a copy of free wine guide brochures at the Blenheim visitor center (p. 323) or check out www.winemarlborough.net.nz. Allow plenty of time for wine tasting and perhaps a delicious platter of local food treats. Plan your afternoon so you end up at one of the vineyard restaurants for dinner. If you'd rather take another wine tour, contact **Sounds Connection** (☎ 0800/742-866; www.soundsconnection.co.nz), which escorts small groups to any requested vineyards. **The Wine Room**, St. Hwy. 1, Grovetown, Blenheim (☎ 03/570-5490; www.thewineroom.net.nz), is another option. They offer blind tastings from five local wineries and also sell gourmet products like chocolate and olive oil. They will organize the shipping of any wine you purchase too. ⏱ Half-day.

The TranzCoastal

The TranzCoastal train (☎ 0800/872-467 or 04/495-0775; www.tranzscenic.co.nz) travels between the port of Picton and Christchurch. This journey is a scenic feast, with the Kaikoura mountain ranges on one side and the rugged Pacific coast on the other. Along the way you pass though the village of Kaikoura (p. 339, ⑭), where, if you're touring New Zealand, you can break your journey to take in the whale watching or swimming with the dolphins. At press time, the TranzCoastal route had been replaced by a bus service making the same trip due to damage suffered by the February 22 earthquake in Christchurch. But by the time you hold this book in your hands, rail service will likely be repaired and operating as normal.

Marlborough Vineyards

★★ **Allan Scott Family Winemakers,** Jacksons Road, Blenheim (☎ 03/572-9054; www.allanscott.com), is home to one of the best vineyard restaurants, Twelve Trees, which has a rustic interior and a beautiful courtyard garden. The winery produces chardonnay, sauvignon blanc, and riesling.

★★★ **Clos Henri Vineyard,** 639 St. Hwy. 63, Renwick (☎ 03/572-7923; www.closhenri.com), was established in 2001 by the internationally recognized French winemaking family of the Domaine Henri Bourgeois of Sancerre. Their intention is to unite 10 generations of traditional French winemaking with the personality of New World varietal character.

No New Zealand winery name resonates quite as much as ★★★ **Cloudy Bay Vineyards,** Jacksons Road, Blenheim (☎ 03/520-9147; www.cloudybay.co.nz). It put Marlborough's sauvignon blanc on the map.

Join a walking vineyard tour of ★★ **Framingham Wines,** 19 Conders Bend Rd., Renwick, Blenheim (☎ 03/572-8884; www.framingham.co.nz), one of the oldest riesling vineyards in Marlborough. The vintners produce white varietals with small amounts of chardonnay and montepulciano.

At ★★ **Grove Mill,** Waihopai Valley Road, Renwick (☎ 03/572-8200; www.grovemill.co.nz), you can enjoy a cheese platter at a wetland sanctuary or browse top New Zealand art at the Diversion Gallery. The unique aroma demonstration is a fun way to learn about the distinct characteristics of Marlborough's world-famous sauvignon blanc.

This is also the world's first carbon-neutral winery.

★★★ **Montana Brancott Winery,** St. Hwy. 1, Riverlands, Blenheim (☎ 03/577-5775; www.montana.co.nz), is New Zealand's largest winery. Their massive building here holds a retail store, tasting rooms, a restaurant, theater, and educational facilities.

★★ **Nautilus Estate,** 12 Rapaura Rd., Blenheim (☎ 03/572-9364; www.nautilusestate.com), is perhaps best known for their Cuvée Marlborough, a non-vintage, bottle-fermented sparkling wine that is widely regarded as one of New Zealand's best.

Architecture buffs should be sure to stop at ★★★ **Spy Valley Wines,** Lake Timara Road West, Waihopai Valley, Renwick (☎ 03/572-9840; www.spyvalleywine.co.nz). The winery is one of the most technologically advanced in New Zealand and the building has won major architectural awards.

State-of-the-art ★★★ **Villa Maria Estate,** corner of Paynters and New Renwick roads, Fairhall, Blenheim (☎ 03/577-9530; www.villamaria.co.nz), has been the country's most awarded winery for over 30 years.

★★ **Wairau River Wines,** corner of Rapaura Road and St. Hwy. 1, Blenheim (☎ 03/572-9800; www.wairauriverwines.com), is one of the largest independent wineries in Marlborough. With a production philosophy of small batches from vine to bottle, they have an excellent reputation for their flagship sauvignon blanc. Their brasserie is one of the best spots for lunch.

Nelson with Kids

Greater Nelson has a host of activities kids will love but in the interests of speed and convenience (and less boring travel time), I have restricted this 3-day itinerary to Nelson city and its immediate surrounds. Kids are usually happy spending the day at the beach and if you've already been on the road a while before arriving here, that's probably the best treat you can give them—freedom, sand, surf, sun, and ice cream.

> Meerkats are one of the most popular animals at Nelson's Natureland Zoo.

START Nelson Fun Park is adjacent to Tahunanui Beach, just around the waterfront to the west of Nelson city. **TRIP LENGTH** About 120km (75 miles) over 3 days.

❶ ★★★ **Nelson Fun Park.** Bumper boats are a great invention—they can keep an entire family amused for hours. Factor in a giant hydro-slide and mini-golf and you can be sure the kids will be happy to stay put. ⏱ At least 2 hr. Turn off Rocks Rd. and drive through the beach car park to the Beach Reserve. ☎ 03/548-6267. Free admission. Hydroslide $7 per half-hour, $10 1 hr; Mini-golf $6 adults, $4 kids 5-15; Bumper boats $8 for 7 minutes. Open daily Sept–Apr; bumper boats and mini-golf open weekends and school holidays May–Aug. Call for hours.

❷ ★★★ **Natureland Zoo.** Small kids will love getting close to the very cute meerkats, monkeys, wallabies, and otters. There are walk-through bird aviaries with native birds and colorful parrots, as well as the chance to spot a tuatara along with other lizards. The park is run by Christchurch's Orana Wildlife Trust. ⏱ 1 hr. Tahunanui Beach. ☎ 03/548-6166. www.naturelandszoo.co.nz. Admission NZ$9 adults, NZ$4.50 kids 2-14, NZ$23 family. Daily 9:30am–4pm.

③ 🍽 **623 On the Rocks.** Wander across the road from the Tahunanui Beach car park and get a paper cone filled with delicious beer-battered fish with chips, or select something else from their lunch or all-day snack menu. 623 Rocks Rd., Tahunanui. ☎ 03/548-6230. NZ$17–NZ$26.

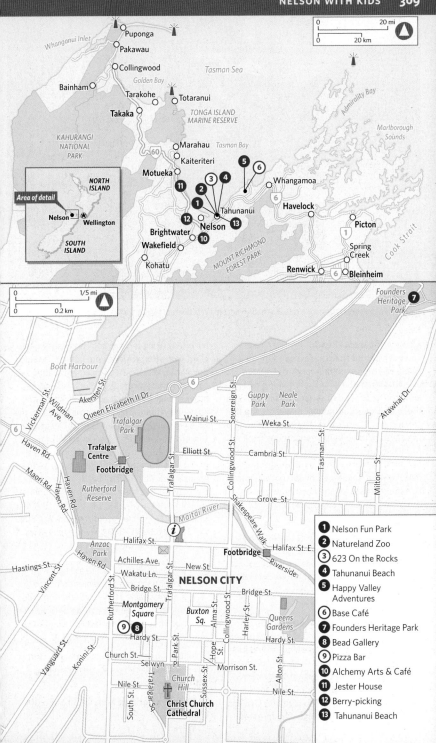

0   20 mi
0   20 km

Whanganui Inlet
Puponga
Pakawau
Collingwood
Bainham
Tasman Sea
Golden Bay
Tarakohe
Totaranui
Takaka
TONGA ISLAND
MARINE RESERVE
KAHURANGI
NATIONAL
PARK
Admiralty Bay
Marlborough
Sounds
Marahau
Tasman Bay
Kaiteriteri
Motueka
5
6
11
3
4
Whangamoa
2
6
1
Havelock
Tahunanui
12
Nelson
13
Picton
Brightwater
10
Wakefield
MOUNT RICHMOND
FOREST PARK
Spring
Creek
1
Kohatu
Cook Strait
Renwick
6
Bleinheim

NORTH
ISLAND
Area of detail
Nelson
Wellington
SOUTH
ISLAND

---

0   1/5 mi
0   0.2 km

Founders
Heritage
Park
7

Boat Harbour
Vickerman St.
Wildman Ave.
Akersten St.
6
Queen Elizabeth II Dr.
6
Haven Rd.
Sovereign St.
Guppy
Park
Neale
Park
Atawhai Dr.
Maori Rd.
Haven Rd.
Haven Rd.
Wainui St.
Weka St.
Trafalgar
Park
**Trafalgar
Centre**
Elliott St.
Cambria St.
Tasman St.
Milton St.
Footbridge
Rutherford
Reserve
Trafalgar St.
Collingwood St.
Grove St.
Maitai River
Shakespeare Walk
Halifax St.
Anzac
Park
Hastings St.
Vincent St.
Haven Rd.
Achilles Ave.
Wakatu Ln.
Footbridge
Halifax St. E.
Riverside
New St.
NELSON CITY
Bridge St.
Bridge St.
Rutherford St.
Montgomery
Square
Buxton
Sq.
Alma St.
Harley St.
Queens
Gardens
Vanguard St.
Konini St.
9 **8**
Hardy St.
Park St.
Collingwood St.
Hardy St.
Alton St.
Church St.
Selwyn
Pl.
Morrison St.
Nile St.
Nile St.
South St.
Trafalgar Sq.
Church
Hill
Sussex St.
Hope St.
**Christ Church
Cathedral**

1 Nelson Fun Park
2 Natureland Zoo
3 623 On the Rocks
4 Tahunanui Beach
5 Happy Valley
   Adventures
6 Base Café
7 Founders Heritage Park
8 Bead Gallery
9 Pizza Bar
10 Alchemy Arts & Café
11 Jester House
12 Berry-picking
13 Tahunanui Beach

> *Ride through forests and valleys and across rivers on 4WD bikes at Happy Valley Adventures.*

❹ ★★★ **Tahunanui Beach.** Now that you know where the snacks are, spend the rest of the afternoon on this wonderful spread of white sand. You'll find safe swimming for kids, plenty of sand to shape into castles, and thousands of other holiday-makers doing the same thing. There's also a small playground in the car park that younger children will enjoy. Mobile espresso carts come and go from the car park, so there will be a ready supply of caffeine to keep parents at the top of their game. End the day with an early dinner at one of the restaurants I've suggested on p. 322. ⏲ Half-day.

On day 2, head north on Trafalgar St., turn right onto Queen Elizabeth Dr., and head west on Atawhai Dr., which becomes Whakapuaka Rd. (St. Hwy. 6). Turn left at Cable Bay Rd. and follow the signs to Happy Valley. It's 16km (10 miles) and about 15 min. away.

❺ ★★★ **Happy Valley Adventures.** You can happily spend most of the day here, although your personal budget constraints may determine how many activities the family decides to do, as each activity is priced separately. You might have to put it to a family vote. Certainly the Skywire is the highlight (NZ\$85 adults, NZ\$55 kids). Set high on a forested

hill overlooking the sea and river valleys, this giant flying fox will take you 3.2km (2 miles) down in a rush, safely buckled into a four-seat carriage. I won't reveal the surprise ending other than to say you'll all love it. There are also lovely, hour-long horse treks (NZ\$65 per rider) for all ages and levels of ability and, for something speedier, 1½ hr-long 4WD drive rides (NZ\$80 per rider, NZ\$20 per passenger) over a number of different circuits. You could also try a paintball battle (from NZ\$25 per player). Twenty-minute Argo (amphibious vehicle) rides are NZ\$15 per person. ⏲ At least a half-day. 194 Cable Bay Rd., Nelson. ☎ 0800/157-300 or 03/545-0304. www.happyvalley adventures.co.nz. Daily 9am–6pm.

---

⑥　🍴 **Base Café.** This cafe at Happy Valley Adventures is a convenient place to grab a quick snack. They have a light menu that should keep you going until you get back into town. At Happy Valley Adventures (see above). NZ\$5–NZ\$10.

Drive back into Nelson on St. Hwy. 6. Before you reach central Nelson, turn left on Atawhai Dr.

❼ **Founders Heritage Park.** ⏲ 2 hr. See p. 300, .

8 ★★ **Bead Gallery.** If you have a family full of boys, this may not be the activity for you, but I'm a great believer in the modern young man being well versed in all areas, so set a challenge—who can make the most creative necklace, perhaps, or the best gift for granny? After all the physical exercise today, you'll be hoping for a quiet wind-down before bed. There are over 10,000 beads and trained staff on hand to point you in the right direction. ⏱ At least 1 hr. 157 Hardy St., Nelson, or 18 Parere St., Nelson. ☎ 03/546-7807. www.beads.co.nz.

9 🍕 **Pizza Bar.** Order some pizza and either eat in or bring takeaway to Queen's Gardens, a park that you can access further down Hardy Street heading east. 105 Hardy St. ☎ 03/548-8990. NZ$12–NZ$19.

On day 3, leave Nelson via Wakefield Quay and Rocks Rd., veer left at Tahunanui, and at the roundabout take the exit onto Whakatu Drive (St. Hwy. 6). Continue on Richmond Deviation and at the roundabout, turn left on Bateup Rd. It's about 16km (10 miles) and 20 min.

10 ★★ **Alchemy Arts & Café.** You're in Nelson, home to dozens of leading potters, so let the kids tap into their creative urges. You can book ahead to secure them a turn on the potter's wheel or simply set them to work decorating pottery with their own designs. Their ceramics will be a great memento or gift. The whole family can join in or just leave the kids to it in the studio while you enjoy a cup of coffee in the cafe. There are swings, a duck pond, and a few animals on site too. ⏱ At least 1 hr. 92 Bateup Rd., Richmond. ☎ 03/544-5853. www.alchemyarts.co.nz. Daily 10am-4pm.

Head back to the roundabout on St. Hwy. 6 and go straight through, then over the bridge to Appleby Hwy. and Coastal Hwy. (St. Hwy. 60). Go through Ruby Bay (24km/15miles and 30 min.) to the Jester House.

11 ★★ **Jester House.** The big attraction here, oddly, is a bunch of tame eels that seem to get bigger and fatter every time I see them. Not surprising I suppose, when you consider that almost every visitor feeds them. Buy the kids a bag of food and let them have a go. The property also has a playground, garden art, a wishing

> *Tahunanui Beach is a giant spread of white sand and safe swimming minutes from the heart of Nelson.*

well, and a giant chess set—plus a nice cafe where you can all enjoy morning tea or an early lunch. ⏱ 1 hr. Coastal Hwy., Tasman. ☎ 03/526-6742. www.jesterhouse.co.nz. Daily 9am–5pm.

Drive back the way you came on Coastal and Appleby hwys.

12 ★★★ **Berry-picking.** There's nothing like being out in the sun, plucking fresh, ripe fruit from the vines. There are a number of options in the district but two of the best are **Berrylands,** 108 Appleby Hwy. (☎ 03/544-2099), and **Best Berry Company,** 8 River Rd. (☎ 04/544-8434), taking the Coastal Highway exit at Appleby Bridge. The latter has fresh berry ice cream too, which is bound to be a draw. The best berry-picking happens December through March. Both are open daily 9am until late. ⏱ 2 hr.

Head back to Nelson the way you came.

13 ★★★ **Tahunanui Beach.** End your afternoon back at the beach. If it's still warm, have a swim, walk along the beach, or let the kids loose in the playground. Plan to have dinner back in the city, or at one of the cluster of cafes, restaurants, and pizza bars across the road from the beach car park. If you get takeaway pizza or pasta, you could have an evening picnic on the beach. ⏱ At least 1 hr.

Nelson for Art & History Lovers

You could easily spend two weeks in Nelson and still not see all the artists and craftspeople who live and work in the region. The Nelson i-SITE Visitor Centre (p. 323) puts out at least six art brochures and many artists have individual brochures stocked at the center. The best investment, though, is the ring-bound *Nelson Art Guide,* which breaks everything down into districts with maps. (It will be a lovely souvenir, too.) Once you've gathered the material you need, follow this itinerary over 3 days to cram in as much as possible.

SHAGUAR

> *Collectible cars and award-winning costumes come together at the World of WearableArt™ & Classic Cars Museum.*

START Nelson Provincial Museum is in the main shopping area, on the corner of Trafalgar and Hardy sts. **TRIP LENGTH** About 100km (62 miles) over 3 days.

❶ ★★★ kids Nelson Provincial Museum. This small museum is an excellent first stop that will give you an overview of Maori history and early European settlement in Te Tau Iho—the Top of the South. There are some beautiful historical books and fascinating Maori artifacts. Look out for the fabulous silver collection, antique furniture, and the new stained glass window featuring native birds and plants. The former museum building in Isel Park, Stoke (see below), now houses the research center, which includes one of the largest historical photograph collections in the country and a comprehensive reference library on local history. ⏱ 1 hr. Corner of Trafalgar and Hardy sts. ☎ 03/548-9588; www.nelson museum.co.nz. Admission by donation; free admission to research center. Museum Mon–Fri 10am–5pm, Sat–Sun 10am–4:30pm; research center Tues–Fri by appointment, Sat 10am–2pm.

❷ ★★ Yu Yu Japanese Calligraphy Gallery. This serene space is dedicated to one of the finest Japanese traditions. Owned by Japanese master calligrapher Akiko Crowther and her husband Tim, it displays both traditional works and those with a local twist, inspired by the Nelson landscape. Paintings, scrolls, prints, posters, cards, and screens all capture an elusive, mysterious beauty. ⏱ 40 min. 129 Hardy St. ☎ 03/545-7487. www.yuyu.co.nz. Tues–Sat 10am–5pm.

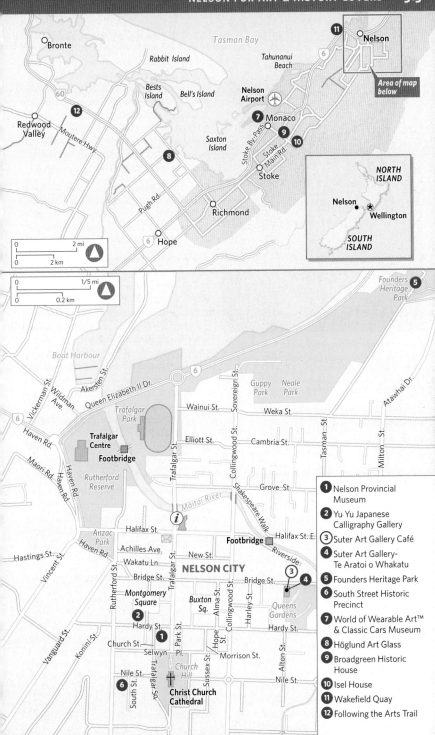

Tasman Bay

Bronte

Rabbit Island

Tahunanui Beach

11 Nelson

6

Area of map below

Redwood Valley

12

Moutere Hwy.

Bests Island

Bell's Island

Nelson Airport

Saxton Island

8

7 Monaco

Stoke By-Pass

Stoke Main Rd.

9

10

Stoke

NORTH ISLAND

Nelson

Wellington

Pugh Rd.

Richmond

SOUTH ISLAND

6 Hope

0   2 mi
0   2 km

0   1/5 mi
0   0.2 km

Founders Heritage Park **5**

Boat Harbour

6

Vickerman St.

Wildman Ave.

Akersten St.

Queen Elizabeth II Dr.

Guppy Park

Neale Park

Sovereign St.

Wainui St.

Weka St.

Atawhai Dr.

6

Haven Rd.

Trafalgar Park

Trafalgar Centre

Footbridge

Trafalgar St.

Elliott St.

Collingwood St.

Cambria St.

Tasman St.

Milton St.

Maori Rd.

Haven Rd.

Haven Rd.

Rutherford Reserve

Maitai River

Grove St.

Shakespeare Walk

Anzac Park

Halifax St.

Haven Rd.

(i)

Halifax St. E.

Footbridge

Riverside

Hastings St.

Vincent St.

Achilles Ave.

New St.

NELSON CITY

Rutherford St.

Wakatu Ln.

Bridge St.

Bridge St.

Collingwood St.

Harley St.

3

4

Montgomery Square

Buxton Sq.

Alma St.

Queens Gardens

Vanguard St.

Konini St.

2

Hardy St.

1

Church St.

Selwyn

Park Pl.

Hope St.

Hardy St.

Morrison St.

Alton St.

6

Nile St.

South St.

Trafalgar Sq.

Church Hill

Sussex St.

Nile St.

Christ Church Cathedral

1 Nelson Provincial Museum

2 Yu Yu Japanese Calligraphy Gallery

3 Suter Art Gallery Café

4 Suter Art Gallery-Te Aratoi o Whakatu

5 Founders Heritage Park

6 South Street Historic Precinct

7 World of Wearable Art™ & Classic Cars Museum

8 Höglund Art Glass

9 Broadgreen Historic House

10 Isel House

11 Wakefield Quay

12 Following the Arts Trail

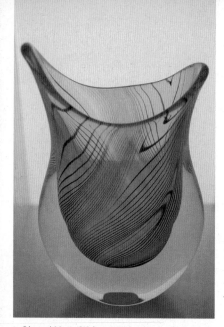

> Ola and Marie Simberg-Höglund trained as glass-blowers in Sweden before coming to New Zealand.

③ 🍽 **Suter Art Gallery Café.** See p. 301, ⑧.

④ ★★ kids **Suter Art Gallery–Te Aratoi o Whakatu.** ⏱ 1 hr. See p. 301, ⑨.

⑤ ★★ kids **Founders Heritage Park.** ⏱ 2 hr. See p. 300, ⑦.

⑥ ★★ kids **South Street Historic Precinct.** ⏱ 2 hr. See p. 301, ⑩.

On day 2, leave the city heading west on Wakefield Quay and Rocks Rd. (St. Hwy. 6). At Tahunanui, veer left onto Tahunanui Dr., then right at the main roundabout onto Whakatu Dr. Get into the right-hand lane; a short distance further, turn right on Quarantine Rd. It's 6km (3¾ miles) and 15 min. to reach the World of WearableArt™ & Classic Cars Museum.

⑦ ★★★ kids **World of WearableArt™ & Classic Cars Museum.** Fancy garments and classic cars may seem like an odd partnership but you're in for a visual feast here. Along with over 50 collectible cars and motorbikes, there is a remarkable collection of past entries and winners of the internationally renowned

World of Wearable Art Awards (or WOW™). Started in 1987 by Nelson's Suzie Moncrieff, the awards show now attracts over 35,000 viewers. A recent addition to the museum complex is the stylish Reflections Art Gallery, which has excellent exhibitions of New Zealand painting, sculpture, prints, photography, glass, ceramics, and jewelry. ⏱ 2 hr. 95 Quarantine Rd. ☎ 03/547-4573. www.wowcars.co.nz. Admission $20 adults, $8 kids 5–14. Daily 10am–6pm in summer, daily 10am–5pm in winter.

Return to Whakatu Dr. (St. Hwy. 6) and turn right. Drive onto Richmond Deviation. Turn right on Lower Queen St. then left on Lansdowne Rd. It's 12km (7½ miles) and about 15 min. to the Höglund Art Glass gallery.

⑧ ★★★ kids **Höglund Art Glass.** This is a place of breathtaking (and very breakable) beauty, where world-renowned glass artists Ola Höglund and Marie Simberg-Höglund make magic with molten colors. Ola and Marie trained at the Orrefors and Kosta Boda studios before emigrating from their native Sweden. Their signed, one-of-a-kind glass treasures have found a place in art collections all over the world. Here you can watch them at work in their studios. In addition, there is a beautiful gallery space where finished works are shown off to perfection. A glassblowing video is shown on the screen in the museum area. ⏱ At least 1 hr. 52 Lansdowne Rd., Richmond. ☎ 03/544-6500. www.hoglundartglass.com. Daily 10am–5pm.

Go back to Richmond Deviation and turn left. At the second roundabout take the first exit onto Salisbury Rd. and continue onto Main Stoke Rd. Turn left on Saxton Rd. W and then right on Nayland Rd. It's 10km (6¼ miles) and about 16 min.

⑨ ★ **Broadgreen Historic House.** This pretty

Ball Games

The first recognized game of rugby in New Zealand was held in Nelson on May 14, 1870, between Nelson College and the Nelson Football Club. The game was staged on grounds below Botanical Hill, which is more commonly known today as the Centre of New Zealand (p. 301).

Victorian home built in 1855 has 11 rooms furnished to faithfully replicate a family home of the period. An excellent example of early cob construction (using clay and straw, then plastered over), it was built for Mr. and Mrs. Edward Buxton and their six daughters. In 1855, Buxton's general store sold "everything from firearms to sausage skins." At the adjacent property you'll find the Samuels Rose Garden. It opened in 1968 and it's a heavenly spot to be when its 3,000 roses are in full bloom (best seen between October and February). ⏱ 1 hr. 276 Nayland Rd., Stoke, Nelson. ☎ 03/547-0403. www.ncc.govt.nz. Admission NZ$5 adults, NZ$2 kids, NZ$8 family. Daily 10:30am-4:30pm.

Head southwest on Nayland St., turn left onto Songer St., then left onto Main Stoke Rd. Turn right on Marsden Rd. then take the third right onto Hilliard St. It's 2km (1¼ miles) to another Victorian home.

🔟 ★★ **Isel House.** This rather grand homestead was built for watchmaker Thomas Marsden and his wife, Mary. Two large ground-floor rooms have been restored, complete with wallpapers imported from England to replicate the Victorian elegance of the day. When it came time to re-carpet, the original carpet was scanned and a special run of the pattern was made in Australia. Today the lower rooms are used as community exhibition spaces. The house is surrounded by 6 hectares (15 acres) of woodland gardens, which include an excellent rhododendron collection in a glasshouse. A great picnic spot. ⏱ 45 min. Hilliard St., Stoke. ☎ 03/547-1347. www.iselhouse.co.nz. Admission by donation. Tues–Sun 11am–4pm.

Retrace your steps back to Nelson.

⓫ ★ **Wakefield Quay.** There are a number of points of historical interest along the waterfront, chiefly the Seafarers' Memorial Wharf, where the annual Blessing of the Fleet is staged every July. It's next to the Nelson Yacht Club and features a bronze sculpture by Grant Palliser, depicting a seaman at the wheel of a boat. Near here you'll also find the bronze Early Settlers Memorial Wall and Statue by Anthony Stones (near Saltwater Café). Also look for the Aotearoa mural painted by artist Christopher J. Finlayson on the side of one of

the buildings. Take a wander along the waterfront before heading back into the city for dinner at one of the restaurant's I've recommended on p. 322. ⏱ 30 min.

⓬ ★★★ **Following the Arts Trail.** On day 3, armed with the *Nelson Art Guide* and any other brochures that appeal, I suggest you hit the road around 9am and spend the day calling on artists, potters, and galleries. To make it easier on yourself, plan the area you'd like to cover so that you're not spending half the day in the car. You'll find a good concentration of studios in Nelson itself and out along the Coastal Highway and the roads leading off it. To give you a head start, some of the top artists and galleries are: paintings at Woollaston Estates Gallery; pottery at Fulmer Gallery; sculptor Darryl Frost; potters Royce McGlashen, Sue Newitt, and Katie Gold; general arts at Cool Store Gallery; furniture-maker David Haig; and potter and sculptor Christine Boswijk. ⏱ 1 day.

Famous Father

Sir Ernest Rutherford, winner of the Nobel Prize for Chemistry in 1908 and internationally known as the father of nuclear physics, was born in Nelson in 1871. Rutherford, who was one of 12 children, attended Canterbury University before moving to England. He died in 1937 at the age of 66 and his ashes are buried in the nave of Westminster Abbey in England.

Nelson Outdoor Adventures

Bicycling

★★ **The Gentle Cycling Company.** Cycling quiet country roads and stopping to visit vineyards, country pubs, and beaches is just as lovely as it sounds. The team at Gentle Cycling Company has several tours to suit different preferences. They'll also pick you up in the city and transport you to the start of the cycling route. 411 Nayland St., Stoke, Nelson. ☎ 03/929-5652. www.gentlecycling.co.nz. NZ$55–NZ$95. Daily Sept–Apr.

★★ **Biking Nelson.** Either hire a bike and set out on your own, or let a guide lead you around the city's major sights. If you're a mountain biking fan, you might also consider this company's tours to hidden trails that will test all levels of ability. ☎ 0800/224-532. www.bikingnelson.co.nz. 3-hr. guided rides NZ$90–NZ$120; bike hire NZ$50 half-day, NZ$70 full day. For collection of rental bikes, meet the Biking Nelson team outside Harry's Pub, near the Cathedral Steps at the top end of Trafalgar Street in Nelson.

★★★ **Abel Tasman Mountain Biking.** If you want to experience some of Nelson's stunning and more challenging backcountry, this is the company for you. Guides are all experienced mountain bikers and they'll lead you through forest trails, through bush, up mountains and down. They're based at Kaiteriteri Beach and their tours run from 2 to 6 hours depending on your preference (NZ$90–NZ$210). An action-packed 2-day option (NZ$295–NZ$350) includes kayaking, water taxis, and hiking. Kaiterieri beachfront kiosk or Marahau beachfront, Franklin St., Marahau. ☎ 0800/808-018; www.abeltasmanmountainbiking.co.nz.

Bird-Watching

Coastal Nelson abounds with bird-watching opportunities. **Mapua Estuary** is always a good spot, as is the **Motueka Wharf** area (from St. Hwy. 60 heading north, turn right on Wharf Rd. just before you head into Motueka town) and **Motueka Sandspit.** There are also numerous quiet bays and estuaries leading off the **Coastal Highway.** Prince among bird-watching areas

> *Join John Moore of Sail Nelson on a day or sunset charter on Nelson Harbour.*

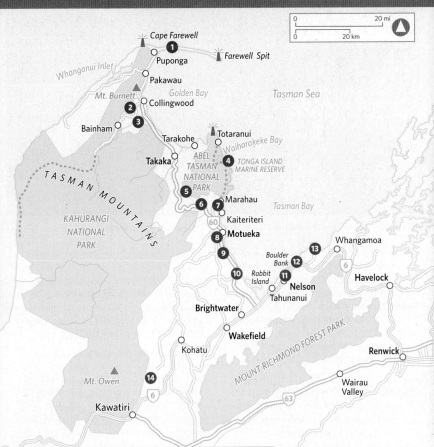

Bicycling

Abel Tasman Mountain Biking **7**, **11**

Biking Nelson **11**

The Gentle Cycling Company **11**

Bird Watching

Mapua Estuary **10**

Motueka Sandspit **8**

Motueka Wharf **8**

Coastal Highway **9**

Farewell Spit **1**

Caving

Ngarua Caves **6**

Te Anaroa & Rebecca Caves **3**

Rawhiti Caves **2**

Harwood's Hole **5**

Cruising

Abel Tasman Wilson's Experiences **8**

Fishing

Boulder Bay **12**

Cable Bay **13**

Connolly's Quay **11**

Mapua Wharf **10**

Motueka Wharf **8**

Tahunanui Beach **11**

Kayaking

Abel Tasman Kayaks **7**

Sailing

Catamaran Sailing
  & Launch Charters **11**

Sail Nelson **11**

Walking

Abel Tasman Track **4**

Boulder Bank **11**

> The Abel Tasman Track, near Nelson, is one of the prettiest walks in New Zealand.

is **Farewell Spit.** You can explore the lower reaches on your own but because the spit is a protected area, you need to join a licensed tour to explore the upper reaches. **Farewell Spit Eco Tours** (☎ 0800/808-257; www.farewellspit.com) and **Farewell Spit Nature Experience** (☎ 0800/250-500; www.farewell-spit.co.nz) both offer excellent experiences year-round starting at around $100.

Caving

Ngarua Caves. These marble caves feature the skeletal remains of New Zealand's extinct flightless bird, the moa, and 45-minute tours are offered on the hour. The caves are 70km (43 miles) from Nelson and 20km (12 miles) from Motueka and are easily negotiated. Takaka Hill, off St. Hwy. 60. ☎ 03/528-8093. Admission NZ$20 adults, NZ$8 kids 5-15. Oct-June daily 10am-4pm.

Te Anaroa and Rebecca Caves. These caves have the best glowworms. They're very beautiful but some of the rooflines are low and narrow, which might put you off if you're claustrophobic. Rockville, Golden Bay (about 140km/87 miles northwest of Nelson via St. Hwy. 6 and St. Hwy. 60). ☎ 0800/832-283. Admission NZ$20 adults, NZ$7 kids 5-15. Guided tour daily year-round at 12:30pm. Arrive 10 min. early for safety briefing.

Rawhiti Caves. You'll need to walk for 40 minutes through bush to get to these caves. Once you've negotiated the huge entrance, there's a steep descent. The experience requires fitness and agility, so it is not suitable for children under 5. This is a natural area open to the public; for more information, contact Department of Conservation, 62 Commercial St., Takaka (☎ 03/525-8026; www.doc.govt.nz). From Takaka, drive east toward Pohara Beach. At Motupipi turn right on Glenview Rd., then left on Packard Rd. The carpark for the caves is signposted near the end of Packard Rd.

Harwood's Hole. You need to be an experienced climber and caver to negotiate this heart-stopping cavity—the deepest vertical shaft in New Zealand. It's an awesome 183m (600 ft.) straight down (with an overall depth of 357m/1,171 ft.) and is a 40-minute walk from the car park. Make sure you have suitable safety gear because people have lost their lives here. This is a natural area open to the public. **Access via unsealed road 11km (6¾ miles) into Canaan Downs. Golden Bay Information Centre, Willow St., Takaka. ☎ 03/525-9136 for details.**

Cruising

Boat charters and cruising opportunities are too numerous to list but by far the biggest and most professional company is ★★★ **Abel Tasman Wilson's Experiences,** 265 High St., Motueka (☎ 0800/223-582 or 03/528-2027; www.abeltasman.co.nz). The award-winning, family-owned business operates buses, launches, beachfront lodges, cruise vessels, and kayaks, and they've been operating since 1977. Their Vista Cruises operation takes you out on the new catamaran, *Abel Tasman Voyager.* They offer numerous walk-cruise-sea-kayaking combination packages (starting around NZ$60).

Fishing

There's good onshore fishing at **Connolly's Quay** on Rocks Road and also at the western end of **Tahunanui Beach, Boulder Bay,** and **Cable Bay.** Keen amateur fishers (kids included) gather on the new pier at **Motueka Wharf** and **Mapua Wharf.** Fly-fishing is also very popular here and numerous rivers are home to plump trout. Motueka River is a top local destination. Check www.flyfishingnz.co.nz for current fishing limits, licenses, and guide details.

Kayaking

From the quiet waters of **Cable Bay** near Nelson to **Abel Tasman National Park** and **Golden Bay,** there are dozens of magnificent kayaking locations. Operators offer everything from seal spotting and paddling in calm bays to more strenuous ocean kayaking adventures. Check out their brochures and ask the staff at Nelson i-SITE Visitor Centre (p. 323) to help you make your choice. The best operators in my opinion are **Abel Tasman Kayaks**, Main Rd., Marehau (☎ 0800/732-529 or 03/527-8022; www.abeltasmankayaks.co.nz), who offer a wide range of guided trips year-round. They will give you an insight into Maori history of the area too. The full-day guided excursions range from NZ$185 to NZ$250.

Sailing

★★★ **Sail Nelson.** John Moore, sailor, maritime tutor, and boatie extraordinaire, has spent most of his life on the water and he takes pride and delight in giving visitors a memorable experience on the *Manaia*, a 34-foot Farr 1020 design. Apart from a range of learn-to-sail opportunities, the *Manaia* is also available for day sails and sunset charters in the Nelson Harbour, or you can design your own charter adventure with John. 385 Wakefield Quay, Nelson. ☎ 03/546-7275 or 027/265-7547. www.sailnelson.co.nz. NZ$100 per hour for boat charters.

★★★ **Catamaran Sailing & Launch Charters.** Martin and Jane-Maree Holmes offer a wide range of skippered charters on sailing bridge deck catamarans and launches. Their four vessels are maintained to a very high standard and have handpicked, friendly crews. Wakefield Quay, Nelson. ☎ 03/547-6666 or 027/441-4853. www.sailingcharters.co.nz. Short sails from 2 hr. to 1 day NZ$50–NZ$100; overnight sails NZ$175–NZ$300.

> *Abel Tasman National Park provides numerous kayaking opportunities.*

Walking

Almost anywhere in Nelson is suited to walking. In the city itself, there are charming walks along Maitai River, off Nile Street, and you can get to the Centre of New Zealand (p. 301) via Nile Street too. **Boulder Bank,** the thin strip of land that reaches out from Nelson into the sea, is also popular. Take water, sun protection, and a jacket for this 2½-hour, 8km (5-mile) walk, which begins at the end of Boulder Bank Drive.

★★★ **Hiking New Zealand.** This multi-award-winning operator offers a range of unique hiking safaris throughout New Zealand. In this area, its 5-day guided Abel Tasman Track experience includes 3 days walking the track and 2 "free days" at beachfront lodges swimming, relaxing, or kayaking. Meals are included ☎ 0800/697-232 or 03/384-3706. www.hikingnewzealand.com. NZ$1,550–NZ$1,750 adults, NZ$1,100–NZ$1,250 kids 8–14. MC, V.

★★ **Top of the South Guided Walks.** Guide Doug Barry-Martin and his team know this part of the country intimately. They offer easy 1-day walks to Abel Tasman, Mount Arthur, and Nelson lakes, as well as more challenging walks up to the bush line of Mount Robert for spectacular views of Nelson Lake, through off the beaten track beech forests, or to forgotten gold-mining towns and extensive caving systems. ☎ 0800/333-552 or 021/0234-3964. www.topofthesouth.co.nz. Prices start around NZ$175.

Where to Stay

> Nick and Jenny Ferrier began renovating Warwick House in 2003 and the couple loves to show guests around their mansion.

Blenheim & Picton

★★★ Escape to Picton PICTON

This exquisitely decorated place is all about romance. It's small but perfect (with an equally perfect restaurant) and sits just up from the Picton Waterfront. All three spacious units are decorated in classic style; my favorite is the large, formal upstairs suite. 33 Wellington St. ☎ 0800/693-7227 or 03/573-5573. www.escapetopicton.com. 3 units. Doubles NZ$450–NZ$650. AE, DC, MC, V. Map p. 303.

★★ McCormick House PICTON

This historic home on a hill is a lovely, restful place to be. I especially like the leafy, botanical Palm Room with its double Jacuzzi and sunroom overlooking the garden. A fascinating photographic display depicts the home's history. 21 Leicester St. ☎ 03/573-5253. www.

mccormickhouse.co.nz. 3 units. Doubles NZ$300–NZ$450 w/breakfast. MC, V. Map p. 303.

★★★ Peppertree Lodge BLENHEIM

This 1901 homestead on the outskirts of Blenheim has large, well-appointed, character-filled rooms. The owners are happy to show you around the tiny vineyard, olive grove, and farmlet. Take up a chair on the shady verandah and forget the world. St. Hwy. 1. ☎ 03/520-9200. www.thepeppertree.co.nz. 5 units. Doubles NZ$470–NZ$595 w/breakfast. MC, V. Map p. 303.

Motueka & Golden Bay

★★ Aporo Pondsider TASMAN

These two cute, self-contained, environmentally friendly cottages overhang an ornamental pond in a peaceful rural environment. Staggered for privacy, each has big beds and modern furnishings with a small kitchen, living room, and balcony overlooking the water. 23 Permin Rd. ☎ 03/526-6858. www.aporo.co.nz. 2 units. Doubles NZ$320 w/ breakfast provisions. MC, V. Map p. 299.

★★★ kids Awaroa Lodge ABEL TASMAN NATIONAL PARK
Tucked away at the northern end of this beautiful national park and only accessible by boat, on foot, or via helicopter, this stunning, award-winning property is the ultimate hideaway. Rooms are spacious, un-cluttered, and stylish. Abel Tasman National Park. ☎ 03/528-8758. www.awaroalodge.co.nz. 26 units. Doubles NZ$295-NZ$450. AE, DC, MC, V. Map p. 299.

★ Collingwood Homestead COLLINGWOOD
This lovely old villa is one of the best home-stays in the region and the friendly, personal-ized hospitality is well worth going the extra miles for. 15 Elizabeth St. ☎ 03/524-8079. www. collingwoodhomestead.co.nz. 3 units. Doubles NZ$265 w/breakfast. V. Map p. 299.

★★★ Edenhouse ORINOCO VALLEY/MOTUEKA
This divine, tranquil retreat is set in acres of beautiful gardens in a quiet and unbelievably pretty rural valley. Choose one of the giant in-house suites or opt for the large, completely private garden cottage. Thorpe-Orinoco Road, Orinoco Valley, Motueka. ☎ 03/526-8174. www. edenhouse.co.nz. 3 units. Doubles NZ$1,050-NZ$1,150 w/breakfast. AE, DC, MC, V. Map p. 299.

Nelson

★★ kids Baywick Inn CENTRAL CITY
This 120-year-old home beside the Maitai River has large, colorful rooms. A new two-story cottage overlooking a stream in the garden is great value for families or two couples traveling together. 51 Domett St. ☎ 03/545-6514. www.baywicks.com. 4 units. Doubles NZ$190-NZ$250 w/breakfast. MC, V. Map p. 299.

★★ Shelbourne Villa CENTRAL CITY
This 1929 villa is a pleasurable oasis offering lovely rooms with plenty of space and balcony views. The charming downstairs Garden Suite has its own living room and kitchenette. It's a short walk into town. 21 Shelbourne St. ☎ 03/545-9059. www.shelbournevilla.co.nz. 4 units. Doubles NZ$295-NZ$450 w/breakfast. AE, DC, MC, V. Map p. 299.

★★★ Te Puna Wai WATERFRONT
This beautiful rooms here are filled with art and antiques and have harbor views to die for. My favorite is the top suite, tucked away up a tiny attic staircase. Its two bedrooms share a divine marble bathroom and you wake to wide sea views. There's a 2-night minimum stay. 24 Richardson St. ☎ 03/548-7621. www.tepunawai. co.nz. 3 units. Doubles NZ$220-NZ$345 w/ breakfast. AE, MC, V. Map p. 299.

★★★ 39 Russell WATERFRONT
This sublime, self-contained, 2-bedroom, hill-side cottage is owned by acclaimed artist Jane Evans, who lives across the lane. Everything about the place is delicious—from the food in the pantry to the suffusion of color and char-acter. Art, ceramics, and art books abound and you have a beautiful courtyard. There's a minimum 2-night stay. 39 Russell St. ☎ 03/548-7621. www.nelsonluxuryaccomodation. co.nz. 1 2-bedroom cottage. Double NZ$495, NZ$25 each extra guest, w/breakfast provi-sions. MC, V. Map p. 299.

★★ kids Warwick House CENTRAL CITY
This huge, 3-story, Victorian home is one of Nelson's landmark properties—a breathtaking architectural statement that is testimony to the industriousness and optimism of early settlers. The lower ground-floor apartment is best for families. 64 Brougham St. ☎ 03/548-3164. www. warwickhouse.co.nz. 5 units. Doubles NZ$300-NZ$400 w/breakfast. MC, V. Map p. 299.

Where to Dine

> *Enjoy fine dining at the Herzog Winery restaurant.*

Blenheim & Picton

★★★ Herzog RAPAURA ROAD EUROPEAN

Dining at Herzog Winery restaurant must be considered one of the singular pleasures of any trip. They have one of the best wine lists anywhere. Enjoy a summer bistro lunch on the grassy lawn or indulge yourself in the fine-dining restaurant. 81 Jeffries Rd. (off Rapaura Rd.), Blenheim. ☎ 03/572-8770. www.herzog.co.nz. Main courses NZ$28–NZ$40. AE, DC, MC, V. Lunch daily, mid-Oct–mid-May; dinner daily, mid-Dec–Apr.

★ kids Le Café PICTON CAFE

There's nothing fancy about this waterfront cafe but it has been Picton's friendliest and most popular joint for years. Green-lipped mussels steamed in white wine are a local specialty and fresh fish is always a good bet. 12–14 London Quay, Picton. ☎ 03/573-5588. Main courses NZ$12–NZ$23. AE, MC, V. Daily lunch and dinner.

★★ kids Raupo BLENHEIM MODERN NZ/BISTRO

This cheery riverside bistro offers terrific big platters to enjoy with a glass of wine on the outdoor terrace. They offer set menus in addition to the delicious bistro menu. The fig, vegetable, and feta salad I enjoyed here one wintry afternoon was one of the nicest meals of my trip. 2 Symons St., Blenheim. ☎ 03/577-8822. www.raupocafe.co.nz. Main courses NZ$18–NZ$34; set menus NZ$45–NZ$55. AE, MC, V. Breakfast, lunch, and dinner daily.

Nelson

★★ kids Boatshed Café WATERFRONT SEAFOOD

This historic boatshed restaurant showcases local seafood and glorious views. Handpick your own wriggly crabs or crayfish and have them delivered to the chef, or choose from award-winning beef and lamb dishes. 350 Wakefield Quay. ☎ 03/546-9783. www.boatshedcafe.co.nz. Main courses NZ$28–NZ$34. AE, MC, V. Brunch, lunch, and dinner daily.

★★★ Hopgoods CENTRAL CITY MODERN NZ

Kevin Hopgood has worked with the Roux Brothers and Gordon Ramsey in London and he brings a welcome style and professionalism to Nelson with his calm, contemporary restaurant. Expect beautifully presented dishes from a short and frequently changing menu based on fresh, organic local ingredients. 284 Trafalgar St. ☎ 03/545-7171. Main courses NZ$28–NZ$38. AE, MC, V. Dinner Mon-Sat, lunch Thurs-Fri.

★ kids Lambretta's Café Bar CENTRAL CITY CAFE

This popular bar-cafe is invariably packed day and night. It's a favorite with the bar crowd and although the meals are not outstanding, they do serve excellent thin-crust pizzas, big steaks, and pasta dishes. 204 Hardy St. ☎ 03/545-8555. www.lambrettascafe.co.nz. Main courses NZ$24–NZ$34. AE, MC, V. Daily breakfast, lunch, and dinner.

★★ kids Morrison Street Café CENTRAL CITY

MODERN NZ You may have to wait for a table at this popular cafe, but it's worth it. I loved the seafood laksa (noodle soup) and they also do a very tasty lamb salad, classic bacon and eggs, beef noodle stir-fry, or crisp salads. They have a very good kids' menu too. 244 Hardy St. ☎ 03/545-8110. www.morrisonstreetcafe.co.nz. Main courses NZ$18–NZ$28. AE, MC, V. Breakfast and lunch daily.

Nelson & Marlborough Fast Facts

> *Over a million passengers a year cross Cook Strait on the Interislander ferries.*

Arriving

BY PLANE Nelson Airport has regular flights
to and from Wellington, Auckland, and
Christchurch and major provincial centers. It's
serviced by **Air New Zealand** (☎ 0800/737-
000; www.airnewzealand.co.nz). Air service
to **Picton Airport** (Koromiko Airport) is via Air
New Zealand and **Sounds Air** (☎ 0800/505-
005; www.soundsair.com). **BY BUS** Nelson,
Picton, and Blenheim are all serviced by
InterCity (☎ 09/623-1503). **BY FERRY**
For timetables and information on the
Interislander, call ☎ 0800/802-802 (www.
interislander.co.nz). For **Bluebridge Ferries,**
call ☎ 0800/844-844 (www.bluebridge.
co.nz). The ferry trip takes 3 hours.

Emergencies & Medical Care

For all emergencies always call ☎ **111.** Local
hospitals are **Nelson Hospital,** Tipahi Street
(☎ **03/546-1800**) and **Wairau Hospital,**
Hospital Road, Blenheim (☎ **03/520-9999**).
For a doctor, try **Lister Medical Practice,** 16
Francis St., Blenheim (☎ **03/578-5599**) or
Stoke Medical Centre, 470 Main St., Stoke,
Nelson (☎ **03/547-7488**). For dental care, try
Nelson Duty Dentist (☎ **027/448-2424**) or
Seymour Dental Centre, 62 Seymour St.
(☎ **03/578-4203**).

Visitor Information Centers

BLENHEIM VISITOR CENTRE Blenheim Railway
Station, St. Hwy. 1, Blenheim (☎ 03/577-
8080; www.destinationmarlborough.com).
NELSON I-SITE VISITOR CENTRE 77 Trafalgar
St., Nelson (☎ 03/548-2304; www. nelsonnz.
com/isite). **PICTON I-SITE VISITOR CENTRE** The
Foreshore, Picton (☎ 03/520-3113).

My Favorite Moments

Christchurch's biggest single selling point is its location, smack in the middle of the South Island. It's less than an hour's drive from ski fields, forests, beaches, lakes, rivers, wineries, and a host of specialty attractions like whale-watching, multiday hikes, and thermal alpine pools.

> PREVIOUS PAGE *Akaroa Harbour sits in the belly of an ancient volcanic crater.* THIS PAGE *The Peacock Fountain puts on a water show next to Canterbury Museum in the Botanic Gardens.*

❶ Wandering through Christchurch Botanic Gardens. I can spend hours walking through this gorgeous green oasis. It's a fine spot for walking, people-watching, or a picnic. See p. 334, ❹.

❷ Visiting the latest exhibitions at Christchurch Art Gallery Te Puna o Waiwhetu. This sparkling architectural icon has a lively, thought-provoking range of exhibitions and a very fine bookstore. See p. 331, ❶.

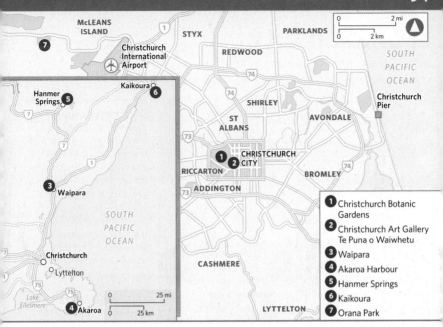

3 Wine tasting in Waipara. There's nothing nicer than driving north on a hot Canterbury summer day, finding a leafy winery with cool verandas, and ordering a big platter of treats and a selection of wines. See p. 336, **10**.

4 Dolphin-watching in Akaroa Harbour. Akaroa Harbour on Banks Peninsula is home to a lively population of rare Hector's dolphins and you can join a 3-hour cruise that also takes you to salmon and paua pearl farms, and bird-life sites. See p. 335, **6**.

5 Soaking in hot mineral pools at Hanmer Springs. Visitors flock to Hanmer Springs for the terrific alpine walks, the family adventures, and the legendary thermal pools and day spa. See p. 338, **12**.

6 Whale-watching in Kaikoura. Started by five local Maori families with one tiny boat, Whale Watch Kaikoura is now a multimillion-dollar enterprise that has completely changed the destiny of the little fishing village of Kaikoura. See p. 339, **14**.

7 Watching the big cats at Orana Park. This park has one of the most successful cheetah breeding programs in the world. I like to come at feeding time and watch them make a dash for their raw meat supper. See p. 345, **7**.

> The hot mineral pools at Hanmer Springs were first discovered by early Maori.

A Shaken City

VISTING POST-QUAKE CHRISTCHURCH

> *The spire of Christchurch's iconic cathedral toppled over during the February 2011 quake.*

On September 4, 2010, Christchurch residents were shaken awake by a violent 7.1 magnitude earthquake. It caused extensive physical damage but no lives were lost. Five months later, on February 22, 2011 the city was struck by an even more devastating 6.3 magnitude quake at 12:51pm. The central city, the port town of Lyttelton, the village of Sumner, and several eastern residential suburbs suffered massive destruction and 182 lives were lost. The city business district was in complete lockdown for many months. Despite ongoing aftershocks, significant progress has been made to get the city back on its feet. Infrastructure, hotels, restaurants, nightlife, and shops took a severe hit, but there are still plenty of options for visitors on the west side of the city; and many key attractions for the region lie well outside the city in Akaroa, Hanmer, Kaikoura, and South Canterbury, which were unaffected by the earthquakes.

There were more than 6,000 businesses in the inner city prior to the quakes. Nearly 75% of those have now opened elsewhere. Around 1,000 inner city commercial buildings and 300 more in the suburbs, many of them architectural icons, will have been demolished by the time you read this. The city cordons are reducing all the time as those demolitions are completed. Cashell Mall will open first and will act as a gateway to the rest of the city center. Re-locatable, expo-style structures will be placed in the mall for retailers and hospitality businesses that are not able to open in their former premises. But Christchurch is constantly changing since the quakes and as this book goes to press more of the city will probably be open. If you are planning a visit here, it is vitally important that you check on the current status of the city and its infrastructure. A good source of information is **Christchurch i-SITE Visitor Centre,** at Christchurch Airport Domestic Terminal (☎ **03/353-7744;** www.christchurchnz.com). Their central-city premises have temporarily relocated to the foyer of **Chateau of the Park Hotel,** corner of Deans Ave. and Kilmarnock St., Riccarton (☎ **03/379-9629** for the visitor center), but this may also change. Their website is the best first stop.

The shopping centers of Lyttelton (over the Port Hills) and the commercial suburb of Sydenham will be the first to be rebuilt. About 60 of the city's 150 suburban centers, which range from large malls to small shopping blocks, were damaged in the February quake. In the meantime, much of the social and commercial business of the city is now conducted in the largely unaffected suburbs of Riccarton (west of Hagley Park), Merivale, and Papanui (north of the central city), and Ferrymead

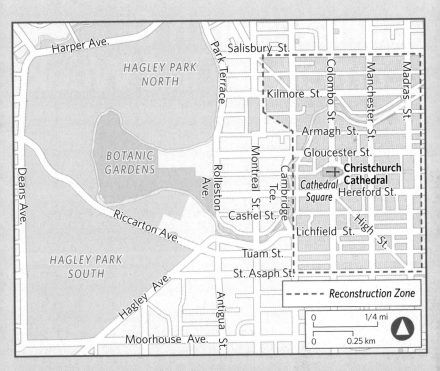

in the east, near Sumner. At time of writing, there were still 26 major city attractions and activities operating, and 7,100 guest beds available at hotels, apartments, and lodges throughout the city. There are another 11,500 guest beds available in the greater Canterbury region, however; so don't worry about not having a place to stay. Earthquake damage is very localized and most of the region is unaffected, so there is no need to cancel your holiday. Just keep checking www.christchurchnz.com for updates.

> The core of historic Christchurch will be undergoing construction for years to come.

The Best of Christchurch & Canterbury in 1 Week

One of the best things about Christchurch (pop. 370,000) is that many of its main inner city attractions are within walking distance of each other within the Cultural Precinct. The first day of this itinerary is planned from a walking perspective, taking you on a tour of key attractions, then out into the countryside to some of the wider-spread attractions via two road trips. This will give you a good idea of the enormous range of attractions that makes this province so popular. You don't have to follow my outline precisely; instead, interchange the days and locations to suit your schedule and preferences. This itinerary presumes you will have a rental car.

> *The Botanic Gardens have one of the finest collections of indigenous and exotic plants in New Zealand.*

START Christchurch is the main entry point to the South Island. It's 336km (209 miles) south of Picton. Christchurch Art Gallery is in the heart of the city at Worcester Boulevard and Montreal Street. **TRIP LENGTH** 664km (413 miles).

> *"Reasons for Voyaging" by Christchurch artist, Graham Bennett stands outside Christchurch Art Gallery.*

❶ ★★★ Christchurch Art Gallery Te Puna o Waiwhetu. This vibrant art gallery, opened in 2003, brings art and architecture together in one setting. Loved or loathed by locals, its flashy glass façade has become a city landmark. During the 2010 and 2011 earthquakes, it served as the Civil Defence headquarters. The gallery has regular exhibitions of leading national and international artists, and changing shows from its collection of more than 5,500 paintings, drawings, and sculptures. The building itself was designed by Melbourne architectural firm the Buchan Group. The large steel sculpture out front is *Reasons for Voyaging*, a collaboration between local sculptor Graham Bennett and architect David Cole. I love the gallery's innovative approach to exhibiting contemporary art in unexpected places (along the corridor leading to the restrooms, for example). You're never quite sure when you'll come upon something wonderful. Don't forget to check the superb book and gift store and the adjacent, privately run craft gallery. ⏱ 2 hr. Corner of Worcester Blvd. and Montreal St. ☎ 03/941-7300. www.christchurchart gallery.org.nz. Free admission; fees may apply to some exhibitions. Thurs–Tues 10am–5pm; Wed 10am–9pm. Free 45-min. guided tours daily 11am and 2pm. ⏱ At least 1 hour.

---

② 🍴 **Alchemy.** Stop here for morning coffee and a muffin to carry you through the next hour or two. Sit outside on the balcony and watch everyone going about his or her business. **Christchurch Art Gallery Te Puna o Waiwhetu. 49 Worcester Blvd.** ☎ 03/941-7311 NZ$10–NZ$12.

Walk west on Worcester Boulevard, passing the Arts Centre building. You'll see the museum straight ahead.

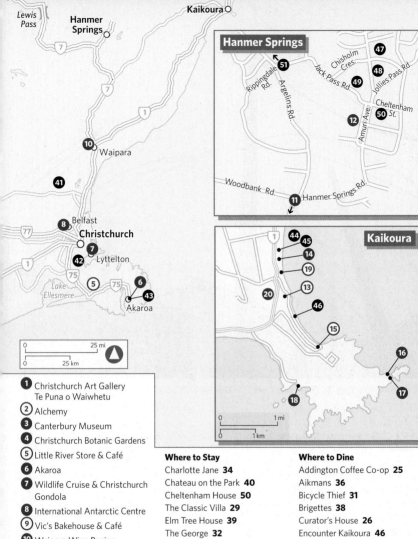

0   1/2 mi
0   0.5 km

NORTH ISLAND
SOUTH ISLAND
★ Wellington
● Christchurch

Normans Rd.
Weston Rd.
Knowles St.
Innes Rd.
Browns Rd.
St. Albans St.
Edgeware Rd.
Heaton St.
Leinster Rd.
Aikmans Rd.
Office Rd.
Rugby St.
Papanui Rd.
Holly Rd.
Springfield Rd.
Colombo St.
Manchester St.
Madras St.
Merivale Ln.
Rossall St.
Holmwood Rd.
Andover St.
Victoria St.
Bealey Ave.
Durham St. North
Colombo St.
Fendalton Rd.
Harper Ave.
Park Terrace
Salisbury St.
HAGLEY PARK NORTH
Kilmore St.
Armagh St.
Gloucester St.
Kilmarnock St.
Riccarton Ave.
BOTANIC GARDENS
Rolleston Ave.
Montreal St.
Cambridge Tce.
Christchurch Cathedral
Cathedral Square
Hereford St.
Picton Ave.
Mandeville St.
Deans Ave.
Clarence St.
Cashel St.
Lichfield St.
High St.
HAGLEY PARK SOUTH
Hagley Ave.
Tuam St.
St. Asaph St.
Blenheim Rd.
Antigua St.
Moorhouse Ave.
Christchurch Railway Station
Whiteleigh Ave.
Lincoln Rd.
Durham St. South
Montreal St.
Colombo St.
Selwyn St.
Brougham St.
Sydenham Park
Lyttelton St.
Barrington St.
Selwyn St.
Strickland St.
Bradford Park

Christchurch

> Akaroa *(long harbour) was the first substantial settlement in Canterbury.*

❸ ★★ kids Canterbury Museum. Wander through the replica streets of early Christchurch; explore the fascinating Asian Gallery, where snuff bottles, Buddha figurines, and samurai swords jostle for space; and marvel at the inventiveness of Fred and Myrtle Flutey's iconic paua shell house that encapsulates so much of the Kiwi kitsch spirit. There are superb Maori collections here, with traditional carving, jewelry, tools, and weapons. If you've always been intrigued by the polar regions, the Antarctic adventures displays are a must-see—they give you an excellent historical overview that is a good prelude to the modern Antarctic Centre displays (p. 336, ❽). I always love the Bird Hall with its big dioramas and kids love the Discovery Centre, where they can pull open drawers, inspect the contents of jars, solve puzzles, count butterflies, dig for fossils, and say hello to live tarantulas. ⏱ 2 hr. Rolleston Ave. ☎ 03/366-5000. www.canterburymuseum.com. Free admission. Discovery Centre NZ$2; fees for special exhibitions. Oct–Mar daily 9am–5:30pm; Apr–Sept daily 9am–5pm. Free 1-hr. guided tours Tues–Thurs at 3:30pm.

❹ ★★★ kids Christchurch Botanic Gardens. Plan to have a picnic lunch in this pretty, verdant core. When you're ready to explore the gardens, start by the museum and the bright Peacock Fountain. The gardens cover 23 hectares (57 acres) and you don't have to be a plant fiend to appreciate them—they're a popular picnicking and walking spot for locals, and there's always lots of activity in summer. Many huge trees are among the 10,000 exotic and indigenous plants showcased here in woodland gardens, colorful bedding displays, herbaceous borders, scented gardens, a stunning central rose garden, a fabulous tropical conservatory, and desert garden glasshouses. Don't forget the leafy fernery, the lovely ponds, and the rhododendron gardens. If you're traveling with kids, they'll love to feed the ducks and let off steam in the big playground. ⏱ At least 1 hr. Rolleston Ave. ☎ 03/941-8999. www.ccc.govt.nz/parks. Free admission; Caterpillar garden tours NZ$15 adults, NZ$6 kids 5–18; guided walk NZ$5. Grounds daily 7am–1 hr. before sunset; conservatories daily 10:15am–4pm; information center Mon–Fri 9am–4pm, Sat–Sun 10:15am–4pm. Caterpillar garden tours every 30 min. daily 10am–4pm, departing from both the museum entrance and gardens kiosk; guided 90-min. walks daily 1:30pm (plus 10:30am Feb–Mar), departing from museum entrance.

On day 2, get onto Moorehouse Avenue, turn left onto Lincoln Road, and drive straight ahead through Halswell and Taitapu. Follow signs to Akaroa on State Highway 75. It's 53km (33 miles) to Little River; if you drive straight through to Akaroa it's 82km (51 miles)—about 1½ hr.

⑤ 🍴 **Little River Store & Café.** Stop here for a quick bite to eat and a browse in the adjacent Little River Gallery, which has some excellent exhibitions and stocks of New Zealand art and jewelry. Main Rd., Little River. ☎ 03/325-1944. NZ$5–NZ$12.

⑥ ★★★ kids **Akaroa.** Pull into the car park at Hilltop Café to get photographs of the famous view, looking down into Akaroa Harbour. Early French explorer Jean Langlois took word of this pretty harbor back to France and in 1840, two ships and a handful of settlers arrived to colonize the site, only to discover the British had beaten them to it. The settlers stayed on, and you'll still see some French names in places. You can check out Akaroa's colorful history at the ★ **Akaroa Museum,** 71 Rue Lavaud (☎ 03/304-1013). Admission is NZ$4 adults and NZ$1 kids; the museum's open November through April daily 10:30am–4:30pm and May through October daily 10:30–4pm. Stop in at **Akaroa Bakery,** 51 Beach Rd. (☎ 03/304-7663), for a takeaway lunch to eat on the waterfront. In the afternoon, head to the wharf for the ★★★ **Black Cat Wildlife Cruise** (☎ 0800/436-574 or 03/304-7641; www.blackcat.co.nz). The 2-hour cruise visits a salmon farm, a paua pearl farm, and bird-life sites. You're likely to see rare Hector's dolphins as well. The cruise costs NZ$71 adults, NZ$25 kids ages 5 to 15; be sure to book ahead. After your cruise, head to ★★ **The Giant's House,** 68 Rue Balguerie (☎ 03/304-7501; www.linton.co.nz). On her 1881 homestead, local sculptor Josie Martin has created a magical world of mosaics amid terraced gardens that will take your breath away. Admission is NZ$20 adults, NZ$10 kids ages 2 to 15; the home is open December 26 through April 25, daily noon to 5pm, April 26 through Dec 24, daily 2pm to 4pm.

Spend the rest of your afternoon wandering around Akaroa's boutique stores and galleries, swimming at the beach, or line fishing off the main wharf. If you'd like to explore further afield, pick up the free brochure *Peninsula Pioneers,* which details the Akaroa to Little River Summit Road Tourist Drive. This is really an all-day excursion but you can use this as an alternate route back to Christchurch and take in a few of the highlights. 🕒 1 day.

On day 3, back in Christchurch, leave the central city, driving east on Moorehouse Avenue. Veer right onto Ferry Road. and follow this to the first large roundabout where the Lyttelton Tunnel is signposted. Drive through the tunnel, then turn left and drive along Norwich Quay. It's 12km (7½ miles) and will take about 25 minutes.

⑦ ★★★ kids **Wildlife cruise and gondola ride.** The great-value Double Deal gives you a 2-hour Black Cat wildlife-spotting cruise and a gondola ride for less than you'd pay to do each separately. The cruise introduces you to fascinating Lyttelton Harbour, where you're very likely to see Hector's dolphins and birds aplenty. From there, you'll be driven to the Christchurch Gondola for a ride with fabulous 360-degree views. Get off at the top for the Time Tunnel Experience—an automated ride that takes you back 12 million years and through to early Christchurch settlement. 🕒 Half-day. Christchurch Wildlife Tours, 17 Norwich Quay, Lyttelton. ☎ 03/328-9078.

An International Biennial

Every two years, Christchurch streets bulge with national and international artworks, as artists from around the world are invited to participate in the **SCAPE Biennial,** staged by the Art & Industry Biennial Trust (www.scape biennial.org.nz) in even-numbered years, usually between September and November. Now recognized as a showcase of established international talent and a springboard for new local talent, the biennial presents a wide array of contemporary installations and sculptures, some of which are purchased for the city of Christchurch at the end of the event. It's a fascinating time to be in town if you're an art lover.

> Multi-media displays at the International Antarctic Centre give an insight into life on the frozen continent.

www.blackcat.co.nz. Double Deal admission NZ$67 adults, NZ$25 kids 5–15.

Drive back to the city. Get onto Bealey Avenue, cross the bridge near Hagley Park, and continue on Harper Avenue. Turn right on Memorial Avenue, following signs to the airport. At the last roundabout in front of the airport, take the Orchard Road exit and follow signs to the International Antarctic Centre. It's about 10km (6 miles).

⑧ ★★★ kids International Antarctic Centre. Romp with penguins, climb aboard a snow-mobile, explore a snow cave, and feel the icy chills of Antarctica. You'll be hooked from the start of the 7-minute introductory light-and-sound show that takes you through four seasons in Antarctica. Snow falls every day (11:30am and 2:30pm) as part of the Snow and Ice Experience, which will give you an idea of what it's like to live in 23°F (-5°C) temperatures. (Warm jackets and overshoes are provided). A colony of rare Little Blue penguins is a real highlight. Also make sure you see the stunning 17-minute movie *Beyond the Frozen Sunset*. For an extra fee, peek behind the scenes with a Penguin Backstage Pass or take the Hagglund Ride, a 10-minute jaunt in an authentic Antarctic all-terrain vehicle. ⏱ 3 hr. 38 Orchard Rd. ☎ 03/353-7798. www.iceberg. co.nz. Admission (all-day pass with unlimited Hagglund rides) NZ$65 adults, NZ$36 kids 5–15, NZ$170 family. Oct–Mar daily 9am–7pm; Apr–Sept daily 9am–5:30pm.

Head back into the city on Memorial Avenue and Fendalton Road Turn left at Hagley Park onto Harper Avenue, then take your second right onto Victoria Street.

⑨ 🍽 ★★ Vic's Café & Bakehouse. Award-winning European-style breads are sold by the loaf, or choose a filled baguette from their cabinet. The salads are also divine. 132 Victoria St. ☎ 03/366-2054. www.vics.co.nz. Around NZ$16 for lunch and coffee.

Set off early on day 4 and travel north of Christchurch on State Highway 1 to the Waipara wine region. It's 60km (37 miles) and about 1 hour.

⑩ ★★★ Waipara wine region. There are more than 80 wineries in the Canterbury region, many of them clustered in the pretty, rolling,

Christchurch Nightlife

Like inner city Christchurch shopping, inner city nightlife ceased with the earthquakes. By the time this book hits the shelves, though, some temporary hospitality venues will be up and running in the Cashel Mall area (bounded by Oxford Terrace, and Hereford, Colombo, and Lichfield sts.) and more will gradually come on stream over the next year or two as the city rebuilds. There are good bars in the Westfield Riccarton, the Palms, and Merivale Mall areas (see "Christchurch Shopping," p. 357); and you will find up-to-date information on bars, restaurants, and events at www. christchurchnz.com. Look for news of films, music, and shows in the "Entertainment" section of the daily newspaper, *The Press* (www.press.co.nz).

> *Waipara's rolling hills are home to one of the fastest growing wine regions in New Zealand.*

limestone country of Waipara Valley. The Christchurch & Canterbury i-SITE Visitor Centre (p. 365) can give you a free copy of *Waipara Valley Wineries Wine Trail* or the *North Canterbury Food & Wine Trail,* which have maps showing the main wineries. Keep in mind that you have to drive on to Hanmer Springs this afternoon and there are steep fines for driving over the legal alcohol limit. Given time constraints, I suggest you call first at award-winning **Pegasus Bay Restaurant & Winery,** 263 Stockgrove Rd., Waipara (☎ 03/314-6869; www.pegasusbay.com), and then **Mud**

House Winery & Café, St. Hwy. 1, Waipara (☎ 03/314-6900; www.mudhouse.co.nz). ⏲ Half-day. Free adminssion. Both wineries open daily 10am–5pm.

Continue north on State Highway 1 and after crossing the river, turn left onto State Highway 7 and follow signs to Hanmer Springs. It's 70km (43 miles) and 1 hour to Thrillseekers Adventures.

⓫ ★★ kids **Thrillseekers Adventures.** There's an assortment of adventures here but I suggest you buckle up for the jet-boat ride, which will

> *The warm waters of hanmer Springs are known to Maori as* Waitapu *(sacred waters.)*

race you along the Waiau River, through narrow gorges, white-water rapids, and braided shallows. It's lovely countryside and there's more than a small thrill involved as you rotate 360 degrees and skim past rock faces. ⏱ 1 hr. Hanmer Springs Rd. ☎ 0800/661-538. www. thrillseekers.co.nz. NZ$115 adults, NZ$65 kids 13 and under. Daily 9am–5:30pm. Children must be large enough to fit safety gear; to participate in the bungy they must weigh no less than 35kg (77 lb.).

Drive 5km (3 miles) on Hanmer Springs Road to Hanmer Springs.

⓬ ★ ★ ★ kids **Hanmer Springs Thermal Pools and Spa.** The natural thermal waters here were first discovered by early Maori and then by early European settlers in 1859. Today the complex has more than a dozen pools ranging in temperature from 91° to 108°F (33°to

42°C). There are lovely rock pools, a cooler lap pool, private indoor pools, and a large family area with water slides. Factor in steam rooms, saunas, and a luxurious spa complex that delivers everything from pedicures and facials to massages, hot stone therapy, and body wraps, and you begin to understand why everyone flocks here. ⏱ At least 2 hr. Amuri Ave., Hanmer Springs. ☎ 03/315-0000. www. hanmersprings.co.nz. Admission NZ$18 adults, NZ$9 kids 3–15. Private pools NZ$28 per person for 30 min.; water slide NZ$10, spectator NZ$2. Daily 10am–9pm.

Spend the night in Hanmer Springs (see p. 360 for recommendations). On day 5, get on the road by 9am, driving back to State Highway 7. Turn left and drive to Waiau Intersection. Turn left onto the Inland Kaikoura Road and follow signs to Kaikoura. It's a 2-hour drive of 130km (81 miles).

⑬ 🍴 **Encounter Kaikoura.** This is a good spot for morning tea. There's a very nice range of cabinet food—all manner of cakes and sandwiches, or salads and pies if you opt for an early lunch. West End, Kaikoura (south of the information center on the waterfront). ☎ 03/319-6777. NZ$12–NZ$18.

⑭ ★★★ kids **Whale Watch Kaikoura.** Get here by midday in time for the 12:45pm tour. Nothing compares to the sight of a giant whale looming up out of the water beside your boat, its beady eye looking right at you. You'll need to book well ahead for this awesome adventure because it's hugely popular. If you are prone to seasickness take medication because Kaikoura waters can get rough. Whale sightings are not guaranteed, but if you don't see any (which is unusual) you'll get an 80% refund. ⏱ 3 hr. The Whaleway Station, Kaikoura. ☎ 0800/655-121 or 03/319-6767. www.whalewatch.co.nz. NZ$150 adults, NZ$70 kids 3–15. Nov–Mar daily 7:15am, 10am, 12:45pm, and 3:30pm; Apr–Oct daily 7:15am, 10am, and 12:45pm.

Drive back through the village and follow the Esplanade around. It's 4½km (3 miles) to the seal colony.

⑮ 🍴 **Kaikoura Seafood Barbecue.** On the way to the seal colony, stop at Jimmy Armers Beach just past Fyffe Quay and pick up a snack at this little beachside shack. They serve up fresh scallops, mussels, whitebait, and crayfish. 194 Torquay St. 027/330-0511. Assorted seafood plates NZ$25 or less.

⑯ ★★ kids **Point Kean Seal Colony.** Continue following the coast road to the seal colony. You can't miss it as the road ends in a large car park and there are information boards about the New Zealand fur seal colony. There is a resident seal population here, though numbers fluctuate at different times of day as the seals go in and out of the ocean to feed. It is imperative that you stay well back from the seals and keep a close eye on your children—the seals can be dangerous when their territory is invaded. ⏱ 1 hr. Free admission.

⑰ ★★ kids **Point Kean Lookout.** It's just a 5- or 10-minute walk up the hill from the seal colony to the Point Kean Lookout. This gives you lovely views of the Kaikoura Seaward Range and South Bay. If you walk another 25 minutes or so, you'll come to Whaler's Bay Viewpoint,

> *A deep off-shore canyon near Kaikoura is a favorite feeding ground for sperm whales.*

> *Once hunted to the point of near extinction, the New Zealand fur seal now thrives in large colonies along the Kaikoura coast.*

which gives you another perspective. This track is part of the 12km (8-mile) Kaikoura Peninsula Walkway, which takes you all the way to South Bay. Allow about 3 hours for the full walk—and then you'll need to get back to your car of course. ⏱ At least 1 hr. to walk part of the track.

Return to Kaikoura for the night. See my hotel and restaurant recommendations starting on p. 360.

🔞 ★★★ kids **Kaikoura Kayaks.** This is one of the loveliest ways of getting a feel for the richness of Kaikoura's marine environment. You'll have fur seals diving around your kayak and seabirds diving down from above. Best of all, you don't have to be an experienced kayaker because you'll be paddling with experienced guides in the calmer waters near the shore. ⏱ Half-day. 19 Killarney St., Kaikoura. ☎ 0800/452-456. www.kaikourakayaks.co.nz. Half-day trips from around NZ$95 adults, NZ$75 kids 12 and under. Daily summer departures 8:30am, 12:30pm, and 4:30pm; winter daily 9am and 1pm.

⑲ 🦞 **Craypot Café.** Treat yourself to a delicious battered blue cod or seafood chowder lunch here. Try to get an outside table so you can watch the busy summer activity. 70 **West End, Kaikoura.** ☎ 03/319-6027. NZ$14–NZ$22.

⑳ ★★★ kids **Maori Tours Kaikoura.** Maurice Manawatu and his wife, Heather, delight in sharing Maori and Pakeha stories with visitors. Maurice will take you around his home environment, giving you an insight into local Maori history, the traditional uses of bush plants, and what various local landmarks mean to his people. Wear sensible walking shoes and take along a sense of humor and a willingness to participate. It's a terrific tour and bookings are essential. ⏱ Half-day. ☎ 0800/866-267 or 03/319-5567. www.maoritours.co.nz. NZ$125 adults, NZ$65 kids 5–15. Daily 9am and 1:30pm. Complimentary pick-up from accommodation, or meet at Kaikoura i-SITE Visitor Centre.

Return to Christchurch on State Highway 1 on day 7. It's 181km (112 miles) and about 2½ hours.

Christchurch for Architecture Lovers

By the mid-19th century the early English settlers had already stamped their mark on a fledgling Christchurch society. Grand houses and hefty Gothic and neoclassical civic buildings were set off by large parks and streets filled with English trees. While many of the earliest buildings have now gone, Christchurch still boasts one of the best collections of Victorian Gothic buildings in the country, and early architects like Benjamin Mountfort have left a lasting legacy. Sadly, most of those heritage buildings sit within the inner city Cultural Precinct and most received significant damage during the 2010 and 2011 earthquakes. However, many have been earmarked for major restoration—a process that will take many years—and even if you can't gain access to them, you can still view the exteriors to get a feel for their original splendor. The best place to start is in Cathedral Square. From there, wander west on Worcester Boulevard to see the following key heritage buildings.

Christchurch Cathedral (Cathedral Square). The cathedral's foundation stone was laid in 1864, just 14 years after the city was founded, and completed in 1904. Original plans by English Gothic designer George Gilbert Scott were later adapted by local architect Benjamin Mountfort, whose work dominates the central city. Also in Cathedral Square, look for two sculptures: *Chalice*, by Neil Dawson, and *The Risen Christ*, by Terry Stringer.

Our City Otautahi (corner of Worcester Blvd. and Oxford Terrace). This Queen Anne–style building, designed by local architect Samuel Hurst Seagar, opened in 1887 as the city's Municipal Chambers and remained the center of local government until 1924. It's currently used as a space for meetings, offices, and exhibitions.

Canterbury Provincial Council Buildings (corner of Durham and Armagh sts.). This architectural masterpiece was designed by architect Benjamin Mountfort and built between 1858 and 1865. Much of the building is now given over to private businesses. It is hoped that some of the complex can be restored.

Christchurch City Council building (53 Hereford St.). The Christchurch City Council building opened in August 2009 after a refit of the old post office structure. The multimillion-dollar project is New Zealand's "greenest" building, with an impressive list of sustainable credentials. If you go around to the main entrance off Hereford Street, you'll see the spectacular glass frontage etched with Maori designs.

The Arts Centre (1 Hereford St.). Home to Canterbury University College from 1873 to 1975, this magnificent cluster of Victorian Gothic buildings, the work of several early architects, including Benjamin Mountfort, is one of the most significant in New Zealand. A major restoration is underway.

Christ's College (Rolleston Ave.). Founded in 1850, the school has a handsome collection of buildings. The oldest is Big School (now the library) on the west side of the quadrangle. It was built in 1863 and was followed by the construction of the chapel in 1867. A number of architects have contributed to the complex, including Benjamin Mountfort, Cecil Wood, and James Edward Fitzgerald.

Christchurch & Canterbury with Kids

There are a ton of things to entertain all the family in Christchurch, many of them free. I've created this itinerary based on a mix of free and paid attractions so that you won't have to spend a fortune—or travel far. It's flexible enough to mix and match if you want to shift things around a little to suit different age groups. Keep in mind that Ferrymead Heritage Park (④) is best visited on weekends, when the steam train and trams are running.

> Orana Wildlife Park—New Zealand's only open-range zoo—sits on 80 hectares just outside the city.

START Christchurch is the main entry point to the South Island. It's 336km (209 miles) south of Picton. The Antigua Boatsheds are on the banks of the Avon River, on Cambridge Terrace, off Rolleston Avenue. TRIP LENGTH 74km (46 miles) over 2 days.

❶ ★★ **Antigua Boat Sheds.** The whole family can join in the fun rowing or paddling through Hagley Park in a kayak (single or double), a Canadian canoe (three to four people), a

Clinker-built rowing skiff (three people) or a two-person paddle boat. The water is very shallow, so even if you topple out you'll be perfectly safe. Two boat builders raised the boat shed in 1882 and it's one of the oldest buildings in Christchurch. ⏱ 1 hr. 2 Cambridge Terrace. ☎ 03/366-5885. www.boatsheds.co.nz. Kayak and boat rentals NZ$10–NZ$30. Summer daily 9:30am–5:30pm; winter daily 9:30am–4pm.

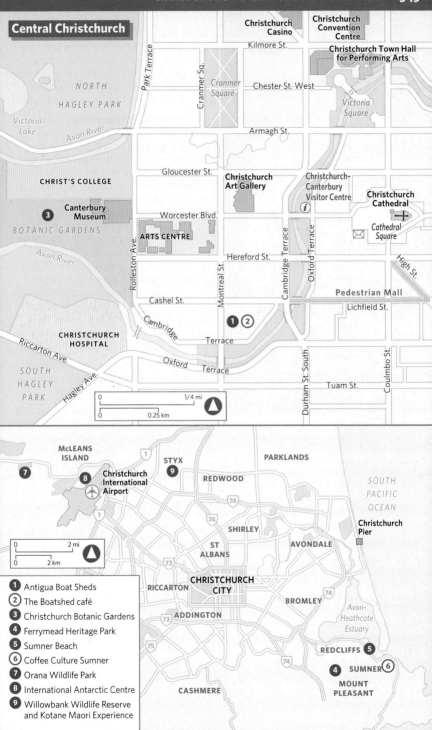

Central Christchurch

NORTH HAGLEY PARK

Victoria Lake

Avon River

Park Terrace

Cranmer Sq.

Cranmer Square

Christchurch Casino

Christchurch Convention Centre

Kilmore St.

Chester St. West

Christchurch Town Hall for Performing Arts

Victoria Square

Armagh St.

CHRIST'S COLLEGE

Gloucester St.

Christchurch Art Gallery

Christchurch-Canterbury Visitor Centre

Christchurch Cathedral

3 Canterbury Museum

Worcester Blvd.

Cathedral Square

BOTANIC GARDENS

Avon River

Rolleston Ave.

ARTS CENTRE

Hereford St.

Montreal St.

Cambridge Terrace

Oxford Terrace

High St.

Cashel St.

Pedestrian Mall

Lichfield St.

1 **2**

CHRISTCHURCH HOSPITAL

Cambridge Terrace

Riccarton Ave.

Oxford Terrace

Durham St. South

Coulmbo St.

Tuam St.

SOUTH HAGLEY PARK

Hagley Ave.

0   1/4 mi
0   0.25 km

McLEANS ISLAND

7

STYX

PARKLANDS

9

REDWOOD

8 Christchurch International Airport

1

74

SOUTH PACIFIC OCEAN

Christchurch Pier

74

SHIRLEY

0   2 mi
0   2 km

ST ALBANS

AVONDALE

73

RICCARTON

CHRISTCHURCH CITY

ADDINGTON

BROMLEY

Avon-Heathcote Estuary

75

73

74

REDCLIFFS **5**

4 SUMNER **6**

CASHMERE

MOUNT PLEASANT

1 Antigua Boat Sheds
2 The Boatshed café
3 Christchurch Botanic Gardens
4 Ferrymead Heritage Park
5 Sumner Beach
6 Coffee Culture Sumner
7 Orana Wildlife Park
8 International Antarctic Centre
9 Willowbank Wildlife Reserve and Kotane Maori Experience

In the afternoon, take Ferry Road east from the city center following signs to Sumner. Take the first right after the Heathcote Bridge onto Bridle Path Road and follow signs to Ferrymead Heritage Park. It's around 10km (6 miles) and 20 minutes to the park.

④ ★★ Ferrymead Heritage Park. This re-created 1900s Edwardian town is made up of old buildings gathered from the Canterbury community. The 8-hectare (20-acre) historical park offers a look at life in colonial Christchurch with old shops, a schoolhouse, jail, houses, a printer, church, and an operating bakery. There are several museums and you'll have to drag children out of the one featuring model trains. A steam train ride or an outing in the electric tram is usually a big hit. These operate weekends and school holidays and unlimited train rides are included in your ticket price. ⊙ Half-day. Ferrymead Park Dr., Ferrymead. ☎ 03/384-1970. www.ferrymead.org.nz. Weekend admission NZ$20 adults, NZ$8 kids 5–15, NZ$48 family. Weekday admission is almost half price but trains and trams are not running. Daily 10am–4:30pm.

Go back the way you came on Bridle Path Road, turn right onto Main Road and follow signs to Sumner. It's 7km (4 miles).

⑤ ★★★ kids Sumner Beach. Take a walk along the Esplanade or on the main ocean beach, watch beach volleyball (usually on weekends) or simply find a seat and watch people going about their business. Let the kids build sandcastles. Everyone flocks to Sumner on summer weekends, so be prepared for traffic jams. Please note that since the earthquakes, raw sewage has been pumped directly into the ocean, so DO NOT SWIM in the sea if signs advise against it. Check with locals when you get to the beach. ⊙ At least 2 hr.

> *Ferrymead Heritage Park is a reconstruction of an early Canterbury town, complete with shops and a tearoom.*

② 🍵 The Boatshed Café. This is a handy spot for a morning snack or an ice cream. You can also buy picnic food for lunch in the park. 2 Cambridge Terrace. ☎ 03/366-5885. NZ$5–NZ$12.

③ ★★★ Christchurch Botanic Gardens. Pick up picnic fare on your way to the gardens—and perhaps some stale buns from the bakery so kids can feed the ducks—and head for the Hagley Park parking area off Rolleston Avenue, close to the kids' playground. Enjoy your picnic and let the kids run off some energy or cool down in the toddlers' pool. When they're bored with the play equipment, buy an ice cream from the kiosk and take them for a walk through the gardens and into the giant conservatory to see tropical plants and enormous cacti. ⊙ 2 hr. See p. 334, ④.

⑥ 🍵 ★★ Coffee Culture Sumner. This friendly local coffee stop serves big, mouthwatering slices of cake and cheesecake, savory treats, biscuits, and handmade chocolates. They're right beside the movie theater and if you say you saw them in Frommer's they'll give you a 20% discount. 28 Mariner St., Sumner. ☎ 03/326-5900. www.coffeeculture.co.nz. NZ$5–NZ$12.

On day 2, get picnic goodies and leave the central city heading north on Victoria Street and Papanui Road. Veer left onto Harewood Road at the suburban Papanui traffic lights and continue to the Johns Road intersection. Turn right, then left into McLeans Island Road. Follow signs to Orana Park; the drive is about 17km (11 miles) and 30 minutes.

❼ ★★★ Orana Wildlife Park. I seldom need an excuse to visit the big cats at Orana. The tigers are my special favorites but there's also a big lion pride, the only successfully breeding cheetahs in Australasia, some beautiful giraffes, large rhinos, and the always-popular lemurs and meerkats. Kids can also touch and feed farmyard animals. A guided tour on the Safari Shuttle helps reduce walking time between spread-out animal shelters. All up, the 80-hectare (198-acre) park features over 400 animals from 70 different species. There are numerous changing animal feeding times throughout the day, so ask about those and the close-up animal encounters (which cost extra) when you arrive. Find a shady place in the park and enjoy your lunchtime picnic before moving on. ⏱ Half-day. 743 McLeans Island Rd. ☎ 03/359-7109. www.oranawild lifepark.co.nz. Admission NZ$26 adults, NZ$10 kids 5–14, NZ$60 family. Daily 10am–5pm.

Return to Johns Road and turn right. At the roundabout, turn right into Orchard Road and follow signs to the International Antarctic Centre. It's around 9km (5½ miles).

❽ ★★★ International Antarctic Centre. The marvelous Snow & Ice Experience is fun and informative for all the family. For a less pricey afternoon, take the kids to New Brighton Beach to build sand castles and let them fish off the end of the Brighton Pier. ⏱ Half-day. See p. 336, ❽.

Return to Johns Road the way you came, cross over to Harewood Road, then turn left on Gardiners Road. Turn right on Hussey Road and follow signs to the Willowbank Wildlife Reserve. It's 6km (4 miles) and will take about 10 minutes.

❾ ★★ Willowbank Wildlife Reserve and Kotane Maori Experience. Kids can get up close with a number of tame animals here. The

> *A live colony of Little Blue Penguins is one of the most popular attractions at the International Antarctic Centre.*

highlight is the Kiwi House, with the country's largest kiwi collection. Your best plan is to enjoy the first 1-hour Kotane cultural performance at 5:30pm, grab a quick bite to eat, and then join the 1-hour New Zealand Kiwi Experience tour at 7:30pm. There are additional later performances and kiwi tours but this way the kids can have the fun and still be in bed at a reasonable hour. Prior booking is essential. ⏱ 3 hr. 60 Hussey Rd. ☎ 03/359-6226. www. willowbank.co.nz. Admission and kiwi tour NZ$30 adults, NZ$15 kids 5–15, NZ$65 family; Kotane performance NZ$60 adults, NZ$30 kids 5–15, NZ$135 family. Daily 9:30am–10pm.

Tekapo & Aoraki/ Mount Cook

Between them, Lake Tekapo and Aoraki/Mount Cook
National Park provide some of the most dramatic and beautiful landscapes in the country. It's rugged country—the land parched and golden in summer with brilliant turquoise lakes and enormous skies; and all snow-white and slightly forbidding in winter. Aoraki means "cloud piercer" and at 3,754 m (12,316 ft.), New Zealand's highest peak does just that. It's where Sir Edmund Hillary honed his mountaineering skills before his successful assault on Mount Everest; and where today, the Sir Edmund Hillary Alpine Centre pays tribute to his incredible life's work. Drag out your trekking boots and all-weather clothing and prepare to be mightily impressed.

> *Bounded by ocean, mountains, rivers, and lakes, Canterbury is the largest region in New Zealand.*

START Tekapo is 226km (141 miles) south of Christchurch and 258km (161 miles) north of Queenstown. Head south from Tekapo on State Highway 8. Turn right on Godley Peaks Road and then right up Mount John. **TRIP LENGTH** 115km (72 miles) over 2 days.

① ★★★ kids **Mount John Earth & Sky Observatory.** The skies above Lake Tekapo are renowned as some of the clearest in the world. That's why the top of Mount John is dotted with assorted international observatories. If you're a keen astronomer then obviously

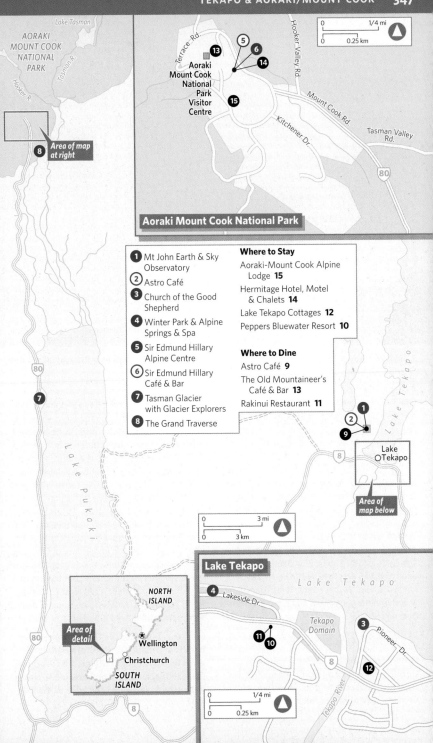

AORAKI
MOUNT COOK
NATIONAL
PARK

Aoraki Mount Cook National Park

Aoraki
Mount Cook
National
Park
Visitor
Centre

Area of map
at right

0 ___ 1/4 mi
0 ___ 0.25 km

Hooker Valley Rd.
Mount Cook Rd.
Kitchener Dr.
Tasman Valley Rd.
Terrace Rd.
80

1. Mt John Earth & Sky Observatory
2. Astro Café
3. Church of the Good Shepherd
4. Winter Park & Alpine Springs & Spa
5. Sir Edmund Hillary Alpine Centre
6. Sir Edmund Hillary Café & Bar
7. Tasman Glacier with Glacier Explorers
8. The Grand Traverse

Where to Stay
Aoraki-Mount Cook Alpine Lodge **15**
Hermitage Hotel, Motel & Chalets **14**
Lake Tekapo Cottages **12**
Peppers Bluewater Resort **10**

Where to Dine
Astro Café **9**
The Old Mountaineer's Café & Bar **13**
Rakinui Restaurant **11**

Lake
Tekapo

Lake
Tekapo

Area of
map below

0 ___ 3 mi
0 ___ 3 km

Lake Pukaki
80
7

Lake Tekapo

Lake Tekapo
Lakeside Dr.
Tekapo Domain
Pioneer Dr.
Tekapo River
8

NORTH
ISLAND
Wellington
Christchurch
SOUTH
ISLAND

Area of
detail

0 ___ 1/4 mi
0 ___ 0.25 km

80
8

> *Aoraki/Mount Cook National Park is a place of mountainous giants, spectacular glaciers, and chilling lakes.*

you'll want to come back here at night and do the 2-hour night tour but firstly, let's get you up here in daylight to take in the dramatic 360-degree views. You'll also be able to see the observatory buildings and take a day or family tour if you choose to get a feel for what goes on up here. New Zealand's largest telescope is housed here and astronomers and physicists from all around the world come here to study. ⊕ At least 2 hr. Godley Peaks Rd., Tekapo. ☎ 03/680-6960. www.earthandsky. co.nz. 35-min. day tour NZ$30 adults, NZ$15 kids 5-15, NZ$80 family; 2-hr. night tour NZ$80 adults, NZ$45 kids 5-15, NZ$225-NZ$260 family. 35-min. day tour departures 10am-3pm (hourly, on the hour), 2-hr. night tour departures 8pm and 9:15pm.

② 🍵 **Astro Café.** See p. 364.

Drive back to Tekapo the way you came. Go through the village and turn left on Pioneer Drive, just past the bridge. The drive is 5km (3 miles) and about 10 minutes.

❸ ★★ kids **Church of the Good Shepherd.** Built in 1935 to commemorate the pioneers of the Mackenzie Country, this little stone beauty is one of the most visited churches in New Zealand, thanks mostly to its dramatic location on the edge of this perfect blue lake with the mountains behind. It is still used as a place of worship by three different faiths and is booked well in advance for weddings. While you're in this area, take a walk around the lakefront. You'll also find the now-famous statue of the sheep dog. He stands in memory of "the hardy mustering dogs, without the help of which, the grazing of this mountainous country would have been impossible." ⊕ At least 1 hr. Lakefront, Tekapo. ☎ 03/655-8389. Summer daily 9am-5pm; winter daily 10am-4pm.

From the Church of the Good Shepherd, go back to the main highway, turn right, and drive through Tekapo village. Just after the main shops, turn right on Lakeside Drive and follow the road around the edge of the lake to the spa.

4 ★★ kids **Winter Park & Alpine Springs & Spa.** The international-sized artificial ice rink at Tekapo is open all year, but from late September through to late May you'll be using roller skates instead of ice skates. After you've spent an hour trying to stay on your feet, cross over to the Alpine Springs for a hot soak in one of their pools. All three pools are in the shape of one of the three lakes within the region and all have lovely views over Lake Tekapo. Finish off with a sauna, massage, and beauty treatments if you feel like truly treating yourself. ⏱ At least 2 hr. 6 Lakeside Dr., Tekapo. ☎ 0800/235-38283. www.alpinesprings.co.nz. Skating NZ$16 adults, NZ$12 kids 3–12, NZ$54 family; pools NZ$18 adults, NZ$10 kids 3–12, NZ$55 family. Ask about combo prices. Hot pools daily 10am–9pm; day spa daily 10am–6pm; skating rink daily 10am–10pm.

On day 2, try to set off by 8:30am, heading south on State Highway 8. Follow signs to Mount Cook Village, turning right into State Highway 80. It's 105km (65 miles) and about 1½ hr. The Sir Edmund Hillary Alpine Centre is inside the Hermitage Hotel on Terrace Drive. Just follow the road up to the clearly visible hotel.

5 ★★★ kids **Sir Edmund Hillary Alpine Centre.** I found this memorial to New Zealand's famous humanitarian, ambassador, and one of the world's greatest explorers profoundly moving. The museum is filled with quirky collectibles and photographs and there is a very touching short film about his early days on Everest with his first wife, who, along with one of their daughters, was killed in a plane crash there. The *Mount Cook Magic* 3-D movie is a must-see experience: it depicts the Ngai Tahu Maori myth about the creation of Aoraki, with spectacular footage. The full-dome planetarium plays high-definition video images on a huge suspended dome. Three separate movies (about 20 min. each) explore the night sky above Mount Cook, space discoveries, and black holes. ⏱ At least 2 hr. Hermitage Hotel, Terrace Rd., Aoraki/Mount Cook. ☎ 0800/686-800. www.hillarycentre.co.nz. Explorer Pass to all 3 attractions (museum, movie, planetarium) NZ$26–NZ$30. Museum daily 9am–7pm. Call or check the website for planetarium and movie showtimes.

6 🍴 **Sir Edmund Hillary Café & Bar.** This light, bright café upstairs from the museum has astonishing mountain views. It serves an excellent range of Panini, sandwiches, pies, pizza, salad, sausage rolls, cakes, pastries, and drinks. Hermitage Hotel, Terrace Rd., Aoraki/Mount Cook. ☎ 03/435-1809. NZ$12–NZ$15 for coffee and a snack.

7 ★★★ kids **Tasman Glacier with Glacier Explorers.** If you do nothing else in this dramatic region, get out on New Zealand's largest glacier—one of the few in the world that terminates in a lake. It is a surreal and unforgettable experience and Glacier Explorers will take you close to towering ice cliffs and huge floating icebergs. This is the only company permitted to operate in this area and one of only three tours of its kind in the world. Make the most of the rare experience and don't forget your camera. You must book in advance and meet 20 minutes prior to departure in the Hermitage Hotel lobby. You're then transferred to the glacier area by bus, followed by a half-hour alpine walk to the glacier. ⏱ 3 hr. Hermitage Hotel, Terrace Rd., Aoraki/Mount Cook. ☎ 0800/686-800. www.glacierexplorers.co.nz. NZ$135 adults, NZ$70 kids 4–15. Mid-Sept–end of May (providing lake is not frozen); departures 10am, noon, 2pm.

Follow signs south about 5km (3 miles) to Glentanner Park Airfield.

8 ★★★ kids **The Grand Traverse.** When you take off from the golden tussocky flats of Glentanner Park and soar high over brilliant blue glacier lakes and mountains, you'll be entering both the Aoraki/Mount Cook and the Westland Tai Poutini World Heritage national parks. It's a remarkable 1-hour journey that takes you 200km (124 miles) over 12 major glaciers, across the Main Divide to the West Coast glaciers, and over some of the most awe-inspiring landscapes in the world. There are a few different types of planes used for the tour, but all passengers have a window seat in all planes. ⏱ 1 hr. Glentanner Park Airfield, SH 80, Aoraki/Mount Cook. ☎ 0800/806-880. www.airsafaris.co.nz. NZ$350 adults, NZ$250 kids 3–13. Tours daily, weather permitting. Reservations required.

SPORTING HEROES

Famous New Zealand Sportsmen   BY ADRIENNE REWI

Sir Edmund Hillary
(1919–2008)

Sir Colin Meads
(1936–)

Sir Peter Snell
(1938–)

CLAIM TO FAME		
Mountaineer, author, humanitarian, first person on Earth to reach both its poles and its highest peak, Mt Everest.	Rugby player and coach, public speaker. Nicknamed Pinetree, he is widely considered one of the greatest rugby players in history.	Track and field athlete who won multiple Olympic and Commonwealth Games medals and broke the world mile record in 1962.
EARLY LIFE & ACHIEVEMENTS		
After he left school he became a beekeeper. He climbed his first peak, Mt Ollivier, in 1939. Joined the British team to Everest in 1959. The attempt failed but he reached the summit in 1953 with Sherpa Tensing. He climbed 10 other Himalyan peaks, visited both poles, and travelled the length of the Ganges.	Brought up in the farming district of Te Kuiti and credits farming with developing his legendary strength and fitness on the rugby field. Played for the All Blacks from 1957–1971. Captained the All Blacks several times and after retiring from the game got involved with rugby administration and public speaking. He often appears in NZ television advertisements.	An all-round sportsman in his youth, Snell excelled at middle distance running. He came to international attention when he won gold and set a new world record for 800m at 1960 Rome Olympics. He dominated at 1964 Tokyo Olympics and in 1962 broke the world mile record at Wanganui, NZ. He moved to USA in 1971 to study exercise physiology and today lives in Texas.
HONORS & TRIBUTES		
Appointed New Zealand High Commissioner to India; first living person to feature on the NZ $5 note; first foreigner to be awarded citizenship by Nepalese government; knighted by NZ government.	Named Player of the Century by NZRFU in 1999. Member of both the International Rugby Hall of Fame and New Zealand Sports Hall of Fame. Knighted in 2009.	Honored with an MBE in 1962, knighted in 2009. As an International Scholar, he was inducted into the Athletics Hall of Fame at the University of Rhode Island in 1999. Statues of Snell stand in Wanganui where he broke the mile record and in his birthplace, Opunake, in Taranaki.

Sir Peter Blake (1948–2001)	**Sir Richard Hadlee** (1951–)	**Caroline & Georgina Evers-Swindell** (1978–)
Yachtsman and Environmentalist who led New Zealand to victory in successive America's Cup races.	Cricketer and one of the greatest fast bowlers and all rounders in international cricket history.	Identical twins and world class rowers, the Evers-Swindell sisters shot to fame as winners of the 2002 and 2003 Rowing World Championship double sculls.
Blake won the Whitbread Round the World Race, the Jules Verne Trophy, setting a new record for the fastest time around the world on the catamaran Enza. Heavily involved in America's Cup racing from 1992, (they won in 1995) he led Team New Zealand to victory in 2000, becoming the first non-American team to successfully defend the America's Cup. In 1997 he became the Cousteau Society's head of expeditions. He later led expeditions to Antarctica and the Amazon on Seamaster and in 2001 was named special envoy for the UN Environment Programme. He was gunned down by pirates during an environmental expedition in the Amazon.	Born and raised in Christchurch, Hadlee was nicknamed Paddles because of his large feet. He has played cricket for New Zealand, Tasmania, and Nottinghamshire, and was the NZ Cricket Blackcap selection manager from 2000–2008. He supports numerous charities, is an after-dinner and conference speaker, patron of the India NZ Business Council, and a consultant for the American Premier Cricket League (2009).	Born in Hastings, the twins were inseparable as children, playing in the same netball, basketball, cricket, badminton, and hockey teams. Caroline started rowing at 14 and Georgina joined her two years later. They later won World double sculls titles in 2002, 2003, and 2005, and Olympic gold medals in 2004 and 2008. Their win at the 2008 Beijing Olympics was the first time in history that a women's double sculls title had been successfully defended. They retired from rowing in 2008 and both married in 2009.
Knighted in 1991. In 2002, the International Olympic Committee posthumously awarded him one of its highest honours, the Olympic Order. The Sir Peter Blake Trust was established in 2003 "to help New Zealanders make a positive difference to the planet." It also funds the annual Blake Medal for outstanding NZ leaders.	1981 awarded MBE and knighted in 1990. Winner of the Winsor Cup 13 times and New Zealand Sportsman of the Year three times. NZ Sportsman of the last 25 years (1987) and Sportsman of the Decade 1990. Inducted into the ICC/FICA World Cricket Hall of Fame in 2009.	2003 and 2008 the twins were awarded the Lonsdale Cup by the New Zealand Olympic Committee for an outstanding contribution to an Olympic sport. They were also twice named the International Rowing Federation's Female Crew of the Year.

Christchurch & Canterbury Outdoor Activities A to Z

Ballooning

★★★ **Up Up & Away.** There's no other place in the world where you can fly from the center of a city, in view of the ocean, toward snow-capped mountains. Seeing the first pink flush of dawn rising out of the Pacific Ocean is worth getting up early for. ☎ 03/381-4600. www.ballooning.co.nz. Trips from NZ$340 adults, NZ$300 kids 5–11.

Biking

Christchurch is renowned as an ideal biking city thanks to its mostly flat terrain. Bike lanes are marked off in several parts of the city and it is compulsory to wear a cycling helmet. You will be fined by police if you are caught without one.

★★★ **City Cycle Hire.** These are the people to contact for rentals. They'll deliver bikes to your accommodation. They also offer an excellent tour of the delightful 21km (13-mile)

★★ **Little River Rail Trail.** ☎ 0800/343-848; www.cyclehire-tours.co.nz. Rentals NZ$35–NZ$45 per day.

★★ **Mountain Bike Adventure Company.** The Port Hills are a favorite spot for mountain bikers, who come to test themselves on the continual network of tracks. This company has a very good package that includes a gondola ride to the summit complex. You'll be set up with your bike and you can choose between a gentle on-road cycle down to Sumner Beach or a much more challenging off-road descent on the Rapaki Track. Both are around 16km (10 miles) and take 1 to 2 hours depending on your fitness. Book ahead. 68 Waltham Rd., Sydenham, Christchurch. ☎ 0800/424-534. NZ$65.

★★★ **Tuatara Tours.** Tuatara Tours is the best company at organizing multiday cycling

> *Set off at dawn for an aerial view of the patchwork of Canterbury Plains at first light.*

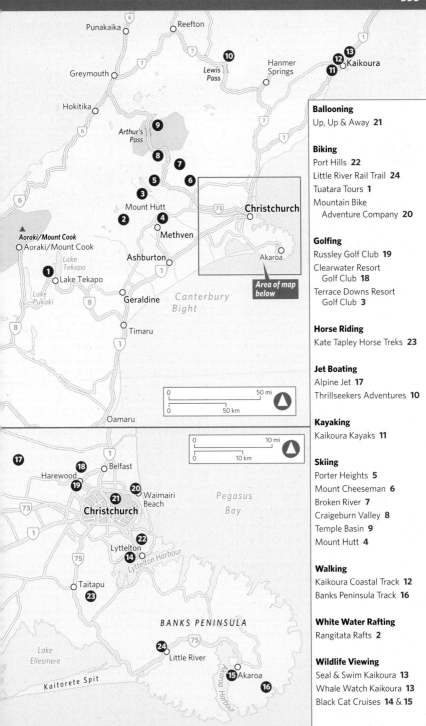

Ballooning
Up, Up & Away **21**

Biking
Port Hills **22**
Little River Rail Trail **24**
Tuatara Tours **1**
Mountain Bike
    Adventure Company **20**

Golfing
Russley Golf Club **19**
Clearwater Resort
    Golf Club **18**
Terrace Downs Resort
    Golf Club **3**

Horse Riding
Kate Tapley Horse Treks **23**

Jet Boating
Alpine Jet **17**
Thrillseekers Adventures **10**

Kayaking
Kaikoura Kayaks **11**

Skiing
Porter Heights **5**
Mount Cheeseman **6**
Broken River **7**
Craigeburn Valley **8**
Temple Basin **9**
Mount Hutt **4**

Walking
Kaikoura Coastal Track **12**
Banks Peninsula Track **16**

White Water Rafting
Rangitata Rafts **2**

Wildlife Viewing
Seal & Swim Kaikoura **13**
Whale Watch Kaikoura **13**
Black Cat Cruises **14** & **15**

> *Speeding down the Waiau River, near Hanmer Springs, will get your heart racing in a hurry.*

and walk-cycle tours. They've chosen all the best spots—Tekapo Lake, Hanmer Springs, Waipara Valley, and Akaroa. ☎ 0800/377-378 or 03/962-3280. www.tuataratours.co.nz. Tours from around NZ$1,500.

Golfing

The wider Canterbury region has dozens of golf courses. In the city, **Russley Golf Club,** 428 Memorial Ave., Christchurch (☎ 03/358-4748; www.russleygolfclub.co.nz), has reasonably flat, well-bunkered greens and is one of New Zealand's premier courses; overseas guests pay about NZ$85 for 18 holes. ★★★ **Clearwater Resort Golf Club,** Johns Rd., Christchurch (☎ 03/360-2146; www.clearwaternz.com), is a par-72 championship course where you'll pay around NZ$140 for a round of golf. ★★ **Terrace Downs Resort & Golf Club,** Coleridge Rd., Windwhistle (☎ 0800/465-373; www.terracedowns.co.nz), is set in spectacular mountain scenery 50 minutes from the city. You'll pay around NZ$135 for a round on the par-72 course.

Horseback Riding

★★ **Kate Tapley Horse Treks.** Take your pick from horse trekking in Akaroa, at Mount Lyford in North Canterbury, or around rural Christchurch, leaving from the beautiful grounds of luxurious Otahuna Lodge. You'll feel miles from anywhere once you get up into the saddle and ride into the hill country. 5 Gracefield Ave., Christchurch. ☎ 03/329-0160. www.katetapley.co.nz. 2-hr. rides from around NZ$90; all-day ride NZ$240.

Jet-Boating

★★★ **Alpine Jet.** This company has been rushing people up the Waimakariri River longer than anyone. The full-day adventure takes you the full length of the river canyon—36km (22 miles) upstream—highlighting historical points of interest and geographical landmarks. ☎ 0800/263-626. www.alpinejet.co.nz. NZ$85–NZ$385.

★★ **Thrillseekers Adventures.** If you're visiting Hanmer Springs, this fabulous 30-minute ride up the Waiau River is well worth doing. It takes you into backcountry you would never otherwise see. Hanmer Springs Rd., Hanmer Springs. ☎ 0800/661-538. www.thrillseekers.co.nz. NZ$115 adults, NZ$65 kids.

Kayaking

★★★ **Kaikoura Kayaks.** This is one of the loveliest kayaking experiences in the region. Nothing beats setting off early in the morning when the Kaikoura waters are still and quiet, and coming face-to-face with cute fur seals who

> Swim with rare Hectors dolphins in Akaroa Harbour for a special take-home memory.

pop their noses out of the water to see what you're up to. 19 Killarney St., Kaikoura. ☎ 0800/452-456. www.kaikourakayaks.co.nz. Tours from around NZ$95 adults, NZ$85 kids.

Paragliding

★★★ **Nimbus Paragliding.** This experienced team of qualified paragliding pilots will see you off from one of their three Port Hills sites on a thrilling tandem ride down toward the beach. ☎ 0800/111-611. www.nimbuspara gliding.co.nz. 5- to 10-minute tandem flight costs around NZ$180.

Skiing

There are at least twelve ski fields within a 2-hour drive of Christchurch. The closest are the five main fields of the Arthur's Pass area: **Porter Heights,** State Highway 73, Porter's Pass (☎ 03/318-4002; www.

skiporters.co.nz); **Mount Cheeseman,** State Highway 73, Castle Hill (☎ 03/379-5315; www.mtcheeseman.co.nz); **Broken River,** State Highway 73, Castle Hill (☎ 03/318-7270; www.brokenriver.co.nz); **Craigieburn Valley,** State Highway 73, Craigieburn Valley (☎ 03/365-2514; www.craigieburn. co.nz); and **Temple Basin,** State Highway 73, Arthur'sPass(☎ 03/377-7788; www. templebasin.co.nz). They're all within 1½ hours of Christchurch. They're all club fields except for Porter Heights, which is a popular commercial field. Further south near Methven, the **Mount Hutt Ski Area** (☎ 03/302-8811; www.nzski.com) is internationally recognized as having the longest number of skiable days in Australasia. It's also the most developed commercial field in Canterbury.

> *There are a dozen well established ski fields within two hours' drive of Christchurch city.*

Skydiving

★★ **Skydivingnz.com.** If you feel the urge to leap out of an airplane, may I direct you into the safe hands of this professional sky diving team. They'll attach you to a highly experienced tandem instructor, who will take that "will-I-won't-I" decision away from you by leaping boldly out into thin air. Locations vary; check at time of booking. ☎ 0800/697-593. www.skydivingnz.com. NZ$335-NZ$440.

Walking

The Christchurch visitor center (p. 365) can furnish you with information about the many easy walks within the city itself. Suffice to say, with so many parks, beaches, streams, hills, and rivers, you're never short of a pretty walking route. Some of the best multiday walks are listed below.

★★★ **Banks Peninsula Track.** If you strike perfect weather, you'll get perfect scenery and perfect photographs. This is one of the loveliest and most popular multiday walks in Canterbury so be sure to book well ahead as space in the cute farm huts is always limited. It features rugged exposed headlands and hill country so a reasonable level of fitness is required for the 4-day walk. ☎ 03/304-7612. www.bankstrack.co.nz. NZ$255 per person. Oct–Apr.

★★ **Kaikoura Coast Track.** This popular and dramatic 3-day coastal walk takes you through high country farmland with farm cottage accommodation along the way. It's steep in parts so you'll need to be fit, but you'll be rewarded with wonderful views across the Kaikoura mountains. ☎ 03/319-2715; www.kaikoura track.co.nz. NZ$205 per person. Oct–Apr.

★★★ **Tuatara Tours.** I've done two or three of the walks offered by this company and they're very professionally run with informed guides

Heading West—A Great Train Ride

The ★★★ **TranzAlpine** (☎ 0800/872-467; www.tranzscenic.co.nz) is rated as one of the five most spectacular train journeys in the world. It passes through beautiful alpine scenery, making its way from Christchurch to Arthur's Pass and then on to Greymouth on the West Coast. There are tunnels, viaducts, huge braided rivers, beech forests, and massive gorges along the way. The train departs daily from the Christchurch Railway Station. If you take the Arthur's Pass option (NZ$165 adults, NZ$115 kids), you'll have 5 hours there to explore before the train returns. If you go to Greymouth (NZ$215 adults, NZ$150 kids), you'll have just 1 hour in the town before returning to Christchurch.

who make your life easy. Your big packs are transported for you and meals are provided in comfortable accommodation each night. Two of their best offerings are the strenuous but extremely rewarding Akaroa Walk and the impossibly pretty West Coast Trail. ☎ 0800/377-378 or 03/962-3280. www.tuataratours.co.nz. Tours from around NZ$1,800.

White-Water Rafting

★★★ **Rangitata Rafts.** Your adventure starts with a relaxed lunch and after safety briefings and practical training, you'll take to the water for the ride of your life down the Rangitata River's Grade V rapids in South Canterbury. In between hanging on and paddling, try to look around at the spectacular scenery as you pass through rugged gorges. At the end of the day you can enjoy a barbecue with your hosts, Tussock and Alex. ☎ 0800/251-251. www.rafts.co.nz. NZ$210–NZ$220.

Wildlife-Watching

With its long coastline and numerous bays and harbors, the Canterbury region is blessed with plenty of wildlife-watching opportunities. The marine environment off the Kaikoura coast includes deep-sea canyons rich in nutrients that attract multiple sea mammals. Whales, seals, and dolphins are in abundance and the pelagic seabird life is just as impressive. When you get to Kaikoura, you have the choice of scenic boat cruises with **Whale Watch Kaikoura** (p. 339, **14**), or flights with **Wings over Whales** (☎ 0800/226-629; www.whales.co.nz). Get a taste of dolphins and seabirds with **Encounter Kaikoura** (☎ 0800/733-365; www.dolphin.co.nz or www.oceanwings.co.nz), and contact **Seal & Swim Kaikoura** (☎ 0800/732-579; www.sealswimkaikoura.co.nz) to get up close and personal with these sleek creatures. In Christchurch and Akaroa, Christchurch Wildlife Cruises and Swimming with Dolphins, both run by **Black Cat Cruises** (☎ 0800/436-574; www.blackcat.co.nz), give you the chance to swim with gorgeous little Hector's dolphins, the smallest and rarest dolphin breed in the world. Akaroa Swimming with Dolphins prices are NZ$72 to NZ$75 for adults and NZ$55 for kids 5 to 15; Christchurch Wildlife Cruises prices (dolphin-watching only) are NZ$57 to NZ$60 for adults and NZ$25 for children.

Christchurch Shopping

Most of the central shopping zone was severely impacted by the earthquakes. About 60 of the city's 150 suburban shopping centers were also damaged. Rebuilding was expected to start on the two worst affected of these suburban areas: Sydenham, in the city, and the small town of Lyttelton over the Port Hills. In the central city, temporary relocatable structures were placed in Cashel Mall so some retailers and hospitality owners could open for business by October 29, 2011. This is the area bounded by Oxford Terrace, Hereford Street, Colombo Street, and Lichfield Street.

Most shopping is now centered on the three major suburban malls largely undamaged by the quakes. These include the giant **Westfield Riccarton**, 129 Riccarton Rd., Christchurch (☎ 03/983-4500; www.westfield.co.nz/riccarton), where there are around 200 stores on two levels, plus movie theaters, a food hall, cafes, restaurants, and bars; **Northlands Mall**, 55 Main North Rd., Papanui (☎ 03/352-6535; www.northlands.co.nz), which has 135 stores, cafes, and a large food hall; and the smaller, more upmarket **Merivale Mall,** 189 Papanui Rd., Merivale (☎ 03/355-9692; www.merivalemall.co.nz), which has 40 stores and surrounding cafes, bars, and restaurants. A fourth large mall, **The Palms,** corner of Marshlands and New Brighton Rds., Shirley (☎ **03/385-3067**; www.thepalms.co.nz), was badly damaged in the earthquakes, but reopened by September 2011. It has 110 stores, movie theaters, a food hall, cafes, restaurants, and bars. All of the malls are open daily from 9am (10am weekends) and close at 6pm (9pm Thurs and Fri at Riccarton, Northlands, and the Palms; 7pm Thurs at Merivale). All have a wide range of stores, from fashion and accessory boutiques to bookstores, shoes shops, and department stores. **Please note that the redevelopment of the central city is an ongoing project and stores will gradually come back on stream over the next three to five years.**

Where to Stay

> *The chic rooms at Akaroa's Maison de la Mer are the perfect end to any day.*

Akaroa

★★★ Maison de la Mer AKAROA

This upmarket bed-and-breakfast has romance, style, and hospitality. If you like privacy, go for the Boathouse, a large self-contained apartment with its own kitchen, set apart from the main house. Inside the house, the Fleur de Lys room has a private sunroom. 1 Rue Benoit. ☎ 03/304-8907. www.maisondelamer.co.nz. 3 units. Doubles NZ$450–NZ$500 w/breakfast. AE, MC, V. Closed July–Aug. Map p. 332.

★★ Wilderness House AKAROA

This peaceful haven set in a large garden oozes old-world charm. A claw-foot bath is a drawcard in the Walker Room and the Shepherd Room has its own balcony. 42 Rue Grehan. ☎ 03/304-7517. www.wildernesshouse.co.nz. 4 units. Doubles NZ$290–NZ$325 w/breakfast. MC, V. Map p. 332.

Christchurch

★★ Charlotte Jane MERIVALE

This stunning old mansion delivers some of the biggest rooms you'll find anywhere, complete with giant Jacuzzis. They have an onsite restaurant and extra accommodation and conference space in the adjacent Henderson House. 110 Papanui Rd., Merivale. ☎ 03/355-1028. www.charlotte-jane.co.nz. 14 units. Doubles NZ$525–NZ$825 w/breakfast. MC, V. Map p. 332.

★ Chateau on the Park RICCARTON

You'd be hard-pressed to find another mid-range hotel in Christchurch with such unique style, such a big garden, and such good rates. Set on 2 hectares (5 acres) of lush greenery, it's a great spot for families, and despite quirky medieval touches, it's aged well over its 30-plus years of business. The Hagley wing gives the best pool and garden views. 189 Deans Ave.Riccarton ☎ 0800/808-999 in NZ or 03/348-8999. www.chateau-park.co.nz. 193 units. Doubles NZ$185–NZ$325. AE, DC, MC, V. Map p. 332.

★★ The Classic Villa ARTS CENTRE

This small boutique hotel offers spacious, character-filled rooms in an original villa wing and modern upstairs rooms in a newer wing—all within a stone's throw of the Christchurch Art Gallery and Canterbury Museum. It has the comfortable feel of home about it and large dining and living areas are a great place to chat with fellow guests. 17 Worcester Blvd. ☎ 03/377-7905. www.theclassicvilla.co.nz. 12 units. Doubles NZ$289–NZ$489 w/breakfast. AE, DC, MC, V. Map p. 332.

★★ Elm Tree House MERIVALE

Built in 1920, this lovely two-story home is just a few steps from Merivale Mall and plenty of cafes and restaurants. Original wood paneling throughout gives it a warm feeling. The upstairs honeymoon suite is huge but all rooms are big and lovely. 236 Papanui Rd., Merivale. ☎ 03/355-9731. www.elmtreehouse.co.nz. 6 units. Doubles NZ$295–NZ$455 w/breakfast and pre-dinner drinks. AE, MC, V. Map p. 332.

★★★ The George HAGLEY PARK AREA

Sleek, cool, and modern, this international-award-winning boutique hotel is Christchurch's finest. Personalized service is paramount, rooms are classically elegant, it has lovely park views, and it's close to the Arts Centre. 50 Park Terrace. ☎ 0800/100-220 or 03/379-4560. www.thegeorge.com. 56 units. Doubles NZ$506–NZ$1,095. AE, DC, MC, V. Map p. 332.

★★★ kids Huntley Lodge UPPER RICCARTON

At the core of this property is a truly grand, 1876 mansion that has been renovated to the highest standards. Rooms here are sumptuous and elegant. The adjacent suite and apartment wings feature more modern, contemporary spaces that are perfect for families or couples traveling together. 67 Yaldhurst Rd., Upper Riccarton. ☎ 03/348-8435. www.huntleylodge.co.nz. 17 units. Doubles NZ$445–NZ$900 w/breakfast. AE, DC, MC, V. Map p. 332.

★ Orari Bed & Breakfast ARTS CENTRE

Built in 1893, this stunning old homestead has

> *Enjoy privacy and old world charm at Akaroa's Wilderness House.*

been beautifully preserved to provide a number of charming rooms just across the street from Christchurch Art Gallery. In addition, there are smart new, contemporary apartments right across the courtyard. Corner of Gloucester and Montreal sts. ☎ 0800/267-274. www.orari.co.nz. 10 units. Doubles NZ$180–NZ$245 w/breakfast. Min. 3-night stay in apartments. AE, MC, V. Map p. 332.

★★★ Otahuna Lodge TAITAPU

This magnificent 1895 mansion set on breathtaking grounds in the countryside, 30 minutes from the central city, gives you an insight into the privileged lives of Canterbury's early landed gentry. Now one of New Zealand's leading luxury lodges, it is a place of exquisite taste and indulgence. Rhodes Rd., Taitapu. ☎ 03/329-6333. www.otahuna.co.nz. 7 units. Doubles NZ$1,2650–NZ$2,2500 w/breakfast, pre-dinner drinks, canapés, and 5-course degustation dinner with wine pairings. AE, DC, MC, V. Map p. 332.

★★ kids Peppers Clearwater HAREWOOD

Surrounded by a championship golf course and 186 hectares (460 acres) of greenery, the modern apartments are cantilevered out over trout-filled lakes. Hotel rooms and suites are great value and larger terrace apartments are perfect for families. There is an excellent restaurant and bar and you're about 20 minutes from the inner city. Clearwater Ave., Harewood ☎ 0800/555-075 or 03/360-1000. www.

> *Antique elegance abounds at The Worcester of Christchurch, directly opposite the Arts Centre.*

clearwaternz.com or www.peppers.co.nz. 97 units. Doubles NZ$255–NZ$600. AE, DC, MC, V. Map p. 332.

★ Sudhima Christchurch AIRPORT
This midrange hotel has big rooms just 2 minutes from the airport. Set in large gardens with a pool and barbecue area, it's popular with both business and leisure travelers and always has good online deals. They run a 24-hour free shuttle to the airport, so it's especially good as a one-night stopover. Corner of Memorial Ave. and Orchard Rd. ☎ 03/358-3139. www.sudhima christchurch.co.nz. 208 units. Doubles NZ$145–NZ$185. AE, DC, MC, V. Map p. 332

★★ The Worcester of Christchurch ARTS
CENTRE The gorgeous two-story Victorian home, filled with paintings and sculptures acquired by the art dealer owners, sits directly across the street from the Arts Centre and features two big, romantic suites. 15 Worcester Blvd. ☎ 0800/365-015 or 03/365-0936. www. worcester.co.nz. 2 units. Doubles NZ$580 w/ breakfast and pre-dinner drinks. AE, DC, MC, V. Map p. 332.

★ YMCA ARTS CENTRE
Three words spring instantly to mind: value, location, and liveliness. There's a constant flow of traffic of all ages here and the modern six-story building is perfectly situated across the road from the Botanic Gardens. The apartments have kitchenettes and deluxe rooms have bathrooms and TVs. Each person in the bunk rooms gets a locker with a key. This is the best of Christchurch's hostels. 12 Hereford St. ☎ 0508/962-224 in NZ, or 03/366-0689. www.ymcachch.org.nz. 105 units (26 with ensuite bathrooms). Doubles NZ$62–NZ$88. Dorm beds from NZ$28 per person per night. AE, MC, V. Map p. 332.

Hanmer Springs
★★★ Cheltenham House HANMER
This charming 1930s home with sunny, spacious bedrooms and garden suites is owned by Len and Maree Earl, long-time Hanmer residents who are always delighted to share their local knowledge with guests. 13 Cheltenham St. Hanmer. ☎ 03/315-7545. www.cheltenham. co.nz. 6 units. Doubles NZ$235–NZ$285 w/ breakfast. V. Map p. 332.

★ kids Heritage Hanmer Springs HANMER
This lovingly restored landmark building is right in the center of the village. It's a modest hotel but has a wide range of room types, a heated pool, and tennis courts. 1 Conical Hill, Hanmer. ☎ 0800/738-732 or 03/315-0060. www.heritagehotels.co.nz. 64 units. Doubles NZ$195–NZ$425. AE, DC, MC, V. Map p. 332.

★★ Rippinvale Retreat HANMER
This modern home near the Hanmer Springs thermal complex features two beautifully appointed suites, each with its own kitchen and sitting room. You also have the use of tennis courts and a big Jacuzzi. 68 Rippingale Rd., Hanmer. ☎ 0800/373-098 or 03/315-7139. www.rippinvale.co.nz. 2 units. Doubles NZ$355–NZ$375 w/breakfast. MC, V. Map p. 332.

Kaikoura
★★★ Hapuku Lodge NORTH OF KAIKOURA
This outstanding small boutique lodge is a great value. Being tucked up in one of their peaceful tree houses is complete bliss—every modern convenience at your fingertips and all the birds right outside your window. It's 12km (8 miles) north of Kaikoura but very definitely worth the drive. There are also rooms in the main lodge building and an Olive House suite. Hapuku Rd., just off State Hwy. 1, Kaikoura North. ☎ 0800/521-568 or 03/319-6559. www. hapukulodge.com. 14 units. Doubles NZ$563–NZ$793 lodge room; NZ$805–NZ$1,095 Treehouse; NZ$920 Olive House. Rates include breakfast. AE, MC, V. Map p. 332.

> *Heritage Hanmer Springs is located in the center of Hanmer Springs Village, a short walk from everything.*

Tekapo & Aoraki/Mount Cook

★ kids Aoraki/Mount Cook Alpine Lodge

MOUNT COOK VILLAGE There's a range of accommodations here, from bunk rooms and family units to suites with lovely mountain views. A big communal kitchen and living room adds to the fun of things in this friendly, independent, modern chalet. 101 Bowen Dr., Aoraki/Mount Cook. ☎ 0800/680-680 or 03/435-1860. www.aorakialpinelodge.co.nz. 16 units. Doubles NZ$160–NZ$230. AE, MC, V. Map p. 347.

★★ kids Hermitage Hotel, Motels & Chalets

MOUNT COOK VILLAGE This old faithful complex is an uneven mix of older motel units, chalets, and new and old hotel rooms, but recent renovations have made it more cohesive and the onsite restaurant is greatly improved. Some rooms have breathtaking mountain views—it's worth paying extra for one of these. Terrace Rd., Aoraki/Mount Cook. ☎ 0800/686-800 or 03/435-1809. www. hermitage.co.nz. 212 units. Doubles NZ$135–NZ$565 hotel rooms; NZ$155–NZ$260 motel rooms; NZ$145–NZ$230 chalets. AE, DC, MC, V. Map p. 347.

★★ kids Lake Tekapo Cottages TEKAPO

This selection of cute, self-contained cottages hosted by Stephen and Amina Hunter is just the thing for the independent traveler wanting a change from hotel rooms. All are well set up and close to the lake, village, and eateries. 12 Sealy St., Lake Tekapo. ☎ 03/680-6865. www. laketekapocottages.co.nz. 4 self-contained cottages, 1 studio unit, 1 large holiday home. Doubles NZ$135–NZ$175. MC, V. Map p. 347.

★★ kids Peppers Bluewater Resort TEKAPO

Among the hundreds of new apartments now available in Tekapo, these are a new, good-value option within walking distance of the lake, village and hot pools. They have a mix of lovely earth-toned, modern studios and one-, two- and three-bedroom apartments that are perfect for families, or friends traveling together. State Hwy. 8, Tekapo. ☎ 0800/680-570. www. peppers.co.nz/bluewater. 142 units. Doubles NZ$240–NZ$400. AE, DC, MV, V. Map p. 347.

Where to Dine

> *You'll have one of your finest dining experiences in New Zealand at Pescatore in The George Hotel, Christchurch.*

Akaroa

★ **kids Ma Maison Restaurant & Bar** AKAROA *MODERN NZ* This pretty, ivy-clad building is a good bet for a tasty meal without too many frills. The courtyard has lovely water views. Meals are based on local ingredients like Canterbury lamb and Akaroa salmon. **2 Rue Jolie.** ☎ 03/304-7668. www.mamaison.co.nz. Main courses NZ$30–NZ$36. AE, MC, V. Breakfast, lunch, and dinner daily. Map p. 332.

★ **kids Vangionis** AKAROA *MEDITERRANEAN* Timber floors and dark walls make for a warm, inviting atmosphere in this little restaurant. There's a large pizza menu plus such choices as paella and rabbit with prunes and bacon. **Rue Brittan.** ☎ 03/304-7714. Main courses NZ$30–NZ$33. MC, V. Dinner daily. Map p. 332.

Christchurch

★★ **kids Addington Coffee Co-Op** ADDINGTON *CAFÉ* This place is all about a fun retro mood and great fair-trade coffee. Filled with old sofas and armchairs, benches, and tables, it's usually packed with people, who overflow to outdoor seats on a fine day. There's a roastery on site and a breakfast menu (French toast, cereals, and the like) that runs until 2:30pm. The food cabinets bulge with gourmet pies, mini pizzas, muffins, and cakes. Definitely a place to linger. **297 Lincoln Rd., Addington.** ☎ 03/943-1662. Main courses NZ$12–NZ$16. AE, MC, V. Breakfast and lunch. Map p. 332.

★★ **Aikmans** MERIVALE *MODERN NZ* I love this place for its terrific sheltered outdoor areas; on cool evenings, you can huddle around the fireplace on a big leather sofa. They serve fabulous big platters—the seafood spread is especially delicious with a glass of Canterbury wine. **154 Aikmans Rd., Merivale.** ☎ 03/355-2271. Main courses NZ$30–NZ$36. AE, DC, MC, V. Lunch and dinner daily. Map p. 332.

★ **Bicycle Thief** LATIMER SQUARE *ITALIAN/PIZZERIA* Dark and moody, this is a popular spot day and night. They serve divine pizzas, rich risottos, and hearty pasta dishes in a relaxed atmosphere with intimate seating arrangements. **21 Latimer Sq.** ☎ 03/379-2264. www.

thebicyclethief.co.nz. Main courses NZ$30–NZ$34. AE, DC, MC, V. Breakfast, lunch, and dinner Mon–Fri, dinner Sat. Map p. 332.

★★ **Brigittes** MERIVALE *CAFÉ/MODERN NZ*
Half the population of upmarket Merivale seems to enjoy weekend brunch at Brigittes, so make sure you book ahead. In addition to being a good coffee and cake stop, it's also worth having lunch in their sheltered courtyard. Salt-and-pepper squid, salads, pasta dishes, curries, and beef dishes all feature on the menu. Aikmans and Papanui roads, Merivale. ☎ 03/355-6150. www.brigittes.co.nz. Main courses NZ$16–NZ$32. AE, DC, MC, V. Breakfast and lunch daily, dinner Tues–Sat. Map p. 332.

★★ **Curator's House Restaurant** HAGLEY AREA *SPANISH/MODERN NZ*   Javier Garcia presents classic Spanish dishes like hearty seafood and chicken paella and house-made chorizo, plus contemporary New Zealand dishes that make the most of Canterbury lamb, seafood, and duck. The elegant restaurant is set in the old Botanic Gardens' curator's house—the perfect setting for a romantic night out. Christchurch Botanic Gardens, 7 Rolleston Ave. ☎ 03/379-2252. www.curatorshouse.co.nz. Main courses NZ$26–NZ$37. AE, DC, MC, V. Lunch and dinner daily. Map p. 332.

★ **Fox and Ferret** RICCARTON *GASTRO-PUB*
Located beside Westfield Riccarton Mall, this is a great spot for a relaxed lunch or dinner, indoors or out, with a local or imported ale. Modeled after modern English-style gastro pubs, it serves excellent stone-grilled meals and big platters. Steak and chips is another favorite and meals can be matched with beers. They have live entertainment on Thursday, Friday, and Saturday nights. 28 Rotheram St., Riccarton. ☎ 03/348-6677. www.foxriccarton.co.nz. Main courses NZ$14–NZ$26. AE, DC, MC, V. Brunch, lunch, and dinner daily. Map p. 332.

★★ **Hays** VICTORIA STREET *MODERN NZ*
Chef Celia Hay sources her high-quality lamb off her own Banks Peninsula farm. Likewise, standards are consistently high when it comes to presentation and service. All choices are matched with Canterbury wines. 63 Victoria St. ☎ 03/379-7501. www.foodandwine.co.nz. Main courses NZ$38–NZ$42. AE, MC, V. Lunch and dinner daily (no dinner Sun–Mon in winter). Map p. 332.

★★ **JDV** MERIVALE *INTERNATIONAL*
This busy, trendy joint is the restaurant of choice for Merivale's movers and shakers (and the rich and slothful). Akaroa salmon with fennel velouté, coq au vin, or grilled lamb rump go well with the attentive service. The Mall, 190 Aikmans Rd. ☎ 03/964-3860. www.jdv.co.nz. Main courses NZ$25–NZ$36. AE, DC, MC, V. Breakfast, lunch, & dinner daily. Map p. 332.

★★★ **Pescatore** HAGLEY AREA *PACIFIC RIM*
The swanky interior and extensive wine list here are the perfect accompaniments for first-class service and culinary brilliance—every plate is a visual triumph. The degustation menu is a great way to get a sample of everything. Definitely Christchurch's best restaurant. The George, 50 Park Terrace. ☎ 03/371-0257. www.thegeorge.com. Main courses NZ$40–NZ$50. AE, DC, MC, V. Oct–June, dinner daily; July–Sept, dinner Wed–Sun. Map p. 332.

★★★ **Rotherhams of Riccarton** RICCARTON *INTERNATIONAL*   Swiss owner/chef Martin Weiss spoils his guests with divine flavors and classic European dishes. It's an elegant, romantic restaurant and every plate is a work of art. The best way to get an overview is to opt for one of the degustation menus. You won't be disappointed. 42 Rotheram St., Riccarton ☎ 03/341-5142. www.rotherhamsofriccarton.co.nz. Main courses NZ$35–NZ$45. AE, DC, MC, V. Dinner Tues–Sat. Map p. 332.

★★ **kids** **Tutto Bene** MERIVALE *ITALIAN/PIZZERIA*   Felice and Paulette Mannucci have been running successful eateries in Christchurch for more than 30 years and this gem is one of my favorites. People queue up for delicious pizzas, rich pasta dishes, risottos, and traditional Italian fare like veal saltimbocca. And let's not forget the tiramisu! 192 Papanui Rd., Merivale. ☎ 03/355-4744. Main courses NZ$32–NZ$35. AE, DC, MC, V. Dinner daily. Map p. 332.

Hanmer Springs

★★ **kids** **Malabar** HANMER *ASIAN FUSION*
This is probably the best and most reliable restaurant in the village. You get a choice of Asian, Indian, or fusion dishes, such as tandoori salmon and Thai beef noodle salad. The ginger-and-lime crème brûlée is the perfect way to finish. Alpine Pacific Centre, 5 Conical Hill Rd. ☎ 03/315-7745. Main courses

> Christchurch restaurants showcase the fine beef, lamb, seafood, and fresh vegetables grown throughout the province.

NZ$28–NZ$38. AE, DC, MC, V. Dinner daily. Map p. 332.

★ **kids The Powerhouse Café** HANMER *CAFE* Located in an old, converted power house, this cafe has the best coffee in town and a tasty array of cabinet food and a light menu to accompany it. There's usually a buzzy, happy atmosphere as locals call in for their daily caffeine shot and I've always found the service friendly and efficient. 8 Jack's Pass Rd. ☎ 03/315-5252. Cabinet food NZ$8–NZ$10, menu NZ$12–NZ$20. MC, V. Breakfast and lunch daily. Map p. 332.

Kaikoura

★ **kids Encounter Kaikoura** KAIKOURA *CAFE* There's always a busy, happy atmosphere in this modern cafe, which is within the En-counter Kaikoura booking office. I like their excellent cabinet food choices, good coffee, and, if it's lunchtime, their light meals listed on the backboard menu. West End, Waterfront ☎ 03/319-6777. Main courses NZ$12–NZ$20, cabinet food NZ$8–NZ$18. MC, V. Breakfast and lunch daily. Map p. 332.

★★ **kids Hislops Wholefoods Café**. KAIKOURA *CAFE* Most of the food is made with an organic focus—and it's divine. It's a great place to buy big muffins and filled bread rolls to eat on the run or to stock up on picnic food. Or sit a while on the sunny veranda with a coffee. 33 Beach Rd., Kaikoura. ☎ 03/319-6971. Main courses NZ$12–NZ$18. MC, V. Breakfast and lunch daily. Map p. 332.

Tekapo & Aoraki/Mount Cook

★★ **kids Astro Café** MOUNT JOHN/TEKAPO *CAFE* Astro Café, not to be confused with the much lesser Observatory Café of State Highway 8, is on top of Mount John and has the most spectacular views of any property in New Zealand. This "glass box" beside the observatories is *the* place to come for photographs. They have delicious coffee and cake and jumbo sandwiches. Make sure you look through the telescopes. Mount John summit, Godley Peaks Rd., Tekapo. ☎ 03/680-6960. www.earthandsky.co.nz. Coffee and cake NZ$8–NZ$10. MC, V. Breakfast, lunch, and afternoon snacks daily (until 6pm summer, 5pm winter). Map p. 347.

★★ **kids The Old Mountaineer's Café & Bar** MOUNT COOK VILLAGE *CAFE* This is the only independent café and bar in the village—all others are part of the Hermitage Hotel complex—and you'll find a friendly, welcoming atmosphere as people gather around the fire. From the big breakfasts to hamburger snacks, pizzas, and full meals (like Mount Cook salmon), they put a big emphasis on organic produce and healthy options. Bowen Dr. (next to DOC), Aoraki/Mount Cook. ☎ 03/435-1890. www.mtcook.com. Main courses NZ$26–NZ$38, light meals NZ$15–NZ$25. AE, DC, MC, V. Breakfast, lunch, and dinner daily. Map p. 347.

★★ **kids Rakinui Restaurant** TEKAPO *MODERN NZ* This is Tekapo's best restaurant—a simple, uncluttered eatery located within Peppers Bluewater Resort. It's nice to dine outdoors in summer and if you like fish you'll adore their signature dish: poached Mount Cook salmon served with cucumber tagliatelle with champagne and watercress sauce. State Hwy. 8, Tekapo. ☎ 0800/680-570. www.peppers.co.nz/bluewater. Main courses NZ$30–NZ$38. AE, DC, MC, V. Breakfast and dinner daily. Map p. 347.

Christchurch & Canterbury Fast Facts

> *The TranzAlpine and the TranzScenic are two memorable train journeys in Canterbury.*

Arriving

BY PLANE **Christchurch International Airport** (☎ 03/353-7783; www.christchurchairport. co.nz), 10km (6 miles) from the central city, receives direct flights from all around New Zealand and from numerous international destinations. BY TRAIN The **TranzAlpine** to Greymouth and the **TranzScenic** to Kaikoura and Blenheim are the only passenger rail services. Call ☎ 0800/872-467; www.tranz scenic.co.nz. Christchurch Railway Station is on Clarence Street in the suburb of Addington. It is about a 10- to 15-minute cab ride from the central city depending on traffic flow. BY BUS **InterCity** (☎ 0800/468-372; www.intercity. co.nz) covers most of the South Island.

Emergencies & Medical Care

Always **dial 111** for fire, ambulance, and police emergencies. The main hospital is **Christchurch Hospital,** Oxford Terrace and Riccarton Ave., Christchurch (☎ **03/364-0640**).

For a doctor, try **After Hours Surgery,** Colombo St. and Bealey Ave., Christchurch (☎ **03/365-7777**). For a dentist, contact **Bealey Dental,** 163 Bealey Ave., Christchurch (☎ **03/366-2912**).

Visitor Information Centers

CHRISTCHURCH & CANTERBURY I-SITE VISITOR CENTRE Temporary premises: Foyer of the Chateau on the Park Hotel, 189 Deans Ave., Riccarton (☎ 03/379-9629; www. christchurchnz.com). For the latest information on their location please check their website. AKAROA VISITOR CENTRE Old Post Office Building, 80 Rue Lavaud (☎ 03/304-8600; www.akaroa.com). KAIKOURA I-SITE VISITOR CENTRE Town Car Park (☎ 03/319-5641; www. kaikoura.co.nz). HANMER SPRINGS I-SITE VISITOR CENTRE 42 Amuri Ave., Hanmer Springs (☎ 03/315-7128; www.alpinepacifictourism. co.nz).

12

Queenstown, Fiordland & The West Coast

My Favorite Moments

There are jaw-droppingly beautiful vistas in every direction in these southwestern regions of the South Island. The West Coast, a narrow strip of land to the west of the Southern Alps, is a place of majestic landscapes, rich pioneer history, colorful characters, and small, laid-back communities. Queenstown, which hosts over one million visitors a year, has a well-deserved reputation for adrenaline-packed activities and carefree partying. Wanaka, just over the Crown Range, is tucked into the southern end of a perfect blue lake, where it acts as the gateway to Mount Aspiring National Park. Fiordland, the southwestern corner of the South Island, is perhaps best known as home to Milford and Doubtful sounds. The whole area is an adventurer's heaven but there's plenty for lounge lizards too.

> PREVIOUS PAGE *Lake Wakatipu is a great place for a cool summer dip.* THIS PAGE *There's a thrill a minute on a Shotover Jet boat ride.*

❶ Biking around Lake Wanaka. Hire a bike from the information center on the lakefront and pedal around the leafy cycle track past the boat marina, lovely private homes, and small beaches. See p. 385, ❾.

❷ Drinking coffee at Joe's Garage. This is quintessential Queenstown—the place where the locals hang out. It's always busy, always boisterous, and always an insight into the social ticking of this hedonistic village. See p. 403.

❸ Gaping in awe at Milford Sound landscapes. Everyone likes a fine day in Milford Sound for those picture-postcard photographs, but when it's raining, waterfalls suddenly spring to life and you feel like you're on the set of *The Lord of the Rings*. See p. 370, ❶.

❹ Wine tasting at Wanaka's Rippon Vineyard. It's hard to play favorites with wineries because they all have good points and dramatic locations, but Rippon must surely have the most picturesque views of any winery in

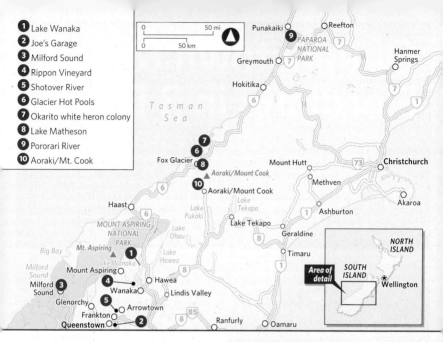

1 Lake Wanaka

2 Joe's Garage

3 Milford Sound

4 Rippon Vineyard

5 Shotover River

6 Glacier Hot Pools

7 Okarito white heron colony

8 Lake Matheson

9 Pororari River

10 Aoraki/Mt. Cook

the country. Make sure you take a camera to a wine tasting. See p. 384, 5.

5 Jet-boating up the Shotover River. There are some things that should be compulsory in everyone's life. A high-speed race up the Shotover River is one of them. You will never forget missing huge rock gorges by inches. See p. 373, 8.

6 Soaking in the Glacier Hot Pools. By the time you've trekked, climbed glaciers, and walked around lakes you will have earned a good long soak in these pretty hot pools tucked away in a natural bush setting. See p. 381, 12.

7 Creeping up on the Okarito white heron colony. The nesting season of the beautiful *kotuku* (white heron) is between November and February and entry is via the only permitted tour. It includes a jet-boat ride and walk through the rainforest. See p. 379, 8.

8 Photographing mirror-like reflections at Lake Matheson. When the water and air are still, you'll get an ideal West Coast shot of the Southern Alps reflected in a perfect blue, bush-fringed lake. See p. 381, 15.

> *Enjoy breakfast and catch up on email at Joe's Garage.*

9 Canoeing on Pororari River. Catch a glimpse of this awe-inspiring wilderness and you'll wonder how the original settlers ever cut through this landscape to make a new life for themselves. See p. 396.

10 A helicopter landing on Aoraki/Mt. Cook. For me, nothing compares to the buzz of hovering over the Fox and Franz glaciers and then landing on the milky-white slopes of Aoraki/Mt. Cook. Well worth the expense. See p. 392.

Queenstown & Fiordland in 3 Days

Because the weather in this region can be extremely changeable, even in summer, and scenic flights can often be cancelled, aim to fly to Milford Sound on your first day. That way, if it's wet, you still have the option to try again. It's cheaper to go by bus but keep in mind that you'll be on the road for 10 of the 12 hours the journey takes—and that's a waste of precious time on a 3-day schedule. I've included most of Queenstown's iconic experiences and a few tours to make the best use of your short time in the area and save on driving time.

> Getting up in the air is the best way to appreciate the vast, untouched wilderness regions of Fiordland.

START Queenstown is 486km (302 miles) south of Christchurch and 117km (73 miles) south of Wanaka. To get to the airport, head east from central Queenstown on Stanley St. (St. Hwy. 6A) and Frankton Rd. Turn right at the roundabout onto Kawarau Rd. and left on Airport Ave. **TRIP LENGTH** 54km (34 miles).

1 ★★★ kids **Milford Sound.** It is impossible not to be impressed by grandeur and splendid isolation of this world-famous place. It is a rare glimpse into the power and beauty of New Zealand's last great wilderness area. Make sure you take wet weather gear and if it does rain (which is likely) don't despair. I think the sounds are far more spectacular when it rains than on a fine day. If you can, fly both ways. There are many flight/cruise/coach packages available and you may decide to fly in and coach out. Both **Great Sights** (☎ 0800/744-487; www.greatsights.co.nz) and **Real Journeys** (☎ 0800/656-503; www.realjourneys.co.nz), offer coach/fly combos. Real Journeys also offers a flight/nature cruise option priced

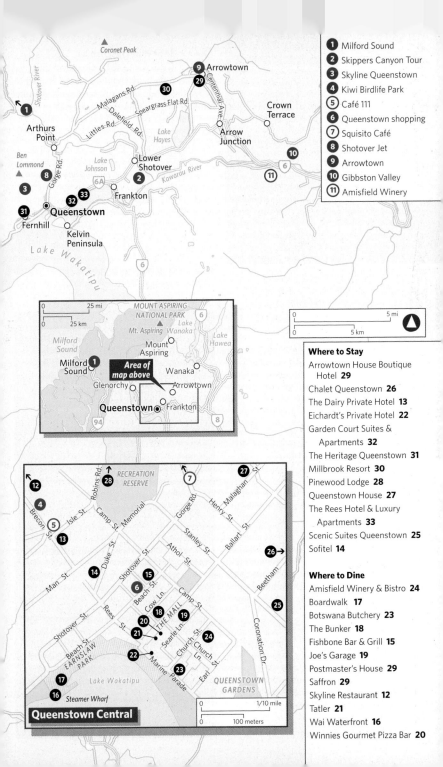

1 Milford Sound
2 Skippers Canyon Tour
3 Skyline Queenstown
4 Kiwi Birdlife Park
5 Café 111
6 Queenstown shopping
7 Squisito Café
8 Shotover Jet
9 Arrowtown
10 Gibbston Valley
11 Amisfield Winery

Where to Stay

Arrowtown House Boutique Hotel **29**
Chalet Queenstown **26**
The Dairy Private Hotel **13**
Eichardt's Private Hotel **22**
Garden Court Suites & Apartments **32**
The Heritage Queenstown **31**
Millbrook Resort **30**
Pinewood Lodge **28**
Queenstown House **27**
The Rees Hotel & Luxury Apartments **33**
Scenic Suites Queenstown **25**
Sofitel **14**

Where to Dine

Amisfield Winery & Bistro **24**
Boardwalk **17**
Botswana Butchery **23**
The Bunker **18**
Fishbone Bar & Grill **15**
Joe's Garage **19**
Postmaster's House **29**
Saffron **29**
Skyline Restaurant **12**
Tatler **21**
Wai Waterfront **16**
Winnies Gourmet Pizza Bar **20**

> *Start your Queenstown adventures with a ride on the Skyline Queenstown gondola to get a good overview of the surrounding landscape.*

❸ ★★★ kids Skyline Queenstown. There is no better place to appraise Queenstown than from the lofty heights of Bob's Peak. From the top of the gondola you can take a free chairlift another 100m (328 ft.) for even better views and then walk the short distance down the track to this complex to enjoy a 30-minute Maori cultural performance. Take time out here for a cup of coffee in the cafe with the best view in town. You can also speed down the luge track (p. 30, ❷) or do a bungy jump (p. 388). ⏲ 2 hr. Brecon St. ☎ 03/441-0101. www.skyline.co.nz. Gondola round-trip NZ$25 adults, NZ$12 kids 5–14; gondola and Maori performace NZ$55 adults, NZ$30 kids. Gondola daily 9am–midnight.

❹ ★★ kids Kiwi Birdlife Park. Get up close to birds and reptiles here, including the kiwi and

from NZ$455 for adults and NZ$296 for kids. There are numerous suppliers of fixed-wing flights from Queenstown to Milford but if you mention Frommer's to either **Air Fiordland** (☎ 0800/103-404; www.airfiordland.com) or **Milford Sound Scenic Flights** (☎ 0800/207-206; www.milfordflights.co.nz), you'll get 10% discount. They're similarly priced—to each other and to Real Journeys—and offer flight/cruise options. This is a pricey adventure but it's one you'll never forget. ⏲ 1 day.

Return to Queenstown for the night.

❷ ★★★ kids Skippers Canyon Tour. This pretty canyon, 22km (14 miles) from Queenstown at the head of the Shotover River, was made famous by the discovery of gold in 1862. Within four months there were over 10,000 miners in the canyon. Today, among the few reminders of this bustling era are an old schoolhouse and an incredible narrow, winding road that was carved out of the rock faces by Chinese laborers. It can be a hair-raising journey, so I'd advise booking a tour and letting someone else do the driving. One of the best is **Queenstown Heritage Tours,** who offer a delightful half-day adventure limited to four to six people, culminating in a delicious picnic on the edge of a cliff overlooking the river. ⏲ 4 hr. ☎ 03/442-5949. www.qht.co.nz. Admission NZ$150 adults, NZ$75 kids 5–15. Includes pick-up from your hotel in Queenstown. Daily 8am and 1:15pm.

A Sound Decision

Everyone asks which of the sounds they should visit—Milford or Doubtful. Here are some facts to help you make your decision. Milford is the most famous and most accessible. Doubtful doesn't have the same jagged peaks and abrupt cliff faces as Milford, but because it's harder to get to, visitor numbers are far fewer and you're more likely to get a better sense of the remoteness. Even father south, Dusky Sound is definitely the most remote and mysterious of the trio. The important thing is to weigh up the amount of time you have and how much money you want to spend. If you can afford it, the best way to go is to fly over Dusky and Doubtful sounds, then drive to Milford Sound and do a cruise. ★★★ **Fiordland Helicopters** (☎ 03/249-7575; www.fiordlandhelicopters.co.nz) has a 1-hour flight over Doubtful Sound (NZ$510 per person) or a combined Dusky and Doubtful flight (1½ hr.) for NZ$750 per person. ★★★ **Air Fiordland** (☎ 0800/107-505 or 03/249-6720; www.airfiordland.com), has several options covering all the sounds, including a 40-minute Doubtful Sound flight for NZ$300 adults, NZ$195 kids. Their 1-hour Dusky and Doubtful combination flight is NZ$595 per person. For more flightseeing options, see p. 392.

> *Once a bustling gold-mining town, Arrowtown is now a shopping mecca selling top class NZ goods.*

the tuatara. If you're in time for the 30-minute Conservation in Action show (11am and 3pm daily), you'll see keepers interacting with free-flying native birds and you'll meet some of our most endangered species. There's a Native Garden Trail and it's always fun to catch kiwi feeding time (10am, noon, 1:30pm, and 4:30pm daily). You can explore the replica Maori hunting village and enjoy Maori dance performances at 11am and 3pm. ⏱ At least 1 hr. Brecon St. ☎ 03/442-8059. www.kiwibird.co.nz. Admission NZ$38 adults, NZ$19 kids; 1 child per paying adult is free. Daily 9–6:30pm in summer, 9am–5pm in winter.

⑤ 🍽 **Café 111.** Just a short walk downhill from the Kiwi Birdlife Park, tucked in by a medical center, is this well-placed spot for homemade goodies like muffins, carrot cake, and very good coffee. 9 Isle St. ☎ 03/441-0561. NZ$8–NZ$12.

⑥ ★★ kids **Queenstown shopping.** There's a constant holiday atmosphere in Queenstown that invariably lulls me into personal extravagance (see "Queenstown Shopping," p. 374). Everything is a pleasant walk in Queenstown, so even if you don't buy anything, a wander around the town will give you a feel for this crazy place. If you'd rather skip the town, spend the rest of your afternoon enjoying a quiet, easy walk to Queenstown Gardens on the edge of the lake (off Park St.) or take one of the lake-edge walking tracks. ⏱ 2 hr. See p. 374.

On day 3, leave Queenstown on Gorge Rd. and look out for the supermarket on your left. Turn left here on Robins Rd. and then take a hard left into the lower car park just past the supermarket.

⑦ 🍽 **Squisito Café.** Begin day 3 with a delicious coffee, fresh breads, and pastries at this cafe in the Mediterranean Market. While you're here, buy some goodies for a picnic lunch in Arrowtown. 53 Robins Rd. ☎ 03/442-4161; www.mediterranean.co.nz. NZ$10–NZ$15.

Rejoin Gorge Rd., turn left, and drive 5km (3 miles) to Arthurs Point. Cross the bridge and take a hard left into the car park.

⑧ ★★★ kids **Shotover Jet.** Imagine racing through narrow canyons just inches from towering rock faces, reaching speeds of up to 85kph (53mph). There are other jet-boat operators in Queenstown but this is the only one operating on this dramatic stretch of river—and it's one of the most exciting. Book in advance to secure a place. It's also a good idea to wear glasses or sunglasses and a warm jacket. ⏱ 2 hr. Shotover Jet Beach, Gorge Rd., Arthurs Point. ☎ 0800/746-868. www.shotoverjet.com. Admission NZ$120 adults, NZ$70 kids 5–15. Daily departures every 15 min.

Get onto Centennial Ave. and continue straight onto McDonnell Rd. Turn left at Gibbston Highway (St. Hwy. 6) and drive east, through the Gibbston Valley.

⑩ ★★★ kids Gibbston Valley. There are a number of attractions in this very pretty, vineyard-filled valley and you can stop at whichever ones appeal to you most. If wine is your thing, stop at some vineyards. My favorites include **Chard Farm,** just past the Kawarau bungy bridge (☎ 03/442-1006; www.chardfarm. co.nz), reached via a perilously skinny cliff-top access road off St. Hwy. 6 and **GVW Winery,** a bit further down the highway (03/441-1388; www.gvcheese.co.nz), with a divine setting and an underground barrel hall and store. (Don't miss the adjacent Gibbston Valley Cheesery, ☎ 03/441-1388; www.gvcheese.

> Spend a day tasting wine in the Gibbston Valley and finish with a cheese platter from Gibbston Valley Cheesery.

Turn left onto Gorge Rd., which becomes Malaghans Rd., and follow signs to Arrowtown. The drive is 15km (9⅓ miles) and takes about 20 min.

⑨ ★★★ kids Arrowtown. Old miners' cottages, the old jail, and other 19th-century buildings are strong reminders that this tiny town (current population around 2,000), was once a busy gold-mining center. Gold was struck here in 1862 and in 1863. The **Lakes District Museum,** 49 Buckingham St. (☎ 03/442-1824; www.museumqueenstown.com), in an 1875 bank building, has excellent displays highlighting the town's mining history. Admission costs NZ$6 adults, NZ$1 for kids 5–14. It's open daily from 8:30am to 5pm; the staff will also arrange visits to the Arrowtown Gaol (1875). You can wander the restored Chinese Miners' Camp at the north end of the town or venture further down Buckingham Street to see the former miners' cottages, now privately owned. Everything is within walking distance and the cute shops along the main street are all part of the attraction. Enjoy a picnic lunch by the river. ⏱ 2 hr.

Queenstown Shopping

★★★ **Toi o Tahuna Fine Art Gallery,** on Church Lane (☎ 03/409-0787; www.toi. co.nz), is tucked away off the main streets but it's worth hunting for if you like art. They stock predominantly work by Maori artists. The iconic ★★★ **Canterbury of New Zealand's** stocks the famous CCC brand of clothing including men's and women's international rugby jerseys. It has two branches, one at O'Connells Shopping Centre, Camp Street (☎ 03/442-4020; www.canterbury ofnz.com), and another at Remarkables Park Shopping Centre, Kawarau Road, Frankton (☎ 03/441-2280). Pearl lovers will adore ★★★ **Pounamu Pearl,** at the corner of Beach and Rees streets (☎ 03/442-9611), which offers an exclusive range of top quality Tahitian black, South Sea white, Chinese natural, Japanese akoya, and New Zealand's unique blue pearls, all sold either loose or handcrafted into jewelry. The shop stocks some beautiful jade (greenstone) pieces as well. ★★★ **Lord of the Rings,** 37 Shotover St., (☎ 0800/688-222; www.lordoftheringsnz. com) is the place to buy a little something for the movie fans who thought they had everything. The shop is filled with Middle Earth memorabilia, from jewelry to books to statues. You can even organize a tour of movie filming sights here. It's open in high season, October to April.

co.nz). Continuing east on St. Hwy. 6 (which changes names from Gibbston Hwy. to Kawaru Gorge Rd.), **Peregrine** winery (03/442-4000; www.peregrinewines.co.nz), is known for its stunning architecture. Even if you're not into bungy jumping, I recommend a visit to the **AJ Hackett Bungy Centre** (☎ 0800/286-4958; www.bungy.co.nz) at Kawarau River Bridge. It's home to the company's original bungy (the world's first commercial bungy site) and the new visitor center is a masterful feat of engineering and architecture as it curls underground. Hackett also offers a very good Secrets of Bungy Tour (adults NZ$45, kids NZ$35). There are excellent viewing platforms for watching jumpers and a cafe if you feel like a snack. ⏱ 3 hr.

⑪　📷 ★★★ **Amisfield Winery.** This is one of the best restaurants and wineries in the region, a lovely place to settle in for a late afternoon glass of wine and a big platter of delicious local treats. If you like, stay on and enjoy dinner here or head back into Queenstown and choose from one of the restaurants I've recommended on p. 402. 10 Lake Hayes Rd. ☎ 03/442-0556. www.amisfield.co.nz. NZ$17–NZ$29.

Queenstown Nightlife

★★★ **Bardeaux,** Eureka Arcade, off The Mall (☎ 03/442-8284), has a cellar full of vintage wines that will set wine lovers up for a good night out. ★★★ **Barmuda,** Searle Lane (☎ 03/442-7300), has long cocktail and wine lists, with an outdoor courtyard and plush lounge to socialize in. Small, intimate ★ **Barup,** upstairs at Eureka Arcade, next to Bardeaux (☎ 03/442-7707), is famous for cocktails —especially their Gin Gimlet and the Brandy Alexander. Settle into small, exclusive ★★★ **Eichardt's House Bar,** Eichardt's Hotel, Marine Parade (☎ 03/441-0450), for tapas and a glass or three of Otago's premium wines. Everything at ★★ **Minus 5 Ice Bar,** Steamer Wharf (☎ 03/442-6050), is made of ice, even the glasses you drink out of. After a few vodka cocktails, you probably won't even feel the cold. Looking for a friendly pub? Try ★★★ **Dux de Lux Craft Brewery Bar,** 14 Church St. (☎ 03/442-9688); ★★★ **The**

Speight's Ale House, corner of Stanley and Ballarat streets (☎ 03/441-3065); or the English-themed ★★★ **Pig & Whistle Pub,** 19 Ballarat St. (☎ 03/442-9055), which features live entertainment and karaoke.

Gamblers can try their luck either at the small, boutique **Lasseters Wharf Casino,** Steamer Wharf (☎ 03/441-1495; http://wharf-casino.co.nz), or at the much larger **SKYCITY Casino,** 16-24 Beach St., (☎ 03/441-0400; www.skycityqueenstown.co.nz), which has live entertainment Friday and Saturday nights.

For a quieter night out, try ★★★ **Dorothy Brown's Cinema & Bar,** Buckingham St., Arrowtown (☎ 03/442-1964; www.dorothy-browns.com). Small-town arthouse cinemas are all the rage in provincial New Zealand and Dorothy's is a classic example of how one theater has reawakened local interest in the movie scene.

The West Coast in 3 Days

To get the best from this skinny stretch of land in just 3 days, you're best to focus on the southern section, nearer the glaciers and the bulk of activities. Be mindful, though, that September through April is New Zealand's main tourism season and here on the West Coast, where accommodations are more limited, you'll need to book well in advance to secure a bed. It is also important not to underestimate driving times; roads are very narrow and winding in some parts of the coast.

> There's something moody and unfathomable about the bush-fringed West Coast lakes.

START Hokitika is 487km (303 miles) north of Queenstown, 245km (152 miles) west of Christchurch, 45km (28 miles) south of Greymouth, and 147km (91 miles) north of Franz Josef Glacier. The West Coast Historical Museum is on the corner of Tancred and Hamilton streets. TRIP LENGTH 226km (140 miles).

1 ★★ kids **West Coast Historical Museum.** The West Coast's largest museum and archive is in the grand old Carnegie Building (1908). Spend 18 minutes watching the audio-visual display that details the history of *pounamu* (greenstone) and gold in the region, then inspect New Zealand's most significant greenstone

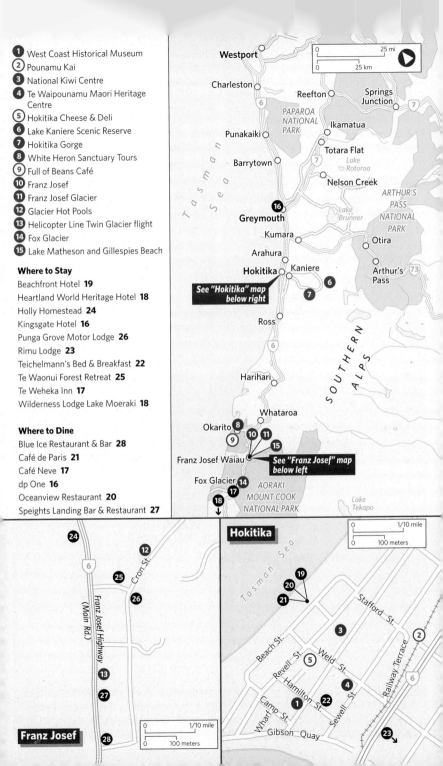

1 West Coast Historical Museum
2 Pounamu Kai
3 National Kiwi Centre
4 Te Waipounamu Maori Heritage Centre
5 Hokitika Cheese & Deli
6 Lake Kaniere Scenic Reserve
7 Hokitika Gorge
8 White Heron Sanctuary Tours
9 Full of Beans Café
10 Franz Josef
11 Franz Josef Glacier
12 Glacier Hot Pools
13 Helicopter Line Twin Glacier flight
14 Fox Glacier
15 Lake Matheson and Gillespies Beach

Where to Stay

Beachfront Hotel 19
Heartland World Heritage Hotel 18
Holly Homestead 24
Kingsgate Hotel 16
Punga Grove Motor Lodge 26
Rimu Lodge 23
Teichelmann's Bed & Breakfast 22
Te Waonui Forest Retreat 25
Te Weheka Inn 17
Wilderness Lodge Lake Moeraki 18

Where to Dine

Blue Ice Restaurant & Bar 28
Café de Paris 21
Café Neve 17
dp One 16
Oceanview Restaurant 20
Speights Landing Bar & Restaurant 27

Westport
Charleston
Reefton
Springs Junction
PAPAROA NATIONAL PARK
Ikamatua
Punakaiki
Totara Flat
Barrytown
Lake Rotoroa
Nelson Creek
Tasman Sea
ARTHUR'S PASS NATIONAL PARK
Lake Brunner
Greymouth
Kumara
Otira
Arahura
Hokitika
Kaniere
Arthur's Pass

See "Hokitika" map below right

Ross
SOUTHERN ALPS
Harihari
Whataroa
Okarito
Franz Josef Waiau

See "Franz Josef" map below left

Fox Glacier
AORAKI MOUNT COOK NATIONAL PARK
Lake Tekapo

Franz Josef

Franz Josef Highway (Main Rd.)
Cron St.

Hokitika

Tasman Sea
Stafford St.
Beach St.
Revell St.
Weld St.
Hamilton St.
Sewell St.
Camp St.
Wharf St.
Gibson Quay
Railway Terrace

25 mi
25 km
1/10 mile
100 meters

exhibition. They also have excellent displays of old horse-drawn vehicles, mining tools, early household items, in all a superb collection of over 16,000 historical photographs and relics from the gold-mining era. ⏱ 1 hr. Corner of Tancred and Hamilton sts., Hokitika. ☎ 03/755-6898. Admission NZ$5. Summer daily 10am–5pm; winter Mon–Fri 9:30am–5pm, Sat–Sun 10am–4pm.

---

② 🍽 **Pounamu Kai.** Choices at this cafe include vegan, vegetarian, and gluten-free options. They serve some of the most consistently good coffee in town. **23 Weld St. ☎ 03/755-8581. NZ$10–NZ$12.**

❸ ★★ kids **National Kiwi Centre.** The stars here are the creepy, yet intriguing, giant eels. There are over 60 of them, several weighing more than 25kg (55 lb.). If you're there for mealtime you can try your hand at feeding the slippery monsters. The center also features the kiwi, of course, tucked away in their nocturnal habitat, along with a huge aquarium and an indoor lake with giant trout, plus birds, reptiles, and tiny tree frogs hiding in ferns. ⏱ At least 1 hr. 64 Tancred St., Hokitika. ☎ 03/755-5251. www.thenationalkiwicentre.co.nz Admission NZ$20 adults, NZ$10 kids 5–14, NZ$45 family. Daily 9am–5pm.

❹ ★★★ kids **Te Waipounamu Maori Heritage Centre.** Come here to get a greater understanding of the beauties of *pounamu*, its history, and what it means to Maori. *Pounamu*, jade, and greenstone are different names for the same stone, but here you'll learn how Maori value different types of *pounamu* for its differing characteristics. The center also features the history of the local Ngati Waewae tribe, one of the Ngai Tahu *hapu* (sub-tribes). Significant occasions are celebrated throughout the year—Matakriki, the Maori new year in June and July; Waitangi Day, which celebrates

The Wild West

Franz Josef and Fox glaciers are just a small part of the 115,000-hectare (284,000-acre) Westland National Park, an impressive area of high mountains, glacial lakes, and rushing rivers. The park is popular for tramping, mountain climbing, fishing, canoeing, hunting, and horse trekking. In 1990, the combined Mount Cook/Westland National Parks, Fiordland National Park, Mount Aspiring National Park, and all significant adjacent natural areas were incorporated into the single vast Southwest New Zealand World Heritage Area–Te Wahipounamu, which contains 10% of New Zealand's total land area, or 2.6 million hectares (6.4 million acres). The World Heritage Highway traverses the northern third of this region and is largely confined to the West Coast side of the Main Divide.

the signing of the Treaty of Waitangi, in February; and Anzac Day in March and April. ⏱ 1 hr. 39 Weld St., Hokitika. ☎ 03/755-8304. www.maoriheritage.co.nz. Free admission. Daily 8:30am–5pm, extended hours in summer.

---

⑤ 🍽 **Hokitika Cheese & Deli.** Here you'll find some delicious cabinet food and deli items like fresh breads, cheese, and cured meats. Buy some extra goodies and cold drinks for an afternoon tea snack at your next stop. 84 Revell St. ☎ 03/755-5432. NZ$10–NZ$15.

From Weld St., turn left onto Fitzherbert St. (St. Hwy. 6), then right onto Stafford St. Continue onto Kaniere Rd., then Lake Kaniere Rd., traveling 20km (12 miles) and 30 min. to Lake Kaniere.

⑥ ★★★ kids **Lake Kaniere Scenic Reserve.** The road meets the lake at The Landing, which is the starting point of two 4-hour walks. Veer to the left here and drive the fern-fringed road through a beautiful reserve that takes you around to the small holiday settlement of Hans Bay on the eastern lake edge. There are picnic, swimming, and camping spots here and several pretty short walks. The lake itself is one of the biggest in the South Island at 8km (5 miles) long and 2km (1¼ miles) wide. If the weather is fine, you'll get some wonderful reflective photographs. If you'd like to go for a drive, carry on around the narrow, unsealed road around the east side of the lake. About 3.5km (2¼ miles) from Hans Bay, take the short, 2-minute walk to Dorothy Falls, which is a nice spot for a refreshing dip. ⏱ At least 2 hr.

Continue around the east side of the lake (the road changes names to Hans Bay Rd. then Dorothy Falls Rd.), then turn right once you've crossed the Styx River Bridge. This will take you to the village of Kokatahi. Turn right and follow signs back to Hokitika. Or, turn left to the Hokitika Gorge.

⑦ ★★★ kids **Hokitika Gorge.** If you still have plenty of hours of daylight left, it's worth traveling the short distance (about 15 min.) to Hokitika Gorge. On the way, you'll pass the large Kowhitirangi Incident Memorial on your left, which marks the scene of New Zealand's first mass murder. At Hokitika Gorge, you'll be

> *White herons (kotuku) are sacred to Maori. The only nesting colony in New Zealand is at Okarito.*

blown away by the huge granite cliffs and the stunning milky-blue river water. It's a 2-minute walk to the short swing bridge and about 5 minutes further on to the best pools, where you'll get some unbelievable photos. ⏱ 1hr.

Drive back along Kowhitirangi Rd., following signs (28km/17 miles) to Hokitika, where you'll spend the night. Leave Hokitika early on day 2 and travel south on St. Hwy. 6 to the village of Whataroa. It's 103km (64 miles) and about 1½hr to Whataroa.

⑧ ★★★ kids **White Heron Sanctuary Tours.** Nesting season at New Zealand's only *kotuku* (white heron) colony is between November and February, but tours run from September to March. It starts with a short minibus ride from the Whataroa office, then a 20-minute jet-boat ride up the Waitangitaona River. You'll then be guided through native rainforest

> *You'll go home with unbelievable photographs if you go hiking at Franz Josef Glacier.*

to spend about 30 to 40 minutes in a colony-viewing hide. Seeing the birds in the native trees is an awesome sight and you'll get plenty of good photo opportunities. You're also likely to see Royal Spoonbills and numerous native birds. This is a popular activity so make sure you book early. ⏱ 3 hr. Main Rd., Whataroa. ☎ 0800/523-456. www.whiteherontours.co.nz. NZ$115 adults, NZ$50 kids 12 and under. Tours 9am, 11am, 1pm, and 3pm daily.

Head south on St. Hwy. 6 again. It's 27km (17 miles) and 30 min. to Franz Josef.

⑨ 🍴 **Full of Beans Café.** This is a great stop for coffee and a quick snack. There's a good selection of cabinet food and they offer dine-in or takeaway meals. If you want a big hearty brunch, see my restaurant recommendations on p. 402. **Main Rd., Whataroa.** ☎ 03/752-0139. NZ$8–NZ$12.

⑩ ★★★ kids **Franz Josef.** To make sense of the jumble of helicopter rides and glacier adventures on offer in Franz Josef and Fox Glacier further south, start at the Westland National Park Visitor Centre and i-SITE (p. 405) in the center of the village. If you plan to fly, book ahead. Your next stop should be Alpine Adventure Centre (Main Rd. ☎ 03/752-0793), to watch the spectacular short movie, *Flowing West.* It runs daily from 10:30am and it will take your breath away. ⏱ 1 hr.

⑪ ★★★ kids **Franz Josef Glacier.** Explorer and geologist Julius von Haast named Franz Josef Glacier after the Austro-Hungarian emperor in 1863. The glacier extends 12km (7½ miles) from its three feeder glaciers high in the Alps to within just 19km (12 miles) of the sea. It is around 7,000 years old. There are plenty of options for guided glacier walks, climbing experiences, and helicopter and fixed-wing flights, with or without landings (see p. 391). ***Remember:*** never go on the glaciers without a guide. Glaciers are constantly moving and several people have lost their lives after ignoring safety barriers and danger signs. If you can't afford a guided experience, drive to the glacier car park, 5km (3 miles) south of the village and either do the Sentinel Rock Walk

(20 min.) for good views of the glacier or the Glacier Terminal Face Walk (1 hr. 20 min.), following the Waihao riverbed to the glacier terminal. Always heed all signs and barriers. Make sure you wear sturdy footwear. ⏲ 2 hr.

⑫ ★★★ kids **Glacier Hot Pools.** Finish your day unwinding in the warm, glacier-fed pools of this leafy haven. There are three public pools, three private pools, and excellent massage facilities on hand. If you don't have swimwear and towels, both are available to hire or buy. ⏲ At least 1 hr. Cron St., Franz Josef. ☎ 0800/044-044. www.glacierhotpools.co.nz. Admission NZ$25 adults, NZ$18 kids 16 and under. Private pools (45 min.) NZ$45 per person. Daily noon–10pm.

Spend the night in or near Franz Josef. See p. 398 for hotel and restaurant recommendations.

⑬ ★★★ kids **Helicopter Line Twin Glacier flight.** Try to get in the air early on day 3. The Helicopter Line is New Zealand's largest helicopter company, with flights to the South Island's iconic locations. Given a restricted timetable, I suggest you do their 30-minute Twin Glacier trip with a snow landing, which takes you over both Fox and Franz Josef glaciers. It's an unforgettable flight and if you mention you saw them in Frommer's you'll get a 10% discount when booking direct. They offer longer flights too. Main South Rd., Franz Josef. ☎ 0800/807-767 or 03/752-0767. www.helicopter.co.nz. NZ$275–NZ$295 per person. Flights are always weather dependent and minimum passenger numbers apply. Ask about kids' discounts.

Get some lunch in Franz Josef (see p. 403), then take your pick of the next two stops for the afternoon. If you haven't had enough of glaciers yet, leave Franz Josef, heading south on St. Hwy. 6. It's 24km (15 miles) and 25 min. to Fox Glacier.

⑭ ★★★ kids **Fox Glacier.** This 13km (8-mile) glacier gets it name from William Fox, a former premier of New Zealand. If you drive just south of the township, you can turn into Glacier Access Road and do the 1-hour **Fox Glacier Valley Walk,** which takes you to the glacier terminus. A little further south, Glacier View Road takes you to the beginning of the 1½-hour **Chalet Lookout Walk,** which gives a good view over the glacier. As at Franz Josef, it is vital that you do not go beyond safety barriers. If you want to do a guided walk on Fox Glacier, hook up with **Fox Glacier Guiding,** Main South Road, Fox Glacier (☎ 0800/111-600 or 03/751-0825; www.foxguides.co.nz), which offers a number of different options. ⏲ 4 hr.

If glacier hiking isn't your thing, drive 5km (3 miles) west of Fox Glacier to the village of Lake Matheson.

⑮ ★★ kids **Lake Matheson and Gillespies Beach.** Lake Matheson is famous for its perfect reflections of Aoraki/Mt. Cook and the Southern Alps. There is a very good walk (about 1 hr.) around the lake, with plentiful bird life and several excellent little bays for swimming. You can enjoy afternoon tea at Matheson Café, to the left of the walkway. If you continue down Cook Flat Road beyond Lake Matheson, you'll get to Gillespies Beach (about another 15km/9⅓ miles). The last 11km (6¾ miles) is unsealed so take care. There's an old gold dredge here, a fabulous driftwood-strewn beach, and farther along the beach, a seal colony. ⏲ 4 hr. www.lakematheson.com.

Taking the High Road

If you're driving to the West Coast from the south, you will pass through one of New Zealand's most spectacular regions, Haast Pass. The Haast Highway took 40 years to build and only opened in 1965. It is 563m (1,847 ft.) above sea level and passes through a moody, often mist-shrouded canyon with high peaks rising either side of the winding road. The route follows an ancient Maori greenstone trail that was rediscovered by gold prospectors in the late 1860s. As you drive through beech forest beside the raging Haast River, look out for green and gold Department of Conservation signs detailing a number of excellent short walks leading off the highway to pretty waterfalls and the Blue Pools (just north of Makarora). They're a nice way to stretch your legs.

Exploring Wanaka

Wanaka is the gateway to the astonishing natural beauty of Mount Aspiring National Park—a place of braided river valleys, native beech forests, lush alpine meadows, dozens of hiking tracks, fishing spots, and wild landscapes. It's an adventurer's dream and a photographer's paradise. There are commercial adventures here too but it's much quieter than nearby Queenstown, which is why so many New Zealanders prefer it. In winter it is a leading ski resort; in summer, a mellow place to while away hot Otago days.

> Be prepared to be confused at the very puzzling (and entertaining) Stuart Landsborough's Puzzling World in Wanaka.

START Wanaka is 145km (90 miles) south of Haast and 117km (73 miles) north of Queenstown. To get to Stuart Landsborough's Puzzling World, leave Wanaka heading southwest on Ardmore St., which becomes St. Hwy. 84. Travel 2km (1¼ miles). **TRIP LENGTH** 50km (31 miles) and 2 days.

1 ★★★ kids **Stuart Landsborough's Puzzling World.** There's a little bit of madness happening here—you will have guessed that from the crazy, tilted houses at the entrance—and more than a few challenges to set you thinking. It's

great for kids but adults will also find a lot to wonder at. Expect incredible illusion rooms, a 1.5km (1-mile) maze, confusing passageways, leaning clock towers, and much more. ☺ 1 hr. 188 St. Hwy. 84. ☎ 03/443-7489. www.puzzling world.co.nz. Admission NZ$13 adults, NZ$9 kids 5–15. Daily 8:30am–5:30pm (5pm in winter).

Turn right onto St. Hwy. 84 and follow signs to Wanaka Airport. Turn left on Airport Way and right on Lloyd Dunn Ave. It's about 8km (5 miles).

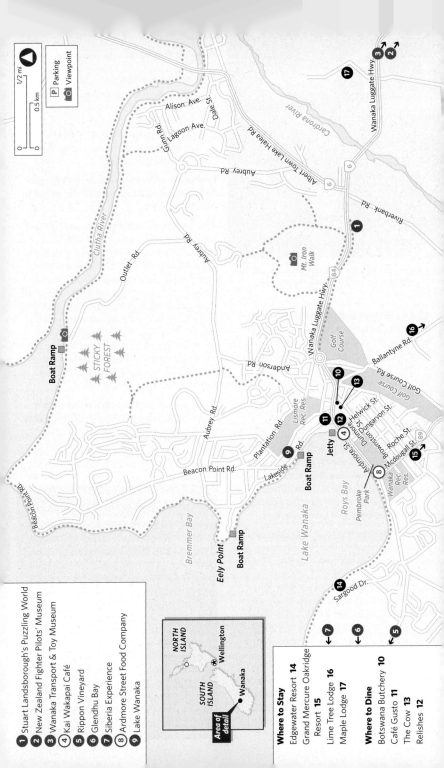

Where to Stay
Edgewater Resort **14**
Grand Mercure Oakridge Resort **15**
Lime Tree Lodge **16**
Maple Lodge **17**

Where to Dine
Botswana Butchery **10**
Café Gusto **11**
The Cow **13**
Relishes **12**

1 Stuart Landsborough's Puzzling World
2 New Zealand Fighter Pilots' Museum
3 Wanaka Transport & Toy Museum
4 Kai Wakapai Café
5 Rippon Vineyard
6 Glendhu Bay
7 Siberia Experience
8 Ardmore Street Food Company
9 Lake Wanaka

NORTH ISLAND
Wellington
SOUTH ISLAND
Wanaka
Area of detail

Alison Ave.
Dale St.
Lagoon Ave.
Gunn Rd.
Albert Town Lake Hawea Rd.
Aubrey Rd.
Cardrona River
Wanaka Luggate Hwy.
Riverbank Rd.
Outlet Rd.
Clutha River
Boat Ramp
STICKY FOREST
Mt. Iron Walk
Aubrey Rd.
Anderson Rd.
Golf Course
Ballantyne Rd.
Golf Course Rd.
Lismore Rec. Res.
Plantation Rd.
Lakeside Rd.
Beacon Point Rd.
Beacon Point Rd.
Bremner Bay
Eely Point
Boat Ramp
Boat Ramp
Jetty
Roys Bay
Pembroke Park
Wanaka Rec. Res.
Lake Wanaka
Sargood Dr.
Helwick St.
Dungarvon St.
Brownston St.
Dunmore St.
Ardmore St.
Roche St.
McDougall St.
Viewpoint
Parking
1/2 mi
0.5 km

Wanaka Luggate Hwy.

> *Allow plenty of time to explore the weird and wonderful at Wanaka Transport & Toy Museum.*

② ★★★ **kids New Zealand Fighter Pilots' Museum.** This is home to the largest collection of flyable World War II fighter planes in the Southern Hemisphere. At time of writing, plans are underway to move the museum to a new, much larger building nearby. The new facility will be very close to this address and signage will indicate the new location. Expect to see all the current memorabilia, the intricate war histories, the stunning photographic collections, and an astonishing collection of aircraft and collectible cars. ⏱ 2 hr. Wanaka Airport, Lloyd Dunn Ave. ☎ 03/443-7010; www. nzfpm.co.nz. Call or check the website for information about the opening of the new facility, including open hours and admission fees.

③ ★★★ **Wanaka Transport & Toy Museum.** If you've ever wondered where to find New Zealand's largest Barbie™ and Star Wars™ collections, wonder no more—it's right here, among the millions of other intriguing collectibles spread over four huge hangars. Along with a wide range of vintage aircraft and vehicles, there are over 30,000 old toys and items that will bring back memories for everyone. Kids will think they've landed in heaven when they get to the toy shop. ⏱ At least 1 hr. 891 Wanaka-Luggate Hwy. (St. Hwy. 6, near Wanaka Airport). ☎ 03/443-8765. www.wanakatrans portandtoymuseum.com. Admission NZ$12 adults, NZ$5 kids 5–15, NZ$30 family. Daily 8:30am–5pm.

Drive back to Wanaka the way you came.

④ 🍴 ★★ **Kai Whakapai Café.** This is a terrific place to fill up on pies, pizzas, burgers, croissants, and more. You can eat in or get takeaway and have a picnic across the road on the lakefront. Corner of Ardmore and Dungarvon sts. ☎ 03/443-7795. NZ$10–NZ$15.

Head west on Ardmore Rd. to join Wanaka-Mount Aspiring Rd. Drive 3km (1¾ miles) to Rippon Vineyard.

⑤ ★★★ **Rippon Vineyard.** Rolfe and Lois Mills pioneered grape growing in Central Otago and their vineyard must have one of the loveliest outlooks of any vineyard in the world. Make sure you take your camera because you will want a lasting impression of their leafy, green vines cascading down the hillside to meet the bright blue waters of Lake Wanaka, with the jagged mountains beyond. They have free wine tasting here too. ⏱ At least 45 min. 246 Wanaka-Mount Aspiring Rd., ☎ 03/443-8084. www.rippon.co.nz. Nov–April daily 11:30am–5pm; July-Oct daily 1:30pm–5pm.

Turn right and continue on Wanaka-Mount Aspiring Rd. 10km (6¼ miles) to Glendhu Bay.

⑥ ★★ **Glendhu Bay.** This is a nice little drive if you want to take in some more of the beautiful landscapes in this area. There's not much to

An Airshow to Remember

Every two years, the Wanaka skies come alive with the sounds of the ★★★ **Warbirds Over Wanaka International Air Show** (www.warbirdsoverwanaka.com). The event draws many thousands of people to the region and the skies are filled with classic vintage and veteran aircraft. The New Zealand Air Force and its aerobatics teams put on dynamic displays overhead. It's one of the top four Warbirds air shows in the world and is held every second Easter in even-numbered years. The next show will be staged from April 6 to 8, 2012, and tickets will be on sale from February 2011. If you're coming to visit during that period, make sure you book your accommodation well in advance.

> *Finish your day in Wanaka with a picnic dinner by the lake, as the sun sets across the mountains.*

Glendhu itself—just a big camping ground—but it's a nice place to stop and take photos of Mount Aspiring across the lake. Take a wander through the camping ground, walk around the lake for a bit, and if it's a very hot day, perhaps take a dip (southern lakes are often very cold). ⏲ At least 2 hr.

Retrace your route back to Wanaka for a spot of shopping or for dinner at one of the restaurants I've recommended on p. 404.

❼ ★★★ Siberia Experience. Spend day 2 on this marvelous wilderness adventure in Mt. Aspiring National Park. You can drive yourself to the start point at Makarora (45 min. from Wanaka on St. Hwy. 6) or catch the 9am Atomic Shuttle from Wanaka (return trip NZ$50 per person). When you've met up with the Siberia team, they'll take you on a 25-minute flight into the remote Siberia Valley, where you'll start a 3-hour walk through river valleys and beech forests. You then rendezvous with a jet-boat in Wilkin Valley and have a racy 30-minute boat ride back to Makarora. The shuttle will have you back in Wanaka around 3 or 4pm. This is a spectacular excursion that takes you into some of the finest wilderness country. Make sure you take plenty of insect repellent to fight off the super-greedy sandflies, and if you're taking children, make sure they're up to several hours trekking through wilderness areas. ⏲ 6 hr. Siberia Experience, St. Hwy. 6, Makarora. ☎ 0800/345-666 or 03/443-4385. www.siberiaexperience.co.nz. Admission NZ$325 adults, NZ$275 kids 3–13.

⑧ ☕ Ardmore Street Food Company. Stop in for an afternoon snack. You can eat in, or buy takeaway coffee and cake and eat it across the road on the lakefront. 155 Ardmore St. ☎ 03/443-2230. NZ$10–NZ$12.

❾ ★★★ Lake Wanaka. You may have walked yourselves out this morning but if you still have the energy, take a leisurely walk around the lake in either direction from the information center. If you'd rather, hire a bike at the information center and pedal around the lake or rent a kayak and end the day with a bit of paddling. Otherwise, browse the shops or relax in your accommodation before heading out for dinner. ⏲ 2 hr.

TE WAIPOUNAMU

The Southwest New Zealand World Heritage Area

BY ADRIENNE REWI

THE SOUTHWEST OF THE SOUTH ISLAND is home to some of New Zealand's greatest natural beauty. This vast tract of land is now enshrined as Te Waipounamu, the Southwest New Zealand World Heritage Area. It covers 2.6 million hectares (6.4 million acres), which equates to 10% of New Zealand's total landmass. This is where you'll find Milford Sound (known to Maori as Piopio-tahi, "a single thrush"), with its thundering waterfalls, glossy green rainforest and steep mountainous walls; the more remote Dusky Sound, New Zealand's largest fjord, which was home to early sealers; and Doubtful Sound, said to be the prettiest of all the southern fjord and home to rare dolphins. The vast Te Waipounamu region includes three national parks:

FIORDLAND NATIONAL PARK
Early Maori called Fiordland Te Rua-o-te-moko—"the pit of Tattooing." This may reference the fact that the glaciers here chisel the land in much the same way a tattooist chisels the skin. It's a lonely, moss-covered landscape covering 1.26 million hectares (3.1 million acres), making it New Zealand's largest national park and one of the biggest in the world. Much of it is impenetrable to all but the toughest explorers but many of its towering mountains, spectacular waterfalls, lakes and rivers, and its vast beech forests and fjord are accessible to visitors. The famous Milford, Hollyford, and Kepler walking tracks are all found here.

AORAKI/MOUNT COOK/ WESTLAND NATIONAL PARKS
Aoraki/Mount Cook, "the cloud piercer" to Maori, is New Zealand's highest peak and the centerpiece of this dramatic region, which covers 70,969 hectares (about 175,000 acres) of alpine heartland. It is also home to the Tasman Glacier, which had some 30 million tons of ice shaved off its terminal face when the devastating 6.3 earthquake struck Christchurch on February 22, 2011. Fox and Franz Josef Glaciers are key tourism features in the adjoining Westland National park, which was formed in 1960. It covers 127,541 hectares (315,000 acres) from sea level to the 3,491m (11,453 ft.) summit of Mount Tasman. Think alpine grasslands, dense rainforest, wild oceans, icy glaciers, rocky rivers, and crystal blue lakes.

MOUNT ASPIRING NATIONAL PARK
This rugged 355,000 hectare (over 877,000 acre) landscape features everything from the deep blue lakes of Wanaka and Whakatipu and the roaring Kawarau and Clutha Rivers to vast tracts of alpine forest, hanging valleys, moraines, glaciers, and the striking 3,027m (9,931 ft.) Mount Aspiring. Birds and native vegetation abound. The easiest access to the area is via the beautiful Matukituki Valley, following the Matukituki River upland from Wanaka.

More Maori Place Names

TITITEA (Mount Aspiring)—the upright glistening one

TE WAI POUNAMU (The South Island)—the water of greenstone

(more correctly it should be Te Wahi Pounamu, or the place of greenstone)

MATUKITUKI RIVER—the white destroyer

AORANGI or **AORAKI** (Mount Cook)—cloud in the sky (more popularly "cloud piercer' or "sky piercer")

POUTINI TE IKA-A-MAUI (The West Coast)–Poutini is a form of greenstone. It is also the fish that legendary Kupe brought with him from Hawaiki.

HOROKOAU (Mount Tasman)–Horo means to swallow; koau is a shag (bird). The mountain is said to have been given this name because its shape resembled the swelling in the long neck of the shag when it is swallowing a fish.

Queenstown, Fiordland & The West Coast Outdoor Adventures A–Z

Biking

Queenstown Bike Hire, 23 Beach St. (☎ 03/442-6039), rents road and mountain bikes, tandems, and scooters. They can set you up with maps that detail popular rides around town. They hire mountain bikes for around NZ$12 per hour and NZ$38 per day. **Vertigo Bikes** (4 Brecon St. ☎ 03/442-8378; www.vertigobikes.co.nz), are mountain bike experts and can arrange heli-biking in the Remarkables among other tours. Bike rentals start at NZ$39 per half-day; heli-tours start at NZ$299. You can also arrange to pick up a bike at the top of the Queenstown gondola to ride the trails there (NZ$69 half-day). At Lake Wanaka (p. 385, ❾) you can rent bikes from **Lakeland Adventures** at the information center and go for a leisurely ride around the lake. They hire mountain bikes for NZ$15 per hour, NZ$30 per half-day and NZ$50 for a full day.

Bungy Jumping

★★★ **AJ Hackett Bungy** started in Queenstown and now has three bungy sites in the area. **Kawarau Suspension Bridge,** at 43m (141 ft.) high, was the world's first commercial bungy jump and is now home to an iconic architectural complex that curls underground through solid rock. It's located 23km (14 miles) from Queenstown. At the top of Bob's Peak in Queenstown, **The Ledge** offers a 47m (154-ft.) jump, which you can also do at night. The **Nevis Highwire Bungy,** further along Kawarau River, is the big daddy of them all. At 134m (440 ft.), it is the country's tallest bungy—a thrill for which you'll pay NZ$250 to NZ$275. Jumps at most other sites cost around NZ$175. Beside Nevis bungy is the Nevis Arc, the world's biggest swing. You'll walk across a 70m (230-ft.) suspension bridge to a launch pad and then free fall

> *You don't have to go it alone at AJ Hackett Bungy—hitch yourself to a friend and scream in unison.*

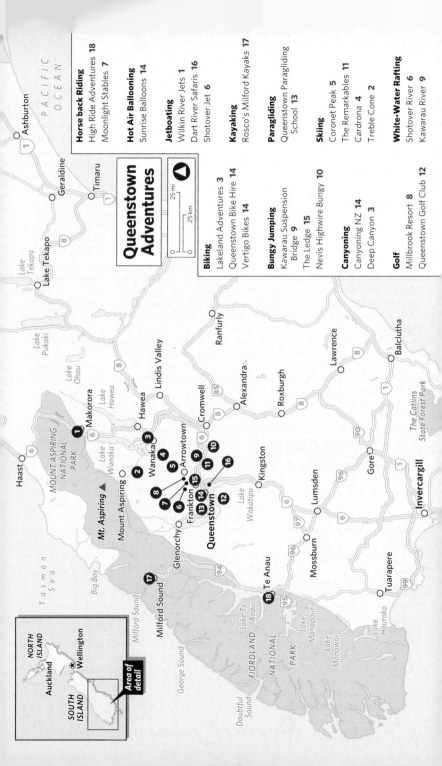

Queenstown Adventures

Biking
Lakeland Adventures 3
Queenstown Bike Hire 14
Vertigo Bikes 14

Bungy Jumping
Kawarau Suspension
Bridge 9
The Ledge 15
Nevis Highwire Bungy 10

Canyoning
Canyoning NZ 14
Deep Canyon 3

Golf
Millbrook Resort 8
Queenstown Golf Club 12

Horse back Riding
High Ride Adventures 18
Moonlight Stables 7

Hot Air Ballooning
Sunrise Balloons 14

Jetboating
Wilkin River Jets 1
Dart River Safaris 16
Shotover Jet 6

Kayaking
Rosco's Milford Kayaks 17

Paragliding
Queenstown Paragliding
School 13

Skiing
Coronet Peak 5
The Remarkables 11
Cardrona 4
Treble Cone 2

White-Water Rafting
Shotover River 6
Kawarau River 9

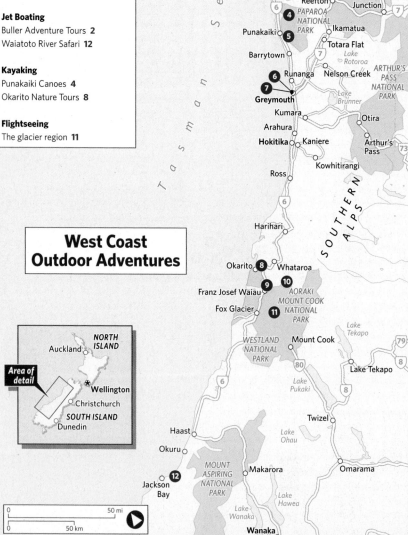

Caving
Oparara Experience **1**
Norwest Adventures **6**
Wild West Adventure Company **7**

Glacier Hiking
Fox & Franz Josef Glaciers **10**

Horseback Riding
South Westland Horse Treks **9**
Buller Adventure Tours **3**
Punakaiki Horse Treks **5**

Jet Boating
Buller Adventure Tours **2**
Waiatoto River Safari **12**

Kayaking
Punakaiki Canoes **4**
Okarito Nature Tours **8**

Flightseeing
The glacier region **11**

West Coast Outdoor Adventures

NORTH ISLAND
Auckland
Area of detail
✳ Wellington
Christchurch
SOUTH ISLAND
Dunedin

0   50 mi
0   50 km

160m (525 ft.) through the air above Doolan's Creek Gorge. Don't forget to ask about the AJ Hackett combos, which will give you significant savings on several thrills. The minimum age for any bungy jump is 13.

Canyoning

Canyoning NZ (☎ 03/441-3003; www.canyoning.co.nz), operates in the Queenstown area from mid-October to mid-April. A half-day trip will cost NZ$155 to NZ$255. In Wanaka, **Deep Canyon** (☎ 03/443-7922; www.deepcanyon.co.nz) offers a range of thrilling day trips that include tobogganing, rappelling, and swimming, from November through April. These trips range from NZ$195 to around NZ$255.

Taking a cruise on the TSS Earnslaw

This iconic Queenstown vessel, commonly called the Lady of the Lake, has been ferrying people across the lake for almost 100 years. She's been undergoing a makeover lately and in 2012 her entire forward deck section will be replaced, so there may be a substitute vessel operating for a period then. Nonetheless, the cruise across the lake is well worth it and kids will love it. Most people take a cruise earlier in the day but there's something special about gliding across Lake Wakatipu in this old beauty as the sun sinks, and you'll have beautiful light for photographs. Try to catch the 6pm Steamship Cruise (NZ$50 adults, $22 kids) so that you're back in time for dinner, although café style food is available on board. Cruises run throughout the day and evening (including dinner cruises; be sure to book these in advance). For information and bookings, contact **Real Journeys,** Steamer Wharf (0800/656-503 or 03/442-7500; www.realjourneys.co.nz).

Caving

★★★ **Oparara Experience.** These people are your ticket into the restricted areas of Oparara Valley and its cave mysteries. The full-day (5-hr.) Grand Eco Tour includes an extensive tour of the basin with the choice of either a Honeycomb Hill cave or a kayak trip. It costs NZ$250 per person. The Honeycomb Hill Cave Tour is 2½ hours and NZ$150 per person. You'll need warm clothes, good walking shoes, and you'll need to be fit. No walking sticks are allowed in the caves. **Karamea Visitor Information Centre, Market Cross, Karamea.** ☎ 07/782-6652. www.oparara.co.nz.

★★★ **Norwest Adventures.** To join this mad crew on their underworld abseiling adventures, you must be over 16 and very fit. If you qualify, you're in for a treat as trained guides take you adventure caving (NZ$300). The Glow Worm Cave Tour (NZ$100) takes you to the huge Nile River glowworm caves, and the Underworld Rafting Experience (NZ$155) takes you along an underwater stream and out via the Nile River rapids. **Main Rd., Charleston, Westport.** ☎ 0800/116-686. www.caverafting.com.

★★★ **Wild West Adventure Company.** The 5-hour Dragon's Cave Rafting Trip (NZ$175) takes you deep into a subterranean wonderland of lakes, glowworms, and waterfalls; and if that's not thrill enough, you can add in rappelling (NZ$285). **8 Whall St., Greymouth.** ☎ 0800/122-283. www.fun-nz.com.

Fishing

Numerous fishing guides operate throughout the greater Wanaka, Queenstown, and Fiordland areas. Your best bet is to call local visitor centers and check out the many brochures on offer. Prices for guides vary but expect to pay anything from NZ$100 an hour to over NZ$1,000 for a full day. Shop around though and ask who the best local guides are at local fishing supply stores.

Flightseeing

Sometimes you need a bird's eye view of a landscape—and when the landscape is as rugged and often impenetrable as the West Coast, a fly-over is the only way to truly appreciate the vastness of the place. Personally, I don't think it matters which operator you fly with; local companies are all excellent and

> *Keen to hook a fat trout? Then partner up with a fishing guide who can take you to the best spots.*

all charge a similar price. Ultimately it comes down to where they fly and how often. Remember, too, that the climate in this part of the South Island is very temperamental and flights can be cancelled at a moment's notice. The operators below all have a range of trips. It pays to book well in advance during the summer months; if you can do this online, so much the better because pricing fluctuates and prices listed here should be considered a guide. There may also be a discount available for kids; ask when you book your flight.

★★★ **Air Safaris.** You get to see over 200km (124 miles) of incredible World Heritage landscapes, mountains, and several glaciers when you join The Grand Traverse, a 50-minute scenic extravaganza that's great value at around NZ$305. Main Rd., Franz Josef. ☎ 0800/723-274; www.airsafaris.co.nz.

★★★ **Air West Coast.** This operator offers great-value deals that fly out of Greymouth. This means you get to see far more than just the glaciers and mountains. The pilots fly as far south as Milford Sound and can tailor a flight to suit your preferences. Flights to Aoraki/Mt. Cook and the glaciers begin around NZ$320 per person; and to Milford Sound, NZ$740 per person. Greymouth Airport. ☎ 03/738-0524. www.airwestcoast.co.nz.

★★★ **Aoraki Mt. Cook Ski Planes.** This company offers the only fixed-wing glacier landing in New Zealand and when you land, the engines are switched off and you're in total silence. It's a breathtaking feeling. Their 1-hour Glacier Magic trip costs around NZ$410 per person and gives you close-up views of Aoraki/Mt. Cook and Mount Tasman. The company operates out of both Franz Josef and Mount Cook. Ski Plane Bldg., Main Rd., Franz Josef. ☎ 0800/368-000. www.mtcookskiplanes.com.

★★★ **Fox Glacier & Franz Josef Heliservices.** This locally owned and operated company runs 4- and 6-passenger helicopters and is licensed to land at all designated landing sites in the Westland National Park. Flights to both glaciers and Aoraki/Mt. Cook range from NZ$190 to NZ$375 per person. Fox Guides Bldg., Main Rd., Fox Glacier and Alpine Adventure Centre, Main Rd., Franz Josef. ☎ 0800/800-793. www.scenic-flights.co.nz.

★★★ **Glacier Helicopters.** Flights to both glaciers, twin glacier experiences, and flights over Aoraki/Mt. Cook with snow landings are all offered and range in price from NZ$200 to NZ$400 per person. Fox Glacier office: Main Rd., ☎ 03/751-0803. Franz Josef office: Main Rd., ☎ 03/752-0755. Toll-free number (NZ only): ☎ 0800/800-732. www.glacier helicopters.co.nz.

★★★ **The Helicopter Line.** This leading company offers scenic flights from 20 minutes (NZ$225) to 40 minutes (NZ$425) long. Snow landings are included and they also offer charter flights and heli-hike combos. Fox Glacier office: Main South Rd., ☎ 03/751-0767. Franz Josef office: Main South Rd., ☎ 03/752 0767. Toll-free number (NZ only): ☎ 0800/807-767. www.helicopter.co.nz.

Glacier Hiking
★★★ **Fox Glacier Guiding.** As in Franz Josef, options here range from a terminal face walk to half- and full-day glacier walks, ice-climbing adventures, and heli-hiking opportunities (prices from NZ$100–NZ$400). The team also offers an overnight stay and climb on Chancellor Dome followed by glacier walking the next day. Main Rd., Fox Glacier. ☎ 03/751-0825. www.foxguides.co.nz.

> *Splash out on a scenic flight and swoop over glaciers before landing on Aoraki/Mount Cook.*

★★★ **Franz Josef Glacier Guides.** This team of experienced guides has a number of different hiking options graded according to your fitness levels. There's a Glacier Valley walk that takes you to the terminal face but not on the glacier, all the way through half- and full-day hikes (NZ$125–NZ$165) to adventurous ice climbing and heli-hiking in pristine areas (from NZ$395). Main Rd., Franz Josef. ☎ 03/752-0763. www.franzjosefglacier.com.

★★★ **Franz Josef Glacier Heli-Hike.** The Helicopter Line offers heli-hiking trips with guided walks among ice caves and pinnacles, in conjunction with Franz Josef Glacier Guides. The trip includes a 10-minute helicopter flight to the Franz Josef icefall, a glacier landing and pickup, and 2 hours walking with professional guides for around NZ$400. All necessary equipment is provided. Main Rd., Franz Josef. ☎ 03/752-0767. www.helicopter.co.nz.

Golf

The ultimate in Queenstown golf is ★★★ **Millbrook Resort Arrowtown,** Malaghans Rd. (☎ 0800/800-604 or 03/441-7010; www.millbrook.co.nz), where you'll pay NZ$65 to NZ$155 for the par-72, Bob Charles-designed course. Carts, equipment, instruction, and a free shuttle from Queenstown are available. The 18-hole **Queenstown Golf Club,** Kelvin Heights (☎ 03/442-9169; www.queenstown golf.co.nz), is a full-service course where green fees are NZ$95. Club rental available.

HIKING GUIDE PAGE 395

Hiking

Hiking is one of the best ways to explore the pristine wilderness regions of the deep south as the area is blessed with some of the finest multi-day hikes in the world. Hiking in New Zealand is best tackled between November to April when the temperatures in these cooler regions are more moderate; most tracks are closed (and impassable) in winter. Even so, you must always come well equipped with broken-in boots and woolen hiking gear, as New Zealand alpine conditions can be treacherous and changeable. For information, reservations, and to arrange transport, contact the **Department of Conservation,** Great Walks Booking Desk, Fiordland National Park Visitor Centre, P.O. Box 29, Te Anau (☎ 03/249-8514; www.doc.govt.nz).

> *You'll feel like you've left the real world behind when you set out into the southern wilderness on horseback.*

If you don't have time to tackle the big walks, or don't want to go it alone, many operators offer everything from one-day excursions to guided multi-day treks that include overnights in lodges, baggage handling, and all your meals. Reputable companies include: Ultimate Hikes (☎ 0800/659-255 or 03/450-1940; www.ultimatehikes.com); Guided Walks of New Zealand (☎ 03/442-7126; www.nzwalks.com); Hollyford Guided Walk (☎ 0800/832-226 or 03/442-7789; www.hollyfordtrack.com); Milford Track Guided Walk (☎ 0800/659-255 or 03/450-1940; www.milfordtrack.co.nz); Trips 'n' Tramps (☎ 03/249-7081; www.milfordtourswalks.co.nz); and Real Journeys (☎ 0800/656-503 or 03/442-7500; www.realjourneys.co.nz).

Horseback Riding
The southern landscapes make for superb horseback riding. Most operators charge between NZ$85 to roughly NZ$150. **High Ride Adventures,** 865 Wilderness Rd., Te Anau (☎ 03/249-8591; www.highride.co.nz), will take riders of all abilities on remote adventures into spectacular backcountry. Queenstown's **Moonlight Stables** (☎ 03/442-1229; www.moonlightcountry.co.nz) is located

on the 325-hectare (800-acre) Doonholme Farm, 15 minutes from town. They have well-mannered horses and experienced guides to take you on half- or full-day treks.

In the deep south, **South Westland Horse Treks,** Waiho Flat Rd., Franz Josef (☎ 03/752-0223; www.horsetreknz.com), offers 1-,2-, 3-hour and full-day treks through wild mountain and bush country. **Buller Adventure Tours,** Lower Buller Gorge, St. Hwy. 6, Westport (☎ 03/789-7286; www.adventuretours.co.nz), has 2-hour treks along the sandy banks of the Buller River. **Punakaiki Horse Treks,** St. Hwy. 6, Punakaiki (☎ 03/731-1839; www.pancake-rocks.co.nz), offers 2½-hour treks through bush and beach environments.

Hot-Air Ballooning
★★★ **Sunrise Balloons** (☎ 0800/468-247 or 03/442-0781; www.ballooningnz.com) will get you up before dawn so you can see the sun rising over lakes, vineyards, gullies, and gorges. It's NZ$395 for adults and NZ$250 for kids 11 and under, including a champagne breakfast on landing.

Jet-Boating
See also **Shotover Jet,** p. 373, **8**.

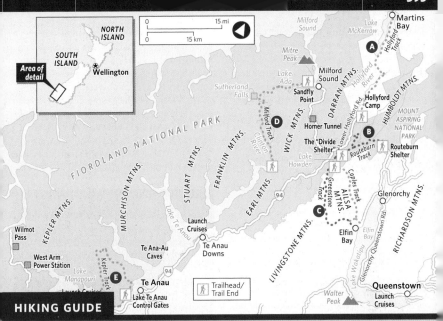

HIKING GUIDE

The Great Walks

The relatively flat, 4-day, 56km (35-mile), one-way **(A) Hollyford Track** follows the Hollyford River out to the coast at Martins Bay. You can walk it as a round-trip or as a one-way with a fly-out option from Martins Bay. This is one of the few Fiordland tracks that can be done year-round. Hut fees are NZ$35 per night.

The **(B) Routeburn Track** is a moderate 2- to 3-day, 39km (24-mile) track that takes you into the heart of unspoiled forests, along river valleys, and across mountain passes, requiring a good level of fitness. Bus transfers are available to the start and from the finish. Hut fees are NZ$50, camping fee NZ$15 per night. Reservations are required.

The 2-day, 40km (25-mile) **(C) Greenstone Valley Track** follows an ancient Maori trail. You'll pass Lake Howden and Lake McKellar and follow the Greenstone River through deep gorges and open valleys to Lake Wakatipu. Boat transfers are available to and from Elfin Bay, where the track begins and ends. You can also start and end the walk at Lake Howden near the Divide Shelter. Hut fees are NZ$40.

Many consider the famous **(D) Milford Track** the finest anywhere in the world. Known for its glacier-carved valleys, alpine flowers,

and waterfalls, the 4-day, 54km (34-mile) walk is closely regulated by DOC staff. You'll walk from Glade Jetty at Lake Te Anau's northern end to Sandfly Point on the western bank of Milford Sound, where you'll take a ferry across the sound. The track is open from late October to mid-April. Reservations are required and accepted a year in advance. The cost is around NZ$300 per person, which includes huts and transportation.

(E) Kepler Track, a 4-day, 67km (42-mile) hike, starts and ends at the Lake Te Anau outlet control gates. You'll pass through beech forests and a U-shaped glacial valley, and walk along the edges of Lakes Te Anau and Manapouri. This is a challenging hike with a lot of altitude variations. Access to the track is via shuttle bus or boat to the control gates. Hut fees are NZ$50 per night and camping is NZ$15 per night; transport costs extra and early bookings are essential.

★★★ **Buller Adventure Tours.** You'll get to see plenty of beautiful scenery on this 1¼-hour high-speed tour as it races you down the lower reaches of Buller River Gorge. It's a great outing for all the family and is very reasonably priced at around NZ$80 for adults, $70 kids 13–16 years, and NZ$55 for kids under 13. Lower Buller Gorge, St. Hwy. 6, Westport. ☎ 03/789-7286. www.adventuretours.co.nz.

★★★ **kids Dart River Safaris.** I cannot imagine anyone not being totally blown away by the full-day Jetboat Safari experience, which combines walks in ancient forests and visits to *Lord of the Rings* sites with one of the most exhilarating jet-boating experiences in New Zealand. It's the longest ride (3 hr.) in the Queenstown region (NZ$245 adult, NZ$145 kids 5–15). The fabulous Funyak Safari includes a jet-boat ride upriver, followed by a spectacular downstream journey in inflatable canoes and even a 4WD stretch (NZ$300 adult; NZ$200 kids). Advance bookings essential. Queenstown Information Centre, Corner of Camp and Shotover sts. ☎ 0800/327-853 or 03/442-9992. www. dartriverjetsafaris.com.

★★★ **Waiatoto River Safari.** This tour operates on the Waiatoto River in the deep south, near Jackson's Bay. It's a spectacular ride that takes you from the coast into the mountains, through rugged, isolated bush-clad landscapes for NZ$199 adults, NZ$129 kids 5–13. Hannah's Clearing, Jackson Bay Rd., Haast. ☎ 03/208-0958. www.riversafaris.co.nz.

★★★ **Wilkin River Jets.** For a reasonable NZ$98, ($59 kids 3–13), you get a 1-hour ride along the Wilkin and Makaroa rivers. They also offer combos that include helicopter flights and bush walks. St. Hwy. 6, Makarora. ☎ 03/443-8351. www.wilkinriverjets.co.nz.

Kayaking

Kayaking is one of the best sports in my view. It's easy and you get to see a landscape from a completely different perspective. My dream kayaking activity in the Queenstown area takes you out on the eerily quiet waters of Milford Sound with **Rosco's Milford Kayaks,** St. Hwy. 94, Deepwater Basin, Milford Sound (☎ 0800/476-726; www.roscosmilfordkayaks. com). They offer shorter trips for those without experience, but if you are experienced and fit you'll love the sunrise paddle (spring and summer only) of the full length of Milford Sound. It requires 4 hours of paddling but you'll be rewarded with amazing scenery. It costs from NZ$175 per person.

The West Coast has numerous waterways especially suited to kayaking and canoeing as well. ★★ **Punakaiki Canoes,** St. Hwy. 6, Punakaiki (☎ 03/731-1870; www.riverkayaking. co.nz), will take you upstream on the beautiful, moody Pororari River just north of Punakaiki.

Keeping Safe

Every year, tourists get into strife in the New Zealand wilderness and many thousands of dollars have to be spent rescuing them. Keep in mind that if it can be shown you've ignored advice, you may be paying that rescue bill yourself. It is vital that you check in with the Department of Conservation (www. doc.govt.nz) to register your intentions and pay your fees. The department maintains more than 12,500km (7,700 miles) of walking tracks and 1,000 backcountry huts throughout New Zealand's 13 national parks and numerous scenic reserves. Don't ignore the advice it gives on its website or at the regional offices:

- Don't hike alone.

- Carry a cell phone and call 111 in emergencies.

- Always tell people where you are going and when you'll be back.

- Hypothermia is a common killer, even in summer, so know the symptoms and wear sensible clothing.

- Always be on the watch for avalanches and never underestimate the power of the sun.

- Avoid river crossings wherever possible, especially after rain.

- Take a small first aid kit with you.

- Get further information from the New Zealand Mountain Safety Council, Wellington (☎ 04/385-7162; www.mountainsafety. org.nz). Its brochures are also available at visitor information and DOC centers.

★★★ **Okarito Nature Tours,** 1 The Strand, Okarito (☎ 03/753-4014; www.okarito.co.nz), takes you through the lovely Okarito Lagoon, which is rich in birdlife (it's close to the white heron colony) and has fabulous mountain views. Both have guided trips starting around NZ$80 and also offer rentals.

Paragliding

Queenstown Paragliding School, (☎ 0800/727-245; www.extremeair.co.nz), will give you a day's course in the basics for around NZ$200. There are approximately 15 tandem paragliding operators in Queenstown (Queenstown Paragliding School also offers tandem flights), most working above the gondola on Bob's Peak. Prices range from NZ$185 to NZ$250.

River Boarding

If you thought surfing was restricted to the ocean, forget it. Now you can cling to a specially designed boogie board, don a helmet, and go for it down churning river rapids. Champions of this silliness are **Serious Fun River Surfing,** (☎ 0800/737-468 or 03/442-5262; www.riversurfing.co.nz), and they'll take you down a 7km (4⅓-mile) stretch of the Kawarau River for NZ$169, progressing from flat water to Grade IV rapids. You may not need experience but you do need water confidence. Trips are conducted October to May; pick-up in Queenstown included.

Skiing

From late June to September, the international ski crowd flocks to Queenstown and Wanaka to enjoy the accessible slopes of **Coronet Peak** (www.nzski.com); the least-crowded slopes of **The Remarkables** (www.nzski.com); the best family fields at **Cardrona** (www.cardrona.com); and the most challenging slopes at **Treble Cone** (www.treblecone.co.nz). For the ultimate rush, try a day of heli-skiing or heli-boarding with **Harris Mountains Heliski** (☎ 03/443-7930; www.heliski.co.nz); **Heli-Guides** (☎ 03/442-7733; www.flynz.co.nz); or **Glacier Southern Lakes Heliski** (☎ 03/442-3016; www.heli-flights.co.nz).

White-Water Rafting

The Shotover and Kawarau rivers are tops for white-water rafting. The Kawarau trips are generally better for those who are rafting for

> *If you can muster up the courage to throw yourself off Bob's Peak you'll enjoy a quiet, peaceful ride over the Queenstown landscape.*

the first time, as the Shotover trips are much more challenging and are usually accompanied by safety kayaks. **Challenge Rafting,** (☎ 0800/442-7318; www.raft.co.nz), has half- and full-day trips from NZ$175 and if you mention Frommer's you'll get 10% discount when booking direct. **Queenstown Rafting,** (☎ 0800/723-846; www.rafting.co.nz), operates similar trips for about the same price. **Extreme Green Rafting,** (☎ 03/442-8517; www.nzraft.com), is a smaller operator that offers some calmer rides in addition to the usual high-energy options. It's also priced around NZ$175.

Some of the most popular rafting excursions on the West Coast are the Hot Rock options offered by **Wild West Adventure Company,** (☎ 0800/122-283; www.fun-nz.com), which combine white-water rafting with guided walks and a soak in natural hot pools. Prices start around NZ$210 per person. **Eco Rafting Adventures,** (☎ 0508/669-675; www.ecorafting.co.nz) specializes in heli-rafting, taking you to wilderness canyons and wild, surging rivers (grades III-V), but they also have flat water scenic floats. Prices start around NZ$375 for a 7-hour excursion. Multi-day adventures are also available.

Where to Stay

> *Eichardt's Private Hotel gives you classic glamour in the hotel, or these modern luxury apartments overlooking the lake.*

Queenstown Area

★★ Arrowtown House Boutique Hotel ARROWTOWN Steve and Jeanette Brough are well-traveled hosts who know just how to achieve that delicate balance of providing guests with both privacy and everything they need. They're both superb cooks and breakfast is a highlight. 10 Caernarvon St., Arrowtown. ☎ 03/441-6008. www.arrowtownhouse.com. 5 units. Doubles NZ$495 w/breakfast. MC, V. Map p. 371.

Chalet Queenstown QUEENSTOWN HILL When you sink into the luxurious big beds here you won't want to get out—but when you do, you'll have a view to die for. All rooms have balconies, there is a comfortable lounge and courtyard garden to enjoy, and prices make it extremely good value. 1 Dublin St. ☎ 03/442-7117. www.chaletqueenstown.co.nz. 7 units. Doubles NZ$270–NZ$295 w/breakfast. MC, V. Map p. 371.

★ The Dairy Private Hotel CENTRAL CITY Bedrooms here all well-appointed (Premier rooms have the best views), and the shared living room with its roaring fire, is a great place to chat with other guests. It's a short walk downhill to town. 10 Isle St. ☎ 03/442-5164. www.thedairy.co.nz. 13 units. Doubles NZ$450–NZ$495 w/breakfast. AE, MC, V. Map p. 371.

★★★ Eichardt's Private Hotel CENTRAL CITY Small, intimate, and first-class in every way. Service is personalized and superb; the interiors are mouthwatering; and the central location is perfect. Marine Parade. ☎ 03/441-0450. www.eichardts.com. 9 units. Doubles NZ$1,195–NZ$1,895 w/breakfast and cocktails. AE, DC, MC, V. Map p. 371.

★ kids Garden Court Suites & Apartments CENTRAL CITY My pick here is the smart, great-value apartments. They feature a private courtyard at ground-level or a balcony upstairs, and provide everything you'll need for a very comfortable, fully self-contained stay. 41 Frankton Rd. ☎ 0800/427-336 or 03/442-9713. www.gardencourt.co.nz. 54 units. Doubles NZ$235–NZ$395. AE, DC, MC, V. Map p. 371.

★★ kids The Heritage Queenstown FERNHILL/
QUEENSTOWN This is a big hotel with an intimate feel. It's one of my favorites because
everyone is always friendly and it's blissfully
quiet, just west of the main town area. The
large, stylish villas across the road from the
main hotel are ideal for families. 91 Fernhill Rd.
☎ 0800/368-888 or 03/442-4988. www.
heritagehotels.co.nz. 211 units. Doubles
NZ$235–NZ$675. AE, DC, MC, V. Map p. 371.

★★★ kids Millbrook Resort ARROWTOWN
Opened in 1992, this award-winning resort is
a fabulous place for families to stay. Rooms
are all beautiful, beds are huge, and in addition to the golf course, day spa, pool, and gym,
there's acres of land for kids to romp around.
Malaghans Rd., Arrowtown. ☎ 0800/800-604
or 03/441-7000. www.millbrook.co.nz. 170
units. Doubles NZ$235–NZ$685 rooms and
suites, NZ$465–NZ$965 cottage, NZ$925–
NZ$1,655 fairway home. AE, DC, MC, V. Map
p. 371.

★ kids Pinewood Lodge CENTRAL CITY
The perfect choice if you want quality budget
digs and a sociable atmosphere. Little houses
dot a tree-covered hillside and a new complex
includes a dorm, kitchen, and lounges. 48
Hamilton Rd. ☎ 0800/746-3966 or 03/442-
8273. www.pinewood.co.nz. 26 units. Doubles
NZ$65–NZ$125. AE, DC, MC, V. Map p. 371.

★ Queenstown House QUEENSTOWN HILL
This delightful B&B offers rooms in the main
house as well as large apartments with their
own decks, kitchens, and living rooms. Owner
Louise Kiely encourages guests to meet for
pre-dinner drinks and her breakfasts are always a lively affair. 69 Hallenstein St. ☎ 03/
442-9043. www.queenstownhouse.co.nz. 11
units. Doubles NZ$250–NZ$495 in main house;
NZ$595 apartment w/breakfast. AE, DC, MC, V.
Map p. 371.

★★ kids The Rees Hotel & Luxury Apartments
FRANKTON ROAD/QUEENSTOWN
The 1- to 4-bedroom apartments here offer
some of the best views of any hotel in town.
The hotel sits on Lake Wakatipu, a short drive
east of the city center (they offer a free shuttle
to town). You'll love extra touches like the
library filled with rare books, a cellar filled with
Bordeaux wines, a gallery of original paintings,

> Rooms at Sofitel are big, glamorous, and sensual.

and a stunning in-house restaurant. 377 Frankton Rd. ☎ 03/450-1100. www.therees.co.nz. 150
units. Doubles NZ$215–NZ$575. AE, DC, MC, V.
Map p. 371.

★ kids Scenic Suites Queenstown CENTRAL CITY
These bright, contemporary, roomy apartments with modern kitchens are close to
town. They have excellent views and great-
value pricing. 27 Stanley St. ☎ 0800/696-963
or 03/442-4718. www.scenicgroup.co.nz. 84
units. Doubles NZ$322–NZ$599. AE, DC, MC, V.
Map p. 371.

★★★ kids Sofitel CENTRAL CITY
At New Zealand's only Sofitel, rooms are classical yet sensual. The bathrooms are orchid-
filled and come with LCD screens over the
bathtub. They also have the best day spa facilities of any hotel in Queenstown. 8 Duke St.
☎ 0800/444-422 or 03/450-0045. www.sofi-
tel.co.nz. 82 units. Doubles NZ$350–NZ$675.
AE, DC, MC, V. Map p. 371.

> *Enjoy views of the Hokitika river from your room at Rimu Lodge.*

Glacier & Haast Region
Heartland World Heritage Hotel HAAST
This modest, recently refurbished hotel is probably your best bet for a stay in Haast. It's halfway between the glaciers and Wanaka and there's a restaurant and bar on-site, which is always a good place to meet a few locals and get a feel for the tough southern life. **Corner of St. Hwy. 6 and Jackson Bay Rd.** ☎ 0800/696-963 or 03/750-0828. www.scenichotelgroup.co.nz. 52 units. Doubles NZ$230. AE, DC, MC, V. Map p. 377.

★★ Holly Homestead FRANZ JOSEF
This friendly B&B just a few minutes north of the main Franz village offers ensuite bathrooms and big upstairs decks with mountain views. St. Hwy. 6. ☎ 03/752-0299. www.hollyhomestead.co.nz. 5 units. Doubles NZ$265–NZ$430. MC, V. Map p. 377.

★★ Punga Grove Motor Lodge FRANZ JOSEF
You feel like part of the bush here, especially in the rainforest studios, which have big Jacuzzis, leather furnishings, and views straight into the undergrowth. The whole complex is just across the road from the Glacier Hot Pools. 40 Cron St. ☎ 0800/437-269 or 03/752-0001. www.pungagrove.co.nz. 20 units. Doubles NZ$190–NZ$300. AE, DC, MC, V. Map p. 377.

★★★ Te Waonui Forest Retreat FRANZ JOSEF
Filled with immaculately finished native timber surfaces, this retreat blends seamlessly with its surrounding rainforest environment. Rooms are large, well-appointed, and comfortable. The property is right next door to the Glacier Hot Pools and there's an excellent in-house restaurant. St. Hwy. 6. ☎ 03/752-0555. www.tewaonui.co.nz. 100 units. Doubles NZ$777. AE, DC, MC, V. Map p. 377.

★ **Te Weheka Inn** FOX GLACIER
This modern complex has spacious rooms with balcony views toward the village. There's a big upstairs guest lounge and library, plus a sunny dining room for breakfast. St. Hwy. 6. ☎ 0800/313-414. www.teweheka.co.nz. 21 units. Doubles NZ$360–NZ$425 w/breakfast. MC, V. Map p. 377.

★★ **Wilderness Lodge Lake Moeraki** SOUTH WESTLAND At this peaceful eco-lodge, daily guided nature trips and numerous outdoor activities are all part of the program. Forest View rooms have pleasant natural timber finishes and views into native bush, and the newer River View rooms (adults only) are larger and more luxurious, with their own decks overlooking the river rapids below. St. Hwy. 6, 30km (19 miles) north of Haast. ☎ 03/750-0881. www.wildernesslodge.co.nz. Doubles NZ$780–NZ$1,050 w/breakfast, dinner, guided nature trips, and use of all lodge facilities. AE, DC, MC, V. Map p. 377.

Greymouth

★ kids **Kingsgate Hotel** GREYMOUTH
This modest hotel has a central location and well-priced rooms, plus an old-world charm that is somehow quintessentially West Coast in spirit. The six-floor hotel tower has the best rooms and there are roomy family suites too. 32 Mawhera Quay. ☎ 0800/805-085 or 03/768-5085. www.millenniumhotels.co.nz. 102 units. Doubles NZ$110–NZ$225. AE, DC, MC, V. Map p. 377.

Hokitika

★★ kids **Beachfront Hotel** CENTRAL HOKITIKA
The Ocean View rooms at this hotel in the heart of the town are very good value. They're spacious and modern with balconies or patios (ground floor) overlooking the ocean. 111 Revel St. ☎ 0800/400-344 or 03/755-8344. www.beachfronthotel.co.nz. 53 units. Doubles NZ$135–NZ$325. AE, DC, MC, V. Map p. 377.

★★★ **Rimu Lodge** CENTRAL HOKITIKA
This superb lodge overlooks the Hokitika River just south of the township in a peaceful rural setting. The modern suites are enormous and smartly furnished. 33 Seddons Terrace Rd. ☎ 03/755-5255. www.rimulodge.co.nz. 4 units. Doubles NZ$300–NZ$375 w/breakfast, pre-dinner drinks & canapés. AE, MC, V. Map p. 377.

★★★ **Teichelmann's Bed & Breakfast** CENTRAL HOKITIKA This light, bright haven is filled with a welcoming, homely atmosphere. If you can, try and nab the cute garden suite with its big Jacuzzi and garden outlook. 20 Hamilton St. ☎ 0800/743-742 or 03/755-8232. www.teichelmanns.co.nz. 6 units. Doubles NZ$215–NZ$275 w/breakfast. MC, V. Map p. 377.

Wanaka

★★ kids **Edgewater Resort** CENTRAL WANAKA
This big lakeside property is an ideal spot for families. They have a wide range of rooms and excellent restaurant and bar facilities. The 1-bedroom suites have bigger bathrooms with double tubs. The 2-bedroom suites are good value for couples traveling together. Sargood Dr. ☎ 0800/108-311 or 03/443-8311. www.edgewater.co.nz. 65 units. Doubles NZ$350–NZ$575. AE, DC, MC, V. Map p. 383.

★★ kids **Grand Mercure Oakridge Resort** CARDRONA VALLEY ROAD/SOUTH OF TOWN Another excellent family spot, this one comes with an outstanding hot pool complex and day spa, and new apartments. They offer great-value packages but the resort as a whole doesn't have the same "heart" as Edgewater. Corner of Cardrona Valley and Studholme rds. ☎ 0800/869-262 or 03/443-7707. www.oakridge.co.nz. 173 units. Doubles NZ$130–NZ$495. AE, DC, MC, V. Map p. 383.

★★ **Lime Tree Lodge** BALLANTYNE ROAD/SOUTH OF TOWN Sink back into luxurious rooms in a quiet rural setting at this modern home set in 4 hectares (10 acres) of beautiful gardens. Much of their organic produce comes from home turf. 672 Ballantyne Rd. ☎ 03/443-7305. www.limetreelodge.co.nz. 6 units. Doubles NZ$495–NZ$695 w/breakfast. Map p. 383.

★★ **Maple Lodge** EAST OF TOWN
This lodge is set in 2.8 hectares (7 acres) of maple plantation, just five minutes from Wanaka. All guest rooms have been designed with privacy and comfort in mind. Every room has its own patio or balcony. Halliday Rd. (off St. Hwy. 6). ☎ 03/443-6275. www.maplelodgewanaka.co.nz. 7 units. Doubles NZ$325-NZ$365 w/breakfast and pre-dinner drinks. MC, V. Map p. 383.

Where to Dine

> Meat-lovers will have plenty of choices at Botswana Butchery.

Queenstown Area

★★★ Amisfield Winery & Bistro LAKE HAYES *MODERN NZ*
A daily menu at this classy bistro focuses on local organic produce, which is often infused with European favors. (You might find seared salmon with cumin couscous, for instance). A fabulous wine room tops it off. 10 Lake Hayes Rd. ☎ 03/442-0556. www.amisfield.co.nz. Main courses NZ$18–NZ$30. AE, DC, MC, V. Lunch and dinner Tues–Sun, brunch Sat–Sun. Map p. 371.

★★ kids Boardwalk CENTRAL CITY *SEAFOOD*
A big seafood platter is the way to start proceedings here, although tempura calamari and prawns are equally delicious. Seafood alternatives include oven-roasted lamb rack with *kumara* (indigenous sweet potato) and rosemary gratin. Sit by the window for great lake views. Upstairs, Steamer Wharf, Beach St. ☎ 03/442-5630. www.boardwalk.net.nz. Main courses NZ$34–NZ$44. AE, DC, MC, V. Dinner daily. Map p. 371.

★★★ Botswana Butchery CENTRAL CITY *INTERNATIONAL* This restaurant is a meat eater's heaven that specializes in fine beef cuts, wild game, and organic foods. Marine Parade. ☎ 03/442-6994. www.botswanabutchery.co.nz. Main courses NZ$30–NZ$80. AE, DC, MC, V. Lunch and dinner daily. Map p. 371.

★★★ The Bunker CENTRAL CITY *INTERNATIONAL* This sexy little restaurant has an air of exclusivity and luxury about it. Meals are world-class, with choices like trio of hare or oven-roasted venison with roasted pear puree, cranberry compote, and juniper jus. Cow Lane. ☎ 03/441-8030. www.thebunker.co.nz. Main courses NZ$44–NZ$50. AE, DC, MC, V. Dinner daily. Map p. 371.

★★ kids Fishbone Bar & Grill CENTRAL CITY *SEAFOOD* Fresh fish is sourced daily here and the blue cod dishes are reliably good. Factor in a lively atmosphere, a good kids' menu, and sensible prices and you have a winner. 7 Beach St. ☎ 03/442-6768. Main courses NZ$20–NZ$30. AE, MC, V. Dinner daily. Map p. 371.

★★ kids Joe's Garage CENTRAL CITY *CAFE*
American roadside cafe meets Queenstown hip in this buzzy, unadorned spot. Sit up at the counter while you wait for a bacon-and-egg breakfast, or a lunchtime panini or burger. Searle Lane. ☎ 03/442-5282. www.joes.co.nz. Most menu items under NZ$20. Breakfast, brunch, and lunch daily. Map p. 371.

★★ Postmaster's House ARROWTOWN
MODERN NZ Come here to enjoy a relaxed atmosphere in a pretty, restored historic building. The menu features such treats as crispy roast duck salad with fennel, or prime beef tenderloin with béarnaise sauce and a merlot and mushroom jus. Buckingham St., Arrowtown. ☎ 03/442-0991. Main courses NZ$28–NZ$38. AE, DC, MC, V. Lunch and dinner daily. Map p. 371.

★★★ Saffron ARROWTOWN *MODERN NZ*
Saffron serves up some of the best plates in the entire region. People come from miles around to enjoy meals like Thai duck and lemongrass curry. Book ahead. 18 Buckingham St., Arrowtown. ☎ 03/442-0131. www.saffronrestaurant.co.nz. Main courses NZ$32–NZ$42. AE, DC, MC, V. Lunch and dinner daily. Map p. 371.

★ kids Skyline Restaurant BOB'S PEAK *MODERN NZ* This place has one of the finest restaurant views in New Zealand. Enjoy the big buffet at your leisure as you look down on Queenstown hundreds of feet below. Skyline Queenstown; take gondola up from Brecon St. ☎ 03/441-0101. www.skyline.co.nz. Meal & gondola NZ$74 adults, NZ$35 kids 5–14. Lunch and dinner daily. Map p. 371.

★★ kids Tatler CENTRAL CITY *INTERNATIONAL*
I never visit Queenstown without a stop here. Try the Fiordland crayfish glazed with garlic butter. 5 The Mall. ☎ 03/442-8372. www.tatler. co.nz. Main courses NZ$28–NZ$38. AE, MC, V. Brunch, lunch, and dinner daily. Map p. 371.

★★ kids Wai Waterfront CENTRAL CITY
MODERN NZ Wai has an enviable location right on the wharf. There's a focus on fresh seafood here; the oysters, either with lime sorbet and vodka or baked in a herb Parmesan crust, are personal favorites. Steamer Wharf, Beach St. ☎ 03/442-5969. www.wai.net.nz. Main courses NZ$32–NZ$45. AE, DC, MC, V. Dinner daily. Map p. 371.

> The Bunker's outstanding cuisine and classy, exclusive atmosphere make it worth hunting out.

★★ kids Winnies Gourmet Pizza Bar CENTRAL CITY *PIZZA* A crazy-busy atmosphere and such kid-friendly options as pizzas covered in crispy bacon, tomato, and cheese; burgers with fries; and chicken wings make this a great spot for families. 7 The Mall. ☎ 03/442-8635. Pizzas from NZ$18; burgers from NZ$19. Map p. 371.

Glacier & Haast Region

★ Blue Ice Restaurant & Bar FRANZ JOSEF *CAFE* There are unexpected treats at this unassuming and friendly restaurant include duck confit, salmon, prime beef, and lamb shanks. Apple and blueberry pie isn't a bad way to end an evening. St. Hwy. 6. ☎ 03/752-0707. MC, V. Dinner daily. Main courses NZ$25–NZ$30. Map p. 377.

★★ Café Neve FOX GLACIER *PIZZA/CAFE*
Pizzas are always a good bet for lunch and dinner here but they serve a wide range of things, including the delicious West Coast whitebait omelet with herbs, plus beef, lamb, seafood, and venison. Main Rd. ☎ 03/751-0110. Main courses NZ$20–NZ$30. AE, MC, V. Breakfast, lunch, and dinner daily. Map p. 377.

★ Speights Landing Bar & Restaurant FRANZ JOSEF *PUB FARE* Enjoy the lively atmosphere and outdoor courtyard while noshing on old favorites like lamb shanks, sirloin steaks, whitebait, and pizza. There's a kid's menu and Speights beer is on tap, of course. St. Hwy. 6. ☎ 07/752-0229. Main courses NZ$25–NZ$32. AE, DC, MC, V. Breakfast, lunch, and dinner daily. Map p. 377.

> *Friendly, relaxed Relishes has long been a local favorite.*

Greymouth

★★ kids dp One GREYMOUTH *CAFE*
This funky, unpretentious little cafe serves great coffee and casual fare like fat, filled bagels and burgers. 108 Mawhero Quay. ☎ 03/68-4005. Most items NZ$8–NZ$14. MC, V. Breakfast and lunch daily, dinner Thurs–Mon. Map p. 377.

Hokitika

★★ kids Café de Paris HOKITIKA *FRENCH/NZ*
This French-owned cafe has been going strong for decades. Service, as in most eateries on the West Coast, is a rather free-form concept, to put it kindly, but I've always found the food tasty. 19 Tancred St. ☎ 03/755-8933. Main courses NZ$26–NZ$36. AE, DC, MC, V. Breakfast, lunch, and dinner daily. Map p. 377.

★ kids Oceanview Restaurant HOKITIKA *SEA-FOOD* This restaurant (which does have an ocean view, as its name implies) serves very tasty seafood meals. One of the better restaurants in town. Beachfront Hotel ☎ 03/755-8344. www.beachfronthotel.co.nz. Main courses NZ$26–NZ$36. AE, DC, MC, V. Dinner daily. Map p. 377.

Wanaka

★★★ Botswana Butchery WANAKA *INTERNA-TIONAL* The menu here focuses on specialty cut meats and game dishes—all cooked to perfection. Expect a big bill at the end as it's the priciest restaurant in town. Upstairs, Post Office Lane, off Ardmore St. ☎ 03/443-6745. Main courses NZ$30–NZ$80. AE, DC, MC, V. Lunch and dinner daily. Map p. 383.

★ kids Café Gusto WANAKA *CAFE*
Gusto's excellent menu includes tasty risottos, curries, soups, and salads, and the cabinets are usually bulging with sandwiches and sweet treats. It's a light, airy spot with a small patio that overlooks the lake. 1 Lakeside Dr. ☎ 04/443-6639. Main courses NZ$18–NZ$25. AE, MC, V. Breakfast, lunch and dinner. Map p. 383.

★ kids The Cow WANAKA *PIZZA*
You'll welcome the cozy, all-wood interior of The Cow after a big day outdoors. Combine that with terrific big pizzas or one of the specialty spaghetti dishes and you (and especially the kids) will be happy. Post Office Lane, off Ardmore St. ☎ 03/443-4269. NZ$20–NZ$30. AE, DC, MC, V. Lunch and dinner daily. Map p. 383.

★★ Relishes WANAKA *MODERN NZ*
This warm, simple, country-style restaurant has endured for years and it's always a good place for a reliable meal. Any smoked salmon or blue cod meals are worth trying. 1/99 Ardmore St. ☎ 03/443-9018. Main courses NZ$30–NZ$36. AE, MC, V. Breakfast, lunch, and dinner daily. Map p. 383.

Fiordland & The West Coast Fast Facts

Arriving

BY PLANE **Air New Zealand** (☎ 0800/737-000; www.airnewzealand.co.nz), provides daily service to Wanaka and Queenstown; between Christchurch, Hokitika, and Greymouth; and between Westport and Wellington. **Qantas** (☎ 0800/808-767; www.qantas.com). **Jetstar** (0800/800-995; www.jetstar.com) flies to Queenstown from Melbourne and Gold Coast. Air services to Te Anau and Fiordland are provided by **Air Fiordland** (☎ 0800/107-505; www.airfiordland.com). BY BUS **Intercity** (☎ 09/623-1503; www.intercity.co.nz), runs between Queenstown, Wanaka, and Te Anau, and Christchurch, Dunedin, and Invercargill. Buses also run between Greymouth, Westport, the glaciers, Queenstown, and Nelson. BY TRAIN The **Tranz Scenic TranzAlpine** route (☎ 0800/872-467; www.tranzscenic.co.nz) runs daily between Christchurch and Greymouth. The Greymouth Railway Station is on Mackay Street.

Emergencies & Medical Care

Call ☎ 111 for all fire, police and ambulance emergencies. Hospitals serving the region include **Lakes District Hospital,** Douglas St., Frankton, Queenstown (☎ 03/442-3053 or 03/441-0015); **Southland Hospital,** Kew Rd., Invercargill (☎ 03/218-1949); and **Grey Base Hospital,** High St., Greymouth (☎ 03/768-0499). Other options for medical care include **Wanaka Medical Centre,** 21 Russell St., Wanaka (☎ 03/443-7811); **Queenstown Medical Centre,** 9 Isle St., Queenstown (☎ 03/441-0500); and **Fiordland Medical Centre,** 21 Luxmore Dr., Te Anau (☎ 03/249-7007; open 24 hr.). For dental care, try **Queenstown Emergency Dentist** (☎ 03/442-7274); or **Fiordland Dental Centre,** Jailhouse Mall, 52 Tower Centre, Te Anau (☎ 03/249-8580).

Internet

Get online at **Dub Dub Dub,** corner of Helwick and Brownston sts., Wanaka (☎ 03/443-7078). **Internet Outpost** has multiple branches: 26 Shotover St. in Queenstown

> The railway station in Greymouth.

(☎ 03/441-3018); corner of Cook Flat Rd. and St. Hwy. 6, Fox Glacier (☎ 03/751-0078); and Main Rd., Franz Josef (☎ 03/752-0288). There's online access at **Greymouth Railway Station**, 164 Mackay St., Greymouth, too.

Visitor Information Centers

DEPARTMENT OF CONSERVATION HOKITIKA 10 Sewell St. (☎ 03/756-9100). **DEPARTMENT OF CONSERVATION FRANZ JOSEPH** Westland National Park Visitor Centre, Main Rd. (☎ 03/752-0796; www.doc.govt.nz). **FIORDLAND I-SITE VISITOR CENTRE** Lakefront Drive, Te Anau (☎ 03/249-8900; www.realjourneys.co.nz). **FIORDLAND NATIONAL PARK VISITOR CENTRE** Lakefront Drive, Te Anau (☎ 03/249-7924; www.doc.govt.nz). **GREYMOUTH I-SITE VISITOR CENTRE** Corner of Herbert and Mackay sts., Greymouth (☎ 03/768-5101; www.greydistrict.co.nz). **LAKE WANAKA I-SITE VISITOR CENTRE** 100 Ardmore Rd., Lakefront (☎ 03/443-1233; www.lakewanaka.co.nz). **QUEENSTOWN I-SITE VISITOR CENTRE** Clocktower Centre, corner of Shotover and Camp sts. (☎ 0800/668-888 or 03/442-4100; www.queenstown-vacation.com). **WESTLAND I-SITE VISITOR CENTRE** Carnegie Bldg., corner of Tancred and Hamilton sts., Hokitika (☎ 03/755-6166; www.hokitika.org).

My Favorite Moments

Dramatic scenery, plentiful wildlife, fine historic buildings, and a testing winter climate make Dunedin unique among New Zealand cities. It has a justly deserved reputation as one of the best preserved Victorian and Edwardian cities in the Southern Hemisphere and a youthful energy thanks to the university students that make up one-fifth of the 123,000 residents. Stunning architecture and prolific wildlife are enlivened by art galleries, cafes, and some of New Zealand's best artists and fashion designers.

> PREVIOUS PAGE *A drive around the Otago Peninsula rewards you with glorious views.* THIS PAGE *The Dunedin Railway Station is as grand on the inside as it is on the outside.*

❶ Exploring Dunedin Railway Station. This giant show-off of a building is one of my favorites. It's Flemish Renaissance style at its best—all pillars, columns, arches, and a mosaic floor made of over 725,000 Royal Doulton porcelain squares. See p. 424, ❺.

❷ Fossicking in the Animal Attic at Otago Museum. The zany stuffed animals, birds, and spiders that have colonized this replicated Victorian timbered gallery make for an old-style museum experience that shouldn't be missed—especially by the kids. See p. 426, ⓫.

❸ Spending the day on Otago Peninsula. Take the low road out and the high road back for two views of this extraordinary peninsula. It's riddled with marine wildlife, boatsheds, beaches, a castle, and a marae. A photographer's paradise. See p. 412.

❹ Finding old tomes at Raven Books. Every time I visit Dunedin I head straight for this wonderful, old-fashioned, secondhand bookshop, where browsing old pages and touching well-loved covers is a singular pleasure. See p. 427.

❺ Admiring the city's magnificent church architecture. I'm a big fan of church architecture and Dunedin is blessed with several ecclesiastical beauties. First Church (p. 424, ❹) and St. Paul's Anglican Cathedral (p. 422, ❷) are

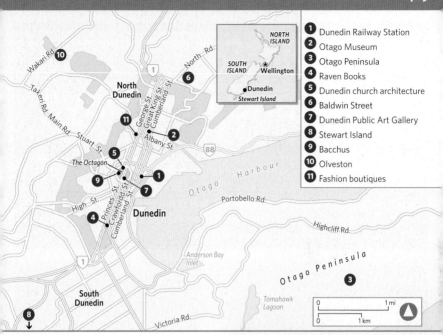

① Dunedin Railway Station
② Otago Museum
③ Otago Peninsula
④ Raven Books
⑤ Dunedin church architecture
⑥ Baldwin Street
⑦ Dunedin Public Art Gallery
⑧ Stewart Island
⑨ Bacchus
⑩ Olveston
⑪ Fashion boutiques

my two favorites near the Octagon.

⑥ **Negotiating the world's steepest street.** If you're hale and hearty, the impossible gradient of Baldwin Street should keep you out of mischief for a while. See "Counting the Steps," p. 427.

⑦ **Checking out the latest exhibitions at Dunedin Public Art Gallery.** This is a great spot to soak up the works by two of Dunedin's (and New Zealand's) greatest artists—Frances Hodgkins and Colin McCahon. There's a big collection of both, along with a surprising hoard of French Impressionists. See p. 422, ①.

⑧ **Spending a day or two on Stewart Island.** New Zealand's third largest island is about the same size as Singapore but instead of 5 million residents, it's home to just 400 people and some of our best birdlife. Come here if you like tranquility and natural beauty. See p. 432.

⑨ **Eating lunch overlooking the Octagon.** Head upstairs to Bacchus before the business lunch crowd, grab the front table overlooking to the Octagon and enjoy fresh, tasty ingredients and modern New Zealand cuisine. Pretty geraniums will wink at you from the window boxes as you enjoy the view. See p. 437.

> *Dunedin Public Art Gallery is located in what was once an old department store.*

⑩ **Drooling over beautiful things at Olveston.** Once a private home, this drop-dead gorgeous Jacobean-style mansion hints at a life of sophisticated colonial refinement. Its rooms are embellished with the finest furniture and over 250 paintings. See p. 426, ⑬.

⑪ **Browsing designer fashion boutiques.** Dunedin is home to some of New Zealand's most innovative fashion houses. Roam George Street and Lower Stuart Street, keeping an eye out for contemporary New Zealand jewelry studios too. See "Dunedin Shopping," p. 427.

Dunedin & Southland in 3 Days

While Dunedin, the largest city of Otago province, has plenty of cultural attractions and ready access to Otago Peninsula's remarkable wildlife, the triangular province of Southland encompasses rich farmland, the smaller city of Invercargill, and sleepy rural towns. Combined, they present an invigorating, friendly slice of New Zealand that is too often ignored in favor of bigger, flashier centers. Forget sophistication and let yourself be won over by dramatic landscapes and southern hospitality.

> *Most people think Stewart Island is quite small, but it's roughly the same size as Singapore.*

START Dunedin is about 360km (224 miles) southwest of Christchurch via St. Hwy. 1.
TRIP LENGTH 280km (174 miles).

1 ★★★ **Dunedin.** Start the morning of your first day with a quick overview of old and new at **the Octagon**, the city's heart. The **Dunedin Public Art Gallery** and **St. Paul's Anglican Cathedral** are all within a few steps of each other. After that first big gulp of history, walk up Stuart Street past the cathedral. Just after a row of quaint houses, turn left into Moray Place, wander down past boutique stores and cafes, cross over Princes Street, and check out the beauties of the landmark **First Church.** Continue down Moray Place, turn right into Lower Stuart Street, and head for **Dunedin Railway Station.** ⏱ Half-day. See p. 424.

Leave the city heading south on Castle Street. Follow signs to Otago Peninsula, which indicate a left turn over the railway

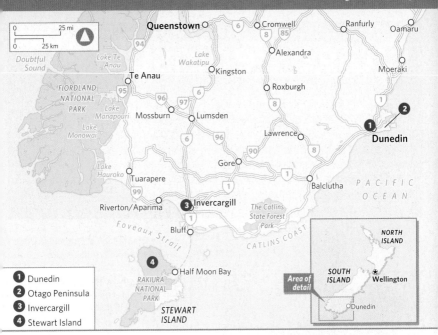

- ① Dunedin
- ② Otago Peninsula
- ③ Invercargill
- ④ Stewart Island

bridge just past the Dunedin Chinese Garden. Veer right into Wharf St., which becomes Portsmouth Dr. Follow signs and take the coastal Portobello Rd. out to the end of the peninsula. The drive is 33km (21 miles).

② ★★ **Otago Peninsula.** Nature lovers, rejoice: You are about to enter paradise. This is where man and wildlife have come to a happy eco-tourism arrangement that allows you close-up encounters at the **New Zealand Marine Studies Centre & Westpac Aquarium** at Portobello (p. 414, ④), the kids **Royal Albatross Centre** (p. 415, ⑨) and kids **Penguin Place** (p. 415, ⑧). You won't have time to do them all in an afternoon but if nature spins your wheels, you might like to switch the morning's historical perspective for more of our feathery friends. Take the high road back to the city for a different outlook, stopping at **Larnach Castle** (p. 415, ⑪) if you have time. ⏱ Half-day.

On your second day, head south from Dunedin on Castle Street. Get into the right lane and follow signs to Invercargill via St. Hwy. 1. The drive is 204km (127 miles).

③ **Invercargill.** Spend a day exploring the southernmost city in New Zealand, then overnight here. ⏱ 1 day. See p. 428.

> *The Royal Albatross Centre features the only mainland albatross colony in the world.*

On day 3, take St. Hwy. 1 south from Invercargill 27km (17 miles) to Bluff, where you'll catch the ferry to Stewart Island. Allow 25 min. driving time.

④ **Stewart Island.** Spend your last day exploring the rugged natural wonders of New Zealand's third-largest island. ⏱ 1 day. See p. 432.

Otago Peninsula

Pack a picnic, grab your camera, and head out to this extraordinary peninsula—a place that celebrated naturalist professor David Bellamy has described as "the finest example of eco-tourism in the world." Take Portobello Road out from Dunedin and wriggle your way around pretty bays, little beach communities, gardens, historic homes, and wildlife attractions. Return to Dunedin city via Highcliff Road, with its spectacular views and New Zealand's only castle. The entire journey is easily managed in a long day but don't rush; this is a place to savor.

> Larnach Castle is the story of one woman's passion for the restoration of an architectural icon.

START Glenfalloch Woodland Garden is about 9km (5⅔ miles) from Dunedin, about a 20-min. drive. Leave the city heading south on Castle Street. Follow signs to Otago Peninsula, which indicate a left turn over the railway bridge just past the Dunedin Chinese Garden. Veer right into Wharf St., which becomes Portsmouth Dr. Follow signs and take coastal Portobello Rd. **TRIP LENGTH** Approximately 80km (50 miles) round-trip.

❶ Glenfalloch Woodland Garden. Just 9km (5⅔ miles) into your peninsula journey, turn right at the sign (on a sharp bend) to find this historic homestead and 12-hectare (30-acre) Garden of National Significance. It's best between August and December when its renowned collection of azaleas and rhododendrons are in bloom, though if you're a garden lover, you'll find equal pleasure in its mature trees and unusual hybrids in any season. You'll also find a cafe, pottery, and jewelry shop. ⏱ 45 min. 430 Portobello Rd. ☎ 03/476-1775. www.glenfalloch. org.nz. Admission NZ$5 adults, free for kids under 15. Guided tours are available (NZ$10, including garden entrance) but must be pre-booked. Daily year-round during daylight hours.

Rejoin Portobello Rd. and continue on to Macandrew Bay.

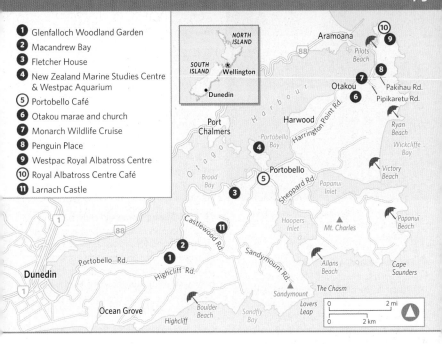

1. Glenfalloch Woodland Garden
2. Macandrew Bay
3. Fletcher House
4. New Zealand Marine Studies Centre & Westpac Aquarium
5. Portobello Café
6. Otakou marae and church
7. Monarch Wildlife Cruise
8. Penguin Place
9. Westpac Royal Albatross Centre
10. Royal Albatross Centre Café
11. Larnach Castle

2 ★ kids **Macandrew Bay.** Pull into the car park beside the boatsheds on your left to take photographs of the harbor and the seabirds perched on jetties. Around the corner there's a tiny beach and a playground. There's a very nice printmakers' gallery (Bellamys Gallery) across the road. ⏱ 20 min.

Continue on Portobello Rd. to Fletcher House.

Travel Tip

Get an early start and make sure your gas tank is full before you leave the city, as there are no gas stations on the peninsula. It's also a good idea to buy picnic food in the city because peninsula eateries are limited and expensive. The coast road is narrow with few stopping places and it gets busy in summer, so take advantage of legal parking spots when you see them. Please note that due to the fragile ecology here, camping is only permitted at Portobello Village Tourist Park, 27 Hereweka St., Portobello (☎ 03/478-0359).

> There are few places prettier than Otago Peninsula on a fine summer's day when you can see for miles.

> *Join Monarch Wildlife Cruises for an excellent day at sea, photographing seabirds, seals, and landscapes.*

❸ Fletcher House. As you wind around tiny Broad Bay, this beautifully restored 1909 Edwardian villa, furnished in period style, is on the right-hand side of a tight bend. Don't stop there. Continue 150m (492 ft.) down the hill to the designated car park and then walk back up to the house via the pathway. ⏱ 30 min. 727 Portobello Rd., Broad Bay. ☎ 03/478-0180. Admission NZ$4 adults, free for kids under 15. Open 11am–4pm daily Christmas–Easter; weekends and public holidays Easter–Christmas.

Around 20km (12 miles) from the start of Portobello Rd., you'll come to the peninsula's biggest settlement, Portobello. Turn left at the store, drive past the small beach, and follow the red fish signs on the private dirt track, Hatchery Rd., for 2.1km (1⅓ miles). You may need to give way to sheep.

❹ ★★★ kids New Zealand Marine Studies Centre & Westpac Aquarium. Part of Otago University's Marine Science Department, this superb facility has the largest touch tank in Australasia, filled with sea stars, crabs, anemones, sponges, and barnacles. When you're done fiddling, you can observe sea horses, fish species, and octopi in the tanks. Don't forget the yellow submersible for a 15-minute virtual descent to the ocean floor. Kids will love the activity room next to the marine-themed shop. Get here early to beat the crowds. ⏱ 1 hr. Hatchery Rd., Portobello. ☎ 03/479-5826. www.marine.ac.nz. Admission NZ$12 adults, NZ$10 seniors and students, NZ$6 kids 2–14, free for kids under 2, NZ$24 family. Daily 10am–4:30pm.

Drive back out to Portobello Rd.

⑤ 🍴 kids Portobello Café. This is my pick for Portobello's best quick snacks and light lunches (coffee, home baking, filled rolls, and the like) at a reasonable price. 699 Highcliff Rd., Portobello. ☎ 03/478-1055. Around NZ$10.

Continue on Portobello Rd. and then veer right on Harrington Point Rd. After about 7km (4⅓ miles) you'll get to the little Maori settlement of Otakou. Turn right at the marae sign (on your left) and drive a few hundred meters.

❻ ★ kids Otakou marae and church. You get excellent views of both the *wharenui* (meeting house) and the church from the road. (They are private property; do not enter the grounds.) Both feature beautiful traditional carving and you can get a close-up view of gate carvings. This is the region's most important marae. ⏱ 10 min.

Continue on Harrington Point Rd. for about 2km (1¼ miles).

❼ ★★★ kids Monarch Wildlife Cruise. Stop at Wellers Rock for some photographs, then join one of the best wildlife-viewing adventures on the peninsula. I recommend pre-booking and note that this is the 1-hour tour; half- and full-day tours depart from Dunedin city. ⏱ 1½ hr. Wellers Rock. ☎ 0800/666-272. www.wildlife.co.nz. Admission NZ$46 adults, NZ$20

Getting Back to Nature

For a personalized peninsula nature experience, spend two nights at ★ **Nisbet Cottage**, 6A Elliffe Place, Shiel Hill (☎ 03/454-5169; www.natureguidesotago.co.nz), and let host/nature guide Hildegard Lübcke and her team take you away from the crowds. You'll get a sunrise penguin walk and a 6-hour tour of the peninsula that focuses on tidal inlet birdlife, native vegetation, and the royal albatross. You need to be reasonably fit but even if you're exhausted after a big day, you can sink into comfort in one of two large, modern suites. Two-night tour packages start around NZ$600 and include breakfast, tour, and picnic lunch. No kids under 15.

kids 5–16. In summer, cruises depart daily at 10:30am, noon, 2pm, 3:15pm, and 4:30pm; in winter daily at 2:30pm.

Continue on Harrington Point Rd., then turn right on Pakihau Rd. and follow the signs to:

8 ★ ★ ★ kids **Penguin Place.** This is your best chance to get close-up photographs of rare yellow-eyed penguins. This highly successful conservation project has dramatically increased penguin numbers and you can watch the world's rarest penguin from an elaborate network of tunnels and hides without disturbing the birds. The tour includes lots of walking (wear sensible shoes) and wonderful coastal views. You may also see fur seals and Hooker sea lions. ⏱ 2 hr. Pakihau Rd. ☎ 03/478-028. www.penguinplace.co.nz. Admission NZ$48 adults, NZ$27 kids 5-14. Tours Nov to mid-Mar 10:15am–7:45pm; reservations required.

Rejoin Harrington Point Rd. and turn right. Travel 5 min. to:

9 ★ ★ ★ kids **Westpac Royal Albatross Centre.** Taiaroa Head has the only mainland colony of royal albatrosses in the world. Although you have a good chance of seeing lots of activity in January and February when the chicks are hatching, there are no guarantees. A 1-hour tour shows you birds only; a 90-minute tour adds in the tunnel complex of old Fort Taiaroa and the last working example of an Armstrong disappearing gun. Make sure you also look into the excellent wildlife displays in the main complex. ⏱ 1½ hr. Taiaroa Head. ☎ 03/478-0499. www.albatross.org.nz. Free admission. Albatross-only tour NZ$42 adults, NZ$21 kids 5-14; tour with Fort Taiaroa NZ$50 adults, NZ$25 kids; Fort Taiaroa-only tour NZ$22 adults, NZ$11 kids. Daily 9:45am–7pm. Tour reservations required.

---

10 🍴 **Royal Albatross Centre Café.** If you didn't bring a picnic, grab a pie or sandwich to go from the cafe and enjoy it on the grassy cliffs overlooking the ocean on the far side of the car park. Royal Albatross Centre, Taiaroa Head. ☎ 03/478-0499. NZ$10–NZ$15

Retrace your steps back to Portobello and turn left up Highcliff Rd. by Portobello Café. Travel about 15km (9⅓ miles) to the tiny settlement

> *A visit to Penguin Place will get you right up close to these cute-as-a-button birds in their natural habitat.*

of Pukehiki. Turn right on Camp Rd. and drive 2km (1¼ mile) to Larnach Castle.

11 ★ ★ kids **Larnach Castle.** Larnach Castle was built over 12 years starting in the 1870s by William Larnach, who was determined to impress his first wife, a French heiress. The Georgian hanging staircase is the only one in the Southern Hemisphere. Admire the fine interior detailing, find out about the original family's tragic history, and keep an eye out for the ghost of a Victorian man many claim to have seen. And don't overlook the 14-hectare (35-acre) Garden of International Significance. The restoration of both castle and gardens is the result of over 40 years of hard work by owner Margaret Barker and her family. There's lodging and a restaurant. ⏱ At least 1 hr. Highcliff Rd. ☎ 03/476-1616. www.larnach-castle.co.nz. Admission to castle and gardens NZ$27 adults, NZ$10 kids 5-14; gardens only NZ$12.50 adults, NZ$4 kids.

EXPERIENCING RAKIURA NATIONAL PARK

Land of the Glowing Skies **BY ADRIENNE REWI**

OPENED IN 2002, RAKIURA NATIONAL PARK is New Zealand's fourteenth national park. It covers an area of 157,000 hectares and dominates 85% of Stewart Island's land mass. It is a glorious world of untouched ecosystems, dense native forest, vast stretches of beach and sand dunes, craggy granite mountains, and freshwater wetlands—in short, the perfect habitat for an abundance of wildlife, much of it rare or endangered. It is a wilderness crisscrossed with 245km (153 miles) of walking tracks, from short, easily managed outings to multi-day tramping tracks that require a high level of fitness, endurance, self-reliance, and navigating skills. The Rakiura Track is one of the Department of Conservation's eight identified Great Walks of New Zealand, and one of the easiest introductions to the splendor of Rakiura National Park. The 36km (22 mile) track requires moderate fitness and can be comfortably hiked in 3 days, year-round. The circuit follows the open coast, climbs over a 300m (980 ft.) forested ridge, and traverses the shores of Paterson Inlet.

Words About Birds

KAKAPO
(Night Parrot, or Strigops habroptila) This fat, funny, critically endangered character, native to New Zealand, is the world's only flightless, nocturnal parrot. The last kakapo on Stewart Island were transferred to nearby Codfish Island between 1982 and

1997. You cannot visit Codfish Island without a permit.

KIWI
(Stewart Island Brown Kiwi, or Apteryx australis lawryi) A distinct subspecies of the brown

kiwi found throughout the rest of New Zealand, this bird thrives on Stewart Island. It has larger legs and a longer beak than its mainland "cousins" and females are generally bigger than males. They can be seen in the wild frequently here, often combing the beaches at night.

KAKA
(Nestormeridionalis) *Kaka* is the Maori word for parrot and this fellow, endemic to New Zealand, is related to both the Kakapo and the mainland Kea. It is relatively common on Stewart Island and can often be seen at close quarters in domestic gardens in Oban village. It's a

rowdy bird with a very sharp beak but they're great performers and make excellent photographs.

TIEKE
(Saddleback, or Philesturnus caruncalatus) The saddleback is one of New Zealand's greatest conservation success stories. Once rare and endangered, it has made a big comeback thanks to conservation programs on predator-free islands like Ulva Island. There

are now around 700 known birds. The Tieke has distinctive wattles hanging beside its beak.

TOUTOUWAI
(Stewart Island Robin or Petroica Australia rakiura) This little fellow has won the hearts of thousands of tourists by hopping close to their feet and "posing" for photographs at close

range. It is a subspecies of the South Island robin and you can encourage one to come close by scratching the forest floor with a stick or your fingers.

The Maori Stories

Maori originally named Stewart Island Te Punga a Te Waka a Maui, which translates as "The Anchor Stone of Maui's Canoe." In Maori mythology, this refers to Stewart Island's role in the legend about Maui and his crew, who from their canoe (the South Island), hooked and raised the great fish (the North Island). Maori also referred to the island as Rakiura, which translates as either (depending on who you ask), "the land of glowing skies" or "the great and deep blushing of Te Rakitamau." Te Rakitamau was an early Maori chief who suffered the indignity of having his requests for marriage declined. It is said the red sunrises and sunsets over Stewart Island reflect his embarrassment.

Dunedin & Southland Outdoor Adventures A to Z

Bicycling

The 150km (93-mile) ★★★ **Otago Central Rail Trail** (☎ 03/474-6909; www.otagocentralrail trail.co.nz) is an adventure through some of Otago's remotest settlements. As you battle against the elements (it can be windy), you can distract yourself with viaducts, old station sites, tunnels, quaint villages, orchards, vineyards, and historic buildings. There are no very steep climbs but the gravel surface does call for a degree of fitness and you'll need clothing for all seasons. The trail stretches from Middlemarch (73km/45 miles northwest of Dunedin) to Clyde (83km/52 miles southeast of Queenstown). Book accommodation well in advance (see the website for lists of hotels in communities along the trail). The website also lists places to rent bikes along the trail. A comprehensive Rail Trail brochure is also available at the Dunedin i-SITE Visitor Centre (p. 439).

Birding

Oamaru (blue penguins), Otago Peninsula (royal albatrosses, yellow-eyed penguins, and dozens of seabirds), the Catlins (more of the same), and Stewart Island (kiwi, back robins, kaka, kereru, and many others) offer some of the best bird-watching in the country. **Ulva Island,** just off Stewart Island, hosts birders from all over the world, who come to see the happy outcome of pest eradication and endangered species enhancement projects first hand. My pick for the best experience here is ★★★ kids **Ulva's Guided Walks** (☎ 03/219-1216; www.ulva.co.nz), with half-day guided walks starting around NZ$115.

The other must-do Stewart Island bird experience is kiwi spotting with Phillip Smith of ★★★ **Bravo Adventure Cruises** (☎ 03/219-1144). He'll take you on a night cruise to remote Glory Bay and lead you to a deserted beach where you'll see kiwi foraging for food in the wild.

> *Visit isolated villages and stay in cute B&Bs on the very popular Otago Central Rail Trail.*

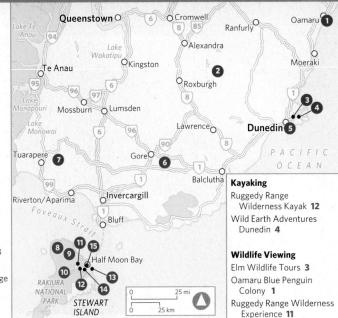

Bicycling
Central Otago Rail
Trail **2**

Bird Watching
Ulva Island **13**
Kiwi spotting **14**

Fishing
Mataura River **6**

Helicopter Tours
Rakiura Helicopter
Services **15**

Hiking
Rakiura Track **9**
Northwest Circuit **8**
Southern Circuit **10**
Tuatapere Humpridge
Track **7**
Esplanade St Clair
Beach **5**

Kayaking
Ruggedy Range
Wilderness Kayak **12**
Wild Earth Adventures
Dunedin **4**

Wildlife Viewing
Elm Wildlife Tours **3**
Oamaru Blue Penguin
Colony **1**
Ruggedy Range Wilderness
Experience **11**

Fishing

Southland's **Mataura River,** just 30 to 40 minutes from Invercargill, has some of the best trout fishing in the world. Many other Southland waterways are home to fat brown and rainbow trout and quinnat salmon. The season in most areas runs from October 1 to April 30 and most local visitor centers can point you in the direction of reliable fishing guides. **Southland Fish & Game,** P.O. Box 159, Invercargill (☎ 03/215-9117; www.fishandgame.org.nz), will also fill you in on license requirements (around NZ$22 a day) and guidelines on preventing further spread of the unwanted organism didymo that is damaging South Island waterways (see "Keeping New Zealand Waterways Clean," p. 458).

Helicopter Tours

There's only one way to get a true feel for the size, the isolation, and the rugged beauty of Stewart Island and that's by joining Zane Smith of ★★★ 🅺🅸🅳🅨 **Rakiura Helicopter Services.** He's a sixth-generation islander and he knows the island like the back of his hand. His 2-hour flight will show you a good chunk of the 700km (435 miles) of coastline and the stark granite peaks of Pegasus. You'll also land on some of New Zealand's most remote beaches.

Fern Gully Heliport. ☎ 03/219-1155. www.rakiura helicopters.co.nz. Flights NZ$165–NZ$600.

Hiking

These regions are flush with spectacular hiking opportunities almost too numerous to mention. On Stewart Island the **Rakiura Track,** the **North West Circuit,** and the **Southern Circuit** will all test even the seasoned hiker. Purchase passes and hut tickets for these very challenging multi-day adventures at **Rakiura National Park Visitor Centre,** Department of Conservation, Main Rd., Oban, Stewart Island (☎ 03/219-0009; www.doc.govt. nz), open daily in summer from 8am to 5pm, winter 8:30am to 4:30pm. They can also tell you about the many short walks on the island ranging from 15 minutes to 7 hours.

Southland's **Tuatapere Hump Ridge Track** is a 3-day guided hike aimed at the moderately fit. You'll see beautiful native bush and huge railway viaducts on this one. For information and reservations, call ☎ 0800/486-774 or visit www.humpridgetrack.co.nz.

In Dunedin, a lovely short walk with kids is a wander along **the Esplanade at St. Clair Beach,** where they can watch surfers, run about, and eat ice cream.

> *The South Island kaka is a cheeky Stewart Island parrot that has brilliant orange plumage under its wings.*

Kayaking

Ruggedy Range Wilderness Kayak. An afternoon of guided kayaking in Paterson Inlet lets you see some of the most photogenic, forest-fringed coastlines and a wealth of wildlife. 170 Horseshoe Bay Rd. ☎ 03/219-1066. www.ruggedyrange.com. Tours start at NZ$180 per person.

★★ **Wild Earth Adventures.** Wild Earth will take you along wild beaches and soaring sea cliffs to the albatross colony at Taiaroa. Have your camera ready because you're sure to see a million birds and seals. ☎ 03/489-1951. www.wildearth.co.nz. Tours start at around NZ$100.

Wildlife Viewing

No matter where you go near water in these three regions, you're bound to see something that flies, wriggles, or squawks—that's the nature of the place. There are numerous places on both Otago Peninsula (see p. 412) and in the Catlins (see p. 418) where you can stop the car and quietly view sea lions, seals, Hector's dolphins, penguins, and seabirds. Just make sure you obey the rules and don't get too close to the wildlife.

★★★ kids **Elm Wildlife Tours.** Twice voted New Zealand's best wildlife tour, the guides here make sure you get an in-depth insight into the habits of various penguin species, fur seals, and sea lions. Tucked away in viewing hides, you'll get great up-close views in a private conservation area. The 6-hour tours require moderate fitness and are limited to 10 people per guide. ☎ 0800/356-563 or 03/454-4121. www.elmwildlifetours.co.nz. From NZ$95 adults, NZ$85 kids 4–18. Not recommended for kids under 4.

★ kids **Oamaru Blue Penguin Colony.** Each night at dusk, a colony of blue penguins—the world's smallest penguins—waddles ashore at Oamaru, an hour north of Dunedin. It may be the cutest thing you'll ever see. This very professional operation is a scientifically monitored breeding colony. Filming and taking photographs are completely banned, even without flash. But you get informative commentary and you can do a 30-minute self-guided tour during the day from 10am to see penguins in their nest boxes. Waterfront Rd., Oamaru. ☎ 03/433-1195. www.penguins.co.nz. Evening

> *Experienced hikers will revel in the challenge of Stewart Island's multi-day walks.*

viewing NZ$21 adults, NZ$11 kids 5–17, NZ$56 family; daytime tour NZ$9 adults, NZ$5 kids, NZ$23 family.

★★ Ruggedy Range Wilderness Experience. As the name suggests, this is a company prepared to take fit adults to the best untouched places for pelagic or native bird-watching, photography, and botany studies. Whether you want a slow amble around the Ulva Island bird sanctuary, a vigorous overnight trek, a boat cruise, or a sea kayaking adventure, they can provide for you. They actively support conservation projects and knowledgeable guides always give you plenty to think about as you push back ferns for a bird's-eye view of a tiny rare robin hopping across the forest floor to your feet. Corner of Main Rd. and Dundee St., Stewart Island. ☎ 03/219-1066. www.ruggedyrange.com. Tours start at NZ$115.

> *Keen wildlife spotters and photographers should take to a kayak to get creative take-home images.*

Dunedin

Dunedin is big enough to be interesting and small enough to be intimate. It's a multi-layered place where student hijinks sit comfortably alongside the sophistication of theater, fashion, and art openings. It's an egalitarian city, where everyone is accepted regardless of occupation or status and the streets teem with interesting-looking people. I like that about a place, and Dunedin gets my vote for one of the best little cities in New Zealand. It is, in fact, our fourth-largest city, with a population of 123,000.

START Dunedin is about 360km (224 miles) southwest of Christchurch via St. Hwy. 1. You can reach the Octagon (an eight-sided plaza in Dunedin's city center) from most city accommodations on foot in about 10–15 min.

❶ ★★★ Dunedin Public Art Gallery. This is where you'll find the only work by Impressionist painter Claude Monet (*La Débâcle*) in a New Zealand public collection—along with a big selection of European art, Japanese prints, and other French Impressionists. Dunedin's own great artists, Frances Hodgkins and Colin McCahon, are also well represented. Don't forget to walk around the back of the gallery on Upper Moray Place to see the window display. ⏱1 hr. 30 The Octagon. ☎ 03/474-3240. www.dunedin.art.museum. Free admission; charges for special exhibitions. Daily 10am–5pm. Tours availableby arrangement.

❷ ★★ St. Paul's Anglican Cathedral. Huge Gothic-style pillars and a lofty, vaulted roof soaring 20m (66 ft.) high give the interior of this hefty cathedral a marvelous sense of grandeur. Look out for the beautiful Great War Memorial Window (above the main entrance), which sprinkles pretty shards of color when the morning sun rises. In the chapel, look at the Maori carving and *tukutuku* (woven) panel created by local Maori of Te Whanau Arohanui o Waitati. The cathedral was started in 1915 but only received its final touches in 1971. ⏱ 30 min. The Octagon. ☎ 03/477-2336. www.stpauls.net.nz. Free admission. Daily 10am–4pm. Enter through the office, around a path to the right of the main marble steps.

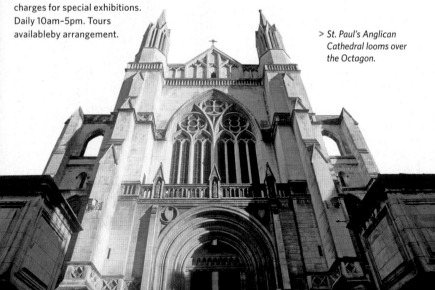

> St. Paul's Anglican Cathedral looms over the Octagon.

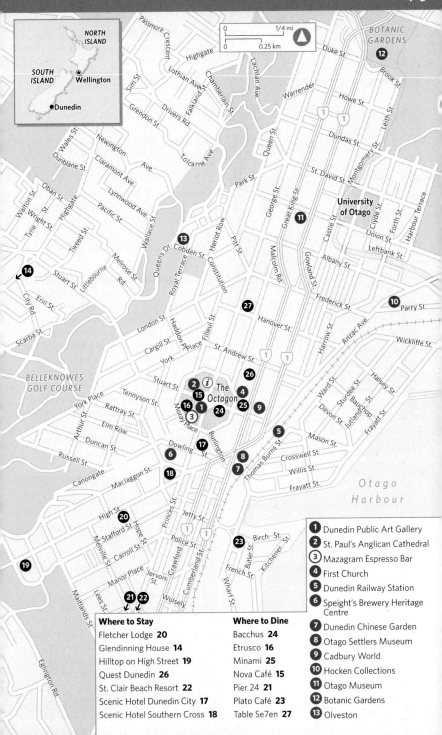

NORTH
ISLAND

SOUTH
ISLAND
★ Wellington

● Dunedin

BOTANIC
GARDENS

Where to Stay
Fletcher Lodge **20**
Glendinning House **14**
Hilltop on High Street **19**
Quest Dunedin **26**
St. Clair Beach Resort **22**
Scenic Hotel Dunedin City **17**
Scenic Hotel Southern Cross **18**

Where to Dine
Bacchus **24**
Etrusco **16**
Minami **25**
Nova Café **15**
Pier 24 **21**
Plato Café **23**
Table Se7en **27**

1 Dunedin Public Art Gallery
2 St. Paul's Anglican Cathedral
3 Mazagram Espresso Bar
4 First Church
5 Dunedin Railway Station
6 Speight's Brewery Heritage Centre
7 Dunedin Chinese Garden
8 Otago Settlers Museum
9 Cadbury World
10 Hocken Collections
11 Otago Museum
12 Botanic Gardens
13 Olveston

> *It's hard to imagine the task of laying 750,000 Royal Doulton floor tiles in intricate patterns at Dunedin Railway Station.*

③ 🍽 ★ **Mazagram Espresso Bar.** This tiny roaster with a few tables is just the place for a quick shot of espresso and a sweet cake—and you can watch the coffee beans roasting at the same time. **Upper Moray Place.** ☎ 03/477-9959. Mon–Fri 8am–6pm; Sat 10am–2pm. Cakes NZ$10–NZ$12.

④ ★★★ **First Church.** One of the city's founders, the Reverend Thomas Burns, wanted "a monument to Presbyterianism" and Melbourne architect R. A. Lawson was hired to create it. Built in 1873, this gorgeous Gothic construction is a fluted fancy compared to the austerity of St. Paul's Cathedral. I love the stained glass rose window above the altar and the Heritage Centre, behind the altar and to the right, is also worth your time. ⏱ 30 min. 415 Moray Place. ☎ 03/477-7150. www.firstchurchotago.org. Free admission. Sept–May 10am–4pm; June–Aug 10:30am–2:30pm.

⑤ ★★★ **Dunedin Railway Station.** Imagine being the tradesmen who had to lay the 725,000 Royal Doulton porcelain tiles that make up the mosaic floor of this magnificent Flemish Renaissance-style building. They're best viewed from the mezzanine, where you can also get a close look at stained glass windows and the replica of Dunedin's coat of arms. Designed by architect George Troup (who earned the nickname "Gingerbread George" thanks to this building) and built between 1904 and 1906, it's the city's foremost landmark. **The New Zealand Sports Hall of Fame** (☎ 03/477-7775; www.nzhalloffame.co.nz) is also upstairs. Entry costs NZ$5 for adults and NZ$2 kids; it's open daily from 10am to 4pm. ⏱ 1 hr. Corner of Castle St. and Anzac Ave. ☎ 03/477-4449.

⑥ ★ **Speight's Brewery Heritage Centre.** Speight's advertising slogan, *Pride of the South since 1876,* says it all. Join a 90-minute tour of the working brewery for a comprehensive overview of the industry and a chance to smell, touch, and taste beer ingredients. The tour involves walking and stair climbing, and covered shoes are required. Adults (18 and over) also get to sample six different Speight's beers. Make sure you watch the stunning Otago video presentation at the end—it made my little Kiwi heart burst with pride. ⏱ 1½ hr. 200 Rattray St. ☎ 03/477-7697. www.speights.co.nz. Admission NZ$22 adults, NZ$10 kids

Counting the Steps

I've never walked up Dunedin's Baldwin Street which, according to the *Guinness Book of Records,* is the world's steepest street. I have however, driven my car up and all I'll say about that is, never again! Don't be fooled by the gentle beginning—the gradient rises sharply. It's a dead end at the top and requires nimble turning to get out again—and the only way out is down the way you came. If you want a certificate to prove you did it, stop by the World's Steepest Street Tourist Shop, 282 North Rd. (☎ 03/473-0923). To get to Baldwin Street, take the Normandy bus to North Road; Baldwin is the tenth street on the right north of the Botanic Gardens.

> *Dunedin Chinese Garden is one of a handful of authentic Chinese gardens found outside of China.*

5–17, NZ$45 family. Tours Mon–Thurs at 10am, 11:45am, 2pm, and 7pm; Fri–Sun at 10am, 11:45am, and 2pm. Please arrive 10 min. before the tour begins.

7 ★★ kids **Dunedin Chinese Garden.** This authentic Chinese garden was created in Dunedin's sister city, Shanghai, by traditional craftsmen, then dismantled, shipped to New Zealand, and reconstructed on the current site. It was supported by the local Chinese community, many of whom have roots back to the Chinese gold miners of the 1860s Otago gold rush. Complete with lanterns, pagodas, willows, and ponds, it's as pretty as picture, especially at night. ⏱ 1 hr. Admission NZ$9 adults, NZ$6 students, free for kids 12 and under; 1 hr. guided tour NZ$20. Daily 10am–5pm; evening viewing Wed 7pm–9pm.

8 ★ kids **Otago Settlers Museum.** If you've ever wanted to ride a Penny Farthing cycle, this is the place for you—they have one for visitors to try. Engine buffs should be happy with the big transport collection. This is a museum of social history that traces the lives of those who made the region home, from original Maori to Scottish settlers to gold miners to the present day. The museum also runs 1- or 2-hour walking tour of the city (NZ$14–$NZ$22). ⏱ 1

hr. 31 Queens Gardens. ☎ 03/477-5052. www.otago.settlers.museum. Free admission. Daily 10am–5pm.

9 kids **Cadbury World.** Chocolate lovers, rejoice! This is your chance to see molten vats of chocolate, a chocolate waterfall, and boxes of bars running off the production line. There are sample treats to eat along the way, which may take kids' minds off the mechanical focus of the tour. The retail outlet at the end offers "tour-only" prices. ⏱ 1½ hr. 280 Cumberland St. ☎ 03/467-7967. www.cadburyworld.co.nz. Admission NZ$20 adults, NZ$14 kids 5–15, NZ$50 family. Daily 75-min. tours start every 30 min. from 9am to 3:15pm.

10 ★★ **Hocken Collections.** This treasure trove of books, photographs, journals, drawings, and paintings make up an impressive research facility based on the donated collections of Dr. T. M. Hocken. They date from the 17th century to the present day and focus on history, development, culture, and the natural environment of New Zealand, Antarctica, and the Pacific, with an emphasis on Southland and Otago. ⏱ 1 hr. Corner of Anzac Ave. and Parry St. ☎ 03/479-8868. www.library.otago.ac.nz/hocken. Free admission. Mon and Wed–Fri 9:30am–5pm, Tues 9:30am–9pm, Sat 9am–noon.

11 ★★★ kids **Otago Museum.** If you don't have time to explore Otago Peninsula's wildlife, this is a good second-best. Kids will love the nature galleries and the Victorian-styled Animal Attic, a nature and collector's nirvana, where zany stuffed animals peer out of glass cases at kid-level, giant bugs and beetles inhabit cases, and a turtle shell awaits the curious. The fun continues in Discovery World, where you step into the Tropical Forest for the hottest tour in town and a live butterfly display. The exceptional Maori carvings in the Tangata Whenua Gallery shouldn't be missed either. ⏱ At least 1½ hr. 419 Great King St. ☎ 03/474-7474. www.otago museum.govt.nz. Museum admission free; Discovery World's Tropical Forest NZ$9.50 adults, NZ$8.50 students and seniors, NZ$4.50 kids 1–15, NZ$20–NZ$24 family. Daily 10am–5pm.

> There are exceptional and rare examples of traditional Maori carving at Otago Museum.

> Olveston is a treasure trove of art and antiques, and an unbeatable example of early settler extravagance.

12 **Botanic Gardens.** Rhododendron enthusiasts should try and visit when the garden's collection of over 3,000 rhododendrons bursts into bloom between October and December. Factor in maples, magnolias, cherry trees, and azaleas, and you can be guaranteed some of the prettiest photos of your trip. The handsome Edwardian conservatory garden, rock gardens, and a comprehensive native plant collection are also worth your time. ⏱ 1 hr. North end of Castle St. ☎ 03/477-4000. Free admission. Daily dawn–dusk.

13 ★★★ **Olveston.** Back in 1907, when the wealthy Theomin family moved into their stately, new, Jacobean-style mansion, they could enjoy rare luxuries like central heating, an in-house telephone system, a shower, and heated towel rails. Today, when you step into this extraordinary home, you'll be transported back to those times. The library is my favorite space—it even has the original embossed leather wallpaper. Look out for all the beautiful clocks; the *pièce de résistance* is the elaborate French lantern clock dating back to 1760. From Japanese weaponry and Chinese urns to Staffordshire earthenware and Venetian glass, this is a taste of colonial sophistication and opulence that shouldn't be missed. Photography is not permitted in the house. ⏱ 1½ hr. 42 Royal Terrace. ☎ 03/477-3320. www.olveston. co.nz. Admission NZ$18 adults, NZ$8 kids 5–15. Reservations are required for 1-hr. guided tours at 9:30am, 10:45am, noon, 1:30pm, 2:45pm, and 4pm daily.

Dunedin Shopping

Dunedin and fashion are synonymous. In addition to hosting the iD Dunedin Fashion Show (www.id-dunedinfashion.com) in March, the Dunedin Fashion Incubator (www.dfi.co.nz) helps emerging fashion designers into business. The top three Dunedin fashion houses are ★★★ **Plume,** 310 George St. (☎ 477-9358), founded by Margi Robertson of the internationally regarded Nom*D label, which also stocks Zambesi, Comme des Garçons, Workshop, and others; ★★ **Carlson,** 106 George St. (☎ 03/470-1982; www.tanyacarlson.com), known for superb tailoring and exquisite hand-beading; and **Charmaine Reveley** (☎ 03/470-1982; www.charmainereveley.co.nz), who is known for flattering cuts and custom-made prints (her pieces are stocked at Carlson).

For contemporary jewelry, my picks are ★ **Bob Wyber Contemporary Jewellery,** 91 Stuart St. (☎ 03/474-9984; www.contemporaryjewellery.co.nz), and ★★★ **lure,** upstairs at 130 Stuart St. (☎ 03/477-5559).

To pick up some reading material, stop by ★★ **Raven Books,** 389 Princes St. ☎ 03/474-5562), for secondhand and rare books.

★★★ **University Book Shop,** 378 Great King St. (☎ 03/477-6976; www.unibooks.co.nz), is the best place for contemporary New Zealand fiction.

One of my favorite Dunedin dealer galleries is **Brett McDowell Gallery,** 5 Dowling St. (☎ 03/477-5260; www.brettmcdowellgallery.com). It's a small space but Brett has a great stable of top New Zealand artists and he runs thought-provoking exhibitions. Just across the road and up a bit is **Milford Galleries,** 18 Dowling St. (☎ 03/442-6896; www.milfordgalleries.co.nz), which also represents an excellent group of New Zealand artists. **Quadrant Gallery,** Bracken Court, 480 Moray Place (☎ 03/474-9939; www.quadrantgallery.co.nz) is a great place to view and buy works by leading New Zealand jewelers, glass artists, ceramicists, and sculptors.

Invercargill

This is the largest city in Southland (pop 53,000) and while many people bypass it altogether, I do think it's worth a visit—for its fine heritage buildings, its friendly people, and the rolling green farmland that surrounds it. Contrary to its apparently slow and sleepy nature, Invercargill sits at the heart of one of the richest provinces in the country, thanks to the nearby Tiwai Point Aluminium Smelter and a successful dairying industry. You'll need to devote 2 days to Invercargill to see all the sites described on this tour.

START Invercargill is 217km (135 miles) southwest of Dunedin on St. Hwy. 1. Southland Museum & Art Gallery and the Invercargill i-SITE Visitor Centre are all in the same building in Queens Park, off Gala St.

❶ ★★★ kids Southland Museum & Art Gallery. You can't miss this distinctive pyramid-shaped museum on the edge of the Queens Park. A highlight is the largest indoor display of live tuatara in the world and chief among them, Henry, who is over 100 years old. The museum's tuatara breeding program has reared more than 110 baby tuatara and if you're lucky, young ones will be playing in their own small aquarium. Upstairs, the natural history gallery is filled with albatrosses, giant spider crabs, and the like. A 26-minute movie on local hero Burt Munro, of *The World's Fastest Indian* fame, is worth watching. The Invercargill i-SITE Visitor Centre is also here; stop in and pick up the Invercargill Heritage Trail brochure. ⏱ 1 hr. Queens Park. ☎ 03/219-9069. www.southlandmuseum.com. Free admission; charges for some visiting shows. Mon–Fri 9am–5pm, Sat–Sun 10am–5pm.

> The Invercargill water tower is a fine example of early Victorian craftsmanship.

Where to Stay & Dine

Ascot Park Hotel **8**

Bonsai Restaurant & Sushi Bar **9**

Kelvin Hotel **10**

Level One **11**

❶ Southland Museum & Art Gallery

❷ Queens Park

❸ Zookeepers Café

❹ Riverton

❺ The Invercargill Heritage Trail

❻ Three Bean Café

❼ Bluff

Invercargill

❷ ★ kids **Queens Park.** The statuary in the children's playground of this verdant 80-hectare (198-acre) park is by English sculptor Sir Charles Wheeler, and was unveiled by Queen Elizabeth II in 1966. Other highlights include the Jessie Calder old rose collection, which includes over 900 plants representing more than 400 cultivars, and the lovely parrot collection in the aviary. The park's main Feldwick Gates feature Invercargill's original coat of arms, which includes a plough, a sheaf of corn, and a bale of wool to depict the province's prosperity. ⏱ 1 hr. Main entrance on Gala St. Free admission. Daily dawn–dusk.

❸ 🍴 ★ kids **Zookeepers Café.** Look for the giant tin elephant on top of this Tay Street cafe. It's a fun place to grab some hot chips and salad or a muffin and coffee. 50 Tay St. ☎ 03/218-3373. NZ$10–NZ$20.

Drive along Tay St. and turn right onto Dee St. at the clock tower. This is St. Hwy. 6, leading north to Fiordland and Queenstown, but you will veer left once you're a few kilometers out of town and follow the signs 38km (24 miles) to Riverton on St. Hwy. 99. Allow 40 min. driving time.

> In spring, Invercargill's Queens Park is filled with nodding tulips in a multitude of colors.

> *Many of the beaches west of Invercargill, like Riverton, are covered in pretty colored pebbles.*

4 ★ kids **Riverton.** Get an insight into how Riverton evolved from early Maori settlement to whaling town to its present-day sleepy seaside presence at the **Te Hikoi Southern Journey** museum, 172 Palmerston St. (☎ 03/234-8260; www.tehikoi.co.nz). Admission to the museum is NZ$12 for adults, NZ$5 for kids; the center is open daily from 10am to 4pm. After checking out the lively displays and stories, continue southwest on Palmerston St. over the main bridge, turn left, and follow the road around the little harbor to Riverton Rocks, a 9km (5⅔-mile) peninsula, and finish the afternoon exploring its pretty beaches. ⏱ At least 3 hr.

Drive back to Invercargill the way you came and spend the night.

5 ★ **The Invercargill Heritage Trail.** This tourist trail provides an excellent overview of the city's best buildings and places of interest. You can pick up a brochure detailing the route at the Invercargill i-SITE Visitor Centre (p.

439). It includes 18 different locations (with a map) that you can choose from, but I suggest you stick to a few highlights. Don't miss the landmark brick **Water Tower,** built of over 300,000 bricks in 1888 (open for tours Sun 1:30–4:30). The Edwardian Baroque **Civic Theatre** (1906), on Tay Street, is also another iconic building. Just across the road, check out the bulk of **First Presbyterian Church** (1915) and its elaborate brick patterning. On Leven Street, stop to admire the beauty of the Victorian, Edwardian, and Baroque **Railway Hotel** (1896). ⏱ Half-day.

6   🍴 **Three Bean Café.** This is an easy spot for a quick snack or a hearty brunch. 73 Dee St. ☎ 03/214-1914. NZ$10–NZ$16.

Continue south along Dee St. and go straight ahead at the clock tower on Clyde St. This is the continuation of St. Hwy. 1. Follow the signs 27km (17 miles) to Bluff. Allow 25 min. driving time.

> *The southernmost sign post in New Zealand points the way to Tokyo, the South Pole, the Equator, and more.*

7 ★ kids **Bluff.** There's plenty of activity on the wharves in this scruffy little fishing village to keep kids amused for an hour. Little fishing boats come and go and the **Stewart Island Experience** ferry to Stewart Island is also based here (see "Practical Matters," p. 434). As you drive into town, turn left over the railway lines—it's well signposted. Bluff has been settled since 1824 so there's plenty of history here. Start at **Bluff Maritime Museum** on Foreshore Road (☎ 03/212-7534). It's open from Monday to Friday, 10am to 4:30pm,

and Saturday and Sunday from 1pm to 5pm; admission is NZ$2 adults, NZ50¢ kids 5–15. You can also pick up the Bluff Heritage Trail brochure from the Invercargill i-SITE Visitor Centre (p. 439) and visit places of interest. Drive around the Foreshore Road to **Stirling Point** to see the famous signpost that attracts many thousands of visitors every year. It marks the beginning of St. Hwy. 1, which runs the length of New Zealand. It also points the way to New York and 11 other international locations. ⏱ **3–4 hr.**

Stewart Island

New Zealand's third-largest island is roughly triangular in shape and at 1,680 sq. km (649 sq. miles), it is about the same size as Singapore. Only 1% of it is inhabited; all the rest is given over to native bush and abundant wildlife. You'll need at least two days here for the best experience and don't forget to take your hiking boots, warm clothes, and a camera. You'll land at the little village of Oban, where the population of 400 islanders lives, and your assorted adventures will introduce you to remote rugged mountains, tranquil bays, and beautiful white-sand beaches completely devoid of people.

> The southern coast of Stewart Island is only accessible by boat, plane, or helicopter, but its fascinating landforms are worth seeing.

START Oban Visitor Centre, near the ferry landing.

❶ ★ **Oban Visitor Centre.** This is a good place to begin your island adventure. The friendly staff can provide all the information you'll ever need on Stewart Island. ⏱ 30 min. The Red Shed, 12 Elgin Terrace. ☎ 03/219-0056. www.stewartisland.co.nz. Daily 9am–7pm summer, 9:30am–6:30pm winter.

❷ ★ kids **Rakiura National Park Visitor Centre.** You'll find more information and good exhibits here that introduce you to various aspects of life (and wildlife) on the island. Of particular interest is the Maori tradition of "birding" for titi on the tiny islands south of Stewart Island—that is, hunting for prized mutton-birds (sooty shearwaters), which Maori still preserve in unique ways. If you plan hiking in Rakiura National Park you should also watch the 4-minute video, which gives you an idea of the often testing environment you'll have to face. This is also where you purchase hut passes and maps and can gather weather information for all National Park walks. ⏱ 30 min. Department of Conservation Building, Main Rd. ☎ 03/219-0009. www.doc.govt.nz. Daily 8am–5pm summer, 8:30am–4:30pm winter.

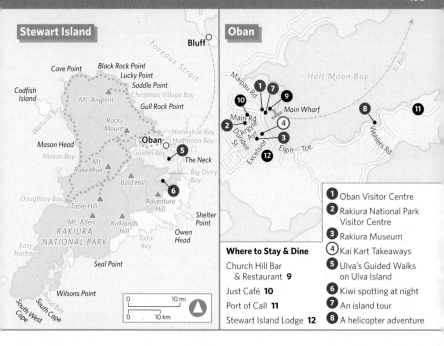

Stewart Island

Bluff

Foveaux Strait

Cave Point
Black Rock Point
Lucky Point
Saddle Point
Christmas Village Bay
Gull Rock Point

Codfish Island

Mt. Anglem

Waituna Bay

Rocky Mount

Mason Head
Mason Bay

Oban
Golden Bay

Horseshoe Bay
Halfmoon Bay

The Neck

Mt. Rakeahue

Big Glory Bay

Doughboy Bay

Bald Hill

Adventure Hill

Table Hill

Mt. Allen
Kirklands Hill

Toitoi Bay

Shelter Point

Owen Head

Easy Harbour

RAKIURA NATIONAL PARK

Seal Point

Wilsons Point

Broad Bay
South Bay
South West Cape
South Cape

0   10 mi
0   10 km

Oban

Half Moon Bay

To Bluff

Maipau Rd.

1   7

10   9

Main Rd.   Main Wharf

2   Argyle St.   4

Dundee St.   Ayr St.   3

Excelsior   Elgin Tce.

12

Wohlers Rd.

8   11

1 Oban Visitor Centre
2 Rakiura National Park Visitor Centre
3 Rakiura Museum
4 Kai Kart Takeaways
5 Ulva's Guided Walks on Ulva Island
6 Kiwi spotting at night
7 An island tour
8 A helicopter adventure

Where to Stay & Dine

Church Hill Bar & Restaurant 9

Just Café 10

Port of Call 11

Stewart Island Lodge 12

---

3 ★ kids **Rakiura Museum.** This may well be one of the smallest, quirkiest museums you'll ever visit. It traces the island's history through sailing, whaling, tin mining, sawmilling, and fishing; with photographic, shell, and Maori artifact displays. ⏱ 45 min. Ayr St. ☎ 03/219-1049. Admission NZ$5. Mon–Sat 10am–1:30pm, Sun noon–2pm.

---

4 🍔 **Kai Kart Takeaways.** Make sure you take a look inside this super-cute operation (in a funky caravan beside the Rakiura Museum) while you wait for one of their delicious hamburgers or fresh blue cod with chips. Eat here or take your meal down on the beach with the seagulls. Ayr St. ☎ 03/219-1225. www.kaikartstewartisland.com. Most items around NZ$10.

From Ayr St., walk up Golden Bay Rd., veer left, and go down Thule Rd. to Golden Bay Wharf to meet Ulva Goodwillie and the water taxi to Ulva Island. It's a good 30–40 min. walk or just 5 min. by car. Arrive at 1:05pm for a 1:15pm departure.

5 ★★★ kids **Ulva's Guided Walks on Ulva Island.** This will be an outing you remember long after the event. Ulva is not the only person doing guided bird-watching tours on Ulva Island but she's the best in my view. It's not just about the birds; you also get an insight into history, flora, and Maori culture. Ulva, who was named after the island, is Maori herself and she has an obvious passion for the protected wildlife that makes this island conservation retreat unique. You're likely to see tiny robins, wood pigeons, tui, rare saddlebacks, and many more birds. You'll also fall in love with the beautiful little beaches. ⏱ 4 hr. Golden Bay Wharf. ☎ 03/219-1216. www.ulva.co.nz. Guided walks NZ$113 adults, NZ$46 kids 12 and under.

Return to your accommodation for a rest before embarking on a late-night adventure.

6 ★★★ **Kiwi spotting at night.** It's pitch dark, the ocean is crashing on the remote beach, and you've never seen so many stars in your life. All of a sudden, your guide Phillip Smith, a fifth-generation islander, spots a moving shadow waddling across the sand. It's the Stewart

> *Elephant seals sometimes visit the southern coasts of New Zealand. Don't get too close—they can be territorial.*

a guided tour, **Village & Bay Tours** (☎ 0800/000-511 or 03/219-0034; www.stewartisland experience.co.nz) visits most of these places, with photo stops and short walks. The tour lasts 1½ hours and costs NZ$44 for adults, NZ$22 for kids 5–14. ◷ 3 hr.

8 ★★★ kids **A helicopter adventure.** If your purse strings will stretch to this pricier option, I'd highly recommend Zane Smith's unforgettable adventure. Zane is the son of kiwi-spotting Phillip Smith and like his father, he has great knowledge of Stewart Island. From the remote beauty of Mason and Doughboy bays to the grandeur of weathered granite domes of Port Pegasus in the south, Zane will fly you over (and land) in remote areas to which you would not otherwise have access. ◷ 3-4 hr. Rakiura Helicopters, Fern Gully Heliport, 151 Main Rd. ☎ 03/219-1155 or 027/221-9217. Price on enquiry.

Island brown kiwi, a distinct sub-species of the brown kiwi found throughout mainland New Zealand. You'll start out for the shores of Paterson Inlet at twilight. After a 35-minute cruise, you'll disembark, walk through the bush with flashlights, and emerge on a pristine beach. In thousands of trips, Phillip has only missed spotting the birds on two or three occasions. ◷ 4 hr. Bravo Adventure Cruises. ☎ 03/219-1144. Admission NZ$115. The trip is subject to weather conditions; you must be relatively fit and no kids under 14 are permitted. Tours depart from an return to the Oban wharf.

7 ★ kids **An island tour.** Start day 2 at the Oban Visitor Centre (**1**). Hire a car (NZ$65–NZ$70 per half-day), pick up some maps, and set off to explore the little bays and beaches. Visit **Lee Bay**, the entrance to Rakiura National Park, and **Horseshoe Bay**. On your way back through town, pick up some picnic supplies from the general store and drive out to **Ackers Point** and walk to the lighthouse. On the way back, turn left into Wohlers Road, left again into Deep Bay Road, and you'll find the very lovely **Ringaringa Beach,** a lovely, quiet beach perfect for a picnic, and the **Ringaringa Heights Golf Course** (green fees only NZ$10–NZ$15 for two people). You can't really get lost on the limited roads but do take care as many are narrow and steep. If you'd rather do

Practical Matters

You can catch the **Stewart Island Experience ferry** (☎ 0800/000-511 or 03/212-7660; www.stewartislandexperience.co.nz) in Bluff (p. 431, **7**). The ferry runs daily September through April from 8:30am to 4pm; from May through Aug it runs from 9:30am to 5pm. Round trip tickets cost around NZ$130 for adults, NZ$65 for kids 5 to 15.

The only other way to get to the island is by plane. **Stewart Island Flights** (☎ 03/218-9129; www.stewartislandflights.com), based at Invercargill Airport, offers round-trip flights for around NZ$200 adults and NZ$115 kids 15 and under. It's a 20-minute flight.

If you're taking the ferry, remember that Foveaux Strait is one of the most unpredictable passages in the world and water can be extremely rough. If you're prone to seasickness make sure you come prepared, or buy homeopathic remedies at the ferry check-in counter. It may be a short trip (1 hour) but it can be notoriously uncomfortable. Also be aware that there are no banking facilities or ATM machines on the island. Some operators accept some credit cards but it's best to come with cash.

Where to Stay

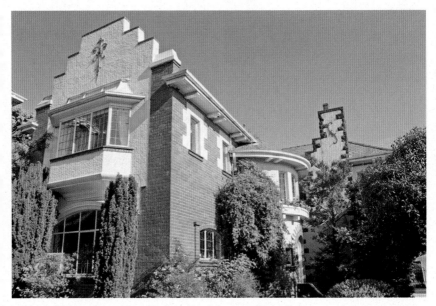

> *Relax in the finery of one of Dunedin's finest historic homes at Fletcher Lodge.*

Dunedin Area

★★★ **Fletcher Lodge** CENTRAL DUNEDIN

Ewa and Keith Rozecki-Pollard, the owners of this stunning historic home, have an eye for detail and a passion for hospitality that flows over into every antiques-filled room. Enjoy breakfast in the music room, notable for its Wedgewood ceiling. 276 High St. ☎ 0800/843-563 or 03/477-5552. www.fletcherlodge.co.nz. 10 units. Doubles NZ$325–NZ$750 w/breakfast. AE, DC, MC, V. Map p. 423.

★★ **Glendinning House** ROSLYN

Sandy Black and Jocelyn Robinson live in an elegant brick mansion in the nicest part of town, a few kilometers northwest of central Dunedin and short walk from local eateries. Two huge, upstairs suites open onto a big balcony. 222 Highgate, Roslyn. ☎ 03/477-8262. www.glendinninghouse.co.nz. 2 units. Doubles NZ$315–NZ$410 w/breakfast. MC, V. Map p. 423.

★★★ kids **Hilltop on High Street** CENTRAL DUNEDIN

Hosts Craig Sherson and Rodney McDonald have converted one of Dunedin's glorious stately homes into an oasis of peace and privacy overlooking the city and harbor. Their elegant, contemporary rooms (two with ensuite bathrooms and balcony) even come with kitchens. 433 High St. ☎ 03/477-1053. 4 units. Doubles NZ$190–NZ$210 w/breakfast. MC, V. Map p. 423.

★ kids **Quest Dunedin** CENTRAL DUNEDIN

These simple, serviced, one-bedroom apartments (with kitchen and laundry facilities) right in the heart of the city are an excellent, great-value stay if all you want is a clean, convenient, no-frills place to sleep. 333 Cumberland St. ☎ 0800/470-1725 or 03/470-1725. www.questdunedin.co.nz. 42 units Doubles NZ$133–NZ$260. AE, DC, MC, V. Map p. 423.

> *The large rooms at Dunedin's Glendinning House have all the comforts of home.*

★★★ kids **St. Clair Beach Resort** ST. CLAIR BEACH Lie back in a room or apartment here, look out over the ocean (often wild and elemental), and you'll think you've landed in good-value heaven. Everything is crisp, clean, light, and new. Eighteen rooms have sea views, 24 have balconies, and all have laundry facilities. The fabulous downstairs restaurant is an added bonus. 24 the Esplanade, St. Clair, Dunedin. ☎ 03/456-0555. www.stclairbeachresort.com. 26 units. Doubles NZ$200–NZ$425. AE, DC, MC, V. Map p. 423.

★ kids **Scenic Hotel Dunedin City** CENTRAL DUNEDIN Small, modern, and just one block off the Octagon, this hotel is a winner for all-round convenience and price. You can opt for city or harbor views and rooms are spacious and fresh. Corner of Princes and Dowling sts. ☎ 0800/696-963 or 03/470-1470. www.scenichotelgroup.co.nz. 110 units. Doubles NZ$253–NZ$276. AE, DC, MC, V. Map p. 423.

★★★ kids **Scenic Hotel Southern Cross** CENTRAL DUNEDIN This is the more stately "big sister" of Scenic Hotel Dunedin City—a centrally located Dunedin icon, with a greater range of room types than the smaller, modern hotel up the street.It has the best beds in New Zealand in my view. Rooms in the Exchange Wing are the newest. Corner of Princes and High sts. ☎ 0800/696-963 or 03/477-0752. www.scenichotelgroup.co.nz. 178 units. Doubles NZ$288–NZ$546. AE, DC, MC, V. Map p. 423.

Invercargill

★★ kids **Ascot Park Hotel** NEAR INVERCARGILL RACECOURSE The 20 apartments and studios here are the nicest part of this large hotel on the edge of town and my pick for the best Southland accommodation. They're roomy and modern, with cooking facilities and ready access to onsite swimming pool and children's play area. Corner of Tay St. and Racecourse Rd. ☎ 0800/272-687 or 03/217-6195. www.ascotparkhotel.co.nz. 116 units. Doubles NZ$119–NZ$340. AE, DC, MC, V. Map p. 429.

★ kids **Kelvin Hotel** CENTRAL CITY This moderately priced old faithful had a complete makeover in 2009 and is the better for it. It's a great central city location and room 601, with its corner views over the city, is the pick of the bunch, although all three suites are very nice. You get free use of the gym next door if you need to work off holiday excesses. Corner of Kelvin and Esk sts. ☎ 0800/802-829 or 03/218-2829. www.kelvinhotel.co.nz. 61 units. Doubles NZ$155–NZ$205. AE, DC, MC, V. Map p. 429.

Stewart Island

★★★ **Port of Call** ACKERS POINT This place is a treasure. Put your feet up in lovely B&B rooms, rest in the privacy of The Bach or enjoy cozy comforts at self-contained Turner Cottage (in Halfmoon Bay). Hosts Ian and Philippa Wilson are great hosts and as local tour operators, they can give you the best advice. Leask Bay Rd. ☎ 03/219-1394. www.portofcall.co.nz. 3 B&B units. Doubles NZ$340 w/breakfast; NZ$190-NZ$260 self-catering; from NZ$210 Turner Cottage. MC, V. No kids under 11. Map p. 433.

★★ **Stewart Island Lodge** OBAN Set against a native bush backdrop on a (steep) hill above the village, this five-room lodge has the best views in town. Rooms all have ensuite bathrooms and king beds and all open onto balconies. You won't get five-star treatment, but you'll be comfortable and happy, I'm sure. 14 Nichol Rd. ☎ 03/219-1085. www.stewartislandlodge.co.nz. 5 units. Doubles NZ$400 w/breakfast. AE, DC, MC, V. Closed June, July, August. Map p. 433.

Where to Dine

Dunedin Area

★★★ Bacchus CENTRAL DUNEDIN *MODERN NZ*

Get a window seat at this little culinary oasis so you can look out over the Octagon while you dine. A compact yet diverse menu specializes in New Zealand beef and lamb with Asian and European influences flavoring fish, chicken, and vegetarian dishes. 1st floor, 12 The Octagon. ☎ 03/474-084. www.bacchuswinebarrestaurant.co.nz. Main courses NZ$35–NZ$39. AE, MC, V. Lunch Mon–Fri, Dinner Mon–Sat. Map p. 423.

★ kids Etrusco CENTRAL DUNEDIN *ITALIAN*

This big, boisterous, friendly, Tuscan pizzeria and spaghetteria is just the place to satisfy a busy traveler's appetite. Their pizzas and pasta dishes are the most popular items, while Italian favorites like tiramisu and gelato complete the picture. It can be noisy but that's all part of the fun. 1st floor, 8A Moray Place. ☎ 03/477-3737. www.etrusco.co.nz. Main courses NZ$20–NZ$32. Dinner daily from 5:30pm. Map p. 423.

★ Minami CENTRAL DUNEDIN *SUSHI*

Everyone from students and businessmen to groups of giggling Japanese girls frequents this place for its casual atmosphere and tasty, well-priced sushi, sashimi, and tempura. It's a tiny, low-key place for a quick tasty lunch. 126 Stuart St. ☎ 03/477-9596. Main courses NZ$10–NZ$15. Lunch Mon–Fri. Map p. 423.

★★ kids Nova Café CENTRAL DUNEDIN *MODERN NZ/FUSION*

This smart, good-value cafe beside the Dunedin Public Art Gallery is a favorite for lunch and pre-show dinners. Somehow, it's quintessentially Dunedin. There's are slight Italian and Asian slants to the menu—risottos, wok-fried vegetables, seafood gumbo and the like—and it's a great people-watching spot. 29 the Octagon. ☎ 03/479-0808. www.novacafe.co.nz. Main courses NZ$18–NZ$35. AE, DC, MC, V. Breakfast, lunch and dinner Mon–Thurs. Map p. 423.

> Join the who's who of Dunedin at lunch at Nova Café.

★★★ Pier 24 ST. CLAIR BEACH *MODERN NZ*

Michael Coughlin, a brilliant, award-winning executive chef, entices diners with a happy marriage of flavors and superb presentation—all this in a modern, classy interior overlooking the ocean. St. Clair Beach Resort, 24 the Esplanade, St. Clair, Dunedin. ☎ 03/466-3610. www.stclairbeachresort.com. Main courses NZ$25–NZ$36. DC, MC, V. Map p. 423.

★★★ Plato Café WHARF AREA *SEAFOOD/MODERN NZ*

This unexpected gem sits in the middle of a raw wharf area bereft of charm. Seafood, in partnership with top Central Otago wines, has always been a high point

> Enjoy fine dining overlooking the ocean at Pier 24.

here and this is the place to try such Kiwi icons as seafood chowder, paua (abalone), and the whitebait omelet. 2 Birch St. ☎ 03/477-4235. www.platocafe.co.nz. Main courses NZ$25–NZ$35. AE, MC, V. Dinner daily, brunch/lunch Sun. Map p. 423.

★★ **Table Se7en** CENTRAL DUNEDIN *MODERN NZ* At this stylish eatery, lamb, veal, beef, chicken, and salmon are given a fresh twist and perhaps an international inspiration—harissa-crusted, herb-smoked venison, for instance. It also has an extensive wine list. Level 1, corner of Hanover and George sts. ☎ 03/477-6877. www.tableseven.co.nz. Main courses NZ$29–NZ$35. AE, MC, V. Lunch and dinner Tues–Sat. Map p. 423.

Invercargill

★ kids **Bonsai Restaurant & Sushi Bar** CENTRAL CITY *JAPANESE* This is a good spot for a quick, authentic Japanese lunch in a low-key setting. There's a huge choice of takeaway sushi but I suggest you linger over a bento lunch box, udon noodles, or delicious, crispy tempura. 15 Esk St. ☎ 03/218-1292. Main courses NZ$10–NZ$16. V. Lunch Mon–Fri (10am–5pm). Map p. 429.

★★ kids **Level One** CENTRAL CITY *MODERN NZ* This delightful restaurant at the Kelvin Hotel hovers happily between fine dining and casual. It presents delicious meals (including vegetarian and gluten-free choices) in a stylish, modern interior. The seared scallops were mouth-watering and local blue cod is a bestseller. Level 1, Kelvin Hotel, corner of Tay and Esk sts. ☎ 03/218-2829. Main courses NZ$22–NZ$32. AE, DC, MC, V. Breakfast, lunch, and dinner daily. Map p. 429.

Stewart Island

★ kids **Church Hill Bar & Restaurant** OBAN *MODERN NZ* On the hill overlooking Oban, this is probably your best chance of decent meal on Stewart Island. Set in a 19th-century cottage, the restaurant offers a good choice of seafood dishes (blue cod and local salmon) and stone-grill dining for those who like a good steak. Sit outside in summer and take in the harbor views. 36 Kamahi Rd. ☎ 03/219-1323. www.churchhillrestaurant.com. Main courses NZ$36–NZ$46. V. Lunch and dinner daily. Map p. 433.

Just Café OBAN *CAFE*

This quirky little place is nothing fancy but it serves delicious counter food, good coffee and juices, and it's handy to the center of town. There's also an Internet service for checking your emails and, oddly, a mixed assortment of handcrafted jewelry. 6 Main Rd. ☎ 03/219-1422. Snacks NZ$10–NZ$14. Hours vary but usually open by 9am. Map p. 433.

Dunedin & Southland Fast Facts

> Arriving at Dunedin International Airport in winter can be a cold business when the snow falls on the Maungatua Ranges.

Arriving

BY PLANE Dunedin Airport (www.dnairport. co.nz) is inconveniently located 45 minutes south of the city. It serviced by regular **Air New Zealand** flights (☎ 0800/737-000 or 03/479-6594; www.airnewzealand.co.nz). Taxis charge around NZ$65 to the city. **Dunedin Taxi Airport Shuttle** (☎ 0800/505-010) charges around NZ$35 to NZ$40 to the city. **Invercargill Airport** (invercargillairport.co.nz) is just a few kilometers west of the city. Air New Zealand has service between Invercargill and Christchurch, Dunedin, Auckland, and Wellington. **BY BUS Intercity** (☎ 09/623-1503) provides coach service between Dunedin, Invercargill, Christchurch, Timaru, Queenstown, Te Anau, and Picton.

Emergencies & Medical Care

Dial **111** for any emergency. The hospitals serving this region are **Dunedin Hospital,** 201 Great King St. (☎ **03/474-0999**) and **Southland Hospital,** Kew Road, Invercargill (☎ **03/218-1949**). For a doctor, try **Travellers**

Medical & Vaccination Centre, 169 Eglinton Rd., Mornington, Dunedin (☎ **03/453-6121**) or **Invercargill Urgent Doctor,** 40 Clyde St., Invercargill (☎ **03/218-8821**). For a dentist, contact **Raymond J. George,** Level 7, corner of the Octagon and George Street, Dunedin (☎ **03/477-7993**).

Internet

Get online at **A1 Internet Café,** Level 1, 149 George St., Dunedin (☎ 03/477-5832). The Dunedin visitor center also has an Internet service (see below). In Invercargill, try **Bits & Bytes Computer Centre,** 55 Dee St. (☎ 03/214-0007).

Visitor Information Centers

DUNEDIN I-SITE VISITOR CENTRE 48 the Octagon (☎ 03/474-3300; www.dunedinnz.com). **INVERCARGILL I-SITE VISITOR CENTRE** Southland Museum & Art Gallery, 108 Gala St., in Queens Gardens (☎ 03/211-0895; www.i-site.org.nz/otago-southland#invercargill); visit the Invercargill site for information on Stewart Island.

New Zealand's History & Culture

> Take a cruise boat or a kayak to see the astonishing (modern) Maori carvings on the rock faces on Lake Taupo.

New Zealand: A Brief History

> Early Maori created elaborate carvings represent-
ing their ancestors on their waka (canoes).

Early Maori Settlement

There's more than one theory as to how New
Zealand's first inhabitants settled here. The
Maori legend tells of Kupe, who in A.D. 1000
sailed from Hawaiiki, the traditional homeland
of the Polynesians. The legend doesn't tell us
exactly where Hawaiiki was located in the vast
South Pacific, but present-day authorities believe it belonged to the Society Islands group
that includes Tahiti.

It wasn't until the mid-14th century that
Maori arrived in great numbers. These settlers found abundant supplies of seafood and
berries, which they supplemented with such
tropical plants as taro, yams, and kumara
(sweet potato) that they'd brought along from
Hawaiiki. Dogs and rats also made the voyage;
they were added to the protein source. The
cultivation of these imported vegetables and
animals gradually led to an agricultural society
in which Maori lived in permanent villages
based on a central marae (village common
or courtyard) and whare runanga (meetinghouse). This is where the distinctive Maori art
forms of woodcarving and tattooing evolved.

Abel Tasman & Dutch Discovery

The first recorded sighting of New Zealand
by Europeans occurred in December 1642.
Abel Tasman, who was scouting territory for
the Dutch East India Company, spied the west
coast of the South Island, entered Golden
Bay, and met the Maori before even reaching
land. As his two ships anchored, several Maori
war canoes entered the water and paddlers
shouted hostile challenges. The next day,
Maori attacked a cockboat, killing four sailors.
Tasman fired at the retreating canoes and
departed. Bad weather forced him to proceed
up the west coast of the North Island. Failing
to find a suitable landing spot, he sailed on to
Tonga and Fiji, and Golden Bay was known as
Murderer's Bay for many years to come.

Captain Cook

When Captain James Cook left England in
1768 on the HMS Endeavour, he carried orders
from King George III to sail south in search of
the "continent" reported by Abel Tasman. If he
found it uninhabited, he was to plant the English
flag and claim it for the king; if not, he was to
take possession of "convenient situations," but
only with the consent of the indigenous people.

On October 7, 1769, Nicholas Young, son of
the ship's surgeon, spotted New Zealand from
his perch in the mast. Naming the headland (in
the Gisborne area) Young Nick's Head, Cook
sailed into a crescent-shaped bay and anchored.
With the help of a young Tahitian chief, Tupea,
who had sailed with the crew as a guide and
interpreter, Cook tried to make contact with the
Maori, but to no avail. They remained hostile
and would not accept Cook's gifts, nor let him
take food and water to his men.

Disappointed, Cook claimed the country for
King George, and named the bay Poverty Bay
because, as he noted in his journal, "it afforded
us not one thing we wanted." Sailing north, he
rounded the tip of the North Island and went on
to circumnavigate both islands. During the next
6 months, he accurately charted the country
and missed only the entrance to Milford Sound
(which is virtually invisible from the open sea)
and the fact that Stewart Island was not part of
the mainland.

The British Arrive

Sealers began arriving in 1792 and essentially stripped the South Island waters of its seal colonies. Whalers, too, discovered rich hunting grounds in New Zealand waters. Oil vats soon dotted the Bay of Islands, which provided safe harbor.

Traders and merchants, attracted by the wealth of flax, the abundance of trees for ship-building, and the lucrative trading of muskets and other European goods with the Maori, were little better than the sealers and whalers in respecting the country's natural resources. Great forests were felled and luxuriant bushlands disappeared as land was cleared.

The immigration of Europeans, mostly from Great Britain, had a devastating impact on Maori culture. Most destructive was the introduction of liquor, muskets, and diseases against which the Maori had no immunity. Muskets intensified the fierce intertribal warfare, eventually becoming so common that no one tribe had superiority in terms of firepower. By 1830, Maori chiefs began to realize the weapon was destroying all their tribes.

Missionaries also began to come during this period. They were responsible for putting the Maori language in writing (largely for the purpose of translating and printing the Bible), establishing mission schools, and upgrading agricultural methods through the use of plows and windmills.

Lawlessness grew along with the number of British immigrants and harm was inflicted on both Maori and the new settlers. The missionaries complained to the British government, which was by no means eager to recognize faraway New Zealand as a full-fledged colony, having already experienced problems with America and Canada. As an alternative, the Crown placed New Zealand under the jurisdiction of New South Wales in 1833, and dispatched James Busby as "British Resident" with full responsibilities to enforce law and order. Unfortunately, he was completely ineffective.

> *Many early Maori did not fully grasp what they had signed when they made their mark on the Treaty of Waitangi.*

The Treaty of Waitangi

Back in Britain, the newly formed New Zealand Company began sending ships to buy land from the Maori and establish permanent settlements. Their questionable methods caused increasing alarm in London. Between 1839 and 1843, the New Zealand Company sent out 57 ships carrying 19,000 settlers, the nucleus of the permanent British population.

In 1839, Captain William Hobson was sent by the government to sort out the concerns. Catering to the Maori sense of ceremony, he arranged an assembly of chiefs at the Busby residence in the Bay of Islands. There, on February 6, 1840, the Treaty of Waitangi was signed after lengthy debate. The treaty guaranteed Maori "all the rights and privileges of British subjects" in exchange for their acknowledgment of British sovereignty, while granting the Crown exclusive rights to buy land from the Maori. Many of the chiefs did not understand what they had signed. Nevertheless, 45 of them ultimately signed the treaty, and when it was circulated around the country, another 500 signed as well.

> *Wellington became the capital city of New Zealand in 1865.*

Instead of easing tensions, though, the Treaty of Waitangi ushered in one of the bloodiest periods in New Zealand's history. The British were eager to exercise their right to purchase Maori land and while some chiefs were eager to sell, others were not. As pressures forced them to sell, the Maori revolted. When Chief Hone Heke (the first to sign the treaty) hacked down the British flagpole at Kororareka (Russell) in 1844, it signaled the beginning of some 20 years of fierce battles. The British finally emerged the victors, but the seizure of that Maori land continues to be the subject of debate today.

From Waitangi to the 1970s

By the time the 1860s arrived, gold had been discovered on the South Island's West Coast. The Gold Rush opened up huge tracts of Central Otago. Cobb & Co, a stagecoach company, extended their coaching operations to link the major towns from Christchurch south. They added to that in 1866, initiating a coach service across Arthur's Pass to the gold fields of Westland. By the end of the 1860s, Dunedin was by far the largest city in the country thanks to gold wealth. Advances in transport flourished during this period and with waves of immigrants keen to seek their fortune in the gold fields, New Zealand entered a period

of lively economic activity that was to see it through to the 1870s and 1880s.

Whaling, too, changed the face of New Zealand during this period. It was one of our first major industries and with the influx of international whalers came traders, missionaries, onshore whaling stations, and new housing settlements. Many whalers left their ships to marry into Maori families—the fact that there are many Maori families today with Scandinavian names is part of that legacy.

In 1892, the introduction of the first shipment of lamb to England heralded a new era in New Zealand beef and lamb exports. History was made in 1893 when New Zealand became the first country in the world to allow women to vote.

By 1914, thoughts had turned to war. One hundred thousand New Zealanders joined the Australia-New Zealand Army Corps to fight in World War I and New Zealand lost more soldiers per capita than any other nation.

The 1930s were colored by the Great Depression, unemployment, riots, and, on a happier note, the beginning of air services across Cook Strait. Our soldiers returned to battle in 1939 with the advent of World War II. In 1947, the Statute of Westminster was adopted by the government, giving New Zealand full independence from Britain.

For many, the 1950s were a golden era. The economy had long since settled, our men were back from the war, and, for the first time, New Zealand's population hit two million. Life was easy in the '50s. Threats were few and achievements began piling up: Edmund Hillary became the first man to climb Mount Everest; we had our first royal visit when the newly crowned Queen Elizabeth stepped foot on our shores; and the Auckland Harbour Bridge heralded a new age of modernity when it opened in 1959.

It's hard to believe it now, but New Zealand had to wait until the 1960s to get its first regional television—in Auckland. We didn't get color television until 1973, by which time the New Zealand population had hit three million and the Auckland International Airport had opened.

The 1970s to Today

For many years, the country's economy had traditionally depended on the success of wool, dairy, and meat exports with protected, unlimited access to British markets. This changed when Britain entered the European Common Market in the 1970s. New Zealand was then forced to diversify and do business with many other countries. By the mid-1980s, meat, wool, and dairy products accounted for just under 50% of our export income.

The mid-1980s also heralded the complete deregulation of the domestic economy. It took a decade of struggle for many industries to come to terms with the changes. (This is the main reason our infamous sheep numbers dropped from 72 million in 1983 to the present low of 44 million.) The stern belt-tightening ultimately bore fruit, however, and by 1993, the economy was flourishing. Today, forestry, horticulture, fishing, tourism, and manufacturing are the leading industries. Tourism is the country's largest single source of foreign exchange. Overall standards and the level of professionalism have improved tenfold in recent years, making New Zealand one of the ripest countries in the world for visitors.

Like any young country, New Zealand is growing rapidly and facing issues associated with progress. Urban drift accounts for 80% of the population living in towns and cities, most north of Lake Taupo, with a full third of the population in the Auckland region alone.

> There has been a huge renaissance in Maori culture since the 1970s.

City infrastructures, transport systems, and housing developments are struggling in some cases to keep up with the pace.

Biculturalism has been the loudest catchphrase of the past decade. From the late-19th century until after World War II, there was a marked decline in the use of the Maori language because schools insisted that only English be taught. Since the 1960s, however, there has been a growing resurgence of interest in Maori identity, language, and tradition, and many Maori are now bilingual, thanks to extensive language programs in schools.

The Waitangi Tribunal, set up by the New Zealand government in 1987 to settle unresolved issues related to the Treaty of Waitangi, has brought Maori grievances to light. Many claim their ancestors were tricked out of much of their land. Today, much of that land has been returned to Maori ownership, including the Whanganui River in 1999, giving Maori the financial means to alter their future.

A Timeline of New Zealand History

EARLY HISTORY

A.D. 950 Estimated date of first New Zealand landfall by Maori (see left).

MID-1300S First major influx of Maori settlers.

1642 Abel Tasman of the Dutch East India Company becomes first European to sight the South Island.

1769 Captain James Cook begins 6-month mapping of North and South Islands.

1792 First sealers and whalers arrive in New Zealand waters.

1800

1814 First Christian missionary, Rev. Samuel Marsden, arrives in Bay of Islands.

1833 James Busby is named as "British Resident" under jurisdiction of New South Wales.

1839–43 New Zealand Company sends 57 ships out of England carrying 19,000 settlers.

1840 Treaty of Waitangi with Maori chiefs is signed in Bay of Islands (see left).

1844 Maori Chief Hone Heke chops down British flagpole in Bay of Islands, beginning a 20-year revolt centered on land rights.

1860s Discovery of gold on South Island's west coast and North Island's east coast, creating several boomtowns.

1860–81 Second Maori War over land rights.

1882 Refrigeration is introduced; first shipment of lamb to England.

1893 Voting rights are extended to women.

1900–1960S

1914–18 100,000 New Zealanders join the Australia–New Zealand Army Corps to fight in World War I; New Zealand loses more soldiers per capita than any other nation.

1939 New Zealand enters World War II.

1947 Statute of Westminster is adopted by government; New Zealand gains full independence from Britain.

1951 New Zealand ratifies Australia–New Zealand–United States (ANZUS) mutual security pact.

1953 Sir Edmund Hillary (see left), along with Sherpa Tenzing Norgay, becomes the first man to climb Mount Everest.

1965 New Zealand troops are sent to Vietnam.

1970S–2000

1973 Britain joins European Economic Community (Common Market), with subsequent disastrous reduction in imports from New Zealand.

1984 Labour Government begins comprehensive reform and deregulation of New Zealand's economy.

1985 All nuclear-armed and nuclear-powered vessels are banned from New Zealand ports; Greenpeace's *Rainbow Warrior* is sunk by French intelligence agents in Auckland harbor, killing a crew member.

1987 The New Zealand yacht *KZ 7* wins the World Championship in Sardinia; at home, the stock market crashes.

1990 New Zealand hosts the Commonwealth Games; the visit of Elizabeth II adds to the festivities commemorating the 150th anniversary of the Treaty of Waitangi.

1994 The decade of belt-tightening starts to pay off and New Zealand's economy is declared one of the world's most competitive economies.

1995 Team New Zealand wins the America's Cup yacht race; Mount Ruapehu erupts for the first time in 8 years; New Zealand's population reaches 3.5 million; economic growth continues.

1996 Mount Ruapehu erupts again; ash clouds disrupt air travel throughout much of the country (see left).

1997 Maoris demand return of Crown lands; racial tensions increase. Maori activist damages the America's Cup.

2000S

2000 The final challenge of the America's Cup is held in Auckland; New Zealand wins again.

2001 The New Zealand government gives the go-ahead for strictly controlled genetic modification research. Legendary sailor and environmentalist Peter Blake (see left), who led New Zealand to the America's Cup championship in 1995 and 2000, is killed aboard his ship by pirates in the Amazon.

2004 New Zealand film director Peter Jackson wins big at the Academy Awards for the third film of his trilogy, *The Lord of the Rings: The Return of the King.*

2005 New Zealand golfer Michael Campbell wins the U.S. Open Championship.

2006 New Zealand's population passes the 4 million mark.

2010–2011 Christchurch is struck by 2 major earthquakes just 5 months apart. See "A Shaken City," p. 328.

The Lay of the Land

> *The Takaka Hills, near Nelson, are characterized by strange marble outcrops.*

The Land

New Zealand is part of a fiery rim of volcanoes that encircle the Pacific Ocean. The last large eruption occurred in 1886—Mount Tarawera near Rotorua left an estimated 150 people dead. Our most recent show-off has been Mount Ruapehu, which did its best to ruin the central North Island ski season for several years in a row in the late 1990s.

Today, New Zealand bears all the fascinating geographical hallmarks of a tumultuous geologic history. It may have a reputation for being green, but most visitors are astonished to discover incredible geographic diversity. There are 500-million-year-old marble outcrops on the top of the Takaka Hills in Nelson, while volcanic ash and

pumice have created a barren, desert-like landscape in the central North Island. Franz Josef is one of the fastest-moving glaciers in the world and the Marlborough Sounds are a labyrinth of islands and waterways. Parched tussock country and strange rocky outcrops cover Central Otago, and the Canterbury Plains spread wide and flat as evidence of pre-human glacial erosion.

Despite all this earthly fury, the land has been blessed with an endless coastline of stunning beaches—white or golden sand on the east coasts, black or gray on the west coasts. Craters have filled to create jewel-like lakes, and endless rivers and streams feed lush flora.

Flora & Fauna

For 70 million years, New Zealand has been completely separate from all other land-masses. We've been left with some pretty strange creatures as a result: four flight-less birds—the kiwi, weka, kakapo, and takahe—along with an ancient reptile (the tuatara) directly descended from the dinosaurs. The kiwi, of course, has been embraced as a national symbol, so much so that many New Zealanders are quite happy to be called Kiwis themselves. And that odd spiky "lizard," the tuatara, is being encouraged to breed itself silly to ensure it'll be around for future generations to marvel at.

Our native birds are a rich lot. The bellbird, plain of feather and easily missed, is the songster supreme. The handsome inky tui, with his white-tufted neck, comes a close second. The flightless weka is rowdy rather than tuneful, and you'll see him in the bush or poking his nose into campsites. The green-and-orange kea is a cheeky mountain parrot with a reputation for mischief on the ski fields and in high-country camps. Attracted to anything shiny, he'll lift things if he can, but not before chewing the windshield wipers on your car. His big beak means business, so don't feed him. You'll be delighted by nesting albatrosses and gannets, elegant white herons, penguins, and many more.

New Zealand has no native mammals. It was the first Polynesian settlers who brought in both the dog and the rat. Captain Cook then arrived with pigs, goats, fowl, and probably more rats. As more foreign animals were introduced, it became necessary to introduce other animals to control those that had become pests. We now have more than 33 introduced species of mammals, 34 species of birds, 14 species of freshwater fish, at least 1,000 species of introduced insects, plus an Australian lizard and frog or two. Unfortunately, a good many of the above are pests.

We have no snakes, predatory animals, or deadly critters of any kind. The only one that comes close is the poisonous katipo spider, which

> *The chubby* kereru *(wood pigeon) is everyone's favorite bird.*

you're unlikely to even see, unless you're on the western beaches of the North Island and spot a small black spider with a bright red stripe on its abdomen. There are sometimes sharks in the waters around New Zealand. Please ask the locals about this, even though shark attacks are rare.

When it comes to flora, we have diverse vegetation—moss-covered rainforests and dense primeval forests

of ancient podocarp trees. Palms and Norfolk pines, bougainvillea, flame trees, and hibiscus are in the far north—not to mention our forest of giant kauri trees. Tortured-looking alpine plants, brilliant lichens, beech forests, and gigantic tree ferns flourish in the south. Some 84% of New Zealand's flowering plants are found nowhere else in the world.

New Zealand in High & Popular Culture

> *Over a decade after the release of* Lord of the Rings, *thousands of visitors still flock to film locations.*

Literature

Katherine Mansfield (1888–1923) put New Zealand on the literary map with her still-admired short stories set in New Zealand (though she spent most of her adult life in Europe). Among contemporary fiction writers, Keri Hulme won the prestigious Booker McConnell Prize for *The Bone People* in 1985; Janet Frame is famous for *Owls Do Cry, An Angel at My Table,* and several others; Owen Marshall is perhaps our finest living short-story writer; and Barry Crump (1935–1996) is a legend of a completely unique, raw, backcountry style, having produced books like *A Good Keen Man* and *Hang On a Minute Mate.*

Top Maori writers include Witi Ihimaera, Patricia Grace, and Alan Duff. In addition, Maurice Gee, Maurice Shadbolt, Fiona Kidman, and Lauris Edmond all warrant attention.

Film

Filmmaker Jane Campion attracted world attention with *The Piano* (1993), which was nominated for nine categories at the Academy Awards. (Anna Paquin of Wellington won the best supporting actress Oscar.)

Director Peter Jackson grabbed headlines when he secured Hollywood funding for *The Lord of the Rings,* which was filmed in 2000 with the biggest film budget ever. Jackson had made a name for himself with *Heavenly Creatures* (1994), winner of the Silver Lion at the Venice Film Festival, and his *Lord of the Rings* trilogy went on to win a cluster of Oscars. Jackson has since added to his success with the blockbuster *King Kong* (2005). Weta Workshop in Wellington (which won numerous Academy Awards for its visual effects, make-up, and costume work on Jackson's films)

operate a mini-museum (Weta Cave, p. 265, ⑪), and there are numerous location tours all over New Zealand.

Two of Maori author Alan Duff's novels have also been made into successful films; *Once Were Warriors* (1994) and its sequel, *What Becomes of the Broken Hearted?* (1999) shocked audiences with their true-to-life violent portrayal of Maori gang society. More recently, *Whale Rider* (2002), about the struggles of a young Maori girl, won international acclaim from movie audiences.

The very fact that we have such diverse landscapes within a small country has also attracted international filmmakers, keen to film here. Much of *The Lion, The Witch and The Wardrobe* (2005) was filmed in the South Island. Tom Cruise filmed *The Last Samurai* (2002) in the North Island's Taranaki district. Indian Bollywood film crews are also regular visitors.

Music

We've also turned out our fair share of songbirds—none more famous than internationally regarded opera singer Dame Kiri Te Kanawa. On the pop scene, Crowded House and Tim Finn had big international hits in the 1980s and 90s. Today we have a slew of Auckland-based rap artists making it big. Last but not least, Hayley Westernra has won hearts worldwide with her pop-opera crossover albums.

Eating & Drinking in New Zealand

> There's hardly a single New Zealander who hasn't dined on fish and chips at some point in his or her life.

My best advice to anyone coming to New Zealand is to plan plenty of exercise so that you'll be perpetually hungry and therefore well able to justify every single indulgence that you're likely to be faced with. Forget restraint and prepare to be surprised by the level of sophistication of the top New Zealand dining experiences. This is a land of edible bounty: Canterbury lamb; Central Otago pinot noir; Bluff and Nelson oysters; Nelson scallops; Kaikoura crayfish (lobster); West Coast whitebait; South Island venison; Waiheke cabernet sauvignon; Marlborough green-lipped mussels; Gisborne chardonnay; Akaroa salmon; Stewart Island blue cod; Central Otago cherries and apricots. You shouldn't miss any of it.

Within the restaurant scene itself, there has been a revolution in the last decade. Fine dining (silver service) still lingers in a few city pockets, but the upmarket trend is toward fine food in more relaxed, contemporary settings. Pacific Rim has been the primary culinary influence for some time, although many chefs have stopped using the term, preferring Modern or Contemporary New Zealand terminology instead. Still, the end result is much the same: a combination of Pacific and Asian ingredients combined to perfection and presented elegantly. You'll be spoiled with all the choices in this category, especially in Auckland, Wellington, Christchurch, and Queenstown (in that order).

For moderately priced, casual meals, including lunches, there are now so many cafes, restaurants, and bars it seems silly to try to define what each delivers. In short, you will seldom be without a choice. Most prepare good soups, salads, and main courses based around beef, lamb, chicken, fish, and vegetarian choices. Many others specialize in counter food rather than menu-based options and include panini, pastries, pies, sandwiches, filled Italian and French breads, and salads. Just be aware that many of the more casual cafe/bar

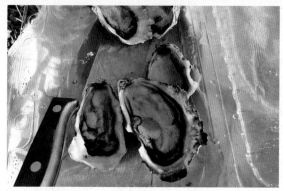

> *When it's Bluff oyster season, fans are prepared to pay exorbitant sums for this juicy delicacy.*

establishments offering lighter meals often turn into rowdy drinking holes after 11pm.

There are a huge number of ethnic restaurants in all the main cities. Indian, Thai, Vietnamese, Chinese, Japanese, and Korean are the most common but you'll also come across Burmese, Afghani, Turkish, Mexican, Spanish, Italian, French, and Middle Eastern choices in Auckland, Wellington, and Christchurch. In Thai, Chinese, Vietnamese, and Indian restaurants in particular, you'll be able to enjoy great meals for a very reasonable price.

On top of the usual restaurant and cafe experiences, you'd be doing yourself a disservice if you miss trying a few of our iconic Kiwi meals. Fish and chips, for instance. The fish and chip shop is still one of the most popular takeaway choices in this country and you'll find one in virtually every town and village in the country. It goes without saying that some are better than others. Many still offer the meal—deep-fried battered fish and fat potato fries—wrapped in newspaper, which is how most New Zealanders prefer them, but some have opted for fancier packaging.

The small meat pie is still a Kiwi favorite too. Every dairy and service station in the country has a pie warmer—perhaps in part because the meat pie is famed as a hangover cure after a night of heavy drinking.

The barbecue is a summer favorite. Almost every family in New Zealand will probably have a barbecue at some point during the summer months. Our balmy evenings lend themselves to eating outdoors and there's nothing quite like it. It invariably includes sausages and steak—often wrapped in bread and smothered in tomato sauce—accompanied by salads. Like most things, though, the barbecue is also changing, and many people now apply as much culinary invention to the once-humble barbecue as they do any meal. I have friends who stay at the beach every summer and they live off freshly barbecued fish, scallops, and crayfish plucked straight from the ocean and enhanced with their own particular sauces and spices. It's as good as any restaurant meal.

Last but certainly not least, the traditional Maori hangi, where food is cooked underground, is a must-do experience while you're in New Zealand. Traditionally, it involves lighting a fire and putting large stones in the embers to heat. Simultaneously, a large pit is dug. The heated rocks are then transferred into the pit and covered with wet sacking and/or wet newspapers. Prepared lamb, chickens, pork, fish, shellfish, and vegetables (most commonly kumara, potato, pumpkin, or cabbage), are wrapped in leaves, placed in baskets, lowered into the cooking pit, covered with more newspaper and earth, and left to steam. The moist, tender, melt-in-your-mouth food is lifted a few hours later.

The distinctive smoky flavors of hangi food can be an acquired taste. If you'd like to try it, ask at visitor centers for tour operators who include a hangi. You'll find this easiest in Rotorua, where a number of hotels offer hangi meals as part of a cultural performance package. Bear in mind, though, that because of modern health and safety regulations, many hotels now prepare their hangi meals using gas-fired ovens, so the meal will lack some of the unique, traditional smoky flavors that, to my mind, make a hangi meal.

Other distinctly New Zealand culinary experiences

include the sheer craziness of the annual Hokitika Wildfoods Festival, where the policy is "if it's not moving, it's edible;" the numerous annual wine and food festivals; and farmers' markets held in individual provinces. All are always well-publicized at information centers.

A word on service

New Zealand has not "grown up" with a long tradition of service in restaurants, so there will be times when you wonder if we even know what the word "service" means. For many young people, being a waitress or waiter is a reluctantly sought holiday job to earn money for university studies—and sadly, it often shows. However, the competitive market is forcing restaurant owners to wake up to the importance of good, friendly, smiling service, and many polytechnics now offer proper training. It is heartening to see a gradual swing toward a belief that restaurant service can be a career option, not just a long-suffering ordeal.

Service glitches are more noticeable in smaller provincial centers and some of that can be attributed to a lack of suitable employees in the district. Areas such as the West Coast face the reality of young people moving out to the cities, while major tourist centers like Queenstown tend to have a very transient population of restaurant employees.

New Zealand restaurants are either licensed to serve alcohol or BYO (bring your own), and some are both. BYO of course is cheaper, as you don't have to pay the

> *There are some 150 different beers available at The Malthouse, in Wellington.*

restaurant's surcharge on the wine. Some BYO establishments do charge a corkage fee (usually NZ$3–NZ$8) for opening the wine bottle. *Note:* BYO means wine only, not beer or any other alcoholic beverages.

Important note

All eateries are now smoke-free. This is a government edict, with smoking banned across the board in all restaurants, nightclubs, and public buildings.

Tipping is not customary in New Zealand, although I've never met a New Zealander who doesn't like a show of appreciation for good service and value. But that's relative. My policy is *don't tip for the sake of it.* You may be used to that in your own country, but I maintain that that does nothing to foster an improvement in New Zealand serving standards, which, let's face it, still need work. If you feel you've had a special dining experience and would like to

reward the staff, then do so by all means, but be aware that many restaurants operate a shared tipping system, so your favorite waitress or waiter may not be the only recipient of your good will. She/he may have to share the goodies with others who may not deserve it—something I personally would like to see changed.

Dining hours vary from one eatery to another. Many cafes and restaurants open for coffee from around 9am to 10am and serve lunch between noon and 2pm or 3pm, reverting to coffee and snack service only after that, then serving dinner from 6pm on. Others open for dinner only and that is almost always from 6pm onward.

Other than that, it's all pretty straightforward—eat and enjoy! Oh, and don't forget New Zealand wine. With the many international award-winners to our credit, I can assure you, you *will* be tempted!

Maori Language & Culture

Taumatawhakatangihangakoauauotamate rip kapikimaungahoronukupokaiwhenuakitanatahu

> Don't worry, even New Zealanders struggle with some Maori place names—especially when they're this long.

The Maori language is a Polynesian dialect. It was first given a written form in the early 19th century by missionaries and British linguists. In the latter part of the 19th century, Maori were forced to adopt the English language in schools, and it wasn't until the 1960s that a strong Maori resurgence began. The Maori Language Act of 1987 really changed things. It made Maori an official New Zealand language along with English and a Maori Language Commission was set up to create authentic Maori names for government departments and major organizations. Today, there are Maori radio stations and television channels. Maori is taught in all levels of the education system.

When you visit New Zealand, you will be surrounded by things Maori: Words, place names, and many tourist ventures are all indications of this revitalized culture. No one expects you to be able to pronounce many Maori names—it's hard enough for those who have spent all their lives here—but the following tips might make it easier for you. Some Maori words are both singular and plural and require no s (like the English words deer and fish). Maori, Pakeha, and kea are all good examples. There are only 15 letters in the Maori alphabet: A, E, H, I, K, M, N, O, P, R, T, U, W, NG, and WH, and every syllable in Maori ends in a vowel. The vowel sounds are of great importance and when two vowels come together, each is given its proper sound. WH is usually pronounced as an F.

In the last ten years, the inclusion of Maori words and phrases in everyday life has become increasingly common. As visitors here, you'll come across a number of words that may seem incomprehensible. Kia Ora (hello) is probably the simplest and the most common. Kai (food), is also in common usage, as are whanau (family), iwi (tribe) and tangata whenua (literally "people of the land," in reference to Maori) .

Tourism New Zealand and many tourism operators have also adopted a number of traditional Maori values as part of their contemporary business practice. These include manaakitanga (hospitality/nurturing), kaitiakitanga (guardianship), rangatiratanga (leadership), and kotahitanga (unity). The two you'll come across most often as a visitor to this country are manaakitangi, which is an all encompassing sense of hospitality, sharing and taking care of, and kaitiakitanga, which is most used (in a tourism context) in relation to the guardianship of treasures (taonga) and the bounty of the land and its resources.

Maori for Beginners

Here's a list of the most commonly used prefixes and suffixes for place names:

Ao Cloud

Ika Fish

Nui Big, or plenty of

Roto Lake

Rua Cave, or hollow, or two

Tahi One, single

Te The

Wai Water

Whanga Bay, inlet, or stretch of water

These are other frequently used words:

Ariki Chief or priest

Atua Supernatural being, such as a god or demon

Haka Dance

Hangi An oven made by filling a hole with heated stones, and the feast roasted in it

Hongi The pressing together of noses in traditional greeting

Karakia Prayer or spell

Kaumatua Elder

Kereru Wood pigeon

Kia Ora Hello, Go well

Kumara Sweet potato

Mana Authority, prestige, psychic force

Marae Courtyard, village common

Mere War club made of greenstone (jade)

Pa Stockade or fortified place

Pakeha Caucasian person; primarily used to refer to those of European descent

Poi Bulrush ball with string attached, twirled in action song

Tangi Funeral mourning or lamentation

Taonga Treasure

Tapu Under religious or superstitious restriction (taboo)

Tiki Human image, usually carved of greenstone

Whare House

A Word on Cultural Protocol

If you want to visit a Maori marae, always make sure you ask permission first but be aware that, unless you are staying with a Maori family, or participating in a commercially run tour, you are unlikely to gain access. You must never eat, chew gum, or take food onto the premises. Some will also request that you take off your shoes and some may have particular rules about visits by women during certain ceremonies. And never take photographs inside a meeting house. If you are uncertain about whether or not photographs are appropriate, just ask. In short, behavior on the marae is governed by strict protocol and you WILL be challenged if you ignore these rules. To save yourself and others a great deal of embarrassment, please do not offend. But don't panic, you will be instructed on what to do and what not to do.

15
The Best Special Interest Trips

Outdoor Activities A to Z

Here's a brief overview of the most popular outdoor activities available in New Zealand. For my recommendations on the best places to go and the best operators to go with, see listings in the individual destination chapters.

Bicycling

Bicycle touring is a breathtakingly fresh way of seeing New Zealand and it's an increasingly popular choice, especially on the South Island, where traffic densities are lower and the scenery is so spectacular. There are numerous companies offering guided cycle tours—everything from short day tours through vineyards to more serious challenges like a month-long tour of the whole country. The best news of all is the current development of **Nga Haerenga, the New Zealand Cycle Trail**, a series of Great Rides to form a national cycleway. The government has allotted more than $NZ50 million to its development over the next three years and work has begun on linking several existing provincial cycleways. The first Great Ride, for instance, opened near South Island's Hanmer Springs in late 2010. Check www.tourism.govt.nz for updates.

Regardless of where you bike, always wear your helmet—they are mandatory in New Zealand and you will be fined for not wearing one. Also, remember the following: Cyclists are not permitted on motorways (freeways); they must always ride on the left side of the road; and all traffic turning left gives way to everything on the right. At night, make sure you have a working white front light and a red rear light and reflector. It doesn't hurt to have pedal and jacket reflectors. A few cities—Christchurch is the standout in this regard—have designated cycle lanes within city limits, which makes pedaling safer.

Fishing

Any prospective fisherman in New Zealand should get a copy of *Sports Fishing Guide*, a free booklet produced by the **New Zealand Fish and Game Council** (☎ 04/499-4767; www.fishandgame.org.nz). This guide supplies you with the myriad rules and regulations you need to know. It also gives details on major freshwater fishing spots. **The New Zealand Professional Fishing Guides Association**

(☎ 06/867-7874; www.nzpfga.com) may also be helpful. Go to www.newzealandfishing.com for *New Zealand Fishing Magazine* online. For assistance in planning a New Zealand fishing holiday from North America, contact **The Best of New Zealand Adventure Travel**, 2817 Wilshire Blvd., Santa Monica, CA 90403 (☎ 800/528-6129 in the U.S. or 310/998-5880). This agency specializes in angler activities and has a 48-page brochure called *The Best of New Zealand Fly Fishing* (which also includes information on saltwater fishing). More information can also be found at www.bestofnzflyfishing.com.

FRESHWATER FISHING

New Zealand is the world's best place to fish for wild brown trout during the season, which lasts from the first Saturday in October to the end of April. During this time, all rivers and streams are open for brown and rainbow trout but local restrictions may apply. Call **Fish & Game New Zealand's Trout Line** (☎ 0800/

Keeping New Zealand Waterways Clean

Sadly, many New Zealand waterways now carry the unwanted organism *Didymosphenia geminate* (didymo), also known as "rock snot," which is a fresh water diatom (type of alga) that was first reported on the Lower Waiau River in the South Island in 2004. Biosecurity New Zealand (www.biosecurity.govt.nz) has since declared the whole of the South island a Controlled Area for didymo. This means that fishermen, boat owners, and others using waterways for pleasure activities are legally required to do everything they can to prevent its spread. Unfortunately didymo is a microscopic pest that can be spread in a single drop of water. You therefore need to ensure that all watersport equipment, including boots, waders, fishing lines, boats, skis, and anything else used in the water is thoroughly clean and dry before moving from one waterway to another. As the name suggests, when didymo takes over a waterway, it forms a slimy brown mass that attaches itself to everything. Please help us contain this pest by taking extreme care not to aid in its spread.

> *PREVIOUS PAGE Tongariro Crossing is one of New Zealand's "Great Walks." THIS PAGE A new national cycleway of Great Rides is under construction.*

876-885; www.fishandgame.org.nz) to get the details. There are several areas where you can fish year-round: the Rotorua district and Lake Taupo on the North Island (chapter 6), and Lake Te Anau and Lake Wakatipu on the South Island (chapter 12).

The Tongariro River, near Turangi (chapter 6), is one of the prime trout-fishing rivers in the world. May through October are the best months to snag rainbow and brown trout, which average nearly 2 kilograms (4½ lbs.). This period is also good for fishing in lakes Taupo and Rotorua. Lake Rotorua is not stocked but it has one of the highest catch rates in the district.

The Eastern Fish and Game region is also an angler's land of opportunity, with a huge range of fishing opportunities and diversity in both lake and river fishing. In particular, you'll find outstanding surf-casting and game fishing along the Pacific Coast Highway (St. Hwy. 35) (chapter 7).

Fishing is good in almost all areas of the South Island. In Nelson (chapter 10), you'll get rainbow trout and also quinnat (chinook) salmon in many places but it's the brown trout that's king of these mixed waters. Canterbury (chapter 11) is best known for its prolific salmon runs that enter the large braided rivers such as the Rakaia and Waimakariri. The region's high-country rivers are known for small numbers of big fish.

In the West Coast region, the Waitaki and Rangitata rivers have been known to land trophy chinook salmon of 15 kilograms (33 lb.). In Southland (chapter 13), dozens of rivers, streams, and lakes hold brown and rainbow trout, plus quinnat salmon. The waters of this region are widely known throughout New Zealand, but you have to be a competent fisherman and know your way around to be successful. Fish and Game Otago has an excellent book, *Guide to Trout Fishing in Otago,* which covers 140 waters and gives information on access and methods. Southland Fish and Game, P.O. Box 159, Invercargill (☎ 03/214-4501; fishgame@southnet.co.nz), will be happy to supply maps, advice, information, and guides.

If fishing is your passion, consider investing some cash in a good guide. Be warned, however, that freshwater fishing guides in New Zealand are not cheap; some run as high as NZ$1,200 to NZ$1,800 per day for one or two people. If you shop around, cheaper deals can be found.

SALTWATER & BIG-GAME FISHING

Deep-sea fishing is at its best along the magnificent 500km (311 miles) of Northland's coastline, slipping down into the Bay of Plenty. Waters less than an hour out from shore can yield marlin, shark (mako, thresher, hammerhead, tiger), five species of tuna, broadbill, and yellowtail. The season runs from mid-January to April and you'll find well-equipped bases at the Bay of Islands in Northland (chapter 4), Whitianga on the Coromandel (chapter 5), and Tauranga and Whakatane in the Bay of Plenty (chapter 5). You can also fish for kahawai, snapper, and more anywhere along the New Zealand coast. Licenses are not required.

Golf

New Zealand is a nation of golfers. There are approximately 400 private and public courses that offer plenty of opportunities. And we're lucky to have some of the best, yet cheapest, golfing facilities you'll find anywhere. Greens fees are well below the world's average—you'll pay anything from NZ$10 to NZ$135 for 18 holes on a good course and up to NZ$150 to NZ$450 for the country's top links. Clubs, equipment, and a motorized cart (trundler) can be rented.

Diehards hit the courses year-round, but the best time to golf is from October to April, when temperatures range from 61° to 70°F (16° to 21°C). Courses tend to be crowded on weekends, less so during the week.

For more information, contact the **New Zealand Golf Association** (☎ 09/485-3230; www.nzga.co.nz). For golf packages, contact **New Zealand Golf Excursions USA, Inc.,** 2141 Rosecrans Ave., no. 1199, El Segundo, CA 90245 (☎ 800/622-6606 in the U.S.), or **Kiwi Golf Tours** (☎ 800/873-6360 in the U.S.).

In New Zealand, try **Golf NZ** (☎ 06/870-8740; www.golfnewzealand.co.nz), which offers multi-day tours for 12 to 36 golfers and partners starting at NZ$1,600 per person including accommodations, travel, and golf; or **Big Boys Golf Tours** (☎ 025/512-020; www.bigboysgolf.co.nz), which offers tours of top golf courses in the Auckland region. Also check www.bestofgolfnewzealand.com for golf holiday planning.

Hiking

Hiking (also known as tramping) is one of the best ways to explore the pristine forests, clear blue lakes, sparkling rivers, fern-filled valleys, and snow-capped peaks of New Zealand. The **Department of Conservation** (DOC), P.O. Box 10-420, Wellington (☎ 04/471-0726; www.doc.govt.nz), maintains more than 12,500km (7,767 miles) of tracks (trails) and 1,000 back-country huts throughout New Zealand's 13 national parks and numerous scenic reserves.

Both short walks and multi-day hikes are available, but much will depend on your fitness level and the amount of time you have. Consider whether you want to be a freedom walker (independent) or a guided walker. Independent walkers can sleep in huts with bunk beds, cooking facilities, and toilets, but they must carry their own food, bedding, and cooking utensils. These overnight huts are sometimes staffed, should you need any assistance or advice along the way.

Hiking in New Zealand is best tackled from late November to April, when temperatures are moderate. From May to October, alpine tracks can be difficult and often dangerous once snow falls. Don't forget to bring broken-in boots, a daypack, water bottles, sunglasses, sunscreen, a flashlight (known as a "torch" in New Zealand), and a hat. **Remember:** You should never attempt any multi-day hikes without first checking in, paying your fees, and giving DOC staff an idea of your plans. Also, always be aware of changeable weather conditions and the very real potential for hypothermia—even in summer. The importance of this cannot be underestimated. Every tourist season dozens of people ignore this sound advice and a good number end up being rescued by emergency services. Be warned that in some circumstances you will now have pay for the rescue services and that is never a cheap exercise.

SHORT WALKS

There are literally hundreds of fabulous short walks through all sorts of landscapes. From a leisurely stroll along a city promenade to deserted beaches, fern-lined bush walks, forest trails, volcanic wanders—you name it and you can probably have it. Every region has its hidden treats. Look in the regional chapters for some of the most popular choices and seek advice from any visitor center or Department of Conservation office, most of which have an extensive array of walking brochures. Short walks tend to range from 45 minutes to a full day.

HIKING SAFARIS

Many companies offer combinations of hiking, kayaking, and other adventures in one or more areas. The **New Zealand Guided Walks Network** (www.walknewzealand.com) was set up in conjunction with Tourism New Zealand to raise the profile of high-quality guided walking experiences available in New Zealand. The Walks Network is a group of independent companies that operate guided walks in our national parks, wilderness areas, and special reserves, providing the best available accommodations with meals, comfortable bedding, and bathroom facilities. Qualified guides provide comprehensive interpretation of natural and cultural history; walkers need only carry personal items—not including food or bedding.

MULTI-DAY WALKS

New Zealand has some of the best multi-day walks in the world. The trails are well maintained and take you through unforgettable scenery. Several can also be done as guided walks, which makes them accessible to people of all fitness levels. Not everyone can agree on which one is the best walk but the Department of Conservation (www.doc.govt.nz) has identified these tramping tracks as the **Great Walks** in New Zealand: the Waikaremoana, the Tongariro Crossing, and the Ruapehu Circuit on the North Island; the Abel Tasman Coastal, Heaphy, Routeburn, Milford, and Kepler tracks on the South Island; and the Rakiura Track on Stewart Island.

If you'd like to strike out on your own, contact the **Department of Conservation,** P.O. Box 10-420, Wellington (☎ 04/471-0726; www.doc.govt.nz). It maintains visitor centers throughout the country. The Milford and the Routeburn are generally the only two tracks where freedom walkers need to make advance reservations. Facilities along other trails are on a first-come, first-served basis. The DOC advises against children under 10 years old attempting any of the serious multi-day hikes. The main multi-day hikes are outlined in the appropriate regional chapters.

Horseback Riding

Like cycling, horseback riding is a beautiful way to see the details of the country. It is the perfect way to get an up-close-and-personal view, rather than flashing through in a fast-moving vehicle. Unlike most cycling tours, though, horseback riding operators will take you off the beaten track, into landscapes you would otherwise never see. Most offer short-term outings—that is, between 1- and 4-hour treks—and cater to a wide range of riding abilities, with horses of varying sizes and temperaments. One of the best providers of longer horseback riding treks is North Canterbury-based ★★★ **Alpine Horse Safaris** (☎ 03/314-4293; www.alpinehorse.co.nz), which offers 3- to 12-day treks covering up to 400 kilometers (249 miles) of some of the most beautiful and testing landscapes in the South Island. Laurie and Jenny O'Carroll are very experienced riders and trekkers and you'll be in safe hands as they guide you across mountain passes and scree slopes, across rivers and through beech forests, spending around six hours a day in the saddle. Accommodation is provided in mountain camps and musterers' huts. **Cape Farewell Horse Treks,** 23 McGowan St., Puponga, Collingwood, Nelson (☎ 03/524-8031; www.horsetreksnz.com), have 1-hour to 7-day horse treks across the farmlands and beaches of the Abel Tasman region, near Nelson.

Kayaking

The prime kayaking spot is Abel Tasman National Park (chapter 10), where the water is so clear that boats appear to float in midair. Sea kayaking is also popular in the Bay of Islands (chapter 4), around Coromandel Peninsula (chapter 5), in Marlborough Sounds (chapter 10), in Milford Sound (chapter 12), and around Banks Peninsula (chapter 11) and Otago Peninsula (chapter 13). You're never far from water in New Zealand and even beginners will find plenty of places for a safe paddle.

Try to book your adventures with members of **SKOANZ,** the Sea Kayak Operators Association of New Zealand (www.skoanz.org.nz), who must adhere to a code of practice covering safety, service, guides, and environment.

Rock Climbing

Rock climbing and bouldering are alive and well in New Zealand. The Canterbury region (chapter 11) is known to provide the highest concentration of great rock climbing routes in the country. If you want to join a rock climbing course, **Wanaka Rock Climbing** (☎ 03/443-6411; www.wanakarock.co.nz), offers 1-, 3- and 5-day courses in the beautiful Matukituki Valley on the edge of Mount Aspiring National Park, near Wanaka (chapter 12).

Sailing

Given the running of the 1999–2000 and the 2002–2003 America's Cup Challenge in Auckland, it's an understatement to say that sailing is popular. For the warmest, balmiest, most subtropical experiences, head for Northland (chapter 4), Auckland (chapter 3), and the Bay of Plenty (chapter 5). There's plenty of excellent sailing farther south, too.

For bareboat and skippered charters, contact **Moorings Rainbow Yacht Charters,** Bay of Islands (☎ 09/377-4840; moorings@onenz.co.nz), or **Royal Akarana Yacht Club,** Auckland (☎ 09/524-9945; www.rayc.org.nz). In Marlborough Sounds, **Compass Charters,** 20 Beach Rd., Waikawa (☎ 03/573-8332; www.compass-charters.co.nz), offers budget to luxury yacht and launch charters. For general information on sailing, contact **Yachting New Zealand** (☎ 09/367-1471; www.yachtingnz.org.nz).

Scuba Diving

With over 32,000km (20,000 miles) of coastline, New Zealand has no shortage of diving opportunities. The best diving seas are around the Poor Knights Islands in Northland (chapter 4). This is where you'll find the wreck of the *Rainbow Warrior,* which is now covered quite nicely with reef formations. Visibility ranges from 20 to 69m (66–226 ft.) in the best months (Feb–June). Another excellent dive spot, renowned for its crystal-clear waters, is the much chillier Stewart Island (chapter 13). Brave divers can also immerse themselves in the murky, tannin-stained waters of Milford Sound (chapter 12) for a unique experience. No matter where you take the plunge, you must have evidence of your diving certification with you. For details, contact the **Dive Industry of New Zealand** (☎ 09/849-5896). Good resources include **Dive New Zealand** magazine online (www.divenewzealand.com); the internationally renowned **Waikato Dive Centre** (☎ 07/849-1922), which offers courses and dive trips; and Napier-based **Adventure Dive** (☎ 06/843-5148) for courses and dive tours.

Skiing & Snowboarding

When the sun warms up in the Northern Hemisphere, skiers and snowboarders come down to the Southern Hemisphere. The ski season generally runs from late June to September. The country has 13 conventional ski areas; as an added bonus at Aoraki/Mt. Cook, you can fly by ski plane or helicopter to the 2,400m (7,874-ft.) head of the Tasman Glacier and ski down the 14km (8⅔-mile) run. For more information on New Zealand skiing, check out the **New Zealand Snowsports Council** (☎ 04/499-8135; www.snow.co.nz), or the websites www.goski.com and www.onthesnow.com. For up-to-the-minute South Island ski details, check out www.nzski.com.

DOWNHILL SKIING

The two major ski fields on the North Island are **Whakapapa and Turoa,** on the slopes of Mount Ruapehu in Tongariro National Park (chapter 6), now both owned by a single company, Ruapehu Alpine Lifts. Ruapehu, with a simmering crater lake, is an active volcano and extends up some 2,760m (9,055 ft.), making it the North Island's highest peak. It erupted in 1995 and again in 1996, effectively ending all skiing activity for about 2 years. Whakapapa (☎ 07/892-3738; www.mtruapehu.com) offers challenges for intermediate skiers and snowboarders and has good beginners' packages. Turoa (☎ 06/385-8456; www.mtruapehu.com) has great terrain for all levels of skiing, plus half-pipes for snowboarders. It also has good packages for skiing and snowboarding schools.

On the South Island, **Mount Hutt Ski Field** (☎ 03/302-8811; www.nzski.com) is 1¾ hours from Christchurch (chapter 11), with a good shuttle service operating from the city. There are numerous club fields close to Christchurch, especially in the Porters Pass region. You'll find information on some of these fields at www.snow.co.nz, www.dobson.co.nz, www.porterheights.co.nz, www.mtlyford.co.nz, www.mtcheeseman.com, www.broken

river.co.nz, www.craigieburn.co.nz, www.templebasin.co.nz, www.mtolympus.co.nz, www.foxpeak.co.nz, and www.skihanmer.co.nz.

Coronet Peak (☎ 03/442-4620; www.nzski.com) is 18km (11 miles) from Queenstown (chapter 12), with moderate to challenging fields. It's the oldest commercial field in the South Island and has several chairlifts including a new six-seater high-speed lift, beginners' facilities, and good variety for experienced skiers. **The Remarkables** (☎ 03/442-4615), 23km (14 miles) from Queenstown, have more diversity for experienced skiers. You'll find a smaller field that's best for intermediate skiers, with three chairlifts, one magic carpet, and a beginner handle tow. **Cardrona Alpine Resort** (☎ 03/443-7411; www.cardrona.com) is a middle-range field with good family facilities, including brand-new social facilities, but it's a bit tame for experienced skiers. It lies 57km (35 miles) from Queenstown and 33km (21 miles) from Wanaka. **Treble Cone** (☎ 03/443-7443; www.treblecone.co.nz),

> International skiers and snowboarders flock to New Zealand ski fields in winter.

23km (14 miles) from Wanaka (about 35 minutes' drive), has the newest and biggest express chairlift in the country, which has improved the flow of skiers on the field. It's one of the more challenging fields and has a lot of variety, with very steep areas and narrow valleys. It also has a good base lodge and the best food facilities of all the southern ski areas. The Treble Cone area backs up against the Harris Mountains, where there are heli-skiing opportunities.

Lift ticket prices in New Zealand range from NZ$99 to NZ$120; ski, boot, and pole rentals run from NZ$40 to NZ$60; and lessons are from NZ$110 for a half-day group class. Costs are lower for children and all ski fields offer a range of day and multi-day passes, plus online specials.

CROSS-COUNTRY SKIING

Snow Farm (☎ 03/443-0300; www.snowfarmnz.com), in the Pisa Range, near Wanaka (chapter 12) is the only Nordic ski field of its kind in New Zealand. The area has ideal terrain for first-time cross-country skiers as well as good conditions for advanced skiers.

Sloping Off to Ski School

The **Mount Hutt Ski School** (☎ 03/308-5074; www.mthutt.co.nz) has an extensive training program that caters to everyone from rank beginners all the way through to advanced skiers. It also offers extensive snowboarding instruction. **Whakapapa Ski & Snowboard School** (☎ 07/892-3410) makes it easy for everyone, with special learning packages and beginners-only slopes. Intermediate or advanced skiers can also improve their skills with group or private lessons. **Cardrona Development Centre** (☎ 03/443-7411; www.cardrona.com) has an extensive program of beginners' lessons, private and group lessons, specialist improvement workshops, ski board instruction, plus an instructor-training program. **Treble Cone Ski School** (☎ 03/443-7443; www.treblecone.com) has everything from the TC Cat Club Junior Ski School, for kids 3 to 12, to middle-range instruction and workshops to women's workshops, carving clinics, snowboard holiday camps, and a Masters program for competitive skiers over 30.

SNOWBOARDING

Treble Cone is "home to some of the best gully runs in New Zealand, which form into awesome quarter pipes, hips, and spines." So says one of the experts on www.board-theworld.com, who rates Treble Cone eighth in the world for freeriding. Treble Cone is rated the top freeriding resort in Australasia and is best for experienced boarders. It has an active training program.

Cardrona is better for beginner and intermediate boarders. It has undulating terrain, lots of gullies, and four half-pipes, and it offers a whole heap of support for snowboarders in general. It also has half-pipe camps throughout the season for all levels. **Coronet Peak** has lots of long groomed runs to tabletops, with quarter-pipes, kickers, and rollers. It's essentially a tourist field and is more expensive. **The Remarkables** offers pretty ho-hum snowboarding on the field itself, but the out-of-bounds territory offers extreme boarding for the daring. There's good stuff up in the backcountry if you're prepared to hike. Generally, though, the Remarkables is not a destination of choice for boarders.

Farther north, there's good snowboarding at **Temple Basin Ski Area,** in Arthurs Pass (☎ 03/377-7788), and at **Turoa** (mentioned earlier, under "skiing").

New Zealand Surf'n'Snow Tours (☎ 09/828-0426; www.newzealandsnow-tours.co.nz) has a wide range of North and South Island snowboard packages. **Gravity Action,** 19 Shotover St., Queenstown (☎ 03/442-5277; www.gravityaction.com), has their finger on the pulse when it comes to all things snowboard-related, including good hire rates.

Surfing & Windsurfing

Every surfer will tell you his or her favorite beach is best, although it does seem unanimous that Eastland and Gisborne (chapter 7) reliably turn out some of the best waves in the country. Whangamata and Mount Maunganui, in Bay of Plenty (chapter 5), and Taylors Mistake, near Christchurch (chapter 11), are others to consider. **New Zealand Surf Tours** (☎ 09/832-9622; www.newzealandsurftours.com) offers 1- to 5-day tours of the Auckland and Northland region.

Windsurfing is popular in many areas around Auckland (chapter 3); at Ferrymead in Christchurch (chapter 11); on Lyttelton Harbour, Christchurch; on Otago Peninsula (chapter 13); at Oakura near New Plymouth (chapter 8); and on Wellington Harbour (chapter 9).

White-Water Rafting

The challenging Wairoa, Mohaka, and Kaituna rivers are popular on the North Island; in the south, you'll find action on the Shotover, Kawarau, and Rangitata rivers. You can do this year-round—wet suits and warm clothing are required in winter, though. Operators give instruction, supply equipment, and arrange transfers to and from launch points.

Rapid Sensations, Taupo (☎ 0800/353-435 in NZ; www.rapids.co.nz), takes 3-day trips on the upper Mohaka River. If you want an all-out 9 days of crazy fun, contact **Ultimate Descents,** Motueka (☎ 0800/748-377 in NZ; www.rivers.co.nz), which exposes you to the serious thrills of the Buller, Karamea, and Clarence rivers on the top of the South Island.

Multi-Activity Outfitters

In the United States, **Artisans of Leisure,** 18 East 16th St., Suite 301, New York, NY 10003 (☎ 800/214-8144 in the U.S.; www.artisansofleisure.com), offers exclusive, highly personalized luxury tours for individuals and groups, with New Zealand as one of their most popular destinations. Their tours run 7 to 19 days and combine top rooms in premium lodges with activities that range from wine-tasting to arts and cultural events and outdoor activities. **Nature Expeditions International,** 7860 Peters Rd., Suite F-103, Plantation, Florida (☎ 800/869-0639 in the U.S.; www.natureexp.com), offers 1 to 15 day guided cultural, wildlife, and soft adventure tours to New Zealand. They cater specifically to small, pre-formed groups.

In New Zealand, there are many companies offering escorted tour options. Some of the reputable tour companies include:

- **Contiki Holidays,** P.O. Box 68640, Newton, Auckland (☎ 0800/266-8454 in NZ; www.contiki.com), offering 3- to 15-day coach tours for 18- to 35-year-olds throughout New Zealand.

- **Thrifty Tours,** P.O. Box 31257, Milford, Auckland (☎ 0800/803-550 in NZ, or

> *Cooking schools are springing up all over New Zealand, and they're a perfect match for our wine tours.*

09/359-8380; www.thriftytours.co.nz), with well-planned 2- to 16-day tours.

- **Discover New Zealand,** 120 Albert St., Auckland (☎ 0800/330-188 in NZ, or 09/356-2190; www.discovernewzealand. com), which offers a range of 3- to 8-day tours.

- **Scenic Pacific Tours,** P.O. Box 14037, Christchurch (☎ 0800/500-388 in NZ, or 03/359-3999; www.scenicpacific.co.nz), which offers a large range of day excursions, short tours, and independent holidays.

- **Navigator Tours,** 553 Richmond Rd., Grey Lynn, Auckland (☎ 09/817-1191; www. navigatortours.co.nz), which offers a diverse range of unique, personalized, guided tours throughout New Zealand, staying at high-end accommodation.

Food, Cooking & Wine Trips

A bounty of fresh seasonal ingredients, limitless supplies of fine wine, and a growing appreciation of both, has seen a number of small cooking schools spring up around New Zealand. Day-long or weekend classes are the main focus. One of the best is ★★ **Ruth Pretty Cooking School,** 41 School Rd., Te Horo, north of Wellington (☎ 06/364-3161; www.ruthpretty. co.nz). Ruth is well known in New Zealand

food circles and most weekends from February through December, she stages classes for a maximum of 34 people. She also teaches private, hands-on classes for small groups.

Auckland Seafood School, first floor, Auckland Fish Market, 22 Jellicoe St., Freemans Bay, Auckland (☎ 09/379-1497; www.afm. co.nz), holds regular short courses in its state-of-the-art facility that includes a 66-seat auditorium and a hands-on kitchen with eight self-contained cooking stations. Also in Auckland, **Main Course,** 20 Beaumont St., Auckland (☎09/302-1460; www.maincourse.co.nz), offers courses in everything from seafood to gluten-free to Italian cooking.

In Queenstown, **Kia Toa Cuisine,** at Punatapu Lodge (☎ 03/442-6985; www.cuisine queenstown.com or www.punatapu.com), offers specialized, short-term classes in a luxury lodge environment. From short demonstration classes to hands-on residential weekend courses for individuals or small groups (8–16 people), the focus is always on New Zealand produce. The courses may include foraging for wild foods and visits to farmers' markets, wineries, orchards, local restaurants, and high-country sheep stations.

You'll find details of local wine tours in each regional chapter. In addition, you should arm yourself with both the *Classic New Zealand Wine Trail Guide* and the *Jasons Taste Traveller* guide, which are free from all i-SITE visitor centers around the country.

16
The Savvy Traveler

> Despite what you might think,
> it's still another 3383 miles to
> the South Pole from Bluff.

EQUATOR
2066 nm
3827 km
VANCOUVER
6059 nm
11222 km
SOUTH POLE
3383 nm
6211 km
LOS ANGELES
5709 nm
10479 km
TROPIC OF CAPRICORN
1220 km
659 nm
SYDNEY
UFF
1452 km
TOKYO
4576 nm
8475 km

Before You Go

Government Tourism Offices

To get started, contact the nearest Tourism New Zealand office for a complimentary copy of its *New Zealand Vacation Planner.*

Tourism New Zealand offices can be found in the United States at 501 Santa Monica Blvd., Suite 300, Santa Monica, CA 90401 (☎ 866/639-9325 or 310/395-7480 in the U.S.); in Canada at 888 Dunsmuir St., Suite 1200, Vancouver, BC V6C 3K4 (☎ 800/888-5494 in Canada, or 604/684-2117); in Australia at Level 8, 35 Pitt St., Sydney, NSW 2000 (☎ 02/9247-5222); and in England at New Zealand House, Haymarket, SW1Y 4TQ, London (☎ 020/7930-1662).

The official Tourism New Zealand website is www.newzealand.com. Click on your home country to see the latest deals, with contact information for travel agents. Other useful sites include New Zealand on the Web (www.nz.com), which offers hundreds of excellent links, and NZSki (www.nzski.com) for up-to-the-minute ski information.

When you arrive in New Zealand, you'll find 80 official i-SITE Visitor Centres scattered around the country. Friendly staff members can book accommodations, activities, and tours; provide maps; and sell stamps and phone cards. Each chapter in this book lists the particular district/city information centers. Check www.i-site.org for more information.

Best Times to Go

New Zealand is in the Southern Hemisphere; therefore, all seasons are the opposite of those in North America, Europe, and other Northern Hemisphere locations.

When deciding when to visit New Zealand, keep in mind that most Kiwi families take their main annual holidays between mid-December and the end of January, which puts enormous pressure on accommodations in major summer beach destinations. During the Easter break and school holidays in April, June to July, and September to October (see "Holidays"), it also pays to reserve well in advance.

Remember, too, that accommodations at ski destinations fill up quickly in winter—reserve early and be prepared to pay higher winter rates. In most other areas, you'll be paying lower rates during the winter months (Apr–Aug). In summer-peak areas, some businesses close down completely for the winter.

Personally, I think the best time to visit is February through April. It's past the summer peak but the temperatures are still pleasant (even hot in some areas). You'll see spectacular autumn colors, especially in Queenstown, Central Otago, and Christchurch. Keep Easter and April school holidays in mind, though, when accommodations may be tight in some areas. Spring (Sept–Nov) is also a lovely time to visit; just be prepared for rain.

Festivals & Special Events

More information can be found in the regional chapters of this book and by going to the Tourism New Zealand website, www.newzealand.com. In particular, if you're interested in **Christchurch-area events,** check to see if the event is still on in wake of the February, 2011 earthquake—rebuilding efforts in central Christchurch are expected to last for a decade or more. For an exhaustive list of even more events beyond those listed here, check http://events.frommers.com, where you'll find a searchable, up-to-the-minute roster of what's happening in cities all over the world.

JANUARY

Two international tennis tour events attract top players to Auckland in early January: The women's **ASB Bank Tennis Classic** (☎ 09/373-3623; www.aucklandtennis.co.nz) and the men's **Heineken Open** (☎ 09/373-3623; www.heinekenopen.co.nz). The **Auckland Anniversary Day Regatta** (☎ 0800/734-2882; www.regatta.org.nz) attracts both local and international sailing competitors and spectators the last Monday in January. In Christchurch, the **World Buskers Festival** (☎ 03/377-2365; www.worldbuskersfestival.com) is a week of zany street entertainment provided by leading international entertainers in mid- to late January. The **Wellington Cup Race Meeting** (☎ 04/528-9611; www.trentham.co.nz) is a leading horse-racing event (galloping), held in conjunction with the National Yearling Sales, late in January.

FEBRUARY

The **Hawke's Bay Wine & Food Festival** (☎ 0800/442-9463 in NZ; www.harvesthawkesbay.co.nz) showcases the region's world-class wines and good food the first week in February. **Speights Coast to Coast** (☎ 03/326-7493; www.coasttocoast.co.nz) is a major multisport endurance race on the South Island, going from Kumara on the West Coast to Sumner, Christchurch in early February. It features a 33km (21-mile) mountain run followed by a 67km (42-mile) kayak race and a 142km (88-mile) cycle dash. The **Garden City Festival of Flowers** (☎ 03/365-5403; www.festivalofflowers.co.nz), in Christchurch in mid-February, features 10 days of garden visits, floating gardens, and floral carpets. **Brebner Art Deco Weekend** (☎ 06/835-0022; www.artdeconapier.com) is a fun celebration of Napier's Art Deco heritage that includes dancing, jazz, vintage cars, walks, and tours held the third weekend in February. The **Devonport Food & Wine Festival** (☎ 09/378-9030; www.devonportwinefestival.co.nz) is a weekend event in late February that includes jazz, classical, and opera performances. The **Auckland Arts Festival** (☎ 09/309-0101; www.aucklandfestival.co.nz) is an extravaganza of national and international dance, music, theater, and visual arts talent held late February to March in odd-numbered years.

MARCH

In early March, Auckland's Pacific Island communities celebrate **Pasifika Festival** (www.aucklandcity.govt.nz/pasifika), the largest 1-day cultural festival in the South Pacific. The **New Zealand International Arts Festival** (☎ 04/473-0149; www.nzfestival.telecom.co.nz), held in Wellington in early March, features top overseas and national artists and entertainers. It's a vibrant mix of all art forms, from contemporary dance to fine music and theater. **Ellerslie International Flower Show Christchurch** (☎ 03/379-4581; www.ellerslieflowershow.co.nz) showcases the best of garden design over 5 days in mid-March in Hagley Park. The 1-day **Hokitika Wildfoods Festival** (☎ 03/756-9048; www.wildfoods.co.nz), held in mid-March, presents the weird and wonderful of New Zealand's wild foods, including wild pig, possum pâté, goat, various bugs and insects, honey, fish, and venison.

APRIL

One of the best Warbirds air shows in the world, **Warbirds Over Wanaka** (☎ 03/443-8619; www.warbirdsoverwanaka.com), held Easter weekend of even-numbered years, combines classic vintage and veteran aircraft, machinery, fire engines, and tractors with dynamic Air Force displays and aerobatic teams in the natural amphitheater of the Upper Clutha Basin. **Arrowtown Autumn Festival** (☎ 03/442-0809; www.arrowtownautumnfestival.org.nz), the week after Easter, features market days, music, and street entertainment celebrating the gold-mining era. The **Fletcher Challenge Forest Marathon** (☎ 07/348-8448; www.rotoruamarathon.co.nz), held late April or early May in Rotorua, attracts over 500 runners.

MAY

The **Bay of Islands Country Music Festival** (☎ 09/404-1063; www.country-rock.co.nz), held the second weekend in May, draws musicians from all around New Zealand plus at least one international act each year.

JUNE

National Agricultural Fieldays (☎ 07/843-4499; www.fieldays.co.nz), held mid-June in Hamilton, is one of the largest agricultural shows in the world. **Matariki** (www.matarikifestival.co.nz and www.matariki.co.nz) is the Maori New Year, which coincides with the time when the Pleiades constellation is visible. A diverse range of cultural celebrations are held throughout the country during late May and throughout June.

JULY

The **Queenstown Winter Festival** (☎ 03/441-2453; www.winterfestival.co.nz) brings a host of zany mountain events and street entertainment to Queenstown every year in mid-July. From July to August, in odd-numbered years, the **Christchurch Arts Festival** (www.artsfestival.co.nz) showcases the best of national and international dance, music, theater, and visual arts.

AUGUST

More than 50 jazz bands from New Zealand and overseas provide live entertainment at various places around Paihia and Russell during the **Bay of Islands Jazz and Blues Festival** (☎ 09/404-1063; www.jazz-blues.co.nz), held early to mid-August.

SEPTEMBER

The **Montana World of Wearable Art Awards** (☎ 03/547-0863; www.worldofwearableart. com) is a creative extravaganza in Wellington held in mid- to late September that should not be missed. The **Alexandra Blossom Festival** (☎ 03/377-2823; www.blossom.co.nz), in late September or early October, is a parade of floats and entertainment celebrating the onset of spring in Central Otago. **Gay Ski Week** (www.gayskiweeknz.com) is a week of celebrations on and around the slopes near Queenstown, held annually the first week of September.

OCTOBER

Kaikoura Seafest (☎ 0800/473-2337; www. seafest.co.nz) celebrates the best seafood and Marlborough and Canterbury wines, with entertainment for the entire family. It's held in Kaikoura in early October. Garden tours and cultural events are highlights of the **Dunedin Rhododendron Festival** (☎ 03/477-1092; www.rhododunedin.co.nz), held in mid- to late October. The **Nelson Arts Festival** (☎ 03/ 546-0200; www.nelsonartsfestival.co.nz) brings 12 days of music, dance, theater, and street performances to the city in mid-October. Over 200 musicians attend and play in bars and restaurants for the **Queenstown Jazz Festival** (☎ 03/442-1211; www. queenstownjazz.co.nz) in late October.

NOVEMBER

Come to Martinborough in mid- to late November for the **Toast Martinborough** (☎ 06/306-9183; www.toastmartinborough. co.nz) wine and food festival.

The **Canterbury A&P Show** (☎ 03/343-3033; www.theshow.co.nz), in Christchurch, includes thoroughbred and standard-bred racing and the New Zealand Cup. It's held the second week of November. **The Southern Traverse** (☎ 03/441-8215; www. southerntraverse.com), in late November, is an adventure race for teams of three to five serious competitors through high ridges, lakes, and river crossings throughout Otago.

DECEMBER

A wide variety of local and national jazz bands perform throughout the **Nelson Jazz Festival** (☎ 03/547-2559; www.nelsonjazz.co.nz). The event culminates in a special New Year's Eve concert.

Weather

New Zealand's climate, especially by Northern Hemisphere standards, is pretty mellow for much of the year. You'll find a far greater seasonal difference in the South Island than in the subtropical North. In Central Otago, winter temperatures are often 14°F (–10°C) and sometimes as low as –4°F (–20°C), with summers up to 100° to 104°F (38°–40°C). By comparison, the northern part of the North Island is subtropical. That means *lots* of winter/spring rain, often daily light showers.

The west coast of the South Island can get up to 100 inches or more of rain a year on its side of the Southern Alps, while just over the mountains to the east, rainfall is a moderate 20 to 30 inches annually. Rain is also heavier on the west coast of the North Island, averaging 40 to 70 inches annually. Milford Sound, though, beats the lot; it's the wettest place in the country, with a phenomenal 365 inches of rain a year.

Strategies for Seeing New Zealand

New Zealand may look like a tiny country on the map but don't be deceived—there is lot to do here and every tourist season, I hear visitors complaining that they haven't allowed enough time. I've outlined a few tips to help you make the most of your time here.

Tip #1: Go in the off season.
If you arrive in New Zealand before the main tourist rush (Sept-Oct) or at the tail end of the season (Mar-Apr), there will be fewer people at main attractions, you won't have to fight for a bed, and the weather will still be plenty mild. You will also find significantly cheaper airfares and hotel rates.

Tip #2: Rent a car.
Having your own vehicle will give you an enormous amount of freedom to take unexpected departures from your itinerary. Our roads are generally good but they're not freeways, so trips between towns, especially in the South Island, can often mean 4 to 7 hours of driving.

Tip #3: Allow plenty of travel time.
Don't fall into the trap of thinking that all the highlights are at the end of a road trip. In New Zealand, the road trip often *is* the highlight. You will pass through a diverse range of

NEW ZEALAND'S AVERAGE DAILY TEMPERATURE & RAINFALL

Temperatures reflected are daily average (°C/°F). Rainfall reflects the daily average in millimeters/inches.

AUCKLAND	SUMMER	FALL	WINTER	SPRING
MAX TEMP	24/75	20/68	15/59	18/64
MIN. TEMP	12/54	13/55	9/48	11/52
RAINFALL	8/0.31	11/0.43	15/0.59	12/0.47

WELLINGTON	SUMMER	FALL	WINTER	SPRING
MAX TEMP	20/68	17/63	12/54	15/59
MIN. TEMP	13/55	11/52	6/43	9/48
RAINFALL	8/0.31	11/0.43	15/0.59	12/0.47

CHRISTCHURCH	SUMMER	FALL	WINTER	SPRING
MAX TEMP	22/72	17/63	13/55	15/59
MIN. TEMP	12/54	10/50	5/41	8/46
RAINFALL	12/0.47	14/0.55	15/0.59	16/0.63

landscapes and many small towns, so stop, walk around, chat with locals, take photographs, or enjoy a picnic.

Tip #4: Book accommodations ahead.
Many accommodation providers are booked up a whole year ahead, so do some Internet research and get your beds sorted well before arriving. You'll also find accommodations are extremely limited in some small towns so if you don't book early, you won't get a bed at all.

Tip #5. If your time is limited, visit one island.
If you have only a week or 10 days in New Zealand, limit yourself to either the North or South Island. Don't try and see them both or you'll spend most of your time traveling and feeling frazzled.

Tip #6. Don't forget the provinces.
Some of New Zealand's true gems are well away from the main tourism beat, so don't be afraid to head away from the cities and into the provinces. That's what we call Heartland New Zealand—the off-beat towns and villages where hard-working Kiwis battle against the elements and just get on with life.

Tip #7. Don't forget the free attractions.
Much of New Zealand's greatest beauty is free. Lakes, rivers, mountains, beaches, forests, and walking trails are all there for your enjoyment and unless you're on a guided walking trail, you won't have to pay a cent. Every town has a park and playground too.

Tip #8. Make the most of the beaches.
New Zealanders have been enjoying summer holidays at the beach for decades. It's an annual ritual—loading up the car, the caravan, the trailer and setting off for a few blissful weeks at the beach of choice. Some families have been returning to the same campsite at the same beach for generations. It is a unique part of New Zealand summer culture and you should definitely get a taste of it, even if it's just a visit and a wander around a camping ground. And don't be surprised if vacationers ask you to join them for a beer or a barbecue.

Getting There

The cost of getting to New Zealand is likely to be your single biggest cash outlay, so shop around. Remember to check out those recommended agents and hot travel offers listed for your country of origin on the Tourism New Zealand website, www.newzealand.com. Also go to Air New Zealand's website at www.airnewzealand.com for special deals.

By Plane

Auckland, Wellington, and Christchurch are all serviced by major domestic and international terminals. There are also much smaller international terminals at Hamilton, Queenstown, and Dunedin. Most cities have domestic terminals. Auckland Airport is the major hub for most airlines coming in to New Zealand, followed by Christchurch and Wellington.

There are at least 20 foreign airlines flying into Auckland. The main ones providing service from the **United States** are: Air New Zealand (www.airnewzealand.com or www.airnewzealand.co.nz), Qantas (www.qantas.com.au), and British Airways (www.britishairways.com).

To and from **Canada,** you can choose from: Air New Zealand and Air Pacific (www.airpacific.com); to and from **Europe and the United Kingdom,** Air New Zealand, British Airways, and Qantas. **From Asia,** options include Singapore Airlines (www.singaporeair.com), Korean Air (www.koreanair.com), Japan Airlines (www.jal.co.jp), Malaysian Airlines (www.malaysianairlines.com), Cathay Pacific (www.cathaypacific.com), and Thai Airways (www.thaiair.com). **From Dubai**, Emirates Airline (www.emirates.com) now flies into New Zealand as well. There are also code-sharing arrangements with Lufthansa (www.lufthansa.com), American Airlines (www.aa.com), United Airlines (www.united.com), and several others.

The timing of your trip can have a tremendous impact on your airline costs. New Zealand's peak season is December through February; the shoulder season includes March and September through November; and the low season begins in April and runs through August.

By Cruise Ship

Most cruises coming to New Zealand also visit Australia and are typically 12 to 16 days in duration. New Zealand cruise ports include Auckland, Tauranga, Napier, Wellington, Lyttelton (near Christchurch), Dunedin, and Milford Sound. You can fly to Australia or New Zealand to join a cruise, or you can take a segment on a world cruise that includes New Zealand.

There are at least a dozen international cruise lines that include New Zealand on their itineraries. Contact details for the main ones are: Cunard Line (www.cunard.com), Silversea Cruises (www.silversea.com), Holland America Line (www.hollandamerica.com), Crystal Cruises (www.crystalcruises.com), Regent Seven Seas Cruises (www.rssc.com), Princess Cruise Lines (www.princess.com), P&O Cruises (www.pocruises.com), Fred Olsen Line (www.fredolsencruises.com), and Oceania Cruises (www.oceaniacruises.com).

Getting Around

By Plane

Air New Zealand (☎ 0800/737-000 in NZ, or 09/357-3000; www.airnewzealand.co.nz), with Air New Zealand Link, dominates the airways, with Qantas New Zealand (☎ 0800/808-767 in NZ, or 09/357-8900; www.qantas.com) servicing the main centers. Jet Star (☎ 0800/800-995; www.jetstar.com), also flies domestically. Several other smaller airlines fly internal routes (see "Fast Facts" sections in regional chapters for details). Air New Zealand is also a good source of special deals. They regularly offer vacation packages and monthly deals, but these must be purchased outside of New Zealand (☎ 800/262-1234 in the U.S.; www.airnewzealand.com).

By Car

Do not underestimate travel times. Distances may seem short in kilometer terms but roads are often winding and sometimes narrow. If you plan to drive, consider joining the Automobile Association (AA) while you're here. In New Zealand, call ☎ 0800/500-213; there are also AA offices in most towns. AA offers excellent breakdown services and advice to drivers. If you belong to a similar organization in your home country, membership is free, so don't forget to bring along your membership card.

Remember to drive on the left and wear seat belts at all times. The open-road speed limit is 100kmph (62 mph), while in towns and built-up areas, it is 50kmph (31 mph). You face heavy fines if you exceed limits. New Zealand has also tightened up its drunk-driving laws and if you are stopped in a random police check for compulsory breath testing for alcohol, you must comply.

CAR RENTALS
You must be 25 years old to rent a car from most companies in New Zealand. You must have a driver's license that you've held for at least 1 year from the United States, Australia, Canada, or the United Kingdom (or an international driving permit). All drivers, including visitors, must carry their license or permit at all times.

Every major city has numerous rental-car companies and international companies like Avis, Budget, and Hertz rent a wide range of vehicles. Most offer good deals that can be pre-booked before you leave home. However, it pays to shop around and compare not only the prices, but also the cars. Some companies offer cheap deals, but their cars may be well over 10 years old. Most companies also require that you take out accident insurance with an insurance company authorized by them. You can rent in advance from the following: Avis (☎ 800/230-4898 in the U.S.; www.avis.com); Budget (☎ 800/527-0700 in the U.S.; www.budget.com); Hertz (☎ 800/654-3131 in the U.S.; www.hertz.com); and Thrifty (☎ 800/847-4389 in the U.S.; www.thrifty.com). Daily costs average about NZ$100 to NZ$150.

By Inter-island Ferry
There are two ferry companies operating on the Cook Strait, with bases in Wellington or Picton; the crossing takes about 3 hours. The **Interislander** ferry system (☎ 0800/802-802 in NZ; www.interislander.co.nz) operates every day year-round with three vessels—*Arahura, Kaitaki,* and *Aratere*—that offer a tourism experience in their own right. You can choose from six daily departure times. The ferries have licensed bar and cafe areas, TV lounges, shops, and play areas. *Kaitaki,* the biggest ferry in New Zealand, has two movie theaters

and room for 1,600 passengers. **Bluebridge Cook Strait Ferry** (☎ 0800/844-844 in NZ; www.bluebridge.co.nz) sails twice daily between Wellington and Picton. The vessel features lounges, cafe and bar facilities, outdoor decks, free big-screen movies, and a shop. Fare bookings are transferable until 24 hours before travel subject to availability, but they're nonrefundable.

Regardless of which ferry you select, keep in mind that Cook Strait is a notoriously changeable stretch of water and high swells can affect those prone to seasickness. Bad weather may also affect scheduled departures.

By Coach (Bus)
Coaches offer a cost-effective way of getting around New Zealand; as a bonus, you don't have to worry about driving on the left and studying maps. Most give excellent commentaries and stop frequently for refreshments en route, but smoking is not permitted. There are three major services in New Zealand, all owned by the same company. **InterCity** (☎ 09/623-1503 in Auckland and 03/377-0951 in Christchurch; www.intercity.co.nz) operates coaches on New Zealand's most comprehensive coach network, visiting 600 towns and cities, with over 170 services daily. **Newmans** (☎ 09/623-1504; www.newmanscoach.co.nz) is also a standard route option throughout the country, except on the South

Taking to the Highways

Some kind and ever-so-thoughtful person—and I think it might be someone at Jasons Publishing (www.jasons.com)—had the good sense to create seven marvelous highway route planners. They include *The Twin Coast Discovery Highway,* covering Northland and Auckland; *The Pacific Coast Highway,* covering Auckland, Coromandel, coastal Bay of Plenty, Eastland, and Hawke's Bay; and *The Classic New Zealand Wine Trail,* roaming between Hawke's Bay, the Martinborough area, and the Marlborough region. These free maps detail the best features of each trip, places to stay and eat, and adventures to sample along the way. They're available at visitor centers throughout the country.

Island's West Coast, where it operates as a tourist service and a code-share with the Great Sights line. **Great Sights** (☎ 0800/744-487 in NZ, or 09/583-5790; www.great-sights.co.nz), New Zealand's premier daily sightseeing operator, providing the most extensive sightseeing network nationwide. *Reminder:* Book coach journeys in advance during peak travel periods (summer and holidays).

For the young and/or adventurous, **Kiwi Experience,** 195–197 Parnell Rd., Parnell, Auckland (☎ 09/366-9830; www.kiwiexperience.com), and the **Magic Travellers Network,** 120 Albert St., Auckland (☎ 09/358-5600; www.magicbus.co.nz), provide something that's between a standard coach and a tour. Popular with backpackers, they travel over a half-dozen pre-established routes. Passengers can get off whenever they like and pick up the next coach days or weeks later. The coaches make stops at scenic points along the way for bush walking, swimming, and sometimes even a barbecue.

By Train

TranzScenic (☎ 0800/872-467 in NZ; www.tranzscenic.co.nz) operates three long-distance train routes through rugged landscapes: the Overlander, which runs from Auckland to Wellington; the TranzCoastal between Christchurch to Picton; and the TranzAlpine, between Christchurch to Greymouth. The trains are modern and comfortable, heated or air-conditioned, carpeted, and ventilated. Service has greatly improved under new management and views of spectacular landscapes are assured.

Tips on Accommodations

Unfortunately, there's nothing standard about accommodations rates here. What you get for NZ$150 can be much better than something for two or three times the price. My words of advice are: ask around; visit websites for photographs; and don't assume that all places in the same price range offer the same standard of accommodations.

New Zealand tourism's official mark of quality, Qualmark (www.qualmark.co.nz), has now been applied to all accommodations types and tourism businesses. This means they have been independently assessed as professional and trustworthy. Businesses are given one star (acceptable), two stars (good), three stars (very good), four stars (excellent), or five stars (exceptional, among the best in New Zealand). Each business has undergone a rigorous assessment and licensing process to become part of the Qualmark licensing system.

If you would like more information when you arrive in New Zealand, pick up the free **Qualmark Accommodation Guide** from information centers (or order it at www.qualmark.co.nz). The guide lists all participating hotels, motels, B&Bs, backpacker lodgings, campgrounds, and tourism businesses.

In addition to the online travel booking sites Travelocity, Expedia, Orbitz, Priceline, and Hotwire, you can book hotels through Hotels.com, Quikbook (www.quikbook.com), and Travelaxe (www.travelaxe.net).

HotelChatter.com is a daily webzine offering smart coverage and critiques of hotels worldwide. Go to TripAdvisor.com or Hotel Shark.com for helpful independent consumer reviews of hotels and resort properties.

There is a multitude of lodging options available in New Zealand—here is a rundown on what you'll find.

HOTELS

A hotel generally provides a licensed bar and restaurant; guest rooms do not usually have cooking facilities. In New Zealand, "hotel" refers to modern tourist hotels, including the big international chains and older, public-licensed hotels generally found in provincial areas. The latter are completely different from the former.

The country hotel, or pub, offers inexpensive to moderate accommodations of a modest nature. It's often noisy and old-fashioned with shared bathrooms down the hall. There are definitely exceptions, but one way or another, they're usually rich in character.

Modern hotels come in all price levels. Several big international chains have two or three grades of hotels, and you can get exceptionally good deals if you book with the same chain throughout the country. In major tourist centers such as Queenstown, competition is fierce and good prices can be found. In major corporate destinations such as Auckland and Wellington, rates will be considerably higher during the week, with weekends bringing superb specials.

APARTMENTS

In the last five years, apartment-style accommodations have become popular. If you'd like to stay in a modern apartment I suggest you contact one of the two following first-class operators. **Touch of Spice,** Queenstown (☎ 03/442-8672; www.touchofspice.co.nz) offers a range of 30 luxury properties from inner city apartments to country hideaways and private island retreats—all with modern furnishings, five-star quality, and full staff if required. **New Zealand Apartments** (☎ 0800/692-727 in NZ; www.nzapartments.co.nz), has a catalogue of 48 stylish apartments in 33 locations nationwide. Most are under 10 years old and go for unbelievably good prices. They're serviced on demand and all have on-site managers to welcome you.

MOTELS & MOTOR INNS

A motel unit is self-contained and usually has cooking facilities, a bathroom, and one or two bedrooms. A motor inn often has a restaurant on the premises.

There has been a major shake-up of standards in the motel industry and many motels and motor inns are now superior to some hotels. Look for the Qualmark sign of quality, which is prominently displayed on signs and promotional material. If you aim for four- and five-star properties I'm sure you'll be happy. **New Zealand Luxury Motels** (☎ 0800/692-727 in NZ; www.nzluxurymotels.co.nz), can save you a lot of time. They have 23 top-end motels nationwide on their books.

BED & BREAKFASTS

As the name suggests, B&B rates include bed and breakfast.

Homestays and bed-and-breakfasts are pretty much the same thing, but the variation in quality within both can be disconcerting—you'll find both the ludicrously cheap and the ludicrously expensive, and price is not necessarily an indicator of what you'll get. Homestays tend to be more family-oriented and modest, especially in rural areas and provincial towns. Be prepared to simply get a bed in a family home. B&Bs, on the other hand, can be as downmarket or as upmarket as you're prepared to pay; some rival the best hotels for quality.

Check websites, or wait until you're in New Zealand to purchase one of the numerous B&B guides. Look for *The New Zealand Bed & Breakfast Book,* which illustrates every property in full color. Another reliable source is *Heritage & Character Inns of New Zealand* (www.heritage inns.co.nz), which details about 90 of the country's best B&B lodgings in heritage homes. Ask for brochures at visitor centers.

You can safely assume that farmstays are located on working farms. They present an ideal opportunity to get a feel for New Zealand's rural life. There are several organizations that will put you in touch with a reliable farmstay, including **Accommodation New Zealand** (☎ 09/444-4895 or 03/487-8420; www.accommodation-new-zealand.co.nz) and **Hospitality Plus, The New Zealand Home & Farmstay Company** (☎ 03/693-7463; www.hospitalityplus.co.nz).

Guesthouses generally offer good value, with modest rooms at modest prices. You can check out a selection of them with **New Zealand's Federation of Bed & Breakfast Hotels, Inc.,** 52 Armagh St., Christchurch (☎ 03/358-6928; www.nzbnbhotels.com).

COUNTRY LODGES

In the truest sense, country lodges in New Zealand are small and highly individual, with 4 to 20 bedrooms. They're fully licensed and have an all-inclusive tariff. They generally offer the very best of everything, including fine dining (three- to five-course dinners). The unspoken factors are the degree of exclusivity that exceeds B&Bs and the degree of personalized service and pampering that exceeds most hotels. For information, go to www.lodgesofnz.co.nz. A luxury accommodations category was also added to the Qualmark program in 2003.

HOLIDAY HOMES

When they're not being used by their owners, holiday homes can be rented by the night or for longer periods. Known as baches in the North Island and cribs in the South Island, they are a good value for independent travelers. You can buy *Baches & Holiday Homes to Rent,* which details over 500 properties, from bookstores or the Automobile Association, 99 Albert St., Auckland (☎ 09/966-8800); 343 Lambton Quay, Wellington (☎ 04/931-9999); or 210 Hereford St., Christchurch (☎ 03/964-3650). For a wider variety—from cozy cottages to superluxury homes—contact **New Zealand Vacation Homes** (www.nzvacationhomes.co.nz), which lists self-catering properties throughout the country.

HOSTELS

Hostels are generally frequented by backpackers but most welcome people of all ages and have single and double rooms as well as dorms. They have shared facilities (some have ensuite bathrooms) and communal lounges and kitchens. Some have cafes and/or bars.

YHA New Zealand National Reservations Centre (☎ 03/379-9808; www.yha.co.nz) has hostels open 24 hours a day that do not impose curfews or duties. **Budget Backpacker Hostels New Zealand** (☎ 03/379-3014; www.bbh.co.nz) lists over 300 hostels around the country. **VIP Backpacker Resorts of New Zealand** (☎ 09/827-6016; www.vips.co.nz) is supported by over 60 hostels. **Nomads** (☎ 0800/666-237; www.nomadsworld.com) offers hostel accommodations at 16 sites.

MOTOR CAMPS & HOLIDAY PARKS

These properties have communal kitchens, toilets, showers, and laundries, and a variety of accommodations from campsites and cabins to flats and backpacker-style lodges. They are very popular with New Zealand holidaymakers during the summer months, so make sure you book ahead. They make an ideal base if you are traveling by motor home. Two contacts for holiday parks are **Top 10 Holiday Parks** (☎ 0800/867-836 in NZ; www.top10.co.nz) and **Holiday Accommodation Parks New Zealand** (☎ 04/298-3283; www.holidayparks.co.nz).

New Zealand Fast Facts

ATMs

ATMs are common throughout most of New Zealand; exceptions include some smaller towns in remote locations such as Stewart Island and some parts of the South Island's West Coast. Otherwise, you'll find them inside and outside all banks, in major shopping centers, in supermarkets, and at gas stations.

Most likely, your ATM card is compatible with New Zealand systems. The Bank of New Zealand accepts ATM cards in the Cirrus system (☎ 800/424-7787 in the U.S.; www.mastercard.com); other banks accept cards in the PLUS system (www.visa.com).

Banking & Business Hours

Banks are open Monday through Friday from 9am to 4:30pm. Shops are usually open Monday through Thursday from 9am (sometimes 8am) to 5:30pm and until 9pm on either Thursday or Friday. Increasingly, shops are open all day Saturday; many shops are also open all day Sunday, with others closing between noon and 4pm.

Car Rentals

See p. 472, "Getting Around."

Customs

WHAT YOU CAN BRING INTO NEW ZEALAND

Customs duties are not assessed on personal items you bring into the country and plan to take with you. New Zealand's duty-free allowances are 200 cigarettes or 250 grams (8¾ oz.) of tobacco or 50 cigars; 4.5 liters of wine or beer (equivalent to six 750ml bottles); three bottles of spirits or liqueur (each containing no more than 1,125ml/about 2½ pints); and goods totaling NZ$700 that were purchased for your own use or for a gift. Make sure you have receipts available for inspection. If you plan to take in anything beyond those limits, contact the embassy or consulate office nearest you *before* you arrive or check www.customs.govt.nz.

Animal products, fruit, plant material, and foodstuffs that may contain plant or animal pests and diseases will not be allowed into the country. Heavy fines may be imposed on people caught carrying these prohibited materials.

Electricity

The voltage is 230 volts in New Zealand, and plugs are the three-prong type. If you bring a hair dryer, it should be a dual-voltage one and you'll need an adapter plug. Most motels and some B&Bs have built-in wall transformers for 110-volt, two-prong razors, but if you're going to be staying in hostels, cabins, homestays, or guesthouses, bring dual-voltage appliances.

Embassies & Consulates

For additional information on embassies in New Zealand, contact the Ministry of Foreign Affairs & Trade in Wellington (☎ 04/494-8500; www.mft.govt.nz).

Auckland has consulates of the United States, Level 3, 23 Customs St. E. (☎ 09/

303-2724); Canada, 318 Shortland St. (☎ 09/309-3690); Ireland, Level 7, 23 Customs St. E. (☎ 09/977-2252); and the United Kingdom, IAG House, 151 Queen St. (☎ 09/303-2973). The U.S. Embassy is at 29 Fitzherbert Terrace, Thorndon (☎ 04/462-6000). The Canadian High Commission is at Level 11, 125 The Terrace (☎ 04/473-9577; www.gc.ca), and the British High Commission is at 44 Hill St. (☎ 04/924-2888).

Family Travel

New Zealand offers hiking, swimming, sailing, whale-watching, and many more activities that children of all ages can enjoy. All cities and towns also have free parks, walkways, and children's playgrounds. If you're here in summer, swimming pool complexes in most towns make for a fun, inexpensive day out for all the family.

Make sure you ask at all visitor centers for advice on the best kids' attractions and summer holiday festivals. Most sightseeing attractions admit children at half price and family prices are usually available too.

Although many of the better B&Bs and up-market lodges do not accommodate children, motels are ideal for families. They are usually cheaper and are regularly equipped with cooking facilities.

Recommended family travel websites include Family Travel Forum (www.familytravelforum.com), a comprehensive site that offers customized trip planning; Family Travel Network (www.familytravelnetwork.com), an online magazine providing travel tips; and TravelWithYourKids.com (www.travelwithyourkids.com), a comprehensive site written by parents for parents offering sound advice for long-distance and international travel with children.

To locate accommodations, restaurants, and attractions that are particularly kid-friendly, look for the kids icon throughout this guide.

Gay & Lesbian Travel

Gay and lesbian travelers will feel at ease in New Zealand, especially in Auckland and Wellington. For information, go to the New Zealand Gay and Lesbian Tourism Association website at www.iglta.org or write to them at P.O. Box 24-558, Wellington 6015, New Zealand (☎ 04/917-9184). Other New Zealand gay and lesbian websites include GayNZ.com (www.gaynz.com), Pink Pages New Zealand (www.pinkpagesnet.com/newzealand), Queer Resources Aotearoa (www.gaynz.net.nz), and Gay Queenstown (www.gayqueenstown.com).

Holidays

National public holidays include New Year's Day (Jan 1), New Year's Holiday (Jan 2), Waitangi Day (Feb 6), Good Friday (varies), Easter and Easter Monday (varies), ANZAC Day (Apr 25), Queen's Birthday (first Mon in June), Labour Day (last Mon in Oct), Christmas Day (Dec 25), and Boxing Day (Dec 26).

Regional holidays include Wellington (Jan 22), Auckland (Jan 29), Northland (Jan 29), Nelson Region (Feb 1), Otago (Mar 23), Southland (Mar 23), Taranaki (Mar 31), Hawke's Bay (Nov 1), Marlborough (Nov 1), Westland (Dec 1), and Canterbury (Dec 16). Regional holidays are always observed on a Monday. If the date lands on a Friday or weekend, the holiday is observed on the following Monday. If it falls earlier in the week, it is observed on the preceding Monday.

School holidays consist of three midterm breaks—in April, June to July, and September to October—that last for 2 weeks each, plus 6 weeks for the December holidays. Kiwi families do much of their traveling during these periods, so be sure to reserve early if you'll also be traveling then.

Insurance

You should always travel with insurance no matter where you go, New Zealand is no exception. For information on traveler's insurance, trip cancelation insurance, and medical insurance while traveling, please visit www.frommers.com/planning.

Internet Access

To find cybercafes in your destination, check www.cybercaptive.com and www.cybercafe.com.

Aside from formal cybercafes, most youth hostels nowadays have at least one computer on which you can use the Internet. Most public libraries across the world offer Internet access free or for a small charge. Avoid hotel business centers, unless access to them is included in your rates; otherwise, you'll find yourself paying an additional charge to use it.

Most upscale accommodations and many B&Bs in New Zealand offer a free high-speed or Wi-Fi service. Wherever you go, bring a connection kit of the right power and phone adapters (the voltage is 230 volts in New Zealand and plugs are the three-prong type), a spare phone cord, and a spare Ethernet network cable.

Lost Property

Be sure to tell all of your credit card companies the minute you discover your wallet has been lost or stolen and file a report at the nearest police precinct. Your credit card company or insurer may require a police report number or record of the loss. Most credit card companies have an emergency toll-free number to call if your card is lost or stolen; they may be able to wire you a cash advance immediately or deliver an emergency credit card in a day or two. Visa's emergency number is ☎ 0508/600-300 in New Zealand. American Express cardholders and traveler's check holders should call collect to the U.S. at ☎ 715/343-7977. MasterCard holders should call ☎ 0800/44-9140 in New Zealand.

If you need emergency cash over the weekend when all banks and American Express offices are closed, you can have money wired to you via Western Union (☎ 0800/005-253 in NZ; www.westernunion.com).

Identity theft and fraud are potential complications of losing your wallet, especially if you've lost your driver's license along with your cash and credit cards. Notify the major credit-reporting bureaus immediately; placing a fraud alert on your records may protect you against liability for criminal activity. The three major U.S. credit-reporting agencies are Equifax (☎ 800/766-0008; www.equifax.com), Experian (☎ 888/397-3742; www.experian.com), and TransUnion (☎ 800/680-7289; www.transunion.com). Finally, if you've lost all forms of photo ID, call your airline and explain the situation; they might allow you to board the plane if you have a copy of your passport or birth certificate and a copy of the police report you've filed.

Mail & Postage

New Zealand post offices will receive mail and hold it for you for 1 month. Have the parcel addressed to you c/o Poste Restante at the chief post office of the town you'll be visiting. It costs NZ$3 to send an airmail letter to the United States, Canada, United Kingdom, or Europe. Overseas postcards cost NZ$2.

Money

The currency in New Zealand is the New Zealand dollar (NZ$). Currency conversion rates fluctuate daily; before departing consult a currency exchange website such as www.oanda.com/currency/converter to check up-to-the-minute rates.

Passports

A passport is required for all entering visitors and it must be valid for at least 3 months beyond your departure date from New Zealand. If you lose yours, visit the nearest consulate of your native country as soon as possible for a replacement. If you do not have a passport, allow plenty of time before your trip to apply.

AUSTRALIA Australian Passport Information Service (☎ 131-232; www.passports.gov.au).

CANADA Passport Office, Department of Foreign Affairs and International Trade, Ottawa, ON K1A 0G3 (☎ 800/567-6868; www.ppt.gc.ca).

IRELAND Passport Office, Setanta Centre, Molesworth Street, Dublin 2 (☎ 01/671-1633; www.foreignaffairs.gov.ie).

UNITED KINGDOM Visit your nearest passport office, major post office, or travel agency or contact the Identity and Passport Service (IPS), 89 Eccleston Square, London, SW1V 1PN (☎ 0300/222-0000; www.ips.gov.uk).

UNITED STATES To find your regional passport office, check the U.S. State Department website (travel.state.gov/passport) or call the National Passport Information Center (☎ 877/487-2778) for automated information.

Pharmacies

Pharmacies observe regular shop hours but most localities have an "Urgent Pharmacy," which remains open until about 11pm every day except Sunday, when there are two periods during the day when it's open, usually one in the morning and one in the afternoon. To find an urgent pharmacy, ask at your hotel or call directory assistance at ☎ 018.

Safety

New Zealand is generally a very safe destination. Still, exercise the same care that you would in any major city. People-oriented dangers—theft, assault, murder—do exist but remember that violent crimes in most countries, especially in New Zealand, occur between acquaintances. As a traveler, it's unlikely you'll be a victim. If you're hitchhiking, however, that may be another matter; women should never hitchhike alone or at night.

Always lock vehicles and rooms, and park your car in a well-populated area whenever possible. If you leave luggage in the car, cover it with a blanket or a coat. *Never* leave handbags or cameras in cars. The simple rule should be, if you can't do without it, don't leave it in the car, locked or otherwise.

The downtown areas of New Zealand's major cities, especially Auckland, Wellington, and Christchurch, are now well covered by closed circuit cameras, which are monitored by police.

Senior Travelers

Discounts for those over 60 are increasingly available in New Zealand so be sure to inquire when making reservations for accommodations and attractions. Don't forget to carry photo identification. Those over 60 are entitled to a 20% discount on InterCity coaches and TranzScenic trains. Newmans Coaches offers a 20% discount to anyone over 60.

Smoking

New Zealand has strict no-smoking laws that apply in all public buildings, restaurants, bars, stores, on all public transport and aircraft, and in all accommodations. Very few accommodation providers now offer smoking rooms, so make sure you check when you book.

Taxes

There is a national 15% Goods and Services Tax (GST) that's applicable to everything. A departure tax of NZ$25 is assessed and can be paid by credit card or in cash in New Zealand currency.

Telephones

The country code for New Zealand is 64. When calling New Zealand from outside the country, you must first dial the country code, then the city area code (for example, 03, 09, or 06) but omit the zero. The city area code in New Zealand is known as the STD (subscriber toll dialing). To call long distance within New Zealand, dial the STD—09 for Auckland and Northland, 07 for the North Island's Thames Valley, 06 for the North Island's east coast and Wanganui, 04 for Wellington, or 03 for the South Island—and then the local number. For operator assistance within New Zealand, dial ☎ 010; for directory assistance, dial ☎ 018.

There are three main kinds of public telephones in New Zealand: card phones, credit card phones, and coin phones. Magnetic strip phone cards for public phones can be purchased from supermarkets, post offices, dairies, and service stations.

The most economical way to make international phone calls from New Zealand is to charge them to an international calling card, available from your long-distance company at home. All calls, even international ones, can be made from public phone booths. (Long-distance calls made from your hotel or motel often have hefty surcharges added.) To reach an international operator, dial ☎ 0170; for directory assistance for an international call, dial ☎ 0172. You can also call home using country direct numbers. They are 000-911 for the U.S.; 000-944 for British Telecom (operator); 000-912 for British Telecom (automatic); 000-940 for UK Mercury; 000-919 for Canada; 000-996 for Australia-Optus; and 000-961 for Australia-Telstra.

Renting a mobile phone in New Zealand isn't cheap. You'll usually pay $40 to $50 per week, plus airtime fees of at least a dollar a minute. You'll get good coverage in most urban areas in New Zealand but be prepared for "black holes" where there is no coverage at all. These areas are usually off the beaten track and are too numerous to list. The West Coast, Arthur's Pass, parts of Eastland, and parts of the far south are notorious for weaker coverage.

True wilderness adventurers should consider renting a satellite phone. Per-minute call charges can be even cheaper than roaming charges with a regular cellphone, but the phone itself is more expensive (up to $150 a week) and depending on the service you choose, people calling you may incur high long-distance charges.

Time Zone

New Zealand is located just west of the international dateline and its standard time is 12 hours ahead of Greenwich Mean Time. Thus, when it's noon in New Zealand, it's 7:30am in Singapore, 9am in Tokyo, 10am in Sydney; and—all the previous day—4pm in San Francisco, 7pm in New York, and midnight in London. In New Zealand, daylight saving time starts the first weekend in October and ends in mid-March.

Tipping

Most New Zealanders don't tip waitstaff unless they've received extraordinary service—and then only 5% to 10%. Taxi drivers and porters are rarely tipped in this country. Do not tip people just because that's what you do at home. Make sure they have done something outstanding to justify it.

Toilets

You shouldn't have any trouble finding a toilet in New Zealand; there are public conveniences strategically located in all cities and many towns.

Tourist Offices

See individual chapters for all local visitor information centers.

Water

New Zealand tap water is pollution free and safe to drink. In the bush, you should boil, filter, or chemically treat water from rivers and lakes to avoid contracting *Giardia* (a waterborne parasite that causes diarrhea).

> *The gannet colony at Cape Kidnappers is the largest and most accessible in the world.*

Index

Photo Credits

Note: l= left; r= right; t= top; b= bottom; c= center